S0-APX-954

HANDBOOK OF HEALTH CARE RISK MANAGEMENT

Edited by

Glenn T. Troyer, MHA, JD

Member, Law Firm of
Locke, Reynolds, Boyd & Weisell
Indianapolis, Indiana

Steven L. Salman, MBA, JD

Director of Risk and Insurance Management
Sisters of Charity Health Care Systems, Inc.
Cincinnati, Ohio

President
MSJ Insurance Company
Denver, Colorado

AN ASPEN PUBLICATION®
Aspen Systems Corporation

1986

Rockville, Maryland
Royal Tunbridge Wells

Library of Congress Cataloging in Publication Data
Main entry under title:

Handbook of health care risk management.

"An Aspen publication."
Includes bibliographies and index.
1. Hospitals–Administration. 2. Risk management. 3. Hospitals–Safety measures. 4. Tort liability of hospitals. I. Troyer, Glenn T. II. Salman, Steven L. [DNLM: 1. Financial Management–methods. 2. Hospital Administration–United States. WX 157 H2363] RA971.H275 1986 326.1'1'068 85-22806
ISBN: 0-87189-248-0

Editorial Services: Jane Coyle

Copyright © 1986 by Aspen Systems Corporation
All rights reserved.

Aspen Systems Corporation grants permission for photocopying for personal or internal use, or for the personal or internal use of specific clients registered with the Copyright Clearance Center (CCC). This consent is given on the condition that the copier pay a $1.00 fee plus $.12 per page for each photocopy through the CCC for photocopying beyond that permitted by the U.S. Copyright Law. The fee should be paid directly to the CCC, 21 Congress St., Salem, Massachusetts 01970.
0-87189-248-0/86 $1.00 + .12.

This consent does not extend to other kinds of copying, such as copying for general distribution, for advertising or promotional purposes, for creating new collective works, or for resale. For information, address Aspen Systems Corporation, 1600 Research Boulevard, Rockville, Maryland 20850.

Library of Congress Catalog Card Number: 85-22806
ISBN: 0-87189-248-0

Printed in the United States of America

1 2 3 4 5

Table of Contents

Foreword .... **xi**

Preface .... **xiii**

Chapter 1—Organization of the Health Care Delivery System in the U.S. **1**
Robert M. Saywell, Jr. and Gerald J. McHugh

Basic Components and Levels of Care 2
The Four Ps 4
U.S. Health Services System: An Overview 5
The Health Care System: A Macroview 6
The Health Care System: Patients' Perspective 11
The U.S. Hospital: Past and Present 26
The Present: 1960 to Now 29
Long-Term Hospitals 40
Nursing Home: Past and Present 43
Summary 48

Chapter 2—The Hospital: Its Organization and Structure **53**
Gerald J. McHugh and Robert M. Saywell, Jr.

Organizing the Hospital's Functional Structure 54
Integration and Coordination of Hospital Activities 56
Authority and Its Delegation 57
The Matrix Organization 59
The Hospital as an Open System 61
The Governing Board 63
The Medical Staff 66

The CEO and the Administration 74
Summary 77

Chapter 3—Financial and Risk Management in Hospitals 81
Richard Rail

The Accounting Formula in Hospitals 82
The Basic Financial Statements 86
Financial Management Systems in Hospitals 91
Managing the Financial Risks 99
How It Ought To Be 100

Chapter 4—Hospital Law: Theory and Application 101
Ralph F. Valitutti and Gregory G. Drutchas

Regulation 102
Hospital Liability 104
Apportionment of Liability 127
Special Statutes Relating to Liability 131
Confidentiality and Investigations 133
Summary 136

Chapter 5—The Concept of Risk 141
Glenn Troyer

Risk Concepts Defined 142
Personal Values and Experiences 144
Group and Individual Attitudes 145
Classification Schemes 145
Management of Risk 146
Summary 147

Chapter 6—Risk Management Processes and Functions 149
Steven L. Salman

A Nontechnical Analysis 149
Generic Model as Outline 150
The 4 Basic Components 153
Risk Identification 153
Risk Analysis 165
Risk Treatment 174
Risk Evaluation 179

Chapter 7—Insurance **183**
William H. Gill and Ronald T. Nelson

What Is Insurance? 183
Types of Insurance 186
Insurance Contract Elements 199
Selecting Brokers and Insurers 203
Insurance Purchasing 206
Insurance Bidding 206

Chapter 8—Alternative Methods of Risk Financing **209**
Ronald T. Nelson and William H. Gill

Analysis of Efficiencies 209
Application of the Analysis 211
Alternatives to Purchased Insurance 216
Advantages and Disadvantages 219
Fronting 222
Pooling Programs 225
Channeling 226

Chapter 9—Noninsurance Risk Transfers **229**
Glenn T. Troyer

Indemnity or Hold-Harmless Agreements 229
Hospitals and Third Parties 231
Legal Responsibility of Parties 232

Chapter 10—Claims Management **235**
Layton Severson and Malcolm S. Parsons

Development of Claims Management 235
General Concepts 236
Incident Reporting System 237
The Foundation: Step 1 238
The Foundation: Step 2 239
Refining the System 242
Legal Liability Defined 245
Liability Evaluation 246
Statements 248
Evaluation of Claims 249
Defense Attorney Involvement 250
The Reserving Process 251
Settlement and Release Considerations 252

Year-Ending Reports 253
Primary Commercial Insurance Coverage 253
Understanding the Self-Insured Concept 254
Excess Coverage above Self-Insurance 256
Potential Conflicts in Self-Insurance 258
The Captive Concept 260

Chapter 11—Structured Settlements 261
Joseph M. O'Reilly and Charles M. Fischesser

Funding Vehicles for Structured Settlements 261
Types of Annuities 262
Pricing of Settlement Annuities 264
Why a Structured Settlement? 266
Structured Settlement Considerations 267
Approaching a Structured Settlement 271
Varieties of Structured Settlements 279
Tax Guidelines and Principles 281
Third Party Assignments 284
Settlement Agreements (Releases) 285
Income Tax Consequences to Defendant 286
Life Insurance Companies 287
Consultants, Brokers, and Specialists 288
The Settlement Conference 288
Closing the Case 290
Communicating with the Plaintiff 290
Appendix 11-A 291
Appendix 11-B 293
Appendix 11-C 296
Appendix 11-D 298
Appendix 11-E 299

Chapter 12—Managing Loss Exposures in Hospitals 301
Paul A. Greve, Jr.

Risk Management Goals 302
Risk Management Functions 302
Selection of the Risk Manager 303
Role of the Medical Staff 304
Nursing Staff 305
Administrative Staff 305
Role of the Board of Trustees 306
Risk Management Committee 306

Educational Programs 307
Patient Billing Department 308
Quality Assurance 309
Processing Patient Care Information 309
Incident Reports 309
Informal Reporting of Problems 310
Claims Information 310

Chapter 13—Organizing a Risk Management Program: The Smaller Hospital 313
Alan J. Mittermaier

Commitment to Risk Management 314
Staff Involvement 314
Development of the Program 317
Use of Consultants 323
Program Evaluation 324
Summary 325

Chapter 14—Organizing a Risk Management Program: The Larger Hospital 327
Charles B. Van Vorst and James A. White

Formal Authority 327
Informal Authority 331
The Inventory 331
Medical Records 337
Bylaws, Rules, and Regulations 338
Credentialing 340
Physician Involvement 341
Dealing with Patients 345
Summary 345

Chapter 15—The Medical Staff and Risk Management 347
Michael B. Guthrie

Functions of the Medical Staff 347
Medical Components of Risk Management 348
Clinicians and Risk Managers 349
Role of Physicians on the Medical Staff 350
Components of Risk Management 351
Being Chicken Costs Money 352
A Model for Change 353

Special Concerns of the Medical Staff 354
Good Guys and Gals Don't Get Sued 356
Informed Consent 357
Summary 359

Chapter 16—Nursing and Risk Management 361
Janine Fiesta

Nursing Liability 361
Risk Management Goals 363
The Need for Documentation 364
Reasonable Standards of Practice 364
Hospitals' Corporate Liability 365
The Nurse as Defendant 367
Other Areas of Liability 368
Refusal of Treatment 369

Chapter 17—Physicians' Office Liability Exposure 371
John R. Tanner

Office Design and Function 371
Workers' Compensation and State Statutes 373
Professional Liability 374
Patient Care by Others than the Physician 378
Credentialing of Employees 379
Transfer of Care to Other Physicians 380
Consultations Involving Other Physicians 381
Bill Collections 381
Loss Prevention and Loss Reduction 382
Risk Management 383
Summary 383

Chapter 18—Management and Leadership for Risk Managers 385
Clayton W. Boringer

Management Structure: Theories and Models 386
Human Needs and Life Style Theories 396
Managers and the Management Process 399
Leadership and Leadership Styles 402
Leadership and Risk Managers 405
Summary 409

Chapter 19—Quality Assurance and Risk Management 411
Steven L. Salman

The AHA Task Force 411
The Circles and Their Roles 413
Similarities and Differences 414
Tools for Joint Use 416
Role of the Board of Trustees 416

Chapter 20—Patient's Personal Items and Valuables: The Bailment Issue 421
Steven L. Salman

Legal Issues 421
Policy Issues 423
Summary 429
Appendix 20-A 430

Chapter 21—Computers in Risk Management 435
Steven L. Salman

Uses in a Hospital 435
Case Files and Other Materials 436
Equipment Management 436
Incident Report Analysis 437
Credentialing, Legal, Insurance 438
Claims Management and Settlements 439
Summary 440

Chapter 22—The Predisposition to File Claims: The Patients' Perspective 441
Irwin Press

Empirical Evidence Lacking 442
Errors not the Sole Cause 442
Patient Perception and Claims 443
Predisposing and Precipitating Factors 445
Patient-Generated Predisposing Factors 445
The Myth of Medical Perfection 446
Illness versus Disease 446
Hospital Values 450
Clinical Organization 452
Recommendations 455
Summary 457

APPENDIXES—MISCELLANEOUS SAMPLE POLICIES AND PROCEDURES **463**

Appendix A—Nursing Policy and/or Procedure: Charting **465**

Appendix B—Nursing Policy and/or Procedure: Informed Consent **471**

Appendix C—Standard Policy and/or Procedure: Authorization for Emergency/Outpatient Treatment **477**

Appendix D—Standard Policy and/or Procedure: Private Duty Nurse Policy **481**

Index **487**

About the Editors **517**

About the Contributors **519**

Foreword

The organization of risk management departments in hospitals and other health care facilities is a relatively recent development. The medical malpractice crisis of the mid-1970s gave considerable impetus to the growth of such departments. Developments since then have heightened the awareness of the importance of this function. The scope of risk management activities has grown continually; few, if any, hospital departments are exempt from potential risk problems.

The rapid growth of risk management departments as well as the increasing scope of their activities have created some uncertainty about the functions that should be under the purview of an organized department. On the other hand, the entire spectrum of activities must be coordinated and monitored if optimal results are to be achieved. The pervasiveness of potential risks requires that a risk management department closely integrate its functioning with all other departments of the hospital. It is extremely important that those managing and working in risk management appreciate how a given department's activities interface with other sectors of the hospital.

Costs of health care, and specifically care in hospitals, continues to be a concern as competition intensifies. As new health services are brought under the umbrella of the hospital organizational structure, the resulting complexities further complicate the type of risk that the institutions must address. The pressure of rising costs requires that hospitals safeguard their assets through measures that minimize the risk of loss of its limited resources. Thus, both internal and external forces are combining to create an ever-changing environment to which the processes of risk management must be ready to adapt.

Employees are entering the risk management arena with a wide variety of experience and education and with an equal variety of expectations. This often results in a lack of common perception of what constitutes a viable and effective program. The potential benefits then are not achieved and a clear direction is difficult to identify.

This *Handbook of Health Care Risk Management* provides a timely resource for those entering the field as well as for those already functioning in it. It is a valuable reference for students and faculty in university programs in hospital and health care administration. It develops a firm foundation in the theoretical principles as well as the practical application of those principles to an organizational setting.

Having identified the salient issues in risk management, the editors, Steven L. Salman and Glenn T. Troyer, have brought together the contributions of many authorities in the field to address these issues. To that they have added their own contributions in several chapters. The early chapters provide a solid insight into the health care system, hospital organization and fiscal management, the concepts, processes, and functions of a hospital risk management program. These stress the structural dimensions as well as the importance of building a program on values held by the organization—its institutional ethics. Troyer's chapter on the concept of risk lays the foundation for an understanding of the importance of risk management. Salman's chapter on quality assurance and risk management (Chapter 19) is especially helpful in clarifying the areas of overlap in the two programs as well as their uniqueness.

A strong thread running through the early part of the book (as well as Chapter 15) is the emphasis on physician and medical staff involvement in the risk management program. The case is well established that the active inclusion of physicians can provide benefits to them and to patients and hospitals. The book stresses a multidisciplinary approach to risk management wherein everyone concerned understands their role and responsibility.

The later chapters (plus Chapter 7) analyze a number of insurance-related issues and how they can be dealt with in the overall risk management program. Without trying to treat the issue of insurance in its entirety, these chapters do lead to an appreciation of the concepts, pitfalls, and complexities of the utilization of insurance in an integrated program. Irwin Press, in Chapter 22, the patient's perspective, gives valuable insight into the predisposition to file claims. His analysis, taken to heart, will go a long way in achieving success in any risk management program.

This *Handbook on Health Care Risk Management* will be helpful in orienting and preparing individuals to function in a risk management program and also will serve as an excellent reference on a continuing basis. To the extent that its overall concepts and processes are put into practice, the ultimate contribution will be improved care for the patient.

Paul R. Donnelly, Ph.D.
Professor, Hospital and Health Care Administration
St. Louis University, St. Louis, Mo.
Chairman of the Board
Sisters of Charity Health Care Systems, Inc.

Preface

For all practical purposes, hospital risk management had its birth during the ''malpractice crisis'' of the mid-1970s. Though risk management had been a concept in other industries prior to that time, it received little acceptance in the health care industry until malpractice claims escalated and malpractice insurance was either unavailable or very costly.

Some states, such as Florida, took drastic measures and required hospitals to employ risk managers. However, the lack of experienced risk managers was not fully appreciated at that time. Before the statutory requirement date, many Florida hospitals advertised in local newspapers, ''Wanted, experienced hospital risk manager'' and were surprised when there was little or no response.

Additionally, those who began to fill these new positions had varied backgrounds. Some had been in hospital administration, some came directly out of graduate programs in hospital administration. Others with no health care background came from the insurance industry, while still others came from the legal profession, the medical profession, the nursing profession, law enforcement, local fire departments, insurance brokerage firms, and many other types of business and health care fields. It became apparent these individuals brought no common body of knowledge to health care risk management. While each may have had expertise in a single area, few had broad expertise in the areas necessary for effective risk management.

In the late 1970s and very early 1980s, ample professional liability insurance was available; premiums became depressed and hospitals' interest in risk management programs began to wane. Because the benefits of risk management were difficult to quantify, premiums became very inexpensive, and hospitals found it difficult to justify risk management programs. However, in the mid-1980s a second malpractice crisis began to appear in proportions that were never dreamed of in the mid-1970s. Risk management was once again recognized as the hospital's tool to begin managing and controlling this crisis. Again, individuals with little or no related background were pressed into service.

In light of this recent history, this book has several purposes. First, it provides guidelines for those thrown into the melee of hospital risk management for the first time, particularly those with no hospital background. A portion of this book attempts to explain to the nonhealth care management professional how the health care delivery and financing system operates in this country. Another portion for those lacking legal background deals with the legal system in this country. The balance of the book deals specifically with risk management, insurance, claims, and related areas that fall within the risk management function.

Some of the early chapters may, indeed, be a review for those who have strong administrative backgrounds or graduate degrees; the later chapters may be more useful to such people. However, someone with an insurance background and no in-house hospital experience may find the early chapters very useful.

The second purpose of this book is to serve as a reference and handbook for experienced risk managers in the field and administrators responsible for risk management programs. It cannot be an answer to all problems, but it can serve as a guideline for the process of problem resolution.

The third purpose is to serve as a textbook that exposes emerging hospital managers to risk management concepts and principals. Typically, those graduating from graduate health administration programs in the past have had little or no exposure to the concept of risk management. This book offers that kind of exposure and background, so that when they assume their responsibilities in hospitals and other health care facilities, they will have a frame of reference from which to operate.

While it was the fulfillment of these three purposes that provided the framework for this book, it was the sincere desire to provide a meaningful publication for today's risk managers that provided the impetus.

Glenn T. Troyer
Steven L. Salman

Chapter 1

Organization of the Health Care Delivery System in the U.S.

Robert M. Saywell, Jr. and Gerald J. McHugh

An ancient Chinese curse often placed on one's enemy reads, "May you live in interesting times." Whether or not people live their "definitely interesting" times under this curse or whether they interpret it as a favorable wish to be placed on their friends depends on how individuals confront and deal with the future and, in particular, the challenges present in the organization and delivery of health care today. What society does today to meet these challenges certainly will affect what occurs far into the future. Many social scientists claim that events in the past serve as a stage for the future and that a thorough understanding of past events is necessary to better understand the present and prepare for the future.

While change has always been present in society, there is no question that the pace of social, economic, political, and technological change has accelerated in the last three or four decades. It is vital, then, that individuals who are working as (or who have plans to become) part of the operations staff of a health care institution have a basic knowledge of the health care system in the United States and the changes that have occurred and probably emerge in the future.

Another ancient Chinese proverb states that "the beginning of wisdom is the ability of a person to state precisely what you mean." With this in mind, a definition of the term system is in order. A system can be thought of as a group of integrated, coordinated, established, specialized components all working together toward some common purpose or goal. Many will argue that the term "health care system" is a misnomer and may be overly ambitious and optimistic in the sense that many critics call the program in the United States a "nonsystem." A system implies a certain set of defined boundaries, a set of established components, and a clearly defined and recognized pattern of interrelationships among the many pieces.

While it can be argued that the system is extremely complex and involves many parts in both the private and public sectors, in the authors' opinion it is not without purpose and is not chaotic to the point that it can be truly classified as a nonsystem.

For this reason, the term "health care system" is used here to describe the mechanism for the provision and delivery of health care services in the United States. While continual evaluation and reorganization are needed, health care still is part of a larger social system and should be thought of and appraised in this manner.

BASIC COMPONENTS AND LEVELS OF CARE

The health care system consists of two principal components: institutional care (hospitals, nursing homes, and other facilities providing inpatient care) and ambulatory care (noninstitutional or outpatient care). Each of these provides service at various complexity levels within the system. For a system to function as a system, it should attempt to meet the health needs of the people in its environment. This goal, then, becomes the purpose of the system.

It has become apparent over time that most health care can be provided on an ambulatory or walk-in basis and ideally should be available to all people within some reasonable time and distance boundary. These ambulatory services comprise what generally is referred to as primary health care. It has been estimated that 80 percent of care can be provided at this level. It includes such activities as the diagnosis and treatment of uncomplicated illnesses and diseases; preventive services; case-finding/screening services; minor surgery (now referred to as ambulatory surgery); home health care services; relatively minor nonemergent injury treatment (not requiring extensive specialized equipment or personnel); and diagnosis, restorative, and preventive dental services.

Some patients, however, will require more specialized care or even hospitalization and thus will need the resources found at the secondary health care level. Secondary health care refers to the medical/surgical treatment or diagnostic care of more complicated chronic and acute conditions and includes such activities as inpatient admission to a hospital or nursing home; emergency care requiring extensive, specialized equipment and personnel; consultation on an ambulatory basis by a medical specialist such as ophthalmologist, neurologist, etc; and medical/surgical dental intervention.

An even smaller number of persons will require services available at the more specialized medical centers, referred to as the tertiary level of health care delivery. Tertiary care generally is available at larger community teaching hospitals or university medical centers and includes services such as open heart surgery, neurosurgery, organ transplants, etc. It is at this level that various resources are joined to meet the combined needs of medical care, medical research, and medical education.

To be complete, a health system must have not only a universally acceptable purpose or goal, e.g., providing quality medical care to all who require it, but also sets of recognized formal and informal linkages (interrelationships) among the various levels of care—primary, secondary, and tertiary. This coordination is vital if the system is to be capable of integrating the services it provides, not only for patient care but also to meet national medical research and education goals.

The individual health care services or activities provided in each of the three levels can be further subdivided into numerous categories depending on what the services are, where they are provided, who provides them, and who receives them. For example, there are services involving public health care, ambulatory care, inpatient hospital care, long-term (extended) care, and mental health care. Each of these activities can be examined along the lines described above—who, what, and where. For purposes here, these terms are defined as follows.

Public Health/Preventive Health Care

This refers to the attempt to control or prevent disease and promote or improve health through organized community efforts. Public health includes activities in which the community offers medical services both to special groups of individuals and to the entire populace at large. These services can be provided by local or state government or by physicians and allied health personnel working in the private sector.

Ambulatory Care

This refers to services provided to individuals presenting themselves for personal health care and who are neither bedridden nor currently admitted to any health care institution. These services can be of a treatment nature or preventive in scope. An ambulatory care visit involves a direct personal exchange between an ambulatory patient and a physician or a staff member working under the physician's supervision for the purpose of acquiring health services.

Inpatient Hospital Care

This refers to the services provided in a hospital setting to persons formally admitted as inpatients to receive observation, care, diagnosis, and/or treatment. The care can be provided at a facility at the primary, secondary, or tertiary level.

Long-Term Care

This refers to the extended-care services provided in a nursing home or other nonhospital setting to patients who require some degree of nursing supervision.

Mental Health Care

This refers to ambulatory care services provided to patients with a suspected or verified diagnosis of a mental disorder. Included in this definition are patients who have psychosis, neurosis, personality disorder (including alcoholism and drug dependence), or any other nonpsychotic mental disorder.

In turn, each of these activities can be divided further into specific categories of treatment for acute and chronic conditions. An acute condition is defined as a morbid condition with a relatively sudden or recent onset (within three months of the visit) and involves either medical attention or restricted activity. A chronic condition can be defined as a morbid condition that has lasted for three months or longer. The care for a chronic condition is of a regular, maintenance nature. The individual acute or chronic condition also could be examined along the lines of what, who, and where the treatment is provided or utilized. However, this chapter does not examine health care at that level of detail.

THE FOUR Ps

The health care system in the United States is not based on any single central governmental organization or authority structure, as is the case in most industrialized nations. However, there are identifiable power and control points and even though it often is difficult to recognize and describe the system, its boundaries, and its linkages, it does exist.

For purposes of both description and evaluation, the individual components of the health care system—from the two major ones, institutional care and ambulatory care—to individuals' use of the service can be described further in terms of the four Ps: patients, providers, payers, and the public. The four Ps provide a more comprehensive view of the system than the what-who-where questions because they include how and who pays for the care. Each level of care (primary, secondary, and tertiary) and indeed down to an individual acute or chronic diagnosis can be analyzed separately in terms of the patients served, the providers involved with the delivery of the care, how the services are paid for, and the extent to which the government or public sector is involved with both the financing and/or provision of the service.

Patients served refers to the general characteristics of the population either served or eligible to participate in a particular component of the health care system. Characteristics of interest include age, race, income, education level, family size, place of residence, program eligibility, etc.

Providers refer both to the actual health practitioner (e.g., the physician, dentist, optometrist, pharmacist, podiatrist, veterinarian, and registered nurse) and/or the site of the visit (e.g., the hospital, physician's office, dental office, outpatient clinic, emergency room).

Payers refer to the broad categories of health care payment:

- private health insurance (e.g., coverage provided by nongovernment sources including consumers, insurance companies, private industry, philanthropic organizations)
- government health insurance (e.g., Medicare, Medicaid, military or Veterans Administration health benefits, Workers' Compensation)
- an assortment of other governmental coverage such as the Title V program, Civilian Health and Medical Program of the Uniform Services (CHAMPUS), CHAMPVA (the Veterans Administration program), no-fault (casualty), vocational rehabilitation, government medical research grant, or legal hold (prisoner in custody)
- self-pay categories in which the major share of the total costs for an episode is expected to be paid by the patient, spouse, family, or next of kin, and not by any public or private third party payer.

Public refers to the extent that the public sector (federal, state, and local government) is involved in the provision or financing of health care.

This chapter concentrates on the institutional component of the health system, essentially excluding the noninstitutional component (e.g., public/preventive health, ambulatory care, etc.). (References at the end of this chapter offer a more comprehensive view of the health care system.) The chapter examines the delivery of health care in hospitals and nursing homes from the perspective of: (1) their historical development and evolution and (2) their present characteristics in terms of size, ownership, utilization, etc. It does not discuss such areas as what makes the overall system perform well or not well, or where—such as in the primary or tertiary care level or within any acute/chronic diagnosis—nor does it provide managers and others with any of the answers, solutions, or techniques that they might use to solve problems.

The goal here is to provide a concise, accurate picture of one part of the large, overall health care system. It is designed to develop a better understanding of the health care environment and to indicate where a specific segment of the system has come from, where it is now, and, perhaps most importantly, to help predict where it is going. How individuals can better prepare for the future is discussed in other chapters.

U.S. HEALTH SERVICES SYSTEM: AN OVERVIEW

Considering the historical development of health services in the United States and the philosophy upon which they are grounded, it is not surprising that the overall system actually consists of a series of somewhat uncoordinated, nonintegrated smaller subsystems. It generally is believed that while some services, such as a segment of primary care, may be viewed individually as being a well-structured, integrated system, the ability of these smaller parts to be coordinated with other subsystems becomes the main problem in attempting to develop and operate a total system.

THE HEALTH CARE SYSTEM: A MACROVIEW

Beginning in the early 1700s, the utilization and provision of health care was viewed by Americans for generations as a private matter resting primarily with the individual. The role of the public sector, until relatively recently, was kept to a minimum. While health care was considered by most to be a right, individuals still were primarily responsible for procuring their own health care, although some free medical care was provided as early as 1700 in facilities called infirmaries or almshouses. The Colonial period's hospitals and nursing homes often were sponsored and operated by churches. By the late 1800s and early 1900s, the rapid advance of medical science and technology led to the establishment of the hospital as the center of the health care system and indeed, by the early 1960s, health care had become "big business" in America.

The health care industry today is the second largest single employer in terms of number of persons at work when compared with 150 others. In 1981 it employed nearly 5.6 million persons, or about 6.1 percent of the nonagricultural civilian labor force.[1] In 1982, health care expenditures totaled $322.4 billion, for an average expenditure of $1,365 per person, and comprised 10.5 percent of the Gross National Product (GNP). These indicators have increased greatly since 1950 (Table 1–1).[2]

In 1983, the Department of Health and Human Services (DHHS) Office of Research and Demonstrations estimated that if the current trend continued, national health care expenditures would consume 12.0 percent of the GNP by 1990. This continued growth relative to other areas (e.g., education, welfare, defense, housing) makes it all the more important to understand the pressures and forces behind the increasing costs of health care and how this increasing demand during a time when the nation and the world are facing ever scarcer resources, will affect the individual and society both in terms of health status and other quality-of-life areas.

An examination of national health care expenditures by source of payment (private sector vs. public sector) reveals that the public share has increased by 55.6 percent since 1950, from 27.2 percent in 1950 to 42.3 percent in 1980 (Table 1–2). That means that the government sector was spending 42 cents of every health-care dollar, and all indications were that this would continue to grow in the next decade.

Table 1–1 GNP and National Health Expenditures, U.S.
(Selected Years 1929–1982)

Year	GNP (in billions)	National health expenditures: Amount (in billions)	% of GNP	Amount per capita
1929	$ 103.4	$ 3.6	$ 3.5	$ 29
1935	72.2	2.9	4.0	23
1940	100.0	4.0	4.0	30
1950	286.5	12.7	4.4	82
1955	400.0	17.7	4.4	105
1960	506.5	26.9	5.3	146
1965	691.0	41.7	6.0	211
1970	992.7	74.7	7.5	358
1975	1,549.2	132.7	8.6	604
1980	2,633.1	249.0	9.5	1,075
1981	2,937.7	286.6	9.8	1,225
1982	3,059.3	322.4	10.5	1,365

Source: Derived from *Health and Prevention Profile—United States, 1983*, p. 177, National Center for Health Statistics, Public Health Service.

Table 1–2 National Health Expenditures, by Source of Funds, U.S.
(Selected Years 1929–1982)

		Source of funds					
		Private			Public		
Year	All health expenditures (in billions)	Amount (in billions)	Amount per capita	% of total	Amount (in billions)	Amount per capita	% of total
1929	$ 3.6	$ 3.2	$ 25	86.4%	$ 0.5	$ 4	13.6%
1935	2.9	2.4	18	80.8	0.6	4	19.2
1940	4.0	3.2	24	79.7	0.8	6	20.3
1950	12.7	9.2	60	72.8	3.4	22	27.2
1955	17.7	13.2	78	74.3	4.6	27	25.7
1960	26.9	20.3	110	75.3	6.6	36	24.7
1965	41.7	31.0	156	74.1	10.8	55	25.9
1970	74.7	46.9	225	62.8	27.8	133	37.2
1975	132.7	76.5	348	57.7	56.2	255	42.3
1980	249.0	143.6	620	57.7	105.4	455	42.3
1982	322.4	185.6	786	57.6	136.8	579	42.4

Source: Derived from *Health and Prevention Profile—United States, 1983*, p. 184, National Center for Health Statistics, Public Health Service.

Expenditures for personal health care include all health services and supplies other than prepayment, administration, and government public health activities. They do not include research and construction activities. Personal health care involves hospital care, physician services, dental services, nursing home care, other professional services, drugs and drug sundries, eyeglasses and appliances, etc. These accounted for 89.0 percent ($286.9 billion) of the 1982 total for such spending. As Table 1–3 demonstrates, this distribution has been fairly stable since 1950.

From 1950 to 1982, the average annual percentage change in national personal health care expenditures was 10.8; from 1950 to 1960, it was 8.1 and from 1960 to 1965 it was 8.6. However, following the passage of the Medicare and Medicaid legislation in 1965, which provided financial assistance to the elderly and the poor in the purchase of their health care, the annual rate increased dramatically to 12.7 percent (1965–1970), 12.4 percent (1970–1975), 13.8 percent (1975–1980), and 14 percent (1980–1982). This trend indicates that Americans are spending greater relative and absolute amounts of money each year on health care.

Table 1–4 shows that government's share of personal health care expenditures increased from 22.4 percent in 1950 to 39.7 percent in 1980. Third party payment (including private, philanthropy and industry, and government-public health insurance) increased its share from 34.5 percent in 1950 to 67.1 percent in 1980; conversely, direct out-of-pocket expenditures (self-pay) fell from 65.5 percent in 1950 to 32.9 percent in 1980. This increase in payments by various levels of government and by public and private third party payers indicates a major shift in the health care industry, both from an economic perspective and from a philosophical/policy view. While individuals still are responsible for choosing and obtaining their own health care, much of the responsibility for payment lies with persons other than the recipients. The philosophy that health care is a right and should be made available to all people who need it, as included in the goals of a health care system, may have produced much of the impetus behind this change.

Hospital expenditures continue to comprise the largest share of the health care dollar—42 percent ($135.4 billion) in 1982 (Table 1–3). This increased from 30.4 percent in 1950, 33.8 percent in 1960, 37.2 percent in 1970, and 40.3 percent in 1980. This is evidence of hospitals' increased role in the delivery of health care. Per capita hospital expenditures can be calculated by dividing the total amount spent for hospital care by the U.S. resident population (227,156,000 in 1980). Per capita hospital expenditures were as follows: $25.53 in 1950, $50.52 in 1960, $136.34 in 1970, and $441.75 in 1980. Again, this shows in part, the increased involvement of hospitals.

Nursing home expenditures, as a percentage of national health care expenditures, had the greatest increase from 1950 to 1980 (1.5 percent to 8.3 percent); expenditures soared from $190.5 million to $26.8 billion (Table 1–3). Per capita

Table 1–3 National Health Expenditures and % Distribution, by Type of Expenditure, U.S.
(Selected Years 1950–1982)

Type of expenditure	*Year*							
	1950	*1960*	*1965*	*1970*	*1975*	*1980*	*1981*	*1982*
				Amount in billions				
Total	$12.7	$26.9	$41.7	$74.7	$132.7	$249.0	$286.6	$322.4
				% distribution				
All expenditures	100.0%	100.0%	100.0%	100.0%	100.0%	100.0%	100.0%	100.0%
Health services & supplies	92.4	93.6	91.6	92.8	93.7	95.2	95.4	95.6
Personal health care	86.0	88.0	85.7	87.3	88.0	88.1	88.8	89.0
Hospital care	30.4	33.8	33.3	37.2	39.3	40.3	41.2	42.0
Physician services	21.7	21.1	20.3	19.2	18.8	18.8	19.1	19.2
Dentist services	7.6	7.4	6.7	6.4	6.2	6.2	6.0	6.0
Nursing home care	1.5	2.0	5.0	6.3	7.6	8.3	8.4	8.5
Other professional services	3.1	3.2	2.5	2.1	2.0	2.3	2.2	2.2
Drugs and drug sundries	13.6	13.7	12.4	10.7	9.0	7.8	7.4	6.9
Eyeglasses and appliances	3.9	2.9	2.8	2.6	2.4	2.1	2.0	1.8
Other health services	4.2	4.0	2.7	2.8	2.8	2.4	2.4	2.4
Expenses for prepayment	3.6	4.1	4.0	3.6	3.3	4.3	3.9	4.0
Government public health activities	2.9	1.5	1.9	1.9	2.4	2.8	2.7	2.7
Research and construction	7.6	6.4	8.4	7.2	6.3	4.8	4.6	4.4
Research	0.9	2.5	3.6	2.6	2.5	2.1	2.0	1.8
Construction	6.7	3.9	4.8	4.6	3.8	2.6	2.6	2.6

Source: Derived from *Health and Prevention Profile—United States, 1983*, p. 187, National Center for Health Statistics, Public Health Service.

Table 1–4 Personal Health Care Expenditures and % Distribution, by Source of Payment, U.S. (Selected Years 1929–1982)

			Source of payment, %							
				Third party payment						
							Government			
Year	All personal health care expenditures (in billions)*	Per capita	All sources	Direct payment	Total	Private health insurance	Philanthropy and industry	Total	Federal	State and local
1929	$ 3.2	$ 26	100.0%	88.4%	11.6%	____%	2.6%	9.0%	2.7%	6.3%
1935	2.7	21	100.0	82.4	17.6	____	2.8	14.7	3.4	11.3
1940	3.5	26	100.0	81.3	18.7	____	2.6	16.1	4.1	12.0
1950	10.9	70	100.0	65.5	34.5	9.1	2.9	22.4	10.4	12.0
1955	15.7	93	100.0	58.1	41.9	16.1	2.8	23.0	10.5	12.5
1960	23.7	129	100.0	54.9	45.1	21.1	2.3	21.8	9.3	12.5
1965	35.8	181	100.0	54.9	48.2	24.4	2.2	21.6	10.1	11.4
1975	116.8	531	100.0	33.4	66.6	25.8	1.4	39.5	26.9	12.6
1980	219.4	947	100.0	32.9	67.1	26.0	1.4	39.7	28.6	11.2
1981	254.6	1,088	100.0	32.2	67.8	26.2	1.4	40.2	29.2	10.9
1982	286.9	1,215	100.0	31.5	68.5	26.7	1.5	40.3	29.2	11.1

*Includes all expenditures for health services and supplies other than expenses for prepayment, administration, and government public health activities.

Source: Derived from *Health and Prevention Profile—United States, 1983*, p. 186, National Center for Health Statistics, Public Health Service.

nursing home figures were as follows: $1.26 in 1950, $2.99 in 1960, $23.09 in 1970, and $90.98 in 1980. This trend indicates the increased use of nursing homes since 1970 in particular, and partly represents expanded sharing of expenditures by the government and the growing age of the population.

THE HEALTH CARE SYSTEM: PATIENTS' PERSPECTIVE

With the four Ps framework as a basis, along with the two major components—institutional care and ambulatory care—the health care system can be described further by viewing it from the patients' perspective. The natural order is to use the payer category to establish subcategories within the population groupings, then examine how each of these payer/patient groups uses the previously defined services. Examination of a population by type of payment defines individuals simply as those who can afford health care vs. those who cannot. Those who can either have sufficient income to be self-pay purchasers (direct, out-of-pocket), have sufficient third party insurance coverage that will pay for their care, or (as in most cases) have both. The group of those who cannot pay includes individuals who do not have the personal resources or third party coverage and thus can be described as being medically indigent.

Obviously, people can move from one category to another at any time and could even be in both categories at the same time. For example, an individual who can afford the most routine primary care could become medically indigent when confronted with a catastrophic illness that results in large expenses at the tertiary level. Some persons have all their care provided in and/or paid for by one system, e.g., the military health care system.

Two population subcomponents must be examined: Medicare and Medicaid recipients. These individuals need to be included, not because they represent participants in an independent, different system but because they constitute a separate population capable of behaving financially as if they were members of the group able to purchase health care out of pocket or with health insurance coverage. The three major patient-based health care system groups (as adapted from Williams and Torrens[3]) are:

1. middle upper-income patients
2. low-income/medically indigent patients
3. government-provided and financed health care patients
   a. Medicare recipients (Title 18)
   b. Medicaid recipients (Title 19).

The Middle/Upper Income Patient System

The middle/upper-income patient health care system is by far the largest of the three and the one with which most Americans are directly involved. For this reason, many refer to it as the one that best represents the true American system of health care delivery. Therefore, it is important to understand its workings not only because of its size and population but because it has been praised as the best medical care system in the United States and, by many, as perhaps the best in the world. It differs from the two other patient-based systems in three ways.

First, as with the overall health care system, it is not a formal, delineated system. Individuals or families combine their own sets of personal knowledge and economic resources to meet their health care needs. The way they combine the health resources to meet these identified needs—that is, the selection and ultimate use of personnel and facilities—will vary with each specific medical situation. Individuals with the same health problem make decisions differently and thus select and use different amounts of services. For example, there are wide variations in individuals' utilization rates of both physicians and institutions on the basis of regional (geographic), cultural (ethnic), and other socioeconomic (income; etc.) differences. To illustrate: in 1981, hospital discharges for all patients per 1,000 population ranged from a low of 26.3 in the West to a high of 55.1 in the South, with a national average of 40.1.

The second difference is that the services offered to participants in this system generally are coordinated and often are provided by a single physician working in a private practice setting as opposed to a clinic in a hospital. This system can be said to concentrate on the private practice physician and the fee-for-service method of payment. The recipient is expected to pay for the service (either out of pocket or through a third party) and the fee is determined by the provider.

The third difference is that the purchase of health care in the middle/upper income system is financed primarily by personal, nongovernmental funds—out of pocket as a direct expense or through third party payers (private health insurance, philanthropy, and industry)—with the premiums paid in part or in full by the individuals. There is little reliance on the government for any form of payment, either for the service itself or for the insurance premium.

The services just defined can be examined further with respect to who delivers them and who pays for them.

Public Health/Preventive Health Care

Such service is provided in this system through two avenues: (1) services aimed at the entire population and (2) services aimed at individuals.

The first involves such services as water purification and fluoridation, waste disposal, air pollution control, and food sanitation that are provided by local and state government through their public health departments. These are available to all people, regardless of their ability or willingness to pay or even to use the services, and thus are found in all three major health care systems.

The second involves such services as well-baby examinations, immunizations and vaccinations, cervical cancer examinations, and family planning. These generally are provided by individual physicians in private practice and paid for with out-of-pocket personal funds because most third party insurance coverage does not include them in its benefit package.

Ambulatory Care Services

These generally are provided by private practice physicians in their offices. While some patients may tend to use family practice physicians for much of their ambulatory care needs, others call on a wide array of medical specialists. For example, they choose to use individual primary care internists, pediatricians, and OB-GYN physicians. Regardless of the medical specialization used, one main characteristic stands out in this system: Much of the payment for ambulatory care is paid as an out-of-pocket expenditure because third party health insurance tends to have limited coverage for such services.

Hospital Care Inpatient Services

In this patient system, these usually are obtained at a local, voluntary, nonprofit hospital (defined earlier as at the secondary health care level). However, as the severity of the medical/surgical condition increases, patients tend to move toward larger, tertiary care teaching hospitals affiliated with a medical school.

One characteristic worth noting in this system is that as the individual moves from outpatient (ambulatory) care to inpatient (institutional) care, there is a distinct shift from out-of-pocket personal expenditure to reliance on a third party payer, typically a nongovernmental source. While patient knowledge and resources are important in making the ultimate decision on service use, the actual decision on where to obtain inpatient care most often made is by the admitting physician and generally is based on where the doctor has hospital privileges.

Long-Term Care Institutional Services

In the past, these were obtained from hospitals, but with increasing utilization review activities during the 1960s and 1970s to monitor the use of hospital resources, there has been increased pressure to shift long-term care patients from the more costly hospital facility to other, less costly settings (e.g., various levels of nursing homes and other extended-care settings). If middle/upper income patients require long-term inpatient care, it generally is provided by nursing homes (skilled nursing or intermediate care facilities of 50 to 150 beds, operated privately and for profit by either a single proprietor or a small group of investors. While there is no uniform definition for a nursing home, since minimum standards vary from state to state, a skilled nursing facility provides the most intensive nursing care available outside a hospital; an intermediate care facility provides nursing services to patients who require neither skilled nursing facility care nor hospital nursing care but do need care beyond that provided at the maintenance level.[4]

Much of the cost of the long-term care is borne by the individual because, as with ambulatory care and individual public/preventive health services, there is relatively limited third party coverage for these nonhospital long-term inpatient needs.

Mental Health Care

Like the other services, this is obtained through a wide array of private sources as the care used by participants in this system tends to be provided by personnel and facilities in the private sector. Unlike the other services (e.g., inpatient hospital care), as the mental health problem becomes more serious, patients tend to rely more on care provided and/or financed by government.

In general, mental health services for a minor episode up to and including medium-term care inpatient services are from a private, nongovernmental unit and it is not until the need arises for long-term extended care for the chronic mentally ill that individuals in this system turn to the state mental hospital facility.

In summary, people in the middle/upper income health system have much control over their individual decisions on care. They tend to choose their own physicians, their own insurance plan, and to some extent to influence the choice of hospital and nursing home they use. In recent years, many new consumer choices in health care have developed, such as preferred provider organizations (PPOs) and health maintenance organizations (HMOs). Members of this health care system are not coerced or even legally mandated in choosing one form of health care delivery over another. It can be concluded that while ability to pay is the key factor that distinguishes between and defines the three systems, it is the actual level of individual consumer choice that becomes a major characteristic and is the primary difference among the three systems.

The Low-Income/Medically Indigent Patient System[5]

The second major health care system frequently is thought of as providing inferior care. As noted earlier, members of this system do not have the economic resources to behave as "typical" consumers since they have neither the income nor the insurance coverage to enter the health care market independently and purchase the needed services. While it has been argued that the poor often do not have the knowledge on which to choose the best or optimum combination of resources, there is little solid evidence of this.

In contrast to the middle/upper income patient system, no formal system is identified here. All persons entering this system in search of health care must create their own informal system and make decisions based on whatever health resources are available and knowledge they have of them. The major problem inherent in this system is that the poor often do not have the economic resources or knowledge of health care or of the system to select and purchase the quality of service that their condition requires. In this system, individuals are forced to consume what is available or offered to them. In other words, they have little or no choice.

The main characteristic of this system that differentiates it from the two others is that the majority of health care is provided by a local government unit (e.g., county or city hospitals, city nursing homes, local government health departments). Individuals in this system generally will not be provided with any degree of continuity of care and, in fact, can expect to be treated by a different provider for each episode of care or for each visit for a single episode.

Public Health/Preventive Health Care

These services are provided to the entire population of this system in the same manner as they are to those in the middle/upper income patient system. However, unlike persons in that system, low-income individuals receive their public/preventive health care services in medical clinics staffed and paid for by the local health department. These services include, for example, the vaccinations/inoculations that middle/upper income system participants typically receive from a private, office-based physician on a fee-for-service basis.

Ambulatory Care

These services are not always provided by an individual family physician, as in the first system, but often are received from allied health professionals and others who are not health providers (e.g., neighbors, friends, pharmacists, public health nurses, etc.) and generally take the form of advice and/or simple treatment remedies. When a physician consultation is required, the individual in this system tends to rely on a hospital emergency room at a city/county hospital. The emergency room serves as the initial point of entry into the medical care system for this individual and serves as the referral point for other ambulatory service locations such as hospital outpatient clinics.

Hospital Inpatient Services

These generally are obtained in a city/county hospital or from a voluntary, nonprofit community hospital that has an affiliated medical teaching program.

Admission to the facility, as noted, usually is through the emergency room or the facility's outpatient clinics.

Long-Term Care Institutional Services

These have been described as somewhat lacking for members of the middle/upper income system but are relatively nonexistent for low-income/medically indigent individuals. Much of such services in this system are provided as hospital inpatient care, as evidenced by the fact that the poor tend to have longer lengths of stay. This finding partially reflects the difficulty in achieving an appropriate and acceptable discharge setting for poor patients. This situation is further aggravated by the fact that some of the long-term care costs of the medically indigent population are absorbed by local welfare funds (not to be confused with Medicaid, Title 19 recipients, who are discussed later) while middle/upper income system individuals tend to be self-pay (out-of-pocket) patients. One of the inherent problems is that low-income/medically indigent individuals do not have the economic resources (either private or public funds) to cover the costs of the long-term care fully. Thus, many providers are reluctant to become involved with these individuals because of low reimbursement rates, the amount of paper work needed to receive public reimbursement, and the relatively high failure-to-pay rate.

Mental Illness Services

Those provided to the low-income/medically indigent individual are similar to the other services used by this group. The service generally is obtained from the public, local government provider without direct concern for the continuity of care.

In summary, it can be concluded that members of this group have little or no choice in their purchase of health services and must rely on others to finance much of their care utilization. Thus, since they do not have much economic power, they are forced to accept whatever health care is available and often may not receive the most appropriate type of services.

The Government-Provided Health Care System

The third system examined—involving government-provided health care—provides the least amount of choice to participants from the standpoint of their selecting providers (personnel and facility). This can be further divided into two parts: the United States military health care system and the Veterans Administration health care system. Each has similar characteristics but has different eligible populations. Selected characteristics of this system are discussed in this section because they are not included in the subsequent sections dealing with health institutions (hospitals and nursing homes) in the private sector.

The United States military health care system provides inpatient and outpatient services primarily to active duty members of the Army, Navy, Air Force, Marine Corps, Coast Guard, and the Commissioned Corps of both the National Oceanic and Atmospheric Administration and the Public Health Service; their dependents; and retired members of these services. Health care is provided in the public sector by Department of Defense medical service resources and in the private sector through the Civilian Health and Medical Program of the Uniformed Services (CHAMPUS).[6] This insurance is designed to supplement the military health care system by paying for care for family members of active duty and retired military service personnel provided by the private sector when these services are not reasonably available at a local military installation.

In general, CHAMPUS pays for most physician charges for both inpatient and outpatient care and for most hospital services and medical supplies. It also pays for medical services obtained from sources other than hospitals. However, some types of care are not covered. For example, CHAMPUS for the most part does not cover dental, eye, or hearing examinations. It does not collect any premium payments from recipients; instead it shares certain medical bills. For example, for outpatient care, there is a 20 percent coinsurance payment after a $50 annual deductible ($100 for a family) for active duty dependents and a 25 percent coinsurance payment for retirees and survivors after the $50 annual deductible ($100 for a family).

The Department of Defense medical service resources include 161 hospitals and 310 ambulatory clinics located worldwide, staffed by more than 151,000 military and civilian health personnel. In fiscal year 1983, DOD requested a budget of $6.7 billion, with $4.5 billion for direct patient care (67.2 percent); $1.1 billion to operate the CHAMPUS program (16.4 percent); and, $1.1 billion for research, construction, and ancillary areas (16.4 percent).

The military health care system serves 9.3 to 10 million persons annually. This figure represents a gross estimate that includes all military retirees, State Department personnel, and civilians working for the Department of Defense, among others; it is only an estimate because many eligible persons may choose not to use this system. While theoretically eligible individuals have a choice whether to use this system, in reality active duty military personnel have little choice, unless of course, they desire to purchase care as self-pay patients. The administration of the system remains with the Surgeon General of each branch who is responsible for the services under that jurisdiction. The Office of the Assistant Secretary of Defense for Health Affairs has a monitoring and overseer function over all of the system. (Tables 1–5 and 1–6 present data on the military health care system.)

The Veterans Administration health care system provides eligible military veterans with free or highly subsidized health services, including hospital, ambulatory, and nursing home care. The Veterans Administration operates 172 hospital centers in the United States, 226 outpatient clinics, 101 nursing home

Table 1–5 U.S. Military Health Care Spending
(Selected Years, 1967–1984)

	(millions of dollars)				
	1967	*1970*	*1975*	*1980*	*1984*
CHAMPUS	$ 106	$ 264	$ 567	$ 712	$1,307
All other	1,453	1,637	2,742	3,940	6,198

Source: Office of the Secretary of Defense, Health Affairs, November 1984.

Table 1–6 Characteristics of Military Health Care Facilities
(FY 1983)

	U.S.	*Worldwide*
Hospital average daily patient load[1]	12,694	14,821
Hospital admissions	783,150	924,501
Outpatient visits	32,456,862	36,581,877
Average length of stay	5.9 days	5.8 days
Operating hospital beds	15,963	19,034
Hospitals (approximate)[2]	131	168
Dental treatment rooms	1,256	1,430
Provider offices	9,118	10,883

1. Gross population served: 9.3–10 million (estimated).
2. Range of hospital size: 112 beds–1,000 beds.

Military Health Care Personnel

Active duty	*1976*	*1980*	*1983*	*1984 projected*
Physicians	10,914	11,695	12,670	12,869
Dentists	5,012	5,049	5,093	5,058
Nurse practitioners	—	—	512	566
Nurses	—	—	10,940	11,289
Optometrists	498	467	535	—

Source: Office of the Secretary of Defense, Health Affairs, November 1984.

units, and 16 domiciliaries (residences and homes). The VA also provides long-term care services under contract with more than 3,000 community-based nursing homes and subsidized care in 48 state veterans' homes when appropriate care is not available at a VA facility or is not economically feasible because of location. Most long-term care is provided in the non-VA facilities.

Most of the three million veterans receiving medical care from the VA either have service-connected disabilities or are financially unable to purchase medical care elsewhere. Eligible veterans are admitted and treated according to a set of priorities:

1. disabled veterans requiring treatment for a service-connected health problem
2. disabled veterans requiring care for a nonservice-connected problem
3. special categories of veterans such as those over age 65 (starting in 1970, all veterans over 65 became eligible for VA medical care regardless of their individual financial need) or those who are medically indigent below age 65.

About 70 percent of patients treated by the VA are not in the first category, having no service-connected health problems, and nearly 67 percent of the service-disabled veterans seen are treated for nonservice-connected problems. Few veterans who apply for medical care are ever turned away or denied treatment unless, of course, they are deemed not to require it. Of the approximately 30 million American veterans, only 10 percent (3 million) utilize VA medical services, as most (75 percent to 80 percent) do not meet the eligibility requirements and many of those who are eligible elect to use other facilities as they most likely have sufficient private or public insurance coverage to pay for medical services in the private sector. A large proportion of the VA patient population has no health insurance coverage. Because of the broad eligibility requirements for Title 18 (Medicare), only 10 percent to 15 percent of veterans 65 or older use the VA system.[7]

In 1982, the Veterans Administration expended $7,155,100 for medical care, up from $1,150,100 in 1965.[8] The VA budget constitutes about 1 percent of the federal budget and 0.2 percent of the nation's Gross National Product. For fiscal year 1984, its budget was $8.3 billion dollars for medical care, or 16 percent higher than 1983.[9] Approximately a third of the agency's budget is for providing and financing medical care. Of the 1982 expenditure of $7.155 billion, 63 percent was spent on hospital services, 19.4 percent on outpatient ambulatory care, 5.3 percent on VA-operated nursing homes and domiciliaries, 2.3 percent on community-based nursing homes, and 10 percent on all other categories (i.e., miscellaneous services and benefits, contract hospitals, education and training, subsidies to state veterans' facilities and the Civilian Health and Medical Program of the Veterans Administration (CHAMPVA).[10]

Comparing 1982 with similar data for 1965 indicates that of the $1.15 billion spent in 1965, 81.9 percent went to hospitals, 12 percent to outpatient services, 2.9 percent to VA nursing and domiciliary homes, nothing to community nursing homes, and 3.2 percent to all the other categories. Among the most apparent trends are: the reduction in the allocation to inpatient hospital services (81.9 percent to 63.0 percent), the rise in outpatient services (12 percent to 19.4 percent), and the increase in long-term care services (2.9 percent to 7.6 percent combined—community and VA-operated). This reflects both an increase in the number of patients being treated by the VA medical system and a rise in the number of veterans being treated in nursing homes and in outpatient clinics.

For example, after 1973, veterans without service-connected disabilities were permitted to use outpatient treatment services if that would eliminate the need for future hospitalization. In 1982, there were 15.9 million outpatient visits in the VA medical centers—a 75 percent increase since 1973. In addition, these medical centers recently began to offer hospital or nursing home alternative care programs such as geriatric day care, hospital-based home health care, and other residential care programs.

All of the 172 agency's medical centers are general medical hospitals, with surgical services provided at 136 of them and acute psychiatric care at 128. From 1973 to 1983, the number of acute care beds in the VA declined from 97,000 to 79,900 while the number of patients increased by 30 percent. Part of the drop in beds resulted from reductions in the need for psychiatric beds and in average length of stay. These declines occurred when the VA became more actively involved in the delivery of ambulatory care/extended care services.

During 1982–1983, the average occupancy rate in VA hospitals was 81 percent. This figure, which is 5 percentage points higher than the rate for community hospitals, is not surprising since 30 percent of the VA beds are devoted to psychiatric care and 30 percent of the designated medical beds are used for long-term care patients, many of whom probably could be treated in other, less costly facilities if more were available. Many VA centers have redesignated their acute care beds to intermediate care in order to provide for the more chronically ill patients.[11]

As noted earlier, the Veterans Administration pays for or subsidizes nursing home care in three settings: (1) VA owned and operated nursing homes, (2) community nursing homes providing care under contract with the VA, and (3) state-operated nursing homes, also under VA contract. In 1982, 35 percent of the agency's long-term care patients were in VA-owned facilities, 39 percent in community nursing homes, and the remaining 26 percent in state-operated nursing homes.

In 1982, the VA operated 9,125 nursing home beds—a 20 percent increase over 1977; the average length of stay was 1.3 years and 62 percent of the patients were 65 or older. An average of 9,525 veterans a day received care at community-based non-VA nursing homes. Reimbursement to these skilled or intermediate facilities is on a per diem basis and is limited to six months for all veterans except for those with service-connected disabilities, who are permitted unlimited time. The number treated in community nursing homes is about 1,000 more than the number residing in VA-owned nursing homes. Approximately 44 percent of the veterans receiving care in community nursing homes had service-connected disabilities; generally, veterans in such facilities do not require the intense skilled nursing treatment available in VA nursing homes.[12]

State veterans' homes are established and operated by individual states and are subsidized by the VA. In 1982, 11,100 veterans received care in state-operated nursing homes, a 29.1 percent increase over the 8,600 treated in 1977. The VA considers this program to be cost effective because the state shares the expense of caring for the veterans with the VA. In 1982, average daily census in state homes for veterans was 6,428. Patients in the state veterans' homes tend to average four years older than those in VA-operated facilities.[13]

Domiciliaries are homes for disabled veterans and are located at VA medical centers. To be eligible for admission, veterans must be chronically or permanently disabled and be unable to work or support themselves. In 1982, the VA provided domiciliary care for more than 14,500 persons and had an average daily census of 7,100, down from the 10,261 in 1977. This decline is caused in part by the increase in the number of nursing homes available to veterans.

VA ambulatory care services have grown considerably in recent years, increasing from about 9 million visits in 1972 to 15.9 million in 1982. The system also provided about 1.9 million patient visits to non-VA physicians, but this practice is available only under special circumstances. The typical veteran in the ambulatory care system utilizes an average of five visits a year. (Table 1–7 presents characteristics of the VA health care system.[14])

Medicaid and Medicare

The Medicaid and Medicare recipient subsystems are included in this description of the health care system because they involve an exception to the three major ones presented earlier. Both the Medicaid and the Medicare programs (P.L. 89–97) allow recipients to enter into and behave as if they were participants in the middle/upper income health care system. Thus, it is important to understand how policy intervention can in fact permit people from one health care system to move into another, and perhaps more desirable, system.

Medicaid (Title 19)

Medicaid is a joint federal-state funded welfare program that provides financial assistance to low-income persons, including the aged, so they can purchase medical care. Medicaid is available in all 50 states. The federal government's

Table 1–7 Selected Characteristics, VA Health Care System, 1982

Facilities:	
Hospital centers	172
Nursing homes	101
Domiciliaries	16
Outpatient centers	226
Expenditures:	
Medical and hospital services	
Hospital	$4,555 (millions)
Nursing home	478
Domiciliary	106
Outpatient	1,383
Construction	429
Other	628
Total	$7,579
Hospitals:	
Acute care beds	79,900
Average daily census	66,000
Average length of stay	20.3 days
Occupancy rate	81%

Source: Congressional Budget Office, *Veterans Administration Health Care: Planning for Future Years*, Washington, D.C., U.S. Government Printing Office, April 1984.

primary responsibility is to share the cost of the program with the states. Eligibility for Medicaid is limited to persons who fall into one of the following categories: (1) Aid to Families with Dependent Children (AFDC), (2) aged—must be 65 years or older, (3) blind, (4) disabled.[15] The states are responsible for defining eligibility requirements and for determining the extent of benefit coverage, subject to federal guidelines. Since the eligibility and benefit packages are set by the individual states, they vary widely.

The primary beneficiary group for Medicaid is the poor; however, it has been estimated that a third to a half of the population below the poverty level is not covered by Medicaid. That population includes the majority of persons in the low-income/medically indigent health care system, described earlier.

Medicaid is financed through general tax revenues collected by both the federal and state governments. In 1967, the first full year after it took effect, the total expenditure (federal, state, and local governments) was $2.9 billion but by 1982 had reached $32.4 billion, a more than tenfold increase in 15 years (Table 1–8). Of particular interest are the rise in the share of expenditures to nursing home care (31.7 percent in 1967 to 40.7 percent in 1982), the decrease in dental services (4.4 percent to 1.9 percent), the increase in other home services (2.6 percent to

4.6 percent), and the gain in other professional services (0.9 percent to 2.2 percent). These changes are thought by the authors to reflect attempts to contain the rapidly increasing costs of the Medicaid program by changing the benefit coverage, the eligibility requirements, and the amount paid to providers of medical care.

Under Medicaid, a state must provide, as a minimum, some institutional and noninstitutional services and some health care for any individual requiring skilled nursing home services. Medical assistance is defined as payment for all or part of the cost of the following, with the first seven items mandated by federal law:[16]

1. inpatient hospital care, except in mental or tuberculosis hospitals
2. outpatient hospital services
3. laboratory and x-ray services
4. skilled nursing home services for persons 21 years or older
5. physicians' services in office, home, hospital, nursing home, or elsewhere
6. medical care or any other type of remedial care furnished by licensed practitioners, other than medical doctors, recognized under state law
7. home health care services

Table 1–8 Medicaid Expenditures[1] and Percent Distribution, by Type of Service, U.S.
(Selected Years 1967–1982)

	Year						
Type of service	*1967*	*1970*	*1975*	*1979*	*1980*	*1981*	*1982*[2]
	Amount in billions						
Total	$2.9	$5.2	$13.5	$21.8	$25.5	$29.0	$32.4
	Percent distribution						
All services	100%	100%	100%	100%	100%	100%	100%
Hospital care	42.3	42.9	34.6	37.3	36.7	36.3	36.4
Physician services	10.9	13.3	14.0	10.1	9.8	9.9	9.0
Dentist services	4.4	3.2	2.9	1.8	2.0	2.1	1.9
Other professional services	0.9	1.4	1.5	2.3	2.0	1.7	2.2
Drugs and drug sundries	7.2	7.9	6.6	5.5	5.5	5.5	5.2
Nursing home care	31.7	27.2	36.0	39.6	39.8	39.7	40.7
Other health services[3]	2.6	4.1	4.4	3.2	4.3	4.8	4.6

1. Expenditures from federal, state, and local funds under Medicaid. Includes per capita payments for Part B of Medicare and excludes administrative costs.
2. Preliminary estimates.
3. Other services include laboratory and radiological services, home health, and family planning services.

Source: Derived from *Health and Prevention Profile—United States, 1983*, p. 199, National Center for Health Statistics, Public Health Service.

8. private duty nursing, if medically necessary, and absorbed through the hospital
9. clinic outpatient services
10. dental services
11. physical therapy and related services
12. prescription drugs, dentures, prosthetic devices (in the patient's home, not in a nursing home), prescribed eyeglasses (one pair per year)
13. other diagnostic, screening (Pap smear—early and periodic), and preventive and rehabilitation services
14. inpatient hospital services and skilled nursing home services for persons 65 and older and who are in an institution for the treatment of tuberculosis or a mental disease
15. intermediate care nursing home services
16. any other medical or remedial health care recognized under state law and approved by the Department of Health and Human Services.

Medicare (Title 18)

The federal Medicare program is a two-part medical insurance program that includes:

1. hospital insurance benefits for the aged, called Medicare—Part A
2. a voluntary supplementary medical insurance program called Medicare—Part B.

Part A, hospital insurance, covers all persons 65 and older who are entitled to monthly retirement benefits under either the Social Security or Railroad Retirement Acts and, under certain conditions, elderly individuals who are not covered by those retirement plans. Also covered are persons under 65 who are permanently disabled, e.g., individuals with end stage renal disease and require either dialysis or transplantation.

Basically, Medicare hospital insurance helps pay for three categories of care: (1) inpatient hospital care, (2) inpatient care in a skilled nursing home when deemed medically necessary after a hospitalization, and (3) home health care. There is a limit on the number of days of hospital or nursing home care and home health visits provided during any one benefit period. A benefit period is started each time an individual is hospitalized and the hospital insurance takes effect and lasts until the individual has been out of the hospital or nursing home for 60 consecutive days. A new benefit period would begin the next time the individual enters the hospital; there is no limit as to the number of benefit periods a person can have during a lifetime. The Part A coverage will pay for most but not all of the services received because each category of care has covered and noncovered services. There are deductible and coinsurance amounts that must be paid.[17]

As of January 1, 1985, the basic coverage during one benefit period was:

1. Up to 90 days in a hospital with all but $400 paid for days 1–60 (the hospital insurance deductible) and all but $100 per day for days 61–90. If a person needs more than 90 days in a benefit period, a lifetime reserve of 60 days is available to cover this excess and will pay all but $200 per day.
2. Up to 100 days in a skilled extended care facility (not an intermediate or non-skilled facility) and will cover all services for days 1–20 and all but $50 for days 21–100;[18] and,
3. Certain home health care benefits for up to one year after discharge from a hospital or extended care facility.

Care in a psychiatric hospital is covered only if the physician certifies that treatment can reasonably be expected to improve the patient's condition and is limited to 190 days during an individual's lifetime. Care in a tuberculosis hospital is covered only if the physician certifies that it is needed to improve the patient's condition or to render the condition noncommunicable. Medicare Part A helps to pay for:

1. a bed in a semiprivate room (2 to 4 beds in a room) and all meals including special diets
2. operating room charges
3. regular nursing charges (including intensive care nursing)
4. drugs furnished during the hospital stay
5. laboratory tests included in the hospital bill
6. x-rays and other radiologic services included in the hospital bill
7. medical supplies, such as splints, casts, and surgical dressings
8. use of appliances and equipment furnished by the hospital, such as wheelchairs, crutches, etc.
9. medical services such as physical therapy, occupational therapy, speech pathology, etc.
10. special care units such as coronary care, intensive care, etc.
11. psychiatric services limited to 190 days per lifetime with no reserve days available.

In general, Medicare Part A does not pay for personal comfort or convenience items (i.e., radio, telephone, or television), private duty nurses, noncovered levels of care and private room unless needed for medical reasons, physician services and the first three pints of blood needed in any benefit period.

Part B, medical insurance, is a voluntary program available to those enrolled in Part A and offers the following coverage:

1. medical and surgical services provided by a doctor of medicine or osteopathy
2. certain medical and surgical services provided by a doctor of dental medicine or dental surgery
3. services by podiatrists who are legally authorized by the state in which they practice
4. other services ordinarily furnished in a doctor's office, such as diagnostic tests and procedures, medical supplies, services of an office nurse, and drugs and other biologicals that cannot be self-administered
5. hospital outpatient services such as emergency room services, outpatient clinic, laboratory tests, x-rays, splints, casts, whether for diagnosis or treatment. After an initial deduction from the first expenses during a year ($75 in 1984), Medicare reimburses for 80 percent of the reasonable charges for all the outpatient covered services.[19]

Services not covered under Part B include routine physical checkups and tests directly related to examinations; routine foot care; eye refractions and examinations; hearing examinations and hearing aids; immunizations, except if directly related to an injury; cosmetic surgery, unless necessary for accidental or malformation problems; and services of a Christian Science practitioner; chiropractors, except for the manual manipulation of the spine, and naturopaths.

As of January 1, 1985, the basic premium for Part A is free for persons receiving Social Security benefits; otherwise, it is $191.40 per month. Also as of 1985, the basic premium for Part B is $14.50 a month.[20]

The actual 1982 expenditure for Medicare was $50.9 billion as compared with $35.7 billion in 1980; $7.1 billion in 1970 and $4.5 billion in 1967, the first year Medicare was in effect. Table 1–9 indicates the percent distribution by category for selected years.

From the inception of Medicare to 1982, the hospital portion stayed relatively stable at approximately 70 percent and physician services at 22 percent, while nursing home care declined from 4.6 percent in 1967 to 1.0 percent, and other services rose from 1.7 percent to 5.3 percent. This last increase is evidence of the increased federal support for home health care and for other attempts to reduce the level of inpatient care costs.

THE U.S. HOSPITAL: PAST AND PRESENT

The Past: 1750s–1950s

The history of American hospitals can be traced to the mid-1700s when such facilities existed in almost every moderate-size city in the country. These hospitals

Table 1–9 Medicare Expenditures and Percent Distribution, by Type of Service, U.S.
(Selected Years 1967–1982)

Type of service	*Year*						
	1967	*1970*	*1975*	*1979*	*1980*	*1981*	*1982*[1]
				Amount in billions			
Total	$4.5	$7.1	$15.6	$29.3	$35.7	$43.5	$50.9
				Percent distribution			
All services	100%	100%	100%	100%	100%	100%	100%
Hospital care	69.0	71.8	74.8	72.1	72.6	72.0	71.3
Physician services	24.7	22.5	21.3	22.1	21.8	22.3	22.4
Nursing home care	4.6	4.2	1.9	1.4	1.1	0.9	1.0
Other health services[2]	1.7	1.4	1.9	4.4	4.5	4.6	5.3

1. Preliminary estimates.
2. Other services include home health agencies, home health services, eyeglasses and appliances, and other professional services.

Source: Derived from *Health and Prevention Profile—United States, 1983*, p. 198, National Center for Health Statistics, Public Health Service.

were only for the poor and usually were referred to as almshouses or, more commonly, pesthouses. They were owned and operated by charitable and religious organizations that provided basic custodial care for the aged, homeless, terminally ill, disabled, insane, and orphans. The hospitals were avoided by most members of the community as it was regarded as a disgrace to enter such a facility. In addition, the health hazards from this type of institutional environment were much greater than those in the home. During epidemics, local governments provided these facilities specifically to isolate people infected by contagious diseases such as smallpox, yellow fever, and cholera, and not necessarily to provide treatment.

By the late 1700s and early 1800s, community-owned hospitals (also called voluntary hospitals) emerged, commonly financed by philanthropies and contributions by local citizens and government. The first voluntary hospital in the American colonies was in Philadelphia (1751), followed by one in New York in 1769 and the Massachusetts General Hospital in 1811.[21] These hospitals admitted both paying patients and indigents and utilized a medical staff that provided care mostly on a voluntary basis rather than by salary. While these voluntary hospitals were an improvement in terms of accessibility, the quality of health care changed little. Surgeons knew enough anatomy to perform basic surgical operations but not how to avoid infection. Thus, about 90 percent of surgical patients died from hemorrhage, infection, and gangrene.[22] Most people continued to avoid voluntary hospitals and provided most of the care for their sick at home, with hospitals remaining as the place of last resort. By 1873, there were only 178 hospitals with 35,604 beds in the country.[23]

Hospitals grew significantly from then to the 1920s as improvements in care convinced people of all economic strata to view these facilities as feasible places to take their sick. By 1909 there were 4,359 hospitals with more than 421,000 beds and by 1929, 6,665 hospitals and 907,133 beds.[24]

Five major forces influenced the growth of the health care system. First, advances in medical (clinical) sciences increased the efficacy of care and improved hospitals' safety procedures and environment. Patients had a better-than-even chance of surviving hospitalization. For example, by the early 1800s, much had been learned about the physiology and anatomy of the human body and several new surgical procedures had been developed. By the 1840s, Long and Morton had discovered ether as the first anesthetic to deaden pain for surgical patients, which also helped increase the precision and success rates of surgery because more time could be allocated to the procedure.

Second, advances in clinical and medical technology led to increased physician and hospital specialization. These included the invention of steam sterilization techniques in 1886, which reduced surgical infection by providing a means of cleansing surgical equipment of microorganisms, as medical researchers first recognized the link between microorganisms and disease. Further scientific breakthroughs included Pasteur's early work with germ theory, rabies, and cholera in the 1880s; Roentgen's 1896 discovery of the x-ray, which created diagnostic images of the human body; the discovery of blood types in 1900, which led to safer transfusions; and the development of the electrocardiogram in 1902.

Third was the improvement in patient care through the development of professional nursing, a result of the growth in medical technology. Custodial care did not require professional training but the new curative aspect of care did. Nursing services were provided by Catholic sisters and other religious orders before the 1850s, and did not become a profession until Florence Nightingale, an English nurse, and Dorothea Dix, an American, led the movement to professional status. Changes included services provided and nurses' education. The first three nursing schools opened in 1873; by 1910, there were 1,129.

Fourth was society's changing view of hospitals. Unsanitary, crowded, and often dangerous conditions in hospitals were slowly eliminated and as a result more people willingly entered these facilities for treatment. Hospitals no longer were viewed as charitable institutions but were considered places for healing.

The final force was the increased time and resources devoted to research and medical education. Scientific discoveries were being introduced into medical school curricula. A major stimulus was the Flexner Report of Medical Education in 1910. Until then, most medical schools did not have laboratories or provide students with clinical training. The Flexner Report documented poor facilities, inadequate staff, lack of scientific and clinical instruction, and low or even nonexistent admission standards. This report had a profound impact on hospital development by changing the context of education to emphasize the scientific basis of medicine. This report also led to the passage of state laws requiring American Medical Association (AMA) accreditation of medical degree-granting institutions and to the establishment of added academic medical training programs and research institutes in and among hospitals throughout the United States.[25]

All of these advancements led hospitals into even greater changes. The number of hospitals declined from 7,370 in 1924 to 6,788 in 1950 but the number of beds increased from 813,000 to 1,456,000, with average hospital size growing from 110 beds to 214.

Two developments had an important impact during this period: the accreditation of physicians and the emergence of private health insurance.

In 1913, the American College of Surgeons was established, leading to the development of criteria to monitor and evaluate the medical staff, medical recordkeeping, and hospitals' diagnostic and therapeutic equipment. These criteria had to be met before a hospital was placed on the ''approved'' list. This function was taken over by the Joint Commission on Accreditation of Hospitals (JCAH) in 1951. This accreditation process led to the closing of many substandard facilities, which helped to improve society's attitude toward the hospital industry.[26]

The second major event, the establishment of private health insurance plans, helped finance patients' hospitalization. Although Baylor University Hospital is thought of as having the first hospitalization plan, in 1929, it was not until after the Depression that such plans went into wider effect. By 1945, there were 87 private hospital insurance plans covering more than 20 million persons. Insurance helped the fee-for-service medical care system grow stronger and make hospitals the major institutions in health care.[27]

THE PRESENT: 1960 TO NOW

Hospitals now represent the hub of the health care system, with expenditures totaling $135.4 billion in 1982, or 42 percent of the $322.4 billion national health care expenditures. If the $286.9 billion spent on personal health care (national health care expenditures expenses for prepayment, government, public health, research, and construction) are included, hospitals received 47 percent. In addition, hospitals employed 4,341,000 persons in 1982—55 percent of the total of 7,863,000 working in the health service industry. In 1981, hospitals (both federal and nonfederal) served 38,417,000 inpatients and had 257,254,000 outpatient visits. Hospital outpatient departments provided 13.3 percent of the total physician visits in the health care industry. Physicians' offices, clinics, or group practice locations accounted for 68.6 percent of the outpatient visits; telephone contacts for 12.2 percent; and all other sources/places, the remaining 4.6 percent. Finally, of the 479,379 federal and nonfederal medical doctors in the United States in 1981, 20.6 percent (98,951) were involved in hospital-based practice; of these, 62,537 (63.2 percent) were residents or interns.

The American Hospital Association (AHA) is one of two major agencies that classifies and counts hospitals in the United States, the other being the National Center for Health Statistics of the Department of Health and Human Services (DHHS). The AHA annually publishes a *Guide Issue* and *Hospital Statistics*, both of which provide descriptive and summary statistics of the industry. The AHA classifies hospitals according to size, type, ownership, and length of patient stay and provides summary distributions by geographic location and medical school affiliation.

The AHA defines size as the facility's number of beds, excluding newborn bassinets. Type of hospital includes four major classifications: (1) mental; (2) tuberculosis; (3) other specialty, including narcotic addiction, eye, ear, nose, and throat, rehabilitation, orthopedic, chronic disease, mental retardation, and alcoholism; and (4) general, which includes all hospitals not in the three other classifications. The ownership classification refers to two major categories, private and public. The public ownership category is broken down into federal, state, and local government.

Private ownership is classified in two categories, depending on how the hospital distributes its surplus income. The first, investor-owned (proprietary) hospitals, return part of their surplus income to the owners. The second, not-for-profit hospitals, do not distribute surplus income. In the final classification, length of stay, long term is defined as a hospital where either the average length of stay for all patients is more than 30 days or more than 50 percent of the patients are admitted to units that have a length of stay greater than 30 days. Short term refers to hospitals with an average length of stay for all patients of fewer than 30 days, or more than 50 percent of all patients are admitted to units with an average length of stay less than 30 days.[28]

For purposes here, community hospitals are defined as all nonfederal, short-term general or other specialty facilities, excluding units of another institution (i.e., prisons or universities) that do not offer medical care services to the public.[29]

Number of Hospitals

As of 1981, there were 6,190 hospitals in the United States, of which 311 (5 percent) were federal. The 5,879 nonfederal hospitals were classified as: nonprofit, 3,356 (54.2 percent of the total); proprietary, 729 (11.8 percent); and state and local government-owned, 1,794 (30 percent). As Table 1–10 shows, in 1960, there were 361 federal hospitals, which by 1981 had declined by 50; 3,291

Table 1–10 Short-Stay Hospitals, U.S.[1]
(Selected Years 1960–1981)

Type of ownership	Year								
	1960	*1970*	*1975*	*1976*	*1977*	*1978*	*1979*	*1980*	*1981*
Hospitals					Number				
All ownerships	5,768	6,193	6,310	6,288	6,307	6,266	6,247	6,229	6,190
Federal	361	334	331	332	334	331	324	325	311
Nonfederal	5,407	5,859	5,979	5,956	5,973	5,935	5,923	5,904	5,879
Nonprofit	3,291	3,386	3,364	3,368	3,371	3,360	3,350	3,339	3,356
Proprietary	856	769	775	752	751	732	727	730	729
State and local government	1,260	1,704	1,840	1,836	1,851	1,843	1,846	1,835	1,794

1. Excludes psychiatric and tuberculosis and other respiratory disease hospitals.

Source: Derived from *Health and Prevention Profile—United States, 1983*, p. 166, National Center for Health Statistics, Public Health Service.

nonprofit hospitals, which dipped by 65; 856 proprietary, which fell by 127; and 1,260 state and local owned, which increased by 534.

From 1960 to 1981, the total number of hospitals increased by 422 (7.3 percent), from 5,768 to 6,190 and the number of nonfederal hospitals by 472 (8.7 percent), from 5,407 to 5,879.

Number of Beds

As of 1981, there were 1,093,370 beds in hospitals in the United States, of which 1,006,774 (92.1 percent) were in nonfederal facilities. Of these, 706,331 beds were in nonprofit hospitals (70.2 percent); 87,743 in proprietary hospitals (8.7 percent); and 212,700 in state and local government-owned facilities (21.2 percent) (Table 1–11).

In 1960, there were 735,451 hospital beds, of which 639,057 were in nonfederal institutions (86.9 percent). The remaining 639,057 in the nonfederal sector were distributed among nonprofits, 445,753 (69.8 percent of the total); proprietaries, 37,029 (5.8 percent); and state and local government, 156,275 (24.4 percent). The 1960–1981 trend indicates that while beds in nonfederal hospitals increased 57.5 percent (639,057 to 1,006,774), nonprofit hospitals continued to supply about 70 percent of the nonfederal beds, proprietary facilities increased their share from 5.8 percent to 8.7 percent, and the state and local government facilities declined from 24.4 percent to 21.2 percent.

As for bed growth rate in ownership type, from 1960 to 1981, nonprofit hospitals increased beds by 58.5 percent, proprietary hospitals by 137 percent, and state and local government hospitals by 36.1 percent.

Occupancy Rates

In terms of hospital occupancy rates, defined as the ratio of the average daily census to the average number of beds (called statistical beds, as opposed to a daily bed count), nonfederal hospitals had a 75.9 percent occupancy rate in 1981, distributed by ownership category as follows: nonprofit, 78.5 percent; proprietary 66.4 percent; and state and local government 71.2 percent (Table 1–12). These are relatively stable when compared with the 1960 occupancy rates: nonfederal hospitals, 74.7 percent; nonprofit, 76.6 percent; proprietary, 65.4 percent; and state and local government 71.6 percent.

Admissions

Admissions to all hospitals in 1981 were 38,417,000 with nonfederal institutions accounting for 36,494,000 (95 percent) (Table 1–13). The nonfederal admissions are distributed by ownership group as follows: nonprofit, 25,955,000 (71.1 per-

Table 1–11 Short-Stay Hospital Beds, U.S.[1]
(Selected Years 1960–1981)

Type of ownership	*Year*								
	1960	*1970*	*1975*	*1976*	*1977*	*1978*	*1979*	*1980*	*1981*
Beds									
All ownerships	735,451	935,724	1,036,025	1,047,912	1,059,903	1,067,566	1,073,671	1,080,164	1,093,370
Federal	96,394	87,492	89,049	86,737	86,037	87,907	85,984	88,144	86,596
Nonfederal	639,057	848,232	946,976	961,175	973,866	979,659	987,687	992,020	1,006,774
Nonprofit	445,753	591,937	658,948	670,939	679,501	683,856	690,278	692,929	706,331
Proprietary	37,029	52,739	73,495	76,416	80,322	81,046	83,338	87,033	87,743
State and local government	156,275	203,556	214,533	213,830	214,043	214,757	214,071	212,058	212,700

1. Excludes psychiatric and tuberculosis and other respiratory disease hospitals.

Source: Derived from *Health and Prevention Profile—United States, 1983*, p. 166, National Center for Health Statistics, Public Health Service.

Table 1–12 Short-Stay Hospital Occupancy Rates, U.S.[1]
(Selected Years 1960–1981)

Type of ownership	*Year*								
	1960	*1970*	*1975*	*1976*	*1977*	*1978*	*1979*	*1980*	*1981*
Occupancy rate				Percent of beds occupied					
All ownerships	75.7%	77.9%	75.0%	74.5%	73.9%	73.7%	74.0%	75.6%	76.0%
Federal	82.5	77.5	77.6	76.4	77.3	76.3	76.3	77.8	76.2
Nonfederal	74.7	78.0	74.8	74.4	73.6	73.5	73.8	75.4	75.9
Nonprofit	76.6	80.1	77.4	77.1	76.3	76.1	76.5	78.2	78.5
Proprietary	65.4	72.2	65.9	64.8	64.6	63.8	63.9	65.2	66.4
State and local government	71.6	73.2	69.7	69.2	68.3	68.7	69.1	70.7	71.2

1. Excludes psychiatric and tuberculosis and other respiratory disease hospitals.

Source: Derived from *Health and Prevention Profile—United States, 1983*, p. 166, National Center for Health Statistics, Public Health Service.

Table 1–13 Short-Stay Hospitals Admissions, U.S.[1]
(Selected Years 1960–1981)

Type of ownership	*Year*								
	1960	*1970*	*1975*	*1976*	*1977*	*1978*	*1979*	*1980*	*1981*
Admissions	Number in thousands								
All ownerships	24,324	30,706	35,270	35,901	36,227	36,433	37,034	38,140	38,417
Federal	1,354	1,454	1,751	1,832	1,874	1,858	1,874	1,942	1,923
Nonfederal	22,970	29,252	33,519	34,068	34,353	34,575	35,160	36,198	36,494
Nonprofit	16,788	20,948	23,735	24,098	24,284	24,443	24,885	25,576	25,955
Proprietary	11,550	2,031	2,646	2,734	2,849	2,880	2,963	3,165	3,239
State and local government	4,632	6,273	7,138	7,237	7,220	7,253	7,312	7,458	7,299

1. Excludes psychiatric and tuberculosis and other respiratory disease hospitals.

Source: Derived from *Health and Prevention Profile—United States, 1983*, p. 143, National Center for Health Statistics, Public Health Service.

cent of all nonfederal admissions); proprietary, 3,239,000 (8.9 percent); and state and local government 7,299,000 (20 percent). From 1960 to 1981, the number of admissions to all hospitals increased by 57.9 percent (24,324,000 to 38,317,000) and to nonfederal facilities by 58.8 percent (22,970,000 to 36,494,000). Nonprofit hospital admissions increased by 54.6 percent (16,788,000 to 25,955,000); proprietaries, 109 percent (1,550,000 to 3,239,000); and state and local government, 57.6 percent (4,632,000 to 7,299,000). The proprietary hospitals showed the greatest growth rate in admissions in those two decades.

Outpatient Visits

Outpatient visits in 1981 totaled 257,254,000 to all short-term hospitals. Nonfederal hospitals had 206,729,000 outpatient visits—80.4 percent of all outpatient hospital visits (Table 1–14). Of these, nonprofit hospitals accounted for 69.6 percent, proprietary hospitals for 4.8 percent, and state and local government hospitals for 25.5 percent. Between 1970 and 1981, outpatient visits to all facilities increased by 48.7 percent (173,058,000 to 257,254,000), nonprofit hospitals by 58.2 percent (90,992,000 to 143,953,000); proprietary hospitals by 112 percent (4,698,000 to 9,961,000); and state and local government by 39.5 percent (37,854,000 to 52,816,000). As with the admission rate growth, proprietary hospitals also had the greatest rate of growth in outpatient visits.

Average Length of Stay

The average length of stay for short-term hospitals in 1981 was 7.9 days, a dip from the 1960 level of 8.4 days (Table 1–15). The average length of stay in federal hospitals was 12.5 days in 1981, a big drop from the 21.4 days in 1960. The nonfederal stay averaged 7.6 days in 1981, with nonprofit hospitals' rate at 7.8 days compared with 7.4 in 1960; proprietary hospitals, 6.6 vs. 5.7 in 1960; and state and local government hospitals 7.6 days vs. 8.8 in 1960. The shorter length of stay for the proprietary section may reflect the many differences in patient case mix between the profit and nonprofit facilities.

Bed/Population Ratio-Geographic Distribution

Since the peak in 1975, the community hospital bed/population ratio has been declining (Table 1–16). In 1981, the beds per 1,000 civilian population was 4.4, as compared with 3.2 in 1941, 3.3 in 1950, 3.6 in 1960, 4.3 in 1970, 4.6 in 1975, and 4.5 in 1980. The annual percent change from 1960 to 1970 was plus 1.8; from 1970 to 1975, plus 1.4; and from 1975 to 1981, −0.7. The bed/population ratio varies widely among the nine geographic regions. For example, in 1981, the ratio ranged from a high of 5.8 beds per 1,000 population in the West North Central region

Table 1–14 Outpatient Visits in Short-Stay Hospitals by Type of Ownership, U.S.[1]
(Selected Years 1970–1981)

Type of ownership	Year							
	1970	*1975*	*1976*	*1977*	*1978*	*1979*	*1980*	*1981*
Admissions				Number in thousands				
All ownerships	173,058	245,938	261,278	254,483	253,896	252,461	255,320	257,254
Federal	39,514	49,627	53,553	50,245	47,434	48,587	48,568	50,524
Nonfederal	133,545	196,311	207,725	204,238	206,461	203,873	206,752	206,729
Nonprofit	90,992	132,368	141,781	139,045	142,617	140,525	142,864	143,953
Proprietary	4,698	7,713	8,048	8,355	8,911	9,289	9,696	9,961
State and local government	37,854	56,230	57,896	56,838	54,933	54,060	54,192	52,816

1. Excludes psychiatric and tuberculosis and other respiratory disease hospitals.

Sources: American Hospital Association: *Hospitals, Journal of the American Hospital Association*, Vol. 35, No. 15, pp. 396–401, August 1961 and August 1971; *Hospital Statistics, 1976–1982 Editions*, Chicago, 1976–82.

Table 1–15 Average Length of Stay in Short-Stay Hospitals by Type of Ownership, U.S.[1]
(Selected Years 1960–1981)

Type of ownership	Year								
	1960	*1970*	*1975*	*1976*	*1977*	*1978*	*1979*	*1980*	*1981*
Average length of stay	Number of days								
All ownerships	8.4%	8.7%	8.0%	8.0%	7.9%	7.9%	7.8%	7.8%	7.9%
Federal	21.4	17.0	14.4	13.2	12.9	13.2	12.8	12.9	12.5
Nonfederal	7.6	8.2	7.7	7.7	7.6	7.6	7.6	7.6	7.6
Nonprofit	7.4	8.2	7.8	7.9	7.8	7.8	7.7	7.7	7.8
Proprietary	5.7	6.8	6.6	6.6	6.6	6.5	6.6	6.5	6.6
State and local government	8.8	8.7	7.6	7.5	7.4	7.4	7.4	7.4	7.6

1. Excludes psychiatric and tuberculosis and other respiratory disease hospitals.

Source: Derived from *Health and Prevention Profile—United States, 1983*, p. 143, National Center for Health Statistics, Public Health Service.

Table 1–16 Community Hospital Beds per 1,000 Population and Average Annual % Change, by Geographic Division, U.S.
(Selected Years 1940–1981)

	Year							Period			
Geographic division	*1940*	*1950*	*1960*	*1970*	*1975*	*1980*	*1981*	*1940–60*	*1960–70*	*1970–75*	*1975–80*
	Community hospital beds per 1,000 population							Average annual percent change			
United States	3.2	3.3	3.6	4.3	4.6	4.5	4.4	0.6	1.8	1.4	−0.7
New England	4.4	4.2	3.9	4.1	4.2	4.1	4.1	−0.6	0.5	0.5	−0.4
Middle Atlantic	3.9	3.8	4.0	4.4	4.6	4.6	4.6	0.1	1.0	.9	—
East North Central	3.2	3.2	3.6	4.4	4.7	4.7	4.7	0.6	2.0	1.3	—
West North Central	3.1	3.7	4.3	5.7	5.8	5.8	5.8	1.6	2.9	0.3	—
South Atlantic	2.5	2.8	3.3	4.0	4.3	4.5	4.4	1.4	1.9	1.5	0.4
East South Central	1.7	2.1	3.0	4.4	4.9	5.1	5.1	2.9	3.9	2.2	0.7
West South Central	2.1	2.7	3.3	4.3	4.7	4.7	4.5	2.3	2.7	1.8	−0.7
Mountain	3.6	3.8	3.5	4.3	4.0	3.8	3.7	−0.1	2.1	−1.4	−1.3
Pacific	4.1	3.2	3.1	3.7	3.9	3.5	3.4	−1.4	1.8	1.1	−2.3

Source: Derived from *Health and Prevention Profile—United States, 1983*, p. 167, National Center for Health Statistics, Public Health Service.

(Iowa, Kansas, Minnesota, Missouri, Nebraska, and North and South Dakota) to a low of 3.4 in the Pacific region (Alaska, California, Hawaii, Oregon, and Washington). There also are variations within regions. For example, the West North Central region's states range from a low of 5.5 in Missouri to a high of 7.4 in North Dakota.

Occupancy Rates—Geographic Distribution

Occupancy rates in community hospitals also have fluctuated since 1940 (Table 1–17). For example, the 1981 average occupancy rate was 75.7 percent, compared with 69.9 percent in 1940, 74.7 percent in 1960, 77.3 percent in 1970, 74.2 percent in 1975, and 75.2 percent in 1980. Between 1970 and 1975, the rate declined by 0.8 percent per year and between 1975 and 1981 increased by 0.3 percent. As with the bed/population ratio, there are geographic variations among the nine regions. The occupancy rates range from a low of 69.9 percent in both the Pacific and Mountain (Arizona, Colorado, Idaho, Montana, Nevada, New Mexico, Utah, and Wyoming) regions to a high of 84.1 percent in the Middle Atlantic region (New Jersey, New York, and Pennsylvania). Again, there are variations among each region's states. For example, the South Atlantic Region states range from a low of 71.4 percent in Georgia to a high of 84.3 percent in Delaware.

Hospital Personnel per Bed

Advances in medical technology have contributed greatly to the recent increases in personnel staffing community hospitals. Data showing full-time equivalent employees (FTEs) per 100 average daily patients are shown in Table 1–18. Full-time equivalents are calculated by adding the number of full-time personnel to half of the number of part-time personnel, excluding medical/dental residents or interns and other trainees.[30]

In 1960, community hospitals had 226 FTEs per 100 daily patients; by 1981, this number had increased to 402. The annual percent change nationally for the periods 1960–1970, 1970–1975, and 1975–1981 has been fairly stable, approximately 2.9 percent; while 1975–1981 increased annually at 2.4 percent. Again, there are variations among regions, with the Pacific region having the most FTEs per 100 patients (479) in 1981, and East South Central (Alabama, Kentucky, Mississippi, and Tennessee) the fewest (354).

LONG-TERM HOSPITALS

There are a number of reasons for the decline in the number of long-term hospitals; for example, changes in medical therapies.

Table 1–17 Occupancy Rate in Community Hospitals and Average Annual % Change, by Geographic Division, U.S.
(Selected Years 1940–1981)

	Year						Period			
Geographic division	*1940*	*1960*	*1970*	*1975*	*1980*	*1981*	*1940–60*	*1960–70*	*1970–75*	*1975–80*
	Community hospital beds per 1,000 population						Average annual percent change			
United States	69.9	74.7	77.3	74.2	75.2	75.7	0.3	0.3	−0.8	0.3
New England	72.5	75.2	79.7	77.6	80.1	80.2	0.2	0.6	−0.5	0.6
Middle Atlantic	75.5	78.1	82.4	81.4	83.2	84.1	0.2	0.5	−0.2	0.5
East North Central	71.0	78.4	79.5	77.2	76.9	76.9	0.5	0.1	−0.6	−0.1
West North Central	65.7	71.8	73.6	70.6	71.2	71.5	0.4	0.2	−0.8	0.2
South Atlantic	66.7	74.8	77.9	73.9	75.5	76.1	0.6	0.4	−1.0	0.5
East South Central	62.6	71.8	78.2	74.0	74.6	74.4	0.7	0.9	−1.1	0.1
West South Central	62.5	68.7	73.2	69.1	69.7	70.6	0.5	0.6	−1.1	0.4
Mountain	60.9	69.9	71.2	68.4	69.6	69.9	0.7	0.2	−0.8	0.4
Pacific	69.7	71.4	71.0	66.2	69.0	69.9	0.1	−0.1	−1.4	0.9

Source: Derived from *Health and Prevention Profile—United States, 1983*, p. 169, National Center for Health Statistics, Public Health Service.

Table 1–18 Full-Time Equivalent Employees per 100 Average Daily Patients in Community Hospitals and Average Annual % Change, by Geographic Division, U.S.
(Selected Years 1960–1981)

	Year					*Period*		
Geographic division	*1960*	*1970*	*1975*	*1980*	*1981*	*1960–70*	*1970–75*	*1975–81*
	Number of employees per 100 average daily patients					Average annual percent change		
United States	226	302	349	394	402	2.9	2.9	2.4
New England	249	351	412	456	471	3.5	3.3	2.3
Middle Atlantic	225	311	352	383	388	3.3	2.5	1.6
East North Central	226	299	343	396	406	2.8	2.8	2.9
West North Central	212	273	305	357	362	2.6	2.2	2.9
South Atlantic	217	295	343	379	389	3.1	3.1	2.1
East South Central	227	275	306	348	354	1.9	2.2	2.5
West South Central	225	297	346	384	398	2.8	3.1	2.4
Mountain	226	299	364	413	411	2.8	4.0	2.0
Pacific	243	327	401	467	479	3.0	4.2	3.0

Source: Derived from *Health and Prevention Profile—United States, 1983*, p. 171, National Center for Health Statistics, Public Health Service.

As of 1981, there were 20 general long-term hospitals, of which 12 were federal and eight were nonfederal (a massive drop from the 75 in 1970) (Table 1–19). They had 9,925 beds, of which 8,823 were in federal facilities and 1,102 in nonfederal hospitals. The average size of the federal long-term hospital was 735 beds, the average nonfederal facility 137. Occupancy rates averaged 86.4 percent—87.6 percent in federal facilities and 77.1 percent in nonfederal hospitals. Of the 75 general long-term hospitals in 1970, 38 were federal and 37 nonfederal; by 1975, the number had dropped to 44, of which 23 were federal. Most of the decline occurred between 1976 and 1978—from 37 to 24. The number of beds in these hospitals also declined, from 42,569 in 1970 (31,403 federal, 11,166 nonfederal) to 17,329 in 1975 (14,406 federal, 2,923 nonfederal), and 9,925 in 1981 (8,823 federal, 1,102 nonfederal).

In 1981, there were 394 psychiatric long-term hospitals, of which 22 were federal, 52 nonprofit, 65 proprietary, and 255 state and local government. As seen in Table 1–19, these numbers remained relatively stable for a decade. The most visible trend has been the increase (from 39 to 65) in the number of proprietary hospitals that have begun psychiatric long-term care. State and local government facilities have declined from 331 to 255. Psychiatric beds have declined significantly from 551,847 in 1970 to 205,003 in 1981. With the exception of the increase in beds in proprietary facilities from 3,399 in 1970 to 6,834 in 1981, other hospitals showed declines, the most dramatic being in federal hospitals (117.8 percent—41,500 to 19,051) and state and local governments (189.3 percent—498,056 to 172,174).

Tuberculosis and other respiratory disease hospitals declined dramatically from 1970 to 1981 (103 to 10) and their number of beds from 19,937 to 1,492. Much of the drop in number of hospitals and beds occurred between 1970 and 1975 (103 hospitals to 34 and 19,937 beds to 5,699).

The final category of long-term hospital—all other—had 139 facilities in 1981, down from 200 in 1970; 34,472 beds, off from 49,152 in 1970; and an average occupancy rate of 67 percent.

In general, the decline in numbers of both hospitals and beds is evidence of a developing new system to care for and treat both rehabilitation and psychiatric patients. The outpatient sector is absorbing more of the patient load, thus reducing the number of inpatient facilities and hence beds that are needed.

NURSING HOME: PAST AND PRESENT

The History of Nursing Homes

Nursing homes emerged about the same time as hospitals. These 18th century facilities evolved from the poorhouses that were community "homes" for the old,

Table 1–19 Long-Term Hospitals, Beds, and Occupancy Rates, by Type of Hospital and Ownership, U.S. (Selected Years 1970–1981)

Type of hospital and ownership	*Year*						
	1970	*1975*	*1976*	*1978*	*1979*	*1980*	*1981*
Hospitals				Number			
General	75	44	37	24	22	17	20
Federal	38	23	21	12	11	9	12
Nonfederal	37	21	16	12	11	8	8
Psychiatric	459	419	394	375	380	381	394
Federal	33	26	25	24	24	23	22
Nonprofit	56	45	43	47	46	47	52
Proprietary	39	51	50	54	57	57	65
State and local government	331	297	276	250	253	254	255
Tuberculosis and other respiratory diseases	103	34	19	13	11	10	10
All other	200	196	183	160	156	150	139
Federal	1	2	2	3	2	1	1
Nonprofit	110	94	84	73	68	66	67
Proprietary	2	9	9	9	10	11	10
State and local government	87	91	88	75	76	72	61
Beds							
General	42,569	17,329	18,664	11,465	9,710	8,253	9,925
Federal	31,403	14,406	16,146	9,305	8,050	7,205	8,823
Nonfederal	11,166	2,923	2,518	2,160	1,660	1,048	1,102
Psychiatric	551,847	344,257	301,374	237,234	232,344	218,400	205,003
Federal	41,500	27,523	25,069	23,158	22,290	20,871	19,051
Nonprofit	8,892	5,366	5,291	6,274	6,951	6,645	6,944
Proprietary	3,399	4,821	4,725	5,162	5,837	5,877	6,834
State and local government	498,056	306,547	266,289	202,640	197,266	185,007	172,174

Tuberculosis and other respiratory diseases	19,937	5,699	3,447	2,641	2,084	1,500	1,492
All other	49,152	49,268	47,469	40,763	39,702	37,911	34,472
Federal	357	968	1,022	1,489	1,024	357	357
Nonprofit	12,638	12,733	11,807	10,120	9,864	10,038	10,328
Proprietary	101	879	1,023	986	1,185	1,356	1,259
State and local government	36,056	34,688	33,617	28,168	27,629	26,160	22,528
Occupancy rate			Percent of beds occupied				
General	79.2%	84.4%	83.8%	83.1%	81.7%	83.9%	86.4%
Federal	80.4	85.2	83.8	82.8	82.0	84.6	87.6
Nonfederal	75.8	80.4	84.0	84.4	80.5	79.0	77.1
Psychiatric	84.9	81.3	80.1	81.7	83.7	85.9	86.7
Federal	83.4	88.3	86.2	85.7	84.8	87.9	87.7
Nonprofit	85.2	84.8	83.5	93.7	86.7	87.2	88.6
Proprietary	78.4	74.1	74.6	75.8	76.8	76.3	80.1
State and local government	85.0	80.8	79.5	81.0	83.7	86.0	86.8
Tuberculosis and other respiratory diseases	61.9	57.6	57.8	59.8	61.9	66.4	67.8
All other	83.3	82.3	82.5	83.3	85.8	85.9	86.3
Federal	73.4	86.3	77.9	65.0	65.2	65.3	65.0
Nonprofit	82.8	83.3	83.1	86.4	87.7	87.3	86.6
Proprietary	87.1	86.0	78.6	80.8	80.8	86.5	87.8
State and local government	83.6	81.7	82.6	83.2	86.1	85.6	86.4

Source: Derived from *Health and Prevention Profile—United States, 1983*, p. 173, National Center for Health Statistics, Public Health Service.

the sick, and the mentally ill. Conditions in those homes were unsanitary, with inadequate patient care and food.

By the end of the 19th century, the mentally ill had been removed from the poorhouses and placed in state institutions. Hospitals were growing rapidly and the sick were being taken to those facilities. As a result, the poorhouses were converted to what were called county homes. Although charitable and governmental contributions made possible environmental and plant improvements from time to time, little progress in modernizing these facilities was made during the late 1800s and early 1900s, when they served as dumping grounds for the elderly and infirm.

Later, government began to place regulations on county homes for the elderly, inspecting them and setting rules and performance standards. Unfortunately, the rules and standards generally were not enforced regularly, so the situation essentially remained the same.

Private nursing homes developed as a direct result of the Social Security Act of 1935, which provided welfare benefits to individuals who could not afford nongovernmental nursing institutions. This forced many county homes for the poor to close, as most inmates elected to use private nursing homes. Congress then responded to the increased demand for nursing home beds by issuing construction grants through the Hill-Burton Act of 1946. Renovation of the health care system for the elderly became reality, and the intense competition that developed between proprietary and nonprofit nursing homes continues today.[31]

The Present

As noted in Table 1–3, Americans spent $8.5 billion dollars for nursing home care in 1982—9.6 percent of the total for personal health care ($89 billion). By comparison, the 1950 figure was $1.5 billion for nursing home care (1.7 percent of the $86 billion spent on personal health care). In 1978, the average daily per capita expenditure for nursing home care was $68, as compared with $12 in 1966 (Table 1–20). From 1966 to 1978, the average annual change in per capita expenditures was 15.6 percent. The 1978 data by geographic region indicate that the spending ranges from a high of $110 in the New England region (Maine, New Hampshire, Vermont, Massachusetts, Rhode Island, and Connecticut) to a low of $44 in the South Atlantic region (Delaware, Maryland, District of Columbia, Virginia, West Virginia, North and South Carolina, Georgia, and Florida). Again, there are variations among states in a region. For example, in the South Atlantic region, the per capita expenditures range from a high of $60 in Delaware to a low of $25 in West Virginia.

As of 1980, there were 14,316 nursing homes with 25 or more beds in the United States compared with 14,129 in 1976 (Table 1–21). Total beds in 1980 were 1,416,757, vs. 1,295,067 in 1976. This 9.4 percent increase in beds (121,690) was

Table 1–20 Nursing Home Care per Capita Expenditures and Average Annual Percent Change, by Geographic Division, U.S. (Selected Years 1966–1978)

Geographic division	*Year*						*Average annual % change*
	1966	*1969*	*1972*	*1976*	*1977*	*1978*	*1966–78*
	Per capita amount						
United States	$12	$19	$31	$52	$60	$ 68	15.6%
New England	20	28	47	86	97	110	15.4
Middle Atlantic	11	18	28	66	74	82	17.9
East North Central	13	20	34	54	63	74	15.5
West North Central	18	28	43	70	83	95	15.0
South Atlantic	8	12	21	33	39	44	15.7
East South Central	7	11	19	35	40	48	17.7
West South Central	12	19	31	49	55	62	15.0
Mountain	10	15	23	35	40	47	13.7
Pacific	13	20	35	49	57	64	14.2

Source: Derived from *Health and Prevention Profile—United States, 1983*, p. 192, National Center for Health Statistics, Public Health Service.

accomplished through an increase in the average size of nursing homes from 92 beds in 1976 to 99 in 1980. The number of beds per 1,000 population over age 65 (referred to as the nursing home bed rate) was 57.5 in 1980 as compared with 56.4 in 1976. As with the geographic distribution of hospital beds in the nation, the bed rate also varies among regions. For example, the South Atlantic region had a 1980 rate of 38.3 beds per 1,000 population over age 65 while the West North Central rate was 79.3.

As of 1977, there were 1,303,100 residents of nursing homes, of whom only 177,100 (13.6 percent) were under age 65. In contrast, 449,900 (34.5 percent) were 85 or older. Of the 1,126,000 over 65, 294,000 were male (26.1 percent) and only 66,100 (5.9 percent) were nonwhite.[32]

In 1977, the average total monthly charge for nursing home care was $719 for nursing care and $514 for personal care with or without nursing (Table 1–22). The average monthly charge in the proprietary facility was $670 as compared with $732 in nonprofit and government nursing homes. Monthly charges increase as the facility expands in size, with homes with fewer than 50 beds charging $546, 50–99 beds $643, 100–199 beds $706, and more than 200 beds $837. Table 1–22 also indicates that 12.9 percent of the residents were in homes with fewer than 50 beds; 30.5 percent, 50–99 beds; 38.8 percent, 100–199 beds; and 17.9 percent, 200 or more beds.

Table 1–21 Nursing Homes with 25 or More Beds, and Bed Rates, by Geographic Division, U.S.
(Selected Years 1940–1981)

	Nursing Homes					
	Number		*Beds*		*Bed rate*[2]	
Geographic division	*1976*[1]	*1980*	*1976*[1]	*1980*	*1976*[1]	*1980*
United States	14,129	14,316	1,295,067	1,416,757	56.4%	57.5%
New England	1,213	1,182	92,189	95,841	66.0	64.8
Middle Atlantic	1,567	1,519	187,435	210,463	44.1	47.3
East North Central	2,899	2,871	284,035	310,149	68.2	70.9
West North Central	1,964	2,086	156,992	171,532	75.7	79.3
South Atlantic	1,475	1,631	142,383	158,888	38.4	38.3
East South Central	856	859	66,994	78,684	45.5	49.7
West South Central	1,742	1,720	157,347	164,596	72.6	70.3
Mountain	493	511	41,874	45,509	47.4	44.9
Pacific	1,920	1,937	165,818	181,095	58.5	58.3

1. The 1980 National Master Facility Inventory (NMFI) excluded certain types of nursing homes that the 1976 NMFI included (nursing homes units of hospitals, nursing homes for the blind, etc.). To make the data comparable, these types of homes and their beds were subtracted from the 1976 figures.
2. Number of beds per 1,000 population 65 years of age and over.

Source: Derived from *Health and Prevention Profile—United States, 1983*, p. 174–175, National Center for Health Statistics, Public Health Service.

Monthly charges vary according to the primary source of payment; in 1977, the average charge was distributed as follows: patient's own income $690, Medicare $1,167, Medicaid $720, public assistance/welfare $508, all other sources $440 (Table 1–23).

SUMMARY

As this chapter has demonstrated, there have been many important changes in the nation's health care system in the last few decades. If people somehow had been transported in time back to the mid-1960s, would they have been able to predict such things as the increase in governmental/regulatory pressures that health institutions now face, the cost crunch in response to many years of spiraling inflation, and the banding together of hospitals as a strategy to promote cost savings?

While such predictions might have been tenuous at best, the need to think about the future environment is an essential part of health administration, planning, and budgeting. This chapter is designed as a springboard for discussing the future of

Table 1–22 Monthly Charge for Care in Nursing Homes and % Distribution of Residents, by Selected Facility and Resident Characteristics, U.S. (1964, 1973–74, and 1977[1])

	Year					
	1964		1973–74		1977	
Facility and resident characteristics	*Average total monthly charge*[2]	*Percent distribution of residents*	*Average total monthly charge*[2]	*Percent distribution of residents*	*Average total monthly charge*[2]	*Percent distribution of residents*
Facility Characteristics						
All facilities	$186	100.0%	$479	100.0%	$689	100.0%
Type of service provided						
Nursing care	212	67.4	495	64.8	719	85.4
Personal care with or without nursing	117	32.6	448	35.2	514	14.6
Ownership						
Proprietary	205	60.2	489	69.8	670	68.2
Nonprofit and government	145	39.8	456	30.2	732	31.8
Size						
Fewer than 50 beds	—	—	397	15.2	546	12.9
50–99 beds	—	—	448	35.1	643	30.5
100–199 beds	—	—	502	35.6	706	38.8
200 beds or more	—	—	576	15.1	837	17.9
Geographic region						
Northeast	213	28.6	651	22.0	918	22.4
North Central	171	36.6	433	34.6	640	34.5
South	161	18.1	410	26.0	585	27.2
West	204	16.7	454	17.4	653	15.9
Resident Characteristics						
All residents	186	100.0	479	100.0	689	100.0
Age						
Under 65 years	155	12.0	434	10.6	585	13.6
65–74 years	184	18.9	473	15.0	669	16.2
75–84 years	191	41.7	488	35.5	710	35.7
85 years and over	194	27.5	485	38.8	719	34.5
Sex						
Male	171	35.0	466	29.1	652	28.8
Female	194	65.0	484	70.9	705	71.2
Level of care received						
Intensive nursing care	224	31.0	510	40.6	758	43.8
Other nursing care	199	28.7	469	42.1	659	40.7
Personal care	165	26.9	435	16.4	586	14.4
No nursing or personal care	109	13.5	315	0.9	388	1.1

1. Excludes residents of personal care homes.
2. Includes live-care residents and no-charge residents.

Source: Derived from *Health and Prevention Profile—United States, 1983*, p. 197, National Center for Health Statistics, Public Health Service.

Table 1–23 Nursing Home Average Monthly Charges by Primary Source of Payments and Selected Facility Characteristics, U.S.
(1973–1974 and 1977)

Facility characteristics	1973–74						1977					
		Primary source of payment						Primary source of payment				
	All residents	Own income	Medi- care	Medi- caid	Public assistance welfare	All other sources	All residents	Own income	Medi- care	Medi- caid	Public assistance welfare	All other sources
	Average monthly charge											
All facilities	$479	$491	$754	$503	$381	$225	$689	$690	$1,167	$720	$508	$440
Ownership												
Proprietary	489	525	754	486	373	406	670	686	1,048	677	501	562
Nonprofit and government	456	427	751	556	397	136	732	698	1,325	825	534	324
Certification												
Skilled nursing facility	566	585	765	567	468	290	880	866	1,136	955	575	606
Skilled nursing and intermediate facility	514	521	719	513	482	396	762	800	1,195	739	623	630
Intermediate facility	376	388	—	375	333	389	556	567	—	563	479	456
Not certified	329	377	—	—	330	89	390	447	—	—	401	155
Bed size												
Fewer than 50 beds	397	429	625	431	296	128	546	516	869	663	394	295
50–99 beds	448	484	786	449	356	186	643	686	1,141	634	493	468
100–199 beds	502	523	787	508	414	256	706	721	1,242	691	563	551
200 beds or more	576	506	689	656	496	307	837	823	1,179	925	602	370
Geographic region												
Northeast	651	637	957	718	538	131	918	909	1,369	975	511	395
North Central	433	449	738	454	360	252	640	652	1,160	639	537	524
South	410	452	615	408	306	278	585	585	1,096	619	452	342
West	454	487	672	442	323	314	653	663	868	663	564	499

Source: Derived from *Health and Prevention Profile—United States, 1983*, p. 195, National Center for Health Statistics, Public Health Service.

health care in the United States. It has provided the authors' insight into the future and the tools with which to progress there.

It now is up to those involved in this field to examine the events and occurrences that ultimately will shape the future health environment—such things as more cooperative efforts among hospitals, the role of regulation and changes in the utilization of health care (i.e., the further acceptance of wellness programming), the role and mission of hospitals and nursing homes, the role of health care marketing and advertising, and coping with an increasingly competitive market. It is a difficult, but essential, task if the national health care goals are to be met.

NOTES

1. U.S. Department of Commerce, *Statistical Abstract of the United States, 1982–83*, 103rd ed. (Washington, D.C.: Bureau of the Census, 1982), 398.
2. National Center for Health Statistics, *Health and Prevention Profile—United States, 1983*. DHHS Pub. No. (PHS) 84–1232, Public Health Service (Washington: U.S. Government Printing Office, December 1983), 229.
3. S.J. Williams and P.R. Torrens, eds., *Introduction to Health Services*, 2nd ed. (New York: John Wiley & Sons, Inc., 1980), 17–19.
4. Williams and Torrens, *Introduction to Health Services*.
5. Ibid., 19–23.
6. U.S. Department of Defense, Civilian Health and Medical Program of the Uniformed Services: *CHAMPUS Handbook* (Aurora, Colo.: January 1983), 9–50.
7. U.S. Congressional Budget Office, *Veterans Administration Health Care: Planning for Future Years* (Washington, D.C.: U.S. Government Printing Office, April 1984), xi–18.
8. *Health and Prevention Profile*, 200.
9. *Veterans Administration*, xi.
10. Ibid., 9–16.
11. Ibid.
12. Ibid., 13–15.
13. Ibid.
14. Ibid., 15.
15. *Indiana Department of Public Welfare Synopsis of Medicaid*. Mimeographed pamphlet, 1984.
16. Ibid., 1–4.
17. U.S. Department of Health and Human Services, *Your Medicare Handbook*, July 1983 (Washington, D.C.: 1984, 3–43.
18. Health Care Financing Administration, Baltimore, personal communication, November 1984.
19. *H.H.S. Medicare Handbook*, 3–43.
20. HCFA, personal communication, November 1984.
21. S. Jonas, *Health Care Delivery in the United States* (New York: Springer Publishing Company, Inc., 1977), 165–66.
22. A.C. McTaggart and L.M. McTaggart, *The Health Care Dilemma*, 2nd ed. (Boston: Holbrook Press, Inc., 1976), 158.
23. Jonas, *Health Care Delivery*, 166.

24. Ibid.
25. M.W. Raffel, *The U.S. Health System: Origins and Functions* (New York: John Wiley & Sons, Inc., 1980), 202–46.
26. Jonathan S. Rakich and Kurt Darr, eds., *Hospital Organization and Management: Text and Readings*, 2nd ed. (New York: Spectrum Publications, Inc., 1978), 2–7.
27. Ibid., 6–7.
28. American Hospital Association, *Hospital Statistics,* 1984 ed. (Chicago: Author, 1984), xi–xv.
29. Ibid., xi.
30. Ibid., xii.
31. Raffel, *U.S. Health System*, 328–32.
32. *Health and Prevention Profile*, 154–55.

REFERENCES

American Hospital Association. *Hospitals in the 1980s: Nine Views*. Chicago: Author, 1977.

Department of Defense, Office of Civilian Health and Medical Program of the Uniformed Services: *CHAMPUS Chartbook of Statistics*. Information Systems Division Statistics Branch. Pub. No. 780–5, Washington, D.C.: U.S. Government Printing Office, July 1984.

Jain, S.C., and Paul, J.E., eds. *Policy Issues in Personal Health Services: Current Perspectives*. Rockville, Md.: Aspen Systems Corporation, 1983.

Joskow, P.J. *Controlling Hospital Costs: The Role of Government Regulation*. Cambridge, Mass.: The MIT Press, 1981.

Lee, P.R.; Estes, Carroll, L.; and Ramsay, N.B., eds. *The Nation's Health*, 2nd ed. San Francisco: Boyd & Fraser Publishing Company, 1984.

Rosenblatt, R.A., and Moscovice, I.S. *Rural Health Care*. New York: John Wiley & Sons, Inc., 1982.

Somers, A.R., and Somers, H.M. *Health and Health Care: Policies in Perspective*. Rockville, Md.: Aspen Systems Corporation, 1977.

Veterans Administration. *Caring for the Older American, Part I: Directions for the Future*. Washington, D.C.: U.S. Government Printing Office, July 1984.

Williams, S.J., ed. *Issues in Health Services*. New York: John Wiley & Sons, Inc., 1980.

Wilson, F.A., and Neuhauser, Duncan. *Health Services in the United States*, 2nd ed. Cambridge, Mass.: Ballinger Publishing Co., 1982.

Chapter 2

The Hospital: Its Organization and Structure

Gerald J. McHugh and Robert M. Saywell, Jr.

This chapter is designed to provide risk managers with an understanding of the formal organization and structure of the community general hospital by presenting the institution as a system that stresses the interrelationships and interdependencies of its internal components (subsystems) with each other and with its external environment. The development of a formal organization follows from the planned structure by which the identified functions and responsibilities form subsystems that are integrated into a synchronous system called the "formal organization."[1]

The formal organization reflects the structure and pattern of formal relationships and the manner in which its functions and responsibilities are differentiated and coordinated. It also defines the authority and administrative systems.[2]

According to Katz and Rosenzweig, the formal structure is of obvious importance in that it provides the framework by which the relationships among and between the various functions can be established.[3] In their discussion of structure and process, they define structure as "the established pattern of relationships among the components or parts of the organization."[4] Thus, structure and process can be examined as the static and dynamic characteristics of the organization. The formal structure also is established as a result of defining the various internal components or subsystems necessary to satisfy the goals and objectives derived from the hospital's strategic planning process.

Georgopoulos and Mann define the community general hospital as "an organization that mobilizes the skills and efforts of a number of widely divergent groups of professional, semiprofessional, and nonprofessional personnel to provide a highly personalized service to individual patients."[5]

A hospital, then, is a formal entity that has been organized to facilitate the achievement of certain generally accepted goals and objectives. These goals and objectives deal almost exclusively with the provision of health and medical services to a defined patient population. They also must sustain and support its stated mission. Through the development of a formal organization, the necessary managerial processes of planning, organizing, staffing, directing, and controlling may be implemented to facilitate the establishment and integration of interdependent organizational relationships. Thus, the organizing process relates to the identification, segregation, and ultimate grouping of specific roles and responsibilities into manageable units. Properly executed, this process should result in well-defined patterns of organizational relationships, roles, and responsibilities that will allow the entity to meet its mission effectively and efficiently.

ORGANIZING THE HOSPITAL'S FUNCTIONAL STRUCTURE

Understanding the process of organizing a hospital's functional structure can be facilitated if certain basic principles are understood. These principles, which describe how activities are organized within the managerial process, can be expressed in terms of organizational differentiation and include the division of work, scalar differentiation or chain of command, and span of control and functional differentiation or departmentalization. Also involved are the concepts of authority and delegation, keys to understanding the process, along with the role of the hospital as an open system and as a matrix organization.

Lawrence and Lorsch describe differentiation as "the state of segmentation of the organizational system into subsystems, each of which tends to develop particular attributes in relation to the requirements posed by its relevant external environment."[6]

Organizational differentiation occurs in two principal directions: vertically and horizontally. Vertical or scalar differentiation occurs as the number of layers or levels of authority are established; this is the process by which the organizational hierarchy, and therefore the authority structure, is created. It is a product of the development of hierarchical positions to which specific levels of authority have been delegated. Horizontal or functional differentiation, on the other hand, is a product of the division of work or labor that results in the functional grouping of certain skills into departments.

Division of Work

The principle of the division of work, also known as specialization of labor, is probably the most important one associated with organizational differentiation. Through the process of dividing the total work effort into smaller, more manageable tasks, the chief executive officer (CEO), as the hospital's organizer, is able to define the functional structure. This is accomplished by grouping specialized tasks into specific departments. The process is dependent upon the accurate definition of the hospital's goals and objectives so that the necessary skills can be identified and grouped logically into specialized, functional departments. According to Katz and

Rosenzweig, the technical and economic advantages of specialization and division of work are achieved primarily through the organization's structure.[7]

Litterer notes that since there is a specific amount of work to be accomplished, the task can be divided and assigned to different persons or groups. The proper assignment of specific tasks will allow employees to specialize, and their efforts will mesh together with those of others to satisfy the goals and objectives.[8]

In this manner, specialized groups of employees, executing designated responsibilities, can increase the productivity of the organization. Health care institutions in recent years have witnessed a startling expansion of technology that has resulted in increased numbers and kinds of specialized personnel and equipment and a transition to larger and more complex hospitals. This proliferation of technology, with its supporting employees, has exacerbated the already serious management problem of integration of service and personnel for the benefit of the patients.

Gulick, however, warns that there are limits to division of work and lists these cautions:

1. Nothing is gained by further subdividing work if the task thus created requires less than the full time of one person.
2. Technology and custom may preclude further subdivision of work at a given time and place. However, this limitation may be modified by invention and education.
3. The subdivision of work must not pass beyond physical division into organic division. Some activities by definition are not divisible.[9]

In summary, the division of work to a great extent determines the formal organizational structure by directly influencing the vertical and functional differentiations necessary to achieve acceptable levels of productivity.

Span of Control and the Chain of Command

Span of control or span of management is defined as the number of persons who report to one manager or supervisor. It is a concept that is difficult to resolve because it simply means that there is some ideal number of subordinates who can be supervised properly by one superior. Nevertheless, it is an important concept because it determines the organization's shape. In other words, depending on the number of levels of supervision developed, the organizational structure may be termed "tall" or "flat." "Tall" structures have several levels of management, "flat" ones relatively few levels. Figure 2–1 represents a "flat" structure, Figure 2–2 a "tall" one.

Classical organizational theory advocates a narrow span of control that will allow managers to integrate and coordinate their subordinate functions adequately. If it is assumed that enough competent managers are available, some

Figure 2–1 Flat Organizational Structure

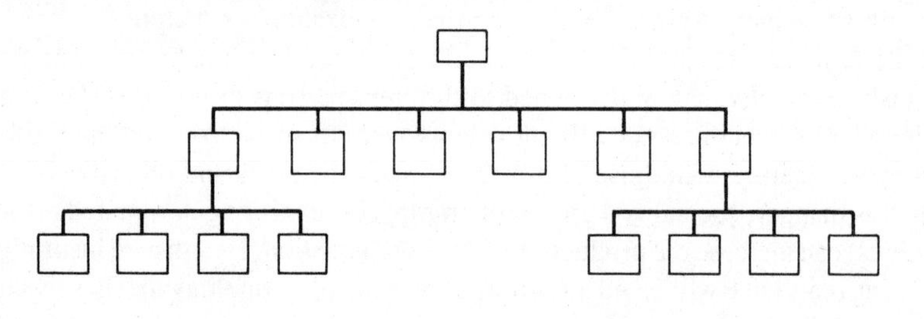

general factors should be considered in implementing or structuring a span of control: (1) a comprehension of the actual amount of working contact between superior and subordinate that will occur on a predictable basis, (2) the level of complexity of the job and the subordinates' level of training and experience, and (3) adequacy of communications channels and geographic proximity. Because of these factors, modern executives have wisely modified some of the classical theorists' attempts at rigidly defining the optimal number of subordinates a superior should supervise.

It is recognized that the most important result of establishing a span of control is that it facilitates the integration of all of the manager's subordinate responsibilities. According to Harrison, once the development of a formal structure has been completed—that is, once the division of work and scalar and functional differentiation have been effected—the process of organizational differentiation is completed and the integration of all the many differentiated functions must now be accomplished to ensure attainment of the corporate objectives.[10]

INTEGRATION AND COORDINATION OF HOSPITAL ACTIVITIES

Because they demonstrate such a broad degree of labor specialization (division of work) and are so highly differentiated (scalar and functional), hospitals are among the most complex organizations known. As a result, coordination and integration of such specialized work generates significant problems in synchronizing the efforts of all levels of activity. Rakich, Longest, and Darr suggest that a well-coordinated organization demonstrates that the harmonious working of one department with another, with each understanding the "share of common tasks it must assume," while ensuring that the working schedules of each are responsive to the present situation.[11]

Coordination and integration of activities thus are major managerial concerns because it is difficult to avoid duplication of effort, "turf guarding," and the inevitable professional conflicts.

It is important to understand, however, that it is the span of control or management that is the principal mechanism for coordination and that coordination is, by and large, confined to the scalar chain (chain of command). Finally, organizational integration is a product of coordination, and it is through the formal structure that differentiation and coordination or integration of organizational activities are effected.

AUTHORITY AND ITS DELEGATION

Authority, as the term is used here, refers to individuals' formal and legitimate power by which they can require those in subordinate positions to perform or not perform certain tasks or duties. It is important to realize that authority is assigned to formal organizational positions and not to specific individuals. Thus, the holder of a certain job, because of that placement, has clearly specified, formal organizational authority. The basis for this authority is its delegation from the position of higher executives to lower hierarchical positions. The authority structure that this process produces provides the framework for assigning jobs and for installing the most appropriate organizational control mechanisms. Weber argues that a manager's authority should be based on demonstrated skill and expertise and that the assignment of ever-decreasing authority to each succeeding lower level creates a chain of command or a scalar chain.[12]

This resulting vertical hierarchy represents one of the more common characteristics of a formal organizational structure and is one of the major tenets of classical organization theory. The chain of command identifies which position is superior and which is subordinate; in other words, who reports to whom administratively—who holds direct authority over subordinate members. Figure 2–2 is an example of a direct line of authority that flows from the president and chief executive officer of a large community hospital to the director of radiology.

Once the division of work has been completed and administration has established a suitable span of control, authority must finally be delegated to the appropriate position. The amount of authority permitted must be commensurate with the amount of responsibility that the subordinate has agreed to assume or is deemed capable of assuming. As more and more responsibilities are accepted, more links are added to the scalar chain. The more authority is delegated throughout the organization, the more decentralized its management becomes.

According to Haimann, delegation of authority is the lifeblood of any organization because without it, there can be no dynamic organizational structure.[13] The authority structure is developed through delegation to facilitate compliance with the established standards of the organization and to induce behavior useful to it. This system of roles and relationships must be prepared and implemented carefully if the organization (the hospital) is to thrive and meet its goals and objectives.

Figure 2–2 Vertical Hierarchy, Senior Management

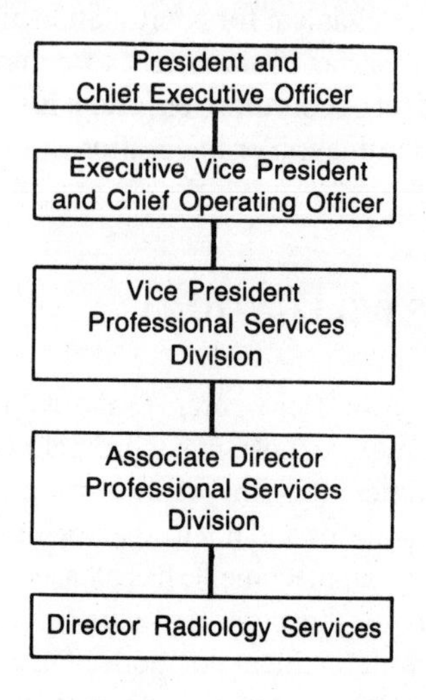

Delegation is a most crucial function of management in the formation or re-formation of an organization. It is, in a large sense, the very essence of the CEO's organizing activities.

The art of delegation is one of the most difficult administrative skills to master, and some administrators are reluctant to turn over some of their duties to subordinates. This reluctance sometimes is caused by a fear of possible mistakes or of loss of power, influence, or prestige. Other managers do not want to invest the time and effort required to train a subordinate to take over a task. However, with increasing complexity of health care facilities and with the growing pressures to operate them more productively, managers do not have time, and sometimes even the skills, to do everything themselves.

Managerial success is dependent upon the administrator's ability or willingness to become less involved in routine duties and details and to focus more on the broader picture of general management.

To be successful, managers must assign the regular, day-to-day operations and activities to others. However, it is imperative that the authority, responsibility, and accountability accepted by an employee is precisely defined and balanced. When a problem arises after a task has been delegated, it frequently means that the superior has not made clear the nature of the assignment and the expected outcome. If the process of delegation is to be successful, the subordinate must receive authority commensurate with the responsibility; otherwise, the superior of necessity will continue to be involved in the task, which will lead to confusion and frustration for both parties. Conversely, too generous an assignment of authority could lead to the subordinate's overstepping boundaries and interfering with another's responsibilities.

This question of the level or amount of delegation is critical in deciding the extent to which the organization will be decentralized. An organization in which the CEO holds most of the decision-making power is considered centralized; that is, little or no delegation has been permitted. On the other hand, an organization in which authority is broadly delegated and decision making is positioned at the lowest possible point is said to be completely decentralized. In many organizations, however, most major policy decisions are retained at the highest levels and the duty of implementing them is delegated to an appropriate managerial level. This is typical of community general hospitals.

There are several additional advantages and disadvantages of delegation. For example, as the organization grows in size and complexity, the CEO can and should be relieved of much of the detail work. Quite probably the delegation of those tasks will improve the quality of the decision because the person making it will be better qualified to do so in terms of detailed, working knowledge. Typically, the delegation of the decision-making process to lower management levels increases morale and interest in the job. However, one possible disadvantage in extensive delegation can be loss of control or a tendency to duplicate effort and therefore to increase waste.[14]

THE MATRIX ORGANIZATION

The hospital's organization, as noted, generally involves functional departmentalization based on the need to somehow manage the numerous kinds of skilled and unskilled employees by assigning them into relatively homogeneous groups with similar backgrounds, training, and interest. Such a basic hospital organizational unit is the department or service appropriate for the small to moderate-sized facility. However, when organizations such as hospitals grow in size and complexity, the traditional functional structure—because of a certain lack of flexibility in coordination and communication—must be modified to accommodate a more precise lateral or horizontal coordination role. This new organizational design has been called a mixed structure or a matrix organization and is designed to provide increased organizational flexibility.

The matrix organization is defined concisely by Neuhauser as: "The existence of both hierarchical (vertical) coordination through departmentalization and the formal chain of command and simultaneously lateral (horizontal) coordination across departments (the patient care team)."[15]

This combination of vertical and horizontal communication among departments recognizes the critically important role of the traditional (vertical) hierarchy while at the same time accommodating the real need for flexibility that often is lost in the traditional structure.[16, 17] The strength of the matrix structure is its unique ability to balance the curious coexistence of stability on the one hand and the need for change on the other.[18]

The matrix organization accomplishes this feat by preserving functional departmentalization while superimposing a "project management" function. Project management, a long-standing device commonly found in such industries as aerospace and marketing, allows a designated manager to be appointed to a special activity or program. This person is permitted to command the periodic use of experts from a variety of functions to complete the project. The emphasis is on direct horizontal communication among specialists, with only rare hierarchical (vertical) communication.[19] When their portion of the project is completed, the specialists return to their functional departments and when the project itself is completed the team is disbanded.

The matrix entity preserves the functional departmentalization while superimposing the project management structure onto the organization's vertical hierarchy. Hospitals have found this structure useful, particularly in patient care team management. Each team consists of nurses and members of various departments involved in the care of an individual patient and is headed by the patient's physician, who directs the care and services needed. Patient care teams are temporary and short-lived since they form around individuals as dictated by their clinical needs and are disbanded when the patients no longer require the team's skill. The team members are accountable not only to the matrix manager but to their functional manager as well.[20]

Figure 2–3 depicts the hospital as a matrix structure and presents a schematic of the coordination process for patient care through functional departmentalization and across the formal chain of command.

While some of the advantages of a matrix organization involve efficiency in eliminating red tape and duplication of effort by sharing information and resources, this teamwork has an additional advantage of providing immediate and appropriate feedback to the manager concerning the patient's (or the project's) status. There also is a tendency to develop mutual respect among employees of different departments.[21]

Many of the problems matrix organizations experience arise from the dual line of authority inherent in the design. Answering to two bosses can cause uncertainty and difficulty in defining accountability and responsibility, which could result in problems of evaluation and compensation for team members.[22,23] Functional and matrix managers find challenges and problems in the matrix organization. As team workers they now must share personnel and other resources. Matrix managers no longer can rely solely on positional power but must turn to persuasion and diplomacy. Functional managers must learn to tolerate role ambiguity, break away from narrow departmental perspectives, and develop an understanding and appreciation of institutional goals.[24]

Figure 2–3 Hospital Matrix Organization

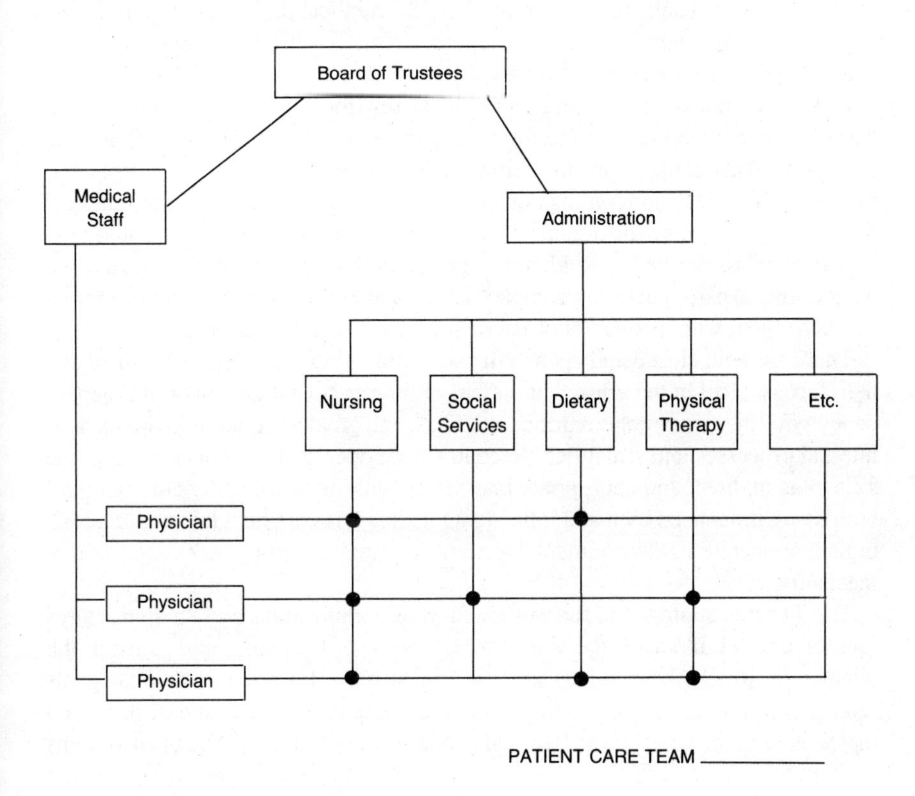

"●" = membership on individual patient's treatment team

Source: Reprinted from *Hospital & Health Services Administration,* Vol. 17, with permission of American College of Hospital Administrators, © 1972.

THE HOSPITAL AS AN OPEN SYSTEM

Traditional or classical organization theory explains some of the important aspects of how entities, including hospitals, are structured. However, the traditional theories have been criticized as being incomplete in their ability to describe adequately the organization's relationship with its external environment and, conversely, its influence on the institution. As a result, theorists have turned to the application of general systems theory to attempt to explain the structure and operation of an organization in its larger environment.

It is important to understand at this point that the use of general systems theory in the study of organizations does not deny the applicability of the traditional or classical management concepts presented already. Rather, the application of general systems theory, in combination with such concepts as authority, delegation, span of management, and hierarchical relationships, goes a long way to describe the development of the formal organization. The utility of applying the general systems concept lies in seeing organizations as open social systems and avoids the general shortcomings of the rather mechanistic concepts of classical theorists who examine the organization in general isolation from its surroundings.

A system is described by Rakich, Longest, and Darr as "a set of interrelated and interdependent parts that form a complex whole, and each of these parts can be viewed as a subsystem with its own set of interrelated and interdependent parts."[25]

There are both closed and open systems. Closed systems are self-contained and therefore isolated in the sense that they have little or no interaction or interdependency with their external environment. Thus, the greatest concern involves their internal processes and structures. In contrast, an open systems concept views the system as in direct and appropriate interaction with its surrounding environment, both being influenced by it and influencing it. It is this continual interaction of the organization with its environment that marks a system as open rather than closed or mechanistic.

The systems approach to the examination of organizations and their structures focuses on such inputs as the work force, materials, financing, and so forth, the manner in which these inputs are used in striving toward institutional goals (conversion process), and, finally, producing outputs (services and/or products) that will enter the social, political, and economic environment. The open systems concept provides a basis for a plausible model that allows managers to depict more accurately the dynamic and increasingly complex internal and external environments in which the organization must survive.

Thus, a department or service such as pharmacy, food service, ambulatory care, or surgery, is a system in its own right and, at the same time, is a subsystem of the hospital. The hospital also can be considered a discrete system as well as a subsystem of a greater system called the hospital field. Finally, the entire hospital field may be viewed as a discrete system, while at the same time, being simply a subsystem of the health system in the United States. The health system is composed of all health providers, third party payers, consumers of health services and products, and the human resources that make it work.

The application of general systems theory and, more specifically, the open systems concept of management have considerable relevancy when used to describe the operational aspects of hospital organization and management. It is important, therefore, for the manager of specific hospital operations such as risk management to be able to identify exactly how that function fits into the framework of the organization and how it supports its general goals and objectives. Managers also must develop a fuller understanding of the role the hospital plays in its external environment so that they will know exactly how their operation affects and is affected by the external and the internal organizational environment. To this end, the following sections examine the principal subsystems of the hospital so risk managers may comprehend the complexity and diversity of the organization they have chosen to help protect.

THE GOVERNING BOARD

The members of a hospital's governing board traditionally have been described as trustees because of the high level of trust a community bestows on each member. Today, trustees have far more responsibilities than their predecessors of even ten to 15 years ago. In the past, numerous trustees frequently were selected because of their social prestige, political persuasion, or financial strength in raising funds. Today, the board's responsibilities go far beyond these functions, embracing essentially total legal, moral, and ethical responsibility, not only for the corporate well-being but also for the quality of patient care and the physical well-being and safety of its employees and visitors.

These responsibilities are derived from the legal powers the organization acquired from the state in which it operates or from the parent organization, if the ownership is located elsewhere. Much emphasis is being focused now on the financial and legal responsibilities borne by the governing body members as they go about the business of establishing and maintaining the policies of the hospital.[26]

Because of the new pressures and the revised perspectives on hospital governance and institutional accountability, it is important for risk managers to understand the roles that are stressed by a board of trustees. Williams and Donnelly provide a comprehensive list of responsibilities that focus on the managerial aspects of maintaining institutional integrity and the quality of performance. These direct administration and medical staff:

1. to maintain a well-qualified management team and to exact accountability for top-level performance
2. to establish and to continually update hospital purposes and objectives
3. to maintain a system in which the fiscal assets of the institution are under constant surveillance, and accountability for these assets is provided to the board at regular intervals
4. to maintain an effective planning process through which both immediate and long-term needs can be identified and resources organized to meet them
5. to maintain a system for the periodic review of operating performance against those plans

6. to maintain and monitor systems to assure that generally accepted controls for the quality of medical care are always in effect and that the quality of medical care is under constant surveillance
7. to exact accountability from the medical staff organization
8. to appoint and reappoint physicians to the medical staff at stated intervals and in a questioning manner that goes beyond just blindly accepting recommendations from the medical staff. (This is not meant to imply that medical staffs routinely recommend incompetent physicians to medical staffs; it is simply that as part of its corporate responsibility, a board must exercise due caution and must challenge and question.)
9. to maintain a formal program of continuing education for all board members
10. to make certain that the board is organized and its meetings structured so that the many tasks required in discharging these responsibilities can be carried out expeditiously.[27]

Traditionally, the governing body or board of trustees of a hospital has been organized into a structure of standing and ad hoc committees through which it conducts its business. While the titles and the nature of the work assigned to these committees is not the same at every facility, most hospitals normally have at least five standing (permanent) committees at the board level. According to Longest, committees normally established to carry out such work are the following.[28]

Executive Committee

This is the most powerful committee of the board in terms of the authority and responsibility assigned to it by the authority of the corporate bylaws. For example, the Executive Committee typically is given the responsibility to act for the board between normally scheduled meetings. It is important to have a deliberative and decision-making body available should an emergency or other critical event take place. The Executive Committee usually is responsible for receiving and evaluating the numerous reports and correspondence coming from subordinate board committees or directly from the hospital's chief executive officer and others authorized to communicate directly with the board. As a result, the Executive Committee typically controls meeting agendas. It normally is chaired by the chairman of the board and its membership includes the officers of the board as well as the chairs of all board committees.

Professional Committee

This group, sometimes known as the Medical Affairs Committee, is the board committee (aside from the Executive Committee) that is concerned most directly with the establishment and maintenance of the highest level of quality of care possible, given the hospital's resources. Its greatest and most demanding function is that of ensuring that the physicians allowed to practice in the hospital are qualified to do so. The Professional Committee discharges this responsibility by working with the medical staff, especially its own executive and credentials committees, and with representatives of administration, to establish and enforce acceptable standards of care.

It is the Professional Committee that makes recommendations to the staff. It also reviews the medical staff's credential renewal recommendations for allowing physicians, dentists, and others to continue to practice in the hospital. The Professional Committee works closely with the committees of the medical staff in coordinating these reviews and appointments. This committee also reviews the need for developing new professional services and programs as well as being responsible for preparing recommendations to the rest of the board concerning the continuation or modification of existing clinical services. Its members should include physicians, either as voting members of the board or as consultants to the committee's membership on matters dealing directly with quality-of-care issues.

Financial Committee

This usually includes the board treasurer in addition to other board members. This important committee has the responsibility for recommending financial policies to the entire board for approval and for implementation by the CEO. It is vital in today's financially difficult environment that the members of this committee be financially astute and capable of understanding the consequences of their recommendations on the very survival of the hospital. This committee has the responsibility for setting the criteria by which the CEO will cause the institutional budgets to be compiled and ultimately reviewed for approval by the board. In addition, it routinely examines the periodic financial operating statements, recommends the hiring of outside auditors on at least an annual basis, and monitors the hospital's investment portfolio.

One of the board's most fundamental responsibilities is to exercise prudent management of and to promote the most appropriate and efficient utilization of the resources it has available. The board has a fiduciary responsibility to invest hospital funds properly so as to acquire additional income. Several lawsuits have established the legal standard that the board must act as any prudent person who would invest funds and not simply to conserve assets. As a result, boards have been devoting even more time than usual to the financial management function. Board members frequently are appointed because of their skill in financial matters and because of the increasing concern of the community that hospital costs be contained as much as possible. A good example of problems in this area is the famous case of Sibley Hospital, Washington, D.C., in which the board was found negligent for not placing funds in an interest-bearing account. In a California case, the trustees were ordered to pay the hospital simple interest on an account after being found guilty of negligence.[29]

Personnel Committee

This has become much more important to the proper management of the hospital in the last decade or so because of labor unions' increasing activity in organizing the facility's work force. Of equal importance, the hospital, like any other employer, must understand the marketplace from which it recruits its staff. The board must be aware of what other facilities in the area are paying for skilled and other personnel and what kinds of benefits are most attractive to prospective employees, and it must understand its incumbent work force and its needs.

To understand all of these requirements, the board must develop and maintain policies and procedures that enhance the organization's relationships with its work force, keep it advised of the hospital's human resource requirements, and apprise it of problems before they get out of hand.

Joint Conference Committee

Properly utilized, the joint conference committee of the board of trustees provides an important avenue of communication among the members of the so-called hospital triad—the board, medical staff, and administration. The purpose normally assigned to this committee is that of liaison between the board and the medical staff, with equal representation from each. The chief executive officer participates either as a full or ex-officio member. While some question the usefulness of this committee, many hospitals have been able to maintain this traditional forum and use it effectively for airing problems and sharing ideas. Longest suggests that this committee may be the preferred avenue for considering issues with overlapping medical and administrative aspects.[30]

THE MEDICAL STAFF

While the board of trustees is ultimately responsible for the provision of the highest possible level of quality of care to patients, it normally delegates this responsibility to the hospital's formally organized medical staff. Since the board does not and cannot relinquish responsibility for the appropriateness of care, it does require that the medical staff be organized to accomplish this. The many mechanisms by which the medical staff organizes itself will vary from institution to institution.

Essentially, the entire organizational structure of the hospital has as a primary purpose the protection of patients. The medical staff, with the approval of the board of trustees, operates under a system designed to ensure patient welfare. This is particularly interesting because medical staff membership is not contingent upon employment by the hospital. In fact, most physicians are in private practice and are not salaried hospital employees. The relationship, then, is one of mutual dependency, because in today's highly technology-dependent therapeutic and diagnostic programs, physicians are dependent to a significant extent on the hospital for services, and the hospital is dependent on those who admit patients to the facility.

Physicians agree, as a condition of membership on the medical staff, that they will abide by the hospital's rules, regulations, policies, and procedures that are known collectively as the hospital bylaws. In the strictest sense, then, the medical staff exists solely by authority of the owners, or the board of trustees, who review and accept the medical staff bylaws as submitted by the medical staff. These bylaws are the rules and regulations by which the medical staff agrees to manage itself, subject to ratification by the board.

As noted, members of the medical staff, with some exceptions, usually are not employed by the hospital. Rather, most physicians are in the private practice of medicine and must apply to the hospital for the privilege of admitting their patients to the facility. As a result, most of the work of the medical staff, as a part of the institution's organizational structure, is conducted by committees. The number of the committees is dictated by the overall organizational complexity of the hospital, the constituency of the medical staff, and other factors.

Categories of Membership

Medical staff members typically are categorized in accordance with the nature of the privileges assigned to them by the board of trustees as recommended by the credentials committee of the medical staff. The Joint Commission on Accreditation of Hospitals (JCAH) requires that the medical staff be structured so that it can accomplish its defined functions. It specifically requires that an ''Active Medical Staff'' be established and recommends other categories of membership be maintained as appropriate. The following, recommended by the JCAH, are the categories most commonly found in a hospital's formally organized medical staff.

Active Medical Staff

This group of physicians and dentists has been assigned full membership status and conducts most of the clinical practice performed in the hospital. It also performs important medical staff organizational and administrative functions such as holding departmental committee and other leadership positions. This is the membership category that is allowed to vote on medical staff matters, although others of the following categories may be permitted to vote in accordance with the medical staff bylaws.

Associate Medical Staff

This designation refers to physicians and others who have advanced through the various categories of membership to the point where they now are being evaluated for advancement to full, active status. The time each physician must serve in this category must be specified in the medical staff bylaws and there must be a mechanism established for consideration for advancement.

Courtesy Medical Staff

Members of the courtesy staff have privileges and can admit patients to the hospital; however, this category is designed to accommodate occasional admissions only. The medical staff will determine the number of admissions that may be permitted before application will be required for some other category. The JCAH also stipulates that these persons should hold active or associate status at another hospital where they are involved in quality assessment activities.

Consulting Medical Staff

Physicians in this category are recognized by their peers as having superior professional knowledge or ability and who come to the hospital on a scheduled or on-call basis. These practitioners are not members of another category of membership at the hospital but remain available to the medical staff for consulting purposes.

Honorary Staff

This category recognizes practitioners who have excelled in their professional practice and now are recognized for their clinical skills as demonstrated by contributions to patient care or for their long-term service to the hospital. Frequently, medical staff members are awarded this status at a certain age and after a certain number of years of service. This automatic change in status must be defined in the medical staff bylaws.

Provisional Status

This status covers practitioners who have been appointed initially to the medical staff. Usually they are placed in this status for a period specified in the medical staff bylaws; it is applied equally to all new members. Assignment normally is made to a specific department or service and the chair or other designated physician is required to monitor the new member's clinical performance and adherence to the bylaws. Should staff eligibility not be achieved during the provisional period, the appointment is terminated in writing and the individual is provided an explanation of any procedural rights. These procedures always should be stated clearly in the medical staff bylaws.

Temporary Status

This status allows the recipient to enjoy temporary clinical privileges for a limited period and may be granted by the chief executive officer after accepting the recommendation of the appropriate clinical department chief or the chief of the medical staff. Temporary status sometimes is given to span the time a specific patient may be admitted if the physician has a legitimate need to provide the necessary care in a hospital where the doctor normally does not practice.[31]

Functional Structure of the Medical Staff

In addition to this categorization scheme or one similarly structured, medical staffs have developed a committee structure over the years that reflects the traditional committee structure used at the board of trustees level. However, while the JCAH is relatively specific about board committee requirements, it lists only the executive committee of the medical staff as a requirement.[32] Several other important quality control functions usually have been conducted by committees of the medical staff, and while they are included within the interpretations of the JCAH Standards, the hospital has some latitude in designating the methods by which these functions are executed. The following are the most commonly identified medical staff committees and their functions.

Executive Committee of the Medical Staff

The most senior of the medical staff committees, its functions and responsibilities parallel those of the executive committee of the board of trustees. This committee, according to the JCAH, should act on behalf of the general medical staff between formally scheduled meetings of the entire staff. In this role, the committee serves as liaison between the medical staff and hospital administration as well as acting as the focus for policy development. Under the JCAH Standards, the committee is required to meet monthly and maintain minutes and other permanent records of its meetings and activities. The Executive Committee must, among other things, perform the following functions:

- receive and act on the reports and recommendations from medical staff committees, departments/services, and assigned activity groups

- implement the approved policies of the medical staff
- recommend to the governing body all matters relating to appointments and reappointments, staff categorization, department/service assignments, clinical privileges, and, except when such is a function of the medical staff, corrective action
- fulfill the medical staff's accountability to the governing body for the quality of the overall medical care provided to patients in the hospital
- initiate and pursue corrective action when warranted, in accordance with medical staff bylaws provisions
- inform the medical staff of the JCAH accreditation program(s) and the accreditation status of the hospital; medical staff members must be actively involved in the accreditation process, including participation in the hospital survey and particularly in the summation conference.[33]

The membership of the medical staff executive committee also reflects its organizational importance in that it includes not only the officers of the medical staff but also those who chair the departments who are accountable for essentially all professional and administrative processes at the departmental level.

For example, the departmental heads are responsible for the maintenance of professional excellence of all departmentally affiliated staff members. This includes evaluating the professional performance of practitioners on a concurrent and/or retrospective basis and recommending to the medical staff clinical and other criteria by which admission privileges to the hospital should be granted. Departmental chiefs are charged with, and held to the duty of monitoring and reporting upon, the performance of individual practitioners so that appointments and reappointments of physicians and others to the medical staff may be made as objectively as possible to protect patients from unnecessary hazards.

Credentials Committee

In this day and age of litigation, the hospital must have effective means by which it can judge the quality of its medical staff. Toward this end the board of trustees delegates the authority to the medical staff to manage the quality assurance and assessment programs within the hospital, recognizing that the ultimate responsibility for the quality of services remains with the board. Internally, the board does hold the medical staff responsible for conducting the programs, while at the same time it assigns the chief executive officer the responsibility and authority for establishing and maintaining the administrative structure necessary to make it work. The credentials committee of the medical staff is a key component of the quality-of-care-management process.

The committee's members usually are elected from the active medical staff. However, it is not uncommon to see members appointed by the chief of the medical staff. The committee's general purposes are to examine the application of physicians, dentists, or other professionals eligible for staff membership; to review the past record of a practitioner who is seeking periodic reappointment; and to determine if that individual should be either continued in current status, have privileges expanded or curtailed, or, as a last resort, recommend denial of privileges.

The JCAH consistently has required that hospitals provide appropriate procedures and criteria by which the medical staff may be evaluated to ensure, to the proper degree, that each member is qualified to practice in the hospital. To this end, the JCAH requires that prospective members supply sufficient evidence of competence by formally submitting an application that complies with the hospital's bylaws. The applicant must allow the medical staff credentials committee access to confidential information, including disclosure of impending or completed lawsuits, history of medical staff membership at other facilities, including the delineation of privileges, and so forth.

Once the applicant's contract has been checked and verified as factual, the Credentials Committee prepares a formal recommendation for delineation of privileges, being certain to get an adequate review by the head of the clinical department to which the individual will be assigned. It is important to understand that the delineation of privileges should be comprehensive and be based on demonstrated competence. Specialty designations by general clinical category, i.e., surgery, medicine, and so on are not recommended. Once this process is completed satisfactorily, the Credentials Committee sends its recommendation to the executive committee of the medical staff for review and approval. The Executive Committee then forwards the application with its endorsement to the board of trustees. The board's professional committee reviews it, then submits it to the full board of trustees for final approval and assignment of privileges to the applicant. Only the board has the final authority to award clinical privileges to a medical staff member.

Medical Records Committee

The medical record is the history of what takes place with regard to the diagnosis, treatment, and eventual disposition of hospital patients. The hospital medical record can be useful should the patient have recurring difficulties and require further treatment. This record frequently is used as a source of data for persons doing biomedical research.

The medical record is a permanent legal record and as such can be subject to court examination in a lawsuit. Because it is the most important evidence of the quality of the medical or surgical care provided, it must be prepared properly and adequately. The committee members must review the written record to verify how well those involved with the care of the patient documented the care and treatment and the results of those efforts. The medical record administrator should always be assigned to this committee for professional consultation to the physicians, nurses, and others who staff this important function.

Medical Audit Committee

This also is an important link in the organizational chain that should be forged to support the quality-of-care review requirements of the hospital. Its principal function, according to Waters and Murphy, is to evaluate the level of performance of medical and other professionals as measured against the standards developed by the hospital's professional staffs. The criteria "must be explicit and measurable and must reflect components of care to enable verification that patients are receiving current technologic and professional services."[34]

Membership in this evaluative committee must include representatives from the clinical specialties, nursing, pharmacy, administration, medical records, and other skills as demanded by the case under study. Thus it can be seen how important it is that the medical record—the committee's principal tool—be completed properly. The documentation in the medical record must be such as to demonstrate clearly the thoroughness with which the clinical team provided care.

This committee will reveal both poor and excellent care and either recommend corrective action in the case of unacceptable care or commend excellent care to the medical staff. Frequently, the attending physician who is responsible for the patient's care will be asked to come before the committee to explain the adequacy of diagnosis and treatment. In large hospitals, the medical audit function is performed at the departmental level, while in small hospitals, it may be combined with the tissue, infection, and utilization review committees, all of which provide additional checks and balances in the medical care evaluation or assessment process.

Utilization Review Committee

This is closely allied to the Medical Audit Committee, the difference being in the focus of the review. The Utilization Review Committee's principal functions are identical to the Medical Audit Committee, plus reviewing the appropriate use of resources in the patient's treatment. Under Medicare, Congress required that, in addition to the need to ensure that the care was appropriate, the committee must determine whether the Medicare patient should have been admitted to the hospital and, if the admission was appropriate, whether there was adequate and effective use of resources. Like the medical audit function, utilization review can be concurrent—that is, while the patient is still considered an inpatient—or it can be performed retrospectively, after patient discharge. Other concerns addressed by this committee include suitability of the length of stay; the effective and efficient use of laboratory, x-ray, and other ancillary services; the need for consultation and/or referral, and whether these were delayed unnecessarily; and abuses of admissions through the emergency department to avoid a wait for a bed.[35]

Tissue Committee

According to Wilson and Neuhauser, this committee reviews the pathological reports prepared by the pathologist or staff concerning specimens removed during surgery. Its purpose is to evaluate the quality of surgical performance.[36] This committee normally includes physicians from the department of surgery and other clinical departments. The pathologist is a critically important member since the main function of this committee is to improve surgical care by reviewing documented procedures, particularly pathology reports.

Infection Control Committee

The JCAH is explicit in its requirement for an effective hospital infection control program: "Responsibility for monitoring the infection control program shall be vested in a multidisciplinary committee. The committee shall recommend corrective action based on records and reports of infections and infection potentials among patients and hospital personnel."[37]

The JCAH prescribes that this be a hospital committee. It does qualify this stance, however, by allowing the medical staff to control the committee's work if there is a proved, effective program in operation that directly involves other professional disciplines and administration. Membership, therefore, must be quite broad and include, at least on a consultant basis, essentially all major departments and services that may have the potential for patient, staff, and visitor infection exposure. Membership by an epidemiologist is particularly useful, if one is available, to direct the committee's surveillance requirements and provide required infectious disease consultation.[38]

In addition, the Infection Control Committee must develop and maintain written hospital and medical staff policies and procedures. These policies would detail the requirements for isolation, prevention, and control procedures necessary for every clinical and other service or department.[39]

Pharmacy and Therapeutics Committee

Members of this committee usually include physicians, nurses, pharmacists, administrators, and other disciplines as may be required on an ad hoc basis. It is, however, a major responsibility of the medical staff to develop, implement, and evaluate such policies and practices as drug utilization and the selection, distribution, handling, and safe administration of drugs to patients. The development and maintenance of a hospital formulary (a list of approved drugs) also is a responsibility of the medical staff and usually is addressed by this committee.

Lastly, each clinical department normally has its own committee structure to deal with its internal management needs. These committees typically reflect the medical staff's general committee structure; thus, such functions as medical audit, privilege delineation, medical records, and so on will be found in larger clinical departments. While not discussed here, some of the other committees that may be found under medical staff control are the critical care, ethics, continuing education, and disaster control committees, all of which have as their major purpose the management of the quality of care provided to the hospital's patients.

THE CEO AND THE ADMINISTRATION

The chief executive officer (CEO) of the hospital is hired by the board of trustees to serve as its agent at its pleasure. It is the CEO who is responsible to the board to see that its policies are implemented properly and that the limited resources available to the hospital are applied intelligently to its day-to-day operation. At the same time, the CEO must ensure that the community's health services needs are addressed properly, taking a proactive position of leadership in the community and sharing the rationale for any decisions that may affect the health and well-being of the population.

It is the CEO who is responsible for installing and maintaining the controls to ensure that the established standards of patient care and safety are enforced, given the quality of available medical and supporting staff. In a word, the CEO is *the* manager of the hospital, bearing the heavy responsibility of establishing and maintaining an organizational structure that is both effective and efficient. A hospital organization chart provides further perspective on the broadness and complexity of the CEO's assigned responsibilities (see Figure 2–4).

The chart shows that two lines of authority coexist in the typical hospital. This duality results from administrative positional authority on the one hand and medical staff's knowledge authority on the other. Physicians and dentists, as noted, usually are not employees of the hospital but operate as private practitioners in fee-for-service arrangements with their patients. However, the rest of those on the staff are employed by and derive income from the hospital. The physicians or dentists, when practicing in the hospital, exercise the authority of knowledge on behalf of their patients and quite properly can direct the nursing staff and others to perform specific functions. Thus, a person who is not an employee can and does exercise considerable authority at specific points, based on the authority of knowledge.

While the traditional role of the CEO has been and remains in the areas of finance, facilities, and personnel, the executive must be deeply involved in the management of the delivery of patient care. It is critical that the organization be established in such a way as to allow the careful coordination of clinical service

Figure 2–4 A Traditional Community General Hospital Structure

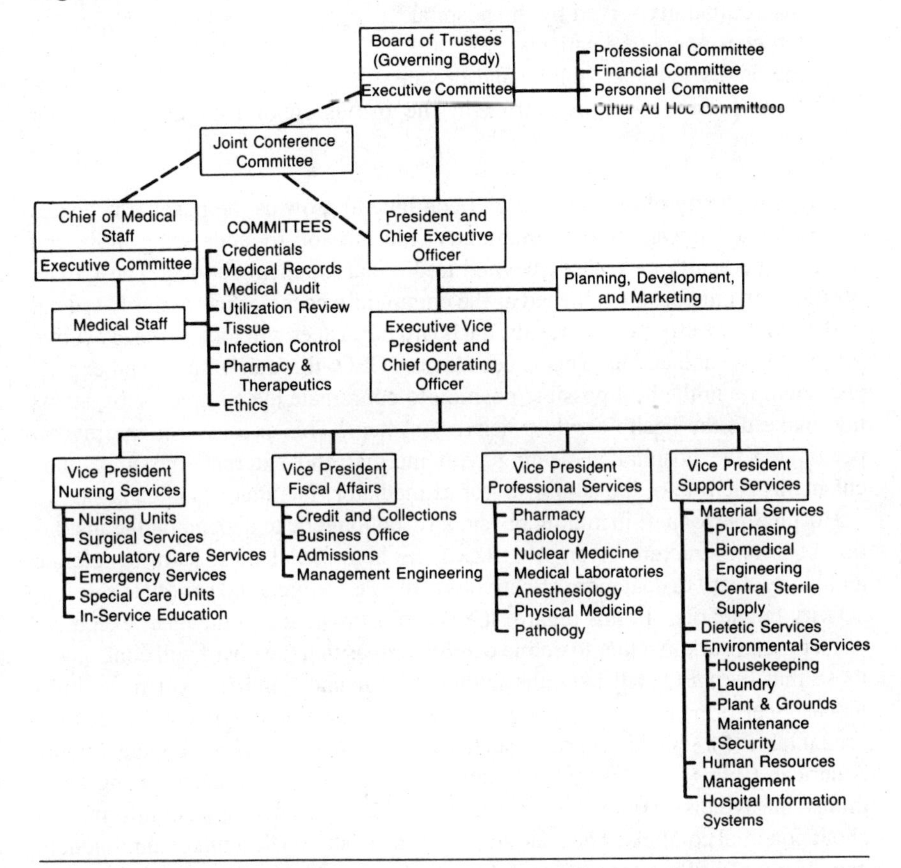

requirements with ancillary and other support services. This role continues to evolve from one of relative passivity to one in which the executive is proactive. McNerney notes that the demand today is for a different, more versatile executive who can adapt to decreasing resources and strong external and internal pressures, all while facing a public that may be questioning the very operation of the hospital.[40]

The role of administrator now demands much greater efforts in strategic planning, marketing, cost containment, productivity, and managing technology while still coordinating and guiding the diverse elements of the hospital toward some common goal. It is the CEO's job to see that cooperation and communication are maintained with the board and the medical staff. The CEO is expected to be an expert in many areas and to be responsible for the total operation of the hospital. Austin offers a partial list of those who hold the executive accountable:[41]

1. the hospital's owners, represented by the board of trustees
2. the community served by the hospital
3. the consumers (the patients)
4. regulatory agencies, public and private
5. third parties—intermediaries in the provision of financial and other resources.

The complexity of the position will continue to grow as the hospital becomes more oriented toward a true communitywide mission by addressing more and more of the health care needs beyond traditional inpatient service. The CEO's position can only be strengthened as the community becomes increasingly critical of the hospital's efforts. As a result, the board of trustees will look to the executive for leadership and action. This is because the CEO, through training and experience, will be in the best possible position to coordinate the complex subsystems that make up the health services delivery system. This executive is the pivotal person for the hospital in dealing with internal and external pressures, thus enhancing the role of the administrator as mediator, facilitator, and catalyst.

Hospital personnel, including physicians, no longer can depend on the institution's formal structure or on what has gone before. All must learn to tolerate ambiguity, learn to deal more effectively with role conflict, and negotiate role and activity boundaries. In this regard, the board of trustees and the chief executive officer must work together to define carefully areas that the board will control and those that the CEO will have the authority to manage and for which the individual's performance will be judged. The board also holds the chief executive accountable for ethical conduct such as the Code of Ethics adopted by the American College of Hospital Administrators. This code requires, among other things, the avoidance of conflict of interest, including the divulging of information about potential conflicts. The code states that there should be a full commitment to and effort in fulfilling the responsibilities and accomplishing the goals and objectives set for the position.[42]

As the hospital becomes more and more complex, the relationship between the CEO and the chief of the medical staff will become more and more critical to the welfare of the organization. This relationship will be tested continually as the hospital addresses the difficult issues of competition in the health marketplace or even the issue of corporate survival. The CEO's role as the senior administrator will continue to evolve from one of relative passivity to that of a much more dominant leader both inside and outside the institution. Unless both the CEO and the chief of the medical staff are generally in complete agreement as to the hospital's future course, serious problems can develop in terms of its effectiveness and efficiency. Not only must there be mutual respect and support; these individuals ideally should share similar management philosophies. Otherwise, critically important managerial processes such as strategic planning and budgeting will be inhibited by professional opposition to some aspect of these programs. The chief executive, in order to avoid or to offset any potential administrative–medical staff conflicts, must establish and constantly update an organized and well-functioning system to provide the strong leadership necessary to allow the physicians to give the quality of medical care demanded by the community. The CEO, therefore, must provide the economic and political support to develop the system that will earn the cooperation of physicians and other professional staff members.

Administrators must realize that the trust and loyalty that they seek from the professions is not earned because they occupy a position of authority. Rather, they must understand that the true source of their influence is their own demonstrated integrity, knowledge, experience, and skills and not the authority conferred on them by their title or by any amount of educational achievement. Since physicians, dentists, and most other professionals detest the regimentation inherent in a bureaucratic structure such as a hospital, the CEO must find an approach by which the professional staffs will offer their cooperation and respect.

Physicians, like everyone else in health services delivery, are coming under closer and closer scrutiny as the public becomes increasingly concerned about the costs and the level of quality of care it can buy. As a result, physicians are taking much greater interest in, and will be much more active in, all aspects of the hospital's operation. It is the chief executive officer's responsibility, as part of the profession's emerging role, to make certain that this involvement is creative and constructive.

SUMMARY

This chapter has presented many of the classical and modern organizational theories and concepts that help explain how organizations are developed to the point where they efficiently and effectively promote their goals and objectives. The development and implementation of the formal structure of a hospital was emphasized by exploring the basic principles of organizational differentiations. Thus, the critically important concepts of division of work, chain of command, and departmentalization were presented.

The study of the concepts of authority and delegation demonstrates to risk managers and others the process of organization in terms of organizational differentiation and integration. The application of general systems theory to explain the modern concept of organization stressed the notion of open systems. The concept of the hospital as an example of a functional matrix organization was delineated. Also provided was an in-depth exposition of the hospital's hierarchical structure, focusing on the formal structure of the board of trustees, medical staff, and the chief executive officer.

NOTES

1. Theo Haimann, *Supervisory Management for Health Care Organizations,* 3rd ed. (St. Louis: The Catholic Health Association of the United States, 1984), 108.
2. Fremont E. Katz and James E. Rosenzweig, *Organization and Management, A Systems and Contingency Approach,* 3rd ed. (New York: McGraw-Hill Book Company, 1979), 198.
3. Ibid., 199.
4. Ibid., 198.
5. Basil S. Georgopoulos and Floyd C. Mann, "The Hospital As An Organization," in *Hospital Organization and Management, A Book of Readings,* ed. Jonathan S. Rakich (St. Louis: The Catholic Hospital Association, 1972), 3.
6. Paul R. Lawrence and Jay W. Lorsch, "Differentiation and Integration in Complex Organizations," *Administrative Science Quarterly* 11, no. 3 (June 1967): 3–4.
7. Katz and Rosenzweig, *Organization,* 203.
8. Joseph A. Litterer, ed., *Organizations: Structure and Behavior,* 2nd ed. (New York: John Wiley & Sons, Inc., 1969), 65.
9. Luther Gulick, "The Division of Work," in *Management, Organizations, and Human Resources: Integrated Readings,* ed. Herbert G. Hicks (New York: McGraw-Hill Book Company, 1972), 4, as it appears in E. Frank Harrison, *Management and Organizations* (Boston: Houghton Mifflin Co., 1978), 128.
10. E. Frank Harrison, *Management and Organizations* (Boston: Houghton Mifflin Co., 1978), 140.
11. Jonathan S. Rakich, Beaufort B. Longest, Jr., and Kurt Darr, *Managing Health Services Organizations,* 2nd ed. (Philadelphia: W.B. Saunders Company, 1985), 146.
12. Max Weber, *The Theory of Social and Economics Organizations,* trans. A.M. Henderson and Talcott Parsons (New York: Oxford University Press, 1947), 341.
13. Haimann, *Supervisory Management,* 135.
14. Ibid., 144–45.
15. Duncan Neuhauser, "The Hospital as a Matrix Organization," *Hospital Administration, 17* (Fall 1972): 10–11.
16. Margaret Timm and Michaelene Wanetick, "Matrix Organization: Design and Development for a Hospital," *Hospital and Health Services Administration* (November-December 1983): 46.
17. Joseph Ryan, "Better Style for Change: Matrix Management," *Hospitals* 54, no. 22 (November 16, 1980): 105.
18. Timm and Wanetick, "Matrix Organization," 49.
19. Rakich, Longest, and Darr, *Managing,* 154.
20. Neuhauser, "Hospital as Matrix," 36.
21. Ryan, "Better Style," 108.
22. Kenneth Knight, ed., *Matrix Management: A cross-Functional Approach to Organization* (New York: PBI-Petrocelli Books, 1977), 82.
23. Timm and Wanetick, "Matrix Organization," 51.
24. Stanley M. Davis and Paul R. Lawrence, "Problems of Matrix Organization," in *Matrix Organization and Project Management,* ed. Raymond Hill and Bernard White (Ann Arbor, Mich.: University of Michigan, 1979), 121, 124.
25. Rakich, Longest, and Darr, *Managing,* 158.

26. Luverne Molberg, "Trustees Take Leadership Role in Community Health Policymaking," *Hospitals* (August 16, 1981): 103.
27. Kenneth J. Williams and Paul R. Donnelly, *Medical Care Quality and Public Trust* (Chicago: Teach 'Em, Inc., 1982), 53–54.
28. Beaufort B. Longest, Jr., *Management Practices for the Health Professional* (Reston, Va.: Reston Publishing Co., Inc., 1976), 13.
29. Lynch vs. Redfield Foundation, 9 Cal. App 3d 293, 1970.
30. Longest, *Management Practices,* 14.
31. Joint Commission on Accreditation of Hospitals, *Accreditation Manual for Hospitals,* 1984 (Chicago: Author, 1984), 95–96.
32. Ibid., 97.
33. Ibid.
34. Kathleen A. Waters and Gretchen F. Murphy, *Medical Records in Health Administration,* in *Hospital Management, A Guide to Departments,* ed. Howard S. Rowland and Beatrice L. Rowland (Rockville, Md.: Aspen Systems Corporation, 1984), 17.
35. JCAH, *Accreditation Manual,* Utilization Review Section, 153–94.
36. Florence A. Wilson and Duncan Neuhauser, *Health Services in the United States,* 2nd ed. (Cambridge, Mass.: Ballinger Publishing Co., 1983), 22.
37. JCAH, *Accreditation Manual,* 70.
38. Ibid., 71.
39. Rowland and Rowland, *Hospital Management,* 16.
40. Walter J. McNerney, "The Role of the Executive," *Hospital and Health Services Administration,* 1, no. 4 (Fall 1976): 12–13.
41. Charles T. Austin, "What Is Health Administration?" in Jonathan S. Rakich and Kurt Darr, *Hospital Organization and Management: Text and Readings,* 2nd ed. (New York: Spectrum Publications, Inc., 1978), 105–116.

Chapter 3

Financial and Risk Management in Hospitals

Richard Rall

Not often can two such seemingly disparate disciplines as financial management and risk management be found to have a highly synergistic commonality of purpose. An often overlooked "truth" is that financial managers and risk managers share one of the most important goals of any hospital—safeguarding its financial assets.

It is the responsibility of the financial manager to oversee the activities of qualified personnel who classify, record, and report upon the financial activities of the hospital in accordance with generally accepted accounting principles applied on a consistent basis and in the context of a system of internal check and control that minimizes the exposure of financial assets to loss through theft or error. The key elements of such a system of internal check and control are qualified personnel, an appropriate approval process, and separation of duties so that errors generally are detected through independent cross-checks and undetected theft generally would require the agreement of at least two persons operating in collusion.

The important synergy between financial managers and risk managers lies in the sometimes obscure fact that the "risk" that the "risk manager" seeks to "manage" is substantially a financial risk—the loss of financial assets, not necessarily through clerical error or theft but more typically through the payment of claims for damages and expenses arising from untoward events that become potentially compensable through judgments or settlements and that, in either case, could tend to erode the hospital's assets and increase the cost of providing health care in the community.

This chapter provides general background on financial management systems in hospitals and addresses the important interrelationships between a hospital's financial management system and the management of its various categories of risk. It offers a general analysis of financial management in hospitals and a clear understanding of the partnership that exists between financial managers and risk managers in circumstances in which the institution's financial assets are safeguarded from all forms of exposure to risk of loss.

Effective risk management requires a basic understanding of the financial aspects of hospital management. This chapter affords an opportunity for such understanding.

THE ACCOUNTING FORMULA IN HOSPITALS

In a financial sense, hospitals are not unlike many other service-oriented businesses. They generate revenue through the provision of services and the investment of idle cash and, they hope, at a cost that leaves some amounts left over to retire the principal portion of debt on a timely basis, purchase new or replacement equipment as needed, finance orderly growth, and provide a cushion for financial stability.

The accounting formula for hospitals is straightforward (Exhibit 3–1). It is through the application of this formula that management can measure (in financial terms) the financial position of a hospital as of a particular date, the results of its operations for a particular period, and the changes in its position during the period under report. The formula elements are described next.

Gross Patient Service Revenue

Gross patient service revenue is the accumulation of individual patient charges for services and supplies arising from care (e.g., room and board, laboratory, x-ray, central supply, etc.). These charges typically are recorded at standard rates

Exhibit 3–1 Accounting Formula for Hospitals

A. (+) Gross Patient Services Revenue
B. (−) Allowances and Provisions
C. (=) Net Patient Service Revenue
D. (+) Other Operating Revenue
E. (=) Total Operating Revenue
F. (−) Operating Expenses
G. (=) Net Operating Income
H. (±) Nonoperating Items
I. (=) Excess (Deficit) of Revenues over Expenses
J. (+) Beginning Fund Balance
K. (+) Contributed Capital
L. (=) Ending Fund Balance

and represent the hospital's business volume expressed in dollars. These also are the amounts that are recorded on the individual patient accounts.

Although there is a broad range of third party payment systems, and many such systems provide for payment of amounts that are different from the hospital's standard rates, it nevertheless is important to make an initial recording of such charges "at standard" to provide a consistent measure (in financial terms) of the volumes of services and supplies provided to patients. The matter of actual payment amounts is dealt with separately (see Allowances and Provisions next).

These payment differences are recognized by recording estimates of the differences between the dollars of revenue or accounts receivable at standard rates and the amounts that ultimately will be collected. These amounts are recorded as adjustments to revenues and as contra (offsetting) accounts to accounts receivable.

Over time, of course, accounts actually are collected (or written off) and these estimates, necessary for fair presentation of financial information on a current basis, are replaced gradually by what finally occurred.

Allowances and Provisions

As described, patient charges are recorded initially at standard rates for measurement purposes. However, for a variety of reasons, patients and third party payers often pay amounts different from these standard rates. Reasons for these differences range from such agreed-upon arrangements as formula-based contracts to mandated arrangements such as Medicare or Medicaid, charity care, and bad debts.

Net Patient Service Revenue

Net patient service revenue is simply the difference between gross patient service revenue and the allowances and provisions.

Other Operating Revenue

Other operating revenue includes such items as cafeteria or snack bar sales, facilities rentals, and perhaps over-the-counter pharmacy or central supply sales. They are revenues related to hospital operations but not directly related to particular hospital patients.

Total Operating Revenue

Total operating revenue is the arithmetic sum of net patient service revenue plus other operating revenue.

Operating Expenses

Operating expenses are the various costs incurred currently in producing the total operating revenue. Although a number of classification methodologies are feasible, one categorization of expenses might be as follows:

- salaries and wages
- payroll taxes and employee benefits
- supplies and services
- utilities and telephone
- insurance
- depreciation and amortization
- interest.

Of course, these general categories usually are recorded in greater detail in the hospital's books of account. For example, insurance might be further subcategorized based on particular coverages (e.g., general liability, malpractice, property, Workers' Compensation, etc.).

Operating expenses, in order to ''match'' the revenue for the same period, are analyzed and amounts paid in advance (for example, advance payment of an insurance premium) are recorded first as prepaid items (so-called wasting assets) and are recognized as current expense on a pro rata basis each month over the term of the policy.

Net Operating Income

Net operating income is the arithmetic difference between total operating revenue and operating expenses. In effect, this is the operating bottom line profit or loss. It measures, in financial terms, the success or failure of the hospital at the operating level, before any nonoperating items are considered.

Nonoperating Items

Traditionally, the most significant nonoperating item in the hospital has been investment income. To greater or lesser degrees, depending upon a particular hospital's financial performance and its operating philosophy, cash balances in excess of amounts required currently are available for investment and the interest or dividend income from these investments is income, but not operating income—hence the separate nonoperating category.

In more recent times, some hospitals have moved into diversified areas to augment the traditional income stream and to meet perceived community needs.

Often these diversified endeavors are through subsidiaries or through participation in partnership arrangements. Gains or losses in these investments are treated as nonoperating items.

Excess (Deficit) of Revenues over Expenses

The excess (or deficit) of revenues over expenses often is referred to as the bottom, bottom line. It is the arithmetic combination of net operating income plus or minus the net of the nonoperating items.

Beginning Fund Balance

The beginning fund balance is the excess of the hospital's assets over its liabilities (see later discussion of balance sheet) at the beginning of the period (e.g., month, quarter, year, etc.). It represents the hospital's equity, the amount by which what it owns (its assets) exceeds what it owes (its liabilities).

Contributed Capital

Under certain circumstances hospitals may receive financial contributions for the purchase of equipment or to pay for construction projects. These specific-purpose capital contributions are not recorded revenues. Rather, they are taken directly into the hospital's fund balance below the line as shown in the formula.

Ending Fund Balance

The ending fund balance is the excess of the hospital's assets over its liabilities at the end of the period under report. It is the arithmetic sum of the beginning fund balance plus or minus the excess (deficit) of revenues over expenses and plus contributed capital, if any.

Risk Management Implication of Accounting Formula

The accounting formula is the profit calculation. Generation of profits is necessary to ensure coverage of debt service, plant replacement, and fixed costs (those that don't vary with patient service volume). The related financial risk of the hospital is the likelihood of an untoward occurrence (e.g., fire or flood) that could interrupt the normal business cycle, resulting in diminished revenues and the inability to meet fixed costs and debt service. Such an event is described as a *business interruption* and is one of the risks for which the risk manager is responsible.

Hospitals generally purchase business interruption insurance coverage to protect against this risk. Such insurance seldom covers gross revenues. Instead, it covers fixed costs, debt service, and similar ongoing cash outlay requirements anticipated to endure throughout a period of business interruption.

A clear understanding of the accounting formula is helpful to risk managers in understanding business interruption risk exposures and the related insurance coverages often written for them. It is of critical importance that carriers be provided with current and accurate information to ensure that adequate coverage is in force at all times.

If the business is not interrupted there are nevertheless risk management exposures arising from the "going concern" that have significance to the risk manager. In general, these exposures are collectively described as liability exposures, the exposure to indemnification claims by others arising from operation of the business. There are five primary exposures:

- general liability (slips, falls, etc.)
- hospital professional liability (often called malpractice)
- Workers' Compensation (statutory provisions related to on-the-job accidents or other disabilities)
- directors' and officers' legal liability (arising from certain acts or omissions on the part of directors and officers in the discharge of their duties)
- auto liability

The risk manager has responsibility for prevention of, or (upon discovery of a potentially untoward incident) mitigation of, damages arising from liability exposures. An understanding of the financial impact of such potential untoward incidents upon financial operating results (either directly or indirectly through experience rated premiums) is essential to an effective risk management program.

THE BASIC FINANCIAL STATEMENTS

Application of the accounting formula to the hospital's transactions provides a basis for preparation of the basic financial statements. Generally accepted accounting principles provide for the preparation of three basic financial statements plus appropriate accompanying notes. This standard of reporting is considered necessary if there is to be adequate disclosure in the financial statements so that a knowledgeable reader can obtain an understanding of what is meant to be reported.

The three basic financial statements are:

1. balance sheet
2. statement of revenues, expenses, and changes in fund balance
3. statement of changes in financial position.

These three basic financial statements are discussed next.

Balance Sheet

The balance sheet is one of the basic financial statements and generally is the one presented first. The purpose of the balance sheet is to present the financial position of the hospital as of a particular date (the balance sheet date). The formula for the balance sheet is simple:

$$\text{Assets} - \text{Liabilities} = \text{Fund Balance}$$

In a general sense, therefore, the hospital balance sheet is divided into three parts: assets, liabilities, and the fund balance.

As noted (see ''beginning fund balance'' discussion), assets are the things that the hospital owns (even if subject to debt). Typically, assets are separated into two general types: current and other (noncurrent) assets. Current assets include unrestricted (as to use or time of use) cash and items expected to be consumed or converted to unrestricted cash and expended during the 12 months immediately subsequent to the balance sheet date.

Examples of other (noncurrent) assets include: property, plant, and equipment (net of accumulated depreciation); investments in subsidiaries and affiliates; and funded depreciation accounts or other restricted cash funds not expected to be spent in the next 12 months.

Knowledge of the special character of funded depreciation accounts and other restricted cash funds (e.g., debt service reserve funds associated with long-term debt) is essential. Hospitals are encouraged to accumulate cash balances in funded depreciation accounts so as to provide an internal resource to pay for renewal and replacement of plant and equipment. Although these funds generally include cash and relatively liquid investment securities (e.g., Treasury obligations, commercial paper, bankers' acceptances, etc.), they are not regarded as ''current'' assets because their purpose is more long-term in nature.

Hospitals that borrow long-term dollars pursuant to a tax-exempt bond issue often are required to set aside (from their own funds or borrowed money) amounts in restricted debt service reserve funds. The purpose of these reserve funds (typically equal to one year of principle and interest payments) is to provide a cushion for the bondholders in the event the hospital experiences financial difficulty and is unable to meet its debt service obligations on a timely basis. These restricted debt service reserve funds are, of course, not current assets because they are not available for current use and because it is not expected that they will be expended at all during the period. Rather, it is expected that such funds will be invested and the interest earned on them will provide cash to help make the principle and interest payments on the outstanding debt.

Liabilities (as discussed earlier) represent amounts the hospital owes. Like assets, liabilities often are separated into current and noncurrent categories based upon whether or not they are expected to be extinguished within a year's time. Examples of current liabilities include short-term (e.g., less than one year) notes payable, trade accounts payable, accrued expenses (e.g., interest, employee leave, etc.), and the principle payments due on long-term debt within the next 12 months. The most common example of a noncurrent liability is the principle portion of long-term debt that is due in more than 12 months.

Fund balance, as noted, is the excess of assets over liabilities and represents the hospital's equity in itself. This equity grows through positive earnings or through the infusion of capital contributions.

A sample balance sheet is set forth in Exhibit 3–2.

Risk Management Implications of Balance Sheet

The balance sheet is the financial representation of the worth of the hospital or what it owns less what it owes. What it owns are assets and they are subject to risk exposures. Certain of these risk exposures are insurable and others are not.

In general, cash and investments are insurable to the extent of risk exposures arising from theft and employee dishonesty. It is not uncommon for hospitals to purchase theft and burglary coverage and require that employees associated with the cash flow cycle be bonded. Poor investment decisions are generally not covered by insurance unless it can be established that directors or officers were negligent (see directors' and officers' legal liability).

Patient accounts receivable are often covered by insurance to defray the cost of reestablishing records in the event of their destruction as part of a casualty loss (e.g., fire or flood). It is not usual to insure the net book value of accounts receivable. However, recent developments have included the availability of "stop loss" coverages to indemnify hospitals against high "outlier" losses under the Medicare Program. This is an emerging risk about which little is currently known.

Property, plant, and equipment are, of course, subject to loss exposure and are generally covered by property insurance for fire, flood, theft, boiler explosion, and similar risks.

An understanding of the balance sheet of the hospital, the costs at which assets are normally carried (original cost less depreciation), and the significance of replacement costs are important to the risk manager who oversees a hospital's property insurance program.

Exhibit 3–2 Sample Balance Sheet

COMMUNITY GENERAL HOSPITAL

Balance Sheet
as of mm/dd/yy

Assets	
Current assets:	
Cash and investments	$xxx
Patient accounts receivable (net)	xxx
Inventories	xxx
Prepaid expenses	xxx
Total current assets	xxx
Property, plant, and equipment (net)	xxx
Investment in subsidiaries/affiliates	xxx
Funded depreciation	xxx
Trustee-held reserve funds	xxx
Total assets	$xxx
Liabilities	
Current liabilities:	
Notes payable	$xxx
Accounts payable	xxx
Accrued expenses	xxx
Current portion of long-term debt	xxx
Total current liabilities	xxx
Long-term debt (net of current portion)	xxx
Fund balance	xxx
Total liabilities and fund balance	$xxx

Statement of Revenues, Expenses, and Changes in Fund Balance

The statement of revenues, expenses, and changes in fund balance is the second basic financial statement. Its purpose is to present the results of operations and their impact on the fund balance for a particular period (e.g., month, quarter, year, etc.) ending on the balance sheet date (see above).

Exhibit 3–3 Sample Statement of Revenues, Expenses, and Changes in Fund Balance

COMMUNITY GENERAL HOSPITAL
Statement of Revenues, Expenses, and Changes in Fund Balance
For the xx Months Ended mm/dd/yy

Gross patient revenue	$ xxx
Less allowances and provisions	xxx
Net patient service revenue	xxx
Other operating revenue	xxx
Total operating revenue	xxx
Operating expenses (normally detailed)	xxx
Net operating income	xxx
Nonoperating items	xxx
Excess (deficit) of revenues over expenses	xxx
Beginning fund balance	xxx
Contributed capital	xxx
Ending fund balance	$ xxx

The formula for the statement of revenues, expenses, and changes in fund balance is the accounting formula presented previously. The elements of this statement are those discussed in conjunction with presentation of that formula. Exhibit 3–3 provides a sample format for the statement of revenues, expenses, and changes in fund balance.

Statement of Changes in Financial Position

The statement of changes in financial position is the third and last of the basic financial statements. Its purpose is to provide a connection between the balance sheet data at the beginning of the period (e.g., month, quarter, year, etc.) and the comparable balance sheet data at the end of the period. Such changes normally include the impact of results of operations for the period, nonoperating items, and changes in the composition of the assets and liabilities. An example is presented in Exhibit 3–4.

Exhibit 3–4 Sample Statement of Changes in Financial Position

COMMUNITY GENERAL HOSPITAL
Statement of Changes in Financial Position
For the xx Months Ended mm/dd/yy

Working capital provided by:	
Income from operations	$xxx
Items not requiring funds (e.g., depreciation)	xxx
Working capital provided by operations	xxx
Nonoperating items	xxx
Proceeds of long-term borrowing	xxx
Capital contributions	xxx
Total working capital provided	xxx
Working capital applied:	
Additions to property, plant, and equipment	xxx
Additions to investments in subsidiaries/affiliates	xxx
Increase in funded depreciation	xxx
Increase in trustee-held funds	xxx
Reduction of long-term debt	xxx
Total working capital applied	xxx
Increase (decrease) in working capital	$xxx

Working capital is the excess of current assets over current liabilities. Typically, the financial statements include a particular note (footnote) that provides an analysis of the working capital changes by element (e.g., cash, receivables, payables, etc.).

FINANCIAL MANAGEMENT SYSTEMS IN HOSPITALS

Application of the accounting formula and preparation of the basic financial statements are facilitated by various financial management systems. Although such systems in hospitals vary in their precise definitions and in the degree to which they make use of automation, there nevertheless is great similarity of data flow, processing objectives, and outputs. Hospital financial management systems are addressed here in a generic sense that presupposes no particular processing methods and no particular level of sophistication.

The total financial management system of a hospital actually is an integrated network of separate elements (or perhaps subsystems). Each subsystem has its own raison d'être and at the same time is an essential element of the total system.

Common elements of a total financial management system for a hospital include:

- budgets
- patient accounting
- payroll and labor distribution
- accounts payable
- materials management
- property records
- statistical records
- general ledger
- management reporting.

The generalized system diagram in Figure 3–1 illustrates the interrelationships of the various elements in a hospital financial management system. These are described next.

Figure 3–1 Hospital Financial Management System

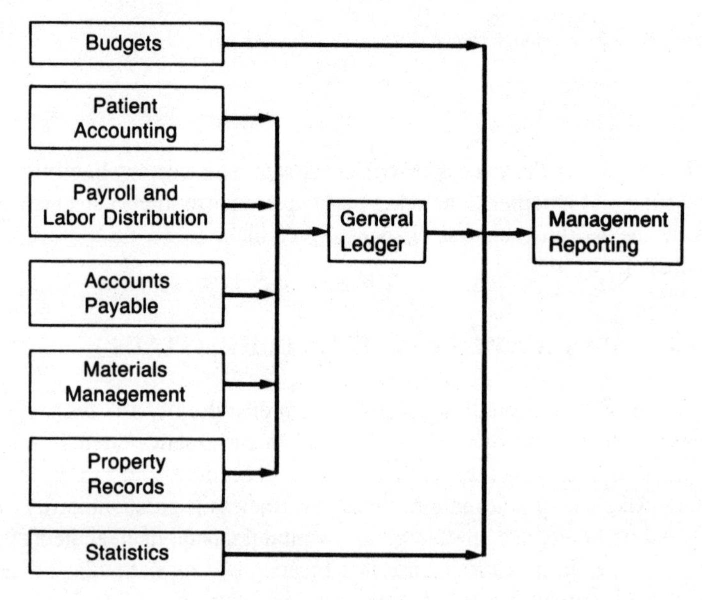

Budgets

Management of a hospital is a complex process. One of the essential ingredients of such management is a well-defined financial plan of action. This plan translates mission statements, goals, and objectives into quantifiable (in terms of dollars and statistics) courses of action and anticipated results. The budget represents the plan of action and its predicted status in terms of pro forma financial statements. Budget data are essential as short-term comparative guideposts (against actual data) for hospital management to use in assessing actual results concurrently and in formulating midstream action plan modifications so as to adapt to changing circumstances.

To be most useful, budgets should be developed through a process that provides for broad participation by all levels of supervisory and management personnel. Without meaningful participation by line managers there may be no "ownership," so administration may lack the grass-roots cooperation it needs to convert the budget to a reality.

In general, there are three separate budgets in the typical hospital:

1. Operating Budget—a pro forma version of the statement of revenues, expenses, and changes in fund balance
2. Capital Budget—a table of approved capital expenditures for plant and equipment
3. Cash Flow Budget—similar to a pro forma statement of changes in financial position but with emphasis on how much cash is expected to be required and where it will come from.

Preparation of the hospital's budget often begins with the development and communication of overall goals and objectives by the chief executive officer. These address such matters as program thrust and direction, facilities plans, overall patient service volume projections, productivity targets, inflation rate assumptions, and any significant financing plans (e.g., hospital revenue bond issue, capital leases, etc.).

Armed with this global guidance, historical data, and experience (plus the telephone number of the chief financial officer) department heads continue the process by developing their individual budgets that incorporate their own (perhaps less global) goals and objectives, staffing patterns, and other operating assumptions based on predicted service volume levels.

The next phase of the budget preparation process involves numerous iterations of consolidation, analysis, negotiation, and restatement. Consolidation and analysis are the responsibility of the financial management staff while negotiation and restatement are line management prerogatives.

Consolidation and analysis functions are primarily administrative in nature and are directed more toward the presentation of data for negotiation than toward actual participation in the negotiation process. Key input to the negotiation process may include information regarding the kinds of rate increases that would be required or the degree to which cash reserves would be invaded under certain budget assumptions. Negotiation and restatement functions are directed toward fine-tuning staffing patterns, compromising on capital equipment acquisitions, and perhaps eliminating or changing proposed programs.

The end product of an effective budget process is a document that addresses financial feasibility, programmatic appropriateness, and a community of support across a broad range of managers within the organization.

Figure 3–2 illustrates the budget process. However, the importance of careful analysis and meaningful negotiation, as discussed, cannot be overemphasized if a process such as this is to be of value to the hospital.

Figure 3–2 Budget and the Budget Process

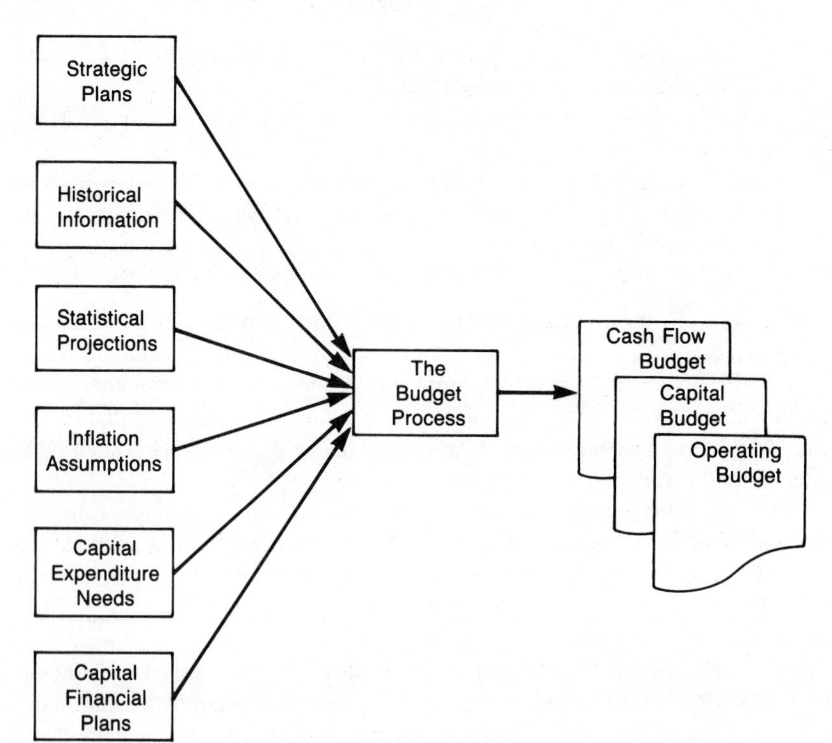

Patient Accounting

The patient accounting system is concerned with the preadmission, admission, and/or registration of patients; the tracking of their physical movement while they are in the hospital; timely acknowledgement of their discharge; and the recording of financial transactions pertinent to their encounter at the hospital (e.g., charges, credits, payments, etc.). The system addresses accounting for revenues and management of accounts receivable. In more technologically sophisticated environments, the patient accounting system is an integral part of the automated patient care system.

The financial objectives of the patient care system are to support census management, accounts receivable management (e.g., billing and collecting), and revenue accounting (dollars and statistics related to patient services and supplies provided).

The diagram in Figure 3–3 illustrates the general concept of the patient accounting system in a hospital.

Payroll and Labor Distribution

The payroll and labor distribution system is concerned with the maintenance of payroll/personnel records, getting people paid, and accounting for payroll and related costs (e.g., payroll tax and fringe benefits) in the hospital's financial

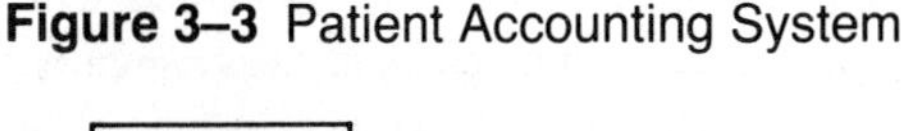

Figure 3–3 Patient Accounting System

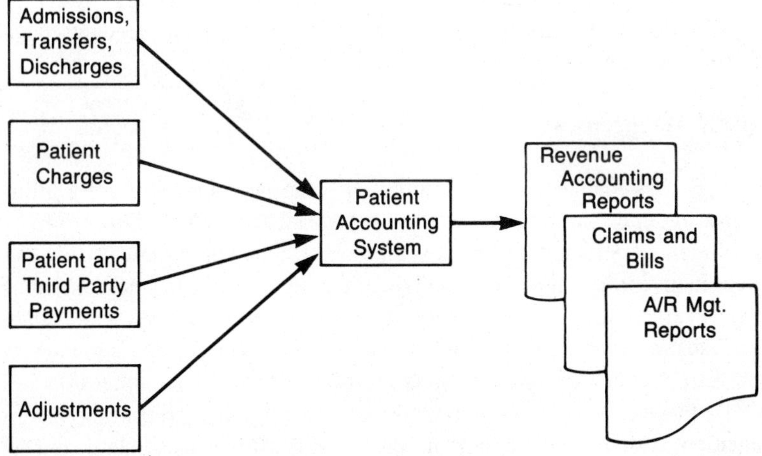

Figure 3–4 Payroll and Labor Distribution System

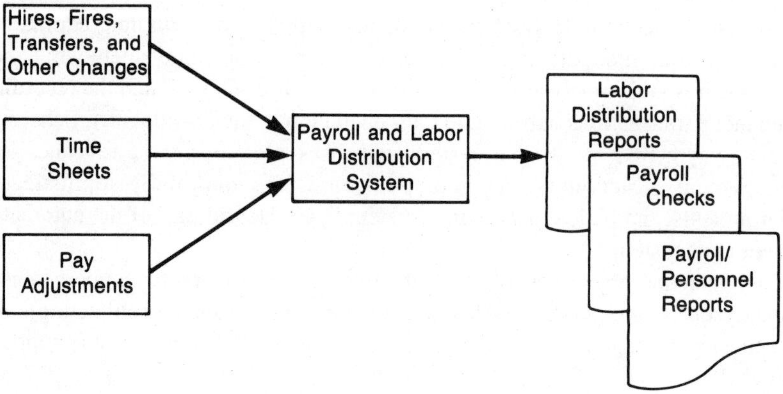

records. It is concerned with hires, terminations, status changes, and time reports for hospital employees. The diagram in Figure 3–4 illustrates the general concept of the payroll and labor distribution in a hospital.

Accounts Payable

The accounts payable system involves the maintenance of vendor files, the verification of vendor invoices, getting vendors paid, and accounting for accounts payable expenditures in the hospital's financial records. It is concerned with purchase orders, receiving reports, and invoices from the hospital's vendors. Typically, this system is closely related to the materials management system. The diagram in Figure 3–5 illustrates the general concept of the accounts payable system in a hospital.

Materials Management

The materials management system handles the negotiation of price arrangements for products and services, the maintenance of supply inventories, the replenishment of depleted inventories, the cost-effective procurement of nonstock (not kept in inventory) items, the receiving of shipments, the in-house distribution of items received, and the certification (to the accounts payable system) of goods and services received so that payment can be made. The materials management system also is concerned with product returns for credit when appropriate. The hospital's Product Standardization Committee often is involved in the materials management system. The diagram in Figure 3–6 illustrates the general concept of the materials management system in a hospital.

Figure 3–5 Accounts Payable System

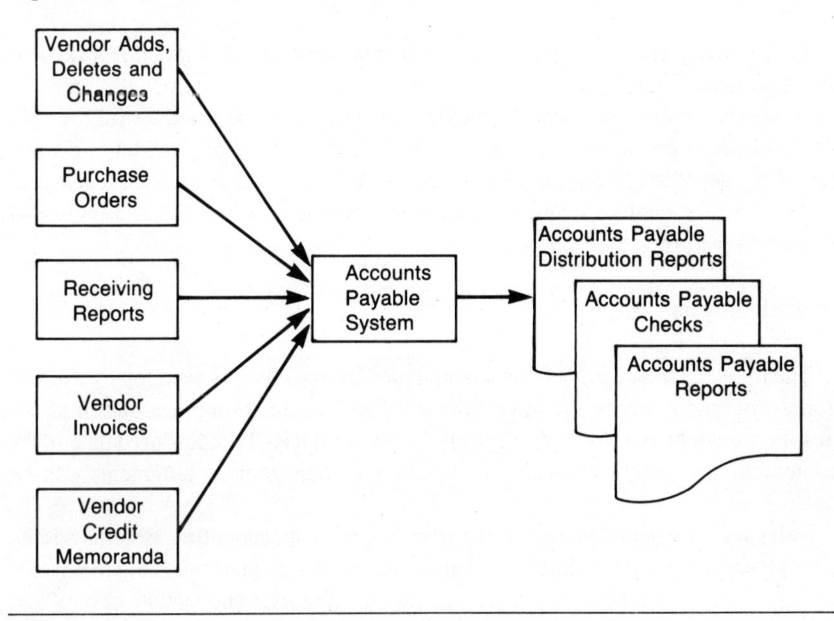

Figure 3–6 Materials Management System

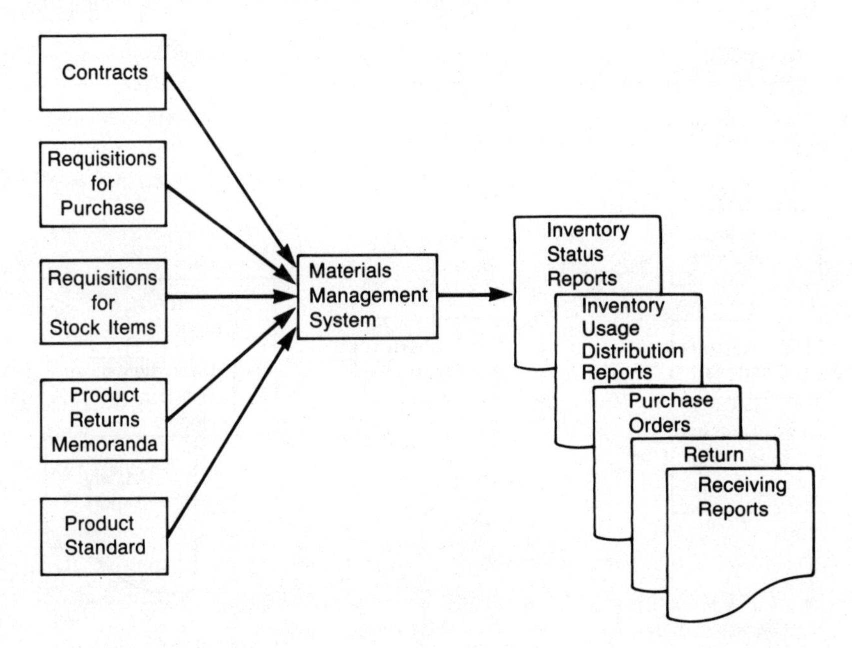

Property Records

The property records system deals with maintenance of detailed information about property, plant, and equipment. This detailed information includes identifying number, description, acquisition date, original cost, expected useful life, and accumulated depreciation. This system also is concerned with providing information about depreciation expense to the hospital's general ledger system. It also may serve as a preventative maintenance control system in some cases. Figure 3–7 illustrates the property records system.

Statistical Records

The financial management of a hospital dictates the obvious need for a variety of dollar-oriented systems. However, the need for accumulating meaningful statistics should not be overlooked. It is only via the analysis of dollar-based data in the context of meaningful statistics that coherent management judgments can be made.

Relevant statistical data are drawn from the patient accounting system (admissions, patient days, procedures, etc.) and the payroll system (hours paid to provide service, etc.). It is only through the analysis of financial and statistical data that management can measure and evaluate the effectiveness of hospital operations. Figure 3–8 illustrates the general concept of the statistics accumulated system in a hospital.

Figure 3–7 Property Records System

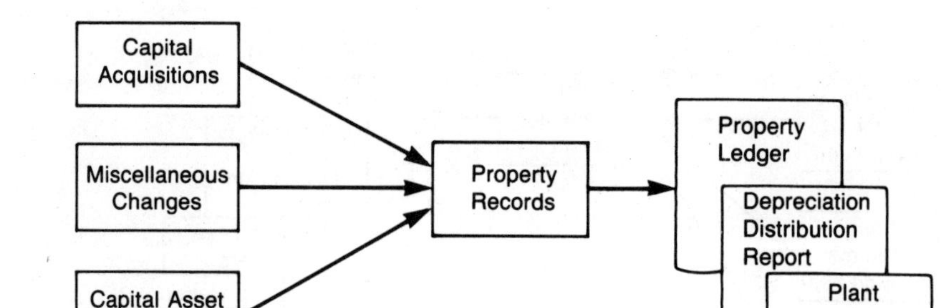

Figure 3–8 Statistics Accumulation System

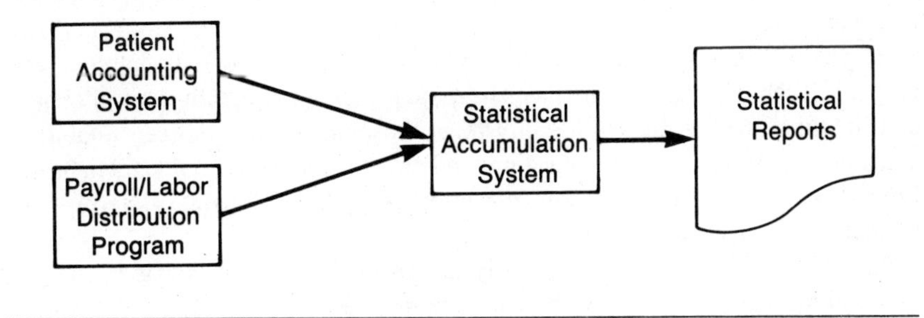

General Ledger

The general ledger is the specific device used in an accounting system to accumulate the aggregate results of financial transactions and to provide the basis for preparation of the basic financial statements and other special-purpose reports as appropriate.

In the general ledger, financial transaction information is classified (according to a detailed chart of accounts) based on the five separate groupings of accounts discussed—assets, liabilities, fund balance, revenues, and expenses. This orderly accumulation of financial transaction data provides the basis for preparation of a variety of financial management reports and for the detailed analysis of financial transactions in order to understand and evaluate operational performance.

Management Reporting

The culmination of the hospital financial management system is the management reporting module. An important part of this module is the production of the basic financial statements discussed earlier. However, other significant, special-purpose reports include budget status reports (budget vs. actual) and special analyses of significant accounts.

MANAGING THE FINANCIAL RISKS

Risk managers direct their efforts toward avoidance or minimization of loss through loss prevention efforts and through effective claims management where losses occur or are alleged to have occurred. In many cases the financial manager can be of meaningful assistance to the risk manager by providing financial management services and the significant information available in the hospital's financial management system. This section summarizes various risk exposures in terms of the ways in which financial managers can be of meaningful assistance to risk managers.

In general, the hospital faces two types of exposures to risk: liability and property. Liability exposure includes hospital professional liability, hospital general liability, special facility liability (e.g., hospital picnic), fiduciary liability, auto liability, Workers' Compensation, and directors' and officers' legal liability. Property exposure includes real and capital property, boiler, business interruption, builders' risk, burglary and theft, and employee dishonesty.

Although these exposures generally are insured, the risk manager and the financial manager share responsibility for prevention of losses and for the mitigation of financial impact when losses occur.

In the area of liability exposure (particularly hospital professional liability) the financial manager can be of assistance because the patient accounting system provides an audit trail of what happened (expressed in terms of patient charges) and when. The record can corroborate or, if appropriate, refute information in the patient's medical chart. With respect to Workers' Compensation exposure, the payroll and labor distribution can provide valuable time and attendance information that may be pertinent to a particular case.

As for property exposure, the property records maintained in the financial management system can be most useful in establishing asset identification, date of acquisition, and net book value. This information can provide a basis for appraisal of assets that become the subject of property losses.

With respect to financial operations, the financial manager can establish and maintain a system of internal control that minimizes the exposure to loss of financial assets through theft or undetected error. The financial manager also can be of significant assistance to the risk manager in providing information as to the cost of various insurance coverages and in negotiation of proposed renewal premiums.

HOW IT OUGHT TO BE

Although the ideal situation is essentially elusive, its pursuit is a laudable goal. With respect to financial management and risk management in hospitals, the ideal situation might be described as one in which there exists a mutual understanding of roles and a mutual appreciation of how common the goals of each discipline really are when compared with one another. Such mutual understanding and appreciation could produce a concerted effort directed toward safeguarding the hospital's assets from exposure to loss from all peril—and, that is how it ought to be.

Chapter 4

Hospital Law: Theory and Application

Ralph F. Valitutti and Gregory G. Drutchas

No major institution in society has been left untouched by the dramatic social evolution and technological advance of the past half century. However, health care in general and hospitals in particular have been the direct focus of many of these changes. The rise of consumerism, increased involvement of government to resolve social and financial problems, and major improvements in the capabilities of medical science at a significantly increased economic cost all have played parts in altering the expectations and demands on the health care delivery system. They also have meant a revolutionary change in hospital law.

The hospital once was perceived as an ''inn'' where patients, too ill to be cared for by family at home, came for palliative medical care and often inevitable death. Now hospitals are viewed as a place where drugs, machines, and health care professionals join to perform miracles for an overwhelming price. When such a miracle cannot be performed, it often is considered a form of failure, not only for the attending health professionals but also for the ''innkeeper,'' which is often held responsible for the quality of care received by patients in the hospital.

To fulfill public expectations, hospitals of necessity have had to rise to big business status. New technology has required new skills to operate technologically complex equipment and to administer treatment. This, in turn, has necessitated large expenditures for capital equipment and facilities and for qualified staff. In this process, hospital facilities have grown from small, barren ''medical inns'' to major complexes with hundreds of thousands of persons working to administer and manage personnel, sophisticated equipment, and large facilities.

As the skills of the traditional supporting health care professionals, nurses, laboratory technicians, radiological technologists, and the like have become enhanced, recognition has developed that not only physicians but also other professionals know something and have a responsibility directly to patients, even if that means in some circumstances outguessing the physician.

As hospital facilities have become larger and medical specialties have developed that often involve little or no patient contact or involvement, the judicial and other branches of government have intensified the search to find a person or entity to assume total legal responsibility. The hospital, as an organization, has been viewed as the most logical choice. Because of public insistence that medical care meets its expectations and the recognition that an ever-increasing portion of the nation's economic pie is being devoted to health care, government as the protector of the people has become much more involved in the operation of hospitals. To be sure, the government's role as the representative of the public has been expanded in many areas other than health care. However, it also is evident that, while hospitals face the general business regulation imposed by government, the health care delivery system of which they are a part has been singled out for additional intensified regulation in many areas.

REGULATION

General Business Regulation

The 20th century has seen a major rise in laws and regulations governing the conduct of business that also have affected hospitals. At one time, a hospital could be opened privately or by a community without an official form of legal existence. A hospital was an entity unto itself. However, with the evolution of corporate law requiring specific filings and other requirements for businesses generally, hospitals, even if nonprofit in nature, were required to incorporate and function like any other corporation. Today, hospitals generally are expected to have a governing board and officially appointed officers, prepare annual reports, and otherwise function as incorporated entities. Although hospital corporations commonly are charitable in nature, in most states they no longer are immune from liability for wrongs that their employees and "agents" are perceived to have committed.

Tax statutes and other regulations have become a force to be reckoned with for newly emerging for-profit hospitals and for traditional and nontraditional or not-for-profit hospitals, which in order to survive economically often have been forced to enter into new enterprises to finance their operational equipment needs. While nonprofit hospitals still are exempt from taxation in their primary operation, they remain subject to taxation for their supplemental economic-enhancement functions such as the rental of facilities and the operation of a cafeteria.

Like any other employers, hospitals today are required to comply with labor laws, including those governing the organization of employees into labor unions and Workers' Compensation for injured personnel. Because hospitals are involved in many activities that present danger not only to patients but also to staff (e.g., disease, drugs, and radiation), they must meet regulations of the federal Occupational Safety and Health Administration (OSHA) (or comparable state agencies).

Similarly, as corporations that may be large enough to affect trade and commerce significantly, hospitals, like other business entities, are bound by antitrust laws and face restrictions on the formation of combinations that have the potential of affecting the cost of goods and services. Should a hospital be found to have violated federal or state antitrust laws, it may be subject to pay double or triple the damages sustained by those who sued them.

As both employers and providers of facilities to the public, hospitals also are bound by civil rights laws involving employment and access without regard to race, color, religion, sex, national origin, age, or handicap. Hospitals thus are subject to administrative action or court litigation for violation of any one of a myriad of restrictions intended to assure individual and group civil rights.

As entities that regularly use in their operation hazardous substances such as chemicals and radioactive materials, hospitals are required to comply with laws designed to protect the environment. Similarly, as owners and operators of buildings, hospitals must comply with building and fire codes.

Special Regulation of Health Care

In addition to generalized business regulation, hospitals face specific regulations directed to health care and the facilities themselves.

Health care increasingly is financed by both governmental (e.g., Medicare) and major private (e.g., Blue Cross) insurers. These insurers have an obvious interest in controlling the cost of health care in order to minimize the draw—from public funds in the case of Medicare and Medicaid or insurance premiums in the case of Blue Cross or other major insurers. As a result, these entities have imposed relatively specific criteria determining the type and amount of services they will compensate; in effect, these criteria often determine the kind of care patients receive.

A hospital may not add to its facilities, obtain new equipment, or expand its range of services merely because it believes such improvements are necessary or helpful. Where expenditures are involved for major changes in facilities, equipment, or services, hospitals are required to obtain governmental authorization known as a Certificate of Need through an administrative process in which the institution must justify its decision before it may be implemented.

To fulfill public expectations, the government has imposed a wide range of requirements on health care providers of all types. Licensure requirements for professionals and hospitals have become more elaborate and exacting. Medications having a perceived significant risk are controlled by restrictive statutes and regulations. Special requirements have been placed on what is considered to be proper human research and what a patient subject to that research must be told with respect to risks and benefits. The requirements for medical and other records maintained by hospitals have been intensified legally. Special reporting requirements regarding infections, child abuse, and vital statistics have been imposed.

Through the elaboration of licensure requirements and the imposition of mandatory requirements by voluntary accrediting bodies such as the Joint Commission on Accreditation of Hospitals and the American Osteopathic Association, hospitals have had placed on them specific minimum requirements for their operations. For example, it is not enough that a hospital have x-ray facilities; rather, it must have a radiology department that complies with requirements designed specifically to assure adequate capabilities and safety of the facilities, equipment, and staff. Through accrediting agencies and statutes, hospitals also have been required to comply with so-called patient rights pronouncements, specifying limitations on their control of patient care in the facility.

All of these, as well as other legal requirements, essentially did not exist before the 20th century. Today, they are basic, and often undesired, ''facts of life'' for hospital operation.

HOSPITAL LIABILITY

These regulatory activities, social changes, and the courts' responses to them have resulted in an expansion of the possible basis of hospital liability.

Regulatory activities by public and private third parties have the effect of increasing the hospital's potential for financial liability in two major respects:

1. They establish directly and indirectly a ''standard of practice'' to which hospitals are obliged to comply; failure to do so will be evidence that the hospital, in effect, has breached its duty of care to patients or staff members and thus will result in liability.
2. They confront hospitals and health care professionals who work there with the problem of trying to strike a delicate balance between the objectives established by the regulatory activity. On one hand, they must be concerned with assuring that patients receive the best quality of care that medical science can provide. On the other, they are constrained by limits on cost, both in the acquisition of facilities and equipment and in their actual utilization, which is subject to being second-guessed as unnecessary.

Even cost-effective quality care may not be appropriate if it is perceived to intrude on patient rights or violate ''new'' duties. It is these ''rights'' and ''duties'' that have been the focus of judicially created law (the so-called common law). While it is a widely held perception that courts are obliged to follow ''the law,'' this is not fully accurate. Courts generally do follow basic legal principles such as the concept of negligence, which is explained next. However, the interpretation of these principles, especially as they relate to rights and liabilities, like the regulatory activity undertaken by the legislative and executive branches of government, are subject to changes in the social, economic, and technological environment.

In recent years, the courts' interpretation of time-honored legal principles has had the effect of greatly expanding the legal duties and liabilities of hospitals. The discussion that follows centers upon these legal principles, including their interpretation by the courts that are of special concern to the hospitals, and suggests how they may be applied by the risk manager.

Negligence

Any determination as to whether conduct will or will not result in liability involves the application of four factors—duty, breach of duty, proximate causation, and damages—to any factual situation that may arise. In each instance of an incident of alleged or actual patient injury, the risk manager therefore must ask the following questions:

1. Duty: Did we have a duty toward plaintiff? If so, what was our duty? Why do we have such a duty? Is the duty one of reasonable care required by law? Is it foreseeable that a failure to carry out this duty could result in the type of injury to others that the plaintiff suffered? Is the plaintiff the type of person that the duty was designed to protect? Did we hire anyone to carry out this duty? Did we presume that someone else would carry out this duty? Was our presumption reasonable?
2. Breach of Duty: Did we breach the duty? Was the breach avoidable or unavoidable? Did anybody know, or should anybody have known, that the duty was breached? Why was the duty breached?
3. Proximate Causation: Did our breach of duty cause the plaintiff's injury? Did other persons or entities contribute to or cause the injury? Was the plaintiff solely or partially responsible? Was the result of our breach of duty directly or only remotely responsible for the injuries sustained or complained of? Would the injury to the plaintiff have occurred irrespective of whether or not we breached a duty to plaintiff? Did we fulfill our duty to the plaintiff but the plaintiff suffered injury anyway? Could the injury have been avoided, by whom, and how?
4. Damages: Was the plaintiff injured? Did the injury preexist the breach of duty? Did a number of factors come together to cause the injury? What were those factors? Did the plaintiff's injury occur immediately after the breach of duty, or years later? Was the plaintiff's injury caused by a breach of duty that would not usually cause injury, or was the injury not the type that normally is

expected to occur as a foreseeable consequence of the breach of duty? What is the extent of the plaintiff's injury?

Answers to these questions can provide risk managers with a preliminary determination as to whether or not hospital liability exists. This question analysis also should assist risk managers in the initial investigation regarding questions that should be answered while the facts are still hot. Early recognition of appropriate issues should allow for preliminary evaluation of a prospective claim and identification of other persons or entities who may share liability and thus be accountable for contribution or indemnity.

Res Ipsa Loquitur/Presumption of Negligence

In a personal injury case, if the plaintiff cannot make out a breach of defendant's duty of care, dismissal will result. This is true because a defendant may be held liable for damages only where they are proximately caused by a breach of a duty owned to a plaintiff.

In the usual case against a health care provider, a breach of duty of care is established by expert testimony supporting the plaintiff's proposition that what the defendant did or failed to do violated the standard of care. In certain cases, however, a plaintiff may establish breach of duty by inference through the doctrine of res ipsa loquitur (translated from Latin: ''the thing speaks for itself''). Res ipsa loquitur is defined by three elements:

1. The injury must be one that common knowledge indicates does not occur in the absence of negligence (leaving a forceps in the abdomen following surgery).
2. The plaintiff must not contribute to the injury (e.g., the patient is unconscious at the time of surgery).
3. The defendant must have been in exclusive control of instrumentalities likely to have caused the injury (i.e., the circumstances of the accident indicate that the defendant might be responsible for any negligence and that the chief evidence of the cause of the accident is accessible to defendant but not plaintiff).

Underlying the doctrine is the recognition that it is unjust to deny the plaintiff any possibility of recovery when the nature of the injury alone speaks so strongly that a reasonable person would presume it probably was caused by defendant's negligence. The key to understanding when the doctrine of res ipsa loquitur applies involves a calculation, upon which, or evidence from which, a reasonable person may conclude that on the whole it is more likely that the event was caused by a breach of duty (negligence) than that it was not. The mere fact that an injury has occurred, with nothing more, is not evidence of negligence on the part of anyone. As long as the conclusion is a matter of mere speculation or conjecture, or where the probabilities are at best evenly balanced between breach of duty and its absence, then the doctrine does not apply and it is the duty of the court to direct the jury that the burden of proof has not been sustained.

It therefore is not enough that counsel for the plaintiff can point to the possibility of breach of duty. The evidence can only sustain the burden of proof. It is necessary to infer the breach of duty as the cause where the evidence makes it appear more likely than not that it was the negligence of the defendant that caused the event. The evidence from which the inference may arise must cover all the elements of negligence and point to a breach of duty. Thus the mere cutting of a ureter during urinary surgery is not sufficient to raise an inference of negligence if cutting of the ureter normally occurs during such surgery. The mere testimony that someone must have been negligent will not sustain the burden in the absence of proof pointing to the defendant.

Since the jury is a res ipsa loquitur case must decide whether the injury is of a type that does not ordinarily occur in the absence of negligence, it must be determined in each case whether a jury of laymen is competent to decide a question concerning professional practice and to make a finding of malpractice without the benefit of professional testimony to support it. As to matters that require the special knowledge or skill of a professional, expert testimony must be presented as to any unskillfulness, negligence, or failure to do what ought to be done.

Consent Issues

Assault and Battery, Basic Consent

Any intentional touching of another's person without consent is a legal wrong (battery). A mere threatening to touch a person that puts an individual in fear of injury also is a legal wrong (assault). Early assault and battery cases against hospitals dealt with situations in which physicians or other care providers had no legal authorization at all to care for or treat the patients or, in other instances, went beyond their legal authorization (consent) to perform medical procedures and/or provide care that was not authorized. In such cases, the dispute presented to the trier of fact was whether or not the patient had, in fact, consented to the procedures that were visited upon the person.

Historically, consent was considered valid whether oral, written, or implied from conduct of a patient that would lead any reasonable person to the conclusion that the individual had no objection to the medical care or treatment involved. In certain instances, mere submission of the plaintiff to medical treatment may be sufficient evidence that the person in fact has consented to treatment.[1] Similarly, silence or inaction may manifest consent where reasonable persons would speak if they objected.[2] However, because of accreditation requirements and a more hostile legal environment, consent generally has become a transaction confirmed in writing. With the development of written consent forms, the problem of assault and battery cases has been reduced greatly.

Who May Consent?

When a patient is a conscious and mentally capable adult, generally only that person may consent to treatment and relatives, regardless of relationship, may not substitute their wishes. This is based on the premise that every "human being of adult years and sound mind has a right to determine what shall be done with his own body."[3]

Given this virtually universal rule of law for capable adult patients, rarely does determination of their consent present a serious problem to the risk manager or other hospital staff members. Where difficult consent issues arise more frequently is with respect to mentally incapacitated adults and minors.

Incapacitated Adults. Some states, by statute or judicial decision, have granted authority, in specified order of preference, to relatives who may consent to elective treatment for mentally incapacitated adults without a guardian. Whether or not such authority officially exists, caution must be exercised in accepting familial consent for incapacitated adult treatment. Those consenting may be found later to have had an interest adverse to the patient, e.g., a spouse who has been estranged for years or a sibling who will inherit a large sum if the patient dies. In such cases, the health care provider relying on authority of family members may be charged with complicity in their wrongdoing. Accordingly, it is important that providers avoid reliance on family member directives that seem contrary to common sense and to seek judicial intervention when the directive seems unreasonable.

When an incapacitated adult has a court-appointed guardian, the guardian's actions, including consent to treatment for the ward, usually are deemed to be fully valid, i.e., the same as if the ward had made the decision had the patient been competent. In this respect, the legal guardian of an adult stands in the same shoes as the parent or guardian of a minor.

Minors. Generally speaking, minors are legally deemed to be incapable of giving valid consent. When a patient is a minor, failure to object to treatment or even an actual request for treatment will not protect the health care provider from assault and battery liability. Thus, in the absence of a bona fide emergency or another special legal exception, hospitals must obtain the consent of the minor's parent or guardian or risk liability.[4]

Among the special legal exceptions to the general rule that minors are legally incapable of providing consent is the doctrine of "emancipation." Most states have statutes that define both the age of majority and the circumstances in which a person under that specified age may be considered emancipated, i.e., an adult for all legal purposes. These statutes provide that factors such as marriage, employment, and ability to maintain and support oneself outside of the home determine whether a person under the legal age of majority is nonetheless competent to enter into a contract or give consent.

Many states also have statutes making even unemancipated minors legally capable of consenting to specified types of treatment, e.g., venereal disease, drug abuse, birth control, and prenatal care. These statutes vary greatly from state to state as to whether parents must, may, or may not be notified when care is given, based on the minor's consent alone.

On occasions, a parent or legal guardian may refuse to give consent to a recommended course of treatment, claiming it violates religious or other personal beliefs. In such an event, proceeding with treatment without the consent of a parent or guardian, in the absence of an emergency or of a statute authorizing a minor to consent to treatment, is an assault and battery. However, where the minor's health, safety, and viability are at issue, providers are put in a "Catch-22" situation. If they go along with the wishes of the parent or guardian, they may incur liability later for failure to act if the minor suffers injury or death. If they go ahead with the necessary treatment, they may incur liability for the unconsented-to care even if the treatment is successful.

In such cases, hospitals must "choose their lawsuit." Obviously, health care providers would rather defend the situation in which they can contend that the patient would be ill or dead if it were not for their actions. However, this reliance on "good judgment" still could be second-guessed by a jury and is dangerous to use without more. The hospital risk managers' responsibility is to reduce the chance of any lawsuit. Therefore it may be important to explore taking advantage of state statutes and/or court rules to seek judicial intervention to protect the minor, provided that a physician attests that medical action is necessary. Many states have adopted neglected child statutes that provide for the transfer of custody and control of a neglected minor from the parents or legal guardian to facilitate needed treatment. Moreover, even in the absence of such statutes, the courts frequently will hear petitions to appoint a special guardian or directly authorize specified treatment where a minor's life or well-being may be at stake.

Decisions ordering or declining to order medical treatment hinge on whether or not there is a danger to the minor's physical or mental health if the treatment is not undertaken. It should be understood that the medical emergency exception to consent does not apply in situations where a patient, the parent (in the case of a minor), or legal guardian (in the case of a "mentally incompetent person or a minor who has a guardian) actively refuses to consent. Along this line, most if not all of the legal decisions in which it has been held that a medical emergency obviated the necessity of consent were cases in which the person involved was unable to consent or refused to do so. Thus, if there is a flat refusal of consent to treatment that is perceived as necessary, medical documentation of that necessity should be obtained and judicial intervention sought.

The question of which medical care or treatment should be given or withheld becomes more complex in the case of the use of life-extending procedures. In the famous *Karen Ann Quinlan*[5] case in 1976, the right of a father, as a legal guardian of his comatose adult daughter, to assert her constitutional right of privacy was determined to be broad enough to encompass the right to withdraw consent for extraordinary medical treatment even though the withholding of such treatment might accelerate death. (After life-support equipment was withdrawn, Miss Quinlan survived in a coma until her death in 1985). In determining that a parent or guardian could oppose the use of life-extending procedures, the court in *Quinlan* set out the following requirements for making determinations involving the withdrawal of such treatment:

1. The attending physician must conclude that there is no reasonable possibility that the patient will emerge into a ''cognitive, sapient state.''
2. The patient's family and guardian must concur in the decision.
3. The attending physician and family, once they have reached agreement, must consult with the hospital's ethics committee or a similar committee of the institution in which the individual is a patient.
4. This committee must agree with the decision of the attending physician.

As in the *Quinlan* case, where competing interests are involved (e.g., physician versus family) and the patient is incapable of making any decision, seeking court action not only is desirable but legally is the most appropriate course. Thus, the procedure chosen should include consideration of the best methods by which to utilize the courts in the ultimate decision. This could include a comprehensive system of recordkeeping through which the hospital could apprise the court of the existence or nonexistence of particular items of the medical criteria previously found important. It must be recognized that many states have statutes defining death that must be complied with before life-sustaining treatment is discontinued.

Whatever approach the hospital does choose to take, it must consider numerous items. The ultimate choice of procedure does remain with the hospital and it should be made upon an informed basis and adequate consideration of the items just noted.

Emergencies. When immediate medical treatment is necessary to prevent death or serious impairment to health, and it is not possible to obtain the consent of the patient or someone authorized to consent on the person's behalf, the attending physician may undertake treatment insofar as it is reasonable and necessary for the preservation of life or limb without the necessity of obtaining the patient's consent. In such an instance, the law implies the patient's consent in conformity with the interest of the state and the preservation of human life and health. It must be remembered, however, that consent is implied in law only in the absence of objection of either a competent, conscious patient, near relative, or legal guardian.[6]

Questions with respect to whether or not an emergency obviates the need for express consent are as follows:

1. Is the health care provider confronted with an emergency that endangers the life or long-term health of the patient, thereby giving rise to a duty on the part of the provider acting within usual and customary practice to take affirmative action on the patient's behalf?
2. Are there medical hazards that would be increased materially by delay in seeking court action, or in the case of a minor or adult with a guardian, obtaining their consent, i.e., the decision to amputate a baby's finger when the only injury that could be caused by delay would be loss of the finger, as compared with the decision to amputate a leg where failure to act immediately might result in a general spread of infection affecting life?
3. Can the need for immediate action be medically supported if challenged?

If each of these questions can reasonably be answered "Yes," then a claim for unjustified treatment is unlikely to succeed. Special caution must be exercised when fewer than all three can be so answered. It thus is important that the risk manager through education of staff and, when the manager is notified, personal action, undertake to be sure these questions are answered appropriately for the treatment decision made; just as important is making sure the basis for the decision is charted fully.

When there exists an emergency justifying treatment without actual patient consent, it still is a good practice to seek the concurrence of relatives if they are available. Even in states where familial consent for adult treatment is not expressly legally authorized, such familial consent is commonly perceived by the public, including prospective jurors, as the right thing to do. Moreover, if the patient should die or become permanently mentally incapable, it is more difficult for family members who concurred with the treatment to bring suit and argue that it was performed unjustifiably.

Informed Consent

By far the largest area of litigation concerning patient consent to treatment involves the informed consent principle. This principle arises from court rulings that a consent was invalid because the health care provider failed to inform a patient adequately of both the risks inherent in a procedure and alternatives to it before obtaining the patient's apparent consent.

In part because of this litigation, there is an increasing trend to require that consent be in writing for various types of treatment involving more than slight risk. Research activities, surgery, and other invasive procedures, as well as the administration of some medications, often require a signed consent form, except in an emergency, to comply with federal, state, and accreditation requirements for informed consent. However, even when written consent forms are used, it is not uncommon for a patient who gave consent to treatment to argue that consent was invalid because the person did not understand its significance.

Because of the almost limitless number of risks attendant to any medical treatment, the traditional rule for informed consent was whether or not a reasonably prudent physician, under similar circumstances, would advise a patient of the specific risk or alternative to medical treatment that the patient contended a right to be informed of. Thus, a physician's duty of disclosure was defined by the standard of professional conduct. A patient seeking to prove that a duty had been violated had to produce expert medical testimony to the effect that the standard of practice would have required the physician in a case such as plaintiff's to inform the plaintiff of information that defendant had not.

Many states still follow the requirement that the plaintiff produce expert testimony regarding the standard of care, following this logic:

1. It would be impossible for a doctor to disclose all information relevant to the proposed treatment.
2. It would be nontherapeutic and/or psychologically improper to advise a patient of all risks when those risks are greatly outweighed by the benefit the treatment will provide to the continued health of the patient.
3. There may be so many risks associated with the proposed medical treatment that patient confusion in trying to sort them out may increase the chance of an unwise decision.

A new rule has emerged from jurisdictions that have broken with the traditional wisdom that "the doctor knows best." In these states, informed consent disputes focus on the information needs of a reasonably prudent patient ("subjective standard") rather than on the professionally established standard of practice ("objective standard") as to what should be disclosed. The subjective standard dispenses with the necessity of producing expert testimony as to what information should be disclosed to a patient, and a question for the jury to decide is presented if the plaintiff offers legitimate evidence that a reasonable person (or patient) would or should have known of the complication before being asked to consent.

It should be recognized, however, that even states that seem to have dispensed with the expert testimony requirement continue to respect the disadvantageous effects of total risk disclosure to a patient. These states therefore seem to have created an exception to the reasonable patient standard in cases in which the defendant can show that the disclosure of risk creates such a potent threat of detriment to the patient (psychological, confusion, etc.) as to become nonfeasible or contraindicated from a medical point of view.

In such instances, the burden apparently is shifted to the health care provider to come forward with expert testimony to establish what is known as a "therapeutic privilege" defense. Once a health care provider establishes that it would be nonfeasible or medically contraindicated to disclose the risks, it appears that plaintiffs' informed consent action will fail unless they submit expert testimony on their own behalf, thereby leaving the factual question for a jury to determine.

Numerous cases have recognized the fact that a physician is in a superior position to that of nurses and other hospital support personnel with regard to informing a patient of the risks attendant to medical treatment the physician is to provide. Consequently, courts generally have been reluctant to charge hospitals with the responsibility of obtaining informed consent to procedures performed by a physician. This conclusion is consistent with the requirement that the testimony of experts is required to establish that a physician has breached the established standard of care in failing to advise a patient of certain risks and/or alternatives, and therefore the standard of care being advanced is the one solely applicable to members of the medical profession.[7]

In the famous *Schloendorff* case,[8] New York's highest appeals court expressly rejected the idea that a hospital has a responsibility to monitor the content of disclosures given by nonemployed health care providers to patients being treated in a hospital. However, the court's opinion appears to recognize that a hospital might well be held responsible for a physician's failure to obtain a proper and "informed consent" when hospital staff members are aware the physician does not have the patient's informed consent to the treatment provided but do nothing.

Since the landmark holding in *Darling* v. *Charleston Community Memorial Hospital,*[9] discussed in greater detail later, it is apparent that a hospital may incur liability even where the physician is not the employee or agent of the institution:

- for failure to have or enforce a procedure requiring physicians to obtain informed consent prior to procedures involving risk
- for allowing a procedure to proceed when nursing or other members of the staff recognize the attending physician has not obtained appropriate informed consent, e.g., the staff becomes aware that the patient does not understand the procedure to which he is submitting
- for patient participation in a research program or for a procedure that is going to be performed by health care providers other than a physician without the attending physician's being actively involved in the decision to carry out the procedure.

Obviously, hospitals always are faced with liability for lack of informed consent where the physician or other provider responsible for obtaining consent is an employee or ostensible agent of the hospital under the respondeat superior doctrine.

The hospital risk manager can serve a vital role in reducing liability exposure arising from the informed consent doctrine by:

- discouraging the adoption of policies that appear to shift the responsibility for informed consent from the attending physician to other support staff members
- seeking policies that require progress notes by physicians reflecting that the risks and benefits and alternatives to more serious types of treatment were explained to the patient
- making sure the hospital's consent form requirements are enforced
- encouraging hospital staff members to advise the attending physician of any indication or claim that the patient does not understand a procedure before it is performed.

Keeping Adequate Medical Records

Medical records are made for the purpose of:

1. providing a basis for planning continuity in the evaluation of a patient's condition
2. furnishing documentary evidence of the course of a patient's medical condition and treatment throughout the hospital stay
3. documenting communication between the physician responsible for the patient's care and any other health care professionals who contribute to the care or treatment while the individual is in the hospital
4. providing a record that may be used to protect the legal interests of the patient, hospital, and/or the health care practitioners involved.

The record also is used regularly by hospitals in their billing, utilization review, and quality assurance functions.

It is the hospital's responsibility to maintain an accurate and complete medical record.[10] Failure to keep adequate records often is pointed to as evidence of its failure to "monitor and oversee" a patient's care. In cases in which patients have sought to hold the hospital responsible for an incomplete record, they have attempted to show that the absence of necessary entries in the record was indicative of the inadequacy of the institution's duty to monitor treatment provided.

For example, a hospital may be held liable if it cannot prove it made sure that a patient was seen by a physician on each day of a stay because hospitals generally are recognized to have an obligation to monitor all inpatients frequently enough to be fully aware of their condition. This duty arises from the hospital's undertaking an obligation to provide not only the patient's room but nursing and supportive staff necessary to observe the person's condition.

Too often efforts of thoughtful and concerned doctors and nurses are made unimportant by gaps or inconsistencies in the medical record. A jury of lay persons generally will believe a black-and-white copy of a record over a person's memory; however, in a contest between the memory of a patient who "knows what happened to his body" and a health service provider who cares for hundreds of patients, the patient usually wins. A failure to keep good records thus can have disastrous consequences by eliminating the provider's best "weapon" in litigation. For these reasons and others, the hospital risk manager must strive for the adoption and enforcement of hospital policies requiring medical and support staff members alike to make and keep accurate medical records.

Communication Responsibilities

While it is generally agreed that physicians have the responsibility to patients to provide care and treatment, their observation between physician visits and/or lack thereof is an area of liability that has given rise to no small amount of litigation. It should be recognized that this duty is distinct from the hospital's duty to assure patients that physicians admitted to its medical staff are competent to provide the requisite quality care, and distinct from a hospital's duty to keep good records. For example, nursing failures to notify physicians of signs of circulatory embarrassment in a patient with a cast on his arm; or to notify a doctor of elevations in temperature, respiration, and pulse; or to communicate information generated by consultants all have led to hospital liability.[11]

Hospital risk managers should be aware that in the majority of instances nurses and other care providers do communicate significant changes to the patients but do not always chart that they did. This is especially true in cases of intense activity where nurses and physicians are "doing everything they can" to save a life but are neglecting the medical chart. In such instances, risk managers, who have educated hospital staff members to alert them to crises having potential liability impact, can play an important role in preserving evidence of exactly what happened by carrying out detailed interviews as close in time to the event as possible.

In many instances, it may be desirable to have the risk manager conduct the interview and investigation as a representative of the quality assurance committee or another committee having a responsibility to investigate morbidity and mortality in order to maximize the likelihood of confidentiality (see later section on Confidentiality and Investigations) and assure that the committees will have the necessary information to make changes that can prevent recurrences.

Failure to observe and report on changes in a patient's condition usually is attributable to the hospital through the actions or omissions of its nursing staff and therefore often involves questions of breach that require expert testimony from qualified nurses and/or physicians as to the required standard of care or observation, monitoring, and/or reporting.

In most of the cases in which hospitals have been held responsible for failure of their nursing staff to communicate changes in patient condition, proximate cause testimony (i.e., testimony that the monitoring would have made a difference in the medical care provided) was provided with surprising frequency by the patient's own attending physician. It thus can be expected that physicians who are codefendants with a hospital in a medical malpractice case will assist the plaintiff by providing requisite expert testimony on negligence and proximate causation. Considering the negative effect that testimony by the hospital's own people can have on litigation against the facility, it is even more critical that the risk manager support policies that minimize the avoidable problem of miscommunication.

Protection of Patients from Harming Themselves

Hospitals have been held liable for a failure to supervise mentally impaired patients from harming themselves. This liability is based on the theory that the institution, through its medical and nursing staff, is in a superior position to assess the condition and tendencies of such patients and to thereby warn, instruct, or supervise the patients so as to prevent injury. Therefore, where there is evidence that patients are incapable of caring for themselves or are so mentally ill as to be hostile and unwilling to comply with a course of human conduct that would avoid injury, hospital employees are expected to establish greater surveillance of such individuals so as to prevent injuries to them as far as possible.

In certain cases, the courts have imposed a duty upon hospitals, through their employees, to anticipate patient needs and prospectively to make proper allowance to assure the individuals' safety. Consequently, hospitals have been found responsible for failing to have bedrails up, notwithstanding the absence of a physician's order to do so, where evidence presented at trial showed that the patients were too mentally infirm to appreciate their orientation. Liability also has been found in cases where patients were not provided with Posey vests or other such devices designed to prevent injury to those in a weakened or impaired mental condition.

If the record without supplementation shows that the patient was largely unattended, a hospital may be held liable on that basis alone, being unable to defend against an allegation that the person was supervised inadequately as an impaired patient.

When a self-inflicted patient injury happens, the hospital risk manager must try to interview as many persons who saw the patient immediately preceding an event as possible and preserve for risk management, as well as for morbidity and mortality review, as accurate a picture as can possibly be developed of what occurred.

Medication Errors

Medication errors result in numerous patient injuries each year. Such errors often arise in the following ways:

1. Medications are labeled improperly on repacking or removal from the hospital pharmacy.
2. Physician instructions are ignored, misunderstood, or miscalculated, resulting in the administration of the wrong drug and/or an inappropriate dosage.
3. Intake and output data are not maintained or monitored properly, resulting in inaccurate information as to the exact level of medication the patient should have, and in turn, leading to overdosages or underdosages.
4. A physician orders medication in a manner that is contraindicated by the drug manufacturer's recommendations, and hospital staff members follow the order, notwithstanding their knowledge that it is inappropriate.
5. Medication is administered for experimental purposes without appropriate precautions or informed patient consent.

Physicians whose patients have received improper medications should be notified immediately so that they may carefully follow such individuals and chart all adverse effects as well as the absence of adverse effects. Nurses can assist by more detailed charting regarding a patient's condition subsequent to medication error so that there will be something to point to in the event that a patient later chooses to exaggerate damages.

The risk manager can play an important role in reducing hospital liability exposure by seeing to it that patients who have received mislabeled prescriptions return all such medications and that they receive the appropriate medicines. Documentation of charts or other statements of facts should be made of all follow-up efforts in the search for patients who have received improper medications and, where possible, an accounting should be made of any mislabeled drugs.

Special Agency Issues

Few if any other businesses, like most hospitals, regularly have nonemployees both performing and directing services that are the integral part of their operation. Because of its dependence on independent staff physicians who are not employed by the institution, yet perform and direct its employees in patient care, a hospital faces unique agency liability issues. Should a hospital be liable for the acts of a qualified doctor merely because the physician performed services within the facility? Should the hospital be responsible for acts of its employees that are directed by a physician the institution does not employ? These questions and their answers have been recurrent subjects of court decisions.

Vicarious Liability for Independent Staff Physicians

A hospital may be held liable for the acts of independent staff physicians notwithstanding the fact that they are not employed by the institution. The principle of law by which a hospital is held responsible for the negligence of an independent staff physician is called vicarious or respondeat superior liability.

A famous legal commentator explained the basis for the theory of vicarious liability:

> ''In multitude, very ingenious reasons have been offered for the vicarious liability of a master: He has more or less fictitious control'' over the behavior of the servant; he has ''set the whole thing in motion,'' and is therefore responsible for what has happened; he has selected the servant and trusted him, and so should suffer for his wrongs, rather than an innocent stranger who has had no opportunity to protect himself; it is a great concession that any man should be permitted to employ another at all, and there should be a corresponding responsibility as the price to be paid for it—or, more frankly and cynically, ''in hard fact, the reason for the employers' liability is the damages are taken from a deep pocket . . . ''[12]

Most courts have made little or no effort to explain the result and have taken refuge in rather empty phrases such as ''he who does a thing through another does it himself'' or the endlessly repeated formula of respondeat superior, which translated from Latin means nothing more than ''look to the man higher up.''

Vicarious liability formerly was limited generally to situations where there was a true employer-employee or principal-agent relationship between the vicariously liable party (e.g., the hospital) and the person who was the wrongdoer. However, in recent years, this vicarious liability theory has been expanded, utilizing an older but seldom-used principle known as ''ostensible agency'' or ''apparent authority.'' This principle is based on the premise that if a person misleads third parties into thinking someone is his agent, he is bound, for liability purposes, as if that someone is his agent in fact.

The principles of vicarious responsibility, and particularly ostensible agency, have been applied to hospitals with increasing frequency as a consequence of the rash of malpractice case verdicts for huge amounts that must be satisfied by uninsured or inadequately insured physicians. In many cases, the application of the doctrine to hospitals appears to be unfair because, as noted, they do not have actual control over physicians' exercise of judgment in most cases.

The courts have done away with the requirement that a plaintiff make any showing that the independent physician in question was under any control of the hospital, instead shifting the entire focus to whether the patient at the time of admission was looking to the hospital for treatment of physical ailments or merely viewed the facility as the place where the person's own physician would treat the problems.[13]

The reasons given by courts in justifying the expansion of the doctrine of vicarious responsibility include the following:

- A hospital holds the physician out as its agent in a manner that leads patients to reasonably believe they are being treated by an agent of the hospital (i.e., the physician is the ostensible agent of the hospital).
- Patients generally look to the hospital to provide treatment, rather than viewing it as the place where the personal physician they hired provides care, leading the patients to believe that the treatment is being provided on behalf of the hospital.
- It would be unfair to require a patient to be familiar with the law of respondeat superior or to inquire whether a doctor is a hospital employee.
- Patients should not be bound by ''secret'' limitations in doctors' contracts with hospitals.[14]

Ostensible agency has been found to exist where a hospital holds itself out as a place where the public an come to see doctors, be cared for by nurses and physicians, and receive all necessary health care required by those doctors and nurses.

The key questions risk managers must ask themselves in making a determination whether the hospital has exposure under this principle for a nonemployed physician are:

1. Did the patient have a physician/patient relationship with the physician prior to admission or was the physician requested by the patient's attending doctor or consulting physician?
2. Was the patient aware of how the physician became involved?
3. Was the patient on notice that the physician seen in the hospital was not an employee or agent of the facility?
4. Did the hospital avoid direct or indirect communication that might lead the patient to believe that the physician was a hospital employee?
5. Was it unreasonable for the patient to presume that the hospital was furnishing the physician?

A "no" answer to any of these questions can mean the hospital faces liability for the actions of the staff physician. The effect of this is to make the hospital a viable defendant and potentially liable in a case where its employees did nothing wrong.[15]

To minimize this exposure it is essential that risk managers propose and encourage hospital policies that:

1. Require patients being treated at the hospital emergency room or by on-call physicians, or physicians selected by the patient or a representative from a list of those available to provide the care, to acknowledge in writing that they recognize that the attending physicians are not agents, servants, or employees of the hospital (where this is a fact); and
2. Require independent staff physicians to carry adequate insurance coverage or be otherwise financially responsible for their own acts.

It must be recognized that neither step will absolutely eliminate hospital risk of vicarious liability for nonemployed physicians. What they do offer is a measure of protection in a case, during trial, and after judgment.

Liability for Employees Directed by Independent Staff Physicians

Even where there is an insufficient basis for a hospital to be held responsible vicariously for the actions of an independent staff physician, liability for the directives of that physician that are carried out by hospital employees still may be a problem. This is sometimes called the "borrowed servant" or "borrowed employee" issue. Many jurisdictions have long recognized that a general employee of one employer may be the borrowed servant of another.[16]

Its underlying premise is that a person in the general employment of one master may be loaned temporarily to another master so as to become a borrowed employee of the second. Under those circumstances, a person may at times serve both "masters" simultaneously and, at others, only one of them. Control and supervision at the time a specific act is performed by the "borrowed employee" are the essential considerations in determining which of the two masters is legally liable for the act. In a hospital context, the Texas Supreme Court approved the following definition of a borrowed servant:

> A "borrowed employee" as used in this charge means one who, while in the general employment of the hospital, is subject to the right of the physician to direct or control the details of the particular work inquired about, and is not merely cooperating with the suggestions of said physician.[17]

Thus, under the borrowed servant doctrine, the essential question is whether or not the putative master (e.g., a surgeon) had the right to control the details of the work the hospital employee performed that gave rise to liability. If the "master" did, the physician may be deemed the captain of the ship and liable to the patient, with or without the hospital's being held jointly liable.[18] The determination of such "control" generally is a factual question for the jury to determine.

Thus, where a nurse, intern, or resident is "borrowed" from the hospital (assigned to work as an assistant to the independent staff physician) to carry out the business of that physician, and it can be shown that the physician directed and controlled the actions of the "borrowed servant," the hospital may be entitled to indemnity from the independent staff physician[19] or to dismissal from the case.

On the other hand, if a hospital resident or nurse is instructed by a physician to independently monitor a patient, and is negligent in doing so, the hospital generally will not be relieved of liability as its agent is carrying out a routine function for which the person normally was employed by the facility. In such an instance, the agent already would be bound to obey the attending physician's orders and there is no true relinquishment of control by the hospital over that employee.

Corporate Liability

As noted, historically a hospital has not been responsible for the direct care of a health care provider it does not actually employ. Although the traditional rule was broken by agency theories, they did not change the underlying premise that hospitals do not practice medicine. However, the premise has been altered by the legal rule, established through case and statutory law, that a hospital has a duty to protect patients from unqualified and/or incompetent physicians and other professionals within its facilities. This is a direct duty owed to patients, giving rise to an independent basis of liability; it is not vicarious or respondeat superior liability. Because the hospital's administrative and governing bodies are involved in the credentialling and review process, a breach of the hospital's duty to act reasonably in this process results in direct corporate liability.

The case generally credited with breaking the traditional policy against direct hospital liability for physician malpractice is *Darling* (1965).[20] Like most landmark decisions, the facts in *Darling* begged the issue as to who is responsible for patient care.

The plaintiff was Pat Darling, an 18-year-old college student who, during football practice, suffered a broken leg. He was taken to the Charleston (Ill.) Community Memorial Hospital where Dr. John R. Alexander was on emergency duty. Dr. Alexander had graduated from medical school in 1927 and gone through a two-year internship. He had no specialty, continuing, or refresher training after his internship.

When the plaintiff was brought in, his unwashed leg was aligned by closed reduction, traction was applied, and the leg was placed in a plaster cast. A heat cradle was applied to help dry the cast. The cast began four inches below the plaintiff's hip and extended to his foot, leaving only his toes exposed. He soon began to complain of pain, apparently excruciating, in the casted leg. Dr. Alexander ordered pain-relieving drugs. There was discoloration of the toes and foot and there was a strong odor emanating from the leg that wafted through the hall. All of this was observed and recorded in the plaintiff's medical record.

Dr. Alexander attempted to relieve the pressure by splitting the cast open with a Stryker saw. Unfortunately, in doing so, he allowed the blade to reach the leg, cutting the flesh. Gangrene set in, many more complaints of pain and odor were recorded, and finally in the second week of the ordeal the plaintiff was transferred to another hospital, where efforts to save his leg were unsuccessful and the lower part was amputated.

Dr. Alexander's negligence was obvious. He settled out of court before trial, leaving his results to be explained by the hospital and administrator. At trial, the hospital was accused of failing to review, supervise, or consult about the treatment Dr. Alexander gave to Darling. The plaintiff presented evidence suggesting that the hospital had the opportunity for such review but failed to exercise it, notwithstanding the fact that its nurses were intimately aware of the patient's suffering. The plaintiff contended that the hospital was negligent in permitting Dr. Alexander to do orthopedic work of the kind required in the case, should have reviewed his operative procedures to make sure that he was up to date, and should have called in a consulting physician to take over the case when it was apparent that Dr. Alexander's treatments not only were ineffective but probably were harming the patient.

The plaintiff further contended that it was the duty of the defendant nurses to inform hospital administration of the deterioration of the plaintiff's leg as proof of Dr. Alexander's incompetence so that administration could intervene in time to have taken remedial action. In affirming a jury verdict for plaintiff, the Illinois Supreme Court concluded as follows:

> The conception that the hospital does not undertake to treat the patient, does not undertake to act through its doctors and nurses, but undertakes instead simply to procure them to act upon their own responsibility no longer reflects the fact. Present-day hospitals, as their manner of operation plainly demonstrates, do far more than furnish facilities for treatment. They regularly employ on a salary basis a large staff of physicians, nurses, and interns, as well as administrative and manual workers, and they charge patients for medical care and treatment, collecting for such services, if necessary, by legal action. Certainly, the person who avails himself of "hospital facilities" expects that the

> hospital will attempt to cure him, not that its nurses or employees will act on their own responsibility. . . .

The court then defined the specific duty of the hospital through its nurses:

> . . . At that point it became the nurses' duty to inform the attending physician and, if he failed to act, to advise the hospital authorities so that appropriate action might be taken. As to consultation, there is no dispute that the hospital failed to review Dr. Alexander's work or require a consultation; the only issue is where its failure to do so was negligence. On the evidence before it, the jury could reasonably have found that it was.[21]

Corporate liability is rapidly becoming a major concern to hospitals because it can be a profitable ground for claimants on which to base liability and has been interpreted in so many ways by the courts that no clear guidelines have emerged. However, despite general agreement that a hospital should be held corporately liable for negligence, selection, and retention of staff physicians, only a few courts have gone so far as to impose liability for a hospital's failure to supervise or oversee a physician's actions, notwithstanding the fact that the doctor's qualifications and credentials are unquestioned.

While facing this duty, hospitals generally are obliged to delegate the selection and review process to a number of committees of the medical staff to assure that the staff is organized so as to be able to collect information about important aspects of patient care, assess this information periodically, and take appropriate steps. When this collection, evaluation, and recommendation process results in the suspension or revocation of staff privileges, affected physicians usually have a right (constitutional, statutory, contractual, or common law) to a fair hearing. The courts have stepped into these discretionary decisions of hospitals and reviewed the governing boards' reasons for the denial or limitation of privileges in order to assure that physicians whose privileges have been suspended or revoked have had due process. Lawsuits by staff physicians alleging wrongful staff privilege decisions are not uncommon.

Hospitals thus find themselves in a quandary between legal duties to patients and to medical staff. Although the courts outwardly seem to have ignored this dilemma, inferentially perhaps it has been recognized and at least partially taken into account.

Thus, while the *Darling* case seems to infer a prospective duty by hospitals to review the care of patients by their independent staff physicians, no other case has gone so far as to actually enforce this as a requirement. In fact, the Illinois courts since seem to have retreated from this position, indicating in other cases that the corporate liability theory in *Darling* was applicable only to physicians who were employees of the hospital.[22]

Other cases have imposed liability upon a hospital only when it knew or should have known that one of its staff physicians was incompetent.

Evidence that may be relevant to a determination as to which physicians should or should not be allowed to practice includes the following:

- evidence of a physician's prior malpractice if the same procedure is undertaken or if the prior incident would have required a review of the doctor's care[23]
- evidence of inaccuracies in a physician's application for staff privileges[24]
- evidence of prior mishaps not resulting in lawsuits as well as incidents of bizarre behavior[25]
- evidence of prior suspension and/or revocation of license or privileges.[26]

These positions are reinforced by the accreditation requirements[27] and hospital licensing statutes of many states.

As a result of the position the courts have taken with respect to the doctrine of hospital corporate negligence, it is essential that an institution be prepared to demonstrate by convincing evidence that it has acted carefully and prudently in the selection and review process. The hospital risk manager can assist by encouraging and participating in the accumulation of accurate documentation that shows that:

1. All credentials submitted were valid.
2. Applicants were required to give sufficient information from which their competency could, in fact, be reasonably determined.
3. References were contacted and meaningful responses were received.
4. Objective criteria were used to determine competency.
5. All negative information was thoroughly investigated or explained.
6. Information as to all malpractice claims or suits against staff physicians were received, reviewed, and evaluated.
7. Current medical information regarding staff physicians was obtained and reviewed to be sure there was no physical or psychological basis that would suggest incompetency.
8. Peer review was conducted for each medical staff member on a regular basis and in a manner that could identify incompetency.
9. The applicant had demonstrated a proficiency in the area for which staff appointment was sought.

While these steps will not necessarily prevent lawsuits or even assure that each staff physician is competent to perform the privileges granted, they at least will provide hospital counsel a solid basis with which to defend a corporate liability claim.

Duty to Third Parties

Since the landmark decision in *Tarasoff,*[28] courts have been extending the health provider's duty to surveil or otherwise supervise mentally ill patients to include a duty to protect reasonably foreseeable third persons who may be injured as the consequence of a mentally or physically ill person's actions.

In *Tarasoff,* a mentally ill person, while a patient in defendant hospital, announced to his psychiatrist that he intended to kill his girlfriend. Later, when the patient was released from the hospital, he went to her house and killed her. The parents sued the hospital on the grounds that it knew that the mentally ill patient was homicidal and knew or should have known that he was likely to carry out the threats he had made while an inpatient.

The California Supreme Court held that the mental health care facility had notice that the mentally ill patient was homicidal and specifically had entertained thoughts of murdering his girlfriend. Based upon this notice, the court presumed a duty arising out of the physician/patient relationship of the hospital to the mentally ill person to protect him from harming not only himself but also others who would reasonably be foreseeable victims.

Other cases decided since *Tarasoff* have expanded the scope of health care providers' responsibility to include not just identifiable victims but the public at large. In one case, a court said a physician could be held liable to a third party injured in an automobile accident with the physician's epileptic patient. The court concluded the physician's duty to third parties included prescribing appropriate anticonvulsive drugs or advising the patient he should not drive.[29] However, most courts seem to have rejected *Tarasoff,* or at least have declined to expand it to anyone but potential victims who are readily identifiable.[30]

It is clear that a hospital must be concerned with the potential that it may be held liable for failure to protect others from its patients. Staff members as part of their function must consider the risk of a patient's injuring (1) identifiable victims known to be specifically at risk (as in *Tarasoff*) and (2) members of the public at large.

In addressing this exposure, key weapons in the hospital risk managers' arsenal are knowledge of local law on duty to third parties and education of hospital staff members (especially those involved in mental health) of this liability potential as well as the desirability of reporting to the managers threats—express or implied—to the welfare of third parties with whom the patient may come in contact. Upon obtaining such information, risk managers must work with health providers to analyze the threat and, when warranted, take action to mitigate it while at the same time maintaining cognizance of provider/patient privilege concerns. Documentation of the rationale for what, if any, action is taken can be critical to managing this exposure.

Premises Liability

Hospitals, like any other landowners, may be held liable for injuries sustained by visitors (including patients) under traditional theories of premises liability. Because of the unique services performed and the population of infirm, disabled, and otherwise dependent people on their premises, hospitals also may be required to be more exacting in offering and maintaining facilities that meet the special needs of their patients. Thus, in certain instances, the standard of conduct in design or premises maintenance applicable to hospitals may be different from that for commercial establishments at large and may require the testimony of expert witnesses to establish that the facilities are safe for people ordinarily expected to be using them within a hospital. For these reasons, hospitals provide nonskid floors, siderails in lavatories, siderails in halls, barrier-free entrances, scald-proof showering systems, and call buttons near commode seats.[31]

Under theories of premises liability, hospitals have been found responsible for failure to periodically salt and/or apply sand to exits and entrances but relieved of responsibility when a slip and fall occurred on ice that accumulated at an exit before the hospital had a reasonable opportunity to salt or sand.[32]

Hospitals also have been found responsible for improper placement of wall mirrors and traffic control signals but have been found not liable when a patient slipped and fell on a soapy substance believed to be shaving cream but the plaintiff offered no evidence that the hospital had actual notice of the condition and no evidence from which it might reasonably be inferred that the hospital was delinquent in not discovering or removing the substance from the floor.[33]

In this regard, an inpatient may rightfully expect the hospital to exercise reasonable care in the selection and maintenance of equipment and facilities furnished for patient use. Accordingly, a hospital may be liable for providing a seat that breaks when the patient sits on it, a defective lamp, Stryker bed, wheelchair, electric fan, or other equipment where it is shown that the hospital knew or should have known of the defect and the patient suffered injury arising out of the defect. Hospitals also have been found liable for injuries caused by the use of defective x-ray equipment and surgical instruments.[34]

In furnishing equipment as in furnishing premises, hospitals must take reasonable care to assure that the equipment is free from defects and reasonably safe for the uses intended. Therefore, if equipment is defectively maintained or repaired or is retained after obsolescence, hospital liability may arise. In the event of patient injury, the hospital risk manager also should be alert to investigate whether the defects involve manufacture and/or design and whether they were not ascertainable by hospital personnel. In such cases, the hospital may be entitled to indemnity or contribution from the manufacturers and/or distributors who provided the equipment originally.

APPORTIONMENT OF LIABILITY

One of the trickiest problems for risk managers and attorneys is sorting out financial responsibility in the event of a patient or visitor mishap that may involve liability. When a patient suffers a ''bad result'' following hospital care, there are numerous possibilities as to responsibility:

1. patient fault
2. hospital employee fault
3. independent physician fault
4. two or more of the above
5. none of the above.

To make a determination as to how a hospital's exposure should be assessed, the following legal doctrines must be considered.

Contributory and Comparative Negligence

Historically, if the actions of a plaintiff were negligent, and such negligence was a cause of the injury, the plaintiff was prevented from obtaining any damages whatsoever from a defendant. This was true no matter how negligent the defendant might have been in comparison to the plaintiff. This rule was called the doctrine of contributory negligence.

Because of the perceived harshness of this rule, over the years juries often ignored plaintiff's fault and the courts began softening the doctrine through the establishment of exceptions. Eventually, the vast majority of states, by statute or court decision, completely changed the rule and adopted a new doctrine called comparative negligence.

Under the comparative negligence doctrine, the jury is asked to determine the total damages suffered by the plaintiff and then to assign corresponding percentages of fault for what happened to the plaintiff and the defendant. Thus, if a jury determined that a patient's slip and fall in a hospital that resulted in $100,000 total damages to the plaintiff was 20 percent caused by the plaintiff's getting up at night without ringing for nurse assistance and 80 percent caused by the hospital for having a wet floor, the hospital would owe $80,000 to the plaintiff.

A difficult question arises with this comparative negligence doctrine when it is found the plaintiff is more than 50 percent at fault, e.g., should a plaintiff who is found to be 90 percent responsible for an injury get anything at all from the defendant? The courts have split on this issue. Some courts, which have adopted the "pure" form of comparative negligence, say "yes;" others, which use the "hybrid" form, deny recovery where the plaintiff is found to be more than 50 percent responsible for the injury.[35]

Whatever approach is taken toward plaintiff negligence, it must be recognized that in a medical malpractice case not everything a patient does "wrong" will necessarily limit a claim. A reformed smoker's long history of smoking may contribute to a constricted coronary artery condition. However, when this condition, along with a physician's failure to diagnose and treat it, results in a heart attack, the patient's earlier smoking probably would not be considered "comparative negligence" in a malpractice case against a physician. On the other hand, modifying the example slightly, renewed smoking by the patient, contrary to the physician's instructions, might be considered "comparative negligence," as would failure to keep appointments or take prescribed medicine.[36]

Thus, in investigating any type of patient incident or claim, it is important for the hospital risk manager to explore and record evidence of relevant patient fault.

Joint and Several Liability

On the surface the concept of joint and several liability appears simple and fair: a plaintiff who has suffered an injury by wrongful acts of two or more persons may sue and/or collect a judgment in full from any one of them. The concept is based on the principle that if two or more persons commit acts that result in a plaintiff's suffering a single injury, the wronged plaintiff's recovery should not be dependent on all of the defendants' being financially capable of paying; if anyone should suffer a loss, it should be one of the wrongdoers who pays more than that individual might owe technically.

It is the rule of joint and several liability that, more than anything, has encouraged plaintiffs to pursue new legal theories against hospitals, such as ostensible agency and corporate liability for the acts of independent staff physicians. By proving to the jury's satisfaction that a hospital is to any degree at fault in a medical incident involving a physician, the plaintiff maximizes the chance that any judgment obtained will be collectible. This approach assumes—for good reason—that even if a physician lacks insurance or assets to pay a judgment, a hospital probably will not.

This problem is not limited to hospitals alone. Physicians, too, face this threat. Not uncommonly, they are made defendants where they merely participated in the care of a patient, in the hope their involvement might also finance a judgment against a colleague whose care is the focus of a lawsuit.

Because of this problem, there is a growing trend among all health care providers to seek remedial legislation that eliminates the concept of joint and several liability, at least as it relates to malpractice claims.

In the absence of such a statute and apart from taking steps to avoid liability in the first place, the best risk management that hospitals can undertake to minimize exposure of joint and several liability is to take steps to assure that staff physicians and independent contractors for whom the institution may be held liable have adequate means or insurance to cover possible losses.

Indemnity

Indemnity is a concept whereby a defendant obtains full reimbursement from other parties for any amounts that may be found owing to the plaintiff. Indemnity can be divided generally into two types: contractual and common law.

Contractual Indemnity

In contractual indemnity, one party (the "indemnitor") promises by contract to pay all losses that a second party (the "indemnitee") may incur by reason of a judgment or otherwise. Unlike common-law indemnity (discussed next) freedom from active fault is not a prerequisite.

The most common form of contractual indemnity is liability insurance—the insurer is the indemnitor who promises to defend and cover all losses the insured, as indemnitee, may be obligated to pay up to a specified limit. However, contractual indemnity may exist in many other situations, usually as a part of a broader contract that relates to services or the sale of goods. Contractual provisions of this kind generally are valid, although courts and legislatures sometimes have established exceptions, especially where because of superior bargaining position the indemnitee was able to obtain indemnity from the indemnitor for sole negligence.[37]

Common-Law Indemnity

Common-law indemnity is implied by law and no contract is required. It arises where a party becomes obligated to pay a loss by reason of the exclusive negligence of another party. The clearest example is the vicarious liability of an employer for the negligence of an employee; the employer is liable even though personally free of fault. However, the employer is entitled to indemnity from the employee.

As a practical matter, because of the availability of insurance, the fact that a claim for indemnity would be "bad business" and pose collectibility problems, employers seldom want to sue their employees for indemnity. However, it is not uncommon for a hospital faced with vicarious liability for an independent contractor or staff physician it does not employ to seek indemnity for losses it incurs for their actions. If a hospital employee and an independent staff physician both are at fault for a patient injury, even if the employee's negligence is slight in comparison with that of the physician, common-law indemnity generally cannot be obtained. This is because freedom from *any* active fault ordinarily is an absolute prerequisite to obtaining common-law indemnity.

Regardless of the type of indemnity involved, its effectiveness is dependent upon the collectibility of the indemnitor. The indemnitor's inability to pay the indemnitee the amount owed does not excuse the indemnitee from the obligation to pay a judgment in favor of the plaintiff. For this reason, where a hospital believes it has a right to indemnity of any kind from a physician or others, it is imperative that the risk manager encourage the facility to adopt policies and practices that assure the collectibility of the prospective indemnitee (staff physician or independent contractor). Usually, this will mean the imposition of an insurance requirement.

Contribution

Contribution, like indemnity, is a remedy for a person who has paid more than a fair share to a plaintiff. However, unlike contractual indemnity, no contract is required and unlike common-law indemnity, freedom from active fault is not required; unlike either type of indemnity, it generally involves partial rather than complete reimbursement.

The concept of contribution developed from the belief that it was unfair for one of multiple negligent wrongdoers to alone pay a plaintiff in full under the concept of joint and several liability. The courts and legislatures decided that even a negligent wrongdoer was entitled to have others who also actively contributed to plaintiff's injuries share in "the misery" (payment of the judgment). Thus, the rule of contribution developed: When one of the multiple wrongdoers paid more than a fair share, that individual was entitled to bring suit against the others to even out the loss.

Since contribution was established, it traditionally tended to be based on a straight pro rata calculation. With this rule, regardless of the degree of fault, each proved wrongdoer was obligated to contribute an equal share.

Today, however, the overwhelming trend is to cast aside pro rata share liability in favor of a relative degree of fault determination, similar to that used for the doctrine of comparative negligence for plaintiffs. When relative degree of fault contribution procedures are used, the jury determines the percentage of fault of each defendant based on the evidence, and each defendant theoretically is required to pay accordingly.

While seemingly more just than pro rata division, unjust results still occur where the traditional joint and several liability doctrine remains intact. For instance, where plaintiff's damages are found to be $1 million as a result of a hospital nurse's being 1 percent at fault and an uninsured uncollectible independent staff physician's being 99 percent at fault, the hospital would be liable to pay the full $1 million without meaningful recourse against the staff physician. On the other hand, if the staff physician has a $1 million dollar insurance limit, the hospital would be in a position to only pay $10,000 after asserting its rights against the physician's insurer.

As with the discussion of indemnity, it is evident that assuring collectibility of those with whom a hospital most likely would share liability (e.g., staff physicians) is an important risk management consideration.

SPECIAL STATUTES RELATING TO LIABILITY

As reflected in the opening section of this chapter on regulation, a multitude of statutes and regulations affect the liability of health care providers. This includes, depending upon the state, statutes defining the standard of practice,[38] informed consent,[39] and minimum licensure requirements. However, two types of statutes are of special risk management attention: the statute of frauds and the statute of limitations.

Statute of Frauds

The name statute of frauds is misleading in that, while it is designed to prevent fraud, it actually is a principle of contract. Although, depending on the state, their provisions may vary, these statutes all in essence provide that specified kinds of contracts must be in writing.

Typically they require that, to be enforceable in court, agreements must be in writing for the sale of real estate, for promises to answer for a debt of another (surety and indemnity), for employment agreements that cannot be performed in one year, and for the purchase of goods having above a specified threshold of value.[40]

Hospital risk managers frequently are involved in contract matters such as physician contracts, patient releases of liability, and insurance policies. It therefore is imperative that they familiarize themselves with their state's statute of frauds or seek out legal counsel when assuring an enforceable agreement is a hospital concern.

Statute of Limitations

What is perhaps "the" statute for risk management purposes is the statute of limitations. Its basic premise is simple and widely recognized: After a legislatively specified period of time (the "limitations period") a claimant no longer may bring a lawsuit (it is "time-barred"). Despite an easily understandable premise, the practical application can be difficult and has been especially confused by the courts in medical malpractice cases.

Historically, statutes of limitations provided that in lawsuits involving medical care, the date that either the wrong occurred (occurrence) or the patient was "last treated" by the health care provider for the same condition was the date that started the statute of limitations clock running. Both usually were relatively easy to use in determining whether or not a claim was time-barred. Judges would decide whether or not the claim was too old upon a motion to dismiss; jury involvement was rare. Under the "last treatment" rule, the analysis became difficult and required a jury only in complicated factual situations such as (1) where multiple health care providers jointly treated the patient at an earlier time and only one of them treated the person later; or (2) the patient continued to see the health care provider after the treatment at issue but for an apparently different condition; or (3) the patient had a basis for claiming "fraudulent concealment" (the health care provider actively taking steps to hide negligence from the patient).

In a fraudulent concealment case, courts generally would extend the starting point of the limitation period to when the effects of the concealment had dissipated (e.g., the patient started seeing another doctor for the same condition). However, courts continued to be concerned that a patient's legitimate claim might be time-barred through a lack of awareness rather than any active concealment by a health care provider. This view emphasized the fact that while any normal persons know when they have been wrongfully injured in an auto accident, they may not recognize that their lasting pain after surgery was caused by physician error.[41]

As a result, many courts (subsequently supported by many legislatures by statute) have adopted what is known as the discovery rule. This rule delays the start of the clock for the limitations period to the time when the patient knew or reasonably should have known that malpractice had occurred. Although this standard is supposed to be objective by including "should have discovered" as part of its definition, in practice most often this determination centers on the patient's statements of what the plaintiff did or did not know at a particular point.

The discovery rule makes the statute of limitations defense—in many, if not most—cases—a question for the jury to decide at trial; many cases that under the last treatment rule would have been dismissed by early motion now are settled or proceed to jury trial with the attendant risk of an adverse jury decision. Practically speaking, the discovery rule thus may have the effect of postponing the running of the limitations indefinitely in certain cases.[42] Some states now use a hybrid of both old and new rules, e.g., they allow a patient to bring suit a specified number of years after last treatment or discovery, whichever is later.[43]

Frequently, a state's statute of limitations will have different time periods for different types of claims. Not only will there be a different limitations period for contractual as opposed to personal injury claims, there also may be different limitations periods for personal injury claims, depending on whether the substance of the claim is based on an intentional wrong or on ordinary negligence, as opposed to malpractice. Furthermore, many states give legally incompetent persons (minors and the mentally incapacitated) additional periods of time in which to bring suit in all kinds of cases. Therefore, the risk manager must know not only the malpractice statute of limitations but also the statutory provisions and limitation periods for other types of claims as well.

Apart from its direct effect on the validity of claims, the statute of limitations provisions' major impact on hospitals' practices and policies is on record retention. As noted earlier, in malpractice cases the medical chart can be the greatest ally of the health care provider. For this reason the statute of limitations must be considered in deciding whether or not medical records should be destroyed, saved, or microfilmed, regardless of what local laws may provide as the legal period for which such records are to be kept. It may be that because of special limitations period rules, medical records of minors and incompetent adults should be identified and kept longer than those of other patients. Similarly, policies and practices regarding retention of contracts, medical staff files, insurance policies, incident reports, and investigative materials all should take into account the relevant limitations period.

CONFIDENTIALITY AND INVESTIGATIONS

Patient Confidentiality

Communications between patient and physician generally are privileged and may not be disclosed to other persons without the express written consent of the patient. The confidential material involves not only the patient's verbal statements to a health care provider but also nonverbal communications, including the results of examination, testing, and monitoring that are necessary for diagnosis or treatment. Information acquired by health care providers in attending a patient in a professional capacity should be presumed confidential until legal counsel advises otherwise.

Since privilege between health care provider and patient generally was not recognized at common law, the rules pertaining to the privilege, its application, and waiver depend upon the many and varied individual state statutes involved. Most statutes make communications between provider and patient privileged from compulsory disclosures in court but tend to differ so much that a hospital risk manager must either become familiar with local statutes or consult with legal counsel.

Where communications between physician and patient are privileged, only the patient may waive the privilege. Therefore, records ordinarily should not be released without the patient's written authorization. Where the patient is a minor, incapacitated adult, or deceased, the written authorization of the patient's legal representative, e.g., parent, guardian, or executor, should be required for disclosure of information.

However, since the privilege is justified as a means of promoting open and frank communication between a health care provider and a patient so as to protect the patient's interest in the privacy of therapeutic matters, any conduct by a patient that is inconsistent with an intent to maintain confidentiality may destroy the privilege permanently.

Thus, the privilege can be waived by testimony in a prior lawsuit[44] or by openly discussing the privileged facts.[45] Generally, if a patient testifies as to privileged communications or puts the condition at issue in a lawsuit, counsel for the opposing party then may ask the health care provider about the same matters. Accordingly, depending upon the type of treatment, a provider may be obliged to provide records, even without authorization, pursuant to a valid subpoena or court order. Some states bar all or part of the privilege in criminal proceedings when the testimony to be derived is unusually important. In such instances, it is has been determined that the state's interest in uncovering and proving crime is superior to a patient's interest in maintaining confidentiality and that the privilege should give way when it is protecting those committing serious crimes.[46]

Many states have statutes with express provisions that make the privilege inapplicable to civil commitment or other similar proceedings involving mental competency. As commitment is thought to be beneficial to the person involved, the patient will not be injured by disclosure.

Hospital risk managers should realize that virtually every state requires physicians to report certain matters (e.g., child abuse, venereal disease, gunshot wounds) despite the fact that such information is revealed during a confidential relationship. As noted, courts also have held that a psychiatrist may have an affirmative duty to breach the privilege and warn particular persons whom the psychiatrist has reason to believe may be in danger.

Information and records relating to the diagnosis, treatment, rehabilitation, or referral of drug or alcohol abuse patients are made confidential by federal statutes and regulations. Except for communications (1) within the hospital among personnel who need such information to perform their duties; (2) between the hospital and qualified service organizations that have agreed in writing to maintain the confidentiality of such information; or (3) that do not contain any patient identifying information, disclosure of such confidential information generally may be made only upon the patient's written authorization. It should be recognized that the authorization executed by the patient for substance abuse treatment information may not be a general form of consent but must comply specifically with the regulations promulgated under the federal statutes.[47] These regulations prescribe rules for the disclosure of confidential information based upon the purpose for which the information is released. Failure to comply with federal regulations pertaining to the release of medical information can result in the imposition of fines.

The courts generally are willing to recognize a cause of action for breach of a confidential relationship, making it clear that hospitals must be careful to avoid nonconsensual disclosures of private information absent a compelling reason or a specified exception in a state confidentiality statute. If, for example, a wrongful disclosure of medical information respecting a patient's drug addiction results in loss of employment, the damages for breach of the privilege can be substantial.

Generally, patients may see their own records, so a release of information to them presents no question of violation of any legal duty. Nevertheless, for a variety of professional reasons, health care providers may wish to withhold information contained in certain records when disclosure to the patient may be damaging to that person. The legal question then becomes whether there is an obligation to provide access. A number of states have passed right-of-access laws that may or may not restrict access where there are reasonable grounds for the exercise of a physician's judgment that access would be harmful. When questions arise that the hospital risk manager is made aware of, the manager should consult first with the patient's attending health care provider and, as necessary, legal counsel.

Hospital Confidentiality and Investigations

Extensive consideration should be given to what is to be done after an incident giving rise to injury occurs. Identifying legal issues is only the beginning of the process that risk managers are responsible for in their investigation of injury-causing accidents.

The next step is to organize and carry out a thorough investigation of the facts. The preliminary investigations must assure confidentiality of the information collected. Confidentiality helps make sure the hospital review function (of which the hospital risk manager must be a part) can go on without fear that information provided to the risk manager will be turned over to outsiders. Confidentiality also can induce the surfacing of truly useful information that otherwise might not emerge, thus giving risk managers and, therefore, review committees reliable material upon which to base policy determinations designed to prevent future injuries.

Despite the best planning and prevention methods, injuries do occur in hospitals. The staff and the risk manager thus must feel comfortable in working hand in hand in addressing such situations. Every effort should be made to guarantee the free flow of information on injuries, actual or complained of, to risk managers and, through them, to appropriate hospital review committees and others responsible for quality assurance.

For these reasons, if investigations are to be meaningful, it is important that those providing information are satisfied that what they say will be kept confidential. The hospital risk manager thus must be familiar with the means of assuring confidentiality.

Under both federal and state law, the attorney-client privilege (completely barring disclosure of private legal communications) generally extends to communications between hospital counsel and hospital employees.[49] However, for this privilege to be invoked, the investigator must be an attorney or a person working under the direction of an attorney. Since many hospital risk managers are not attorneys and work independent of hospital counsel, this privilege is not always available or useful.

Federal laws and those of many states provide that information acquired by a party in anticipation of or in preparation for litigation is ''work product'' regardless of whether or not the person obtaining it is an attorney.[50] While work product theoretically is confidential and routinely not subject to disclosure in legal proceedings, the courts have applied exceptions, such as when the information cannot be reasonably acquired by the opposition from a witness without ''undue hardship.'' It often is inappropriate, therefore, for risk managers to rely too heavily on the work product doctrine to assure confidentiality of investigatory materials.

Many states have statutes that make confidential any information collected for or by committees or individuals assigned to a peer, professional, or morbidity and mortality review function. If the hospital risk manager's work is officially designated to be and consistently is carried out as part of such a review committee's work, there is greater likelihood that a claimant's legal discovery of the risk manager's investigation and reports will not be allowed. Accordingly, where hospital risk management activities and reporting exist, every effort should be made to place them within the scope of these review statutes. This may require that risk managers serve as members of, or at least under the official supervision and control of, patient care review committees so that the information such managers acquire during an investigation is kept confidential.

SUMMARY

In concluding, the authors emphasize that this chapter has only touched upon the field known as hospital law. Practical space limitations and outstanding legal texts available, such as the *Hospital Law Manual,*[51] make it both unfeasible and superfluous to try to address every significant issue meaningfully.

The effort instead was directed toward accomplishing two things:

1. To explain briefly the evolution of hospital law, and particularly the intensive societal scrutiny and broad regulation that providers face. These have

had and in the future will have impact on hospital risk management. Moreover, in their frequent role as hospital liaison to its legal counsel, hospital risk managers' acquaintance with these issues is helpful, if not essential.
2. To provide insight and recommendations on the liability and legal exposures that risk managers may perceive prospectively and thus influence effectively. While supervision of the handling of a claim after it is made usually is the responsibility of risk managers, this is not the kind of risk they can meaningfully put under full control.

Because of these factors, many important issues have been addressed in summary fashion or excluded altogether. As to the former, it is most important that hospital risk managers check local laws and, when appropriate, consult with hospital counsel. As to the latter—excluded issues—obviously matters such as alternative dispute resolution mechanisms (arbitration and malpractice screening panels) and proposed remedial laws that tend to be very locally specific are important but did not fit into the space limitations or perspective of addressing matters risk managers may influence before the fact. However, their omission is, not to imply they are unimportant; clearly, hospital risk managers should take the opportunity to become thoroughly familiar with them as they relate to their home state.

NOTES

1. *O'Brien v. Cunard S.S. Co.*, 154 Mass. 272, 28 N.E. 266 (1891).
2. *Restatement (Second) of Torts* § 50 (1964). *Wright v. Starr*, 43 Nev. 441, 179 P. 877 (1919). *Schulman v. Lerner*, 2 Mich. App. 705, 141 N.W.2d 348 (1966).
3. *Schloendorff v. Soc'y New York Hospitals*, 211 N.Y. 125, 105 N.E. 92, 93 (1914).
4. *Luka v. Lowrie*, 171 Mich. 122, 136 N.W. 1106 (1912); *Delahunt v. Finton*, 244 Mich. 226, 221 N.W. 168 (1928).
5. *In re Karen Quinlan, An Alleged Incompetent*, 70 N.J. 10, 355 A.2d 647 (1976).
6. *Id.*
7. *Roberts v. Young*, 369 Mich. 133, 119 N.W.2d 627 (1963); *Goven v. Hunter*, 374 P.2d 421 (Wyo. 1962); *Visingardi v. Tirone*, 178 So. 2d 135 (Fla. 1965).
8. *Schloendorff, supra*, note 3.
9. *Darling v. Charleston Community Memorial Hospital*, 33 Ill. 2d 326, 211 N.E.2d 253 (1965).
10. Joint Commission on Accreditation of Hospitals, *AMH/85 Accreditation Manual for Hospitals*. (Chicago: JCAH 1984), 63.
11. *Sandhofer v. Abbott-Northwestern Hospital*, 283 N.W.2d 362 (Minn. 1979); *Brannan v. Lankenau Hospital*, 490 Pa. 588, 417 A.2d 196 (1980); *Darling, supra* note 9.
12. Prosser, *Law of Torts* § 69, p. 458 (4th ed., 1971).
13. *Grewe v. Mt. Clemens General Hospital*, 404 Mich. 240, 273 N.W.2d 429 (1978).
14. *Id.*

15. *Mduba v. Benedictine Hosp.*, 52 A.D.2d 450, 384 N.Y.S.2d 527 (1976); *Mehlman v. Powell*, 281 Md. 269, 378 A.2d 1121 (1977); *Arthur v. St. Peters Hosp.*, 169 N.J. Super. 575, 405 A.2d 443 (1979); *Adamski v. Tacoma Gen. Hosp.*, 20 Wash. App. 98, 579 P.2d 970 (1978); *Magwood v. Jewish Hosp. and Medical Center of Brooklyn*, 96 Misc. 2d 251, 408 N.Y.S.2d 983 (N.Y. Sup. Ct. 1978); *Davidson v. Conole*, 79 A.D.2d 43, 436 N.Y.S.2d 109 (1981); *Capan v. Divine Providence Hosp.*, 287 Pa. Super. 364, 430 A.2d 647 (1980); *Howard v. Park*, 37 Mich. App. 496, 195 N.W.2d 39 (1972); *Schagrin v. Wilmington Medical Center, Inc.*, 304 A.2d 61 (Del. Super. Ct. 1973); *Bing v. Thunig*, 2 N.Y.2d 656, 163 N.Y.S.2d 3, 143 N.E.2d 3 (1957); *Stanhope v. Los Angeles College of Chiropractic*, 54 Cal. App. 2d 141, 128 P.2d 705 (1942).
16. Restatement (Second) of Agency §227 (1958).
17. *Sparger v. Woorley Hosp., Inc.*, 547 S.W.2d 582 (Tex. 1977).
18. *McConnell v. Williams*, 361 Pa. 355, 65 A.2d 243 (1949).
19. *Hollant v. North Shore Hosp., Inc.*, 24 Misc. 2d 892, 206 N.Y.S.2d 177 (N.Y. Sup. Ct. 1960); *Shutts v. Siehl*, 109 Ohio App. 145, 164 N.E.2d 443 (1959).
20. *Darling, supra* note 8.
21. *Id.*
22. *Lundahl v. Rockford Memorial Hospital Ass'n*, 93 Ill. App. 2d 461, 235 N.E.2d 671 (1968); *Stogsdill v. Manor Convalescent Home, Inc.*, 35 Ill. App. 3d 634, 343 N.E.2d 589 (1976); *Collins v. Westlake, Community Hosp.*, 12 Ill. App. 3d 847, 299 N.E.2d 326 (1973), *rev'd on other grounds*, 57 Ill. 2d 388, 312 N.E.2d 614 (1974).
23. *Purcell v. Zimbelman*, 18 Ariz. App. 75, 500 P.2d 335 (1972).
24. *Johnson v. Misericordia Community Hosp.*, 97 Wis. 2d 521, 294 N.W.2d 501 (1980), *aff'd*, 99 Wis. 2d 708, 301 N.W.2d 156 (1981).
25. *Crumley v. Memorial Hosp., Inc.*, 509 F. Supp. 531 (E.D. Tenn. 1979), *aff'd*, 647 F.2d 164 (6th Cir. 1981).
26. *Lewis v. Columbus Hosp.*, 1 A.D.2d 444, 151 N.Y.S.2d 391 (1956).
27. Joint Commission on Accreditation of Hospitals, *AMH/85 Accreditation Manual for Hospitals*. (Chicago: JCAH, 1984), 73.
28. *Tarasoff v. Regents of Univ. of Cal.*, 17 Cal. 3d 425, 131 Cal. Rptr. 14, 551 P.2d 334 (1976).
29. *Duvall v. Goldin*, 139 Mich. App. 342, 362 N.W.2d 275 (1984).
30. *Leedy v. Hartnett*, 510 F. Supp. 1125 (M.D. Pa. 1981), *aff'd*, 676 F.2d 686 (3rd Cir. 1982).
31. *Mikel v. Flatbush Gen. Hosp.*, 49 A.D.2d 581, 370 N.Y.S.2d 162 (1975).
32. *Grundmeyer v. Argonaut Ins. Co.*, 341 So. 2d 634 (La. App. 1977).
33. *Bonds v. Brown*, 368 So. 2d 536 (Ala. 1979).
34. *Runyan v. Goodrum*, 147 Ark. 481 228 S.W. 397 (1921); *South Highlands Infirmary v. Camp*, 279 Ala. 1, 180 So. 2d 904 (1965).
35. *Placek v. City of Sterling Heights*, 405 Mich. 638, 275 N.W.2d 511 (1979).
36. 70 C.J.S. *Physicians and Surgeons* § 51 (1951).
37. 41 Am. Jur. 2d *Indemnity* §§ 6–18 (1968).
38. E.g., Mich. Comp. Laws § 600.2912 (1948).
39. E.g., Ohio Rev. Code Ann. § 2317.54 (1977).
40. 72 Am. Jur. 2d *Statute of Frauds* § 3 (1974).
41. Annot., 80 A.L.R.2d 368 (1961).
42. Annot., 70 A.L.R.3d 7 (1976).
43. Mich. Comp. Laws § 600.5805 (1978); Mich. Comp. Laws § 600.5838 (1975).

44. *Hamilton v. Verdow,* 287 Md. 544, 414 A.2d 914 (1980); *D. v. D.,* 108 N.J. Super. 149, 266 A.2d 255 (1969).
45. *Rudnick v. Superior Court of Kern County,* 11 Cal. 3d 924, 114 Cal. Rptr. 603, 523 P.2d 643 (1974).
46. *People v. Doe,* 107 Misc. 2d 605, 435 N.Y.S.2d 656 (N.Y. Sup. Ct. 1981); *People v. Lowe,* 96 Misc. 2d 33, 408 N.Y.S.2d 873 (N.Y. Crim. Ct. 1978).
47. 42 U.S.C. § 290ee-3 (1983); 42 U.S.C. 4582 (1976).
48. 42 C.F.R. § 2.1 et. seq. (1974) (revised Oct. 1, 1984).
49. *Upjohn Co. v. U.S.,* 449 U.S. 383 (1981); *U.S. Steel Corp. v. U.S.,* 730 F.2d 1465 (Fed. Cir. 1984).
50. Fed. R. Civ. P. 26(3).
51. Paul C. Lasky, Patricia A. Younger, and Melanie J. Karsh, eds., *Hospital Law Manual* (Rockville, Md.: Aspen Systems Corporation, 1983).

Chapter 5

The Concept of Risk

Glenn Troyer

For today's hospital administrator, the institution's environment presents many risk situations that to a greater or lesser extent affect the effectiveness and cost of providing health care services. Because these risk situations arise under a variety of circumstances, the managerial skills to control risks must be equally varied. For example:

- Nurse A executes Dr. B's discharge order for Patient S even though the patient is experiencing a fever and other symptoms suggestive of a possible undisclosed complication or lack of resolution of the admitting problem.
- Hospital X is constructing an eight-story medical office building. The contractor places a nine-story boom crane at the site. The tallest building in the hospital complex of five square blocks is only six stories high. The crane remains in its fully extended position (nine stories) without warning lights, both day and night, even though the hospital conducts a helicopter emergency medical flight service with the landing pad on top of a six-story hospital building two blocks away.
- Hospital Y has an active Institutional Review Board set up in accordance with federal statutes and regulations. As part of those regulations the panel is required to assess the risks to patients who could become involved in a research project and determine the extent of disclosure that should be made in a written consent form. The form should describe the risks of this project as well as the alternative forms of treatment available. At an Institutional Review Board meeting, the chairman of the department of surgery, who has a dynamic and domineering personality, convinces the board to authorize his research project even though the protocol and information available to the members does not contain any written consent form or disclose the risks and alternative forms of treatment.

- Hospital Z was to sell tax-exempt bonds in order to finance a new building construction program. Its management prepares a rosy picture of the hospital's future as well as its increasing percentage share of the market and its anticipated growth for the years during which the bonds would be amortized. Some middle management personnel believe certain "material risks" have not been disclosed in the official statement for the bond issue but their attempt to make additional disclosures is unsuccessful.
- The board of directors of "Weakness Memorial Hospital, Inc." continues to permit the physician credentialing process to be conducted solely by the medical staff based on the rationale that the board members "were not physicians" and therefore could not question the competency of doctors.
- Contrary to federal statutory and regulatory requirements, a secretary employed at a substance abuse center releases certain medical records of a patient to the attorney for the patient's employer without the individual's consent or knowledge.

These situations illustrate but a few of the risks facing hospitals on a daily basis. However, in many organizations, these risks go unnoticed. Why? Is it because the concept of risk is so elusive that people do not identify a risk situation when one has developed? Or is it because the hospital employees do not perceive the identification of risks and the management thereof as their responsibility? Whatever the answers, or whatever other questions may suggest appropriate answers for a particular hospital organization, the first question any organization must answer is how to define the concept of risk. This chapter deals with conceptual definitions of the term *risk*.

RISK CONCEPTS DEFINED

The concept of risk can be defined as "exposure to the chance of injury or loss; a hazard or dangerous chance."[1] However, C. Arthur Williams, Jr., and Richard M. Heins define it as "a variation in the outcomes that could occur over a specified period in a given situation."[2] While the dictionary is more general, the Williams/Heins definition provides a clearer understanding of the application of the concept.

Probability

In order to proceed further, it is necessary to review the notion of probability. Probability generally is defined as the likelihood that a particular outcome will occur during the study of a particular event being repeated numerous times. The formula for determining the probability (P) of a particular event (x) is equal to the results of the event under study (m) divided by the total number of different results (n) that have an equal chance of occurring. Thus the formula is

$$P(x) = m/n$$

For example, if the event under study is the number of uncomplicated deliveries in the obstetrical unit of a particular hospital during one year, and there were 500 deliveries in the hospital during that period, of which 20 were considered complicated, then the probability of having a complicated delivery in that particular hospital would be:

$$20 \div 500, \text{ or } .04 \text{ (4 percent)}$$

Variation

The Williams/Heins definition also uses the concept of variation, which differs from probability even though it is related. Variation is the estimated probability distribution. For example, if out of 100 hip replacement procedures performed in a hospital in a year, five patients experienced a post-operative infection localized to the hip area, then the probability would be:

$$5 \div 100, \text{ or } .05$$

Thus, a person contemplating hip replacement surgery might be said to have a theoretical 5 percent chance of having a similar infection result.

Of course, the danger of using such statistical probabilities is that they do not consider the unique facts and circumstances under which those particular infections arose but rather provide only a statistical ballpark guide to predicting outcomes. The variation that might occur among those 100 patients might be considerably different from one in every 20 procedures—perhaps the five infections occurred with the last ten patients in December rather than being spaced evenly throughout the year. The concept of variation thus becomes an important consideration in understanding the concept of risk.

Uncertainty

Yet another concept associated with risk is uncertainty. One definition of uncertainty is "not definitely or surely known; doubtful."[3] Thus, a person who cannot predict an outcome is uncertain or is consciously aware of the risk of unpredictable outcomes. The degree of uncertainty depends on that person's estimation of the risk involved with the activity and confidence in those beliefs or estimations.

Therefore, an individual who is quite confident in the ability to estimate the risk would have little uncertainty concerning the estimate. However, where confidence in ability to estimate risk is lacking, uncertainty may be high. Probabilities, then, help the person to reduce uncertainty in a particular risk situation.

PERSONAL VALUES AND EXPERIENCES

Other aspects of assessing risk are the values, experiences, and beliefs of the person making the evaluation. A person's degree of uncertainty about approaching a particular risk situation may not always predict the individual's behavior. For example, people respond to uncertainty in different ways, depending on the potential gain or loss from the risk situation as well as the effect on their economic status. Therefore, personality, a person's environment, values, etc., all play important parts in the way an individual deals with the uncertainty of risk.

For example, a hospital may adopt a position that even though there is a low frequency of helicopter crashes and accompanying fatalities, even one such incident is one too many. Such a value approach may cause the hospital not to enter into a helicopter transport program or, if it does, to expend large sums to make certain that the program is operated using the ultimate safety principles.

Another example would be that of a high-frequency but perhaps acceptable risk. This could involve a recurring patient property loss situation such as when patients lose dentures as a result of going either to surgery or to some ancillary diagnostic service in which their dentures are removed. The dentures frequently end up being lost, producing intense patient dissatisfaction. However, given this particular property risk in such circumstances, hospitals continue these activities even though a number of dentures will be lost in the process. It would have to be assumed that the hospital has made a value judgment that losing dentures is far outweighed by the benefits that the patient will receive from the surgical or diagnostic test procedures. In addition, from the hospital's standpoint, it is important to remember that the facility is in the business of generating revenue on surgical and diagnostic procedures that produce far more income from patient charges than the cost of replacing the dentures. Hospitals typically do not spend a great deal of time in making sure that dentures are protected before patients are anesthetized, medicated, or otherwise prepared for some surgical or special procedure.

It thus is important for the person charged with the decision-making activities involving risk situations to understand the hospital's values before shaping an organizational attitude of whether to accept certain risks and to undertake certain activities.

GROUP AND INDIVIDUAL ATTITUDES

An interesting point about attitudinal concepts concerning risk taking is raised by Russell D. Clark, III.[4] Describing the difference between group and individual behavior in facing the same risk, he concludes that group behavior and committee decisions tend to be riskier than those made by individual members of the group outside the group experience. Based on this conclusion, hospitals should be concerned about using committees to deal with incident reports, quality insurance issues, risk assessment for research projects, and ethics committees, to name a few.

Although Clark indicates that in certain situations, groups demonstrate more risk-taking behavior than do individuals, his research may not be generalizable to every risk-taking situation in which a committee is involved. Therefore, committees should be properly oriented, should have objective criteria to guide them in their decisions, and should be able to assess the risk from a corporate perspective, given the best interests of the organization and the patients and public to whom the facility will provide services.

CLASSIFICATION SCHEMES

Managers should be able to distinguish between the concepts of risk, probability, and uncertainty as well as understand factors that affect risk attitudes so they can evaluate risks in accordance with the various researchers' classification schemes. Perhaps the most-used classification is one developed by A.H. Mowbray, R.H. Blanchard, and C.A. Williams, Jr.[5] Their system divides economic risks into pure and speculative. Essentially, pure risks are those in which the only chance is of loss. When a hospital is sued by a former patient, the nature of the risk giving rise to the suit is pure in form because the hospital stands to suffer a loss if the plaintiff is successful. In contrast, speculative risks present chances of gain as well as of loss. A hospital that attempts to develop a new health care service may show a financial gain from utilization of that service or it may suffer a loss if the service is not used.

A second typology divides risk into static and dynamic.[6] Static risks are those that result from unusual or irregular activities of nature or the malfeasance of people; they frequently affect only a few persons in the nature of a loss to society. The annual flooding of a river causing property losses to adjacent property owners is one example of a static loss. Dynamic risks or losses result from changes in the economy or society, such as technology advancements. A nuclear power plant would pose dynamic risks to its owner and to nearby inhabitants. While the latter usually are speculative types, the former are pure risks.

The third classification scheme describes two types: fundamental and particular.[7] Fundamental risks are group oriented, impersonal, unpreventable, and associated with uncertainties in the economic and social systems and with natural disasters. They include both pure and speculative types of risks. Particular risks are personal ones such as death or disability from nonoccupational causes; property losses by fire, explosion, or theft; and legal liability for personal or property damage. These usually are pure risks and are more easily controlled.

Perhaps the most significant purpose behind understanding these and other classifications is that risk managers can conceptualize better the nature of risks and categorize them in ways that they can explain easily to others to facilitate management comprehension and acceptance.

MANAGEMENT OF RISK

Risk also must be viewed as a concept that needs to be managed. In hospitals, managing the concept of risk involves dealing with factors that can be somewhat elusive and changing. However, some basic principles in the management of risk should not vary from organization to organization.

For example, a hospital's neonatal intensive care nursery cannot be useful in accomplishing the organization's objectives of delivering health care services if, as a result of hepatitis infection, the unit is closed for days or weeks. Similarly, the hospital may lose a significant share of the health care market if one physician repeatedly is involved in medical malpractice actions that reduce the facility's image in the public's eye. Thus, the handling of such loss exposures lies at the crux of the risk management program of any hospital.

The first step in establishing a risk management program is to identify its objectives clearly and to make certain that they are not at cross-purposes with those of the hospital. In recent years, the hospital industry, which had been characterized primarily by nonprofit entities, has been transforming itself to more for-profit corporations. This has caused boards of trustees to reevaluate the purpose or mission of the hospital corporation.

Perhaps in the late 19th century, it was sufficient to define the purpose of a children's hospital as providing health care to the poor and the orphans of a community regardless of their ability to pay. However, that purpose today could cause that hospital to become insolvent quickly if its literal meaning were carried out on a daily basis.

A management-by-objectives system in a hospital can be an effective way of communicating the corporation's goals to the various departments (such as risk management) so that the results of the risk management program will be positive and supportive of the overall goals and purposes.

For example, an objective of the risk management department might be to reduce or even eliminate slips and falls on nursing unit 5-Y by installing carpeting in corridors and patient rooms. However, it might be quicker and less expensive to install handrails and increase the quality of nursing staff to provide faster assistance to patients.

Risk management program objectives can be categorized as preloss and postloss. Preloss objectives concern how much effort the hospital will expend on the risk management program to reduce or prevent losses. Postloss objectives deal with how the institution can recover from a loss, given the fact that the primary aim is survival of the hospital. If the loss would produce certain effects that could injure the corporation's reputation, the preloss objective may be changed to put more emphasis on loss reduction and loss prevention efforts.

For example, a hospital long-term care facility may place more emphasis than an acute care facility would on reducing or eliminating slips and falls because of the long-term custodial nature of the treatment that is provided. As another example, a hospital management company acquires a small facility that is in need of support and better management of its emergency room. Before the acquisition, the hospital being acquired had significant emergency room patient injuries as a result of what the local community perceived as poor quality of care. From the acquiring hospital's standpoint, it would be worthwhile to spend large amounts of money to make certain that that poor care was not provided after the acquisition.

Another preloss objective is providing management a relatively anxiety-free mental state regarding potential losses. One way of measuring a risk management program is to determine how well such preloss objectives reduce administration's potential loss concerns. For example, when a hospital decides to operate a helicopter ambulance service, administration may feel uncomfortable with the potential catastrophic losses should the aircraft crash into a crowd or even into the hospital. One way to reduce that anxiety is to make certain insurance coverage is adequate for such an eventuality. Other objective alternatives might be to obtain a helicopter with two engines so it could fly on one engine if necessary, or provide a pilot and a copilot to reduce the possibility of error by a single pilot.

SUMMARY

Whatever the organizational goals are—efficiency, growth, improvement of reputation in the community, reduction of anxiety over potential loss exposures, or being a good citizen in the community—they all should guide the specific objectives of the risk management program. Thus, the determination of these objectives and organizational values lies at the heart of the risk management program.

The concept of risk must be understood on both the conceptual and the organizational level if it is to be used successfully on a daily basis.

NOTES

1. Random House, Inc. *The American College Dictionary,* (New York: Random House Inc., 1963): 1048.
2. C. Arthur Williams, Jr., and Richard M. Heins, *Risk Management and Insurance*, 3rd ed., (New York: McGraw-Hill Book Company, 1976).
3. *The American College Dictionary,* p. 1318.
4. Russell D. Clark, III, ''Risk Taking in Groups: A Social-Psychological Analysis,'' *Journal of Risk and Insurance*, 41, no. 1 (March 1974): 75–92.
5. A.H. Mowbray, R.H. Blanchard, and C.A. Williams, Jr., *Insurance*, 6th ed., (New York: McGraw-Hill Book Company, 1969), 6–8.
6. H. Willett, *The Economic Theory of Risk and Insurance* (New York: Columbia University Press, 1901, and Philadelphia: University of Pennsylvania Press, 1951), 14–23.
7. C.A. Kulp and J.W. Hall, *Casualty Insurance*, 4th ed., (New York: The Ronald Press Company, 1958), 3–7.

Chapter 6

Risk Management Processes and Functions

Steven L. Salman

Many of the chapters in this book deal with theoretical exploration of the specific subjects. This chapter offers a more hands-on, operational view of risk management and its processes and functions in the hospital or health care environment. The elements described, and their operations, will help risk managers in the development and implementation of the hospital's program. A general description of terms leads to more specific or detailed applications, concentrating on the hospital environment.

A NONTECHNICAL ANALYSIS

First a nontechnical definition of "what is risk management." Everyone, as part of employment, arrives daily at the hospital or office by some means of transportation—most by automobiles, some by bus, others by train, and those with multihospital systems with locations in various states by plane. Few consider what risk they are exposing themselves to with their choice of transportation. They thus assume the risk of those modes of transportation by default.

This is similar to the way hospitals have been run in the past. No consideration was given to the risk the organization would be exposing itself to by adding a new building, a new service, a new physician, a new practice, new equipment, supplies, etc. These were added without any consideration or attempt to measure or control the potential risks.

The risk management process is nothing more than a formalization of the thought process to include risk management as part of the institution's decision-making process. Therefore, before a change or decision is made, the risk management implications should be identified and explored and that information should become part of the decision-making process.

Sometimes in health care the term risk management is associated exclusively with the risk of medical malpractice or professional liability. Unfortunately, in the medical malpractice crisis of the mid-1970s, it became the greatest risk for hospitals. The crisis tapered off somewhat but a new one arose in the mid-1980s that in both frequency and severity far exceeded anything in the past. Once again, medical malpractice was the greatest risk and often was the exclusive focus of risk management programs in hospitals. As discussed later in the risk financing sections of this chapter and in the chapters on insurance, hospitals should be concerned about many considerations other than professional liability. Many of these are discussed later. Even though much of this chapter and others concentrates on medical malpractice, it should be realized that the situation involving product liability, Workers' Compensation, directors' and officers' liability, and most of the casualty areas is approaching the crisis in medical malpractice.

GENERIC MODEL AS OUTLINE

Figure 6–1 is a generic model of risk management.

Risk Identification and Analysis

The lower left corner asks managers to identify the risks the organization is exposed to. (Useful tools available to hospital risk managers for identifying such

Figure 6–1 Generic Model of Risk Management

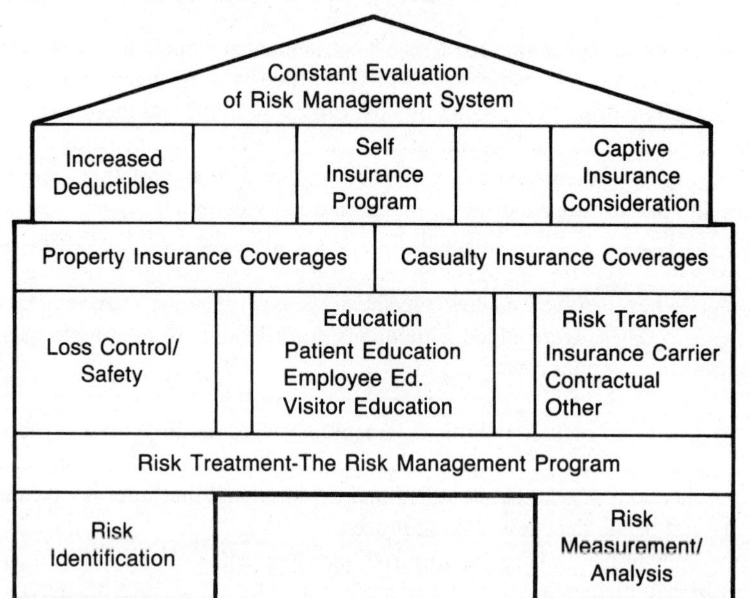

risks are discussed later.) The next step to the right is to measure and analyze the risks. Hospitals, like other organizations, have limited resources available for any program, risk management being no exception. Therefore, by measuring and analyzing the identified risks, managers are in a better position to allocate resources to areas that will produce the best return for the time, efforts, and funds invested. This also helps prioritize and quantify risks for others usages.

Risk Treatment

The next step is to treat the risk with tools such as loss control or safety programs. Loss control can be defined as organizational safety, an attempt to prevent harm to the hospital's resources—financial, human, or intangible.

The primary focus in risk management historically has been on preserving the financial resources of the institution. However, today, particularly in a high-technology industry such as health care, human resources are a valuable asset. Intangible resources include public relations, position in the community, etc. Even though this is important to all hospitals, it is particularly valuable in a small community. The hospital's relationship with its medical staff and the ability to develop and maintain a good rapport with it constitutes an important resource. If the hospital is unable to maintain that rapport, the medical staff members will be in a position to either threaten to or actually take their admissions to another hospital in town. Therefore, hospitals must protect that resource.

Education

Another risk treatment tool is education—of patients, employees, and visitors. Employee education in the health care industry is much like that in other industries: it's old hat. Most employers, be they hospitals or otherwise, have been educating their employees for years, although visitor and patient education are somewhat newer.

Visitor education includes such simple things as signage in the hospital that tells visitors what hours they can visit, where they can partake of certain activities such as smoking, and where they can obtain information. Visitor education also involves the patient's significant other—the spouse, adult child, parent, or other adult involved in the decision-making process with the patient. Hospitals have found that during these difficult times problems often are initiated not by the patient but by this significant other.

For example, in the informed consent process, a patient may have provided a valid informed consent. The individual may have been told that there might be an 8 percent or 10 percent chance of a particular outcome and the patient may, indeed, have anticipated that as a potential result. However, when it does materialize and the patient is unable to articulate the knowledge to the significant other, then the latter may not have anticipated it. When this occurs, the other is unhappy, and this displeasure can lead to litigation. Therefore, involving the significant other in some of the educational processes, such as the informed consent process, may go a long way to dispelling the outcome.

If the significant other has a feeling of being a part of the decision-making process and is well aware of the potential outcome, then such a person is less likely to complain and feel that the patient has been wronged.

Patient education is at different levels in different hospitals. There is informal patient education every time a health care provider, be it nurse, physician, or other, has a contact with the patient. Formal patient education can include the informed consent process, videotapes, closed circuit television, the patient library, and many other print and other types of media. In today's environment, hospitals are dealing with patients who are far better informed than those of even 1970. The burden is on the health care team to further educate today's patients and help with the process of making their contact with the system at least informed, if not beneficial.

Risk Transfer

The next tool is risk transfer. Many managers came to realize that the concept of transferring risk through insurance, at least during the mid-1970s, was a misnomer in that hospitals were not transferring the risk, only postponing it. That probably is even truer today than in the mid-1970s; that is, as premiums rise back to the point where hospitals are paying almost dollar for dollar for coverage (if they want a million dollars' worth of coverage, they pay a million dollars in premiums) they find that they have not transferred that risk—at best they have postponed it and now it is back to haunt them.

Another risk transfer method that is popular, particularly in hospitals, is that of contractual transfer. The hospital may contract out services such as dietary, housekeeping, and laundry. Some clinical areas also may be contracted out: the emergency room, clinical laboratory, radiology, anesthesiology, and so forth. One of the hopes in doing this is to try to transfer the liability to the contractor so hospitals can escape liability for these activities. As the courts began to look beyond these contracts, in some cases they held hospitals liable for the acts of the contractors.[1] Again, the hospitals were not, indeed, transferring liability. With the courts acting thus, hospitals' only hope may be to require the contractors to provide some kind of contractual indemnification and hold-harmless agreements.

Two major types of insurance are property and casualty. Property insurance coverages have not presented a major problem for most hospitals, with the exception of an occasional large inner-city facility. Most hospitals, even today, are able to find reasonable rates for their property. They often are classified under what is called an "HPR" (highly protected risk) rating and find their risk is rated well below that of the average industry.

That is not the case with casualty insurance. Again in the mid-1980s, as in the mid-1970s, casualty liability premiums are running away, reinsurance and insurance are nonexistent for some, and a similar crisis once again exists for hospitals. As premiums increased 300 percent to 1,000 percent in one year and hospitals were required to accept more of the risk, it became apparent that the new crisis was far worse than in the 1970s.

Hospitals have dealt, and will continue to deal, with these in many ways. One way is through increased deductibles. This is much like individuals' auto insurance: if they wreck their own car, they pay the first $100 of the repair bill. Hospitals have done the same thing; they have used deductibles. For example, if a hospital has a claim, it will pay the first $100,000 and the insurance company the balance. Others have opted to go to a self-insurance program, in which they may establish a trust with an independent fiduciary, an actuarially sound deposit base is determined, and the hospitals deposit into this self-insurance fund that is available to pay claims and claims expenses. Still others form captive insurance companies, that is, companies in which the owners are the insureds as well. Captive insurance companies have been popular among multihospital systems, state hospital associations, or other naturally aggregated groups of facilities. The whole method requires constant evaluation because it is a dynamic process. The swift pen of an appellate court in a given state can change the rules overnight. Therefore, hospitals must be in a position to react quickly and change the entire process when necessary.

THE 4 BASIC COMPONENTS

The risk management process, as do many other processes, has four basic components:

1. risk identification
2. risk analysis
3. risk treatment
4. risk evaluation.

RISK IDENTIFICATION

The first element in the risk management process is risk identification. In the hospital, it is important for the risk manager, particularly one who may not have had prior exposure at this institution, to first become intimately knowledgeable about the facility and its organization in general. It is essential to know the hospital's type of legal structure: a not-for-profit corporation, a for-profit corporation, a proprietorship or partnership, or a combination thereof. What is its organizational structure? That has a lot to do with its objectives and the conflicts they may create.

Next it is essential to know the type of services offered. In today's medical malpractice environment, whether or not a hospital has an obstetrical service will have a major impact on its exposure to risk. A risk manager must learn the hospital's employees and employee structures and the medical staff, whether employees are acquired from outside sources, either as a contract service providing the entire department or supplied by a pool service or other type of employment service. These can have a major impact on the hospital's risk potential.

Other key questions: Are physicians employed by the hospital or are they private attending doctors? Is there a teaching program at the hospital? Is it part of the teaching program at another institution? Are residents on 24-hour call? Do residents only rotate through the organization? Do residents moonlight as staff members in the emergency room? Are there contract physicians in various departments?

In the nonpersonnel area, questions include: Where does the hospital get supplies? How does it predetermine which supplies to purchase? Is there a prepurchase review process for buying supplies and equipment? Is there a biomedical engineering department? Is it a part of the prepurchase screening process? Does it provide any preventive maintenance? Does the facility contract out preventive maintenance and repairs for medical equipment? All these come under the heading of "know thyself."

Claims History

Once managers know the services, the actors, the tools, the supplies, and the equipment available, it is vital to be fully aware of past claims information and the hospital's claims experience. For facilities that are commercially insured, such historical data can be acquired from the insurance carrier. Managers also must be familiar with national claims experience. This can be acquired from studies such as the National Association of Insurance Commissioners' Closed Claims Study, State Closed Claims Studies and a perusal of the literature, which today is filled with what is happening nationally in the area of medical malpractice claims.

Organizations such as National Health Lawyers, American Academy of Hospital Attorneys, American Society of Law and Medicine, and many others provide a regular service to their members identifying cases in the various states. Hospitals would do well to learn from others' mistakes, as well as their own. Claims statistics vary from state to state. Some state hospital associations will do "claims surveys," others will compile data of one type or another. This is important for risk managers to understand.

What is happening locally? Local claims experience may be a little more difficult to determine, but major cases often are reported in the local newsmedia. This can be valuable information for risk managers because the circumstance or peculiarities in other localities may lead to unusual experiences in their own communities. For example, if a local plaintiff's attorney also happens to be a pharmacist, there may be a disproportionate number of pharmaceutical and medicine cases in the community. If managers were to solely rely on national experience, they would find such cases might be far less frequent than in their own area. The question is, if this is so, why? It also is true that a number of physicians also are attorneys. If a physician is an orthopedic surgeon and also a plaintiff's attorney, there may be a disproportionate number of orthopedic cases, etc.

These are offered only by example, but knowing what is happening in the community and knowing the plaintiff's bar in the locality can go a long way to explaining any anomalies as compared with national or state experience.

The Incident Report

Another source of risk identification is one that probably has varying value to hospitals: the traditional incident report. Typically, this has provided minimally useful information to most hospitals in identifying true loss-producing events on a timely basis. This is not a function of the concept, but is the way it is administered in some hospitals. Other institutions found that through the expansion of what they title "An occurrence or an incident," they have had far greater success in identifying these events on a timely basis. An occurrence may be an event that has no effect on the patient involved but is important from a loss prevention standpoint. Too often, hospitals do not learn of an occurrence until lawsuit papers are served.

Despite such problems, incident reports can be extremely useful tools when designed and administered properly. First, it is preferable to call them occurrence reports rather then incident reports because many of them are occurrences that do not rise to the level of incidents.

The first element that should be reviewed is the hospital's policy and procedure on incident reports. For incident reports to be valid tools, they must be encouraged.

The hospital should not worry about the numbers of incidents being reported; the objective should be to have reports on as close to 100 percent of the incidents as possible. Therefore, any successful new system will receive a far greater number of reports than before. There should be no more incidents occurring than before, just a larger percentage being reported. Therefore, everything should be done to encourage occurrence reporting not only by employees but also by medical staff members. In reality, medical staffs have not been cooperative in reporting incidents. That will not change materially, but as the process matures and gains creditability, that number will increase somewhat.

The policy must do all it can to protect the reports from legal discovery in any way available. In some states they are open to discovery, while in others they can be protected by involving the hospital attorney in the process or invoking state statutes for protection of quality assurance or peer review type of activities. The design of the system and of its policies and structure may go a long way toward affording the hospital all protections available in the state.

However, as discussed later, if these reports are filled out and handled properly, this protection from discovery should be an unimportant issue.

Encouragement of Reporting

The first step in the policy revision is to issue a statement encouraging employees to fill out incident reports, such as: "No employee will be terminated for reporting a nonmalicious, nonintentional incident; however, failure to report an incident may be grounds for disciplinary action and/or termination." This puts a high priority on reporting incidents and makes it a nonpunitive act, while failure to report an incident may be grounds for termination. However, this causes great consternation in many hospitals because it is read (erroneously) to say that if an employee does something wrong and hurts a patient, that the person is not going to be counseled and, in the extreme case, may be fired. That is not true.

The responsibility of management, be it the head nurse on the nursing unit, a supervisor in respiratory therapy, or anywhere else, is to review the quality of services and the work performed by their employees. When there are problems in this area, it is a normal management function of supervisors to counsel the employees even in the absence of an incident reporting system. This should not change just because the organization happens to be a hospital. The supervisor still should review the quality of work performed by employees and when they make mistakes, they should be counseled. The filing of the incident report should have no relationship to that situation.

The sample hospital policy (Exhibit 6–1) does all it can to encourage the reporting of incidents. Many hospitals worry about reporting an event that does not cause injury and contend that it should not be reported. The importance of reporting is critical.

For example, if the pharmacy sends the wrong medication to the floor, and, through proper procedures, the nurse identifies it as wrong, never gives it to the patient, sends it back, and the proper medication is sent up prior to the patient's receiving it, many hospitals feel this should not be an incident. However, it could easily have been missed on the floor and given to the patient; therefore, the fact that the wrong medication was sent is sufficient to make this an incident.

An incident can be defined as any happening that is not consistent with the routine operation of the hospital or the department. Injury does not have to occur; its mere potential is sufficient. If there are five or six of these events, something

Exhibit 6–1 Policy and/or Procedure for Incident Reporting

Purpose

To establish the policy and outline procedure for reporting unusual incidents that occur in or around Your Hospital and any of its facilities and properties.

Policy

1. It is the policy of Your Hospital to document and report all unusual incidents on the Hospital Attorney's Confidential Notice of Occurrence form [see Exhibit 6–2] and to channel the report to the specified personnel for necessary follow-up.
2. Employees and staff must be cautioned against committing the hospital to liability through their acts or statements in the presence of patients, visitors, or others at any time.
3. No employee will be terminated for an unintentional nonmalicious incident, if it is reported; however, failure to report an incident will be grounds for disciplinary action or termination.

Definition

An incident can be defined as any happening that is not consistent with the normal or usual operation of the hospital or department. Injury does not have to have occurred. The potential for injury and/or property damage is sufficient for an occurrence to be considered an incident.

Text

A. *Reporting Responsibilities*

Your Hospital has adopted an incident reporting mechanism to enable the hospital to carry out its responsibility for providing quality care in a safe environment. Procedures shall be established and observed in order to implement reporting of all incidents.

1. All incidents involving patients will immediately be reported to the Risk Management office. If the incident has extreme circumstances, the Risk Management office should be notified by phone.
2. In the case of personal injury to a visitor on hospital property, the Security Department should be notified immediately through the hospital operator, and an officer will complete the report.
3. In case of theft, disturbance or solicitation, Security should be notified, and an officer will investigate and make the report.

B. *Procedure*

1. The employee involved in, observing, or discovering the unusual incident is responsible for initiating the incident report. The supervisor will assist in the completion of the notice if necessary.
2. The supervisor of the department involved has the responsibility to forward all incident notices (*within 24 hours*) to the Risk Manager.
3. The Risk Manager will review all notices.
4. The Risk Manager will forward reports of nonpatient incidents to the Director of Safety.
5. The Risk Management Committee will meet as needed in order to review each patient incident on a timely basis.

Exhibit 6–1 continued

6. Follow-up responses, when necessary, will be kept on file in the Risk Management office.
7. The patient incident notice from a department or a clinical service will be maintained only in the Risk Management office files and is not to be photocopied or carbon copied.
8. Risk Management will follow up with patient, visitors, employees, or medical staff on necessary matters.
9. The Director of Safety will follow up on all miscellaneous, employee, visitor, and safety incidents. This may involve working with the Employee Health Department to determine the cause of employee injuries or safety problems that are reported.
10. In cases of employee injury, the incident notice should be completed in full, with the exception of the doctor's statement, and sent with the employee to Emergency Services or to the Employee Health Clinic. Where emergency care is required, all forms should be completed after emergency medical attention has been received.
11. In cases of medication loss, the Director of Pharmacy will be advised.
12. Risk Management will keep statistical data of incidents for analysis purposes.

Note: This policy assumes that the safety director works for the risk manager.

obviously is wrong with the process and it should be identified and dealt with, not postponed until a patient is seriously injured. The objective is not to have fewer incident reports filed but, ultimately, to have fewer incidents occurring.

The California Study

The California Medical Insurance Feasibility Study (CMIFS) in the mid-1970s sought to develop the basis for designing a no-fault medical malpractice system. In this study, some 22,000 medical records were reviewed to determine what percentage of the hospital admissions experienced "a potentially compensable event." The study showed that among hospitals of all sizes, 4.6 percent of admissions experienced a potentially compensable event. Therefore, if a hospital has 10,000 admissions a year, 460 patients will experience a potentially compensable event and will have grounds for a lawsuit. Fortunately, in actuality these numbers do not occur. If 4.6 percent of all admissions ultimately filed claims against the hospitals, few institutions would be able to survive.

However, the real value of the CMIFS is that it divided these potentially compensable events into 17 categories that became what is called the Generic Occurrence Screening Criteria. If these are monitored concurrently, they will permit hospitals to deal with the problems identified while the patient is still in the hospital, thus reducing the likelihood of a claim. It also can serve as a source of risk identification and a check-and-balance system to determine whether many of these events are reported through the incident reporting systems or otherwise. These screens thus can be used as an additional input of occurrences. The 17 categories designated in the CMIFS study are:

1. patients admitted for conditions suggestive of potential adverse results of outpatient department or emergency room services
2. readmissions to the same hospital within six months for complications or incomplete management of problems treated on previous admission
3. hospital-incurred incidents, including drug and transfusion reactions
4. transfer from general care unit to special care unit
5. transfer to another acute care facility
6. cardiac or respiratory arrest, including newborns
7. organ failure not present on admission (kidney, liver, heart, lung, etc.)
8. death
9. neurological deficit not present on admission but evident on discharge
10. newborn with an Apgar score less than or equal to 6 in the delivery room
11. operation for repair of lacerations, perforation, tear, or puncture of an organ, or injury incurred during an invasive or operative procedure
12. unplanned return to the operating room on this admission
13. unplanned removal, injury, or repair of an organ or part of an organ during an operative procedure
14. acute myocardial infarction during or within 48 hours of a surgical procedure on this admission
15. general morbidity indicators
16. parenteral analgesics administered last full day prior to or on day of discharge
17. hospitalization for complications of adverse results of prior emergency room or outpatient department care.

Since these were published, many organizations have developed expanded generic screens that apply to nearly all patients in the hospital. The list can be anywhere from the original 17 up to the 40 or so that some organizations use. It should be understood that the occurrence of any of these events does not indicate malpractice or poor care, only that there has been an occurrence. Therefore, it should be reviewed to determine whether or not malpractice or poor care has indeed taken place.

Many organizations have developed specific screens for use by some of the high-risk departments such as labor and delivery, psychiatry, emergency services, surgery, postanesthesia recovery, etc. The individuals who may be reviewing the charts for occurrences should be provided with exceptions so that if they can find an exception (justifying factor) to a particular occurrence screen, they should do nothing. If the stated exceptions do not exist, then they should be reviewed by the quality assurance and risk management departments and in the rare cases where there are, indeed, problems, further investigation and corrective actions should be undertaken.

The Chicago Screens

An example of a set of specific screens is one designed by the Chicago Hospital Risk Pooling Program that deals with the screens for emergency service activities. Coincidentally, it also has 17 screens:

1. emergency room patient discharged from hospital or seen in emergency room within past seven days
2. patient discharged or admitted to hospital without being seen by a doctor
3. patient arrives DOA
4. patient dies in emergency room or within 24 hours of admission
5. patient refuses treatment, hospitalization, or leaves against medical advice (AMA)
6. final x-ray report differs substantially from emergency room diagnosis and/or x-ray interpretation in emergency room—especially fractures, foreign bodies, and abnormal air
7. unexpected abnormal diagnostic tests results obtained after patient is discharged from emergency room
8. patient or visitor falls, resulting in injury
9. medication error
10. transfusion error
11. treatment/procedure error
12. lack of informed consent
13. patient and/or family complains about present or past treatment
14. cardiac arrest
15. respiratory arrest
16. patient with complaint of head trauma discharged with altered state of consciousness or with neurological deficit
17. patient discharged from emergency room on narcotics without an adult present.

The Chicago Hospital Risk Pooling Program also has developed a list of 21 specific screens for surgery and postanesthesia recovery. The screens for these are:

1. wrong patient operated on
2. wrong procedure performed
3. no written consent or improper consent

4. unplanned removal or repair—organ or body part—not in consent
5. patients injured during transfer to/from operating room and/or recovery room
6. patient burned from equipment
7. unplanned disconnection of equipment where potential for injury exists
8. incorrect needle, sponge, sharp, or instrument count
9. instrument breakage
10. foreign object or material found
11. break in sterile technique
12. patient operated on for repair of laceration, perforation, tear, or puncture of organ(s) subsequent to invasive procedure
13. return to operating room for repair or removal of organ or body part damaged in surgery
14. adverse results of anesthesia
15. intubation resulting in injury, including teeth
16. postoperative nerve damage
17. cardiac arrest
18. respiratory arrest
19. acute myocardial infarction during or following surgery
20. death
21. any untoward patient reaction in operating room/recovery room.

Once again, these do not indicate poor care or negligent care, only events that should be evaluated to determine the level of care. The person doing the screening should be provided with a list of exceptions for many of these factors. If the exception exists, then nothing needs to be done concerning the event.

Screens have been developed for many other high-risk areas. This information can be valuable input into the system to identify all types of occurrences, whether picked up on generic or specific screens. These are the types of occurrences that can be included in the input for the expanded incident or occurrence reporting system. Therefore, these can provide concurrent reporting of such events while the patient is still in the hospital, which is the ideal time to have this information.

Costs Not a Major Factor

One of the frequent concerns is that occurrence screening and the obtaining of this information will be expensive. However, the original 17 screens demonstrate that it is not difficult to determine that much of this information can be acquired without any additional cost to the hospital. For example:

- The occurrence screen for transfer from general care unit to special care unit: Most hospitals provide a daily computerized analysis of room activities.

Therefore, if a patient is transferred from general care to an ICU bed or a CCU bed, this will be indicated on that form. Daily review by the quality assurance or risk management department(s) can pick up this information at no additional cost.

- Readmissions to the hospital within six months from discharge: These can be picked up through the medical records department. Typically when a patient is admitted, the first thing requested is previous charts. The clerk in medical records can keep a log of these, send the log of patients readmitted within six months to risk management daily, and risk management can review these on a timely basis.
- Cardiac or respiratory arrest: When a code is called in the hospital, the operator is notified to announce it over the public address system. The operator can keep a log of the room numbers and once a day send them to risk management or quality assurance, which could review them to determine if there are any problems that should be of concern.

Almost all the others can be determined through a similar type of system and most of them through existing systems in the hospital. The cost for such a system should be small and the benefits in reduction of malpractice claims, early notification of potential claims, and improvement of the quality of care can be great.

Other Input Sources

Additional input sources should include many of the hospital departments:

- Public relations: This may be the department to handle the patient questionnaires and patient complaints. Those data should be put into the system, as well, so that when a complaint is received, it can be identified as an event that should be included in the data base; it also may require a claims file to be opened.
- Patient accounts: It is amazing how many patients never complain about the care received until collection activities heat up. Then they complain and say, "The reason I didn't pay my emergency room bill is because you missed my daughter's fracture in the emergency room and I had to take her across the street to have her properly diagnosed." That type of information can be valuable for loss prevention activities, as well.
- Patient representatives making regular patient visitations can help provide data for the system to improve the quality of care.
- Administration: Many complaints go directly to administration, so a unified system for analyzing such data can be valuable.

- Volunteers: Patients often talk more freely to volunteers, whom they perceive more as peers than as employees of the hospital. Volunteers thus can be a good input source on patient complaints.
- Patient escorts: Those who push patients around the hospital in wheelchairs and carts often receive comments about problems.
- Various departments: Patients will go back to the department head to discuss a complaint on care received in the department. That should be put into the system so that such occurrences can be reported and files developed where appropriate.
- Chaplain service: This is another area of frequent patient contacts and high exposure to complaints.
- Social services: These often are involved in discharge planning. Difficulty may arise with a family that feels that the only reason the patient has to be placed in a nursing home is because of a fracture suffered when the patient was dropped in x-ray. This information may be the only source of learning of the occurrence.
- Biomedical engineering and maintenance departments: They need to be called to repair a piece of equipment once it injures a patient. Again, their reporting of this event may be the only way of learning of the injury to the patient.
- Students: Nursing, medical, and the other types of students in the hospital are important sources.
- Infection control: This is an excellent source of learning of patient infections, which may lead to a claim.
- Radiation safety committee: This group receives reports on misadministrations in nuclear medicine.
- Admitting and bed control clerks: They can report information that overlaps into generic screens, but again they may be a source of learning of occurrences on a continuing basis.
- Quality assurance and utilization review: These should be a primary source of information. Risk management can help quality assurance in identifying problems it may not be aware of, and vice versa.
- Medical records: This department is the primary source of information. It contains most documentation of substandard care or medical malpractice and its chart review during coding can be valuable. It also can (should) report any time an attorney wants a copy of a chart or to review one.

The incidents or occurrences referred to here are beyond the classic falls from bed and medication errors that are typical of the classic incident reporting system.

If all these resources are utilized, and all this information is compiled into one source, the material will make it far easier to identify problems.

Statistics and Reports

National statistics show that hospitals have an average of 4.5 reported incidents per bed per year. This may be only a small percentage of those occurring, but this is only the number reported. Therefore, a 100-bed hospital would have 450 incidents reported a year. It should be obvious that even for a hospital that size, it is almost impossible for a risk manager or a quality assurance coordinator to spread these reports out on a table and do any type of meaningful analysis without spending a third of their time just aggregating the data.

Therefore, it is important to have some electronic or computer method of analyzing the reports. This can be done through an in-house (or time-sharing) computer or available through insurers, insurance brokerage houses, or independent companies such as the American Institute of Hospital Risk Management, Control Data, and many other organizations. These systems also will take the hospital's data, analyze it in a variety of ways, and help the institution focus on where loss prevention activities should be undertaken. They are also valuable tools for working with department heads, such as head nurses on individual nursing units, heads of clinical or support departments, vice presidents/administrators, medical staff, department chairmen or boards of trustees to determine their experience.

Such analyses can produce meaningful reports for meetings of the board, medical staff, hospital departments and nursing units, or on rounds. The reports can identify trends, patterns, and where problems exist so that steps can be taken to improve care and reduce the likelihood of loss-producing events. They also show that incident reporting is a two-way process since typically, once an incident report is sent in, the reporter never hears any feedback unless the patient dies. Two-way communication will improve the quality and quantity of incident reports, if the follow-up is handled appropriately.

Incidents should be reported for two purposes: (1) to help develop a case file to assist in the defense of the hospital if a suit materializes; (2) to learn of problems that can be corrected before another patient is injured. This is the theme of loss prevention. For example, while effective claims management activities can save the hospital $100,000 on a given case, a good loss-prevention program can prevent the next ten events of this nature from occurring. This is where the hospital can gain the most. However, it also is the hardest area to quantify. It is difficult to find a specific answer for a question such as: "How many claims did you prevent today and how much would they have been worth?" An understanding of the loss-prevention concept and its worth will help the administrator support the risk management program. The ability to analyze the data is essential to loss prevention; it is impossible if the data are analyzed manually.

Many computer programs are available and can be handled internally by purchase or licensing of software and training of individuals on how to use it. The better computer and/or software firms will show the hospital how to analyze the data because the information can be wasted if not used appropriately. It is important, too, to take steps to improve the quality of the data received.

In addition to the internal sources, there are numerous external sources for identifying problems: product alerts, warnings from the U.S. Food and Drug Administration and other governmental agencies, and published items of many varieties.

Other aids that overlap between the risk identification and risk analysis functions are items such as flow charts. Figure 6–2 is a hospital flow chart demonstrating how physician medication orders flow from the time the doctor writes the order on charts to the time the patient receives the prescribed medication and it is documented. This type of chart helps managers locate potential sources of medication delays and visualize the process in a way that will help them look for corrective measures. (This chart is not necessarily a good process for the flow; rather, it is just a sample of analyzing the process.)

Another example is the hazard logic tree, which identifies a causal relationship between the hazard and the loss events (Figure 6–3). A third tool is a fault tree analysis that allows managers to determine the process and how many events, either cumulatively or independently, can cause the loss-producing event to occur.

RISK ANALYSIS

The analysis process can be approached from many different directions. A typical example might be a statistical or mathematical process in which the manager attempts to identify the exposures and analyze them in an effort to manage particular risks.

Probability is the likelihood a given event will occur. The concept of probability is used in understanding the law of large numbers. The concept is that in the long run, the probability will determine the likelihood a particular event will occur. It must be realized that this may not necessarily be true for a single event but if this event is repeated a sufficient number of times, there is a high likelihood that it will reach the number expected. The studied occurrence should be looked at in several ways:

- the probable frequency of the occurrence of the loss
- the probable severity of the loss
- the possible severity of the loss
- the effect the potential loss would have on the organization clinically as well as financially.

Figure 6–2 Flow Chart—Physician's Medication Order

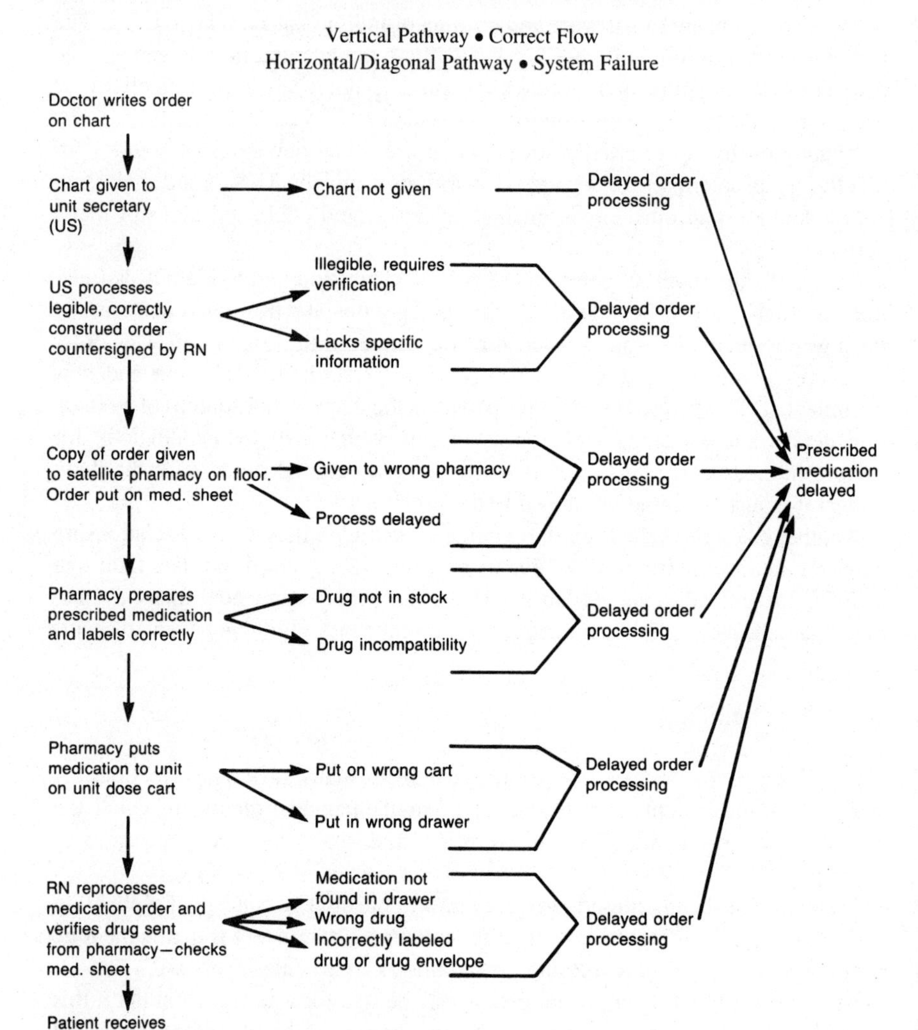

The first step is to look at the maximum probable and possible losses. The maximum probable loss means the worst loss that would be anticipated under average conditions. The maximum possible loss assumes the worst possible conditions and looks at the worst loss that could arise. Typically, one would look

Figure 6–3 Hazard Logic Tree: Physician Medication Order Process

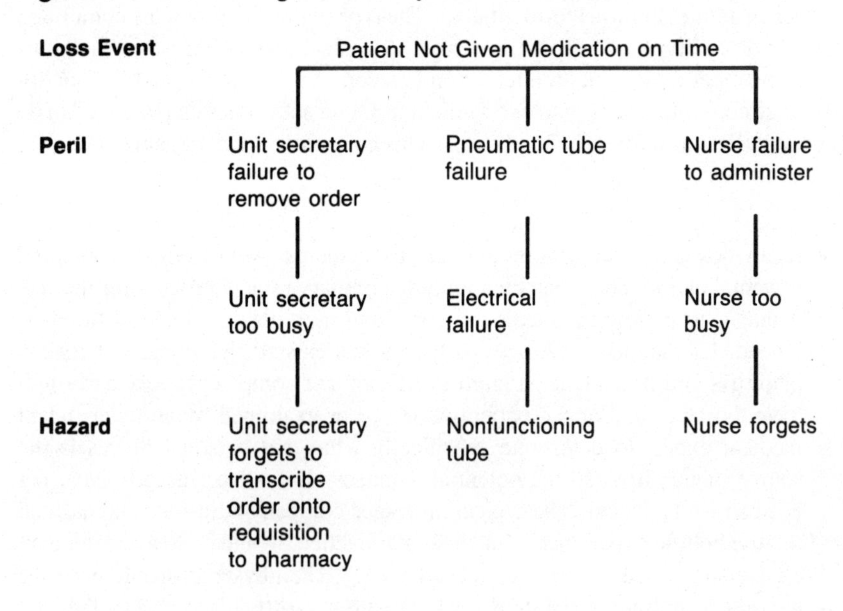

at the maximum possible loss in dealing with a single hospital, since the facility might not have an experience base large enough to spread the loss and therefore would lack the spread among a large number of events to determine the maximum probable loss.

Once the probable and possible outcomes have been determined, the next step is to determine the effects of those potential losses on the organization, both from a clinical and financial standpoint. In today's environment, what effect will it have on (1) the assets of the organization, (2) on its future creditworthiness if the hospital plans to be in the capital market in the future, and (3) the goodwill of the hospital in the community, once the public learns of the losses.

These are some of the factors to be considered in determining the impact on the organization. Other factors include employee morale, medical staff morale and referring patterns, goodwill, image in the community, ability to attract and retain good management and directors or trustees, and the relationship with patients.

Risk Management Committee

Many hospitals have established a risk management committee to assist the risk manager in analyzing data. A committee should be multidisciplinary, composed of physicians, nurses, a pharmacist, the risk manager, a representative from the hospital's insurance company if the facility is commercially insured, legal counsel, and an administration representative. The type of physicians on the committee depends on the type of hospital involved. A typical short-term acute care full-service hospital may want an internist, a surgeon, a psychiatrist, and the quality assurance committee chairman or coordinator. Other specialists can be called in on a consultation basis for individual cases. This committee, once organized, can do several things:

- It can look at individual cases and serious incidents—for example, a potential or actual claim. There can be a multidisciplinary review process for the risk manager to review the medical records and help obtain advice as to what, indeed, has happened. A great disparity has existed, historically, between plaintiffs and defendants. Plaintiffs, if they are competent, very early will have the chart and/or the patient reviewed or examined by an independent medical expert to determine specifically what that person believes is the source of liability and the potential damages. Defendants usually have not been so well advised. The typical insurance company adjuster, who has had relatively little experience in medical malpractice, would go to a codefendant physician and ask, "What happened here?" The physician would describe the case as nothing more than a patient who was difficult to please, the care that was provided was great, the patient's life was saved, and the patient should be happy with the medical services and should not be complaining about them. The adjuster would be surprised, late in the process, to learn that the care was not, indeed, as ideal as the hospital's insurer had been led to believe and there were, indeed, problems. Therefore, this risk management committee can give the risk manager and the insurance company representative semiobjective advice. The term semiobjective is used because as long as the physicians and nurses are on the same staff with those involved in the case, complete objectivity cannot be expected. Referral patterns, social contacts, and business contacts are occurring regularly, which obviously would somewhat taint complete objectivity. However, this information at least would be sufficient to let the risk manager know that there is trouble with this case. At that point, the risk manager can have the case analyzed by an independent physician not involved in the referral patterns or social activities with the individuals involved.
- It can analyze occurrence data to find systems and patterns so that procedures can be evaluated, equipment changed, staffing patterns altered, educational programs undertaken, or whatever may be necessary to correct problems with the care that may be identified.
- It can be a good source for going back to get information from the individual departments or people involved in a problem, such as the nursing member(s)

back to the nursing department or individual nurses having difficulties, the physician member back to medical departments or staff members, etc. This will help those thus approached to understand that the objective of this committee is not to cause problems for them but to help increase the quality of care and reduce the exposure and the frequency of claims against them and the hospital. When there is a problem with a particular medical staff member, depending upon rapport with the medical staff in general or the particular person, the manager may rely on the physician committee member to work with the individual in resolving the situation.

- It can provide educational programs for committee members on risk management and claims processes.

The committee members will become supporters of the program once they understand the process and the benefit individual staff members and the hospital can derive. This message will be taken back to the departments and staff.

Protection of Information

Care should be taken to protect the committee's information in any way possible. If having legal counsel on the committee and having the group in turn serve as a resource to the attorney will afford protection, then that is the structure that should be created. If the committee must be a medical staff committee to be protected under the state's peer review statutes, that step should be taken. If there is no way of protecting the information, then minutes should not be taken at committee meetings and the group should only be an informal resource to the risk management program.

Concerning whether incident reports can be open to legal discovery, Exhibit 6–2 presents an example of a report. It first asks for general information at the top of the form, most of which is available on the chart. It then asks for a brief narrative of what happened, without editorial comments—information that should be similar to that in the nursing notes or the notes of other clinical departments. The medical staff's comments at the end of the form should be nothing more than those available in the progress notes. Therefore, the kind of information that should be in the narrative section is information such as: "Went into room 502, found Mrs. A on the floor, cuts and contusions on forehead, placed her back in bed, took vital signs, called Dr. X."

This is nothing more than what would appear in the nursing notes. Dr. X's comments should be to the effect: "Examined Mrs. A after an apparent fall, found minor cuts and abrasions on forehead. Cleaned and dressed wound, ordered x-rays, and took vital signs. X-rays were negative." This note follows the information that probably would be in the progress notes. Therefore, if this report

Exhibit 6–2 Example of an Incident Report

HOSPITAL ATTORNEY'S CONFIDENTIAL NOTICE OF OCCURRENCE

IDENTIFICATION (CHECK ONE BOX ONLY)	SEX	EXACT AGE	MARITAL STATUS	EMPLOYEE INJURY/ INCIDENT ONLY
☐ 1 PATIENT ☐ 2 EMPLOYEE ☐ 3 VISITOR ☐ 4 MISC.	☐ 1 FEMALE ☐ 2 MALE		☐ 1 MARRIED ☐ 2 SINGLE ☐ 3 WIDOWED ☐ 4 DIVORCED	TIME LOST ☐ 1 YES ☐ 2 NO ☐ 3 UNKNOWN HOSPITAL #

INCIDENT DATE	REPORT DATE	INCIDENT TIME	INCIDENT LOCATION
(DIGITS ONLY)	(DIGITS ONLY)	TIME ☐ A.M. ☐ P.M. SHIFT ☐ 1=1ST ☐ 2=2ND ☐ 3=3RD	

CONDITION BEFORE (PATIENT ONLY)

☐ 1 NORMAL
☐ 2 SENILE
☐ 3 DISORIENTED
☐ 4 SEDATED
☐ 5 UNCONSCIOUS
☐ 6 OTHER (DISCUSS BELOW)

BED ADJUSTMENT (NOT BED RAILS) (PATIENTS ONLY)

☐ 1 NOT ADJUSTABLE
☐ 2 UP
☐ 3 DOWN

CAUSE IF MORE THAN ONE CAUSE, CHECK THE PREDOMINATE ONE AND DESCRIBE THE OTHERS IN THE LOWER PART OF THE REPORT.

A – FALLS

☐ 001 BED BOTH RAILS UP
☐ 002 BED BOTH RAILS DOWN
☐ 003 BED: 1RAIL UP, 1RAIL DOWN
☐ 004 FALL FROM CHAIR OR EQUIPMENT
☐ 005 FALL FROM DIFFERENT LEVEL
☐ 006 FALL FROM SAME LEVEL

B – MEDICATION

☐ 007 PATIENT IDENTIFICATION
☐ 008 DOSAGE
☐ 009 ROUTE
☐ 010 UNORDERED
☐ 011 DUPLICATION
☐ 012 OMMISSION
☐ 013 TRANSCRIPTION
☐ 014 TRANSFUSION
☐ 015 WRONG MEDICATION
☐ 016 LABELING
☐ 017 TIME GIVEN

C – OTHER

☐ 018 I.V. INJECTION TECHNIQUE
☐ 019 STRUCK BY PATIENT
☐ 020 STRUCK BY EQUIPMENT
☐ 021 STRUCK EQUIPMENT
☐ 022 STRUCK BY TOOL OR OBJ.
☐ 023 OVEREXERTION HANDLING PT.
☐ 024 LIFTING OR MOVING
☐ 025 LOSS OF PERSONAL PROP.
☐ 026 PATIENT CARE NURSES
☐ 027 PATIENT CARE OTHERS
☐ 028 ANESTHESIA
☐ 029 SURGICAL/O.B. COUNTS
☐ 030 PATIENT IDENTIFICATION
☐ 031 CAUGHT IN, ON, BETWEEN
☐ 032 VEHICLE ACCIDENT
☐ 033 NEEDLE STICKS
☐ 034 MISC. (DISCUSS BELOW)
☐ ____________

(NOT PART OF MEDICAL RECORD OR PERSONNEL RECORD)
NAME AND ADDRESS OF PERSON INVOLVED; GIVE MEDICAL RECORD NUMBER. USE ADDRESSOGRAPH IF AVAILABLE.

IDENTIFICATION #

NATURE OF INJURY (INJURY SUSPECTED AS A RESULT OF INCIDENT)

☐ 100 ASPHYXIA, STRANGULATION, OR INHALATION
☐ 110 BURN OR SCALD
☐ 120 CHEMICAL BURN
☐ 130 HEAD INJURY
☐ 140 CONTAGIOUS OR INFECTIOUS DISEASE
☐ 150 CONTUSION, CUT, LACERATION, OR ABRASION
☐ 155 PUNCTURE
☐ 160 FRACTURE OR DISLOCATION
☐ 165 INFECTION
☐ 170 VISCERAL INJURY
☐ 180 SPRAIN OR STRAIN
☐ 185 DEATH
☐ 190 NO INJURY
☐ 200 NO APPARENT INJURY
☐ 210 OTHER – NOT CLASSIFIED (DISCUSS BELOW)

REPORTING EMP. DEPT.#	PROVIDER

IF PATIENT, REASON FOR VISIT/HOSPITALIZATION/DIAGNOSIS

ATTENDING PHYSICIAN:
(IF OUTPATIENT)

IF EMPLOYEE INJURY/INCIDENT
DEPT. # DEPT.
JOB TITLE
DATE RETURNED TO WORK
☐ FIRST AID ONLY ?
SOC. SEC. NO. ____________

IF VISITOR INCIDENT
REASON FOR PRESENCE:
HOME PHONE:
OCCUPATION:

LIST ALL PATIENTS IN THE ROOM. GIVE NAMES AND ADDRESSES OF WITNESSES, INCLUDING EMPLOYEES:

GIVE BRIEF DESCRIPTION OF INCIDENT. NO EDITORIAL COMMENTS OR OPINIONS.

NAME, TITLE, AND DEPARTMENT OF PERSON PREPARING REPORT DATE:

VITAL SIGNS AFTER INCIDENT:

REVIEWED BY SUPERVISOR ☐ YES ☐ NO SUPERVISOR'S SIGNATURE DEPT. #

WAS PHYSICIAN NOTIFIED ? ☐ YES ☐ NO NAME OF PHYSICIAN

WAS PERSON SEEN BY A PHYSICIAN ? ☐ YES ☐ NO TIME SEEN: : ☐ A.M. ☐ P.M. WHERE

PHYSICIAN'S STATEMENT REGARDING CONDITION OF PERSON INVOLVED AFTER THE INCIDENT:

RESULTS OF LABORATORY AND X-RAY EXAMINATIONS:

TREATMENT PRESCRIBED:

NAME OF PHYSICIAN (PRINT) ____________ PHYSICIAN'S SIGNATURE ____________ ultimately is discoverable, there is no damage done to the hospital or its personnel because the information is available from other easily obtainable sources, primarily the medical record.

Investigations subsequent to filing this notification should be under the direction of legal counsel, quality assurance, or peer review based on state law. Therefore, great effort should be taken to educate the medical and employee staffs as to the actual purpose of the form and the proper way of completing it, without editorial comments.

Blame shifting in the incident report is a dangerous activity. If the purpose is to relieve the chart writer of liability by blaming another, it seldom if ever serves that purpose. If it is to vent anger, it should not be put in the chart—it may be necessary to explain it six years later. It may be impossible to explain why one put in the chart: "Dr. X is a quack and should be working in a veterinarian clinic." Whether or not it ultimately becomes discoverable is not the point; it is important to have a chart or report that facilitates the flow of communications on a patient and that objectively documents treatment, diagnosis, and observations.

Some hospitals add corrective actions taken to the incident report but managers who review many of these will find that 99.9 percent of them say, in effect: "I counseled Nurse Y and she told me this will never happen again." That is not useful and may be damaging. Extremely damaging are comments such as: "This is the third time that Nurse Y has made a mistake like this and she should be taken out and shot." The final tiny percentage of information is useful. For that limited benefit, the exposure of having this kind of material on the form is not beneficial and thus should not be included. That kind of follow-up can be done by the risk manager with the department on an individual case basis, particularly on the critical incidents. In serious incidents, there will be investigations anyway.

Risk Treatment Priority Chart

Another tool is the Risk Treatment Priority Chart (Exhibit 6–3). This can be completed by either an individual or a group. Users begin by giving the appropriate rating to each of the factors, then weighting it. An example is falls. Most hospitals would agree that falls occur every day. The manager begins in the frequency column, placing a 5 in the small box in the upper right corner of the fall block. This is done with each of the factors. Then, in each large block, that 5 is multiplied by the weighting factor at the top of the column, in this case 5 for frequency, producing 25. The points are added across to the right, with the sum in the total exposure block. The points are rank ordered and the risks prioritized.

This chart's usage varies according to the department involved. Department members as a group should analyze the exposures/risks based on the same frame of reference. This will develop the weightings and will help the members understand

Exhibit 6–3 Risk Treatment Priority Chart

Exposure	*Frequency*	*Severity*	*Estimated Correction Cost*	*Estimated Correction Time*	*Public Interest*	*Exposure Total*	*Exposure Priority*
	Wt. 5	Wt. 10	Wt. 8	Wt. 4	Wt. 6		
Foreign body in operative site							
Post-op wound infections							
Falls							
Medication errors							

Frequency

5 — Each day
4.5 — Each week
4 — Each month
3.5 — Every two months
3 — Every six months
2.5 — Every year
2 — Every two years
1.5 — Every five years
1 — Every 10 years
.5 — Every 25 years

Severity

5 — Catastrophic
4.5 — Severe
4 — Major
3.5 — Serious
3 — Minor
2.5 — Marginal
2 — Negligible

Estimated Correction Cost

5 — Up to $500
4 — $501–$1,000
3 — $1,001–$5,000
2 — Over $5,000

Estimated Correction Time

5 — Within 1 day
4 — Within 1 week
3 — Within 1 month
2 — Within 1 year

Public Interest

5 — Extremely visible
4 — Highly visible
3 — Moderately visible
2 — Not visible

why risk managers spend so much time worrying not about minor problems but about the major ones.

With nursing, falls will show a high frequency but a fairly low exposure. Therefore, that department will understand why, even though falls are of critical importance for a nursing unit from a total exposure priority, they are well down on the list. Since falls are rated lower than other, more serious problems, risk managers will spend less time dealing with them. This is important to those on the nursing unit because of the criticism they receive from patients' families. The unit will be surprised, too, that the numbers will usually support what the risk manager has been saying all along.

This tool certainly involves a fair amount of subjectivity but by the same token it provides an appearance of objectivity in a process that health care people think is a black-box operation. It is remarkable how effective an awareness instrument this can be for medical staffs and similar groups when the risk manager sits down with such persons and goes through this exercise. Members of the nursing or medical staff departments often will argue over what number goes in a particular block. Once this happens, awareness of the entire problem grows and the manager has won the battle.

RISK TREATMENT

Loss/Risk Control

The next step in the risk management process is risk treatment. This section deals with two types:

1. loss/risk control
   a. loss prevention
   b. loss reduction
   c. risk avoidance
2. risk financing.

Loss Prevention

Loss prevention can be defined as an attempt to reduce the frequency of loss-producing events. In medical malpractice situations, this is an attempt to look at the standard of care and to assure that it is met in providing care and services to patients. This may be as simple as establishing a count procedure in the operating room for surgical instruments or as technical as reviewing the care provided by some of the medical departments to determine that it is acceptable.

Loss Reduction

Loss reduction, however, involves decreasing the potential severity of loss exposure. This often is a function of sound claims management. The general concept of claims management is handled in detail in Chapter 10. It is mentioned here only superficially. One key to loss reduction is evidence preservation. More and more, tangible items are found to be involved in patients' claims. A sound evidence preservation program can enable the hospital to receive contributions from the manufacturer to help pay the claim. This can be accomplished only if the procedure immediately identifies, tags, and properly preserves the evidence so the manufacturer can be shown the exact item involved.

The product also should be evaluated independently by an outside engineering firm when necessary and appropriate. This is not to imply that the internal biomedical engineering staff does not have the competency to evaluate the equipment. However, if serious injuries are involved, it is essential to have an independent third party evaluate the equipment to determine whether there was a malfunction and, if so, whether it was caused by a defect in the product's design or manufacturing or in the way it was used by hospital personnel. The answer can help to shift much of the burden of loss to the manufacturer. However, this evaluation must be undertaken on serious cases before the equipment has been altered/repaired by hospital personnel.

Also in loss reduction, after an event occurs, risk managers must follow all loss notice provisions in the insurance contract and cooperate fully with the insurer. In addition, with the long tail on medical malpractice claims, it is important to retain expired policies so they are available at time of claim.

Risk Avoidance

Risk avoidance is another step in the loss/risk control function. The concept is simply to avoid risk. For instance, if the organization is building a new hospital and the risk manager is consulted as to which services the facility should have and should not have, it might be worthwhile to consider not including an OB service, since this is the highest risk area. If that is a motivating factor and the manager prevails, then the hospital will have avoided the risk of brain damage or defective newborns in the new institution.

Risk Financing

Once the loss risk/control techniques are established, the next consideration is how to finance that risk. This deals primarily with methods of paying for losses. It became popular in the mid-1970s and again in the mid-1980s for hospitals to retain or assume portions of the risk; that is, they retained the financial burden of a certain portion of the risk exposure rather than attempting to transfer it to an insurance carrier (in effect, partial self-insurance).

Risk assumption may be intentional or accidental. If it is assumed accidentally, that would imply poor risk identification and analysis. The hospital is not aware of the risk and therefore assumes the risk because of ignorance. The wiser decision is for hospitals to make a conscious decision to retain the risk.

There are many ways of retaining risk. One is unfunded self-insurance. Under this method, the hospital provides no financing in advance, only at that time of loss. Even though this system offers many benefits, particularly low administrative cost, it can be catastrophic if the hospital were to experience a $3 million unfunded loss. Therefore, funded self-insurance has become the more popular of the two methods.

In that system, anticipated levels of losses are funded in advance, typically deposited with an independent fiduciary in a trust account. These funds accumulate and are available to pay claims as they materialize. Considering the long tail of medical malpractice claims, it may be a number of years from a given year before funds are drawn upon and, with interest, the hospital may find that it can pay losses out of interest without touching the principle if the self-insurance has been funded properly. This allows the hospital great freedom over claims management. In addition to the interest income, administrative costs are far below those of commercial insurance. The primary disadvantages are the inability to spread the risk among a large group of insureds and the difficulty in acquiring reinsurance for the fund, or excess insurance in some cases.

Another popular method of handling retention is through a captive insurance company, with either a single or multiple ownership. For example, an individual hospital under the single-owned or a multihospital group under the multiowned captive insurance company forms its own insurance company to insure the owners of the insurance company. There are substantial advantages under this method. An insurance company that is properly licensed and admitted in the various states will have access to reinsurance. Reinsurance is a method of selling part of the risk to a number of other companies so that the hospital is not totally at risk for the full amount of its policy. Nearly all casualty insurance companies do this to protect themselves from catastrophic loss. There also would be a good underlying basis for excess insurance. There is some risk spreading, even though it usually is among a small group. The disadvantages include the required premium taxes; depending on the type of organization, the inability to acquire tax exemptions; and the general overall operating expenses of running an insurance company and meeting the requirements of a given state or foreign government.

Another method of retention is pooled self-insurance funds. This is nothing more than a joint venture with several organizations to pool self-insurance funds. It is similar to self-insurance, except that it spreads the risk among a larger group, even though it is small by insurance standards. It also spreads the cost of administrative expenses. However, this may come under some state insurance regulations and there may be some Internal Revenue Service implications making the pool taxable. There can be difficulty in getting agreement among individually unrelated hospitals as to shares of losses and required loss-prevention activities.

Still another example is the fronting arrangement. This typically involves the hospital purchasing an insurance contract through a commercial carrier but agreeing by contract to take back a certain portion of the risk from the insurer. Thus, the risk is transferred back to the hospital. This can be done by taking back all of the risk, or a portion of it. It gives the appearance to outsiders of commercial insurance through a commercial insurer. It would increase the hospital's ability to obtain excess insurance and the fronting organization may have the ability to acquire reinsurance. However, such an approach usually requires a substantial fee, which would include taxes and expenses, and the fronting company may place numerous restrictions on the hospital. There also may be requirements for different types of letters of credit to the insurance company to assure it that if a claim is made, the hospital will be able to repay the losses to the fronting company. Some of the footnotes on financial statements required by auditors may outweigh any advantages gained. Such footnotes may have a negative effect on credit worthiness. Many of the advantages that once existed have been reduced considerably in today's environment.

Risk transfer is done primarily through the purchase of commercial insurance, which probably is still the most popular form of risk financing, even though the insurance may be purchased through a captive that is owned by the state hospital association or some other group. In today's environment commercial insurance is costly.

In addition to professional liability, many other areas should be included in analyzing insurance and risk treatment:

Property:

- buildings owned and leased;
- hospital's personal property;
- business interruption, which includes extra expense, loss of income, and rental value;
- boiler and machinery;
- builders' risk;
- bonding of construction projects;
- outdoor signage and glass;
- personal property, including motor vehicles, aircraft, and watercraft;
- inland marine to cover movable equipment, particularly in home health care where expensive equipment is moved about on a regular basis;

- computer and data processing records; and reconstruction costs of billing and medical records.

Liability:

- hospital professional liability, medical malpractice;
- comprehensive general, premises and operations;
- druggist;
- employee benefit;
- fiduciary responsibility insurance;
- products and completed operations;
- owners' protective, contractual;
- personal injury;
- directors and officers;
- products liability;
- excess;
- umbrella;
- aircraft (owned and nonowned);
- airport (heliport);
- premises owned but not utilized as hospital;
- safe deposit box;
- garage keepers' legal liability;
- Workers' Compensation;
- excess Workers' Compensation;
- unemployment compensation;
- motor vehicle.

Miscellaneous:

- blanket crime insurance;
- employees' dishonesty;
- ERSA bonds;
- alcohol bonds;
- self-insured Workers' Compensation bonds;
- many others.

Many of these risks involve aspects of medical malpractice. Two expanding areas are product liability and directors' and officers' liability. The latter is growing rapidly and becoming costly as hospitals are sued under antitrust, EEOC, and many other new and innovative theories of liability.

RISK EVALUATION

The final step in the risk management process is risk evaluation. There is a need for constant evaluation of the entire system to make sure it is current and up to standards in individual states. These standards can change dramatically because of court decisions, so risk managers must be able to adapt the system as needed.

Figure 6–4, Internal Elements of Hospital Risk Management System reviews much of what has been discussed.

Figure 6–4 Internal Elements of Hospital Risk Management System

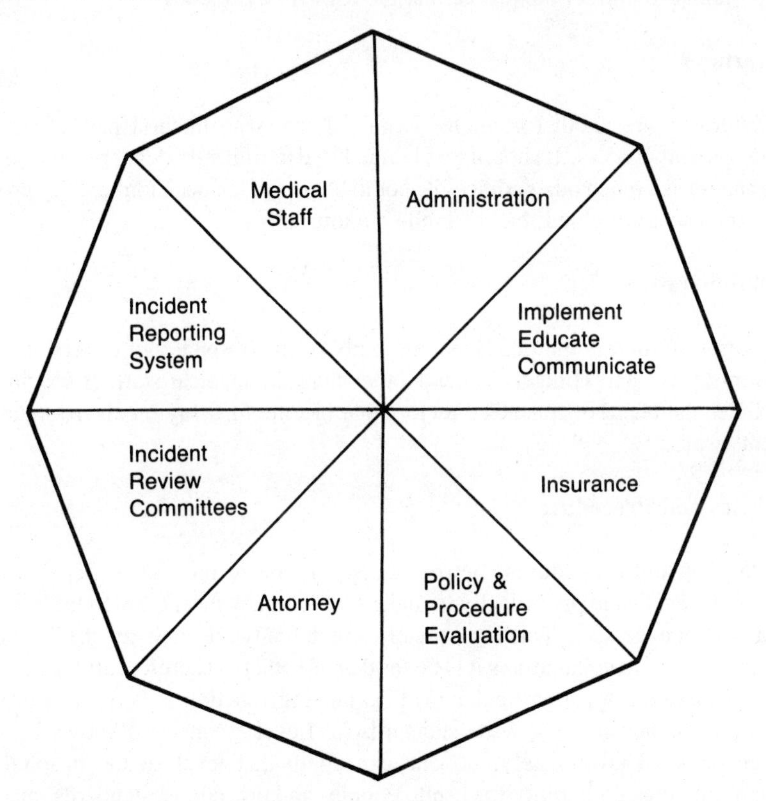

Incident Reporting

This begins by looking at the incident reporting system as a form of identifying risks that goes beyond the classic incident report. The next element is the incident review committees, part of risk analysis.

Medical Staff

Then comes the medical staff, which can both create and resolve many of the problems, with the focus on trying to handle them at the lowest possible level. When a specific physician has caused care problems, either the risk manager or a physician member of the risk management committee should go to the individual and offer an opportunity to correct the situation. If the physician chooses not to do so, the process can advance to the section or department chairman, chief of staff, quality assurance committee, medical executive committee, joint committee, and ultimately the board if necessary. Again, the individual must always be given the opportunity to correct the problem at the lowest possible level.

Attorneys

Attorneys are another element. Legal advice is an integral part of the risk management process. It should be obtained to determine the legal peculiarities in the state. Like much other advice, it should be part of the decision-making process and should be weighted, based on the circumstances.

Administration

Administration is the policymaking body of the hospital and covers all of its administrative and clinical elements other than the medical staff. It specifically includes the board of trustees/directors that has the final say on all risk management issues.

Policies and Procedures

Policies and procedures, be they hospitalwide or individual departments, should be evaluated periodically to make sure that they meet the standards of care and are not excessive. This is an area in which many hospitals get themselves in trouble. Every hospital thinks it is better than all others. Therefore, if the standard of care required for a particular medical/nursing function is, say, a theoretical Level 2, the hospital will write standards for Level 7, since it "knows" it is so much better. Unfortunately, no one can attain that level so the hospital has voluntarily created liability for itself. Policies and procedures standards must not be written so high that they cannot be met. They should be set at the minimum required unless it is certain that they can be met without fail. For example, if Level 2 is the one required and the hospital wants to set its policies and procedures at Level 3 and can attain that without fail, then it is safe to do so. From a legal standpoint, where a hospital is required to achieve only Level 2 but says it will do Level 3 and does so, it should have no liability under the concept of negligence, as discussed in Chapter 4.

What does all this mean? What is a practical example of this? An absurd example may make this point clearer. Every hospital has procedures on the medical and surgical units to provide for suicide precaution for patients who may indicate such tendencies. The safest procedure to be written would be that any patient who is placed on suicide precaution on a medical/surgical floor must be checked by a nurse every three minutes. This would make it very difficult for patients to kill themselves while under suicide precautions. However, that is not realistic. No hospital could provide staffing to make checks every three minutes. The hospital thus has created an excessive standard for itself. It may be reasonable to check patients every 15 or 30 minutes or transfer them to a psychiatric unit if it is believed they are extreme risks. It may be sufficient to have a procedure that calls for a consultation by a qualified psychiatrist to determine what level of suicide precaution is necessary. If it is felt safe for patients to be on a medical/surgical unit with checks every half hour, that may meet the standard of care. Thus, hospitals should not write policies that are excessive; policies are not a place to state goals or define what optimal care is.

Implementation, Education, Communication

The next area is implementation, education, and communication. If the hospital changes a policy or the way in which something should be done, it is imperative to communicate these changes to appropriate individuals. It cannot be assumed that just because a nurse walks by the procedure manual once a day, that person will know automatically what changes have been made. Employees then must be educated so they will know what is required of them today that was not required yesterday, or what no longer is required.

Insurance

Insurance is the area people most think about when discussing risk management. It involves the purchasing of insurance, the developing of bid specifications, policy and premium management, and numerous other elements, including the selection of insurance agents and brokers. (Another viewpoint on this issue is discussed in Chapter 7 in the section titled "Selecting Brokers and Insurers.")

In times when insurance is readily available and inexpensive, the need for sophistication and expertise of brokers in being able to access the various insurance markets and develop creative packages is of relatively little importance. However, when the insurance environment is tight, premiums escalate, availability is lessened, insurers' capacity is reduced, and demands by prospective insurers are onerous. In such situations, the insurance brokers' competency is of critical importance. In that kind of environment, the hospital needs a broker with tremendous expertise in the health care industry. Regardless of how large brokers may be, hospitals should be interested only in their ability to access the markets; it is irrelevant whether they represent General Motors, General Electric, or Shell Oil. Therefore, hospitals should be very select in choosing brokers that have extensive health care experience and access to the worldwide markets necessary during a tight environment.

In a tight insurance environment, when a hospital places its brokerage out for proposals, the best way to handle the procedure is not to allow prospective brokers to go to the insurance markets but to require them to provide information on their access to markets and to demonstrate their internal expertise. If those on the bid list have been selected properly, the assumption is that any two or three of the top candidates will have comparable access to the markets. What the bidders need to sell is their ability to provide service to the hospital organization and their creativity and expertise in the health care industry. This is of critical importance, and the more difficult the insurance environment is, the more important this becomes.

Brokers' services can be helpful not only in acquiring and maintaining insurance but also in negotiating contract provisions, exploring the feasibility of alternate risk financing programs, assisting at the time of claims, and advising on other methods for broadening the hospital's risk-spreading technique. Creativity is the watchword.

NOTE

1. *Adamski v. Tacoma General Hospital,* 20 Wash. App. 98, 579 P.2d 970 (1978); *Hannola v. City of Lakewood,* 426 N.E.2d 1187 (Ohio 1980); *Grewe v. Mt. Clemens General Hospital,* 404 Mich. 240, 273 N.W.2d 429 (1978).

Chapter 7

Insurance

William Gill and Ronald Nelson

WHAT IS INSURANCE?

Although the decision to insure often is presented as the last step in the risk management process, nothing should be permitted to reduce the importance of insurance in the overall program. The intelligent purchase of insurance may be the single most important action undertaken by risk managers. It is important, therefore, that they not only know all the other skills that go with their jobs; they also must understand the nature of insurance and how to use it as a part of their overall program.

Adam Smith offered a definition of insurance more than 200 years ago: "The trade of insurance gives great security to the fortunes of private people, and by dividing among a great many that loss which would ruin an individual, makes it fall light and easy upon the whole society."[1]

Although the economic nature of today is very different from that of Smith's, little change is needed in his definition to make it fit the current situation. However insurance may function in various circumstances, it remains a mechanism permitting the shifting of a potentially unbearable loss cost from the individual to a pool composed of many individuals, then averaging the total cost of loss paid by the pool across all its members.

In the interest of precision, some concepts introduced elsewhere in this book should be reviewed in the context of the insurance mechanism.

"Risk" is a word that has many connotations. From an insurance point of view, managers are concerned only with a special kind of risk that exhibits all of the following characteristics:

- It offers only the opportunity for financial loss. It is characterized by one of two possible outcomes: if it does not happen, there is neither financial loss nor financial gain or profit; if it does happen, only financial loss results. The best of outcomes in the event of risk is neutral as respects the financial result of operations involving it. If the event of the risk does happen, it produces loss, and the loss could be large enough to ruin the enterprise involved.

- The occurrence of an event producing this kind of risk of loss is beyond the control of the persons or organizations carrying out activities whence the loss arises. In the clearest sense of the term, the loss-producing events are fortuitous or random in their nature. Mathematically, the probability of the loss event occurring is equal to the probability of its not occurring in any randomly selected unit of time.
- The activities out of which the risk of loss-producing events arise are not carried out with the intent of producing the risk or the event. The intent of the activity may be isolated from the event even though the risk of the event's happening cannot be eliminated from the activity, whether or not the event occurs. It thus may be inferred that every human activity contains the risk of the occurrence of just such a fortuitous, unintended, loss-producing event. This kind of risk is a necessary byproduct of activity.

A risk that exhibits these characteristics is called "pure" risk. Only pure risk is the proper subject of an insurance transaction, just as it is the subject for risk management in general.

With this understanding of pure risk, it is possible to establish a new definition of insurance and the insurance mechanism: "Insurance permits the individual to transfer his pure risk of loss to a pool formed by a large number of similar individuals, and to distribute equitably the cost of the loss transferred to the pool amongst all the members of the pool."

To understand how this mechanism works, underlying concepts related to the word "pool" need to be examined:

- A pool is composed of a large number of similarly situated individual members. "Similarly situated" is a key phrase: while no two members of the pool will be exactly alike, they must be in a similar situation—that is, doing the same kinds of things, even though the process by which they do them may vary somewhat from member to member.
- The pool must be large enough that, while it is impossible to predict for any one member that a loss will occur in any precise period of time, it becomes possible to predict of the pool as a whole that a definable amount of loss will occur within that same period.

For example, it is not possible to predict that loss will occur to any one member of the pool within one year, but it is possible to predict with some level of confidence that the pool as a whole will experience losses and the total of those losses within the same year. It follows from this that the number of members of the pool should be large compared with the amount of loss predicted for the pool. The larger the pool, the more stable its results and the more predictable its outcome. This principle is sometimes referred to as the Law of Large Numbers.

The average loss cost per pool member becomes the basis for charging all the members for their participation. If the method of allocating this cost among the members were based on the number in the pool, some inequities would arise quickly: very large pool members would pay the same amount as very small ones. To avoid this, another step is added to the process to define an exposure base for the members. An exposure base is something that is objectively measurable, common to all members of the pool, and accurately reflects their level of activity. For example, for a Workers' Compensation pool, the normal exposure base is the amount of remuneration paid to a member's employees. For hospital professional liability, the exposure bases used are occupied beds and outpatient visits. For property insurance, the exposure base is the value of the property insured.

After an exposure base is selected, a determination is made as to the unit of exposure. For Workers' Compensation, the unit of exposure is each $100 remuneration; for hospital professional liability, each occupied bed and each 100 outpatient visits; for property insurance, each $100 of insured value.

Hence, in determining what to charge members, the loss cost is averaged not on the basis of the number of members but on the basis of the number of exposure units in the pool. The rate obtained by dividing the loss cost projected for the pool by the number of exposure units projected for the same time interval is called the pure rate. A premium obtained by multiplying the pure rate by the number of exposure units is called the pure premium.

Operating the pool is not inexpensive. People must be employed to select and evaluate risk, adjust claims, operate accounting systems, and go about trying to encourage people to join the pool. The pool and its attendant activities require overall management and direction. Taxes and license fees must be paid. And overall the pool must make a profit. All of these costs must be charged back to the members. This is done by dividing these costs and allowances by the number of exposure units in the pool. The result is called the expense rate. Adding the expense rate to the pure rate produces the manual rate charged the pool members. The ratio of the pure rate to the manual rate is called the expected loss ratio and of the expense rate to the manual rate the expense ratio. The manual insurance premium is obtained by multiplying an insured's number of exposure units by the manual rate.

As a result of this discussion, a final definition of insurance may be offered: "Insurance is a mechanism permitting the individual to substitute the certainty of small, defined loss (the insurance premium) for risk of a large fortuitous loss that is predictable neither as to size nor as to time of occurrence."

TYPES OF INSURANCE

Several broad categories of insurance exist, each containing many subsets. They relate in general to the kinds of loss insured against. The classifications used here do not necessarily reflect those used by others in discussing insurance but they appear to be helpful in understanding the different kinds of perils that may underlie a particular policy. The categories used here are:

1. life and health insurance
2. first party insurance
3. third party insurance
4. social insurance.

Life and Health Insurance

These policies either insure against the death of the insured persons, or against the cost of restoring to health ill or accidentally injured insured persons. A subcategory of this type also replaces income lost by an insured person as a result of accident or sickness.

This class includes individual life insurance policies, annuities, individual sickness and health policies, hospital and medical benefit plans, most employee benefit plans, and special failure-to-perform type of coverages that recognize that a unique talent or ability of the insured may be destroyed by accident or sickness, resulting in injury to or loss of income, even though the person is not disabled in an ordinary definition of this term. An example would be a policy guaranteeing a hospital the continuation of its revenue from a specially skilled surgeon in the event that individual is prevented by accident or illness from performing duties as a surgeon even while remaining able to practice medicine.

Workers' Compensation clearly lies in this category of insurance although it often is classified as social insurance (as is done here) since it is mandated by statute.

When coverage is provided for medical benefits on a group basis to the employees or one employer, self-insurance may become an attractive option, especially if the number of persons involved is large. When self-insurance is used, employers often find it desirable to establish maximum cost limits for the obligations they assume. Two types of insurance policies are used to achieve this goal: excess-specific and stop-loss coverage.

Excess-specific policies provide insurance for the portion of each and every claim that exceeds the maximum cost that the employer is willing or able to pay from the self-insurance program for an individual claim. These policies provide coverage up to a stated limit excess of the insured's retained level of loss for each individual claim exceeding the per-claim retained-loss limit. No coverage is provided for claims not large enough to exceed the insured's retained-loss limit per claim. Excess-specific insurance also is used frequently in conjunction with Workers' Compensation self-insurance programs.

Excess-specific insurance may be one way in which reinsurance is provided a health maintenance organization (HMO) with respect to its own exposure to loss arising from the protection it provides its membership. The term reinsurance in this connection really is improperly used: Reinsurance refers specifically to financial arrangements made by an insurance company to limit the loss it assumes under its policies so as to stabilize its operating statements and balance sheets.

The other type of coverage, stop-loss insurance, also is called excess-aggregate insurance. In excess-specific insurance, as noted, the amount of loss less than the insured's elected per-loss retention limit is never covered, even if a portion of a claim is greater than that limit and is covered. As the year goes by, substantial retained loss may accumulate and be paid by the self-insurer. To control the total amount of retained loss the self-insured will pay in any one fiscal year, an aggregate stop-loss retention limit may be established and insurance purchased that pays the amount by which the sum of retained losses in one annual fiscal period exceeds the aggregate stop-loss limit elected by the underwriter and the insured. The name of this kind of policy is based on the fact that it promises the insured that the cost of the retained loss will be stopped at a preagreed point (the aggregate retention limit). As with excess-specific insurance, the excess-aggregate policy has a stated limit of liability, which is the maximum level of protection that will be offered the insured in any one year. Again, as with excess-specific coverage, this kind of policy also is used in conjunction with Workers' Compensation.

A final point about these policies: They are flexible concepts and the principles underlying them permit their use in areas other than those described. In addition, the way coverage is applied may be varied to suit the nature of a particular risk situation. For example, the insured may be required to continue to share in the loss covered by these policies. Such a loss-sharing device is called insured's participation in loss, and should be distinguished from self-insured retention. In a retained loss, the insured stands by itself. An insured who participates in loss shares on a stated basis (usually expressed as a percent) in the loss paid by the underwriter. These participations are used by an underwriter as a means of maintaining an incentive for the insured to work actively to minimize the amount of loss.

First Party Insurance

This type of policy involves situations where insurance attempts to restore the injured party (the named insured) to the condition it occupied before the loss. It usually covers the cost of loss to the named insured's own property or resulting from destruction of that property. Examples are insurance against fire, automobile physical damage, ocean marine or aircraft hull, earthquake, and the various kinds of crime coverage.

Perhaps the most important type of first party insurance covers the destruction or injury of the insured's own real or personal property as a result of fire or other named perils. This insurance also is called direct damage coverage.

Fire and Extended Coverage Insurance

One of the largest exposures to loss faced by any hospital is direct damage to owned buildings and business personal property. Buildings are subject to losses from fire, windstorm, hail, explosion, smoke, water, sprinkler leakage, riot, vandalism or malicious mischief, falling aircraft or other vehicles, earthquake, flood, and other perils. Building contents are exposed to burglary, theft, disappearance, breakage, and other perils. These various causes of loss are called perils.

Coverage to protect against direct damage losses may be purchased in two ways—the named peril basis and the all-risk basis.

Named perils coverage provides that the loss must fall under one of the perils named in the contract for coverage to exist. True all-risk coverage provides that a loss will be covered unless it is caused by a specifically excluded peril or property.

Often, policies sold as all-risk really are simply named peril policies with an expanded list of insured perils. True all-risk coverage usually is found only in comprehensive all-risk policies, a new development in property insurance. The philosophy underlying these new forms is different from that involved in most other policies. The difference shows up most of all in response to claims. Under the standard property coverage, the insured must prove that coverage exists for a loss if the claim is to be paid. Under the comprehensive approach the insurance company must prove that coverage does not exist if the claim is denied.

Time Element or Consequential Loss Insurance

In addition to direct damages losses, the hospital faces the peril of losing income or revenues as a result of a fire or some other peril insured under such a policy. Coverage for this kind of loss is provided by consequential loss or time element insurance.

A major fire, flood, or building collapse could result in either a partial or total shutdown of the hospital's operation. During the shutdown, revenues generated by those operations are lost and there could be additional expenses in attempting to continue as nearly as possible the normal conduct of business. For example, a fire could force partial closing of a portion of the premises, necessitating the evacuation of patients to other facilities. Ambulance costs for the transfer would be additional expense incurred in continuing business operation.

Business interruption insurance covers the loss of revenues from such a disaster. It also is possible to buy rents insurance, which protects a lessor against loss of revenue when a leased building is shut down by an insured direct damage peril.

Extra expense insurance will reimburse necessary extraordinary expenses incurred if the insured is continuing to function when the normal operating pattern has been halted as a result of a direct damage insured peril. "Extraordinary expenses" are expenses above and beyond the insured's ordinary expenses of operation for the time from the interruption of ordinary operations by the insured peril to the time ordinary operations are restored.

Consequential loss insurance reimburses damages to the insured's other property by, or brought about by, a direct damage loss. An example would be the spoilage of food or supplies as a result of the loss of refrigeration as a result of fire even if the refrigerator itself was not burned.

The loss of rents or revenues as a result of the same fire would be the basis of a business interruption claim and the cost of obtaining temporary refrigeration would be the basis of an extra expense claim. Since those losses take place over a period of time this coverage is called time element insurance.

Boiler and Machinery Insurance

Fired vessels and objects often are required to function under high temperature and to withstand different levels of pressure. Many times the ability of the institution to continue to operate depends on continued successful functioning of its steam boilers and the ancillary equipment relying on them.

Hospitals also make heavy demands on air conditioning equipment and may have substantial requirements for refrigeration at very low temperatures.

Many pieces of equipment essential for the operation of a hospital are subject to accidental damage or mechanical breakdown. A peril often overlooked in this class of business is the cost of replacement or repair of electronic medical equipment or tubes. The cost of repairs, or the extra expense of the cost of operating around this broken or damaged equipment, may be substantial.

A valuable adjunct to the purchase of boiler and machinery insurance is the engineering service provided by the insurer. Boiler insurers often offer top-notch loss control services that alone are worth the premium paid for the policy. Such services take the place of and satisfy local government requirements for inspection of operators of boiler and machinery. As with ordinary property insurance, time element and consequential loss coverages are available in conjunction with boiler and machinery insurance.

Dishonesty Insurance

The hospital is subject to financial loss through the dishonesty of employees such as the theft of money, securities, or other property; fraud or dishonesty of one employee, or a number of them working in collusion; and robbery, burglary, or other similar crimes. Coverage should be purchased to provide protection against this type of loss.

A related loss exposure may arise as a result of the kidnapping of a patient or an employee or staff member. Ransom demands may be sizable and create dislocations in the hospital's financial results. Extortion threats—to destroy hospital property or do bodily injury to the families of key personnel unless sizable sums or controlled substances are provided—may be expected from time to time.

Each of these types of acts also may result from activities by terrorists or political extremists. If hospital personnel travel overseas on its behalf, these risks are increased materially. In some parts of the world the danger is so great as to make it foolhardy for United States citizens or their families to go there without some form of insurance. A key benefit offered by this coverage is the service of organizations skilled in hostage negotiation and related activities in dealing with kidnappers for the release of detained persons.

The purchase of kidnap, ransom, and extortion insurance should be reviewed, with the decision to purchase or not purchase this coverage made at the highest administrative levels. It is important to remember that this is a confidential cover, and policies require that knowledge of the purchase be restricted to management persons designated by the chief executive officer as having a need to know.

Electronic Data Processing Equipment and Media

Electronic data processing (EDP) equipment is subject to loss from all of the perils to which other equipment is exposed: fire, lightning, windstorm, building collapse, and so forth. In addition, it is sensitive to perils that have little effect on other kinds of property. Dust, temperature, and humidity are crucial environmental factors that could affect it enough to result in actual loss.

EDP media (discs and tapes) and their recorded data are vulnerable to loss from all sorts of perils, including magnetic storms. They also can be lost, stolen, erased, or tampered with.

In addition to direct loss, the temporary loss of data processing facilities could result in a serious interruption of business, loss of profit, and substantial additional expense. That extra expense could involve equipment rental or use of time-sharing facilities, additional payroll, extra office equipment, temporary help, and rental quarters. This extra expense could well be the most significant exposure.

Difference In Conditions Coverage (DIC Coverage)

The hospital's building and equipment are subject to direct loss by the perils of earthquake, landslide, mud slide, or flood. Geological faults capable of producing earthquakes exist throughout the United States aside from California: serious faults exist in the Southeast, Missouri, Arkansas, New England and southeastern Canada. The potential for flood exists in many areas.

Since these exposures are specifically excluded under the normal property contract, it may be necessary to purchase insurance under a separate coverage known as Difference In Conditions. This covers perils that are not or cannot be covered elsewhere. These policies also represent an effort to provide true all-risk coverage in conjunction with the more limited coverage of other property insurance contracts. In this respect, a difference in conditions contract is similar to an umbrella third party liability contract. A DIC policy is not normally required if the basic contract is one of the new, comprehensive, all-risk forms.

Third Party Insurance

Liability insurance protects the insured from loss arising out of its liability to others for their injury caused by negligence. Unlike the first two classes of insurance just described, the named insured is never a direct recipient of the payment for loss responded to by a third party liability policy; the injured party made whole by the insurance is always some person other than the insured.

Examples include general and automobile liability insurance, directors and officers liability insurance, and all the other insurance that promises to pay on behalf of or to indemnify the named insured for loss arising from a legal liability to other persons.

An important consideration in third party insurance is the nature of the coverage trigger. Two kinds of coverage triggers are in use in third party insurance—occurrence basis and claims made.

Occurrence basis policies provide the most favorable terms from an insured's point of view. The standard definition of an occurrence is "an accident, including injurious exposure to conditions resulting in loss neither expected nor intended by the insured." In these policies, the occurrence out of which the loss arises must happen during the time the policy is in force. Any claim resulting from that occurrence is covered (unless specifically excluded by the policy), regardless of when the claim is discovered. The fact that the claim may not become known or discovered until years after the policy period is over will not void coverage. For example, some claims honored by the courts in recent years have originated in events happening 20 or 30 years prior to their discovery (certain chemicals, asbestos, brown lung, radium watchmakers) and several different insurers may have written the coverage during the time between the expiration of the policy providing coverage and the date the claim is discovered who are not involved in the claim at all.

This characteristic of occurrence basis coverage is the chief benefit it confers on the insured. Once the premium for the policy has been paid, its protection is always there. This same characteristic makes it a nightmare for the underwriter.

Where long tail business—such as product or professional liability—is involved, guessing the ultimate amount of loss that must be paid becomes almost impossible. As a result, the underwriter is unable to price the coverage in such a way as to cover loss expenses and make a profit. The pattern of the underwriting market is to have got it wrong more often than to have got it right in the last 20 years.

One result of this fact is the pressure by insurers to require liability coverages to be written on a claims made basis.

Claims made insurance applies only to claims first made during the term of the policy. If a loss event happens during that term but the resulting claim is not reported until after the policy expires, the policy will not cover it. A pure claims made policy includes no provision for a retroactive date; hence, it covers all claims first made during the policy term, regardless of when the event producing the loss happened.

Even though at first glance the result does not appear too dissimilar from occurrence basis policies, there is one important difference for the underwriter: when the policy expires, no further claims may be brought against it—ever. Hence, the underwriter's cost of providing coverage for that year may be determined much more accurately than under an occurrence form, and the underwriter has a better opportunity to write the coverage profitably than under occurrence basis.

If all claims made policies were written on the basis described—that is, with no retroactive date—the problems arising out of the coverage could be lived with. Unfortunately, most such policies include a retroactive date provision. The retroactive date usually is the inception date of the first of an uninterrupted string of renewals of claims made policies issued by the same underwriter. This provision states that it will cover only claims first made during the policy term, providing the event producing the claim happened on or after the retroactive date. If underwriters are changed, the new underwriter establishes a new retroactive date that coincides with the inception date of the new policy.

When this happens, no coverage exists anywhere for claims arising from events occurring during the time the earlier underwriters provided coverage. This creates a serious coverage gap for those who change carriers. In order to avoid this gap, the insured must buy tail or reporting endorsement coverage from the underwriter whose policy is being replaced.

A reporting endorsement extends the time during which a claim may be reported for a specified period after the termination date of the policy it is attached to. An additional premium charge is required. Despite extending the reporting period, no increase in the available policy limit is offered. When a carrier is changed and a reporting endorsement purchased, careful attention must be paid to the effect on the underlying limit provisions of any excess policies. Extending the reporting period may result in the reduction of the limit available to pay claim. This reduced limit availability may create an uninsured gap between a claim covered by reason of the reporting endorsement and the point at which an excess policy commences to provide coverage.

The cost of tail coverage is determined by the abandoned underwriter on the basis of circumstances applying at the time that insurer's coverage is being terminated. When this happens, the underwriter whose coverage is being terminated has no incentive to be fair or reasonable to the insured and the latter has no bargaining power to use against the underwriter to obtain fair and reasonable costs. The only recourse is for the insured to throw themselves on the mercy of the spurned underwriter and hope for the best.

There are two possible solutions to this problem, neither of which may be achievable. The first is to obtain from each underwriter of a claims made policy, before accepting an offer of insurance, a specific endorsement to the policy establishing a specific formula on which the tail coverage premium and terms will be calculated. The second is to obtain an agreement from the superseding underwriter not to use a retroactive date in the policy or, if a retroactive date is used, that it will be the earliest retroactive date expressed in any prior claims made policy. This latter kind of agreement is referred to as prior acts coverage.

The same sort of circumstance also arises when a firm goes out of business, or when an individual personal insured retires or dies. Specific arrangements must be made to obtain reporting endorsement coverage. These arrangements often can be expensive.

Automobile Insurance

Automobile accidents can result in high costs for repairs to vehicles and medical care for injured persons. The hospital is exposed to this type of loss through the use of owned, hired, leased, or nonowned vehicles. With the high costs of cars today, a multicar or chain reaction type of collision could result in repair costs totalling $100,000 or more. These costs often are a minor part of a claim, with the primary loss being from bodily injury to persons and the resultant medical bills. It should be recognized that most states by statute impose on the owner and the operator of a motor vehicle the obligation of financial responsibility.

Automobile insurance protects against this type of exposure to loss. A business auto policy provides protection against losses arising from the ownership, maintenance, and use of owned automobiles. Coverage should be included for hired and nonowned automobiles. The policy should protect the hospital automatically against loss from newly acquired or long-term leased vehicles, including those used for emergency purposes. Automobile physical damage coverage should be included for any vehicle owned or leased by the insured.

Note that the business auto policy does not insure the owner of a vehicle rented by or leased to the named insured. If employees or volunteer workers are involved in an accident while operating their personally owned automobiles on behalf of the hospital, the hospital's policy will not protect them. No employees or volunteer workers should be permitted to operate a personally owned auto on behalf of the hospital until after they have provided the hospital with a certificate of their personal auto insurance.

Other General Liability Insurance

The hospital is subject to claims from members of the public (other than patients) for injury to their person or their property arising out of negligence in connection with the facility's premises or nonmedical operations. Losses from slips and falls, faulty elevator doors, or falling objects are examples of general liability loss. Often, when contracts with suppliers or service providers are executed, the hospital is asked to assume the liability of others as a part of its obligations under the deal. Claims could be brought against the institution because of this agreement. Claims also may be made against the hospital because of goods sold through its gift shop or other stores. Product liability coverage would protect it against such claims; it is a form of general liability insurance.

The hospital should purchase a comprehensive general liability insurance policy that should include broad-form coverage. This will protect the hospital against many of the kinds of claims resulting from the perils discussed. Broad-form CGL insurance is a special extension of general liability coverage to include coverage for many hazards that are normally not included in the printed policy. Some of these extensions of coverage include host liquor liability; advertiser's liability; contractual liability; personal injury coverages (libel, slander, and defamation of character, wrongful entry, invasion of privacy, wrongful eviction, false arrest, illegal detention, and imprisonment are typical personal injury hazards); and nonowned watercraft coverage.

Directors and Officers Liability Insurance

The board of trustees has the ultimate responsibility for the affairs of the hospital. The board delegates authority to conduct those affairs on a day-to-day basis to the administrative and medical staff officers of the institution. The board is ultimately responsible for the establishment and maintenance of appropriate standards relating to medical professional activities conducted in the hospital. The authority to establish and enforce protocols relating to credentialling, standards of care, professional discipline, and the responsibility to supervise their day-to-day implementation may be delegated to the medical staff and its officers and committees. The board also has ultimate responsibility for appointments (or refusals to appoint) to the medical staff, although the authority to act in these areas may be delegated to the medical or administrative staff, or both.

A common pattern may be seen in each of these items. While authority may be delegated, the board's responsibility to make sure that the authority is used properly and in the best interest of the institution and of the community cannot be delegated. The holders of this authority bear the responsibility to act solely on behalf of the institution so as to further the best interest of the facility and the community.

The common phrase linking the responsibilities and authority of the board, administrative staff, and medical staff while acting on behalf of the institution is the obligation imposed on each individual by law to act solely in the interest of the institution and not contrary to the interest of the institution in relation to the surrounding community area served. Failure to meet these standards of conduct may result in claims against the individual trustees and officers of the institution or its medical staff. These claims may seek redress in damages or equitable relief in the form of an injunction. They may allege violation of the standards because of improper actions on an application for privileges; violations of law or regulations, to the detriment of the institution; improper interference in contractual rights; price fixing or other anticompetitive acts in restraint of trade; or that an individual officer or trustee has acted out of concern for personal rather than corporate interest.

Those who serve in positions of responsibility and authority are expected to act prudently and to recognize that they have special skills and knowledge to bring to the performance of their duties. As such, they are accountable for their acts, mistakes, and failures to act, in accordance with what is expected of a person with similar special skills and knowledge, not just ordinary persons. In short, they are recognized as professionals in the performance of their managerial duties and as such have a managerial professional liability exposure. Insurance coverage for these exposures is provided by directors and officers liability insurance.

Fiduciary Liability Insurance

The need for insurance protection for persons who exercise management or administrative responsibilities for employee benefit plans was emphasized by the Employee Retirement Income Security Act of 1974 (ERISA).[2] Although state law and prior federal law already imposed strict accountability on fiduciaries, ERISA:

1. defined the principal responsibilities of individuals who are fiduciaries of employee benefit plans
2. established a requirement for personal financial responsibility of the fiduciaries for actions as such
3. defined who is a fiduciary in a new and broadened manner
4. established a more widespread body of persons who have standing to bring suit against a fiduciary.

Every employer (except churches and political subdivisions) with more than 25 employees is subject to ERISA. Every employee benefit plan (except Workers'

Compensation plans, unemployment compensation plans, Social Security, and nonoccupational disability plans required by statute) maintained by an employer subject to ERISA is also subject to ERISA.

Every plan subject to ERISA must be controlled by a written plan document that defines the benefits provided, the eligible participants, and vesting rights (if applicable); identifies by name individuals responsible for the management of the plan; and establishes the claims process.

Fiduciaries are defined by ERISA as individuals named as fiduciaries in the plan documents, and any other person, whether or not named in the plan, responsible for administering benefits or claims or collecting or handling monies relating to the plan. Coverage for this management peril is provided by fiduciary liability insurance.

Employee Benefit Legal Insurance

In addition to management responsibilities, individuals charged with duties relating to the administration of employee benefit plans can create situations in which either they personally or their employer may become liable for misadministration of the program. Administration of an employee benefit plan is defined as:

1. counseling employees on their dependents and beneficiaries with respect to employee benefit programs
2. handling records in connection with an employee benefit program
3. effecting or terminating any employee's participation in a plan.

Administrative risks arising from Workers' Compensation, Social Security, unemployment compensation, or statutorily required nonoccupational disability benefit programs exist even though ERISA does not apply to them. State statutory or common law also may create legal responsibilities with respect to such plans.

Insurance against such administrative risk is called employee benefit legal liability insurance and often is included in the comprehensive general liability insurance policy.

Professional Liability (Malpractice) Insurance

Hospitals provide a place where medicine is practiced. In most instances, the circumstances that produce an admission to a hospital indicate a serious illness, the need for a surgical procedure, or a response to a medical emergency. Under such circumstances, the likelihood that something will go wrong in the course of the treatment of a particular individual patient is much higher in hospitals than in other places where medicine is practiced.

Hospitals also maintain large, sophisticated, and necessary medical apparatus, both for testing and treatment purposes. Improper maintenance or improper operation of this equipment may produce patient injury.

The California Medical Insurance Feasibility Study (CMIFS) undertook an extensive analysis of patient medical records as part of a study to determine the feasibility of no-fault malpractice insurance.[3] The study indicates that whenever a patient receives medical treatment, either in a hospital or in a physician's office, there is a 4.7 percent probability that the person will be injured or killed as a result of a mistake, error, or negligent act or omission in the course of the treatment. These events often do not surface as claims. The CMIFS report estimates, based on its rather extensive sample, that only 5 percent of such adverse outcomes that are result of negligence actually become claims.

The public has come to perceive the hospital as having a paramount duty to select, supervise, and retain members of its medical staff in such a way as to minimize the occurrence of these potentially compensable events. In addition, it perceives the hospital as having a duty to establish standards of care and protocols relating to its own employees, as well as to attending staff members, that ensure the maximum level of safe patient care.

When a perception exists on the part of an individual patient, or a member of the family, that there has been a failure by the hospital, its medical staff, its employees, or its administration to perform this perceived duty, and a patient is injured or killed as a result (or apparently as a result) of medical treatment, a malpractice suit or claim probably will ensue. The hospital's assets are protected from exposure to this type of claim by hospital professional liability insurance or self-insurance.

Umbrella Liability Insurance

Catastrophic loss can be defined as one so large that the institution could not survive it without financial support of one kind or another. Umbrella liability insurance is designed to provide that type of support.

For a hospital, the principal danger of a catastrophic loss arises not from its malpractice risk but from its "hotel" exposure. Patients often are bedridden and unable to move themselves. Large numbers of visitors are on the hospital premises and are susceptible to panic if something serious happens.

Two catastrophic losses in recent years have shocked the nation—the fire at the MGM Grand Hotel in Las Vegas (1980) in which 84 persons died from smoke inhalation and flames and the collapse of a catwalk during a tea dance in a Hyatt in Kansas City in 1981, killing 114 and injuring 239. Claims from these two losses totaled in the hundreds of millions of dollars. It is easy to imagine how much more severe these losses could have been had they occurred in a hospital.

The hospital also faces exposure to a catastrophic event in connection with the operation of an automobile owned by the hospital or by employees or volunteers while being used on its behalf.

The potential for a catastrophic loss from a malpractice claim is more remote but could occur in the form of food poisoning or the spread of some type of fatal nosocomial disease. Miscalibration of radiation devices could result in radiation injury to large numbers of patients. Recently, there have been circumstances in which hospital employees have deliberately killed or seriously injured groups of patients, the fatal or injury-producing acts spread over a long period of time. Although larger awards are being made in connection with this type of loss, the possibility of a catastrophic impact on the hospital at present appears to be less than the hotel type situations described.

Social Insurance

Social insurance may be defined as an insurance program established by the government for the benefit of broad classes of beneficiaries, the cost of which is met by mandatory premium charges spread across the widest possible number of payers. Often, as in Social Security, the premium becomes a tax that must be paid by almost everyone.

Social insurance is designed to provide protection against risks perceived by society as an otherwise unrelieved burden on those who can least afford it. In most instances, social insurance programs are perceived as uninsurable by the private insurance industry, so direct governmental action becomes the only means of responding to the perceived needs.

Workers' Compensation Insurance

In the early years of this century, the cost of industrial injury was recognized as part of the price that must be paid in order to achieve the benefits of relatively sophisticated technology and industrialization. Imposing the cost of industrial injury on the employer allowed this cost to be transferred to society as a whole by means of the selling price for goods and services manufactured or provided by the employer.

Every state therefore developed a statute designed to cause the sharing of workplace injury costs on the widest possible basis. These are the Workers' Compensation statutes of the various states. In addition, where appropriate, the federal government has established similar Workers' Compensation laws.

All employers are subject to the Workers' Compensation statutes of the states in which they operate or, under the appropriate circumstances, to federal statutes. Failure to comply with these laws can result in fines and penalties, one of which is statutory removal of the employer's defense to suit by employees alleging injury as a result of their work.

Employers come under the Workers' Compensation statute if they elect to purchase insurance or obtain permission from the state to be self-insurers.

Workers' Compensation insurance is an example of no-fault protection. All that has to be proved for employees to collect such compensation is that they were injured at work or in the course and scope of their duties as employees. "Course and scope" is a phrase that broadens the work injury exposure substantially beyond the boundaries of the workplace. Employees stricken by coronary or cerebral infarcts at home have been held to be engaged in the "course and scope" of their employment if the infarct is in any way attributable to the pressure of job duties.

Unemployment Compensation

Social policy has recognized the disastrous effects on individuals of being laid off or discharged. The cost of ameliorating this effect is perceived to be one that must be spread as widely as possible throughout the economic structure of society. Insurance is seen as the most efficient method of doing so. Because it is regarded as social insurance, private insurers are not allowed to provide such coverage. As a result, every employer (except a not-for-profit corporation) is required to participate in state-administered unemployment compensation insurance programs. Not-for-profit corporations may be granted permission to self-insure.

The other principal social insurance programs are Social Security (old age and survivor's disability insurance), Medicare, Medicaid, and, in some jurisdictions, mandatory nonoccupational disability income benefit insurance that employers must provide as an employee benefit.

INSURANCE CONTRACT ELEMENTS

Legal Background

Insurance policies are legal contracts and hence are subject to the specific principles underlying any contractual agreement. Without getting deeply into a complicated area, five essential elements underlie a valid contract:

1. The offer: Generally, completing the application for coverage and submitting it to the insurer constitute the formal offer of insurance to the insurer and the first step of the contractual process. The insurer usually will reply by proposing prices, terms, and conditions under which it will agree to accept the risk. This is a counteroffer and supersedes the original offer. This process continues until both parties are satisfied, at which time the next formal element occurs.
2. Acceptance: This is the formal acceptance by one party of an offer or counteroffer proposed by the other. It is a formal accepting act that effectu-

ates the contract agreed to, providing there has been a true meeting of the minds.

3. Meeting of the minds: This means that both parties understand the terms of the contract and their rights, privileges, duties, and obligations to one another arising from it. It is important that neither party have any reservations or withold germane information; the contract should both be negotiated and entered into on the basis of the utmost good faith.
4. Binding: The contract is made binding by a valuable consideration. In an insurance contract, the payment of the premium is the consideration.
5. Legal purpose: The last element is that the contract must be for a legal (not illegal) purpose.

There are some unique aspects relating to the insurance contract. The most important of these is the reliance the underwriter places in the truthfulness and honesty of the insured in completing the application. The application is not just a proposal offered to the insurer; it also is an inducement to accept the insured's risk. If the insured withholds a fact or piece of information that if discovered at the time of the examination of the application would have caused the underwriter to reject the risk, and a loss later occurs as a result of the withheld information, the underwriter may have the privilege of voiding coverage. Hence, every care must be taken to be complete and accurate in providing information to the underwriter.

Also important is the fact that an insurance contract is a contract of adhesion. In a contract of adhesion, the basic contents of the agreement are established by one of the parties, and that same party is responsible for the language used to express the agreement. The other party has little or no opportunity to negotiate or amend the agreement and simply must adhere to the terms and conditions proposed by the maker of the contract. In the insurance contract, generally the insured has little influence over the actual language of the contract. The document normally is designed by the insurer and the insured has little opportunity to amend it to suit any particular situation. Under these circumstances, ambiguities in the contract generally are interpreted against the insurer.

Reading the Insurance Contract

All insurance contracts have five basic divisions. An understanding of these and how they relate to one another will simplify the task of reading an insurance policy. The five divisions are:

1. the insuring agreements
2. the exclusions
3. the conditions
4. the definitions
5. the declarations.

Insuring Agreements

This is the most important part of the policy since it is the one containing the insurer's promises to the insured. The language of the insuring clause defines the coverage granted by the policy. It usually is organized in accordance with the coverages specified on the declarations page of the policy. Each coverage is identified by its name, followed by language expressing the insurer's duties and obligations as respects such coverage.

In some, notably third party liability policies, a part of the insuring agreements may be titled supplemental payments. This defines duties and responsibilities of the insurer arising out of its obligations created by the other part of the insuring agreements but not subject to the limits of liability applicable to the insuring agreements. In the past, this portion of the insuring agreements involved the insurer's obligation to provide legal defense to the insured at the insurer's cost. Under the newer contracts, the cost of providing this defense is often made subject to the policy limit.

Exclusions

Exclusions are specific kinds of acts or events that the insurer eliminates from the coverage of the policy. Exclusions usually exist for one or more of the following reasons:

1. Another kind of insurance provides coverage for the excluded exposure, and the insurer does not intend to provide that coverage other than by that other kind of insurance.
2. The exposure excluded is not normal to the operations generally covered by the policy. If coverage is desired, it must be bought back by a special endorsement and premium charge.
3. The exclusion eliminates a hazard or peril the insurer deems uninsurable.

For example, all liability policies exclude damage to property owned by or in the care, custody, or control of the named insured. Such damage is properly covered under a property insurance, not liability, policy. An example of the third type is the pollution or war exclusions found in most liability policies; an example of the second type would be the exclusion relating to liability assumed by contract.

The exclusions and the insuring agreements must be read together in order to define the coverage of the policy.

Conditions

The conditions are a series of clauses defining the rights, privileges, and duties of the insured and the insurer. For example, one condition defines how the policy may be cancelled by either the insured or the insurer. Another establishes the insured's duties in the event of loss. Another sets the insured's obligation with respect to premium.

The conditions establish the mechanical and administrative framework necessary to make the policy work for both the insured and the insurer.

Definitions

Special meanings often are assigned to special words or phrases in the insurance contract. The meanings of these words and phrases are established by the definitions portion of the policy.

Since these key words can include the meaning of words such as "occurrence" and "insured," which are vital to understanding the insurance coverage, the definitions should be studied closely as a part of the process of reading the policy.

Declarations

The declarations section contains fundamental information relating to particular insurance contracts. This includes the name and address of the insured, the effective and expiration date and time of the policy, the coverages purchased and their limits, the amount of the premium charged, the way the premium is to be paid, and any other detailed information required to identify and account for the insurance policy.

Final elements are endorsements or riders. These are documents attached to the policy to amend the coverage in some way. They may be attached either at the inception of the policy or after the policy is issued, when they may represent an afterthought about the basic contract. Endorsements are used to correct an error made in the original contract or an earlier endorsement or can reflect changes in the insured's circumstances since policy was issued. In any event, the language of a validly executed endorsement is held to supersede language in conflict with it in the policy or in earlier dated endorsements.

The declarations, the policy, and the endorsements attached to it constitute a single document. Amendments may be made only by validly executed endorsements—oral amendments are not binding on either the company or the insured unless reduced to writing and issued as an endorsement.

Before leaving the subject of the insurance policy, a word need be said about binders. These are temporary evidence that insurance has been placed in effect and are subject to all the terms and conditions of the policy that replaces them. Oral binders are valid only temporarily until they may be replaced by written ones. They may be issued only by agents of the company involved. To be valid, a written binder must:

1. identify clearly the kind of insurance being bound, including any applicable limits on the liability of the insurer

2. identify explicitly the name and address of the named insured and all locations subject to the coverage
3. specify the name of the insurance company with which the coverage has been placed
4. provide specific inception and termination dates for the binder itself.

Binders may be issued only by contract agents of the company involved.

A cover note or covering note is a particular form of a certificate of coverage issued by a broker who is not an agent of the underwriter. The cover note also may be issued to stand in place of the policy when, for one reason or another, a long time may lapse between the effective date of cover and the actual issuance of the policy. When this happens, a duplicate of all policy and endorsement language is attached to the cover note.

SELECTING BROKERS AND INSURERS

By and large, the most important part of this task is broker selection.

It is important to distinguish between a broker and an agent. An agent legally and contractually is a representative of an insurer, not of the insured. An agent has the legal authority to act on behalf of an insurance company, and the courts normally will force the company to honor the commitments made on its behalf by the agent. In a situation where the interest's of the insurance company and the insured are in conflict, the agent by law must act on behalf of the company, not the insured. On the other hand, a broker legally represents the insured, not an insurance company.

In American practice the distinction becomes fuzzy. Most brokers have one or more companies with which they have the kind of contractual relationships that makes them an agent; most agents under various circumstances will place business on behalf of their clients with companies with which they have no contractual arrangement.

In either case, the buyer's primary point of access to the insurance marketplace is through the broker/agent. For this reason, the greatest care must be exercised in selecting a broker/agent. That individual will represent the hospital to the insurance provider and act as a valuable, continuing consultant in the management of the insurance program. Good broker/agents relate well to the hospital and to its needs, making the risk manager's job and relations with administration much easier.

Some important requirements must be fulfilled by the broker if that person is to serve the hospital effectively:

- First and foremost, the broker must be a skilled professional in the field of insurance, with an adequate, well-trained supporting staff, and must be constantly in the insurance marketplace in order to keep the risk manager advised of developments and changes that may reflect on the hospital's insurance program.

- The broker must have a deep and abiding understanding of the nature of the hospital business and its particularities both from the point of view of operating the hospital business successfully in its own field and from the point of view of understanding and resolving the special insurance problems that arise solely because of the particular nature of the health care business. The broker also must know how the hospital, as an individual risk, is both like and unlike other organizations engaged in the health care business.
- The broker must be able to provide imaginative and innovative concepts that permit the risk manager to anticipate coverage problems and plan effective responses to them.
- The chemistry of the relationship among the risk manager, administration, and the selected broker must be a beneficial and satisfactory one for everyone.

Today, the least effective way to select a broker for a long-term relationship is through bidding the insurance program. While bidding may have a place in the overall insurance buying picture, using it as a means of broker selection is counterproductive.

The best way to select a broker is for the risk manager to:

- Identify a small number of individual brokers or firms that appear to have the desired level of professional skills. This process is best achieved by word of mouth informal discussions with professional peers.
- Ask each of the selected firms to prepare a presentation relating to the hospital's insurance program. Do not seek pricing; seek concepts and approaches, recognition of problems, and ideas. Imagination and innovation should be important parts of this kind of presentation.
- Interview the finalist firms carefully as a part of the presentation process. Try to develop a realistic sense of their interests, strengths, and concerns and how these relate to the hospital's needs. Usually, it is better if this process is carried out by a panel including more than the risk manager; it may involve the chief financial officer or some other senior administrative person. Often, a double interview process is used in which all but two contenders are eliminated in one set of interviews and a final selection made through a second interview.
- Check all references given by the firm carefully. In particular, an adverse reference should be requested and checked, as well as favorable references.
- Examine the results of this process carefully, then select one broker/agent to work with the hospital.

Once the broker/agent has been selected, there should be a mutual understanding that as long as that broker performs ably on the hospital's behalf, that individual will be retained as the facility's representative.

After the selection, the risk manager and the broker should work together to establish the minimum qualification level applicable to the insurers. Generally, it is suggested that no insurer should be used with an A.M. Best rating of less than B+:XI, but exceptions may be in order from time to time. A.M. Best and Co. is a firm whose principal business is reviewing and reporting upon the financial strength and management skills of insurance companies. A shorthand notation has been developed by this organization for use in this area. The meanings of this notation are given in Exhibit 7–1.

The broker must understand that it is necessary to clear with the risk manager any company falling outside the normal guidelines before it is used. In the event

Exhibit 7–1 Best's Policyholders' Ratings

A+	Excellent	B	Good
A	Excellent	C+	Fairly Good
B+	Very Good	C	Fair

Financial Size Category

Companies recipient of ratings reflecting a group business pooling arrangement, starting in 1982, are assigned financial size categories based upon the consolidated pool results.

(Categories of foreign companies are based upon their home office balance sheets)

Class I	$250,000	or less	
Class II	250,000	to	$500,000
Class III	500,000	to	750,000
Class IV	750,000	to	1,000,000
Class V	1,000,000	to	1,500,000
Class VI	1,500,000	to	2,500,000
Class VII	2,500,000	to	3,750,000
Class VIII	3,750,000	to	5,000,000
Class IX	5,000,000	to	7,500,000
Class X	7,500,000	to	12,500,000
Class XI	12,500,000	to	25,000,000
Class XII	25,000,000	to	50,000,000
Class XIII	50,000,000	to	75,000,000
Class XIV	75,000,000	to	100,000,000
Class XV	100,000,000	or more	

Source: Reprinted from *Best's Key Rating Guide* with permission of A.M. Best Company, © 1984.

that there are certain companies that the risk manager feels must be used or must not be used as a part of the program, the broker should be informed of this position.

INSURANCE PURCHASING

As a part of the overall risk management plan, the manager has identified where insurance is to be purchased and where the hospital plans to self-retain risk, either through the use of deductibles or self-insurance. The next step is a careful review with the broker of the areas to be insured. Based on this review, the broker will prepare specifications to be used by the insurance market in responding to the hospital's specific needs. A good broker will be able to provide a wide representation of the available markets and to utilize them in their most efficient way on the facility's behalf.

The question of bidding insurance needs to be addressed specifically. Whether or not bidding is advantageous depends largely on whether or not the line of insurance involved is relatively easy to place. If it is easy to place, that means that insurers perceive it to be profitable and therefore one to be sought after. A line is difficult when there are few insurers offering the coverage and none of them perceive it to be desirable. In the first case, bidding may produce beneficial results, providing it is not done too frequently. In the second case, bidding is likely to result in all the insurers' refusing to offer quotations. Part of the reason for relying on the broker is to allow that expert to control both when and how to exercise the market on the hospital's behalf, whether by requiring responses to bid specifications or by negotiation.

INSURANCE BIDDING

If after careful consideration of the advantages and disadvantages of bidding the decision is made to make a general offering by means of a bid, several actions need to be taken.

The process of broker qualification should proceed as described earlier. The only difference is that the process should be used to qualify not more than three brokers, one of whom normally should be the current broker. If one of the goals of the exercise is to eliminate the present broker, this is the time to do so. Generally, the hospital's best interest will be served by keeping the holding broker as a part of the selected bidding group.

While the broker qualification process is proceeding, the coverage specifications should be prepared by the risk manager. All of the supporting underwriting data, including at minimum five years of loss and exposure data experience for each line, should be accumulated. The specifications and the data provided to each competing broker should be exactly the same.

After the brokers have been qualified and given the specifications and underwriting data, each should be asked to list in order of preference at least five markets for each line of insurance. The market requests should be returned by a specified date and time; the date and time they actually are received should be recorded on each.

Markets are assigned to brokers in the following manner:

- The holding broker automatically is assigned the market the coverage is presently placed with unless there are unusual contrary circumstances. Such circumstances could result from a cancellation request by a particular underwriter.
- The market requests are sorted on a time-and-date basis, from the earliest to the last received. Markets are assigned in rotation in this order. Once assigned, a market is striken from all the market requests.
- Each broker is assigned that individual's first-choice market for each line of insurance unless that market already has been assigned to another broker. If the first-choice market is assigned, the broker is assigned his or her next highest unstricken market choice. This process is continued until all the requested markets by line of insurance are assigned.
- Broker of Record Letters are issued to each broker for each market assigned by line of insurance.

With this process, no one market ends up being approached by more than one broker; the widest possible spread of bidders also is received.

After this process has been completed and the brokers have submitted the underwriting data and specifications to the market, the underwriters probably will have questions. These questions should be submitted to the risk manager by a fixed date. Answers to all the questions should be distributed to all the brokers, whether or not the questions were raised by any one broker.

From the initial submission of underwriting and specification data to the brokers, to the market request date, not fewer than 30 days should be allowed. It will take the brokers this long to line up and obtain expressions of preliminary interest from the markets they wish to use. Preparing conceptual proposals and determining that they are concepts that can be implemented, as well as the interview processes, will require this amount of time. From the market assignment date to bid closing date should be not fewer than 60 days. Underwriters will require inspections by their loss prevention and inspections departments; they may have to arrange special reinsurance. Also, the ordinary workload and pace of the insurance industry indicate that 60 days is the minimum time in which they can respond to a request for quotation. The bid closing date should not be closer than 30 days to the inception date of coverage. Review and analysis of the bids received and the process of finally selecting the broker and market take time. The brokers and selected underwriters, in turn, will require at least that much time to be able to find coverage. Broker qualification should take another 60 days. The decision to undertake bidding of the insurance program thus needs to be made at least 180 days—six months—in advance of the coverage anniversary date.

As may be seen from this description, bidding is a time-consuming and laborious process, both for the risk manager and for the insurance industry. It also is expensive for both sides. Too frequent use of the technique will result in the insurance marketplace's losing interest in responding to the bids. Bidding done every renewal loses its effectiveness. If bidding must be done—and the authors still maintain it to be the least efficient way of purchasing insurance—it should be done not less often than every six years and preferably every nine years.

NOTES

1. Adam Smith, *An Inquiry into the Nature and Causes of the Wealth of Nations,* Book V, Modern Library Edition (New York: Random House, 1937), 715.
2. *Employment Retirement Income Security Act of 1978,* 29 U.S.C. 1001, 88 Stat. 829.
3. Don Harper Mills, *A Medical Insurance Feasibility Study* (Sacramento: The California Medical Association and California Hospital Association), 1977.

Chapter 8

Alternative Methods of Risk Financing

Ronald T. Nelson and William H. Gill

From the material reviewed in Chapter 7, it is clear that insurance is a method of financing the payment of loss. It then follows that insurance offers a broad range of efficiencies as a risk-financing method.

ANALYSIS OF EFFICIENCIES

It should be remembered that insurance is intended to convert an unintended random large loss into a fixed stable cost. Insurance never was intended to provide protection in the area of anticipated loss. Hence, the more insurance, as a mechanism that is asked to respond to anticipated loss, the less efficient it becomes as a means of financing that loss. On the other hand, the more insurance is perceived as a method of financing unexpected large losses, the more efficient it becomes as a financial tool. In the case of the largest losses of all—catastrophic events that by themselves could cause the failure of the enterprise—literally no other means of loss financing is effective at all.

These principles can be illustrated with some practical examples.

The Lowest Level

In Workers' Compensation insurance, a substantial portion of the losses that occur are small medical-only events. In any given Workers' Compensation risk where a sufficient number of employees are involved, it will be possible to identify a loss-size point where the annual sum of all losses equal to or less than the loss size examined (including the portion of loss less than the examined point, in those losses larger than the examined size point) varies little from year to year. This level becomes the anticipated loss for this employer.

As noted in Chapter 7, expected loss is a term having a precise definition for premium establishment purposes. In this chapter, the new term anticipated loss is used to mean the aggregate annual level of loss for an individual risk involving minimal variation from year to year.

The cost of insuring this level of anticipated loss (including the cost of loss adjustment) will always be at least 146 percent of the cost of paying these losses directly. But since prediction of anticipated loss is likely to err on the side of conservatism (i.e., too much loss is projected rather than not enough) this ratio of insurance cost to loss and loss adjustment expense cost is more likely in any year to be greater than 146 percent rather than less. It also should be recognized that Workers' Compensation is the most efficiently managed line of ordinary property and casualty insurance. If the same example were to be drawn from automobile insurance, the equivalent ratio of premium to loss and loss adjustment expense at the point of anticipated loss would be at least 158 percent, and for general liability insurance at least 185 percent. If these examples were revised to reflect the usual difference from estimated anticipated loss, the cost of insurance would be 195 percent to 250 percent of actual incurred loss, where the size of each actual loss is limited to the level underlying the projection anticipated.

The Catastrophic Level

At the other extreme are cases of catastrophic loss similar to the 1981 collapse of the balcony during a tea dance in a Kansas City hotel. The ultimate claims cost arising from that accident exceeded $250 million. Even at the historical interest assumption of 8.5 percent, funding for that amount of loss as if it were a sinking fund goal would have required a payment of $3,177,921 in each of 25 years. In the real world, the liability would have had to have been funded over no more than 10 years, which at the same 8.5 percent interest assumption would require annual payments of $16,851,926. The actual premiums for insurance coverage protecting the hotel against such a loss were less than $1 million a year. In addition, with the purchase of insurance coverage for this amount, full payment of the loss would be available as soon as it could be proved; if the hotel attempted to fund the loss out of its operations, full payment would be available only at the end of the funding period. During the time the loss remained unpaid, it would have to be carried as a liability by the hotel—a liability that would be offset only partially by any asset. The efficiency of insurance as a method of financing this extreme is clear.

Unfortunately, the real world does not often permit distinctions to be drawn as clearly as the example. Establishing anticipated loss is a statistical and actuarial exercise and by its very nature is inexact and imprecise. The real future never is predictable and since risk managers are dealing with random events, none of which they intend to occur, it is difficult to identify the real level of loss they can anticipate and, therefore, handle most efficiently by budgeting.

The Middle Level

In addition, in examining again the two extreme positions described, it is possible to identify still a third or middle area, where the anticipated loss is less likely to occur and where each loss event is likely to be larger than those of the anticipated loss area. It is characteristic of this middle zone that its individual losses probably are not going to be so large as to cause the failure of the enterprise but still large enough to cause serious pain. Losses in this zone happen much less frequently than those in the expected loss layer and are much less predictable as to when they will occur. In this middle zone, a reasonable financing method may be established with the expectation that, even if the worst were to occur, the organization could survive.

It now is possible to define these three levels of loss and draw some conclusions about them.

The smallest zone of anticipated loss can be called the level of deductibles in the insurance program. Losses in this zone are characterized by high frequency (many individual cases) and low severity (each individual loss is small). Deviation (a term discussed later in this chapter) in the total annual values of loss is small. Losses or portions of larger losses falling in this zone should be insured only rarely.

The middle zone can be called the optional zone of risk retention. In this zone, the decision to insure or not insure is made on the basis of an actuarial evaluation of the cost of self-handling loss, compared with the cost (and other benefits) of purchasing insurance. As noted later, this zone occupies the difference between the upper limit of the deductible zone and the lower portion of the catastrophic loss area. In nearly every case, a decision not to insure in this zone involves a careful cost-benefit analysis, with a clear demonstration of deriving greater benefits from not insuring than insuring before the insuring-noninsurance decision is made.

Last is the zone of catastrophic events. While the lowest end of this zone may be included in a self-insurance program, the upper area should always be insured. The amount here that can be self-insured safely is a function of the deviation associated with the level of anticipated loss and of the financial ability of the organization to absorb loss without aid from insurance.

APPLICATION OF THE ANALYSIS

These concepts are so fundamental to any analysis leading to the best use of insurance and self-insurance that it is worthwhile describing how risk managers can use them as tools in the decision-making process. In doing so, it is necessary first to introduce some basic techniques both of loss and of statistical analysis.

The first step in this analysis is to prepare separate size-of-loss distribution tables for each of the five most recent annual periods. Table 8–2 is an example of such a table. This table is based on the amount of loss incurred. Incurred loss includes both paid and open case reserve claim values. This table does not include the value of loss-adjustment expenses. To be effective for this analysis, each policy period must be analyzed separately and the separate analyses then compared with one another.

A size-of-loss distribution table is easy to prepare. Fundamentally, it is a means of grouping losses together by size brackets, called size cells. The first step is to establish the cell boundaries. The establishment of cell boundaries is a judgment call. Little is gained in making the cell too small with boundaries too close together. On the other hand, if the cells are too large and their boundaries separated too widely, the desired stability patterns may be distorted and hidden. The proper selection in any particular case can be arrived at only by a process of trial and error. There are some principles that may be used in making the first try:

- A key point is the number of claims that are closed without payment. Technically, these claims fall into the cell whose upper and lower boundaries both equal zero.
- There is little point in subdividing a cell whose lower boundary is zero and whose upper boundary is $1,000, except in unusual cases.
- One approach is to decide that for any cell whose lower boundary is equal to or greater than $1,000, the upper boundary should be not less than twice the lower boundary. This does not mean that every such cell should have an upper boundary twice the lower boundary; rather, that should be the minimum interval used. Whether or not wider intervals are used depends on the specific nature of the loss experience being analyzed.
- In another technique, the cell sizes are uniform to the greatest extent possible. For such a table, the technique just described may be used until an upper cell limit of, say, $25,000 is reached. After that level, the upper limit of each cell should be $25,000 greater than its lower limit, until an upper limit of $100,000 is reached. Thereafter, each cell should encompass a range of $250,000, until an upper limit of $1 million is reached. Once this level has been attained, each cell should have a range of $1 million until $5 million is reached.
- The last cell needed for analysis may be titled ''Over *N*,'' where *N* is the first upper cell limit equal to or larger than $5 million. The two examples of cell boundaries shown in Table 8–1 illustrate these principles.

It should be remembered that we are not dealing with precise results that can be accurately quantified or predicted. The best we can hope to achieve is a

Table 8–1 Two Examples of Cell Boundaries

Cell number	*Example 1 Lower boundary*	*Example 1 Upper boundary*	*Example 2 Lower boundary*	*Example 2 Upper boundary*
1	0	0	0	0
2	0	$1,000	0	$1,000
3	$1,000.01	5,000	$1,000.01	5,000
4	5,000.01	12,000	5,000.01	10,000
5	12,500.01	25,000	10,000.01	25,000
6	25,000.01	50,000	25,000.01	50,000
7	50,000.01	75,000	50,000.01	100,000
8	75,000.01	100,000	100,000.01	250,000
9	100,000.01	250,000	250,000.01	500,000
10	250,000.01	500,000	500,000.01	1,000,000
11	500,000.01	750,000	1,000,000.01	2,500,000
12	750,000.01	1,000,000	2,500,000.01	5,000,000
13	1,000,000.01	2,000,000	5,000,000.00 and up	
14	2,000,000.01	3,000,000		
15	3,000,000.01	4,000,000		
16	4,000,000.01	5,000,000		
17	5,000,000.01 and up			

glimpse of what some of the many possible futures of our hospital may look like that has some basis in the past. Cell boundaries vary depending on how fine a tune you wish to give the process—bearing always in mind that the fewer claims you have to work with, the less you are likely to predict the future from your work.

Example 1 cuts the division finer and extends the defined larger loss division further upward than example 2 does. Example 1 also has the advantage of following normal layer sizes for insurance or reinsurance programs structured on a layered basis. Example 2 seems less practical in terms of useful information. However, these examples are not intended to be all-encompassing; risk managers should feel free to develop their own tables, based on their own loss experience.

Once the cells have been established, what are they used for? The analysis can answer several important pieces of information, such as the following:

1. What is the number of claims where the size of each individual claim falls within a particular cell?
2. What is the sum of the amount of loss incurred in each cell for all claims where the size of each individual claim falls within that cell?

3. What is the sum of loss incurred within the cell as a result of all claims' having loss within the cell, even if the individual claim size is larger than the upper limit of the particular cell?
4. What percentage of the total loss incurred is incurred:
    a. within any particular cell?
    b. cumulatively, as regards a particular cell and those cells smaller than it?

A typical loss size distribution table is shown in Table 8–2. The table displays the required data vertically within columns. Each cell will occupy one row of data, across all the columns.

Once the size distribution tables are prepared, how are they used? Earlier, it was recommended that risk managers prepare separate tables for each of the five most recent policy years. The next step is to prepare a table displaying the information in Column 6 of the annual size distribution tables for each year side by side for all the cells. A new form can be developed that will have column headings like Table 8–3. Again, in Table 8–3 each cell occupies a row to itself.

The calculations of Column 8 and 9 are done on a row-by-row basis, with each row calculated separately. Column 8 in Table 8–3 is derived by adding the entries for each cell in Columns 3 through 7 and dividing the sum by the number of entries.

Column 9 is a little more complicated and requires the use of a calculator with a square root function. For any one row, the steps involved are:

Table 8–2 Column Headings for Loss-Size Distribution Table

Policy Year xxxx

Lower cell boundary	*Upper cell boundary*	*Number of claims with size of each claim lying in the range cell*	*Total value of claims with size of each claim lying in the range cell*	*Number of claims with loss in cell regardless of ultimate size of claim*	*Total value of all loss incurred in cell regardless of ultimate size of claim*	*% total loss in cell*	*Cumulative % of total loss*
(1)	*(2)*	*(3)*	*(4)*	*(5)*	*(6)*	*(7)*	*(8)*
0	0	22	0	52	$ 0	0 %	0 %
0	1,000	10	8,220	30	38,220	14.9	14.9
1,001	5,000	4	12,892	20	76,892	29.9	44.8
5,001	10,000	8	49,904	12	89,904	35.0	79.8
2,500,001	5,000,000	0	0	0	$0	0	100.00
	over 5,000,000	0	0	0	$0	0 %	100.00%

Table 8–3 Column Headings for Analysis Form

Lower cell boundary	*Upper cell boundary*	*(Year) Total loss incurred*	*(Year) Total loss incurred*	*(Year) Total loss incurred*	*(Year) Total loss incurred*	*(Year) Total loss incurred*	*Average total loss incurred*	*Standard deviation*
(1)	*(2)*	*(3)*	*(4)*	*(5)*	*(6)*	*(7)*	*(8)*	*(9)*
0	1,000	38,220	27,432	11,568	5,742	17,689	20,130	11,704
1,001	5,000	76,892	56,233	112,582	68,633	62,498	75,368	22,160
5,001	10,000	89,904	126,342	115,986	98,345	121,332	110,382	15,575
2,500,001	5,000,000	0	0	0	0	0	0	0
over	5,000,000	0	0	0	0	0	0	0

1. Subtract Column 8 from Column 3; multiply the difference times itself (square the difference).
2. Do the same operation again for each column in which an entry appears, for Columns 4 through 7.
3. Add all the results calculated by steps 1 and 2. This will result in a sum of the square of all the differences. Divide the sum of the squares for a given row by the number of entries on the same row in Columns 3 through 7.
4. Take the square root of the answer obtained by the division performed in Step 3. This value should be entered in Column 9.

While Column 9 is here called "deviation," those with some statistical background will recognize that the full name of this value is the "standard deviation." The standard deviation measures the consistency of data with respect to themselves. The smaller the standard deviation, the more likely future results-producing data classified in the same manner as those in the sample are classified are to be similar to the known data in the sample. It thus is also a measure of the stability of the data being examined.

When all the deviations have been entered in Column 9, it will be noticed that they probably will display one of two patterns:

1. The standard deviation will become larger as the upper cell boundary becomes larger and as the cell average becomes larger.
2. The deviations will grow smaller as the upper cell limit becomes larger and then, after reaching minimum, will commence to become larger, the higher the upper cell limit is.

Each of these suggests a possible answer to the question of determining the anticipated loss.

If the first pattern emerges, managers should look for the cell in which the cell standard deviation is closest to but less than 25 percent of the average cell value. Multiply the standard deviation by 2 and add the result to the average cell value. The total normally is a good estimate of the upper limit of the hospital's annual aggregate anticipated loss. If the cell deviation never reaches 25 percent of an average cell value, the test should be tried again at half of 25 percent and, if necessary, again at one-quarter of 25 percent. In the example given in Table 8–3, this analysis would suggest that the hospital's annual anticipated loss would be 15,572 × 2 + 110,382, or 141,526.

If the second pattern emerges, the average cell value of the cell with minimum standard deviation should have twice the standard deviation for the cell added to it. The resulting value will be an estimated upper limit of annual aggregate anticipated loss.

The anticipated losses resulting from these estimates are annual, not per-loss, values. Hence, as a rule of thumb, the value of anticipated loss obtained by this means should always fall in a cell whose upper limit is less than or equal to $5 million. To obtain an estimate of the best level of a per-claim limit, the average cell value of the cell in which the aggregate anticipated loss falls should be divided by 3 since industry practice is to limit a per-claim level of loss to not more than one-third the annual level of loss limitation. The resulting value should be entered in the cell within which it fits; the lower boundary of that cell, rounded to the nearest $100,000, should become the per-loss anticipated limit. These calculations indicate the lowest level of loss that should, whenever possible, be maintained by the hospital as deductibles or retentions. Insurance should not be purchased for the loss limits indicated by this calculation.

Further tests must be applied to the anticipated aggregate and per-loss limits to determine that the values indicated by this analysis are financially feasible for the institution. Still further examination must be made to determine the most fruitful levels for entering the excess insurance marketplace. Various alternative levels of self-retention will produce different funding costs to the hospital and these, combined with the costs of purchased insurance and externally supplied services, must be analyzed to determine the most favorable cost-benefit outcome for the institution.

ALTERNATIVES TO PURCHASED INSURANCE

If as a result of the cost-benefit analysis, the decision is made to not insure, either in whole or in part, several alternatives open to risk managers. These alternatives, and some of their advantages and disadvantages, follow.

Noninsurance

This also is called "going bare" or nonfunded self-insurance. This occurs when insurance is not purchased and no advance provision is made for a loss-producing event. No formal or uniform financial technique is used to anticipate and prepare for the cost of the loss-producing event. Institutions can go bare inadvertently or for lack of an ability to find an alternative. Going bare may be acceptable at a deductible level and somewhat justifiable at lower levels of anticipated loss as calculated by the previously described methodology; at the higher (including catastrophic) levels, going bare also may be compared to a game of Russian roulette.

Self-Insurance

This may be defined as consciously and deliberately retaining the risk of loss within the financial structure of the organization and simultaneously developing, adopting, and following a formal financial plan to accumulate funds with which to pay for a loss-producing event when it occurs. Many times this will involve the use of a trust fund. When that is the case, it may be referred to as trusteed self-insurance. Self-insurance nearly always involves limiting the institution's ultimate exposure to loss by the purchase of appropriate insurance or reinsurance in conjunction with the self-insurance program.

Single-Owner Captive

This involves formation of the organization's own insurance company to insure its own risks. This approach has several attractive features as well as some possible disadvantages (discussed later).

Multiowner Captive

In conjunction with one or more organizations of like size and exposures, the hospital participates in forming a jointly owned captive insurer to cover the exposures of the member institutions.

Risk-Pooling Mechanism

A risk-pooling mechanism is a noninsurance device used by several different organizations with similar risk characteristics to fund in common their loss exposures. All losses involving each of the members are paid by the pool and the cost of these losses then is divided among the members. A pooling mechanism is similar to a group captive, with many of the same advantages and disadvantages.

From these definitions, it may be seen that from a fiscal standpoint, the difference among insurance, noninsurance, and self-insurance lies primarily in the method of financing the payment of loss cost. When loss arises in noninsurance, the cost is paid as it occurs; in self-insurance, an effort is made to anticipate the amount of future loss that must be paid and, by setting aside appropriate funds and recognizing the time value of money, to minimize and stabilize the effect of that loss on the financial administration of the institution. From this point of view, captives (or limited-purpose insurance companies) are just another form of self-insurance; the same statement may be made about risk pooling programs and multiowner captives.

It is appropriate at this point to point out an easy trap to fall into when discussing any form of self-insurance, whether it be trusteed self-insurance (that is, self-insurance using a trust fund as the device in which funds to pay loss are accumulated) or a captive: the phrase "limits of liability", applied to self-insurance, may give a flavor of comfort and protection that does not really exist. Two examples indicate why:

1. The institution becomes a self-insurer with an elected trust fund limit of $1 million for each claim, $3 million in the annual aggregate. An initial contribution of $250,000 is made to the trust fund. No excess insurance is purchased. Shortly after the inception of the self-insurance program, a $2 million claim is filed and judgment is returned against the hospital for that amount. While the trust fund pays its $250,000, the assets of the hospital are directly at risk for $1,750,000.
2. The same circumstances apply except that the hospital purchases umbrella excess insurance with limits of $5 million/$5 million attaching over the trust fund. The schedule of insurance in the umbrella shows underlying self-insured limits of $1 million/$3 million. The same claim is filed, with the same judgment. The trust fund pays $250,000 and the excess insurance $1 million, with the assets of the hospital paying $750,000.

Limits of liability established for any self-insurance program, by themselves, constitute only a statement of intent that permits a reasonable calculation of the cost of funding the program. In terms of actually controlling or containing the hospital's exposure to loss, such limits become effective only to the extent that they are confirmed by becoming the point at which purchased insurance or reinsurance commences to apply or attach. As long as this principle is understood, and as long as it is further understood that, absent any protection from purchased insurance, the ultimate responsibility of a self-insuring institution to its claimants lies against its total assets, it is permissible to use the phrase limits of liability in conjunction with a self-insurance program. Otherwise, it is more correct technically to use the phrase, "limits established for funding purposes."

ADVANTAGES AND DISADVANTAGES

Each of the alternatives to purchased commercial insurance has advantages and disadvantages.

Purchased Insurance

The advantages of purchased insurance include these:

- It provides protection against catastrophic loss that would result in the financial destruction of the insured organization (this, of course, is the primary reason for insurance).
- Insurance premiums permit advance costing, thus permitting accurate budgeting.
- Insurance companies provide ancillary services such as adjusting claims of third parties, loss prevention engineering, and development of statistical reports.
- Insurance premiums are paid with pretax dollars and are recognized as a legitimate business expense deduction.

On the other hand, there are disadvantages to purchased commercial insurance, including these:

- The device of insurance involves a complicated mechanism that requires an expense burden for the cost of operating the insurance carrier.
- Insurance involves advance funding of losses, depriving the insured of the use of funds that are then held by the insurer in the form of premium reserves and loss reserves.
- Insurance involves time and expense in negotiating with carriers as to premiums, policy provisions, and loss adjustments.
- Loss prevention requirements of the insurer, while frequently to the benefit of both the insurer and insured, sometimes involve a set of priorities different from those that the insured would see as in its own interest. The amount and nature of such service provided by an insurer may be neither adequate nor appropriate to the needs of the insured.
- The insured may be in a noncompetitive insurance market and forced to pay an unrealistic premium.

Going Bare

Other methods of financing loss also have advantages and disadvantages. The first of these methods is going bare. The advantages of this approach include these:

- No payment is required until a loss-producing event has actually happened and the cost finally determined.
- Loss cost that is nominal or relatively definable may make going bare the least expensive way of handling a payout. This is the theory and practice (from an insured's point of view) behind most uses of deductibles.
- No administrative burden is placed on the organization until a loss-producing event occurs, so administrative expenses are minimized.
- Costs actually paid may be deductible as business expenses in the year in which they are paid.

There are, of course, disadvantages of noninsurance, too:

- widely fluctuating and unanticipated loss costs
- difficulty in budgeting, arising from the lack of consistency in loss or loss adjustment costs from year to year
- the danger of financial embarrassment (including ruin) resulting from a serious loss for which no provision has been made
- the lack of tax deductibility for monies set aside to be used later to pay losses (reserves), with these funds treated as taxable income. (This disadvantage occurs in all other self-insurance mechanisms if the sponsoring organization is subject to federal income taxation.

Funded Self-Insurance

As with all the alternatives, funded self-insurance has both advantages and disadvantages. Its principal advantages include these:

- The amount required to operate a self-insurance plan is less than would be required to operate an insurance company. The expense of the insurance mechanism, including the profit element and underwriting and acquisition costs, are eliminated in favor of simply the costs necessary for claims administration, loss prevention, and administration of the self-insurance fund.
- The investment return on monies held in the self-insurance program before loss payment accrues to the benefit of the self-insurer.

- Claims administration and loss prevention can be tailored to the needs of the self-insurer. It is important, however, that the quality of these services not be diminished in the transition to a self-insured program.

The principal disadvantages of a funded self-insurance program include these:

- There is no spread of risk so the self-insurer has not really transferred any risk of loss away from its own operations.
- It may not always be possible to obtain excess insurance coverage above the self-insured layer. Thus, the organization may be subject to potential catastrophic loss.
- Contributions required to fund the self-insurance program are not tax deductible.

Single-Owner Captive Company

A single-owner captive company achieves essentially the same results as a funded self-insurance program and has the same advantages, plus these additional ones:

- A captive has the ability to enter the true reinsurance market, which often is more stable and committed to long-term relationships than is the retail insurance market.
- It may be feasible for single-owner captives to join together in reinsurance pools to develop risk-sharing/transfer devices that function at excess loss levels. This advantage may be particularly desirable when commercial reinsurance is difficult or impossible to obtain.

The disadvantages of a single-owner captive are these:

- There still is no spread of risk, although losses may be limited by reinsurance, as noted.
- Premiums paid to a single owner captive by its for-profit owner are not tax deductible. They must be treated as capital contributions to a subsidiary.
- The capitalization of the captive is not tax deductible. This may involve a significant expense, depending on the location of domicile and extent of regulation.
- Losses paid on behalf of a for-profit owner by the captive are not treated as losses. While the actual amount of loss paid is a deductible expense, the reimbursement for that loss from the captive must be treated as a capital gain.

Multiowner Captive

The next alternative is the multiowner captive. Its advantages include these:

- It is operated, as is a self-insurance fund or a single owner captive, at much lower overhead than a conventional insurer.
- The investment return earned from premium and loss reserves accrues to the benefit of the captive.
- Tailored claims administration and loss prevention services can be arranged.
- Access to excess insurance and reinsurance markets can be provided through the captive.
- A spread of risk can be obtained.
- Capitalization costs and operating expenses can be split several ways instead of being loaded onto a single organization.
- A geniune transfer of risk from an individual owner to a pool (the captive) and a sharing in the risks of that pool by many separate owners may make the premiums paid tax deductible as business expenses—i.e., they may be recognized as true insurance premiums.
- Losses are treated as those paid by any other insurer and are recognized as such in the captive's own accounting formulas by the tax authorities.

The disadvantages of a multiowner captive are these:

- The spread of risk carries with it the possibility of paying a portion of someone else's losses. This also can be limited by the method used to transfer risk to the pool. Some pools, for example, transfer to the pool more large losses than small losses. This disadvantage also can be limited and controlled by the purchase of reinsurance for the captive.
- There always are problems inherent in getting several different organizations to agree on the establishment and management of any joint venture.
- Formation of such a captive puts its owners in the insurance business. Whether or not they wish to be in this business is something they may want to think deeply about.

A risk-pooling mechanism enjoys the same advantages and disadvantages as a multiple-owner captive, with the additional advantage of not being required to raise substantial sums of money before it may start operations.

FRONTING

A technique that should be examined under certain circumstances is the use of a "fronting" carrier in conjunction with a self-insurance fund, captive, or risk-pooling program. When a fronting carrier is utilized, to all external appearances the organization has continued to purchase commercial insurance while in fact it is permitted to enjoy all of the benefits of its selected alternative method of financing loss. How the fronting technique works, and its advantages and disadvantages, are discussed next.

In fronting, an ordinary commercial insurer issues a policy to the organization just as if the company were going to insure it normally. All the usual endorsements and policy provisions apply, as in any other situation where the company issues a policy.

A premium is charged on the policy, is entered in the insurance company's books, and normal certificates of insurance are issued to satisfy certificate holder requirements, as with any other insurance policy. State premium taxes are paid. As far as any organization external to the organization, its insurer, and its broker are concerned, the organization has purchased an insurance policy. This document is the "front" or fronting policy, and the company issuing the policy is the fronting or issuing carrier. The policy also is referred to as the "paper"—as in "Whose paper is it on?" meaning "What issuing company is being used to issue and service the policy."

This technique is called fronting because the issuing carrier has entered into a reinsurance agreement with the self-insurance program or captive insurer to cede to the self-insurance mechanism (or the captive or pool) most of the losses covered by the fronting policy. In pure fronting, no risk is retained by the front or issuing carrier—it is all transferred by the reinsurance agreement to the selected self-insurance mechanism. A fronting fee is paid to the fronting carrier for the use of its facilities and name. The premium shown on the face of the policy is the sum of the charge made to the fronting carrier by the assuming reinsurer (the captive or trust fund) for the risk of the fronting carrier, the fronting fee, and any premium tax due the state.

Despite all the care taken by the issuing carrier to insulate itself from the risks arising from the fronting operation, the policy issued bears its name and the signatures of its officers. Courts and insurance regulators have no difficulty in treating the issuing carrier as the insuring carrier. Legally, the obligations of the policy can be enforced on the issuing carrier, regardless of whether or not these are honored by those backing up the issuing carrier. The fronting carrier and the fronting policy are subject to all appropriate regulatory processes regardless of any arrangement between that carrier and the device it is fronting for. These facts cause many insurers to regard fronting as a subterfuge that may expose them not only to unsecured loss but also to licensure difficulties. As a result, issuing companies are not easy to find.

At least one other point must be made about the general nature of fronting. In ceding reinsurance to the kind of reinsurance source represented by a trust fund or a captive insurer, the fronting carrier is using what is technically referred to as nonapproved reinsurance, and hence is unable to reflect a credit for the effect of this reinsurance on its balance sheet. To avoid any adverse effect on its policyholders' surplus, the fronting carrier will require a clean, irrevocable, automatically renewable letter of credit with an "evergreen clause" in its favor in the amount of both case reserves and IBNR reserves ceded to its reinsurer. Such letters of credit unconditionally obligate the assets of the issuing bank to the amount of the letter of credit. An evergreen clause obligates the issuer of the letter of credit to automatically renew the letter without restriction or change until the holder of the letter releases it by drawing funds against it or by mutual agreement. "IBNR" means "incurred but not reported" losses; that is, loss events have already happened, but no one is yet aware of the fact that a claim has occurred, and no report yet exists of the claim. Most banks will require 100 percent collateralization for such a letter of credit. This kind of letter of credit constitutes an admitted asset, that may be shown on the fronting carrier's balance sheet to offset the liability it assumes but transfers under the reinsurance agreement to a captive or trust fund.

Fronting, too, has advantages and disadvantages. The advantages include these:

- A normal commercial insurance policy is purchased by the self-insurer, as far as lienholders, bond trustees, excess underwriters, and the general public are concerned.
- The premium for the commercial policy is basically the sum of the cost of the self-insurance trust fund contribution, the fronting fee, and premium taxes. Hence, control of the cost of the program resides with the hospital's self-insurance fund or captive.
- Most of the advantages of either self-insurance or a captive are retained.
- In certain states and lines of insurance—including professional liability and Worker's Compensation—fronting is the only legal way to become a self-insurer.

The disadvantages of the fronting technique are:

- The cost to the sponsor organization, while less than ordinary insurance, is higher than a self-insurance fund, captive, or pool.
- The requirement of a letter of credit may be difficult to satisfy. The need for 100 percent collateralization may cause substantial dents in the financial structure of the self-insurance mechanism or may strain the parent corporation.
- The technique is more complicated and complex than either self-insurance or a captive utilized without fronting.
- Fronting as a device is frowned upon by many insurance regulators. In New York, the state appears to be trying to prohibit any company licensed there from participating in any fronting arrangement anywhere.

- The fronting carrier may seek to impose difficult or onerous conditions as a basis for utilization of its facilities.

POOLING PROGRAMS

An insurance pool comes into existence when two or more insurance companies agree to share premiums and losses resulting from insuring some specially defined activity or risk.

The task of running the pool is assumed by a pool manager, who accepts or declines risks, issues evidence of insurance, establishes premium rates, collects premiums, manages the adjustment of claims, pays adjusted loss, maintains the necessary pool accounting records, and provides periodic underwriting, premium, and claims records and accounts for the members. Each member company executes a contract with the pool manager and with one another defining the authority of the pool and its manager.

At the time the pool is formed, the insurance companies that are members establish the level of participation in premiums, losses, and expenses of the pool each will accept. This level is expressed as a percent. All policies issued by the pool list the companies that are members and the percentage of the business written by the pool that each one accepts. Once this participation percentage has been agreed to by a member company, it automatically participates for that amount in all risks written by the pool, surrendering its ability to pick and choose among risks.

The pool manager may be a member company of the pool or an independent contracting entity. The pool manager in turn may retain active involvement in all its management functions or it may delegate portions of those functions to other outside entities or to one or more member companies.

Pooled programs often are used by the insurance industry as a means of developing the capacity to handle situations that no individual company feels able to cope with comfortably by itself. The Nuclear Energy Liability Insurance Association is an example of a pool formed for this purpose. Another use for pools is in dealing with special reinsurance or risk situations.

As noted earlier, a group of single-owner captives, each engaged in insuring similar risks (for example, a group of single-owner captives, each of whose parent was a chain of related health care institutions) could form a reinsurance pool for the purpose of providing reinsurance protection to their members when acceptable terms for such reinsurance could not be obtained from the commercial market. In this case, each captive would agree to assume a percentage participation in the risk of all the other members of the pool.

For example, ten captives agree to take part in a pool formed to provide stop-loss reinsurance to each member. This class of reinsurance is chosen because it is difficult to place in the commercial market. The pool operates this way:

1. Each captive agrees to contribute $200,000 capacity per reinsured company. Hence, with ten members, the total capacity per reinsured company available from the pool is $2 million in any one year.
2. It is agreed that the stop-loss point will be not less than 150 percent of the reinsured captive's retained earned premiums for each year.
3. Each captive then issues each other captive a reinsurance policy (called a reinsurance treaty) committing the issuing captive to 10 percent participation in the amount of which the sum of the reinsured captive's retained loss exceeds 150 percent of the reinsured captive's retained earned premium for the year, providing that the maximum amount of loss payable under the treaty shall not exceed $200,000 in any one year.
4. Each captive charges the others to which it issues its treaty a premium agreed as applicable by all the members. The premium normally is a percentage of the reinsured's earned premium for the year.
5. The ten companies participating in the pool each actually receives $1.8 million in reinsurance from the other members. Each company therefore must maintain a 10 percent participation in its own risk. This level of participation, from an underwriting point of view, maintains a level of incentive to the reinsured company to actively control its own loss and not simply take advantage of its partners by turning over to them without care its loss in excess of the treaty attachment point.

When used in this manner, the pooling concept has the advantage of stabilizing the balance sheet of each reinsured captive as well as broadening the risk base written by each. When used cautiously and with careful planning, the methodology provides a valuable tool for achieving reasonable results not readily available from the commercial market place.

CHANNELING

Channeling is not a new concept. In the crisis of 1975, the then commissioner of insurance in Virginia attempted to have legislation passed requiring that malpractice insurance there be provided on a channeled basis; that is, that the hospital be made responsible for the physician's malpractice liability insurance.

"Channeling" and "channeled programs" refer to methods of providing physicians' malpractice insurance coverage that use the hospital as a primary integrating tool. At the least, such programs include common claims adjustment and loss prevention services. At the most, the hospital and the physicians are subject to only one policy, one premium, and one set of limits, with the premium paid by the hospital.

By mid-1985, the jury still appeared to be out on channeling. One clear success story exists—the Harvard Medical Group/Crico program. Several equally clear failures can be spotted, such as the New York City approaches based on commercial pooling techniques. Most of the other programs being tried have not been in existence long enough to have been tested fully.

Basically, the assumptions underlying channeling programs can be verified only as losses emerge. Hence, entering into channeling requires long, careful study and a cautious assessment. All of the actuarial and marketing assumptions should be extremely conservative. Every effort must be made to avoid failure of the program and to avoid raising expectations beyond the point of a reasonable chance of realization.

Perhaps the most important task for the hospital is to determine the goals it really wants to achieve from channeling, and then to test them against models of reality to see whether they will work. The authors suspect that the goals usually set for channeling may not, in the long run, be the correct ones—in other words, hospitals may not be able to tell what they really hope to achieve by channeling. It also is easy for the institution to allow its staff to set the goals for channeling for it—and that approach may result in unmitigated disaster.

As the nature of the insurance business changes, some of the new problems being created—for instance, those resulting from the change from occurrence basis to claims-made forms—may well find effective solutions through channeled programs. Certainly, continuing evaluation of channeling in this context remains well worth the substantial effort it will require.

Chapter 9

Noninsurance Risk Transfers

Glenn T. Troyer

Risk transfer is a concept describing the act of passing risk exposures from one party to another. The most common method of transferring is the insurance contract. This requires one party (the insured) to transfer the risk to a second party (the insurer) in exchange for paying a premium. However, there are several noninsurance/risk transfer mechanisms in use; these will be the subject of this chapter.

One noninsurance form of transfer is the bailment contract in which one party (bailee) leaves an item (i.e., automobile, ring, clothing, etc.) in the control and safekeeping of another (bailor) and the latter, by operation of personal property bailment law principles, assumes certain obligations.

Still another form is in the construction contract. Under cost-plus construction contracts, the contractor agrees to build a structure for the costs involved plus a percentage for the profit and overhead. Thus, depending on the specific language, the contractor usually bears little or no risk for shortages, strikes, bad weather, etc. In essence, much of the risk has remained with the owner. However, if the contract is on a fixed-price basis, then the risks assumed by the owner under the cost-plus contract usually are transferred to the contractor. A discussion of the various ways in which contracts deal with risk transfer requires a more complete analysis of contract law. For that reason, the examples here serve simply to illustrate the importance of understanding how contracts can be useful means of transferring risks even in the absence of indemnification or hold-harmless clauses.

INDEMNITY OR HOLD-HARMLESS AGREEMENTS

Another common method of transferring involves indemnity or hold-harmless agreements. Because insurance and bailments are discussed more completely in Chapters 7 and 20, the focus here is on indemnification and hold-harmless policies.

Indemnification agreements usually are referred to as hold-harmless contracts and for all practical purposes are considered one and the same. That is not to say, however, that there is not a distinction between a hold-harmless clause in a general commercial contract and a detailed indemnity insurance agreement. While the two may be based on similar legal principles, their content, terms, and conditions can vary significantly in scope and meaning.

For purposes here, however, the references are to the indemnification and hold-harmless clauses frequently inserted in sales and other business transaction agreements. One such clause might read as follows: "Your Hospital agrees to indemnify and hold harmless Dr. X from any and all liability, claims, or damage arising out of the activities of the Hospital, its employees, or agents in the operation of the emergency room."

To understand the basic concept of an indemnity agreement, it is useful first to distinguish it from similar types of agreements—the surety contract and the guarantor contract. In a surety contract one party (a surety) agrees to be bound, along with the principal, to a third party in the same agreement, executed at the same time, and on the same consideration with the third party. In such contracts, the surety becomes a promisor, along with the principal, to a third party promisee. These transactions usually involve the surety's agreeing to be obligated to the promisee third party on the debt or obligation of the principal. Thus, the third party would be able to collect the obligation either against the principal or against the surety during the time the debt is owing, regardless of whether the principal is in default.

In contrast, the guarantor arrangement usually involves two contracts: one in which the principal obligates itself to the third party and the other between the guarantor and the third party promisee. In this case, while the consideration for the guarantor's contract often is the same as for the principal's agreement with the third party, the terms and conditions are not the same. The third party, in contrast to rights under a surety contract, may not seek payment from the guarantor but first must find the principal in default before being able to assert rights under the guarantor contract.[1]

In contrast to these two types of agreements, the contract of indemnity obligates the indemnitor to indemnify or to make good any loss for damages the indemnitee has incurred or may incur; it involved only two parties. There are two types of indemnity contracts: (1) against liability that arises irrespective of whether the indemnitee has suffered actual loss or damages and (2) against indemnitee loss that does not obligate the indemnitor until the indemnitee actually has incurred some loss or injury.

Hold-harmless or indemnification agreements often are in the form of clauses in supply and equipment contracts executed between vendors and purchasers. Thus, in many hospital purchase contracts, it would be common to find hold-harmless agreements in which the seller is asking the hospital to hold the seller harmless for any loss that would arise from the hospital's use of a particular product. The hospital itself may ask the seller to indemnify it for any claims the hospital subsequently may be forced to pay as a result of product defects. Unfortunately, with the fast pace of business transactions in today's hospitals, purchasing agents frequently agree to such indemnification agreements without necessarily considering the legal and insurance ramifications that result from such obligations.

Leases between landlords and tenants frequently contain hold-harmless agreements that attempt to shift the landlord's liability to the tenant for defects in the building or for any act or neglect by any tenant or occupant of the building, often including even actions of the landlord.

HOSPITALS AND THIRD PARTIES

Hold-harmless agreements appear in agreements between hospitals and third parties for professional and nonprofessional services. As with the previous types of contracts, these hold-harmless clauses tend to shift liability for certain activities back and forth between the hospital and the service provider, whether the latter be a physician or a provider of some other service.

A typical hold-harmless agreement might require a medical equipment supply company to indemnify and hold harmless the hospital from any and all losses ensuing from the failure of such equipment to perform as intended by the manufacturer. Thus, should a claim arise against the hospital resulting from a malfunction of the equipment, by this hold-harmless agreement the medical equipment supply company would be required to pay the amount of the loss suffered by the hospital.

Often, parties to a contract seek to reduce the effect of a broad indemnification agreement by including a cross-indemnification agreement, whereby the hospital would agree to hold harmless and indemnify the medical equipment supply company from any losses arising from the use of the equipment and which resulted from the sole negligence of one of its employees. This would provide protection by limiting the obligation of the medical equipment supply company in the event the equipment failed as a result of the sole negligence of the hospital employee.

An Ohio case involved a claim by the deceased's wife against not only the hospital but also the city of Lakewood and an emergency room physician alleging that her husband died as a result of malpractice on the part of all three defendants.[2] The trial court granted summary judgment dismissing the hospital from the case. However, the appeals court reversed that decision on the basis that evidence submitted to the lower court indicated the existence of a material fact on whether the plaintiff in taking her husband to the hospital had relied upon the appearance of the physician as an agent of the hospital. The appellate court further indicated that a full-service hospital cannot contractually insulate itself from liability for acts of malpractice committed in its emergency room by entering into an agreement with a third party (physician) for the operation of the emergency room.[3]

In cases such as this one, even though the hospital may include seemingly exculpatory language in a contract with an independent physician, the relationship in fact is one in which the hospital is employing an independent contractor, so the institution may want to require an indemnification hold-harmless clause from the physician. The effect of such a clause would be to require the physician to indemnify the hospital for claims arising out of care in the emergency room. Without the hold-harmless agreement, the hospital would not be entitled to indemnification from the contracted physician and therefore would bear the cost of such a claim by itself even though the facility, per se, might have had little or no involvement in the care of the patient.

LEGAL RESPONSIBILITY OF PARTIES

One of the basic policy principles behind the use of hold-harmless agreements is to require each party to bear legal responsibility for its own actions and its actions only. Because the Ohio *Hanola* case would permit a jury to decide whether the hospital should be responsible for the negligent professional action of an independent physician contractor over whom the facility had no right or control, either by contract or by virtue of the physician's medical license, the hospital might be forced to pay for injuries it did not cause. Thus, a hold-harmless indemnification agreement would allow the hospital a contractual method of seeking recovery from the physician for claims and injuries caused by the doctor.

However, an important point is whether the parties have sufficient resources to finance such hold-harmless clauses. One way of doing so is through the purchase of contractual liability coverage, which often is easily acquired as an addendum to a general liability policy. Of course, another way is through some self-insuring mechanisms.

If the hospital has agreed to indemnify and hold harmless some other party in whatever transaction, that prudence would indicate that the institution should have some mechanism for funding such potential liability situations should they arise. Similarly, the hospital should be cautioned to make certain that if the other party has agreed to indemnify and hold the facility harmless under certain circumstances, but without sufficient financing of that agreement, it may be only as good as the assets of the other party. Thus, while it may be easy to extract from the other party a sufficiently broad indemnification clause to give comfort to the hospital, unless that clause is supported by the other party's contractual liability insurance coverage or significant assets, the bare promise to indemnify may be, in a practical sense, virtually worthless.

In conclusion, the drafting of indemnification and hold-harmless documents requires a lawyer who understands the hospital transaction in which the agreement is being considered, and will give specific attention to the nature of the arrangement, the types of claims or injuries expected to be covered, the time period involved, the requirement for carrying contractual liability insurance, the inclusion of attorney fees and other costs, and whether cross-indemnification agreements should be used.

NOTES

1. C.C.A. 8, 69 F.2d 447, 450.
2. *Hanola v. City of Lakewood*, 426 N.E.2d 1187 (Ohio).
3. *Ibid.*, 1192.

Chapter 10

Claims Management

Layton Severson and Malcolm S. Parsons

Since the infamous malpractice crisis of the 1970s, hospitals and physicians have been forced to seek alternatives to rising insurance premiums. Self-insured trust funds have been established, insurance companies have been formed, and the captive insurance company concept has grown. Lobbyists have been active in seeking legislation to protect medical professionals and many states have passed professional liability measures. Mandatory arbitration or mediation statutes have been enacted in many states. Iatrogenic prevention has been emphasized. The practice of ''defensive medicine'' has become commonplace. From the time patients enter the hospital until they are discharged, the possibilities that medical-legal problems can arise are countless.

While a claims management system is not a solution to the causes of problems, it is a positive control mechanism that must be established if resolution of claims is to be cost effective. An efficient claims management system cannot, in and of itself, prevent actual or potential medical malpractice. However, an effectively run system can reduce the overall cost of claims substantially.

Because all health care institutions differ in size and have unique characteristics, a claims management control system must take numerous factors into account. Legal counsel, corporate structure, hospital administration, and the insurance company's relationship all must be evaluated in the establishment and creation of the system.

DEVELOPMENT OF CLAIMS MANAGEMENT

This chapter explores claims management in the hospital environment and some of the insurance-related considerations. Since the mid-1970s, more and more hospitals have become either self-insured for a substantial exposure or have increased deductibles to the extent that the exposure has become a capital budget item. Both of these approaches have created a need to develop a more professional and informed approach to insurance concepts. Many hospitals have diversified to the extent of creating or buying captive insurance companies. These alternatives mandate the need for expertise in traditional insurance areas such as risk management, loss reduction, loss retention, underwriting, actuarial and financial projections, and the ability to manage and control claims. Modern hospital risk and claims managers also must understand the insurance principles of excess and reinsurance and position themselves to manage such policies with some degree of expertise.

Risk management has made substantial progress in the areas of identification and reduction of financial exposures to the hospital and medical staff. From a financial viewpoint, proper and timely claims management is a separate and distinct entity in the health care arena that can improve the hospital's profitability and affect its long-term stability. This is true whether the hospital uses a self-insured concept of risk retention or a risk transfer method such as commercial insurance.

In hospitals, one main thrust of any such program involves professional and general liability exposures. The claims management concepts and philosophies discussed here could be applied as well toward property, inland marine, D & O, Workers' Compensation, employee benefits, and other insurance coverages.

It is appropriate to approach claims management from a professional liability standpoint because: (1) this is a major and unstable financial exposure for a hospital, (2) this area deals with unique, difficult, and sometimes uncontrollable factors, and (3) insurance premium costs for these coverages are extremely volatile.

Each hospital is structured somewhat differently so managers must ''restructure'' this material to relate to their particular institution. Claims management is one loss reduction process used in risk management. This is further explored in Chapter 6.

GENERAL CONCEPTS

The claims management system outlined here is a generic method of implementing, maintaining, and processing claims. The system will work on all types of claims, although the examples cited relate to professional liability. The chapter is designed as a guide for hospital claims representatives in the handling of cases coming under the jurisdiction of the Risk or Claims Management Department.

Claims representatives should be ever mindful that prompt, efficient, and courteous service is a factor necessary for the promotion of risk management programs in the health care setting. Such persons, in implementing a claims management system, must have the full approval and support of legal counsel, hospital administration, and the governing board.

The primary objective of the representatives in conducting an investigation of a claim is the collection of the essential data that will permit them to arrive at proper conclusions and resolve cases. The investigation will require contact with many individuals and the information to be obtained from these contacts depends not only upon a thorough knowledge of the problem but also upon the manner in which the interviews and the investigation are conducted. The investigator should never adopt a superior attitude toward anyone as that will operate to the detriment of a proper disposition of the claim. The claims representative should never lose sight of the fact that to claimants, a loss or liability case is a major event in their lives. The importance of maintaining an impartial and unbiased attitude in an investigation is of paramount importance.

INCIDENT REPORTING SYSTEM

While a review of the incident reporting procedures will be elementary for most of our readers, we feel that the basics in risk management should never be overlooked or taken for granted. Incident reporting is, after all, the foundation of any risk management program. In order to take any action, risk managers first must be made aware of the fact that something has happened.

Initially, minor occurrences will be reported: falls, nonadverse medication errors, and the like. Eventually, as trust is built, the reporting of incidents involving physicians, medical/legal questions, and surgical events will become commonplace. It should not be surprising if reports of serious events are verbal rather than written.

An incident form (sometimes called an occurrence form) should be developed that answers basic questions pertinent to investigations. Questions such as who, what, when, where, and how must be addressed. Cause of injuries and connection to the incident itself must be noted. Nationally, several varieties of the incident report are available. Tailoring one to an individual hospital's needs is a minor task.

Instructions on completing the form should be written and reinforced constantly. New employees and house staff as well as attending physicians should be advised of its importance.

Incident forms should be readily available at all locations in the hospital. This basic instrument will provide enough data to screen the events and determine which ones require investigation. It is important to follow up significant events with the individuals who report them. This will provide core information and, at the same time, reinforce the need for reporting by employees or medical staff members. Not all incidents require follow-up, but in the beginning all reports should receive attention from the risk department.

THE FOUNDATION: STEP 1

Basically, all claims progress from an incident. The typical progression is from incident to claim to lawsuit. Therefore, a three-pronged management system must be instituted. After that system is in place, it becomes a clerical function to add or delete claims.

The incident report log will provide a ready reference to all events reported. Ideally, each month this log should be reviewed to identify trends that require analyzing; i.e., delay in the time of risk management awareness of an incident, incident location, type of incidents, type of errors being committed, severity, frequency, etc.

Therefore, Step 1 of the claims management system is to receive the incident report and log it with date, patient name, description of incident, location, etc. Space should be left for future progress in the incident—date of creation into a claim file, date closed, date of suit, and final disposition.

Investigation and General Handling of Claims

The importance of prompt and efficient investigation of claims cannot be overemphasized. An immediate inquiry to determine the facts and circumstances of the occurrence and a careful check on injuries, disability, and potential damages is important. If the Risk or Claims Management Department has not been informed properly of the facts, it is put at a substantial disadvantage.

The ability to complete a thorough investigation becomes increasingly difficult as time passes. Any initial difficulty in locating witnesses is aggravated by delay; memories become less accurate and facts distorted. A preliminary investigation should be completed within ten days after notice of a potential claim.

The claim representative then should determine what disposition should be made of the case. If it is one for adjustment and the amount involved is within the authority of the Risk or Claims Management Department, it should be settled. If the amount is beyond the authority of the claim representative, the investigation report should be sent at once to the appropriate authority with the representative's recommendations and the claimant advised that others must make the decision.

As all of the facts come together, the importance not only of a prompt investigation but also a complete, accurate, and timely one will be evident. The flow of data helps form the claim representative's opinion as the investigation proceeds. The timely decision as to liability of a claim is related directly to a prompt investigation.

Creation of a claim file does not constitute an admission of guilt or imply liability; it is only an indication that an "incident" has progressed to "claim" status. Thereafter, the flow of information will slow down. File creation, clerical duties, evaluation of potential liability, reserve setting, implementation of system procedures, follow-up, medical reports, and communication with counsel will take place. Claim reports on an as-needed or as-discussed basis will follow. Ideally, claim review will occur every 30 days. Many potential claims gather dust and are closed without payment. Others, for many reasons, develop into litigation. The investigator should keep detailed notes of the claim activities and discussions with hospital counsel regarding the development of the file.

Investigative Considerations

To complete the investigation, the claim representatives must gather the proper information upon which to base a decision. Complete investigation and knowledge of the facts will allow the representatives to make recommendations, offers, give instructions, etc. They must consider questions such as these:

- Have statements been taken or fully noted conversations held with all parties involved, including witnesses, nurses, interns, residents, orderlies, department personnel, medical staff, etc.?
- Have conflicting stories been resolved?
- Have conversations been held with claimant, family, next of kin, plaintiff counsel?
- Have next of kin been interviewed and claims and identification made in a death case?
- Is the person being dealt with a professional claimant?
- Is the injury permanent in nature?
- What were the claimant's true losses?
- Are all actual or potential defendants involved?
- Has an in-house medical opinion been rendered as to the claim, injury, standard of care, and medical documentation?
- Will an outside expert be needed before a decision can be made?
- Has hospital counsel reviewed the claim/suit and provided a written opinion?
- Does a legal liability exist?

THE FOUNDATION: STEP 2

Step 2 includes several administrative and clerical tasks. The decision to create an active claim file is made and the system is used to monitor and develop the file into a complete investigation. This step includes basic clerical duties such as the making of a file jacket with the claimant's name, date of incident, and risk management file number. Data and investigation activity sheets to date are placed in this file for confidential handling (potential exposure to discovery is discussed later).

The log should contain the date of file creation and a simple diary card should be created for control purposes and placed in a diary card file. This card also may include allegation, date opened, closed, closing status, amount paid, physician, department, attorney's name, expenses paid in the investigation, and legal costs. Any file, regardless of status, should be reviewed every 30 to 60 days to maintain awareness of the claim itself.

Claim Development

As time passes, the claim may develop into a lawsuit. At that point, legal discovery will begin. Medical charts will be reviewed again, medical opinions obtained, expert witnesses acquired, reinterviews and possibly statements gathered. A seemingly endless flow of file correspondence will begin. All of these activities need to be noted and the file activity sheets updated and kept current. The flow sheet diagram in Figure 10–1 indicates the time necessary to develop a complete defense file and the steps in a case. Depending upon the aggressiveness of the attorneys involved, the backlog of suits awaiting trial, the temperament of the judge assigned, and various other factors included in the term *due process*, the trial usually will take place two to five years after the suit is filed, and after trial, the verdict might be appealed.

Claim Brief

For claim management purposes, a claim brief should be dictated and added to the file. After receiving all available data, the claims representative should prepare the file for review. To prevent long hours of reviewing medical charts, information from witnesses, etc., a capsule version of the claim should be prepared. This short summary will provide a case review and reference for all parties.

This brief should denote points of interest such as claimants, possible defendants, date and description of the incident, allegations, legal status, legal issues, offers, demands, and comments. The claims representative should identify which items need to be completed in the investigation itself.

The outline in Exhibit 10–1 is concise and self-explanatory. When completed, the brief will provide a two- or three-page summary that will save countless hours of review. Minor deviations from the outline often are necessary to review the entire scenario of a given claim. The outline is to serve only as a guide. The sample of a completed claim brief outline shows that minor deviations from the outline itself are often necessary to encompass all the circumstances of a claim (Exhibit 10–2).

Figure 10–1 Claim Development Flow Sheet

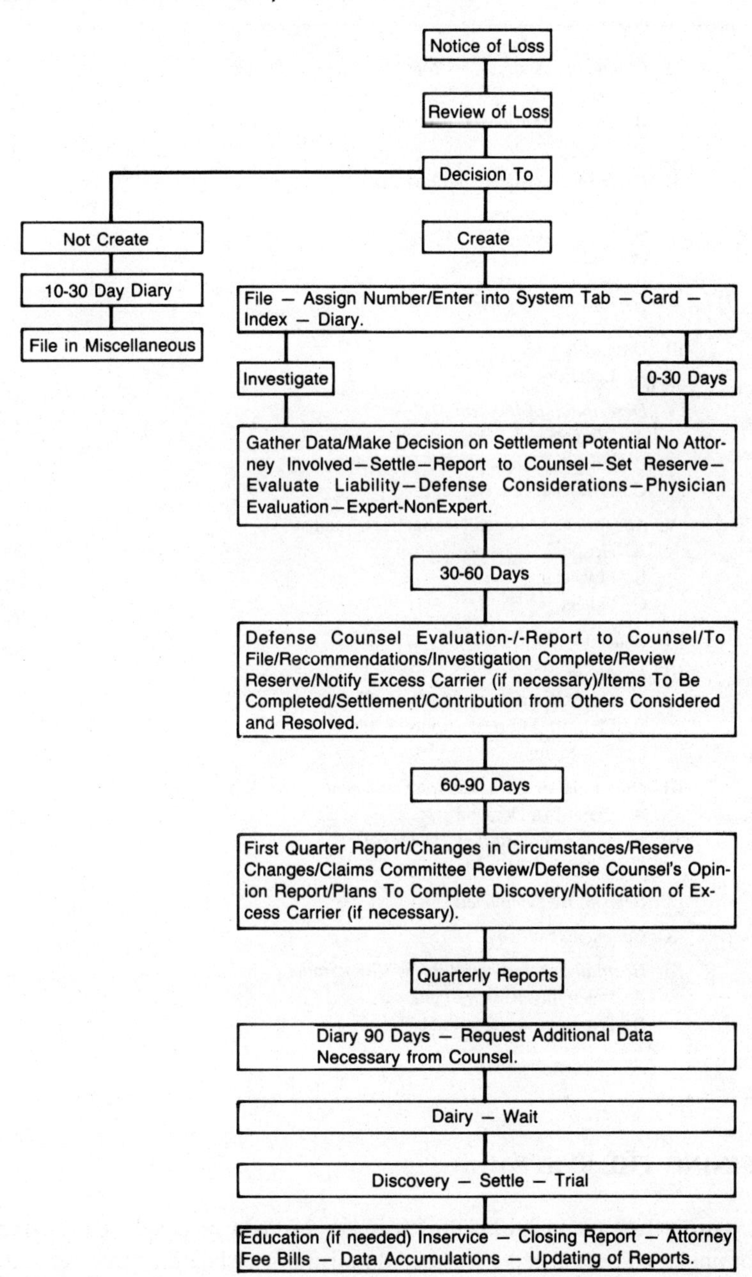

Exhibit 10–1 Claim Brief Outline (Capsule Version)

I. *Claimants:* Address M/F Age Phone
   A.
   B.
   C.

II. *Defendants:* (Actual and Possible)
   A.
   B.
   C.
   D.
   E.

III. *Date of Incident*
   A. Location

IV. *Description of Incident*
   A. Who, What, When, Where, and How
   B. Hospital/Employee Involvement
   C. Physician Involvement

V. *Allegations* (Alleged Negligence) Against
   A. Hospital
   B. Physician
   C. Others

VI. *Issues* (To Be Defended)

VII. *Legal Status*
   A. Defense Attorney, Address, Phone
   B. Plaintiff Attorney, Address, Phone
   C. Suit Status

VIII. *Offers and/or Demands for Settlement*
   A. Plaintiff's Demand
   B. Value Per Attorney (Defense)
   C. Value Per Risk Manager

IX. *Items to Be Completed*

X. *Comments*

XI. *Hospital Self-Insured Reserve (SIR) Status*
   A. Indemnity Reserve/Paid
   B. Expenses Reserve/Paid

REFINING THE SYSTEM

A year-by-year tracking of claims accrued must now be developed. This report is not unlike an annual report to the administrator or board of trustees and will show the claims history of the institution. As time permits, old claims should be

Exhibit 10–2 Completed Claim Brief (Sample)

RM FILE NO. 1001
April 14, 1985
RM Advised

I. *Claimant*

Jean Jane Doe, 2056 Gruber Road, Small Town, USA 12345
Telephone No. 1–234–567–8910

II. *Defendant*

Possible defendants include: (Suit not filed at this time)

a. Your hospital, employees, and staff
b. Emergency Room physician (Corp.)
c. Fire Department A
d. Fire Department B

III. *Date of Incident*

January 6, 1985

IV. *Allegation*

IV infiltration caused nerve damage to the patient's left arm and severe scarring that subsequently resulted in two skin grafts.

V. *Description of Incident*

On January 6, 1985, Township Emergency Life Squad A was called to the patient's office at 1111 Broadway in Small Town, USA, where it found the patient sitting at a desk unconscious and shaking vigorously.

The life squad found the patient to be very combative, especially during the establishment of an IV. The patient was taking six different medications, none available at the scene, and had a history of being a diabetic. An EKG showed arterial vigeminy. The patient was transported to the Emergency Room, having been restrained, and the IV was lost en route.

At the East facility, Dr. X examined the patient and transferred her to the West Hospital for a CT scan of the head (the patient subsequently was discharged from East Hospital ER and transported to West Hospital via Township Life Squad B and accompanied by an Emergency Room nurse.

Dr. X's discharge diagnosis from East Hospital was intercranial bleed.

At West Hospital the patient was received via the Emergency Room and transported to CT and subsequently to ICU.

It was in the ICU that the patient's IV infiltration was noted and changed by nursing staff in the ICU unit.

VI. *At Issue*

At issue here is who in fact caused the IV to infiltrate: the hospital, employees and staff, or Township Life Squad A. It is not a contention that the IV did not infiltrate; moreover, conversations with the attending physician revealed that in his opinion the IV had infiltrated and the injury was caused by the Township Life Squad A in its attempt to transport the patient while establishing an IV that was lost en route.

Exhibit 10–2 continued

VII. *Legal Status*

The claimant is represented by John Attorney of Attorney and Attorney, 580 Main Street, Suite 100, Small Town, USA 12345.

Inasmuch as this file is not in suit, there is no defense counsel at this time.

VIII. *Offers and Demands*

Via my meeting with John Attorney on March 10, 1985, this claim may be settled for $25,000 for the claimant, $12,000 to $15,000 for the attorney and the payment of the unpaid medical bills to date as well as a guarantee against subrogation of the medical bills already paid.

Medical bills to date total in excess of $18,999.66 while lost wages (unconfirmed) are established at $1,955.00 gross.

When questioned concerning a demand, Mr. Attorney demanded $60,000 that could be broken down as previously mentioned.

IX. *Items to Be Completed*

To meet with the Township A trustees and advise them of the potential damages on this claim and that our investigation reveals that they may be negligent in this matter.

After contacting Chief William Z, it is known that the Township Fire Squad A paramedic and emergency personnel were uninsured as of January 1985.

The township has since purchased a malpractice paramedic policy from Western World Insurance Corp.

X. *Comments*

John Attorney, counsel for the claimant, has prepared a package that includes medical statements, lost wage verification, plaintiff's physician's narrative report, and photographs to substantiate this injury.

While this package is not yet included in the Risk Management file, Mr. Attorney has advised that it will be forwarded to our office as soon as possible.

Addendum

Package received from Mr. Attorney as outlined in Paragraph X.

entered into the system. The incorporation of claims into a system begins with arrangement for a series of claims numbers. If the system start-up date is now, adequate numbers of some coding mechanism should be instituted to allow for the older, presystem claims and lawsuits to be added later.

The system must be accountable for reserves (both indemnity and expenses) as well as expenses already incurred. The medical date of the incident, notice of claim date, date closed, and claimant's name, along with indemnity (paid and reserved) and allocated expenses (paid and reserved) should be entered. This one- or two-page summary on a year-by-year basis outlines the financial picture of the hospital's medical professional liability exposures.

First-year data for the claims history form will flow from the log sheets. Subsequent years will be derived from additions/subtractions from the first-year report. The process of setting reserves on claims, and their classifications, is discussed later.

With the basic system in place, risk and claims management personnel will have an accurate record of experience, claims history, reserves (both indemnity and expense), and monies already expended that are to be charged against the reserves.

Claims management personnel next begin the long, often-delayed task of gathering information through detailed investigation. All competent adjusters are aware of the fact that if they cannot control the claim, it may well go to litigation—resulting in a long and expensive process. Control of this situation remains generally in the risk manager's hands. Every reasonable attempt to resolve the claim should be made or there will be additional costs charged against adjustment plus legal expenses. Conversely, the claims manager has a duty to defend against nonmeritorious claims or allegations.

In refining the system, the claims manager is charged not only with obtaining the facts and resolving claims but also with improving the various skills needed, producing policies and procedures to deal fairly and uniformly with claims, and continuously obtaining more education to remain competent in the rapidly changing environment of the profession. The hospital claims, risk, or insurance manager needs additional skills and knowledge tailored to the institution's insuring status or mechanism.

The sections that follow are designed as guidelines for hospital risk or claims managers. They are general in nature because each institution's system must be tailored to its own needs and responsibilities.

LEGAL LIABILITY DEFINED

The prerequisites of legal liability in negligence cases are: (1) a legal duty owed, (2) a breach of the duty owed, (3) injury or damages, (4) proximate cause. The plaintiff must prove all four elements of negligence.

Historically, contributory negligence by the claimant has been a complete bar to recovery. Most states now have comparative negligence statutes. A sample condensed version follows:

> In negligence actions, contributory negligence does not bar the person from recovering damages if their contributory negligence was no greater than the combined negligence of all other persons from whom recovery is sought. However, any damages shall be diminished by an amount proportionately equal to the percentage of negligence on the part of the

> claimant: (1) A plaintiff whose negligence is 50 percent or less recovers but the damages are reduced in proportion to the claimant's negligence. (2) A plaintiff whose negligence is 51 percent or more recovers nothing.

A sample condensed version of the statute for computing defendant liability is as follows:

> If recovery is allowed, each person against whom recovery is allowed is liable for a portion of the total damage. The portion is calculated by multiplying the total damages by a fraction in which the numerator is the person's percentage of negligence and the denominator is the total of the percentage of negligence attributable to all persons from whom recovery is allowed. Any percentage of negligence attributable to the plaintiff shall not be included in the total that is the denominator of the fraction.

The legal liability of the health care facility for payment of a claim against it is based on the percentage of negligence exhibited. All hospitals should check with legal counsel as to the comparative negligence specific statutes applicable in their state.

LIABILITY EVALUATION

General Considerations (Negligence and Liability)

In considering liability, many questions must be asked and data developed through the investigation. The following laundry list can be used as a base to stir the imagination and give rise to a solid, factually based case:

1. Did the hospital, physician, or employee have a legal duty? Was there a breach of that duty?
2. Did the individual fail to use the required degree of care?
3. Was the act one of absolute liability?
4. Was the person negligent per se?
5. Did the person violate the acceptable standard of care?
6. Was the act willful, wanton, or grossly negligent?
7. Did the physician fail to accept/entertain a second opinion?
8. Did the hospital have a legal duty owed by the physician, hospital, or employee such as relevant information on allergies, prior injury, current treatment elsewhere, etc.? (Did the physician/employee have requisite knowledge?)
9. Was the act or occurrence an accident?

10. Was the act of the physician, employee, or staff members the cause of the injury?
11. Was the injury the natural probable consequence of the occurrence?

Other Considerations

A number of other general considerations also are at issue:

1. Do individual personalities have an effect on the case?
2. Are the parties related? Does this have an effect?
3. Do physical defects of claimant have an effect?
4. Does the degree of carelessness have an effect?
5. Does the character (moral and ethical) of the parties have an effect?
6. Does the place of happening have an effect?
7. Does the physician's or claimant's reputation have an effect?
8. Is other insurance available to the hospital, physician, or employee?
9. Was the claimant paid damages by others or by Workers' Compensation?
10. What personal injuries were involved:
    - What was the extent of pain and suffering?
    - What is the extent of permanent injury?
    - How much are the medical bills?
    - What is the loss-of-time expense?
    - Was a special nurse or maid employed?
    - What was the prior physical condition of the injured party?
11. In a death case:
    - Was death the result of the injury?
    - What was the life expectancy of the deceased?
    - What was the occupation and earnings of the deceased?
    - Is loss of companionship to be considered?
    - Is conscious suffering to be considered?
    - Is burial expense to be considered?
    - Is last illness expense to be considered?
    - What was the station in life of deceased and beneficiaries?
    - What was the deceased's family position?

Legal Aspects

In addition to points already raised, there are other legal considerations:

1. Are legal expenses to be considered?
2. Will there be a long and costly discovery period?
3. Will expert witnesses be employed?
4. Will adverse results have an effect on parties involved?
5. Is the public relations aspect of the defendants (particularly the hospital or physician) to be considered?
6. Is precedent on the side of defendant or plaintiff?
7. Is settlement the better economic consideration, i.e., nuisance payment?

Fraudulent Claims

Defendants always must be on the alert for possibly suspicious elements in a case:

1. Are claimant's facts too perfect?
2. Are important witnesses closely related to claimant?
3. Is claimant closely related to the insured or his representative or insurance agent/company?
4. Is claimant a repeater?
5. What is the reputation for honesty of the persons involved?
6. Is there anxiety for a quick settlement by the claimant?
7. Does the claimant refuse to submit to a medical exam?
8. Was there a ready admission of liability by insured (representative)?
9. Does the claimant refuse to submit proof of special damages?
10. What is claimant's financial standing?

STATEMENTS

The policy on the taking of statements should be approved by defense counsel and the insurance carrier. Statements, regardless of how well they are taken and prepared, must be a permanent part of the record. If the data depicted in the statement place the hospital in a liability situation, the institution nonetheless must live with it. Many risk managers and defense experts feel that flawless notes from verbal conversations and interviews are better than a long-hand, signed statement. Depositions later should produce basically thc samc points. Activity notes should be clearly marked ''Attorney's Work Product'' to attempt to prevent discovery by plaintiff's counsel. It is assumed that the case is proceeding based on instructions from defense counsel, thus protecting the investigation and claim files from discovery by plaintiff's counsel.

Statements from or interviews with all parties who have any knowledge of any aspect of the claim are of great value. A proper statement or interview, reflecting the exact and complete knowledge of the person giving it, allows anyone who is called upon to handle the file to know what the individual may be expected to say, should the claim become the basis of a lawsuit. Statements or interviews should be obtained as early as possible in the investigation, while memory is fresh.

Preliminary considerations in the taking of a statement are basic in nature: Is the giver competent? Is it necessary to obtain permission to take the statement? Is the statement necessary? Other rules include avoiding the use of leading questions. Conclusionary questions should be asked last and should use the exact words of the giver. The interviewer should not draw conclusions. However, analysis of the attitude, demeanor, reliability, or unreliability of the person giving the statement is of great importance. They should take a separate statement from each person, write legibly, and avoid leaving blank lines on which someone could insert damaging material later.

The content of the statement should include the following: The full legal name of the giver, address, age, Social Security number, and telephone number. If the giver is married, the name of the spouse and number of dependents are helpful. The occupation and name and address of the employer are important for locating witnesses after the fact. Obtaining names and addresses of close relatives or friends for location purposes is recommended.

After these basic items are obtained, the statement should proceed with the occurrence/incident itself with emphasis on who, what, when, where, and how the event occurred. The nature and extent of injury to the claimant should be noted in the giver's own words. The conclusion of the statement should note that the giver has read, understands, and agrees with the statement given. The review of the statement and its particulars should be completed to ensure that nothing is missed and that the giver is in total agreement. Local law will determine if statements are available through legal discovery. Work with local counsel to design the process to best prevent discovery.

EVALUATION OF CLAIMS

After all pertinent data are gathered and analyzed, it is time to consider a conclusion based on liability and values. Proper evaluation of the claim must rest upon a consideration of all of its elements balanced one against the other.

One of these considerations is the evaluation of liability. From that standpoint, claims fall into three categories: (1) those of liability, (2) those of questionable liability, and (3) those of no liability. When the claim is one of clear liability, the only question to be resolved is the amount of damages sustained. Where it is of questionable liability, sound judgment dictates that the liability element be weighed against the damage element in an effort to arrive at a reasonable and equitable value for settlement purposes. Where the claim is of no liability, it theoretically has no value. Many factors, some insubstantial, must be considered carefully since they may add to or detract from the value of the claims in the first two categories and, out of necessity, may affect a claim in the third category.

The fear of offending a physician sometimes has caused claim representatives to be hesitant or to fail in obtaining adequate, factual information. No one should take offense when claim representatives act within their duties. If there is dissatisfaction, it usually results from misunderstanding, and a careful explanation by the claim representatives usually can eliminate the problem. Attitude, appearance, demeanor, and behavior are the most frequent culprits causing confrontation between individuals.

DEFENSE ATTORNEY INVOLVEMENT

The claim evaluation to this point has been performed by claims personnel with knowledge of the facts and circumstances. Nevertheless, experienced defense attorneys see trends, verdicts, and effects of the legislative and judicial system that often are beyond the knowledge of the claims personnel. It is for this reason that defense counsel's opinion of values, liability, and possible additional data must be solicited. As circumstances change, so may values, etc.

Reports other than those that accompany depositions, answers, etc., should give the hospital risk or claims manager a good idea of how the claim is being handled and place the manager in a position of being able to set reserves accordingly.

Attorney reports should include the following:

- allegations
- issues that will have to be defended (legal and factual)
- plaintiff's position and defense counsel's thoughts on percentages of the win/loss scenario
- current demands for settlement
- possible jury verdict outcome
- defenses to allegations and issues (legal and factual)
- defense counsel's thoughts on case scenario and settlement values
- attorney's recommendations
- favorable or unfavorable legal points.

THE RESERVING PROCESS

Risk and claims personnel understand that claim reserves represent only an opinion based on experience and knowledge of a given claim.

From a financial standpoint, no aspect of claims information requires closer attention than the reserving process. This process enables financial success or failure to be measured. For self-insured and captives accounting, the paid claims and expense ratio allows the actuary to set funding levels. Reserves must be set accurately and timely. Self-insureds do not have the benefit of the insurance principle of large numbers, under which the losses of a few are spread over the cost of many). Their claims history is based on smaller numbers and thus, from an actuarial standpoint, the need for accuracy in setting reserves is critical. Preliminary reserves should be set within 30 days, based upon prompt investigation and evaluation of a claim.

The underreserving of actual or potential claims for medical malpractice for a self-insured can have disastrous results over a period of years. It is imperative that reserves be created with a realistic, if not pessimistic, point of view. To offset national trends and the attitudes of society such as large jury awards, the hospital must, with proper evaluation from defense counsel and medical experts, set proper reserves early and determine the course of the claim. These trends, news articles, and media reports of huge awards will continue to affect professional liability and the values of various claims. Defense attorneys should be encouraged to assist in establishing reserves on claims/suits they are reviewing or handling.

In addition to the escalating costs of indemnity paid in this field, defense costs are increasing rapidly. Reserves, per claim, should be established for both indemnity and expense. Reserves should be updated as necessary with appropriate documentation reflecting the reasons for changes. All reserves should be reviewed at least twice a year.

The need for accurate and timely reserves cannot be overstated. On occasion, claim circumstances change and reserves require revision, with explanations. As a business principle, properly stated reserves should, over an extended period, reflect the paid claim and expense experience cost in a reasonably accurate manner according to accepted accounting principles. This result can only be obtained with due diligence and attention by professionally competent individuals with expertise in the area of professional liability.

Expense reserves, on the other hand, are influenced by hourly fees, discovery costs, court/deposition costs, and the length of the trial itself. Claims handled in house will require lower reserves than those referred to outside counsel for trial preparation and discovery.

Direct handling and settlement by hospital or contract claims personnel will help to minimize defense costs. A complete handling/investigation from the onset of the claim/suit by risk/claims management personnel will reduce the overall costs. Defense counsel assignments and opinions should be limited to serious cases.

SETTLEMENT AND RELEASE CONSIDERATIONS

The final element of claims handling is basic in nature but often made complex by the present status of the legal system. In years past a full and final release was standard throughout the insurance industry. It now is common to find legally specific releases—that is, with numerous details addressing specifically (and only) the case or issue. These often are two or three pages in length.

Before actually disposing of a claim by payment of money, the hospital and the claims/risk manager should review every fact surrounding the case and take that information into consideration before making payment. This double-check scenario will prevent potential problems in the future. Policy limits or retention amounts should never be discussed with plaintiff's counsel. The presence of insurance theoretically neither adds to nor detracts from the value of a claim. However, in no event should the claim representative misrepresent the coverage to the claimant or attorney because doing so may create a fraudulent misrepresentation that would furnish adequate grounds for setting aside a release.

While all phases of claim handling require skillful, courteous, and tactful action, this is particularly true in negotiations for settlement. The exercise of patience and perseverance, and a zeal for a full investigation, usually will result in a fair and equitable settlement. Definite rules of settlement technique cannot be listed, but there are some general considerations for guidance.

In any case where the liability of the hospital is clear and the demand is fair, settlement should be made as quickly as possible. Experience has shown that time adds unwarranted value to an injury case. This means that prompt and preferred attention must be given to the investigation of claims to determine whether or not settlement is justified and at what monetary level.

Good claims practice insists that the claimant or the attorney state an estimated value (demand) before negotiating a settlement. This is particularly true where the claimant is represented by an attorney. If this is not done, claim representatives are faced with the problem of negotiating against themselves.

When settling a claim, the claim representative must be certain that all persons having an interest are joined in the release; for example, a release for an injury to a married person must bear the signature of the spouse.

In cases involving minors and incompetents and in cases of death, the nonattorney claims representative should consult with the legal department or counsel for instructions on the method of settlement and release. Generally speaking, where the claim is small and there is no danger of an increase or recurrence of a disability, the claim of a minor may be settled by taking a parent's indemnifying release, whereby the parents, guardians, or next of kin indemnify future losses or claims, and which must be executed in the same manner as a general release. Such releases should be signed by both parents. In such instances, the age of the minor permitting, the claim representative also should have the minor sign a regular general release (full and final).

A hospital professional liability account with a separate account number to ensure compliance with reporting procedures should be used for professional liability claims. All payments from the account should be reflected in financial reports. Actuarial services and insurance carriers are interested in paid professional liability exposures. If the self-insurance trust fund or captive insures various lines of business, separate coding or account numbers should be established for each line of business.

YEAR-ENDING REPORTS

The year-ending annual report of open/closed claims and report of expenditures is the synopsis of the entire claim management program. This report provides administrative personnel and the board of directors with an accurate reference and picture of the hospital's liability exposures. The report should be factual, accurate, and require little explanation. The bottom line is the potential loss to the hospital and/or the self-insured retention fund.

This report also serves as the self-insured hospital's actuarial base for claims history upon which excess insurance premiums are charged and justified. Accurate reserving will prove to the excess-insurance company that claims personnel are not underestimating losses.

If the system is automated (via computer), entries are current daily and internal status reports can be printed out instantly. There will be occasions when the chief executive officer will need this information for board meetings and progress reports to board committees.

Ideally, the report on pending claims should include the following: Claimant name, plaintiff attorney's name, date of incident, suit status, physician and/or hospital department involved, and the allegation of the complaint. Depending upon the intended use of this report, reserve figures also may be reflected. CEOs, defense counsel, and board members usually are the only persons who need to have access to this information. (Disclosure to board members of claimants' names and details is not without risk.)

PRIMARY COMMERCIAL INSURANCE COVERAGE

Many hospitals still purchase first-dollar or no-deductible commercial insurance for their professional and general liability coverage. They pay their premium as submitted by their agent or broker and send all claims to their agent. As their premiums increase, they ask their agent to "shop" or contact other carriers for coverages at a lower premium. As premiums continue to increase, facilities consider allowing another agent or broker to represent them. These hospitals, when asked about their claim experience, will refer the question to their agent or broker. When questioned about paid claims and expense factors, they reply that the information must be obtained from their agent or insurance company. The hospital thus has little or no information on its indemnity or expense factors or the reasons for them.

An escalating problem, from a financial planning standpoint, is that many hospitals have no active claims management programs to control and guide the claims process. They have little input and no control in their claims costs expenses, exposures, and their reduction. This places them at a disadvantage in relation to insurance (premium) pricing. Modern hospitals have both a financial and professional need to implement a risk and claims management system if they are to review professional liability financial security and profitability properly.

Most hospitals enjoy an excellent relationship with their insurance agent or broker. With encouragement, the agent or broker will share information on premium breakdown, insurance rating concepts, underwriting rules, loss history, and claim data. Insurance premiums are the end result of cost factors such as underwriting, claims handling, acquisition costs (commission), marketing, overhead, growth, actuarial services, profit, etc. Once management understands the factors comprising the insurance premium, it will be in a better position to comprehend some of the cost elements that must be assumed if the hospital is considering a self-insured program.

Hospitals that carry primary commercial insurance should become actively involved in the claims-handling system of the carrier. This will allow them input in resolving their own claims and they can develop a claims management system while providing valuable assistance to their insurer. Hospitals that understand their true exposure from an insurance viewpoint will be better informed and able to make intelligent decisions regarding the choices of first-dollar commercial insurance coverage, deductibles, expense-excluded policies, self-insurance, captives, etc.

There are many valid reasons for carrying first-dollar commercial coverages. However, as health care facilities become more knowledgeable about insurance mechanisms, cost factors, and financial alternatives, they will find additional opportunities to alter the traditional commercial insurance policies. Moreover, they will discover that the insurance industry often is willing to share or change the risk-bearing relationship if the hospitals are willing to work toward changing the risk exposure.

UNDERSTANDING THE SELF-INSURED CONCEPT

The hospital professional and general liability self-insured concept started in the mid-1970s and is directly related to the nonavailability or excessive premium charges for professional liability coverages that emerged during the malpractice crisis. As professional liability insurance became unavailable at an affordable rate, many hospitals were forced to consider either going bare or funding a special trust account to handle professional liability exposures (as discussed in Chapter 8).

Insurance agencies and brokerage houses, responding to this new need, assisted hospitals in creating trust funds and offered service contracts. Hospitals for the first time discovered that their insurance policies included a variety of services. In analyzing this process, they learned that these services could be unbundled and contracted separately. They could obtain actuarial services from a variety of special organizations, contract on a fixed (annual) fee or per-claim basis with insurance adjustors, contract legal fees in a similar manner with law firms, etc. Further exploration revealed that insurance company premium costs were related to commissions, overhead, margins, profits, actuarial expenses, etc. All of these charges are added to the costs of paid claim and claim expenses.

Because of the nature and the circumstances of the insurance market, many hospitals became self-insured. To their surprise, many discovered that they were good actuarial risks and that their trust funds could be managed internally and could indirectly increase their net worth. Many began to take an active role in lowering their risk exposure through sophisticated risk and loss reduction programs controlled through risk management and quality assurance professionals.

Self-insurance now has expanded into areas such as excess and reinsurance, rate-making decisions, creation of captive insurance or reinsurance companies, in-house claims departments, and sophisticated risk and claims management systems. Educational programs for board members, medical staff professionals, and hospital employees now are commonplace.

Thus, the self-insurance concept provides an alternative for some hospitals. To be feasible, the concept needs experienced and qualified insurance/claims management personnel and a priority commitment by administration and board toward increasing the quality of care at all levels. As noted earlier, managers should be qualified to manage claim exposures, educate, adjust claims, and handle the special relationships with the insurance agent/broker as well as the excess and reinsurance carriers. To establish these relationships properly, risk/claims managers must demonstrate the ability to handle and resolve claims exposures in a professional manner and to negotiate rates with various insurance markets.

Caution is counseled for health care institutions considering self-insurance. For such an endeavor to be successful, total commitment is required from the board of trustees directors, administration and the professional staff. If this commitment is genuine, active, and administered properly, the trust and cooperation of medical staff members will be forthcoming. Their commitment and cooperation will form the cornerstone of any self-insured program related to professional liability exposures.

Self-insured programs should not be undertaken without definitive research covering the past claim history of the hospital and its medical staff members.

Consideration of procedures performed, review of medical staff activities, evaluation of the community, and current legal and medical standards is a must. The study should include the evaluation of outside resources and the costs related to services offered by the agent or broker, excess insurance carrier, defense counsel, actuarial services, outside experts, etc.

In summary, hospitals considering self-insuring professional liability exposure should be well versed in the problems that have caused many insurance companies to withdraw from the marketplace. In other words, hospitals should ask: If all this is so good, why did so many insurers drop such coverage or raise rates prohibitively? Hospitals should be aware that insurance industry efforts to reduce physician and hospital liability exposures have had questionable results. Conversely, many hospitals have enjoyed substantial financial success following the creation of self-insured trust funds or captive insurance companies. Examination of successful hospitals will show that they properly researched the project and committed substantial internal resources to assure the success of their program.

Key factors in the prolonged success of these programs involve the professional handling of claims, an organized claims management system, and the overall cooperation of everyone at all levels. Continuing educational efforts and communication at all levels also are of paramount importance.

EXCESS COVERAGE ABOVE SELF-INSURANCE

Hospitals that have elected to self-insure for a primary layer of professional liability (malpractice) exposure have the following concerns:

1. assuring effective and appropriate claims handling and reporting
2. avoiding conflict with members of the medical staff
3. coordinating major claims exposures with the excess or umbrella commercial insurer that underwrites the coverage above the self-insured retention
4. monitoring and negotiating the cost of commercial excess coverage
5. setting realistic reserves, to be charged against that self-insured retention
6. accumulating appropriate actuarial data to determine funding requirements.

Hospitals that self-insure professional liability exposures must employ (either internally or externally) qualified claims handling and management expertise, as noted earlier. A major concern is to understand and predict the excess and reinsurance markets. Several factors are important in understanding the commercial insurance market when dealing with professional liability coverages:

1. The insurance market contains many often perplexing variables.
2. The excess market in professional liability is limited; i.e., there are relatively few excess insurers worldwide.

3. The reinsurance market for commercial insurers (in professional liability) is today severely restricted in capacity.
4. High-value exposure/specialty insurance (such as medical malpractice) is rapidly becoming an unpredictable market.
5. Insurance industry predictions indicate that only four to five major domestic carriers may remain in the near future.
6. Indications are that traditional occurrence coverage will be replaced by claims-made coverage.

In evaluating these factors, it must be remembered that premium cost is directly related to loss and expense experience. Data accumulation by the self-insured hospital must be statistically accurate.

Understandably, the insurance industry prefers to write good risks and often will negotiate favorable rates for a statistically proved good risk. Of course, there are exceptions, and medical professional liability coverage is one area in which negotiations are somewhat hampered. This problem is related in large part to the concept of spreading the risk through many exposures (i.e., the insurance law of large numbers). It is further complicated by legal trends and jury attitudes. It takes only one multimillion-dollar verdict to eliminate the premium from many hospitals.

Conversely, however, responsible insurers are in the business of underwriting good risks for a fair rate. If the self-insured hospital is able to demonstrate an acceptable loss ratio and effective claims and risk management through proper reporting, the commercial excess insurer will consider rate adjustment. Reporting results and claims history in some instances can be improved greatly with the assistance of the agent or broker.

When dealing with the excess insurer through the hospital agent or broker, the following negotiating factors should be considered:

1. The agent/broker receives a commission (fee) for services. The fee should relate to the activity performed on the hospital's behalf.
2. An effective and accurate claims management system is necessary to report accurately the results of the hospital's experience.
3. The self-insured hospital has unbundled the insurance premium components. The hospital is paying directly for adjuster services, actuarial projections, claims management costs, legal services, etc. Therefore, the commercial insurance costs (premium) should be adjusted accordingly.
4. Insurance premiums are based on projected losses as determined by experience. If the hospital demonstrates that its claims management system performs well, the rates should decrease over time. Conversely, if the loss ratio is high and affects the excess insurer, the rates will increase.
5. There is direct financial risk exposure in self-insuring.

6. A properly structured self-insurance program should provide for a flexible level of insurance. A properly evaluated self-insurance program should be able to deal with the fluctuating rates of the excess commercial market; i.e., it is important to be able to adjust the retention and excess commercial insurance costs based on experience and business considerations.
7. The relationship with the agents or brokers cannot be overstated. They must keep the hospital risk and/or claims manager fully informed of the changing market well in advance of renewal dates. This will allow for preplanning and adjustments in the program.
8. Self-insurance is not risk transfer, it is risk retention. Finance personnel will be able to increase the retention trust fund through interest accrued on the unused portion of that retention only if the hospital enjoys a reduced claims cost.

In summary, purchasing excess insurance over a retention program need not be a mystery. The risk/claims manager must fully understand the insurance industry mechanisms for rate setting. If industry standards and concepts are observed, the hospital, performing within these standards, will find itself in a more favorable position to obtain excellent rates. The strength of its position in negotiating cost is related to the statistical reporting of its paid claims and expense factors. If the institution has experienced adverse claims costs, it can safely assume that the excess insurance company will review that claims history and increase premiums.

As stated earlier, not all hospitals should self-insure. Each should carefully review its claims experience, financial capabilities, and legal trends in the area.

POTENTIAL CONFLICTS IN SELF-INSURANCE

As in all business considerations, the possibility of conflict within a self-insured retention program poses many potential problems. These should be identified, isolated, and resolved in advance of the actual implementation of the program. This will greatly enhance the chances for the success of any self-insured program. Actual or potential conflicts raise the following questions:

1. Are there potential conflict situations between any board member and the hospital's self-insured programs? This could involve, for example, insurance agents, adjusting firms, legal counsel, etc. No conflict exists if the board is aware of, understands, and approves these relationships. Many times these arrangements can be beneficial to the hospital and strengthen the system.
2. Will any board member or hospital employee receive compensation for services? If so, the roles should be outlined clearly to convert potential conflicts into strengths to enhance and clarify the program.

3. Are there potential or actual conflicts between the management system and key personnel in hospital administration? For example, would a claims investigation following an incident related to equipment failure prove embarrassing to a particular department or division? Could this conflict be resolved in a positive manner to avoid a recurrence?
4. Will the personalities involved clash? For example, would the nursing department view a claims department investigation of one of its employees as assisting or hindering its overall goal?
5. Will the facility use outside independent adjustors? If so, confidentiality and tact are major factors to be considered. Are the adjustors related to the hospital in any way?
6. Will the claims personnel for the self-insured hospital (whether internal or external) have access to sensitive and sometimes embarrassing situations? There may be some unavoidable conflicts between what is the best approach in resolving a claim and what may be in the best interest of the hospital as viewed overall. For example, an emergency room physician may be performing marginally at best. The hospital will view it as necessary to keep the emergency room open until it can replace the physician with one more experienced or competent in emergency medicine (or until a contract expires).
7. How can claims managers work effectively if they cannot balance the relationships among the board, administration, and medical staff? There are frequent built-in conflicts that must be resolved.
8. Can (or should) the claims management system protect critical sources and delicate claims information from high management or board members? For example, defense counsel may feel that it is important to keep certain facts about a case completely confidential.
9. Are there actual or potential business conflicts between a board member or an employee of the hospital that can affect the claim outcome? For example, is the company contracting to provide services (such as maintenance or equipment) owned or controlled by a hospital employee or board member?
10. If the hospital is required to pay a claim because of the negligence of a medical staff member, will administration and the board allow the hospital to sue the doctor for indemnification?

These are examples of possible conflict considerations that should be analyzed before it is decided to self-insure. The hospital must evaluate both the cost and personnel factors required by self-insurance. If actual or potential conflict situations exist, they should be dealt with honestly before the hospital self-insures. If handled properly, potential conflicts almost always can be resolved to the hospital board's satisfaction.

THE CAPTIVE CONCEPT

Captive insurance or reinsurance companies usually are special interest entities owned by a parent corporation, association, or special interest group. From a pure claims management viewpoint, they do not differ significantly from any other type of insurance carrier except that they usually have closer financial and interpersonal relationships among the owners, insureds, and employees.

The claim-handling functions can be done either by employed members of the company or by an outside contractor. The structure of the captive, advantages and disadvantages, tax considerations, etc., are important but are not discussed here.

As most captives have a limited or restricted goal, special areas of claims management expertise may be required. If the captive company is created to insure medical professional liability, the claims department may need substantial assistance from members of the medical profession in addition to firms having expertise in medical malpractice law. The adjusters and claims manager need to be familiar with medical terminology and state laws involving areas of concern such as informed consent, statutes of limitations, and other special knowledge areas.

As with self-insurance or retention programs, captive insurance companies usually make the insureds more aware of their risks and introduce more sophisticated loss and risk control efforts in the hospital. The claims management system often is involved in identifying these risks from claims files and in assisting in the search for ways to change a situation or procedure to prevent a similar claim situation from recurring.

In considering the claims management function for a captive insurance company, the relationship of the adjuster and claims system to the insured should be considered carefully and the anticipated role in risk reduction and/or risk control outlined carefully before the adjuster handles any claims. The adjuster's role with hospital counsel also must be defined carefully to avoid any potential conflicts or problems within administration.

Chapter 11

Structured Settlements

Joseph M. O'Reilly and Charles M. Fischesser

Traditionally, personal injury and wrongful death cases have been resolved by a lump sum cash payment to the plaintiff. However, since the early 1970s, structured settlements have been used with increasing frequency as an effective technique. Many casualty insurers and self-insurers use this settlement option, not only in multimillion-dollar catastrophic losses but in claims as low as $5,000.

A structured or individualized settlement can best be defined as an arrangement where one or more payments will be made to the plaintiff in the future. These can be made in conjunction with cash payments at the time of settlement to cover out-of-pocket expenses, payment of attorney fees, etc. Future payments can be made monthly, quarterly, semiannually, annually, or at agreed-upon dates.

FUNDING VEHICLES FOR STRUCTURED SETTLEMENTS

Self-Funding

An insurer or corporation can agree to make periodic payments out of general operating or corporate funds. Sufficient reserves would have to be maintained in anticipation of the agreed-upon payments. This also is known as a self-insured annuity. Certain tax deductions are allowable under this method.

Bond/Trust

Under this arrangement, current funds are invested in government bonds, with the proceeds accruing to the plaintiff. A trust is established and the trustee invests the money, collects the income, and distributes it subject to the contingency requirements of the settlement or judgment. For example:

Principal invested: $100,000
U.S. Treasury Bond: 10% rate of return
Term of investment: 30 years
Annual investment yield: $10,000
Principal returned at end of 30 years: $100,000
Total settlement proceeds: $400,000.

Annuity

The instrument used most frequently for managing the payout of settlement funds over long periods is the annuity. A settlement annuity is an insurance contract purchased from a life insurance company that provides predetermined periodic payments in return for a single premium paid at settlement. In simple terms, the settlement annuity works in the reverse of life insurance. Whereas life insurance pays *upon* the death of a policyholder, the settlement annuity generally pays *until* the person's death. The annuity can be made for a period certain, for life, or a period certain and life.

TYPES OF ANNUITIES

Life Annuity

Standard Life Annuity

This is a policy under which payments are made for life. Its cost depends on the age and sex of the annuitant at the date of purchase. Life insurance companies generally provide quotes on a cost per $1,000 of monthly income. The cost (as of March, 1985) of $1,000 of lifetime monthly income for a 25-year-old male, level payments, is $110,715 (Connecticut General Life Insurance Company).

Substandard Life Annuity

This policy agrees to make payments for what appears to be a diminished life expectancy. The chief price determinants here are age, sex, and general health of the annuitant at the date of purchase. Companies generally use a rated-up age approach to substandard life annuities. In the example above, the lifetime annuity for a healthy 25-year-old male costs $110,715 per $1,000 of monthly income. If this same individual suffered a spinal cord injury, his life expectancy would be diminished by *X* years, the *X* to be determined by a life insurance company underwriter or physician. If the life expectancy is diminished, the payout period should be shorter than normal and the carrier's quote will be less per $1,000 of monthly income. If the same 25-year-old were rated as having the life expectancy of a 51-year-old male, $1,000 of monthly income would cost $101,645.

Annuity Certain

This policy will make payments for a stipulated or guaranteed period. Age, sex, and general health have no bearing on the cost. Thus, a $1,000-per-month level for 20 years certain would cost $99,679, be it paid to a 15-year-old male or an 18-year-old female.

Period Certain and Life

In this policy, payments are made for life with a stipulated period of payments being certain or guaranteed. Because it is a life annuity, its price is determined by the individual's age, sex, general health, and by the designated period certain. The cost of $1,000 of monthly income for a 25-year-old male, 20 years certain and life, is $112,045.

Lump Sum Certain

This policy provides a single payment or a series of payments at agreed-upon dates—all at one time, annually, every two years, every five years, etc., for a stipulated period. Age, sex, and general health are not considerations in pricing; $10,000 paid every five years for 30 years would cost $12,160.

Lump Sum Life Contingent

Under this policy, payments are made at a designated date, contingent on the annuitant's being alive on that date. Age, sex, and general health are price determinants and the cost should be less than a lump sum certain to be paid on the same date.

Installment Refund

This policy makes payments for life, but if the annuitant dies before the amount being paid out equals the amount paid in (the premium), the purchaser will receive installment payments until both are equal. The cost of $1,000 per month for life for a 25-year-old male, installment refund, is $111,204.

Cash Refund

This policy is similar to that of an installment refund, except that instead of the purchaser's receiving installment payments, the difference is paid out in a single cash sum.

Joint and Survivor

This policy agrees to make payments for life (and period certain) jointly to two individuals. Age, sex, and general health are price determinants and payments generally are made as long as either individual is living. The cost of $1,000 per month for life, 20 years certain, for a 25-year-old male and a 22-year-old female is $116,152.

Increasing Annuities

Compound Annuities

These policies make payments for life and/or period certain, with the monthly or annual payments increasing at a stipulated annual compound rate of interest. Age, sex, and general health are price determinants for life annuities only. The cost to provide a 25-year-old male $1,000 of monthly income for life, 30 years certain, increasing at 6 percent annually, is $225,687. The increased cost over a level annuity reflects the 6 percent increasing annual payments. Increasing annuities generally are used to offset the impact of inflation.

Step-Increasing Annuities

These are payment plans that remain level for a period and increase in a step pattern.

PRICING OF SETTLEMENT ANNUITIES

It was demonstrated previously that the pricing mechanisms for settlement annuities are based on different criteria. Generally, annuity pricing models include the following considerations.

Life Annuities

Mortality or Life Expectancy

Based on life insurance company experience as well as general population experience, each prospective annuitant or insured has a predetermined life expectancy. This is not to say that an individual will live a specific number of years; rather, the expectancy is based more on the law of averages taken over a particular population or members of a particular group who have purchased annuities or life insurance. Some annuitants will not live to their presumed life expectancy while others will live longer than expected.

Investment Considerations

Life insurance companies are major investors in the American economy, typically in instruments that have a consistent record of achievement. In other words, they invest conservatively. A typical life insurance company's portfolio might include U.S. government bonds, state bonds, special revenue and public utility bonds, preferred and common stocks, mortgages, and real estate. A company's ability to invest wisely and provide a good rate of return will go a long way in determining how competitive it will be in the insurance marketplace.

Expenses

As with all companies, life insurers are subject to a cost of doing business. These costs include normal operating expenses, taxes, marketing expense, etc. Expenses vary from company to company, but those that can keep expenses to a minimum will be more effective in maintaining a competitive pricing mode.

Profit

Life insurance companies, as with all businesses, expect to make a profit for their shareholders or policyholders. If their pricing considerations are accurate, the average profit on annuities will be approximately 2 percent of the premium. As should be expected, mortality, return on investment, and expenses all have a bearing on profitability and determine where a company will place competitively in the marketplace.

Certain Annuities

In that certain or guaranteed annuities pay sums at or over a stipulated period of time without mortality considerations, the pricing model would include only the considerations of investment, expenses, and profit that were included in the life annuity analysis. The pricing of certain annuities involves little more than what a life insurance company can earn on its investment over a specific period of time, with considered expenses and a profit percentage included.

WHY A STRUCTURED SETTLEMENT?

Structured settlements provide plaintiffs with advantages that are not generally available through lump sum settlements. Foremost of these advantages are the savings of federal income tax dollars to the plaintiff, not only on the principal sum but also on the investment income inherent in the annuity. The guiding principle to this tax-free concept is the doctrine of "constructive receipt."

Constructive receipt can be described simply as making the principal sum of the settlement available to the plaintiff, either at the time of settlement or in the future (see later section on "Tax Guidelines and Principles"). Section 1.451-2(a) of the Income Tax Regulations provides that income, although not actually reduced to a taxpayer's possession, is constructively received by that individual in the taxable year in which it is credited to that person's account, set apart for that person, or otherwise made available so that the individual may draw upon it at any time.

Structured settlements provide other advantages to the plaintiff:

- protection against mismanagement of funds
- guaranteed income for life
- financial planning vehicle
- inflation protection through step-annuities, compounding annuities, or increasing lump-sum payments at designated intervals.

Advantages for the defendant include:

- reduced cost of claim
- promotion of settlement
- possible reversionary interest
- elimination of excessive judgment exposure.

Other beneficiaries include:

- The courts: (1) These settlements appeal to judges in guardianship cases. (2) They clear calendars by encouraging settlements.
- The public: There is no concern for the dissipation of funds requiring the plaintiff to be a ward of the state.
- The plaintiff's attorney: (1) The need to provide investment advice to the client is eliminated. (2) Structuring of fees can provide for savings and/or sheltering.
- The policy beneficiary: Payments can flow free of income tax to the plaintiff's estate if arranged properly.

- The life insurance company: The carrier receives the advance premium and can evaluate its long-term investment considerations more appropriately.

STRUCTURED SETTLEMENT CONSIDERATIONS

In negotiating a cash settlement, a number of questions must be asked before a settlement offer is advanced, among them the following:

- What is the liability?
- What are the special damages?
- What is the plaintiff's economic loss?
- What is the verdict potential?
- What is the settlement value?

The assessment in a structured settlement is no different. Once a settlement value has been placed on a claim, the question is: ''Does this case present the possibility of a structured settlement?'' If the answer is yes, then steps can be taken to initiate the process.

There are two ways of analyzing the potential of a case: 1) value analysis and 2) needs analysis.

Value Analysis

A value analysis situation assumes that a plaintiff has fully recovered from injuries and has no expenses or damages to claim in the future. Damages such as medical expenses, lost wages, pain and suffering, etc., are assessed and a value is placed on the claim. Generally, a value analysis situation will require a minimum claim value of $40,000 to present a reasonable lifetime income plan.

For example, David A. was a 22–year–old male who was injured in an automobile accident. His claim was valued at $60,000 and lifetime income seemed appropriate. An initial settlement proposal was developed at $40,000.

Benefit	*Cost*	*Certain Payout*	*Yield to normal life expectancy*
1. Cash at settlement of $17,500, inclusive of counsel fees	$ 17,500	$ 17,500	$ 17,500
2. Immediate annuity of $200 per month for life, 30 years certain	22,500	22,500	144,480
Totals	40,000	89,500	161,980

This proposal was developed using the following methodology.

Generally, the first consideration, once an offer value has been reached, should be the attorney fee. Unless otherwise indicated, the fee should be one-third of the offer value. On a $40,000 offer, the fee would be $13,333.

Cash at settlement, or upfront cash as it often is referred to, also is an important consideration—sometimes the most important. The amount of cash that should be made available is descretionary but for a first–time offer, 10% of the offer value is appropriate. In David A.'s case, the cash at settlement is $4,000. The cash at settlement and attorney fees should be combined into a single benefit amount for purposes of the offer sheet. Subtracting the cash at settlement and attorney fees from the offer value leaves approximately $22,500 for annuity purposes. The type of annuity chosen is left to the discretion of the designer of benefits.

In David A.'s case, a life annuity with a 30–year certain feature was selected. The $22,500 invested produces $200 of monthly income, which is the minimum monthly amount that should be considered for a life income situation. Amounts under $200 are difficult to sell in most situations. Thus, with $200 of monthly income and $17,500 paid in cash, the minimum value to be considered is $40,000.

If David A.'s case were valued at a higher figure, and a proposal developed at $150,000, it might look as follows:

Benefit	*Cost*	*Certain Payout*	*Yield to normal life expectancy*
1. Cash at settlement of $65,000, inclusive of counsel fees	$ 65,000	$ 65,000	$ 65,000
2. Immediate annuity of $500 per month for life, 30 years certain	56,320	180,000	361,200
3. Lump sums certain as follows: $10,000 in 5 years; 20,000 in 10 years; 30,000 in 15 years; 40,000 in 20 years; 50,000 in 25 years; 60,000 in 30 years	28,682	210,000	210,000
Totals	150,002	455,000	636,200

With the offer value at $150,000, the cash at settlement and attorney fees were assessed at $65,000. It was decided to provide monthly life income supplemented by periodic lump sums every five years for 30 years. If the designer of benefits wished, the total annuity premium ($85,000) could have been deposited into the life annuity.

Both of these settlement proposals were developed assuming that there was no input from the plaintiff and that each proposal would be negotiated further beyond the initial proposal. As can be seen in the $150,000 proposal, there is greater flexibility in benefit development than the $40,000 case because of the higher case value. Nonetheless, the $40,000 case produces the same proportionate yield assuming no reinvestment.

In initial structured settlement offers, the defendant generally does not know what benefits the plaintiff might accept and the plaintiff might not know what to request. It is left to the discretion of the designer of the settlement plan to use ingenuity to make the initial structured settlement offer attractive.

Needs Analysis

Needs analysis is precisely what the title implies: It is a structured analysis based upon the needs of the plaintiff. This type of situation can occur in both catastrophic and noncatastrophic injury situations.

In a noncatastrophic injury situation, for example, the plaintiff or attorney may be approached first about considering a structured settlement and may be solicited for ideas as to how the benefits could be packaged, i.e., monthly income, annual income, periodic lump sums, a single lump sum, etc. In a case where a plaintiff might wish to use the monthly income toward a mortgage payment, a double tax benefit could result. Assuming a $500 mortgage payment and a $500 monthly annuity, the annuity would be appropriate to use as a payment source for the mortgage payment. Thus, the $500 would be paid as tax-free income and a deduction could be taken at tax time for any mortgage interest included in the monthly payment.

In like situations, a substantial lump sum could be paid at the age of majority as a nest egg to begin a work career or a business venture or, as another alternative, grandparents could establish education funds for their grandchildren. The opportunities are limitless.

It is in the catastrophic situation, however, that structured settlements far outweigh the benefits of an equivalent cash settlement. A factual situation offers a good example.

Marcia M. was an energetic and athletic 16–year–old girl who not only was an all-state high school softball player but also excelled at track and field. Her goal was to be a world–renowned distance runner. She entered a hospital for surgical repair of cartilage torn in training. While under anesthesia, Marcia suffered a cardiac arrest that rendered her quadriplegic. At the time of settlement considerations, a $252,000 hospital lien had been filed, hospital per diem was $178, monthly physical rehabilitation was $2,200, and miscellaneous expenses were running $12,000 annually.

The jury potential of a case of this nature could be anywhere from $1 million to $10 million, depending upon the jurisdiction. However, this can be analyzed from a needs standpoint to develop a settlement value.

1. Assume the lien will be repaid in full, although it may be negotiated by the plaintiff attorney.
2. Assume that the parents have brought a claim of their own for loss of society and affection.
3. Assume that Marcia would have graduated from college and entered the work force.

Medical records were submitted to a number of life insurance carriers for underwriting consideration. Marcia was rated as having the life expectancy of a 74–year–old female. The settlement considerations were as follows:

1. The medical lien would be paid in full.
2. Cash of $100,000 would be offered for future miscellaneous expenses.
3. Cash of $50,000 would be offered to the parents as part of their claim.
4. Marcia would have entered the work force at $20,000 annually; inflation was computed at 4 percent per annum.
5. Future medical expenses would have to be accounted for.
6. Attorney fees would be one-third of settlement value.

Settlement benefits would be developed accordingly:

1. Cash at settlement to Marcia would be $350,000 (cost $350,000).
2. Cash at settlement to the parents would be $50,000 (cost $50,000).
3. A monthly annuity to Marcia woiuld be $1,833 for life, increasing at 4 percent annually, 15 years certain for loss of earning capacity (cost $215,735).
4. An installment refund annuity would be $5,414 per month for life, increasing at 4 percent annually to cover the per diem hospital costs—$178 × 365 days divided by 12 months (cost $567,241).
5. An installment refund annuity would be $2,200 per month for life, increasing at 4 percent annually to cover physical rehabilitation costs (cost $230,500).
6. An installment refund annuity would be $1,000 per month for life, increasing at 4 percent annually to cover miscellaneous expenses (cost $104,773).
7. A $1,500 monthly annuity would be provided for the 40–year–old parents, increasing at 3 percent annually for life (cost $226,704).

One method of determining a one-third attorney contingency fee is to total the cost of cash and annuities and divide by two. This figure will be equal to one-third of the combined cost of cash, annuities, and attorney fees. Using this method in Marcia's case, the attorney fee amounts to $872,500. The settlement value and subsequent proposal was concluded as shown in Exhibit 11–1.

Exhibit 11–1 Settlement Value and Subsequent Proposal

Benefit	*Cost*	*Certain Payout*	*Yield to normal life expectancy*
1. Cash at settlement to Marcia of $350,000, inclusive of liens	$ 350,000	$ 350,000	$ 350,000
2. Immediate annuity to Marcia of $1,833 per month for life, increasing at 4 percent annually, 15 years certain	215,735	400,470	7,921,130
3. Installment refund annuity to Marcia of $8,615 per month for life, increasing at 4 percent annually	902,619	902,619*	40,944,320
4. Cash at settlement to Marcia's parents of $50,000	50,000	50,000	50,000
5. Joint and survivor annuity to Marcia's parents of $1,500 per month for life, increasing at 3 percent annually, 20 years certain	226,704	483,665	1,953,730
6. Counsel fees of $100,000 at settlement and $206,775 per year for 5 years	872,500	1,133,875	1,173,875
Totals:	2,617,558	3,320,629	52,393,055

*The amount will be paid minimally to the plaintiff or to the annuity owner in the event of premature death.

Annual annuity increases, annual income, and cumulative totals are delineated in Exhibits 11–2, 11–3, and 11–4.

APPROACHING A STRUCTURED SETTLEMENT

Occasionally, defendants try to sell the future value of structured settlements as an important reason why plaintiffs should accept them. It is precisely this approach that has caused some plaintiff attorneys to be skeptical of the concept.

In a reported case, a New York plaintiff attorney demanded $600,000 in settlement of a products liability claim on behalf of his client. The defendant insurer offered to settle on a periodic payment basis of $20,000 per year for 40 years certain. The cost to the defendant to purchase an annuity to fund these payments was $176,000. The defendant insurer then tried to impress upon the plaintiff attorney that while the settlement demand was $600,000, an offer of $800,000 in benefits actually was being made. The transparency of the offer is evident. If, in fact, the settlement value was indeed $600,000, an investment of

Exhibit 11–2 Example of Life Annuity and Lump Sum

Annuitant: MARCIA M.
DOB: 05-01-69
Normal Life Expectancy: 71.66 years

Compound: 4.00%
Certain Period: 15 years

Year	*Annuitant's age*	*Monthly annuity*	*Lump sum*	*Annual income*	*Cumulative total*
1	16	$ 1,833 *	$350,000 *	$ 371,996	
2	17	1,906 *		22,872	
3	18	1,983 *		23,796	
4	19	2,062 *		24,744	
5	20	2,144 *		25,728	$ 469,136
6	21	2,230 *		26,760	
7	22	2,319 *		27,828	
8	23	2,412 *		28,944	
9	24	2,509 *		30,108	
10	25	2,609 *		31,308	614,084
11	26	2,713 *		32,556	
12	27	2,822 *		33,864	
13	28	2,935 *		35,220	
14	29	3,052 *		36,624	
15	30	3,174 *		38,088	790,436
16	31	3,301		39,612	
17	32	3,433		41,196	
18	33	3,570		42,840	
19	34	3,713		44,556	
20	35	3,862		46,344	1,004,984
21	36	4,016		48,192	
22	37	4,177		50,124	
23	38	4,344		52,128	
24	39	4,518		54,216	
25	40	4,699		56,388	1,266,032
26	41	4,886		58,632	
27	42	5,082		60,984	
28	43	5,285		63,420	
29	44	5,497		65,964	
30	45	5,716		68,592	1,583,624
31	46	5,945		71,340	
32	47	6,183		74,196	
33	48	6,430		77,160	
34	49	6,687		80,244	
35	50	6,955		83,460	1,970,024
36	51	7,233		86,796	
37	52	7,522		90,264	
38	53	7,823		93,876	
39	54	8,136		97,632	
40	55	8,462		101,544	2,440,136
41	56	8,800		105,600	

Exhibit 11–2 continued

Year	*Annuitant's age*	*Monthly annuity*	*Lump sum*	*Annual income*	*Cumulative total*
42	57	9,152		109,824	
43	58	9,518		114,216	
44	59	9,899		118,788	
45	60	10,295		123,540	3,012,104
46	61	10,707		128,484	
47	62	11,135		133,620	
48	63	11,581		138,972	
49	64	12,044		144,528	
50	65	12,526		150,312	3,708,020
51	66	13,027		156,324	
52	67	13,548		162,576	
53	68	14,089		169,068	
54	69	14,653		175,836	
55	70	15,239		182,868	4,554,692
56	71	15,849		190,188	
57	72	16,483		197,796	
58	73	17,142		205,704	
59	74	17,828		213,936	
60	75	18,541		222,492	5,584,808
61	76	19,282		231,384	
62	77	20,054		240,648	
63	78	20,856		250,272	
64	79	21,690		260,280	
65	80	22,558		270,696	6,838,088
66	81	23,460		281,520	
67	82	24,398		292,776	
68	83	25,374		304,488	
69	84	26,389		316,668	
70	85	27,445		329,340	8,362,880
71	86	28,543		342,516	
72	87	29,684		356,208	
			350,000		9,061,604

*Represents Certain Payments.

Source: Structure One, Brokers' Service Corp., Providence, R.I., © 1983.

that amount over a 40–year period in a settlement annuity would produce $68,120, annually or $2,724,800 for the 40–year term.

Both the plaintiff and defendant must benefit from a structured settlement if it is to work properly. The plaintiff's primary benefit is the tax-free nature of the funds; the defendant should benefit in a cost of claim lower than that of a cash settlement. The defendant generally purchases and maintains ownership in an annuity to fund its obligation to the plaintiff. A single premium is paid to a life insurance company

Exhibit 11–3 Example of Installment Refund Annuity

Annuitant: MARCIA M.
DOB: 05-01-69
Normal Life Expectancy: 71.66 years

Compound: 4.00%

Year	*Annuitant's age*	*Monthly annuity*	*Lump sum*	*Annual income*	*Cumulative total*
1	16	$ 8,615		$ 103,380	
2	17	8,960		107,520	
3	18	9,318		111,816	
4	19	9,691		116,292	
5	20	10,078		120,936	$ 559,944
6	21	10,481		125,772	
7	22	10,901		130,812	
8	23	11,337		136,044	
9	24	11,790		141,480	
10	25	12,262		147,144	1,241,196
11	26	12,752		153,024	
12	27	13,262		159,144	
13	28	13,793		165,516	
14	29	14,345		172,140	
15	30	14,918		179,016	2,070,036
16	31	15,515		186,180	
17	32	16,136		193,632	
18	33	16,781		201,372	
19	34	17,452		209,424	
20	35	18,150		217,800	3,078,444
21	36	18,877		226,524	
22	37	19,632		235,584	
23	38	20,417		245,004	
24	39	21,234		254,808	
25	40	22,083		264,996	4,305,360
26	41	22,966		275,592	
27	42	23,885		286,620	
28	43	24,840		298,080	
29	44	25,834		310,008	
30	45	26,867		322,404	5,798,064
31	46	27,942		335,304	
32	47	29,060		348,720	
33	48	30,222		362,664	
34	49	31,431		377,172	
35	50	32,688		392,256	7,614,180
36	51	33,996		407,952	
37	52	35,355		424,260	
38	53	36,770		441,240	
39	54	38,240		458,880	
40	55	39,770		477,240	9,823,752
41	56	41,361		496,332	

Exhibit 11–3 continued

Year	Annuitant's age	Monthly annuity	Lump sum	Annual income	Cumulative total
42	57	43,015		516,180	
43	58	44,736		536,832	
44	59	46,525		558,300	
45	60	48,386		580,632	12,512,028
46	61	50,322		603,864	
47	62	52,335		628,020	
48	63	54,428		653,136	
49	64	56,605		679,260	
50	65	58,869		706,428	15,782,736
51	66	61,224		734,688	
52	67	63,673		764,076	
53	68	66,220		794,640	
54	69	68,869		826,428	
55	70	71,623		859,476	19,762,044
56	71	74,488		893,856	
57	72	77,468		929,616	
58	73	80,567		966,804	
59	74	83,789		1,005,468	
60	75	87,141		1,045,692	24,603,480
61	76	90,626		1,087,512	
62	77	94,251		1,131,012	
63	78	98,021		1,176,252	
64	79	101,942		1,223,304	
65	80	106,020		1,272,240	30,493,800
66	81	110,261		1,323,132	
67	82	114,671		1,376,052	
68	83	119,258		1,431,096	
69	84	124,028		1,488,336	
70	85	128,990		1,547,880	37,660,296
71	86	134,149		1,609,788	
72	87	139,515		1,674,180	
				40,944,264	

*Represents Certain Payments.

Source: Structure One, Copyright Brokers' Service Corp., Providence, R.I., © 1983.

to fund the agreed–upon benefits. If the life insurer becomes insolvent, the defendant still has the obligation to the plaintiff for the payments. This is known as a defendant's contingent liability, and it is because of this that the defendant should realize a discount off the full cash value of the settlement. If a plaintiff attorney is unwilling to provide such a discount, the defendant should reassess its position as to the viability of a periodic payment approach.

Exhibit 11–4 Example of Parent's Life Annuity

Annuitant: LAURA AND STEVEN
DOB: 03-10-55 (LAURA) Compound: 3.00%
Normal Life Expectancy: 56.73 years (LAURA) Certain Period: 20 years

Year	*Annuitant's age*	*Monthly annuity*	*Lump sum*	*Annual income*	*Cumulative total*
1	30	$1,500 *	$50,000 *	$ 18,000	
2	31	1,545 *		18,540	
3	32	1,591 *		19,092	
4	33	1,639 *		19,668	
5	34	1,688 *		20,256	$ 95,556
6	35	1,739 *		20,868	
7	36	1,791 *		21,492	
8	37	1,845 *		22,140	
9	38	1,900 *		22,800	
10	39	1,957 *		23,484	206,340
11	40	2,016 *		24,192	
12	41	2,076 *		24,912	
13	42	2,139 *		25,668	
14	43	2,203 *		26,436	
15	44	2,269 *		27,228	334,776
16	45	2,337 *		28,044	
17	46	2,407 *		28,884	
18	47	2,479 *		29,748	
19	48	2,554 *		30,648	
20	49	2,630 *		31,560	483,660
21	50	2,709		32,508	
22	51	2,790		33,480	
23	52	2,874		34,488	
24	53	2,960		35,520	
25	54	3,049		36,588	656,244
26	55	3,141		37,692	
27	56	3,235		38,820	
28	57	3,332		39,984	
29	58	3,432		41,184	
30	59	3,535		42,420	856,344
31	60	3,641		43,692	
32	61	3,750		45,000	
33	62	3,863		46,356	
34	63	3,978		47,736	
35	64	4,098		49,176	1,088,304
36	65	4,221		50,652	
37	66	4,347		52,164	
38	67	4,478		53,736	
39	68	4,612		55,344	
40	69	4,751		57,012	1,357,212
41	70	4,893		58,716	

Exhibit 11–4 continued

Year	*Annuitant's age*	*Monthly annuity*	*Lump sum*	*Annual income*	*Cumulative total*
42	71	5,040		60,480	
43	72	5,191		62,292	
44	73	5,347		64,164	
45	74	5,507		66,084	1,668,948
46	75	5,672		68,064	
47	76	5,843		70,116	
48	77	6,018		72,216	
49	78	6,198		74,376	
50	79	6,384		76,608	2,030,328
51	80	6,576		78,912	
52	81	6,773		81,276	
53	82	6,976		83,712	
54	83	7,186		86,232	
55	84	7,401		88,812	2,449,272
56	85	7,623		91,476	
57	86	7,852		94,224	
			50,000		2,634,972

*Represents Certain Payments.

Source: Structure One, Brokers' Service Corp., Providence, R.I., © 1983.

As an example of how a structured settlement can be negotiated to a successful conclusion, a defendant hospital evaluated a negligence action against it by an injured plaintiff at $500,000. The defendant felt that this was the full value of the plaintiff's loss, and if any larger amount demanded were demanded, the case would be allowed to proceed to trial. The hospital's attitude was that if it could save 10 percent off the full value of the claim (i.e., $50,000), a structured settlement would be an appropriate consideration.

The dollar value to begin a structured settlement offer is important to a successful negotiation. A figure of 60 percent to 65 percent of full cash settlement value is a credible first offer in most situations. (However, it should be noted that the individual facts of each case should be considered before arriving at the value of a first offer). Based on $500,000 full value, and a 65 percent first offer value, a structured settlement should be developed at a cost of $325,000 to the defendant. With this approach, a credible offer can be made and the defendant still has a range of $325,000 to $450,000 for further negotiation.

Once an offer of structured settlement is made, the plaintiff attorney will determine the present value or cost to the defendant and negotiations will then begin.

Exhibit 11–5 Example of a First–Time Offer

Benefit	*Cost*	*Certain payout*	*Yield to normal life expectancy*
1. Cash at settlement of $140,000, inclusive of counsel fees	$140,000	$140,000	$ 140,000
2. Immediate annuity of $1,025 per month for life, 30 years certain, with payments increasing at 3% annually	155,306	585,177	1,804,500
3. Lump sum certain payments as follows: $10,000 in 5 years; 20,000 in 10 years; 40,000 in 15 years; 95,000 in 20 years	29,785	165,000	165,000
	325,091	890,177	2,109,500

A $325,000 first–time offer could be developed as shown in Exhibit 11–5 for a 25–year–old male with a normal life expectancy of 57.06 years.

The plaintiff's counterproposal could be presented as follows:

Benefit	*Cost*	*Certain payout*	*Yield to normal life expectancy*
1. Cash at settlement of $250,000, inclusive of counsel fees	$ 250,000	$ 250,000	$ 250,000
2. Immediate annuity of $2,000 per month for life, 30 years certain, increasing at 3% annually	303,026	1,141,809	3,513,319
	$ 553,026	1,391,809	3,763,319

A suitable counteroffer could be proposed as follows:

Benefit	*Cost*	*Certain payout*	*Yield to normal life expectancy*
1. Cash at settlement of $175,000, inclusive of counsel fees	$ 175,000	$ 175,000	$ 175,000
2. Immediate annuity of $1,485 per month for life, 30 years certain, increasing at 3% annually	225,004	847,793	2,608,639
	$ 400,004	$1,022,793	$2,783,639

At this point in the negotiations, the $400,004 offer represents a 20 percent saving off the defendant's full cash value assessment of the claim's worth. The defendant continues to be in a position of evaluating how to proceed in order to achieve a saving off the full cash value of the settlement. The skill and knowledge of the defendant's negotiating team will play a large part in arriving at the final settlement figures. For example:

Benefit	*Cost*	*Certain payout*	*Yield to normal life expectancy*
1. Cash at settlement of $200,000, inclusive of counsel fees	$ 200,000	$ 200,000	$ 200,000
2. Immediate annuity of $1,575 per month for life, 30 years certain, increasing at 3% annually	$ 238,641	$ 899,175	$2,766,738
	$ 438,641	$1,099,175	$2,966,738

The final settlement amount represents a 12.4 percent saving off what the defendant was willing to pay in cash to settle the action. At the same time, the plaintiff will receive nearly $3 million in tax-free benefits if the person lives to full life expectancy. Both parties have derived a benefit and the settlement amount makes sense.

VARIETIES OF STRUCTURED SETTLEMENTS

The types of structured settlements are as varied as the collective imaginations of those who propose them. Some examples follow.

Lifetime Income

The most common form of periodic payment offers involves paying a monthly sum for a fixed period (period certain) or life. Combinations of these two can be made for a period certain and life. While payments under $100 a month are not generally accepted, any amount over $100 a month can be structured quite easily. Often, in Workers' Compensation situations, the insurer or self-insurer may wish to commute a long-term series of weekly payments to a monthly annuity. Assuming weekly Workers' Compensation payments of $120 per week for a 25-year-old male, settlement value can be determined as follows:

1. Cost of $480 monthly life annuity, 30 years certain	$53,378
2. Cash at settlement	5,000
Total	$58,378

The counsel fee is determined by taking the sum of 1 and 2 and dividing by .8 (the assumption is that in Workers' Compensation cases the attorney fee is 20 percent of the settlement amount). Counsel fee is $14,594. Thus the value of the settlement would be $72,972.

Conversely, if the commutation value is assessed at $75,000, the structuring of benefits can be developed as follows:

1. Counsel fee (20% of 75,000)	$15,000
2. Cash at settlement (10% of value)	7,500
	22,500
3. The remaining amount of $52,500 can be deposited into a life annuity that will provide $472 per month for life, 30 years certain for a 25-year-old male	52,488
Total	$74,988

If a counsel fee is to be paid, and cash at settlement is a consideration, again monthly payments at less than $100 are not attractive. Depending on the amount of the fee and cash, the base settlement value for an immediate monthly annuity payout should begin at about $40,000.

Lump-Sum Approach

If monthly income is not a consideration, but periodic lump-sum payments are, cases can be structured at under $40,000 of settlement value. For example:

	Cost	*Benefit*
Cash at settlement	$ 4,000	$ 4,000
Counsel fee	7,500	7,500
Lump-sum certain payments as follows:		
$ 5,000 in 5 years		
10,000 in 10 years		
15,000 in 15 years		
20,000 in 20 years	11,135	50,000
	$22,635	$61,500

The determining factor in this example is whether or not the plaintiff wishes to forgo monthly income in lieu of periodic lump sums at 5-year intervals.

Education Fund Approach

Cases involving minors can be ideally suited for the structuring of deferred payments. For example: John M., age 6, was struck by a car while riding his bicycle. Suit was brought against the car owner and case value was assessed at $15,000. A structured settlement was concluded as follows:

	Cost	*Benefit*
1. Cash (in trust) to the injured child of $2,500	$ 2,500	$ 2,500
2. Counsel fee	5,000	5,000
3. Education fund paying $8,425 annually at ages 18, 19, 20, and 21	7,498	33,700
Totals	$14,998	$41,200

By deferring the annuity 12 years to age 18, a substantial education fund was established. If John M. decides not to seek higher education at that time, the payments will be made in any event.

Deferred Approach

Charles F., a 47-year-old farm worker, used the structured settlement approach to establish a retirement fund for himself. Never vested in a retirement account, his settlement was concluded as follows:

Benefit	*Cost*	*Certain payout*	*Yield to normal life expectancy*
1. Cash at settlement of $15,000, inclusive of counsel fees	$ 15,000	$ 15,000	$ 15,000
2. A deferred annuity of 1,000 per month for life, beginning at age 60, 7 years certain	19,373	84,000	267,120
Totals	$ 34,373	$ 99,000	$282,120

This case was reserved at $45,000 and settlement authority was granted at $40,000. The insurer saved 14 percent off the settlement authority and Charles F. now had a retirement fund available, free of income tax.

TAX GUIDELINES AND PRINCIPLES

The tax principles for structured settlements relate to gross income as defined and how it relates as compensation for injuries and sickness. Section 104 of the Internal Revenue Code, Revenue Ruling 79-220, and the Periodic Payment Settlement Act of 1982 (Pub.L. 97-473) are the guiding tax principles relating to structured settlements.

Rulings and Decisions under the Internal Revenue Code of 1954

Section 61.–Gross Income Defined
26 C.F.R. § 1 61-1: Gross Income
Whether the recipient must include in gross income any part of monthly payments received in settlement of a damage suit. See. Rev. Rul. 79-220, below.

Section 104.–Compensation for injuries or sickness.
26 C.F.R. § 1.104-1: Compensation for injuries or sickness. (Also sections 61, 451; 1.61-1, 1.451-1.)

Damages; monthly payments; amount excludable. An insurance company purchased and retained exclusive ownership in a single premium annuity contract to fund monthly payments stipulated in settlement of a damage suit. The recipient may exclude the full amount of the payments from gross income under section 104(a)(2) of the Code rather than the discounted present value. Payments made to the estate after the recipient's death are also fully excludable.

Rev. Rul. 79-220

Issue

Does the exclusion from gross income provided by section 104(a)(2) of the Internal Revenue Code of 1954 apply to the full amount of monthly payments received in settlement of a damage suit or only to the discounted present value of such payments?

Holding

The exclusion from gross income provided by section 104(a)(2) of the Code applies to the full amount of monthly payments received by a plaintiff, so long as the plaintiff only has the right to receive monthly payments and did not have the actual or constructive receipt or the economic benefit of the lump-sum amount that was invested to yield the monthly payments. If a plaintiff predeceases the end of certain period annuity payment, any payments made to the plaintiff's estate under the settlement agreement are also excludable from income under section 104.

Elements of constructive receipt then are:

1. power over the money or investment of funds
2. availability upon demand

3. ability to change beneficiary once designated
4. deferment of funds upon request of taxpayer
5. authority to commute future payments to a lump sum
6. plaintiff can only be general creditor of defendant as insurer for future payments.

Periodic Payment Settlement Act of 1982 (Pub. L. No. 97-473)

In January of 1983, President Reagan signed into law the Periodic Payment Settlement Act, which had been passed into law by Congress in 1982. The PPSA codified the existing Rev. Rul. 79-220 and provided certainty as to the tax treatment of periodic payments settlements.

A new section of the Code (section 130. dealt with the tax treatment of assignees who assume the responsibility of periodic payment settlements on behalf of the defendant or its insurance carrier. (Third party assignments are discussed in the next section.)

Revealing Cost of Settlement to Plaintiff (Private Letter Ruling 8333035)

On March 21, 1983, the Internal Revenue Service issued a ruling that you will have neither actual nor constructive receipt, nor the economic benefit of the present value of the amount invested in the annuity, and the periodic payments will be excludable from your gross income under section 104(a)(2) of the Internal Revenue Code. In that ruling we cited Rev. Rul. 79-313, 1979-2 C.B. 75; and Rev. Rul. 79-220, 1979-2 C.B. 74; for the proposition that a corporation will be considered the owner of an annuity if the annuity is subject to the general creditors of the corporation, the corporation can change the beneficiary of the policy, and the beneficiary does not have the right to accelerate any payment or increase or decrease the amount of annual payments specified.

You have asked for a clarification of the above ruling because of your concern that your knowledge of the existence or cost of the annuity might cause you to be in constructive receipt of that annuity.

Section 1.451-2(a) of the Income Tax Regulations provides that income although not actually reduced to a taxpayer's possession is constructively received by him in the taxable year in which it is credited to his account, set apart for him, or otherwise made available so that he may draw upon it at any time, or so that he could have drawn upon it during the taxable year if notice of intention to withdraw had been given.

Based on the language in section 1.451-2(a) of the regulations, the Service has consistently taken the position that knowledge is not determinative in deciding a question of constructive receipt, but that unqualified availability is decisive. Rev. Rul. 68-126, 1968-1 C.B. 194; Rev. Rul. 73-99, 1973-1 C.B. 412; Rev. Rul. 74-37, 1974-1 C.B. 112; and Rev. Rul. 76-3, 1976-1 C.B. 114; as set forth conclusions consistent with this position.

Rev. Rul. 74-37 takes the position that interest accruing in a Uniformed Services savings account subsequent to the time principal and interest on deposit exceeds $10,000 (at which time such interest may be withdrawn at request) is constructively received at that time since it is available within the meaning of section 1.451-2(a) of the regulations. There is no exception to this rule in the case of POW's or MIA's who would not be in a position to know of the triggering event.

Based on the information submitted in the original ruling request, we conclude that disclosure by defendant of the existence, cost, or present value of the annuity will not cause you to be in constructive receipt of the present value of the amount invested in the annuity.

This ruling is directed only to the taxpayer who requested it. Section 6110(j)(3) of the Code provides that it may not be used or cited as precedent.

THIRD PARTY ASSIGNMENTS

Use of Assignments

The opportunity for a defendant or casualty insurer to assign its obligation to a plaintiff to make periodic payments should not be overlooked. Section 130 of Pub. L. No. 97-473, as referred to in the preceding section, clarified the tax status of assignees who accept periodic payment obligations. Depending on the perspective of the plaintiff and the defendant, assignments can be used as follows:

1. where a defendant, casualty insurer, or self-insurer agrees to structure a series of benefits, purchases a life insurance annuity to fund the agreed-upon benefits, and does not wish to be responsible for the life insurance company's continuing ability to meet the required obligation
2. where the casualty insurer has a less-than-desired A.M. Best's rating
3. where the defendant is an administrative or statutorily created entity that can be politically or legislatively put out of business
4. where the plaintiff would feel more secure by having a third party with a more favorable financial position than the defendant or insurer be responsible for future payments.

Qualified Assignment

In a qualified assignment, a third party assumes the liability from a defendant in a suit or agreement (tort-feasor or insurer) and where the following requirements are met:

1. The periodic payment must be fixed and determinable as to amount and time of payments.
2. They must not be subject to acceleration, deferral, increase, or decrease by the recipient.
3. The third party must not provide the recipient with rights against it that are greater than those of a general creditor.
4. The third party's obligation cannot be greater than that of the person whose liability is assumed.
5. The periodic payments must be excludable from the recipient's gross income under I.R.C. § 104(a)(2).

Qualified Funding Assets

The law limits the funding asset for a structured settlement to an annuity contract issued by a life insurance company and purchased within a 120-day period from the date of the assignment, or United States government obligations purchased within the same 120-day period.

SETTLEMENT AGREEMENTS (RELEASES)

Settlement agreements are long-term contracts between the defendant (or insurer) and the plaintiff releasing the defendant from the alleged negligence in exchange for the defendant's (or insurer's) promise of future payments. Appropriate settlement agreements are crucial to the long-term preservation of the defendant's and plaintiff's interests.

Appropriately drafted agreements should:

1. include release of all claims against the defendant, whether past, present, or future, including unknown injuries
2. state clearly that the casualty insurer or self-insured (or assignee in the event of assignment) promises to make the periodic payments
3. provide no incidence of ownership by the plaintiff in the annuity contract
4. fix all payments by date, term, amount, and payee

5. provide for "certain" payments to be paid to the plaintiff's estate or beneficiary in the event of death
6. protect the payments to the fullest extent from attachment or liens by creditors of the plaintiff
7. provide that the periodic payments may not be accelerated, deferred, increased, or decreased by the plaintiff
8. prohibit the assignment, pledge, or sale of the benefits by the plaintiff to a third party
9. provide for the termination of the contract on a specific date or upon the death of the plaintiff
10. avoid mentioning the cost or present value of the periodic payments so as not to convey constructive receipt to the plaintiff; the knowledge of the cost or present value by the plaintiff should not convey constructive receipt (Private Letter Ruling, Appendix 11–A), but it is best to avoid even the hint of conveyance.

Appendix 11–B is an example of a Release and Indemnification Covenant spelling out the terms of the settlement agreement in detail. Appendix 11–C provides the same information plus third party assignment language.

INCOME TAX CONSEQUENCES TO DEFENDANT

The Periodic Payment Settlement Act (Pub. L. No. 97-473, 1982) provides no guidance as to defendant's tax consequences. However, the administrative position is well settled in a business context. It provides that settlement or damage payments are deductible under I.R.C. 162 as ordinary and necessary if they arise within the scope of the trade or business.

For the cash method taxpayer, a deduction is proper in the year of payment. No distinction is made between direct cash payment and the purchase of an annuity contract to fund payment.

For the accrual method taxpayer, deduction of expense is permitted in the year in which (1) all events have occurred that determine the fact of the liability and (2) the amount of the liability can be determined with reasonable accuracy. (Treas. Reg. § 1.461-1(a)(2))

The Deficit Reduction Act of 1984 provides that the all-events test is not met until economic performance occurs with respect to the item. (I.R.C. § 461(b)). Unless the regulations provide exceptions, economic performance as to payment arising out of a tort occurs as payments are made.

LIFE INSURANCE COMPANIES

As of mid-1985, there were no fewer than 30 insurance companies from which structured settlement annuities could be purchased. Some of the largest in the life industry provide competitive products from which to choose. In evaluating a life insurance company and its position within the industry, A.M. Best and Company is a reliable source. Best provides annual reviews of both the life and casualty companies in the United States and rates them according to performance: A+ Excellent; A Excellent; B+ Very Good; B Good; C+ Fairly Good; C Fair. It is recommended that structured settlement annuities be purchased only from companies rated A+ Excellent or A Excellent.

Another category to be considered is the financial size of the insurance company. Financial size is the amount of policyholder surplus plus conditional reserves and the estimated equity in unearned premiums. Categories range from Class I to Class XV:

Class I	$250,000	or less
Class II	25,000 to	$500,000
Class III	500,000 to	750,000
Class IV	750,000 to	1,000,000
Class V	1,000,000 to	1,500,000
Class VI	1,500,000 to	2,500,000
Class VII	2,500,000 to	3,750,000
Class VIII	3,750,000 to	5,000,000
Class IX	5,000,000 to	7,500,000
Class X	7,500,000 to	12,500,000
Class XI	12,500,000 to	25,000,000
Class XII	25,000,000 to	50,000,000
Class XIII	50,000,000 to	75,000,000
Class XIV	75,000,000 to	100,000,000
Class XV	100,000,000 to	or more

Class size of XIII or higher is recommended for structured settlement annuity providers.

Finally, servicing and reputation within the industry also are important factors. It does no good if a company has favorable rates, such as an A+ Best's rating and a Class XV financial size if it takes three months to obtain a policy or payments are issued late. Structured settlement brokers can provide a broad cross-section of companies from which to choose. Brokers also can provide information on service provided by life companies, premium taxes, etc.

CONSULTANTS, BROKERS, AND SPECIALISTS

It should be apparent by now that a structured settlement is an arrangement both complex and dynamic in nature. The structuring of a periodic payment settlement should not be undertaken without the requisite expertise at hand, either developed internally within the company or law firm or through a broker or specialist who is well experienced in the design of settlement options and the negotiation of claims. Simply requesting a price quotation from a broker will not put a defendant on a par with a sophisticated plaintiff attorney. A specialist should be able to provide the following services:

1. analysis of the economic loss sustained by the plaintiff(s)
2. analysis of the economic, medical, and related needs of the plaintiff and the plaintiff's family
3. the ability to design settlements and alternatives to meet the needs of the plaintiff within the confines of the likely settlement figure
4. access to and knowledge of the most favorable insurance and financial markets—at least five
5. the ability to explain all of the features and options of a structured arrangement
6. willingness to assist in the negotiation of a structured offer between the defense and the plaintiff
7. services cost free to the defendant (including travel expenses) if the structured arrangement is not negotiated successfully
8. training services to companies wanting to learn more about the structured settlement approach.

THE SETTLEMENT CONFERENCE

It is rare that a defendant, insurer, or broker will have the opportunity of presenting a structured settlement offer directly to the plaintiff. Offers of settlement usually are made to the plaintiff attorney who, in turn, discusses the proposal with the client. While some attorneys have concluded a number of structured settlements formally, most have not. The initial settlement conference, then, presents the most significant opportunity to convince the plaintiff attorney that a structured settlement is the best way to proceed.

The defendant's negotiating team (adjuster, claims supervisor, defense attorney, and broker) should meet in advance to determine each party's role in the negotiation process: Who will present and explain the offer? Who will handle the negotiations? What role will the settlement broker play? These and other questions should be discussed in advance of the settlement conference so as not to detract from the primary objective of settling the claim.

Generally, the adjuster or defense attorney will contact the broker requesting that a settlement proposal(s) be developed. Once an appropriate initial offer has been prepared, the method of transmitting the offer should be determined. It is suggested that the initial offer be sent to the plaintiff attorney by mail (Appendix 11–B is a sample of such a letter). Included in the cover letter should be the recommendation that the parties meet to discuss the offer and other pertinent information. This allows the parties to meet face to face—the most effective means of negotiating structured settlements. In the meantime, the plaintiff attorney should do two things: (1) determine the present value or worth of the defendant's offer; (2) discuss the form of the offer with the client. Once these tasks are accomplished, the proper groundwork will have been established for meaningful negotiations.

At the settlement conference, the claims person or defense attorney may want to set the tone by discussing the liability, special damages, pleadings, etc. Once the tone has been set, the offer can be described in detail by the settlement broker. Such topics as method and term of payments, funding vehicle, guarantees, etc., should be discussed. In most situations the plaintiff attorney will ask what the defendant has spent to fund the initial offer. The purpose of the question is twofold; seeking to determine whether (1) the offer is credible and of sufficient worth in light of the facts of the case, and (2) the issue of plaintiff attorney fees has been addressed properly with respect to the attorney's contingency arrangement with the client and the percentage of fee as it relates to the offer value.

At this point the defense team must decide whether or not to release the cost of the initial offer. (This should have been discussed in preparation for the settlement conference.) Certainly the plaintiff attorney has enough sources available so as to assess the cost with reasonable accuracy. Releasing the cost to the plaintiff should not constitute "constructive receipt" so long as an equivalent cash amount is not offered as a settlement option. Generally the defendant does not reveal the cost and the plaintiff attorney is left to develop it unilaterally.

Once the cost or present value of the offer is determined by the plaintiff attorney, the parties enter into what can be referred to humorously as "the mating dance." The plaintiff may counterpropose a periodic payment format; the defendant then will have to determine its value. The defendant may make a counteroffer, with the plaintiff again counterproposing. The process can be limited to a simple offer and acceptance or it can go on for a rather long time. It may be necessary to end the initial settlement conference and resume negotiations later. Much of what goes on in the conference depends on such variables as scheduled trial date, amount of defendant's settlement authority, knowledge of the opposition, etc., and negotiations may not be limited to a single meeting. Flexibility is the key and all parties should be prepared to negotiate at more than one conference.

Assuming the case can be negotiated and settled satisfactorily to both parties, the defense attorney and settlement broker then prepare the closing papers. These may include the annuity application to the life insurance company, the schedule of payments, the settlement agreement (release), third party assignment forms, a copy of birth certificate(s), establishment of trust agreements, etc.

CLOSING THE CASE

All stages of a structured settlement negotiation are important, none more so than the closing process. Closing considerations may include the following:

- obtaining biographical information on the claimant(s)
- obtaining a copy of the birth certificate
- satisfying the plaintiff attorney of the financial stability of the life company
- developing appropriate release language
- discussing the need for third party assignment of benefits
- arranging for reinsurance of the settlement
- deciding whether the settlement will require a separate surety arrangement
- determining the correct annuity price at the time of application
- setting up a trust account, if required
- obtaining court approval.

The claims specialist, defense attorney, and settlement broker may be involved in any or all of these transactions. The key is communicating who will perform what function so the process will go smoothly and payments can begin on time.

COMMUNICATING WITH THE PLAINTIFF

As noted, it is rare that the defendant's negotiating team will have an opportunity to deal directly with the injured party. Most plaintiffs involved in structured settlement opportunities are represented by legal counsel who may or may not be familiar with this process. Appendix 11–E describes the structured settlement process in layman's terms. It is included here to demonstrate that there is a way to communicate with plaintiffs, whether or not they are represented by counsel. A description such as this can be added to the settlement offer papers so that the claimant can fully understand, along with advice of counsel, the benefits derived from a structured settlement opportunity.

Appendix 11–A

Private Letter Ruling 8333035

REVEALING COST OF SETTLEMENT TO PLAINTIFF

On March 21, 1983, the Internal Revenue Service issued a ruling stating that you will have neither actual nor constructive receipt, nor the economic benefit of the present value of the amount invested in the annuity, and the periodic payments will be excludable from your gross income under section 104(a)(2) of the Internal Revenue Code. In that ruling we cited Rev. Rul. 79-313, 1979-2 C.B. 75; and Rev. Rul. 79-220, 1979-2 C.B. 74 for the proposition that a corporation will be considered the owner of an annuity if the annuity is subject to the general creditors of the corporation, the corporation can change the beneficiary of the policy, and the beneficiary does not have the right to accelerate any payment or increase or decrease the amount of the annual payments specified.

You have asked for a clarification of the above ruling because of your concern that your knowledge of the existence or cost of the annuity might cause you to be in constructive receipt of that annuity.

Section 1.451-2(a) of the Income Tax Regulations provides that income although not actually reduced to a taxpayer's possession is constructively received by him in the taxable year in which it is credited to his account, set apart for him, or otherwise made available so that he may draw upon it at any time, or so that he could have drawn upon it during the taxable year if notice of intention to withdraw had been given.

Based on the language in section 1.451-2(a) of the regulations, the Service has consistently taken the position that knowledge is not determinative in deciding a question of constructive receipt, but that unqualified availability is decisive. Rev. Rul. 68-126, 1968-1 C.B. 194; Rev. Rul. 73-99, 1973-1 C.B. 412; Rev. Rul. 74-37, 1974-1 C.B. 112; and Rev. Rul. 76-3, 1976-1 C.B. 114; as set forth conclusions consistent with this position.

Rev. Rul. 74-37 takes the position that interest accruing in a Uniformed Services savings account subsequent to the time principal and interest on deposit exceeds $10,000 (at which time such interest may be withdrawn at request) is constructively received at that time since it is available within the meaning of section 1.451-2(a) of the regulations. There is no exception to this rule in the case of POW's or MIA's who would not be in a position to know of the triggering event.

Based on the information submitted in the original ruling request, we conclude that disclosure by defendant of the existence, cost, or present value of the annuity will not cause you to be in constructive receipt of the present value of the amount invested in the annuity.

This ruling is directed only to the taxpayer who requested it. Section 6110(j)(3) of the Code provides that it may not be used or cited as precedent.

Appendix 11–B

Release and Indemnification Covenant

The parties to, and the consideration for, this Release are as follows:

I. RELEASORS:
John S.

II. PAYORS:
Jane D.
Northeast Property & Liability Insurance Co.

III. CONSIDERATION:
In consideration for this Release, Northeast Property & Liability Insurance Co., on behalf of all PAYORS, agrees to make the following payments:

Cash at settlement to John S. paying One Hundred Forty Thousand Dollars ($140,000), inclusive of counsel fees.

An immediate annuity to John S. paying One Thousand Twenty-five Dollars ($1,025) per month for life, increasing at three (3) percent annually, with payments certain for thirty (30) years. In the event John S. predeceases any certain payments due, such payments will be made to his estate.

Lump-sum certain payments to John S. as follows: Ten Thousand Dollars ($10,000) in five (5) years, Twenty Thousand Dollars ($20,000) in ten (10) years, Forty Thousand Dollars ($40,000) in fifteen (15) years, Ninety-five Thousand Dollars ($95,000) in twenty years. In the event John S. predeceases any certain payments due, such payments will be made to his estate.

In consideration of the payments made and to be made by and on behalf of the PAYORS as above stated, the RELEASORS do hereby release said PAYORS, their heirs, executors, administrators, successors, and assigns from any and all actions, causes of action, debts, dues, claims, and demands of every name and nature, both at law and in equity, which against said PAYORS the RELEASORS and/or the said John S. ever had, now have, or may have for or by reason of any matter or thing to the day of the date of these presents, and especially from all claims and demands arising out of any and all personal injuries, damages, expenses, loss or damage, known or unknown, apparent and not apparent, present and future, alleged to have been caused by any of the said PAYORS to the said John S. at any time prior to the date hereof.

FURTHER, FOR THE CONSIDERATION AFORESAID, the RELEASORS do expressly stipulate and agree to indemnify and hold forever harmless the said PAYORS, jointly and severally, against any and all claims, demands, or actions which may hereafter at any time be made or instituted against the said PAYORS, or any of them by the RELEASORS or by the said John S. or by anyone on their behalf for the purpose of enforcing a claim for damages on account of the injuries described in the foregoing premises.

It is further understood and agreed that this release represents a settlement as the result of compromise of a doubtful and disputed claim, and that the aforesaid payments are not to be construed as an admission of liability on the part of the PAYORS, or any of them, by whom liability is expressly denied. It is further agreed that this release expresses a full and complete settlement of a liability claimed and denied and, that regardless of the adequacy of the compensation or the extent or character of the injuries, known and unknown, this release is intended to avoid litigation and that there is absolutely no agreement on the part of said PAYORS, or any of them, to make any payment or to do any act or thing other than is herein expressly stated and clearly agreed to.

The parties hereunto stipulate and agree that the agreements contained herein are confidential and will not be revealed by any party hereto, or their representatives, in whole or in part, or to any third party by any means whatsoever.

It is understood and agreed by and between the parties hereto that the PAYORS may, as a matter of right and in their sole discretion, assign their duties and obligations to make such payments to ABC Reinsurance Company pursuant to an Assumption-Reinsurance/Assignment agreement. Such assignment, if made, is hereby accepted by the Releasing Party hereto without right of rejection and in full discharge and release of the duties and obligations of the PAYORS and all parties released by this agreement with respect to such future payments. In the event the PAYORS assign the duties and obligations as provided herein, it is understood and agreed by and between the parties that ABC Reinsurance Company or their designee shall mail said future payments to the Releasing Party hereto.

It is further understood and agreed by the undersigned that, with the exception of the $140,000 payable upon approval of this agreement as provided below, all future payments hereunder may, at the option of the PAYORS, or their assignee, ABC Reinsurance Company, be funded by the purchase of an Annuity from Acme Life Insurance Company which, by its terms, will provide for payment of the above amounts. The Releasing Party hereto shall have no legal interest, vested or contingent, in such Contract.

The parties hereto expressly understand and agree that if an assignment of the duties and obligations to make such future payments is made by the PAYORS to ABC Reinsurance Company pursuant to this agreement, all of the duties and responsibilities otherwise imposed upon the PAYORS by this agreement with respect to such future payments shall instead be binding solely upon ABC Reinsurance Company and that the PAYORS and the released parties shall be released from all obligations to make such future payments and ABC Reinsurance Company shall at all times remain directly and solely responsible for the future payments. It is further understood and agreed that, if such an assignment is made, ABC Reinsurance Company will assume the duties and responsibilities of the PAYORS with respect to such future payments.

Notwithstanding any other provision of this agreement, the PAYORS shall at all times remain directly responsible for the payment of all sums and obligations contained in this agreement unless an assignment is made in accordance with this agreement, in which event PAYORS shall remain liable for all sums and obligations not so assigned.

It is further understood and agreed that the RELEASORS hereto have no right to accelerate, defer, increase, or decrease any payments due under the terms of this agreement and are prohibited from the assignment, pledge, or sale of the described benefits to any third party.

I/We the RELEASORS further state that I/we have carefully read the foregoing release and know the contents thereof, and that I/we sign the same as my/our own free act and deed.

In presence of: ______________________ By: ______________________

______________________ ______________________

______________________ ______________________

Date: ______________________

Appendix 11–C

Release and Indemnification Covenant—3rd Party Assignment

The parties to, and the consideration for, this Release are as follows:

I. RELEASORS:
John S.

II. PAYORS:
Jane D.
Northeast Property & Liability Insurance Co.

III. CONSIDERATION:
In consideration for this release, Northeast Property & Liability Insurance Co., on behalf of all PAYORS agree to make the following payments:

Cash at settlement to John S. paying One Hundred Forty Thousand Dollars ($140,000), inclusive of counsel fees.

An immediate annuity to John S. paying One Thousand Twenty-five Dollars ($1,025) per month for life, increasing at three (3) percent annually, with payments certain for thirty (30) years. In the event John S. predeceases any certain payments due, such payments will be made to his estate.

Lump-sum certain payments to John S. as follows: Ten Thousand Dollars ($10,000) in five (5) years, Twenty Thousand Dollars ($20,000) in ten (10) years, Forty Thousand Dollars ($40,000) in fifteen (15) years, Ninety-five Thousand Dollars ($95,000) in twenty (20) years. In the event John S. predeceases any certain payments due, such payments will be made to his estate.

In consideration of the payments made and to be made by and on behalf of the PAYORS as above stated, the RELEASORS do hereby release said PAYORS, their heirs, executors, administrators, successors, and assigns from any and all actions, causes of action, debts, dues, claims, and demands of every name and nature, both at law and in equity, which against said PAYORS the RELEASORS and/or the said John S. ever had, now have or may have for or by reason of any matter or thing to the day of the date of these presents, and especially from all claims and demands arising out of any and all personal injuries, damages, expenses, loss or damage, known or unknown, apparent and not apparent, present and future, alleged to have been caused by any of the said PAYORS to the said John S. at any time prior to the date hereof.

FURTHER, FOR THE CONSIDERATION AFORESAID, the RELEASORS do expressly stipulate and agree to indemnify and hold forever harmless the said PAYORS, jointly and severally, against any and all claims, demands, or actions which may hereafter at any time be made or instituted against the said PAYORS, or any of them by the RELEASORS or by the said John S. or by anyone on their behalf for the purpose of enforcing a claim for damages on account of the injuries described in the foregoing premises.

It is further understood and agreed that this release represents a settlement as the result of compromise of a doubtful and disputed claim, and that the aforesaid payments are not to be construed as an admission of liability on the part of the PAYORS, or any of them, by whom liability is expressly denied. It is further agreed that this release expresses a full and complete settlement of a liability claimed and denied and, that regardless of the adequacy of the compensation or the extent or character of the injuries, known and unknown, this release is intended to avoid litigation and that there is absolutely no agreement on the part of said PAYORS, or any of them, to make any payment or to do any act or thing other than is herein expressly stated and clearly agreed to.

It is further understood and agreed that the Releasors hereto have no right to accelerate, defer, increase, or decrease any payments due under the terms of this agreement and are prohibited from the assignment, pledge, or sale of the described benefits to any third party.

The parties hereunto stipulate and agree that the agreements contained herein are confidential and will not be revealed by any party hereto, or their representatives, in whole or in part, or to any third party by any means whatsoever.

I/We the RELEASORS further state that I/we have carefully read the foregoing release and know the contents thereof, and that I/we sign the same as my/our own free act and deed.

In presence of: ______________________________ By: ______________________

______________________________________ ______________________

______________________________________ ______________________

Date: ______________________________

Appendix 11–D

Sample Letter to Attorney

(When Annuity Plan Is to Be Mailed for Settlement Consideration)

Dear Mr. ______________________________:

We acknowledge your (demand and/or ad damnum) in the above-captioned case and have given careful consideration to the facts that give rise to your allegation of negligence on the part of Dr. ______________________________ in treating (claimant).

While we feel that a number of your allegations are without merit, we recognize that an offer of compromise settlement may well be in order so that the matter can be concluded in an appropriate manner.

Our offer is in the form of a periodic payment settlement individually designed for (claimant). An offer sheet is attached along with various illustrations for your review.

As you can see from the attached copy of the IRS Code, section 104, Revenue Ruling 79-220, the tax benefits to (claimant) from this settlement are most advantageous. In addition to a lifetime of tax-free income, there are no brokerage fees, investment adviser, trustee, or bank administrative fees that can occur with a lump-sum settlement.

The benefits to you as counsel to the plaintiff are twofold. With an annuity plan approved by your client, you can eliminate a potential legal liability that can result from investment advice to (claimant).

In addition, the structuring of your fees over a four-year period provides a balanced compensation level without undesirable income fluctuations. Variance in compensation levels is inefficient from a tax standpoint, and the proposed method will allow you more flexibility in your financial planning and investment considerations. The fees as outlined are taxable to you as gross income only as they are received and you may want to consider the benefits of structuring your fees as opposed to accepting a lump-sum amount.

After you have had an opportunity to review the attached proposal, perhaps we can get together to go over it in greater detail. I'll call you in a few days to set an appropriate date.

Very truly yours,

Appendix 11–E

Explanation of Structured Settlements in Simple Terms

(To Be Included with Initial Offer)

Generally, a structured settlement involves a combination of an immediate cash payment and a series of agreed-upon payments in the future. These periodic payments are funded through an annuity purchased from a major life insurance company. By using reputable and well-known life insurers, you can be assured of financial security throughout the period that the payments are due under this proposal.

The use of structured settlements has increased dramatically in recent years, and tens of thousands of cases are concluded in this manner annually. The Internal Revenue Service has ruled that a properly designed structured settlement will flow income tax-free to the recipient, providing that certain guidelines are met. Payments made to an estate after a recipient's death also are income tax-free (Rev. Rul. 79-220). President Reagan signed into law The Periodic Payment Settlement Act of 1982, turning the administrative ruling of the IRS (79-220) into law. Thus, we now have certainty under law that a properly arranged structured settlement, as paid, is entirely free from income taxes.

While there are tremendous tax advantages to a structured settlement over a lump-sum settlement, there are other advantages as well:

1. Structured settlements can focus on specific needs and can provide guaranteed income for life.
2. An annuity purchased from a major life insurance company permits the schedule to be flexibly arranged to make periodic payments monthly, quarterly, semiannually, annually, every two years, every five years, etc.
3. Payments can be level or increase annually to offset the impact of inflation and can be guaranteed for 10, 20, 30 years, or longer.
4. Education funds can be established for children or grandchildren that also are free from income tax.
5. Retirement funds can be established to supplement Social Security income as well as qualified retirement plans and Individual Retirement Accounts (IRAs).
6. Payments can be directed to a bank or lending institution for accumulation in an account or payment of an outstanding debt such as a mortgage payment.
7. A structured settlement reduces the potential of the dissipation of funds over a short period of time. Indeed, surveys have shown where people received large sums of cash in insurance settlements, lotteries, etc., in 90 percent of the cases the money was dissipated in five years.
8. Structured settlements do not require any annual administrative or investment adviser fees. Money management services are not required because the necessary income flow was developed before settlement.

9. Annuities have provided high investment yields over the years and, coupled with the tax-free nature of the structured settlement annuity, the return is greater than the taxable vehicle you may invest in privately.

You may be asking yourself, ''Why can't I settle the case in cash and invest in a structured settlement on my own?'' The IRS has determined that once you receive a lump-sum settlement, you cannot enjoy the same tax benefits by investing the money on your own as you would under a properly arranged structured settlement offered by an insurance company. The reason for this is that once a lump-sum settlement is made and conveyed to you, you are in actual or constructive receipt of the economic value of the settlement and thus you are subject to taxes generated from the investment of the settlement proceeds.

You should be aware that once a structured settlement has been agreed to, it must be maintained for the term of the agreement. However, this should not be a problem if you are interested in gaining maximum income and tax advantages in the settlement of your claim. The following example illustrates how a properly arranged structured settlement can prove beneficial over an equivalent lump-sum settlement.

Lump-Sum Settlement—$100,000

1. $100,000 invested in a 30-year Treasury bond
2. Bond rate—13.09% (7/17/84)
3. Tax bracket—25%
4. Term of investment—30 years
5. Adviser and management fees—1% annually for 30 years

$ 13,090	(annual interest payment)
× 30 years	(term of investment)
392,700	(yield on investment)
× .25	(tax bracket)
98,175	(tax due on investment)
294,525	(after-tax proceeds)
− 30,000	(adviser and management fees)
264,525	
+ 100,000	(return of principal)
$364,525	(proceeds of investment return and principal)

Structured Settlement—$100,000

1. $100,000 invested in annuity (7/17/84)
2. Term of investment—30 years
3. Annual payment—$12,507
4. $100,000 returned in 30 years (lump-sum payment)

$ 12,507	(annual payment)
× 30 years	(term of annuity)
375,210	(nontaxable income)
+ 100,000	(lump-sum payment in 30 years)
$475,210	
$110,685	(net difference, structured over lump sum)

Chapter 12

Managing Loss Exposures in Hospitals

Paul A. Greve, Jr.

As noted in earlier chapters, the 1970s saw a drastic increase in the number of malpractice lawsuits against hospitals and physicians and in the size of settlements and jury awards. Malpractice premiums for physicians and hospitals became prohibitively expensive and insurance coverage was difficult to find as numerous carriers cancelled policies and withdrew from the market.

Out of that so-called "malpractice crisis," which reached its peak in the mid-1970s, came attempts to control the problem. These included numerous study efforts, legislation to reduce the statutory period for filing malpractice lawsuits, legislative caps on damage awards, informed consent statutes, and the creation of many new carriers to provide coverage for physicians and hospitals. It was in this atmosphere that the concept of hospital risk management was introduced in an attempt to reduce the incidence of patient injury. By the 1980s, risk management was an established component of hospital administration.

The malpractice problem continues to be a great concern of physicians and hospitals. In 1985, an American Medical Association report revealed that 16 malpractice claims were filed for every 100 doctors in 1983, an increase of 20 percent over 1982.[1] By contrast, in 1975 at the height of the "crisis," fewer than five malpractice claims were filed for every 100 doctors.

With so many malpractice claims filed originating in a hospital setting, it is clear that the problem requires significant management effort and hospital resources to control and reduce patient injuries.

The keys to an effective risk management program are the support of management, the support and cooperation of the medical staff, and the selection of a risk manager who has a full working knowledge of techniques in that field and strong interpersonal skills.

This chapter provides a brief review of risk management goals and functions; selection of a risk manager candidate; the role of medical, administrative, and nursing staffs and the hospital board in the program; the composition and function of a risk management committee; educational programs; and interaction with the patient billing and quality assurance departments.

RISK MANAGEMENT GOALS

In the hospital setting, two primary risk management goals are closely related: the prevention of patient, employee, and visitor injury and of financial loss.

Prevention of Patient Injury

The prevention or reduction of patient injury must be the primary focus of hospital risk management as this is one of the greatest threats to the financial viability of any facility. The risk management of property losses and employee and visitor injuries should be secondary goals. Hospitals err when risk management is considered a safety function that addresses only environmental safety concerns and reviews incident reports from the nursing department. Some hospitals assign the function to the quality assurance department. In reality, risk management and quality assurance both are important functions that must be integrated but they must receive equal commitment by administration through support, resources, and personnel. (See Chapter _____).

Prevention of Financial Loss

The protection and preservation of hospital assets is another primary risk management goal. In an imperfect world, not all patient injuries can be prevented, nor can employee/visitor liability or property losses. Risk control efforts seek to minimize loss, which also involves risk financing functions such as purchasing commercial insurance, self-insurance programs, and captive insurance programs, to name a few.

RISK MANAGEMENT FUNCTIONS

Risk management functions can be divided into two basic classifications: risk control and risk financing. Risk financing functions involve:

1. supervision of the hospital's insurance program
2. maintenance of a claims filing system
3. monitoring the resolution of all insurance claims
4. analysis of risk transfer and risk retention decisions
5. review of hospital contracts for liability exposures
6. coordination with the hospital's insurance brokers/agents

7. coordination with hospital board and administration on the comprehensive insurance program.

Risk control functions involve:

1. development of a comprehensive risk management plan
2. development of a risk management manual
3. participation as a member of key hospital committees (i.e., Credentials, Quality Assurance, Risk Management, Safety, Infection Control, Pharmacy, Bylaws, Administrative Policy)
4. provision of assistance and consultation to hospital staff in all situations with liability potential
5. review of significant patient care information generated by incident reporting, generic screening, and formal and informal notification by staff.

SELECTION OF THE RISK MANAGER

When hospitals began risk management programs, and many of their managers came to this new field, their prior experience having been in either hospital administration or insurance claims work. Others had experience in personnel, safety, security, nursing, or had a legal background.

It probably is impossible to find a candidate who has a strong educational background and experience in all the areas of risk management. For that reason, hospitals need to budget educational expenses and consulting fees in order to provide new appointees with sufficient skills, support, and knowledge. This is especially true in those that are selecting a risk manager for the first time. The hiring of an experienced consultant to the new risk manager may prove to be most productive at the inception of the program.

Regardless of the education and experience of the manager, no one can succeed in this field without strong interpersonal skills. First and foremost, risk managers must be communicators. They must be able to deal with all hospital employees, from the housekeeper to the chief of surgery, and do it at the others' level. Risk managers must have the support and respect of the administrative and medical staffs. Chief qualities here are self-motivation and a confident, but not overbearing, demeanor. These managers must be diplomats because they must deal with many sensitive and confidential matters in relation to administration and the medical staff.

All in all, successful managers will be those who can learn and apply risk management, legal, and insurance concepts, and through developing high visibility and credibility, are able to interact successfully with the hospital's employees and staff.

ROLE OF THE MEDICAL STAFF

The hospital risk management program cannot succeed without the support and cooperation of the medical staff. Top management must convey to that group the need for such a program and that risk management can improve the quality of patient care by reducing incidents of injury. It also must be made to understand the mutuality of interest between the hospital and its medical staff members in preventing malpractice lawsuits, since both entities probably will be named in any suit arising out of a patient injury.

Physician membership on the risk management committee is essential to provide timely and objective review of malpractice liability exposures. These physicians should be able to provide a review of incidents both retrospective and prospective. Retrospective focus on claims must be objective in offering opinions on the appropriate standard of care and the causation of injuries. In prospective review, the physicians should be able to suggest how the injury could have been prevented and how similar ones can be avoided in the future.

The medical staff should formally designate one of its officers or its member of the risk management committee to work closely with the risk manager. The physician liaison has two important roles: (1) serving as a sounding board to the risk manager and suggesting remedial action after a patient injury; (2) interceding with peers in sensitive issues such as patient relations, patient injuries, and professional competence.

The risk manager must have visibility with the medical staff. Two of the best ways to ensure this are (1) risk management rounds to the patient care units and (2) participation of the risk manager as a member of medical staff committees. Risk management rounds necessarily will invite informal risk management consultations, particularly if they are carried out in the morning when most physicians make patient rounds. While the risk manager cannot be a member of all medical staff committees, it is helpful to be on such committees as Quality Assurance, Credentials, Pharmacy, Medical Records, and Operating Room. At the least, the manager should be on the Quality Assurance Committee so as to be able to identify trends and patterns of substandard care.

The risk manager—and department, if there is one—must provide educational programs to the medical staff, raising staff awareness that patient care injuries should result in efforts to prevent recurrences. The manager or the hospital's defense counsel should make presentations to the medical staff on risk management and medical/legal subjects such as informed consent, malpractice, brain death, and withdrawal/withholding of life-supporting equipment. In this way the risk manager can be seen to assist physicians in their daily practice and the medical staff will view the manager as an ally.

NURSING STAFF

Because members of the nursing staff are always present in patient care areas, they can be the best source of information on problems. Their timely reporting of problems and injuries will facilitate remedial action and correction of liability exposures. The risk manager must interact on a formal and informal basis with nursing administration personnel. Head nurses and supervisors must know that patient injuries, especially serious cases, must be reported promptly to risk management. Nursing administration personnel are essential in gathering formal documentation, including incident reports, to assist in preparation for potential litigation. These individuals must receive specific education in the risk management process and their role in it and also must know that they can rely on the risk manager to (1) provide the education and (2) advise them on the handling of sensitive issues involving consent, confidentiality, and other patient care factors.

ADMINISTRATIVE STAFF

Risk management issues can surface through administrative channels, usually in one of two ways:

1. Most hospitals have a system in place for administration to respond to patient concerns or complaints. This frequently involves the use of an administrator who takes calls on a weekly basis.
2. Members of the administrative staff will have risk management and liability issues brought to their attention through other means and in turn will request the assistance and advice of the risk manager in assessing the problem.

In the first instance, administrative staff members must know that they are required to contact the risk manager immediately when any serious patient injury is reported. The manager should monitor any patient complaints to administration to detect trends or patterns. Therefore, hospitals should have a log for entries by administrative staff members when they field patient complaints or concerns. As with the medical and nursing staffs, the risk manager must develop trust, confidence, support, and understanding of the administrative staff. The manager should make a formal presentation to the administrative staff on the structure and goals of the hospital's risk management program. That program cannot succeed without the support of all administration members.

The risk manager obviously needs an adequate budget to carry out assigned functions. Since most new managers come to the job with varying degrees of skill and expertise in law, insurance, and basic risk management principles, the hospital must expect to budget for educational expenses and for consulting fees as needed.

Administration also must impress on the medical staff that a risk management program is an integral component of the hospital's operation. This can be demonstrated in numerous ways, including formal educational programs, creation of a risk management committee, and placement of the risk manager in the organization structure with the authority to accomplish the program goals. This should mean that the risk manager reports to an administrator at the vice presidential level or above.

ROLE OF THE BOARD OF TRUSTEES

The hospital board of trustees has legal responsibility for the quality of care in the institution. The board must be instructed in the goals of the risk management program and must understand that the presence of such an effort can raise the quality of care by helping reduce or eliminate problems. The entire board, or at least a committee, should have up-to-date knowledge of the function, particularly when it must make decisions on risk financing for insurance purchases or on becoming self-insured. The board also must be kept apprised of claims activity, including trends or patterns of substandard care and how these are being dealt with. It should adopt a formal policy for the approval of all settlements or decisions to take cases to trial.

Most importantly, the board should establish a policy indicating that it supports the risk management program and identifying the reasons why this approach is needed in the hospital. Without board and administrative support, it is difficult for the program to gain the cooperation and support of the medical staff. The board and the administrative staff must stand behind the program when it deals with sensitive physician practice problems.

RISK MANAGEMENT COMMITTEE

The board's establishment of a risk management committee requires administration support and medical staff participation. The committee should have a formal statement of purpose or goals, delineating its functions, composition, and frequency of meetings.

The committee's goals should be comprehensive, stressing risk control and the assurance of quality care. In practice, this means that the committee must review serious incidents and claims and must attempt to detect system failures and trends or patterns of problems in care. These reviews will be based on incident reports, claims data, quality assurance audits, and referral of patient care problems identified by other hospital committees. The committee also is an appropriate forum for the discussion of such risk management issues as informed consent policy, incident reporting, and professional liability insurance, including minimum levels of coverage for medical staff members.

The composition of the committee is important. Members should be appointed by the chief executive officer or an officer of the medical staff such as its president or the medical director. This will serve to enhance the stature and importance of the group.

Administration representatives on the panel should include the risk manager, the chief executive officer, or at least the vice president responsible for the risk management function, the director of nursing, pharmacy director, and the chief financial officer if risk financing decisions, including the purchase of insurance, are made by that executive. Key medical departments represented can include emergency, surgery, intensive care, obstetrics, and medicine. If the hospital has a medical director who is ultimately responsible for the quality of care, that individual should be a member. If there is no such title, the president-elect or past president of the medical staff may serve. Unquestionably, the hospital's defense counsel should be represented. So also should the head of the quality assurance committee, which can implement risk management committee requests for the study of recurring problems and can provide reports on instances of substandard care uncovered by audits.

At the outset, the committee chair must address the need for both confidential and candid discussion of risk management issues. Ideally, this should not involve hospital policies or personalities; rather the chair should focus on analysis of each serious incident from the perspective of what could have been done to avoid that potential claim and what can be done to prevent a recurrence. The risk manager should have an important role in assisting the chair in the preparation of an agenda. The chair should not hesitate to delegate tasks to committee members, including the physicians, that may include meeting with representatives of other hospital committees to discuss a problem or perhaps requiring additional investigation and reporting back to the risk management committee on the status of the case.

EDUCATIONAL PROGRAMS

Educational programs are important for hospital risk management programs. They are effective preventive tools because they heighten staff awareness of risk management problems, especially patient injuries. Such programs also help give the risk manager visibility and credibility. These programs are a continuing responsibility of the risk manager. Medical, nursing, and ancillary department staffs directly involved in patient care all require regular educational programs.

Programs for the medical staff can include presentations to individual departments:

- periodic review of state statutes on informed consent for members of the department of surgery
- presentations to the entire medical staff at grand rounds or at meetings of the group
- presentations by the hospital's defense counsel on medical/legal topics such as informed consent, brain death, withholding/withdrawing of life support, malpractice, and others
- programs on medical/legal topics for physicians.

In teaching hospitals, risk managers should be included in the orientation program for new residents. Many risk management and legal topics are important for the nursing staff, which also will help in the prevention of patient injuries and the improvement of nursing documentation. At the very least, risk management should be included in the orientation program for all new staff nurses. This should include an explanation of the function: who to call, when, and what to do when there are patient care problems that have risk management implications. There also should be periodic programs on such topics as documentation, confidentiality, professional liability insurance, incident reporting, no-code orders, and others. Often these programs are most effective when presented in small groups.

Ancillary departments that regularly administer patient care should receive periodic presentations by the risk manager. This includes radiology, respiratory care, physical therapy, and laboratory personnel. For these departments, a review of case law and/or reports of insurance company losses, elements of good documentation, and other topics are useful in raising staff awareness, thereby helping prevent patient injuries and improving charting.

PATIENT BILLING DEPARTMENT

The risk manager must develop a protocol for cooperation with the patient billing department. Considerations should include the risk manager's authority to write off entire patient bills or portions of them, the need to hold patient bills until a thorough risk management investigation has been completed, referral of patient complaints of poor care, and use of patient billing information in settlement negotiation.

Any such protocol also should designate administrators (including the risk manager) who have the authority to write off charges, especially those associated with patient injuries that are potentially compensable events. Protocols also should be developed for dealing with patients who may be billed by private physicians or their corporations for services subsequent to injury. Risk managers should keep a record of all patient bills written off or paid for by the hospital. This is an important risk management statistic.

QUALITY ASSURANCE

Many hospitals have combined the risk management and quality assurance functions. Although these have somewhat different goals, they have enough commonality of interest to justify combining them in one department. This simplifies the exchange of important patient care information.

When these functions are separated, there must be sufficient integration and interaction between them to further the purposes of each. This can be achieved in a number of ways:

- an exchange of patient care information such as generic screening data and incident report data (retroactive and concurrent)
- the use of claims data to generate audit topics, using audit findings to generate risk management recommendations
- inclusion of the risk manager on the quality assurance committee
- inclusion of the head of the quality assurance committee or the director of the quality assurance program on the risk management committee
- risk management committee requests for audits by the quality assurance department or committee
- action by the quality assurance program or committee in calling problems to the attention of the risk manager or the risk management committee.

These constitute an effective way to demonstrate problem focus and resolution under the requirements of the Joint Commission on Accreditation of Hospitals for quality assurance activities. They also will help reduce and eliminate substandard care, which of course is a common goal for both risk management and quality assurance.

PROCESSING PATIENT CARE INFORMATION

Once the hospital's risk manager (and department, if there is one) has become well established, the high volume of patient care information will be submitted on a daily basis and must be processed in a meaningful manner. This information will be generated in many ways: from incident reports, informal reports by phone, generic screening data, patient complaints, claims information, committee members, etc.

INCIDENT REPORTS

The hospital must have an up-to-date policy on the handling of patient incident reports that mandates that the risk manager receive all such reports within

24 hours. This allows for timely investigation of potential claims against the hospital. Important considerations here include:

- physician examination of patient subsequent to injuries
- protection of the incident report from discovery by law
- recording of the facts involving injuries in an objective manner in the patient's medical records
- detection of trends and patterns in patient injuries through monthly compilation of incident reports
- holding of a patient's bills until a risk management investigation is completed
- establishment of criteria for completion of the incident report.

Generally, an incident report should be filed any time there is a patient injury, no matter how slight, or an unsafe condition exists that could have caused a patient injury. (See Chapter 6.)

INFORMAL REPORTING OF PROBLEMS

Traditionally, incident reports have been used primarily by nursing and ancillary department personnel. Physicians have been reluctant to record patient care problems on incident reports. Therefore, risk managers must encourage physicians to report problems by telephone, memorandum, or by consulting the risk manager directly.

Through educational programs, committee participation, and personal contacts, the risk manager must encourage physicians to report patients' injuries and adverse reaction to medications, treatment, and surgery. Head nurses and nursing supervisory personnel should be encouraged to contact the risk manager immediately when a serious patient injury occurs. This will allow the risk manager to obtain information and interview witnesses while the facts of the incident are still fresh in everyone's mind. This can be crucial in preparing a defense to litigation.

The risk manager should develop a printed form for recording all patient care information received informally. This so-called problem sheet can be just as vital as incident reports. In fact, more serious problems are likely to be reported informally in this way, particularly by members of the medical staff. Problem sheets can be used while interviewing staff members, then placed in a claim file should one be created; otherwise, they can be placed in a log.

CLAIMS INFORMATION

The risk manager must develop a filing system and a handling protocol for claims. This usually can be done in conjunction with the hospital's insurance carrier and trial counsel. Important considerations here include a diary system, establishment of claim reserves, preparation of witness statements, expert review of medical records, compilation of claims information on a semiannual or annual basis. This compilation should be reported to the risk management committee and the appropriate committee of the board of trustees.

Claims investigations constitute one of the most time-consuming and important functions of risk management. Timely investigation can prevent unfounded claims from being filed and will assist defense counsel in preparation for litigation. The time-consuming aspects include interviewing and preparing witnesses; preparing legal documents, including interrogatories and depositions; meeting with defense counsel to discuss strategy; reviewing hospital medical records; and referring medical records to outside experts.

The risk manager should have sufficient staff to be able to carry out these activities. The larger the hospital, the greater the need for additional individuals to carry out this vital role. This function can be implemented most efficiently and effectively by the risk manager (department), rather than using expensive outside legal counsel.

NOTE

1. American Medical Association (Chicago: Author, 1985),

Chapter 13

Organizing a Risk Management Program: The Smaller Hospital

Alan J. Mittermaier

Hospital risk management is the product of today's realities in the health care industry. Just as larger hospitals and medical centers around the country have responded to conditions in their environment, so also must smaller hospitals be prepared to deal effectively with risk in their milieu.

This chapter addresses the development of risk management in smaller hospitals (fewer than 200 beds) that do not have a staffed risk management department. Such facilities account for 75 percent of the country's nearly 7,000 hospitals. In addition to the typical general acute care institutions, many specialty hospitals fall into this category: pediatric, psychiatric, chemical dependency, and rehabilitation facilities. In recent years, many general acute care hospitals have converted unused beds to long-term care, which can be considered a specialty. While risk management programs in specialty hospitals may focus on types of risks and losses different from those in general acute care hospitals, the same risk management principles apply to each.

All hospitals are exposed to a wide variety of risks in their daily operations. Although this chapter deals only with risk management associated with patient care, other areas of risk should be included in a hospital's program, most notably those involving employees and visitors.

Risk management should not be viewed as simply another separate function, whether organized as a department (as in larger hospitals) or on a less-defined basis (in smaller hospitals). Instead, the program must be integrated into virtually all of the medical, administrative, and management functions of the organization. Risk management by itself can offer dramatic improvements in the handling of unplanned occurrences. When integrated into all hospital functions, it will have maximum impact and benefit.

COMMITMENT TO RISK MANAGEMENT

Before a program can be developed, there must be commitment to risk management from all levels of the organization, including the governing body, medical staff, and administration. It is critical that the board of trustees recognize its legal and moral responsibility not only for the quality of patient care provided in its facility but also for the inherent risks associated with providing such service.

Traditionally, the board has recognized and sought to minimize the hospital's risks involving building and equipment, malpractice, and Workers' Compensation through conventional insurance mechanisms. As the result of numerous landmark court decisions since 1965, starting with the famed *Darling v. Charleston Memorial Hospital*, 33 Ill. 2d. 236, 211 N.E. 2d 253 (1965), the board now bears ultimate responsibility for the quality of care, including the acts of omission and commission by employees and the medical staff. The commitment to a risk management program is one means for the board to discharge those responsibilities.

Since the board is not in a position to direct the daily activities of a risk management program, it must delegate that authority to the medical staff and administration. The medical staff must make the same commitment to the program in order to discharge its responsibility to the board. Because this program relies on peer review activity and information emanating from various medical staff committees, the support of that staff is essential to its success. Hospitals with good working relationships between the medical staff and administration will have little difficulty in gaining such support, but others with less optimal relationships will need patience and persistence in winning medical staff cooperation.

Finally, administration must emphasize its commitment to risk management by establishing the program as a management priority throughout the institution. This will require the direct involvement of the administrator/chief executive officer (CEO) since the smaller hospital has no department or, possibly, even an individual, i.e., risk manager, to assume responsibility for the program. In these facilities, the administrator/CEO should not be discouraged about this since so many of the daily administrative functions already are related to risk management.

The risk management program will require the commitment of all levels of hospital resources and information, particularly in communicating the information effectively. While this is everyone's responsibility, the administrator/CEO should be particularly alert to communicating the results of the program to both the medical staff and the board in order to reinforce their support.

STAFF INVOLVEMENT

Before the risk management program can be developed and implemented, certain individuals in the organization must be designated for specific responsibilities and critical functions. In general, all individuals who have the authority to influence patient care outcomes directly or through other persons should be actively involved in risk management. Of the five individuals discussed next, the first three also have the authority to initiate corrective actions to minimize identified risks and potential losses.

Administrator/CEO

The administrator/CEO provides the overall direction to the development, implementation, and maintenance of the risk management program. Unlike the larger hospital, which may have a risk manager, in a smaller facility the administrator (or designee) must assume daily involvement with the program since a multitude of daily events and occurrences have direct impact.

The administrator/CEO should be intimately familiar with all facets of the effort in order to be able to troubleshoot when necessary and minimize difficulties in the communication of information that is essential to the performance of the program. This individual also has the critical responsibility of exercising the authority delegated by the board to act in the best interests of the hospital when the risk management program has identified adverse situations that may require immediate response or correction.

Medical Director/Chief of Staff

Depending on the organization of the medical staff, either the medical director or chief of staff will have to assume specific responsibilities for risk management functions. In organizations with hospital-based physicians, the medical director ordinarily is responsible for their performance. This responsibility may be shared with department heads or directors in hospitals with medical staffs organized by departments or clinical services. Hospitals that do not have hospital-based physicians must work closely with the elected chief of staff and other voluntary medical staff officers.

In either type of organization, the designated physicians should be thoroughly familiar with the credentials and performance of all doctors on the medical staff. In addition, the medical director/chief of staff must be knowledgeable in areas such as delineation of clinical privileges, peer review mechanisms, disciplinary action, and standards of acceptable medical practice. This individual also has the responsibility of exercising the authority delegated by the board to protect the interests of the hospital and its patients when either are at risk.

Nursing Director

The nursing director has a crucial role in risk management, given that nursing personnel have the greatest daily contact with patients, families, and visitors.

Since nursing personnel generate up to 80 percent of the patient incident reports in a hospital, all of the nursing management staff must reinforce the importance of identifying adverse occurrences or potential risk situations.

Just as important is the need for continually monitoring the accuracy and timeliness of the information documented by such personnel. The director of nursing also should be familiar with the credentials and clinical experience of all nursing staff members and with state statutes or regulations that apply to nursing practice.

Medical Records Director

Since the patient medical record is the primary source of risk management information, the medical records director is a pivotal member of the program. In smaller hospitals, this individual is likely to have contact with patient charts following discharges from the hospital. Many smaller hospitals may assign the responsibility for utilization review to the medical records department, providing additional contact with patient charts during the hospitalization.

The director of medical records must be knowledgeable of applicable federal and state laws regarding discovery, patient confidentiality, and release of medical information. The department will be able to provide valuable assistance in the collection of data for a variety of risk management purposes, including the screening of various adverse occurrences.

Chief Financial Officer

The chief financial officer (CFO) provides the important fiscal dimension necessary to support risk management activities. The CFO can provide the historical information and trend data essential for documenting costs associated with insurance coverages, insured losses, and other miscellaneous claims incurred by the hospital. With the wide variety of insurance coverage available, the CFO must be involved directly in the program in order to be assured that the risk management activities complement the hospital's insurance plan. The CFO has the responsibility of working closely with the hospital's insurance representatives to translate the multitude of risk factors into a plan that best protects the facility and its assets.

Smaller hospitals must rely on each of these individuals to integrate the various risk management functions throughout the organization. While other staff members may need to be involved in selected areas of the program, the bulk of the responsibility will be in the hands of these persons.

DEVELOPMENT OF THE PROGRAM

The development of an effective risk management program requires the preparation of a plan or model that can be implemented over a period of six to 12 months. This can require an even longer time in smaller hospitals since they lack an in-house risk manager to implement the program. In addition, medical staff resistance may be encountered and participation by physicians may be difficult to accomplish. Regardless of the hospital environment, a basic risk management program can be established by incorporating the following five steps in the planning process.

Education

Although risk management may be difficult for physicians and hospital personnel to conceptualize alone, it can be understood more easily when divided into four fundamental activities or functions:

1. identification and assessment of loss potential
2. loss prevention
3. loss funding and risk financing
4. claims control and litigation management.[1]

Each of these contributes to the purpose of risk management, which is to minimize the effects of loss. The inability to communicate these functions and to execute each one will result in an ineffective program.

Regardless of the specific methods for educating physicians and hospital staff, there will be concerns and anxieties about this program. By anticipating this reaction, the administrator/CEO and other key individuals can incorporate a variety of means to overcome myths with facts. Several common misconceptions should be expected to surface, including one or more of the following.

> "This is just another way to blame the physicians and employees for incidents that involve patients."

Some physicians and personnel will consider risk management a "witch hunt" intended to place fault on unsuspecting or undeserving individuals for patient incidents. An effective response to this misconception is to relate the program's purpose—i.e., minimizing the effects of loss—to carowners and homeowners who seek the most protection for their insurance value.

> "This just means more paperwork and another committee meeting to attend."

In most hospitals, the implementation of a risk management program will not entail additional commitments of time or an avalanche of useless paperwork. It will be important to emphasize that most risk management activities can be accomplished by using existing sources of information and committees.

> "Why does the hospital need this program when it already has attorneys and insurance companies to handle its claims and losses?"

The education of physicians and personnel about loss prevention is essential and requires continuing reinforcement. Loss prevention consists of two facets: (1) eliminating or controlling the circumstances that can cause adverse outcomes before they can occur; (2) taking appropriate actions to minimize the loss that may result after an adverse outcome does occur. The program gives the hospital the means to directly deal with adverse outcomes before they are placed in the hands of attorneys and insurance carriers. Hospital counsel and insurance representatives both have roles in risk management but should become involved only after internal mechanisms for handling adverse situations have been exhausted.

> "This is a duplication of the quality assurance program that already is involved in handling patient care problems."

It is important to establish the relationship between the risk management and quality assurance programs and to educate physicians and other personnel accordingly. Each program can benefit by the presence of the other and probably will include many of the same individuals and sources of information. The most important aspect of the relationship should be the exchange of information and data to aid in accomplishing the purposes of both programs.

The board and top management should remember that the purpose of educating physicians and personnel is to increase their awareness of risk management. The time and effort spent to do so will improve the program's chances for success.

Program Scope and Objectives

The risk management program must include statements that identify its scope as well as objectives against which results can be measured. This is of particular importance in the smaller hospital without a risk manager, since the scope and objectives will be the basis on which staff members determine what duties and tasks to pursue. These statements must be in simple and concise terms, presenting objectives in measurable terms whenever possible.

The program's scope can be stated inclusively or may be more detailed if desired. A broad, all-inclusive statement is preferred since it will allow the most latitude in dealing with a variety of situations and circumstances of interest to the program. For example: "The risk management program will pursue all occurrences and circumstances that may result in a loss."

Program objectives should be realistically achievable. The hospital should not be hesitant to revise, add, or delete objectives when necessary to keep them current with the program's status. Initially, it may be advisable to state objectives in two categories, process-oriented and results-oriented: (1) to screen all incident reports within 24 hours of occurrence for loss potential (process-oriented); (2) to reduce the total dollar loss per patient claim by 25 percent from last year (results-oriented).

There is no substitute for clear, well-developed program objectives. They provide everyone with the means to perform their responsibilities effectively and contribute to the program's success.

Identifying Risks

The foundation of the program is risk identification. The hospital must be able to develop a systematic means of detecting potential losses and a thorough, reliable approach for determining what loss events could occur.[2] The key to identifying such situations is the completeness and accuracy of the information. Incomplete or inaccurate identification of loss or potential loss can cause the misdirection of valuable time and energy by physicians and staff members responsible for responding.

The successful approach to this key activity requires a thorough understanding of the entire hospital organization, its daily operations, and the delivery of patient care. This is particularly important since a significant number of specialty facilities fall within the smaller hospital category. Each type of hospital, i.e., general acute, pediatric, psychiatric, or rehabilitation, should be able to easily identify the areas or services that pose the greatest threat for potential loss. As indicated, general acute care hospitals also may be providing certain specialty services, including long-term care. The most likely areas for potential loss that should be carefully evaluated are:

General acute
- Emergency room
- Operating room
- Labor/delivery/nursery
- Nosocomial infection
- Falls
- Informed consent

Psychiatric
- Medication
- Electrotherapy
- Patient rights
- Informed consent
- Staff abuse

Pediatric
- Neonatal nursery
- Emergency room
- Operating room
- Informed consent

Long-term care
- Medication
- Falls
- Emergency care
- Patient rights
- Staff abuse

Rehabilitation
- Medications
- Falls
- Emergency care

Another effective means of identifying risks is to review past insurance claims and patient incident reports. To establish reliable trends with these historical data, it is recommended that at least five years of insurance claims and two years of incident reports be evaluated and classified. The data collected can be classified by type of occurrence (e.g., fall, medication reaction, infection).

Upon completing the evaluation and classification of these data, the hospital's attorney and insurance representatives should be invited to review the information to identify which occurrences represent the greatest potential for loss. The next step is to compare the relative frequencies of claims and incident reports by type of occurrence. This can be done in a format such as this:

Type of occurrence	*$ Cost per claim*	*Ranking*	*Incident report frequency*	*Ranking*
Medication reaction	—	NA	120	6th
Fall from bed	$5,000	7th	50	9th

The findings from this analysis of historical information can have a direct impact on hospital policy and procedure as well as insurance coverage before the rest of the risk management program is implemented. With this information, the staff members involved in the program must develop a strategy for implementing a risk identification system to detect patient-related occurrences at the earliest possible point.

The reliability of the hospital's incident reporting system should be evaluated critically and, where necessary, modified to provide documentation of incidents on a timely basis. The incident report will be useful in identifying risks only if the following guidelines are met consistently:

- The report must give the user a clear understanding of what occurred, why, and the consequences to the patient immediately following the event.
- The report must be initiated by the person(s) who witnessed the occurrence or the immediate consequences.

- The report must be routed to the immediate supervisor to review for accuracy and completeness, then sent to administration within 24 hours. This guideline should be followed even if the incident has been resolved satisfactorily.

A recently developed means of identifying risk is through generic outcome screening, which focuses only on those occurrences that pose potential malpractice risk to the hospital. A generic outcome screening procedure can be developed in-house by selecting examples of adverse or unplanned results that may expose a patient to unexpected or additional risks, such as:

Drug reaction
Transfusion reaction
Fall
Return to surgery
Seclusion or restraint
Return to emergency room (within 24 hours)

Generic outcome screening can be incorporated easily into the postdischarge review of patient charts by the Medical Records Department. Patient charts so identified by the screening should be forwarded to the individual or committee designated to review these cases. An additional benefit of generic outcome screening is to verify the accuracy of the incident reporting system throughout all areas of the hospital.

Sources of Information

The risk management program is dependent on many sources of information that provide details of patient occurrences as well as monitor the degree of compliance with loss prevention activities. As noted, the patient chart and patient-related incident report are two sources of information vital to the program. Other sources can be equally significant:

Operating room log
Emergency room log
Nursing shift report
Autopsy report
Utilization review findings
Quality assurance monitoring
Infection report
Tissue review findings

Their common characteristic is that they all exist for other purposes and do not require additional effort to collect for the risk management program. Each hospital, however, should judge the quality of these sources of information against the program's needs. The sources can be tailored to meet the specific needs of the program.

Incident Review and Claims Management

Depending on each hospital's organization and method of financing risk along with funding loss, there are numerous ways to review incidents detected by the risk identification system and to manage occurrences that materialize into claims.

All incident reports should be screened to determine what, if any, immediate action may be required to protect the patient or the hospital. Generally, this should be the responsibility of the administrator (or designee). Other individuals may be requested to assist as necessary. The objective of the incident review process, however prescribed, should be to establish the most appropriate means to assess risk and minimize loss.

Hospitals with conventional indemnity insurance coverage must follow a prescribed incident or claim reporting mechanism established by their insurance carrier. After notification of an occurrence, the insurance company will initiate its investigation. If hospital liability is established, the carrier proceeds to determine a reasonable settlement. This method relieves the hospital of the control of the settlement and introduces a third party to deal with the patient and family.

Other hospitals have opted for various risk financing packages that generally involve some form of self-insurance with or without secondary coverages purchased from an insurance company. With such coverage, the hospital assumes full or partial liability for losses that it must fund internally through its operations. By assuming some degree of funding of losses, the hospital also can control the management of the occurrences and eventual claims.

One mechanism for evaluating incidents and claims is a Medical Incident Review Committee (MIRC).[3] Its composition should be multidisciplinary, with representation from the medical staff, administration, nursing, and legal counsel. Consideration also should be given to including the insurance company representative if the hospital does not self-insure 100 percent of losses. The MIRC also may designate other individuals to serve when special expertise is necessary to review specific incidents or claims.

The MIRC should have clearly defined responsibilities that may include:

- investigation of the facts related to an incident or claim
- evaluation of the circumstances and facts to determine the severity of the incident or merit of the claim
- recommendation(s) for minimizing the immediate loss and preventing occurrences or future claims.

It is essential that the MIRC have full access to patient and hospital records in order to fulfill its investigation and evaluation responsibilities. Because of the access to such records and information, the hospital should obtain legal counsel regarding whether the MIRC and its activities can be protected from discovery by the peer review statutes in most states. Regardless of the insurance coverage mechanism used, the MIRC should enhance the visibility and effectiveness of the risk management program throughout the hospital.

This section has dealt primarily with the methodology for managing patient-related incidents and claims. A comprehensive risk management program should be prepared to deal with other categories of losses. These categories may include Workers' Compensation claims, general liability claims, and claims made on behalf of visitors or the general public. The appropriateness of including these categories of loss in the risk management program will depend largely on the insurance coverage chosen and the mechanisms already established for managing these claims.

USE OF CONSULTANTS

Smaller hospitals occasionally will encounter situations when certain expertise or information is not available through in-house sources or available information must be verified or substantiated by an authoritative third party. It is no secret that there is a plethora of consultants and experts available with varying degrees of competence in the fields of medicine, insurance, law, and, of course, risk management.

When it is necessary to seek the services of a consultant, the hospital should be certain to follow four simple, but often ignored, rules. It should:

1. Specify the services required by the hospital.
2. Identify the qualified consultants who are available, and their fee arrangements.
3. Select, whenever possible, the consultant who is most available and most conveniently located.
4. Enter into a written agreement or contract for the services requested.

The judicious use of consultants can be a valuable and cost-effective means of accomplishing the risk management program objectives. The types of consultants' services can vary as much as their fees. Typically, attorneys, accountants, physicians, and other hospital consultants expect payment for professional time and expenses. Most insurance companies provide their consultation services as a courtesy to their accounts. Medical and legal consultants may be referred to the hospital by state and national professional associations, e.g., bar associations, medical societies, and by other hospitals that have used such specialists.

PROGRAM EVALUATION

Once the risk management program has been implemented and has survived its first year, time should be allocated to review and evaluate the initial objectives. The evaluation process may involve (1) measuring the degree of achievement of objectives and (2) assessing by subjective means the impact on a variety of hospital activities and services.

Measurement of degree of success or failure must be honest, but the program must be given credit where it is due when it has achieved even a minimal degree of success. Difficulties encountered in cases where objectives were not achieved also should be identified. It should be remembered that the evaluation also is an opportunity to consider and make improvements to enhance the program's effectiveness. The evaluation should be particularly sensitive to the feedback and interests of the medical staff, giving credit to that staff and to the individual physicians involved in the program where appropriate in order to maintain their continued support and participation.

The subjective assessment should evaluate the program's impact on the total hospital operation. Although the program may have failed to achieve all of the process-oriented and results-oriented objectives, other significant benefits can be attributable to it.

Many hospitals will recognize immediately that the risk management program enhances the effectiveness of medical staff credentialing and peer review by aiding physicians in understanding the consequences of permitting substandard medicine to be practiced in the facility. At the very least, physicians will be more aware of their own exposure to risk as the result of the acts of omission, commission, malpractice, and malfeasance by other doctors on the medical staff.

Another benefactor of the risk management effort is likely to be the quality assurance program. The identification of both actual and potential risks can aid the quality assurance program greatly in establishing its priorities for improving patient care and services.

A fundamental component of the program, identified previously, is loss funding and risk financing. The creation of the risk management program by necessity will entail the evaluation of the facility's insurance portfolio. The hospital may discover that it is either overinsured or underinsured. In either case, it may benefit by realizing substantial savings in insurance expenditures or be able to increase its coverage for the same cost. Other insurance options (e.g., self-insurance, pooled interest, captive) now available to smaller hospitals may provide a more cost-effective means of insuring risk and funding loss. Once the risk management program demonstrates the ability to prevent loss as well as control claims, the hospital will be in a position to take advantage of an even greater variety of insurance options.

The risk management program can be expected to produce positive results in employee health and safety. Even though conventional Workers' Compensation insurance is relatively inexpensive, the other costs associated with employee injury or illness can be significant. The most important include loss of productivity and the cost for continuation of employee benefits during the recovery period. With appropriate training of employees, many of their injuries can be prevented by supervisors who can identify risk factors associated with each job and worker. Even when injuries do occur, supervisors can be instrumental in minimizing their severity by taking immediate actions.

Finally, the most elementary risk management program can be expected to improve patient relations. By early detection and prompt communication of patient-related incidents, the program can dramatically reduce the hospital's response time to incidents in which patients and families expect rectification of an unplanned occurrence. The improvement in response may not prevent lawsuits but may make possible the opportunity to settle certain claims for substantially less than might be the result otherwise.

These are but a few of the many benefits that can be realized by an effective, well-organized program. Upon completion of the program evaluation, the hospital should not overlook the value of sharing the results with key personnel and the medical staff. The board should make the final review and provide guidance for its overall future direction.

SUMMARY

As stated at the outset, risk management is a product of today's realities in the health care industry. On the one hand, hospitals strive to deliver the most current patient care and services daily to thousands of patients and their families. Because of the volume of the services and care, unplanned or adverse occurrences will always result to varying degrees. On the other hand, patients seek hospital care with an expectation that they will be alive and well when discharged. Any outcome that falls short of this expectation may result in potential financial loss to the hospital. When adverse outcomes occur, the hospital should be in the position to control the consequences, i.e., to minimize the effects of loss.

By viewing risk management in the same context as preventive medicine, a strong analogy appears. Both disciplines rely on the philosophy that "an ounce of prevention is worth a pound of cure." Both are effective because they rely on early detection and immediate intervention to minimize harm or loss. Both result in substantial long-term savings of resources. It is no coincidence that both risk management and preventive medicine can reap significant returns from minimal investment of resources.

NOTES

1. William Ryan, ''Risk Management Checkup: Hospitals Still Have a Way to Go,'' *Business Insurance* (October 22, 1984).
2. Charles M. Jacobs, *Hospital Risk Management and Malpractice Liability Control* (Chicago and Bethesda, Md.: Interqual, 1980), p. 67.
3. Steven L. Salman, ''Committee Is An Important Tool In Risk Management,'' *Hospitals* 54 (September 16, 1980): 45–50.

Chapter 14

Organizing a Risk Management Program: The Larger Hospital

Charles B. Van Vorst and James A. White

> *"I had never appreciated the complex nature of the hospital. . . . The hospital, I learned, had a variety of turfs, of which personnel became very possessive and defensive . . ."*
>
> *"The challenge is clear. There is a need to pull everything together to coordinate and integrate existing accountability systems without disrupting them . . ."*[1]

While the author of those comments was referring to hospital quality assurance programs, the same sentiment holds true for risk management programs. In most hospitals, the essential parts of a good risk management program already are in place, needing only some individual to organize these elements effectively. "The development of a risk management program does not necessarily mean starting from scratch. It does, however, generally involve a change in emphasis, a reorganization and better coordination of existing activities."[2]

FORMAL AUTHORITY

Before assessing existing activities, it is important the risk manager develop the authority necessary to implement a risk management program. Authority comes to the program in two ways: (1) formal authority that gives the risk manager the power to perform certain essential functions and (2) informal authority that allows the manager to influence others to provide the program with their assistance.

Formal authority comes from the board, administration, and medical staff. Without their endorsements, the risk manager has little or no power base to launch any ideas or programs.

The Role of the Board

The board must acknowledge its legal and moral responsibility to provide quality medical care. It must realize that a well-organized risk management program is an effective way to monitor that responsibility. In turn, the board must be willing to adopt, implement, develop, and maintain a risk management program for loss detection, prevention, and control to protect the assets of the institution from unexpected financial loss and to generally publicize its responsibility and support to the hospital staff.

Publicizing a risk management program is a requirement if it is to be accepted by the organization. Another requirement is for the risk manager to display an enormous amount of friendliness, tact, and good humor. Good judgment also is required, and the risk manager must convey these traits in moving into the various "turfs" noted at the start of the chapter.

The Role of Hospital Administration

No less fundamental to the success of the program than the board is the hospital administration, which should not require being educated in the risk manager's organizational philosophy. After all, administration hired the person to do the job and its cooperation and support should be expected. However, the risk manager must pinpoint the needs in order to win administration help.

Committee involvement is one of those needs. The risk manager's presence makes it obvious to everyone that administration supports this new program. The risk manager should be a voting member of committees dealing with such issues as patient care, employee and patient safety, fire safety, internal and external disasters, and, most importantly, quality assurance.

The Quality Assurance Committee is designed to assure a consistent attempt to provide high-quality services; to ensure cost effectiveness; to assure the interaction of all professional, managerial, technical, and support personnel; to assure identification and correction of problem areas; to evaluate quality assurance activities; and to provide a system of accountability to administration and the board.

Membership on that committee usually consists of the medical director, the director of quality assurance, the vice president of the medical staff, and other physicians who serve on an as-needed basis. The committee is prestigious by virtue of its membership and since it receives its responsibility and authority from the board of trustees, it is important that the risk manager be heavily involved in its activities.

As the risk management program develops, the manager should encourage the formation of its own committee, which in some hospitals is known as the Medical Malpractice Committee. Membership usually consists of several surgeons as well as the medical director and president of the medical staff. (This committee is discussed later.)

Administration should encourage the sharing of information between the director of quality assurance and the director of risk management, expressly to integrate (not necessarily combine) the programs to enable the hospital to provide a higher quality of care through proper identification and correction of services that are of less than optimum quality. These are ingredients of a loss-prevention and a loss-control program that will evolve after the loss-detection program is firmly in place.

Other actions reflecting a strong administration commitment to its risk management program include:

- providing the risk manager the authority to review any and all medical records as necessary
- demonstrating a consistent desire for the interaction of all professional, managerial, technical, and support personnel in the risk management process.

The Role of the Medical Staff

The third major component in establishing formal power is the medical staff. Physician involvement is imperative. Although it is unlikely the physicians will provide the risk manager with any immediate assistance, they need to be informed of what the individual is trying to accomplish. An excellent rule to follow (also used in other contexts) is: ''Don't surprise the doctors.''

To begin cultivating this valuable resource, the president of the medical staff should be given a set of screening criteria for potential malpractice claims that, when they occur, trigger action to inform the risk manager, preferably by telephone or personal visit. The following screens have been developed by Interpol and several other organizations for both retrospective and concurrent use. They serve one major purpose in allowing the hospital to deal with problems identified while the patient is still in the hospital, thus reducing the likelihood of a claim. Seventeen such criteria have been developed[3] but the risk manager should consider limiting the criteria at the outset to six or seven important events. As the manager develops expertise and as the program becomes more oriented to quality care, the criteria can be expanded. Some recommended criteria involve:

- Patients admitted from an outpatient area: This criterion is suggestive of potential adverse results in a doctor's office, emergency department, or outpatient surgery. The resource persons are the nurse supervisors on the admitting floor, in the emergency department, and in outpatient surgery.
- Hospital-incurred incidents, including drug and transfusion reactions: These usually reach the risk manager through the formal reporting process. Informally, the manager needs to know whether the reaction forced a longer

hospital stay or resulted in other unexpected costs to the patient. Did the incident cause a severe burn or sloughing of the skin, requiring unplanned surgery? The nursing supervisors and operating room supervisor are the resource persons.

- Unplanned return to the operating room on this admission: An event of this type can indicate a sponge, instrument, or needle was left in the patient and additional surgery was necessary. The OR supervisor is the resource.
- Operation for repair of injury incurred during an invasive procedure: This is straightforward. When it occurs, the hospital probably is going to have to pay some money for injuries such as laceration, perforation, tear, or puncture of an organ in surgery. It is less expensive in the long run to admit the error and make amends by paying for any additional hospital stay than it is to hope the patient will let the matter pass. The OR supervisor is the resource.
- Hospitalization for adverse results of prior emergency department care: This could indicate a failure to diagnose acute appendicitis or a myocardial infarction during a first emergency room visit. The Emergency Department nursing supervisor is the resource.
- Any patient who threatens to sue because of alleged mismanagement: This usually comes when a patient receives the bill, especially if the person is unhappy with the results of the hospital stay. Plastic surgeons and those who perform gastric stapling have more than their share of unhappy patients. The business office is the resource person.

After receiving this information, at the very least the president of the medical staff will update its members about the risk management program and activities at the next meeting. It is recommended that the risk manager be invited to make a presentation. The medical staff president may be elected for only one year and has many duties, ministerial in nature, but still is the risk manager's opening to other members vital to developing formal authority, including the director of medical affairs and the heads of the surgery, obstetrical, and emergency departments. These physicians represent the high-risk areas in the hospital and their aid is indispensable to the success of the risk manager's program.

The director of medical affairs is a vital link because of close ties with administration and usually is highly regarded by other staff members. This director generally is a long-term hospital appointee, receives a salary from the hospital, and routinely is involved in the more serious problems such as physician incompetency. The director tends to be thick skinned, knows where all the skeletons are buried and, over the long haul, will be the one to eventually sell the risk management program to the medical staff.

The director can be asked to set up a meeting that includes the three key department heads. At this meeting, the risk manager presents the generic screening criteria and reviews all pending malpractice claims against the hospital, highlighting problem cases in each department's area of responsibility. A follow-up meeting should be set for a few months later to analyze the program's progress. Whether or not these physicians realize it, an elite group now has been established with which the risk manager can discuss problems, needs, and possible solutions. From all this, the manager develops the physicians' confidence and trust, important ingredients in the program's future. In addition, the risk manager has formed the malpractice committee referred to earlier.

INFORMAL AUTHORITY

Once it is perceived by the hospital and medical staff community that the risk managers have the formal authority to launch the program, their ability to sell themselves, their professional aptitudes, and their honesty will be the elements on which to establish their informal power. The informal influence is important to evolve a change of emphasis cited earlier; the logical place to start is with an inventory of areas where informal authority or influence is important.

THE INVENTORY

The sine qua non in developing a risk management program is with a thorough inventory of existing activities. All hospitals have a myriad of activities related to risk management that together consist of a network of relationships, reports, and records. It is important to understand each of these segments and how they can help the risk manager in developing the program, beginning with emphasis on loss detection. Activities such as loss control and loss prevention will follow naturally as the program matures.

Only 15 percent of all hospital malpractice suits are reported prior to the institution's being sued. If the lawsuit constitutes the detection system, several years may have elapsed since the actual event. This provides the risk manager with precious little time to develop the facts of the case, a problem compounded by fading memories, people leaving, and lost or destroyed records.

In the ideal setting, once a risk management program is endorsed by the board, administration, and medical staff, there should be a virtual parade of physicians, nurses, and others beating the proverbial path to the risk manager's door, revealing their innermost problems such as errant sponges, perforations, infiltrations, failures to diagnose, and unexpected bad results. Since that will not occur for several years (if ever, in some respects), an early detection system is the risk manager's responsibility.

Relationships

This is the risk manager's most important asset and it begins with the physical location of the office. Visibility is important. An office located in an isolated area of the hospital or, even worse, in a building not contiguous to the facility, makes being visible difficult. If the office is strategically located near administration, the doctors' lounge, or other high-traffic areas, the door should be left open as an invitation and reminder to those who might need the manager's services (although occasionally the open door attracts the curious visitor who will tax the incumbent's ingenuity by asking what a risk manager does).

Insurance Company

With the issue of visibility settled, the risk manager can devote full attention to the other relationships necessary for the program's success, beginning with the individuals who can provide a historical perspective, such as identifying the hospital's malpractice insurance carrier(s) the previous five or ten years. Usually, the financial department and/or the hospital's insurance broker can help with company names, policy numbers, dates of coverage, policy limits, and the actual policies. A master listing of all policies then should be prepared as a reference.

The next project is to develop a background on prior and pending claims, starting with a visit to the regional claim office of the insurance carrier(s). Before the visit, the risk manager should contact the claims manager there requesting the opportunity to review all claims files, as far back as possible. (This is the beginning of a crucial report—a claim log—that the risk manager should provide to administration at least quarterly.) The following information should be sought from the claims manager:

1. Name of plaintiff(s).
2. Plaintiff's attorney. (This is useful in the preparation of a second important report to administration and the medical staff—the names of plaintiffs and law firms that sue hospitals and doctors.)
3. Names of all defendants.
4. Plaintiff's allegations. (The risk manager should ask to read the actual summons and complaint filed by the plaintiff in a court of law.)
5. Plaintiff's financial demand. (Some courts limit the amount that can be demanded to eliminate sensationalism.)
6. Date the alleged event took place (date of occurrence).
7. Date the claim was filed in a court of law.
8. Date the claim was settled. (Items 6, 7, and 8 are useful in determining the length of time from the inception of the incident to the date the claim was

filed and the time elapsed before it was settled. These periods can range to four or five years.)

9. Claim payment. (This should be compared with the claim reserves by the insurance company when the suit was filed to determine the carrier's ability to estimate its liability accurately. If the reserve figure is consistently high, the hospital may be paying too much premium.)
10. Paid legal fees. (This also is useful in understanding the significance of legal fees in a malpractice case even in suits settled without any claim payment.)

Attorneys

The next relationship is with the attorney who represents the hospital in the defense of malpractice suits. The attorney will describe the chronological events that occurred since the suit was filed, including an explanation of such arcane words as respondent superior, *res ipsa loquitor,* interrogatories, discovery, depositions, requests to produce, summary judgments, dismissed with (or without) prejudice, and affidavits. During this visit, the risk manager should offer to serve as a liaison between the attorney and the employees.

In the event of a lawsuit, the risk manager can help reduce legal fees and increase personal credibility with hospital employees by providing the attorney the following services:

1. Identifying, from the medical record, the names, titles, dates, and times hospital employees treated the plaintiff.
2. Introducing the attorney to each employee the lawyer decides is necessary to interview in defending the lawsuit.
3. Attending all meetings and depositions with the attorney and hospital employees. This increases the employees' confidence that administration supports them.
4. Assisting employees in answering interrogatories. The risk manager will be able to answer certain questions found in nearly all interrogatories, e.g., name and address of insurance company at the time of the occurrence, the policy number, amount of insurance, and dates.
5. Establishing a mutually convenient time and place for employees' depositions.
6. Coordinating the copying of medical records and x-rays through Medical Records Department.
7. Coordinating the safekeeping (a locked file) of all medical records and x-rays through the Medical Records Department.
8. Obtaining signatures for all of the employee depositions.

Some attorneys may hesitate, expressing a preconceived concern that the information the risk manager obtains may be discoverable by the plaintiff's attorney. However, there is sufficient law today to protect the risk manager from revealing privileged information.[4]

In addition, in a July 27, 1984, docket entry in the Sixth Judicial Circuit Court of Illinois, Judge Creed D. Tucker ruled that "based on the Affidavits submitted: the court finds 'that the conversation between the named employee and the director-Risk Management is privileged in that the director is in a position to control or take a part in the decision upon any action the corporation might take.' Plaintiff Motion to Compel Answers to Questions is denied."[5]

If the hospital attorney still remains uncooperative, the risk manager should not be reluctant to inform the insurance company. The attorneys are hired to represent the hospital and are paid by the insurance company from the hospital's premium dollars. There should be no hesitation to recommend the dismissal of a law firm that refuses to allow risk management involvement.

The risk manager has now gathered some of the necessary facts and established contact with some of the important players, knows the names of some of the attorneys who sue the hospital and the reasons they sue, the specialties that are sued most frequently and the specialties sued for large dollar amounts. The risk manager should prepare this information in chronological form and file it for convenient future reference. It is now time to begin developing other important relationships.

The Role of Nursing

The Nursing Department represents entry to several important hospital activities. The director of nursing needs to be fully aware of how the risk manager plans to achieve the initial goal of loss detection. The explanation is made that the traditional incident reporting system is important in discovering the routine slips, falls from bed, cuts and burns, but the program frequently is deficient in detecting severe cases of patient neglect.

The director should be given the same set of screens as was presented earlier to the medical staff.

The nursing director now is fully aware of the plans to implement the detection system, realizes the risk manager's dependence on the nursing staff to make the program operable, and will assist in meeting the necessary nursing supervisors to ensure discovery of problems of neglect. In addition to the supervisors in the operating room, emergency department, and outpatient surgery, the risk manager should meet with the infection control nurse and the nursing supervisors (day, evening, and night) responsible for the patient care floors to explain the detection program. The director should be asked to add the risk manager to the agenda for the orientation of all new employees.

This key hospital department now is ready to assist the risk manager in accomplishing the difficult task. The manager should not disappoint these persons but should follow up on the smallest of problems, return phone calls, and visit patient care units (yes, even in the operating room, on occasion). The risk manager's conscious effort of support must be constantly and consistently apparent.

The Role of Others

Other personnel significant to the risk management program are:

1. The librarian, who can provide important resource material such as articles on risk management in medical publications, as well as reference material, including but not limited to, the *Physicians Desk Reference, Dorland's Illustrated Medical Dictionary,* and *Manual of Medical Therapeutics and Infection Control in the Hospital.*
2. The director of infection control (or epidemiologist), who is committed to the investigation of infectious diseases occurring in the hospital and can assist the risk manager in learning more about epidemiology and biostatistics.
3. The director of social services, who deals with problems of all sorts, frequently involving inadequate patient care.
4. The director of medical records, who honors requests for copies of medical records. This director can be invaluable in notifying the risk manager of all such requests. Some will be made by attorneys who have sued the hospital in the past. All these requests should be checked out; they may involve only an auto accident or they may indicate a malpractice suit. Some requests for medical records may come from attorneys inquiring about patients discovered in the generic screening process. This usually is a tipoff that a malpractice action is being considered so, if the investigation process has not yet begun, it must be started now.
5. The director of the business office, who can tell of patients unhappy with their bills and who threaten to sue for alleged poor medical management.
6. The director of medical education, who can enroll the risk manager in medical terminology and medical abbreviations courses. These courses are crucial to learning to read a medical record.

Much has been written so far about the importance of intrahospital relationships with risk management. The risk manager, in turn, must stress the importance of the hospital's relationship with its customers. A friendly, helpful, and competent staff can do much to reduce the number of malpractice claims. It is not uncommon for a patient to sue an unfriendly, aloof physician yet exclude the hospital because "they were so nice to me there."

Reports

The generic screening criteria have been established and the risk manager has convinced nursing and a few doctors to send in information on medical misadventures in their treatment areas. The beginning of the program has been successful but there may be an uneasy feeling that things still may be going on about which the risk manager is unaware.

Some checks and balances are available to allow the risk manager to determine the degree of the program's success. The manager, who already has explained the goals to the operating room supervisor, should stop by and ask to be added to the list of those receiving a daily copy of the surgical schedule—not the one with which surgery begins the day but the one completed at the end of the day, the one that records all the day's activities, including patients returned to the operating room to correct problems from earlier surgery.

Another record that can be used in conjunction with the surgical schedule is the daily admitting log. The following abbreviated example shows how both records can inform the risk manager of possible inadequate patient management. The surgical schedule usually is a computer printout describing the day's planned activity:

Date	*Time*	*Name*	*Age*	*Outpatient inpatient to be admitted*	*Surgeon*	*Procedure*
9/1	0730	Wilson, A.	81	IP	JCC	Resection & Graft AAA
9/1	0730	Smith, B.	32	OP	SN	Vasectomy
9/1	0730	Jones, C.	30	OP	JWP	Laparoscopy

As the day progresses, unplanned surgeries are added to the schedule. These are handwritten additions and one might read:

9/1	0800	Davis, D.	46	OP	TRN	Repair L. Ring Finger Index

However, one of the handwritten entries reads:

9/1	0830	Jones, C.	30	TBA	HEW	Repair Perforated Bladder

That may indicate a potential problem. Jones originally had surgery for a laparoscopy at 0730, and the risk manager needs to investigate with the doctors involved exactly what occurred during both the first and second surgeries. Was the first unexpectedly difficult? Was the repair difficult? Was it a success? Was the patient told about the perforation?

The risk manager also can check whether any surgical outpatients were admitted unexpectedly. By comparing the names on the admitting log with the names of those who had outpatient surgery the previous day, the risk manager might find:

Patient	Room #	Date Admitted
Smith, B.	7711	9/1/84

The original plan was to do Smith as an outpatient; what happened? Again, the manager checks with the surgeon involved. There may be a legitimate reason why the patient was admitted, but the risk manager needs to be aware of it.

MEDICAL RECORDS

Previous sections have dealt with areas in which the hospital community can provide measurable assistance in detecting and reporting circumstances that later give rise to a malpractice claim. Once a potential malpractice is detected, there begins the tedious process of reviewing all records pertaining to the events leading up to, during, and after the reported incident.

Primary among the records is the patient's medical record. For those being exposed to the bewildering world of medical terminology, the record at first will be more foreign than Sanskrit. As a beginning, the record can be summarized into the following sections:

- History and Physical: The history includes information about the patient's family, personal diseases, operations, and allergies. The physical is an entry by the physician listing the patient's complaints, review of the patient's system (ears, nose, chest, etc.).
- Physician Progress Notes: These are the daily notations of the physicians' impressions and procedures during the patient's hospital stay.
- Nurses' Progress Notes: These are notations of the nurses' impressions and procedures during the patient's hospital stay.
- Physicians' Orders: These are the daily written (and notations of verbal) orders given by the physician to the nurses, regarding IVs, medications, and caring for the patient's general welfare.
- Operative Reports: This is a complete document indicating the patient's name, preoperative diagnosis, operation to be performed, name of the anesthesiologist, name of the surgeon, time the anesthesia began and ended, time

the operation began and ended, and postsurgical diagnosis. This is a technical document that indicates all the steps performed during the surgical procedure.

- X-ray Reports: These are typed reports indicating the radiologist's impression of x-rays and CAT scans taken of the patient's chest, abdomen, esophagus, etc.
- Lab Report: This is an interpretation by the lab of tests taken of the patient's blood and urine. Many times these reports will indicate not only the patient's chemical profile but also which profiles are outside the expected limits of a normal value range according to the person's sex and age.
- Flow Sheets: These cover intake and output of liquids and urine, dates, times, type and rate of IV solutions, and medication records indicating type of medication given, when it is to be given, and the route, such as intramuscular, intravenously, or orally.
- Discharge Summary: This indicates the patient's name, date of discharge, history before admission and the hospital course.

After becoming acquainted with the medical record, the risk manager will understand that all of the sections listed are extremely important in determining the course of events that may or may not have caused the patient to suffer the injury that occurred or was alleged. Each section will contribute to a report to file on potential claims. The outline in Exhibit 14–1 will assist in preparing a complete record.

Once this report is completed, the facts have been fully documented, including the people involved and basic information about the patient and the injury. If at some later point a malpractice action is filed, this document can be used to refresh memories and to assist all the parties in more clearly recalling the actual events as they occurred.

A copy of the medical record also should be made for filing in the risk manager's office. The original medical record should be maintained in locked file (usually in the Medical Records Department), to be released only in the event the patient visits the hospital for additional treatment.

BYLAWS, RULES, AND REGULATIONS

Every hospital is required to maintain bylaws that list the purposes for which it was organized; how physicians qualify as members of the medical staff; how they can be terminated; the qualifications, tenure, and number of trustees who can serve on the hospital's board; the officers and terms of office for the board, the medical staff, and administration.

The rules and regulations identify the type of qualifications necessary for being a member of the medical staff; the procedures for appointment and for reappoint-

Exhibit 14–1 Example of a Staff Report

TO: FILE
FROM: Director - Risk Management
DATE: PATIENT/VISITOR:
DATE OF OCCURRENCE: DATE OF CLAIM:
CLINIC NUMBER: ADMISSION NUMBER:
DEDUCTIBLE:
EXCESS:
RESERVES: LEGAL EXPENSE:
COMPANY:
POLICY NUMBERS:

Attorney

Name, address, telephone number, and reputation.

Facts/Medical Record

Brief synopsis of the medical record abstracted from the summary of the medical record or brief description of events for a nonmedical occurrence. If, for example, the case involves a perforated colon, the writer may wish to give a brief description of the facts surrounding the perforation in the first paragraph and a brief summary of the medical record in the second paragraph. This portion of the report should be flexible to allow for a variety of occurrences.

Injury and Subsequent Medical Treatment

This describes the injury being alleged and discusses any permanent disability that may result. It briefly summarizes any subsequent records on the patient.

Patient

Name, address, age, and marital status. Includes number and age of dependents and employment information such as job title and net income. This would be an appropriate place to discuss damages, if known. Any information about the claimant that would have an effect on determining the claim's value should be presented here. An example of such a situation would be an injury to the hand of a guitar or piano teacher.

Witness

Each witness interviewed is identified and the most important portions of the meeting are highlighted briefly, as given in the conclusion section of interview summary.

Liability

Opinions on the hospital's liability and exposure are stated, with reasons for them based on the factual situation and/or judicial climate.

Reserves

Opinions on the adequacy of existing reserves are presented, based on the factual situation and, if appropriate, the litigation and judicial climate. Injury should be considered an important factor in analysis of the reserves.

Other Defendants

The names of the other defendants are given, along with their exposure if known. Also, if known, the names and addresses of their carriers are listed, as well as any other known policy information.

ment; emergency and temporary privileges; the appointment of limited health practitioners (anesthetists, physicians' assistants, psychologists, etc.); corrective action in the event of professional misconduct; suspension and disciplinary procedures, hearing and appellate review procedures for physicians whose appointments or reappointments are denied; and medical staff divisions, departments, officers, and committees.

The medical staff rules and regulations include admitting practices; standards of practice; rules involving consultations; resuscitation protocol; documentation in the medical record, including information necessary for a complete record and on the history and physical exam; specimens required to be sent to the hospital pathologist, etc.; limits of professional liability insurance; and definitions of licensed health practitioners.

This risk manager must become familiar with the bylaws and the rules and regulations because, in a malpractice action, that will be one of the first items plaintiff attorneys will request be produced. They will be interested in determining whether or not the hospital deviated from its bylaws and rules and regulations in the treatment of the plaintiff. If it is determined that there was a deviation and that it contributed to the plaintiff's injury, the hospital's attorneys will have a difficult time explaining to a jury why physicians and/or other persons did not follow their own rules of care and treatment.

CREDENTIALING

Getting to know the hospital's medical staff can be accomplished by reviewing each member's appointment application, which includes educational and professional background, a record usually found in administration.

Several key questions should appear in the application. If they are not, or if they are not in the list outlined next, or if no one is checking to see whether these important questions are being answered, the risk manager should recommend changes in the credentialing process. The key questions to be asked of physicians are (any "yes" answers should require a full explanation of the details on a separate sheet):

1. Have any disciplinary actions been taken or are pending against you by any state licensure board?
2. Has your license to practice in any state been limited, suspended, or revoked?
3. Have you ever been suspended or otherwise restricted from participating in any private, federal, or state health insurance program?
4. Have you ever, to your knowledge, been the subject of an investigation by any private, federal, or state agency concerning your participation in any of those agencies' health insurance program?

5. Has your Drug Enforcement Agency (DEA) number ever been limited, suspended, or revoked?
6. Have you ever been denied membership, or renewal thereof, or been subject to disciplinary proceedings, in any professional organization?
7. Insurance: Please attach a Certificate of Insurance that contains the following information:
   a. present insurance company
   b. policy number
   c. amount of coverage
   d. effective date
   e. termination date
8. Has your insurance coverage ever been terminated by action of the insurance company? If so, why?
9. Have any professional liability suits ever been filed against you?
10. Have any judgments or settlements been made against you in any professional liability case?
11. Have you any professional liability suits pending against you at this time?

As can be seen, risk management involvement in the credentialing process is critical. It is not unusual for a physician to refuse to answer some or all of these questions because "it is none of your business." In those cases, the Credentialing Committee must decide whether or not the hospital needs such persons on staff. A wise course would be to deny privileges, but practical considerations may dictate otherwise.

Experience will reveal that few physicians can answer "no" to all questions. In today's environment of high government involvement in the practice of medicine and with the patient clientele being increasingly litigation minded, it is unusual to find a practitioner now who has not been either investigated or sued. As a matter of fact, those falling in these categories are more likely to accept and defend risk management programs, and so it may be helpful in the future for the risk manager to know who they are.

The risk manager's main concern is to make certain there are no physicians on staff who are continually in trouble with the government, continually sued, or fail to purchase malpractice insurance. The risk manager has enough troubles without such individuals.

PHYSICIAN INVOLVEMENT

Administrators are increasingly realizing that hospitals can be held liable for certain acts of nonemployee physicians. The hard question that needs answering is how administrators can control the physicians' quality of care without telling them how to practice their licensed skills.

Administration needs to establish an environment of teamwork and cooperation. A bond of unification is created with the medical staff through the latter's involvement in committees on patient care; quality assurance; bylaws, rules, and regulations; medical practice; ethics; and utilization review as well as service on the board of trustees. A strong risk management program can enhance this relationship.

As discussed earlier, involving physicians in a risk management program is not easy. Physicians, by training, do not reveal things they consider inviolable, and making an error in treatment and discussing it with a stranger would be unconscionable. It will take time for this stranger to become accepted as a confidant, but until then the risk management program will never be an unqualified success.

Some risk managers suggest appealing to the physicians' logic and the importance of letting people know early of a medical misadventure so a thorough investigation can be made while memories are fresh. Others argue that if physicians do not notify their insurance company when they know they have a problem, the carrier might reserve the right to defend but not pay damages if the doctor loses. While these certainly are legitimate reasons, physicians do not consider them so when it comes to telling some hospital employee about their latest misadventures.

It is important not to let this attitude affect the early stages of the development of a risk management program. It will take time to stop being a stranger and to become a friend; to stop being a hospital employee and to become an important resource person. Following are some suggestions how.

Legal Opinions File

Over a period of years, administrators have had need to obtain legal opinions on a number of topics. As might be suspected, for problems recurring every few years, there probably are several opinions on the same topic, by the same attorney, saying the same thing. This creates an opportunity to provide a valuable document for physicians and hospital employees. By asking the hospital's attorneys for copies of all their legal opinions, the risk manager can create such a file. Its myriad of topics will be invaluable as a resource. A typical file has an index that covers many often-asked questions such as:

- consent for treatment of minors
- parental permission for an autopsy for a child
- consent to emergency treatment, such as for Jehovah's Witnesses
- confidentiality of quality assurance studies
- statute of limitation in medical malpractice
- release of child's medical record to a noncustodial parent

- who can practice acupuncture in the state
- subpoenas—when are they not valid
- who can give permission for an autopsy.

Information of this type also can be useful to physicians, who frequently encounter such problems. The risk manager can be helpful to physicians by publicizing the permanent location of the file and its index. It is beginning evidence that the risk manager is interested in their problems and is providing a real service to them.

Visibility

In the early stages of the program, if the physicians will not go to the risk manager, that individual should go to them. With the help of the president of the medical staff and the director of medical affairs, a medical staff meeting can be scheduled when the risk manager can give a *few* words about self and program. Later, when the program has developed more fully, the manager can go more into details.

After physicians can relate a face to a name, the manager should begin appearing at the hospital at various times before or after normal working hours. Making rounds with the administrator on call is an excellent way to show the medical and nursing staff an earnest interest in their work. The administrator can introduce the risk manager to those not met previously and provide an opportunity to briefly explain the program one on one. The manager should spend extra time in the emergency department, being careful to stay away from the action but continually observing the pressure on the staff in this important service. It is easy to find fault with less than optimum care if one has not observed at first hand what factors sometimes cause inadequate treatment.

The risk manager also should visit the operating room, the area with the most potential for medical misadventures. The head of the surgery department can be asked for the opportunity to observe an operation. If the chair approves, the manager should go through the entire process—gowning, scrubbing in, and observing. Like anything new, observing surgery takes getting used to, and risk managers may want to avoid certain steps until they are certain they are ready.

One approach is to sit in a corner, away from the action, observing the anesthesiologists, surgeons, and technicians at work, watching the method used for calling for and passing instruments, how sponges are accounted for, and the relaxed nature of the participants. Only after becoming totally relaxed in the surgeon's milieu, should the risk manager attempt to observe the operative site. This step is not essential, as one can have a genuine interest and education in the overall process without getting involved in the actual surgery. Even so, after having gone that far, the risk manager probably will decide to watch what actually is occurring.

A risk manager in a hospital should have curiosity equal to that of counterparts in a manufacturing plant. The risk manager does not actually need to become physically involved in the product but does need to know all the activities necessary to make a product serviceable.

Information

Another method of making physicians aware of and appreciate the risk manager's presence on staff is to keep them informed of what is going on in the malpractice field. What are the latest statistics, articles, or documents that might be of interest to them now or in the future? Occasional memos on the latest legal opinion on informed consent, or ruminations of other surgeons on documentation, are of interest to physicians. Such memos should be kept brief and not too frequent. Numerous magazines, periodicals, and articles also provide the risk manager with a steady supply of items of interest. These reference materials include:

- "Keeping a Lawsuit in Perspective" by Robert V. Wills, J.D., encourages physicians to treat a malpractice claim as an economic nuisance, not a personal assault, "much in the nature of an IRS assessment or audit." (*Exchange Commentary,* January 1983, volume 6, no. 1, a publication of the Illinois State Medical Services, Inc., 55 East Monroe Street, Chicago, Ill. 60603.)
- "How to Handle a Deposition: A Primer for Defendant Doctors" by Douglas Danner gives physicians expert insight into what to expect during a deposition. This article can be used with nonphysician employees as well. (It was published in the *Medical Malpractice Cost Containment Journal,* unfortunately now out of print. Danner can be contacted at Powers and Hall, P.C., 100 Franklin Street, Boston, 02110, for copies of the article and permission to reproduce.)
- *Hospital Risk Management* encourages hospital risk managers to publish their successes, concerns, and problems. (This is issued monthly by American Health Consultants, Inc., 67 Peachtree Park Drive, N.E., Atlanta, Ga. 30309.)
- *Medical Liability Advisory Service* reports on the legal aspects of medical malpractice and cases of interest. (This is published monthly by Capitol Publications, Inc., 1300 North 17th Street, Arlington, Va. 23209.)

There are many other helpful publications that the risk managers should consider as their budgets permit—yet they need not seek them out, as the publishers are resourceful and will find them soon enough.

DEALING WITH PATIENTS

In an article in *Hospital Risk Management,*[6] several of the industry's most respected risk managers, attorneys, and physicians discussed the merits and defects of the proposed Alternative Medical Liability Act (H.R. 5400 98th Cong., 2d Sess., 1984) sometimes referred to as a modified form of a no-fault method of compensating immediately patients who incurred an economic loss because of inadequate care while in a hospital.

One commentator, Charles Baggett, risk manager of Mercy Hospital, Miami, made a statement that should be the philosophy of every hospital risk management program. When discussing whether or not H.R. 5400 would reduce the length of time patients need to wait to be compensated for their damages, Baggett said: "If a patient is injured in my hospital, and we know it, we will be nose to nose with that patient within the week, if not sooner. We tell the patient the truth. We lay it on the line and do everything we can." Baggett believes that most hospitals "don't do it that way . . . but why not try it?"

It is important for the risk manager to discuss with physicians the necessity of dealing with their patients in the event of an adverse outcome. Physicians should understand that the risk manager is not addressing issues regarding bad results that have a definite etiology and negligence is not involved. The manager is most interested in dealing immediately with cases in which joint negligence (hospital and physician) is obvious, such as a retained sponge or instrument, a perforation, a wrong site, or a bad result where the etiology is unknown and negligence may be inferred.

In indemnifying a patient, an offer to reduce hospital and doctor charges may be enough. Sometimes no offer is enough. But the risk manager (and the physician) will be surprised how often the impact of a concerned administration will dissipate the anger in a patient and/or the family and allow the dispute to be settled in a short time. It is a well-tested philosophy and it works. As Baggett suggested, "Why not try it?"

SUMMARY

This chapter has explained organizing a comprehensive risk management program in a larger hospital. Little or no reference is made to quality assurance, negotiation of insurance contracts, review of contracts or leases, Workers' Compensation or safety, which are covered in other chapters. The tasks here seem endless and become increasingly more so as the risk manager's credibility and value increase.

The authors consider loss detection the No. 1 function of a quality risk management program. Consequently, it is the most difficult function to implement. Risk managers should not despair. They should use good judgment, follow up events, follow through, be persuasive, learn the language, avoid finding fault, display openness and trust, and maintain a problem-solving attitude. Above all, they must be discreet.

NOTES

1. Stanley A. Skillicorn, *Quality and Accountability* (San Francisco: Editorial Consultants, Inc., 1981), 12.
2. Ibid.
3. National Association of Insurance Commissioners.
4. *Galminas v. Fred Feitelbaum Const. Co.*, 112 Ill. App. 2d 445, 447 (1st Dist., 1969); *Sierra Vista Hosp. v. Super. Ct. for San Luis Obispo County,* 56 Cal. Rptr. 387 (Cal. Ct. App., 1967); *Insurance Co. of N. Am. v. Super. Ct. for Los Angeles County,* 166 Cal. Rptr. 880 (Cal. Ct. App., 1980); *People v. Knuppenberg,* 66 Ill. 2d 276 (1977).
5. *Cassady v. Strode,* 6th Jud. Dist. Ill., No. 82-L-1207 (1984).
6. "Legislation Proposes Reform in Malpractice Legislation," *Hospital Risk Management* 6, no. 7 (July 1984).

Chapter 15

The Medical Staff and Risk Management

Michael B. Guthrie

Risk management in health care was developed by safety engineers and insurance underwriters in the late 1960s and early 1970s to deal with the management of hospital exposures to potential plant and property liability. This definition of risk management is a bit limited today, given the expansion of the concept as presented in this book, but the original direction of hospital control of liability exposures emphasized elements that were easy to deal with first, specifically general patient safety. From that point, the concept and practice broadened to include the management of professional liability for nurses and other paraprofessional personnel.

Now, risk management has been redefined and focused on the principal cause of hospital risk exposure: physician professional liability and malpractice. It is a general rule that about 80 percent of the time a hospital is sued, a doctor is involved or named. Thus, the individual physician and ultimately the entire medical staff play a vital role in risk management in any modern hospital.

FUNCTIONS OF THE MEDICAL STAFF

In any hospital the medical staff organization discharges two essential responsibilities:

1. It strives to assure the quality of medical care provided by all its members and recommends privileges, changes in status of privileges, and, if necessary, disciplinary action or peer education to maintain the standards of quality patient care.
2. It advises management and the board of trustees on hospital policies and operations.

Table 15–1 Relationship Continuum

↓	*Voluntary Association/Membership*	
	Open Staff	
	Closed Staff	
	Contractual Arrangements	
	Part-Time	Stipend
	Full-Time	Salary
		% Fee
	Employee Relationship	

These functions are discharged not by individual members of the medical staff but are the responsibility of the whole organizational unit. This is done through implementation of well-written and well-constructed bylaws that reflect the organization, design, and controls accepted by the individual practitioners who make application to and become members of the medical staff. Individual practitioners' responsibility for practicing medicine within the constraints of their licenses and their awarded privileges is not a function of the medical staff but rather is the practice of medicine. These functions are separate.

There are numerous models for medical staff organization in hospitals in the United States. Table 15–1 depicts a continuum of the relationships between physicians and a hospital depending on its ownership and its organizational structure. The continuum runs from the more traditional voluntary medical staff organization to one of employed physicians. This chapter focuses primarily on the voluntary medical staff. However, it is important to recognize the varying approaches to risk management that the different models of structure require.

With a voluntary medical staff, it is more difficult to impose risk management requirements since the structure tends to be dominated by consensual decision-making processes rather than hierarchical decision making by management. Even so, there are opportunities for risk management to be a resource to the medical staff. Where differences are important in the process of making change or improvement in the management of risk, these are noted.

MEDICAL COMPONENTS OF RISK MANAGEMENT

Risk management is made up of two principal components: risk control and risk financing. This chapter emphasizes the risk control elements that are the function of the medical staff in collaboration with administration. There are possible roles for physicians and medical staff in risk financing programs, but these are relatively limited in scope.

A form of risk financing is the general approach of buying relief from professional liability exposure from a third party such as an insurance company that agrees to accept this exposure in return for payment of a fee in the form of premiums. This has been a traditional approach to dealing with professional liability. After the early 1970s, the malpractice crisis drove premium rates too high for many hospitals and physicians to pay and limited the availability of coverage in some areas. In that period, hospitals intensified risk control.

Risk control involves activities designed to identify risks, analyze their patterns, prescribe specific treatments or interventions to eliminate or minimize them, and evaluate the impact of the interventions. It is basically a systematic approach to potential loss detection and avoidance in the context of a comprehensive monitoring system.

The theory behind risk control elements parallels the medical ethic of prevention of patient injury and peer review of the quality of care. It is in this context that the medical staff organization can collaborate effectively with risk management in an approach to screening, analysis, and intervention to protect patients from untoward events, repetitive patterns of poor care, and preventable suffering.

Since risk control fits well within this context of the principal functions of the medical staff and parallels the concerns of physicians to assure the quality of patient care, then the risk manager has many opportunities to assist the physician in these efforts. Understanding physician motivation becomes a critical skill in these activities.

CLINICIANS AND RISK MANAGERS

There also are specific role differences between clinicians and managers that have an impact on the acceptance of risk management techniques by the medical staff. Practitioners, for their everyday dealings with patients, have been trained to behave in a certain role and pattern that is most effective and adaptive for clinical decision making. This set of behaviors includes an emphasis on one-to-one interactions, a propensity to be reactive as opposed to proactive, and to avoid any intervention that might do harm without appropriate cause—that is, risk avoidance. Physicians tend to be action oriented, though conservative in goals. Once they have exercised their judgment concerning the nature of a difficulty and have summarized and analyzed the data presented by a situation or patient, they then act, generally on the basis of that judgment alone, not often in consultation with others. This is the traditional and appropriate clinical model for the practice of medicine with individual patients.

Managers, on the other hand, practice their profession more often with groups of individuals. Their decision making addresses problems identified on a larger scale, usually not an individual case or person. Managers tend to be designers of functions, activities, and processes rather than doers themselves. The role of management is to plan for the possibility of future actions, not simply to react on the basis of experience or history.

These essential differences pose difficulties for the integration of risk management concepts into the medical staff organization. The differences are embedded in the models of activity and expected behavior as well as in the approaches to the analysis and solution of problems. Physicians have a difficult time changing hats from a clinical to a managerial role when asked to collaborate with risk managers because of these differences in outlook and habit.

The successful integration of risk management concepts thus must recognize these conflicts among physicians. This recognition will encourage the education of medical staff leaders in management skills and perspectives. Risk managers also will support improved organization of the medical staff; try to bring physicians into the management of the hospital; emphasize communications that are clear, frequent, and consistent; and respect physicians' need for autonomy in decision making wherever possible. Knowing these differences will help managers adapt the introduction of risk management techniques into the expectations and behavior patterns of physicians in their clinical roles.

ROLE OF PHYSICIANS ON THE MEDICAL STAFF

Physicians, as medical staff members, play a variety of roles within that organizational unit. Many are simply passive and, at best, may object to their colleagues' imposition of certain rules, regulations, and protocols on their behavior. Others are informal leaders whose opinions and activities influence the outcome of most major decisions concerning bylaws, rules and regulations, and patient care standards but they are not visible in committee meetings or the executive committee. Finally, there are the formal, visible leaders who are the workhorses on most medical staff committees and who chair the departments. Even where a formal employee relationship exists with the hospital, such differences in informal and formal organizational structure have a powerful influence on the outcome of most decisions on quality of patient care and must be understood by risk managers.

Standards of patient care are established by physicians through both the informal and formal mechanisms of the medical staff organization. The role of physicians on the audit or medical care evaluation committees of the medical staff is to establish these standards of patient care in the review of the treatment provided by their colleagues.

Frequently physicians in this role adapt a "clinical" approach, again focusing on single cases, making rapid individualistic decisions, and expecting immediate action with little consideration for outside encumbrances such as the legalities of due process or rights. They often are frustrated by hospital administrators who do recognize these external constraints. On the other hand, peer pressure in the informal medical staff structure may slow the decisional process in some quality assurance areas to the extent that hospital administrators will be frustrated by the lack of action from the medical staff leadership.

Risk managers, too, must recognize and deal with these problems in medical staff review of clinical issues. They must assist the medical staff in the assessment of risk exposures and their historical relation to risk control but respect the informal constraints that may limit formal action. Risk managers have a supportive role to play in the medical staff's quality assurance and peer review activities.

Physicians have a formal role in many areas that affect risk control and claims management such as reviewing audit and medical care evaluation studies, analyzing patient or physician complaints, and meeting the accreditation standards established by the Joint Commission on Accreditation of Hospitals.

In a hospital with a formal risk management program, physicians may be involved in the review of everyday problems and incidents, trend analysis of incident reports and other historical experience, the review of the outcome of generic screening (see Chapter 6), and participation in the safety program.

The most frequent involvement of individual members of the medical staff is when a claim is filed blaming both them and the hospital.

All of these roles pose special problems for risk managers. Passive members of the medical staff can be influenced and their opinions shaped by consistent, reliable information and data. The formal leadership must be assisted in reaching solutions that help in the identification and prevention of risk exposures. The physician who is unfortunate enough to be the subject of a specific claim usually will be eager to participate in a program for claims management or defense.

COMPONENTS OF RISK MANAGEMENT

It is the defense of a specific claim that most physicians see, incorrectly, as the definition of risk management in the hospital. This is an unfortunate narrowing of the definition, and dealing with this perception becomes the first objective of a successful manager and risk management program.

It is not difficult to broaden the perception to mutually acceptable goals in the medical staff. To improve the quality of patient care, to decrease the harm potential for individual patients or groups of them, and to manage the costs of medical care are goals that most reasonable physicians can accept readily. These then lead fairly logically to the specific functions of risk control, claims management, risk financing, and the administrative aspects of risk management or quality assurance.

The medical staff obviously plays a role in specific areas of risk management: The detection, analysis, and prevention of inappropriate or inadequate care to patients; the education of physicians in the avoidance of preventable misunderstandings and mistreatment of patients; the analysis of specific types of occurrences; the evaluation of trends and other historical experience; and the recommendations concerning interventions, policy changes, and sanctions.

In addition, the physician leadership has a substantial role in advising the risk manager and administration on policies, protocols, procedures, and other administrative aspects of the implementation of an effective program.

The establishment of comprehensive monitoring; the imposition of generic screening devices; the implementation of specific loss prevention, loss reduction, or risk reduction activities; and the etiquette of claims management or defense activities are appropriate focuses of physician collaboration and advice. Risk managers should create and encourage such collaboration.

Thus, physicians can participate in the risk management program not only in their individual care of patients in the hospital but also as members of the medical staff and, if they are leaders of the staff, in their communication with administration.

Ordinarily risk management programs are established on the authority of the board of trustees. This approach to the implementation of an administrative program can pose difficulties for risk managers since they will not have the immediate acceptance of most physicians in a voluntary medical staff organization as to the appropriateness or necessity of such activities. Sophisticated risk managers thus must set as their first task the achievement of widespread understanding, then formal acceptance, of general risk management procedures. This acceptance can be aided by the support of key medical staff leaders. This assistance must be actively sought and the leaders' support made explicit within the medical staff.

BEING CHICKEN COSTS MONEY

Probably the most dramatic role of the medical staff in risk management involves disciplinary actions against physicians who are deemed to be practicing substandard medicine and who may repeatedly expose the hospital and other physicians to claims.

Quality assurance programs, a part of the medical staff's responsibilities, have as one of their tasks the identification of individual practitioners or groups of them who are treating patients in what their peers consider to be inappropriate, substandard, or harmful ways. These practitioners also pose a specific malpractice exposure risk to the hospital and to other physicians and must be dealt with promptly, decisively, and fairly.

Physicians ordinarily have some difficulty dealing effectively with their peers when it comes to discipline. This caution derives from many sources. One is physicians' empathy for a colleague who fails or performs badly. This empathy many times clouds the peer physicians' ability to vote for a sanction.

The risk manager must be positioned to assist and support medical staff peer review committees in taking appropriate action in sequenced steps from education to discipline in order to intervene when a physician is deemed to be practicing substandard medicine. The effect of the exposure of this kind of practice, once it has been identified and analyzed, is immense. The courts have held consistently that the medical staff and board of trustees may be held liable both individually and collectively where they fail to act according to their own bylaws to sanction individuals and to protect the quality of patient care when they knew or should have known that a physician was practicing in a manner less than the standard of care.

Risk managers must develop an approach to effectuating change and assisting and supporting appropriate action by the medical staff and hospital management. To do less is to encumber the organization with tremendous potential cost.

A MODEL FOR CHANGE

Risk managers and the medical staff leadership thus must have some model for change that is applicable to their dealing with individual physicians and groups of them. One model for change, as proposed by an organizational psychologist, Kurt Lewin, in the early 1960s, is a basic framework for discussing behavioral and organizational change in a three-stage process. For a change program to be effective, each of the following stages must be internalized by the individual or accepted and embedded in the group.

Stage 1—Unfreezing

In this initial stage an environment for change is created and some type of reason or pressure for change is applied to bring about a change (or unfreezing) in an individual's or group's attitudes, habits, or behavior, and awareness of the need for motion. The unfreezing stage is critical to the process since inadequate acceptance of the need for change will prevent movement toward the desired result. For example, a hospital proposes a malpractice insurance requirement to the medical staff. If unfreezing were insufficient, the medical staff executive committee would not vote for this as a bylaws provision or as criteria for application to the staff. It might end up as a debate between the board of trustees and the medical staff. If the unfreezing stage has been handled appropriately, key medical staff leaders will come to understand the importance of the risk to the hospital and to themselves of the exposure caused by uninsured physicians. They will be able to push similar need awareness among the informal leadership. This paves the way for movement through the next stage.

Stage 2—Moving/Change

In this stage, attitudes and behavioral habits are changed or moved toward the desired state. The movement occurs in the direction envisioned by the leadership or management as a result of the preparation and logic of the education presented during the previous stage.

Stage 3—Refreezing

In this stage, attitudes and habits are refrozen in the desired state by consistent reinforcement and support. Attempts to implement change toward another state require another round of unfreezing and movement of attitudes and habits. Reinforcement usually takes the form of rewards—personally satisfying outcomes that encourage repetition of the new behavior.

Within that three-stage framework, change must have the backing of top management and medical staff leadership. More important, however, change should be self-motivating. Individuals who take responsibility for the change must be committed to the program, otherwise the desired movement will not occur. There also must be an accommodating environment that is supportive of the change and assists the refreezing once the change has occurred. These are important implications for designing and implementing any policies or procedural changes or other systems.

SPECIAL CONCERNS OF THE MEDICAL STAFF

As physicians become involved in the hospital risk management program some specific areas must be addressed early. Most physicians are worried about how to avoid being named in a malpractice suit. The more conscientious ones also are concerned about how to help the hospital avoid such risk exposures.

Physicians need to be educated concerning the areas of their practice that affect the probability that they will be named in a lawsuit. What many do not seem to understand clearly is that many of these areas have nothing to do with the technical quality of their work. Factors that affect these probabilities include:

- their interpersonal skills with patients and families
- the depth and frequency of their communication with patients concerning their disease, the rationale for the treatments recommended, and any questions patients may have.

It also is important to help physicians put into perspective the adequacy of their practice as compared with their peer group or the standards of care in their community. Problems in this area involve:

- the occurrence (and frequency) of previous suits
- the results of the peer review committee's evaluation of the care provided
- the physician's recognition of failures with hospital's policies and procedures.

Deficiencies in any of these areas have a price.

By studying malpractice episodes in their own hospital, medical staff members may be able to identify potential problem areas that are broadly applicable to all or many physicians and to recommend specific procedural system changes that will help prevent patient injury. Physician audit committees can examine allegations of malpractice incidents or mishaps in an attempt to uncover elements that could be prevented and thus avert harm to other patients.

Risk managers have an important role in assisting clinicians in this assessment and in helping keep the focus broad rather than physician-specific. For example, this analysis can stimulate concern for good recordkeeping. When physician record documentation in a potential litigation case is evaluated, it is an opportunity for the risk manager to educate practitioners as to the importance of good records. Nursing and paraprofessional documentation also is critical. Consistency in the record and adequate notes by all members of the treatment team can assist in successful defense of many claims.

Failure to diagnose a specific condition and inadequate evaluation (usually reflected by the absence of documentation concerning the physician's thought processes or judgment) frequently result in claims based on diagnostic errors. Detailed record documentation is essential in such situations.

Good records properly kept are the physicians' protection as well as the principal means of communications concerning patient care plans to other professionals. Risk managers should assist physicians in educating each other on the importance of documentation, despite the unpopularity of this kind of recordkeeping and paperwork. Positive record protections need to be outlined for physicians:

- keeping track of data in the record
- showing their judgment (even if they may subsequently be determined to be wrong)
- timing their entries
- being up to date in their entries
- indicating follow-up plans when patients are discharged.

Legibility is an issue for some physicians when their notes, comments, judgments, and construction of records cannot be deciphered by any member of the treatment team or any outside expert because they are unreadable.

Risk managers can remind physicians about certain things that should not be done in the medical record. Specifically, it is important to emphasize that physicians:

- should never alter anything
- should write additional comments as addendums or dictate and date them to add or to retract from previous statements
- should line out with a single linc actual errors in writing and note them as "errors"; they should not be scratched out, inked over, or whited out.

Physicians also should be reminded not to insert information in the record between other entries. This usually is done in tiny handwriting totally uncharacteristic of the physician and is an obvious attempt to reconstruct the record in a more favorable light. If this record then appears in court, this behavior becomes almost prima facie evidence of a physician's guilt.

Physicians must refrain from the urge to make editorial comments in the medical record to express their personal opinions about other people's work. These remarks and commentary are totally inappropriate in any medical record. They allow the plaintiff's attorney wide opportunity for divide-and-conquer tactics in any legal action.

Finally, the risk management program must emphasize the integrity of the medical record. Physicians must not tear out sections or parts of it. The importance of maintaining the record as a whole, safely, and confidential, is critical.

GOOD GUYS AND GALS DON'T GET SUED

The technical areas are important but not essential in the prevention of claims against most medical staff members. The truism in the subhead above implies that communication with the patient and the family and the physician's interpersonal skills are as much protection against both justified and unjustified malpractice suits as any of these other strategies.

Good doctors do get sued now and then, but physicians who are good guys and gals rarely do. The physician's good intentions are not enough; neither is being a high-quality physician. However, being a good physician who talks to patients and who clearly evidences concern about their level of information, dignity, and privacy is a major step in the direction of preventing lawsuits.

In addition, many claims situations can be managed without litigation if there is proper use of good communication among the hospital, the physician, and the patient. This communication must emphasize providing correct and accurate information; evidence of concern and understanding for the patient's plight after an untoward event; the acceptance by the physician and/or hospital of some responsibility, when applicable; and cooperation in arriving at a just solution without recourse to litigation.

It is the last factor that gives most physicians the most anxiety. They must have support and be encouraged to take this responsibility for participating personally in the management of incidents as they occur. It is here that a risk manager's function is the most sensitive. A tactful approach to the physician and assisting in approaching the patient constitute skills that are learned through example and experience.

Although prevention of injuries or events obviously is the key, nonetheless injuries will occur. Rapid handling then can help minimize the cost of claims and the probability of litigation. As time goes by, the costs of claims and their handling increase. Thus, the later the situation is addressed and the later the claim is closed or settled, the more likely it is to go on to a costly litigated settlement. The costs thus will include not only the damages requested by the plaintiff but also the legal fees involved in preparing and defending the case.

INFORMED CONSENT

The medical staff organization may participate in defining norms of communication with patients and families through a variety of rules, regulations, procedures, and protocols as well as through the climate of expectations established by the formal leadership. Within this context, informed consent is an additional important area of concern for every physician.

Most physicians conceive of informed consent as a document, usually filled out by nurses, that grants the legal right to do whatever the physician thinks is in the best interest of the patient while the individual is unconscious, asleep, or too sick to object. Of course, this is a fallacy that results in many claims but it is not unrepresentative of many physicians' behavior and attitude about informed consent. This misunderstanding and efforts to correct it have led to much frustration among physicians. They feel that informed consent documentation is so worthless that it is impractical to try to improve it.

Risk managers must work to develop physicians' understanding that informed consent is essential and is the patient's right. This is a process between physician and patient, not between hospital and patient. From this beginning, the medical staff must be led to understand the interpersonal nature of informed consent as the primary basis for the protection that it affords to both physicians and hospital. Informed consent is a process of negotiation and education in which the physician outlines the recommendations, rationale, and risks involved in any treatment or intervention and expects the patient to make some form of conscious decision about the care and choices.

Patients naturally vary in their responsiveness to this kind of process and education. Some habitually will agree with whatever their physician suggests, leading the doctor to the unfortunate conclusion that the patient does not care about understanding what is going on in the treatment. What this is likely to reflect is more of the patient's respect for the physician than indifference to what happens. Many patients today are demanding accountability from their physicians for interventions and treatment planning. They expect more information, candor, and an opportunity to question the physician explicitly about the recommendations. Physicians who want to avoid medical and legal difficulties are wise to invest this time in communicating effectively with patients.

This communication, however, has little to do with its subsequent documentation by the physician as a matter of business record. This is where the informed consent documents of one kind or another play a role. The risk managers' role in explaining these documents should follow only after physicians have a clear understanding of the process involved. But the consent documents do become a critical part of the paper trail that provide evidence that this physician-patient communication took place.

The first informed consent documentation involves the physician's detailing the conversations with the patient, either in the office or in the hospital, as to recommended treatments or interventions. This process can be assisted by preprinted forms that are filled out by the physician, signed by the patient, and witnessed by some other competent adult. These informed consent documents frequently are confused with older and inadequate hospital documents that were called "op permits" or the like.

Hospitals used to provide physicians with such preprinted permits or informed consent sheets that were signed by the patient, then by a nurse as a witness to the patient's signature. However, this process inadvertently led some physicians to believe that nurses already had obtained informed consent from the patients for the procedures ordered and performed. This is not true but has led to numerous situations in which physicians have written an order that nurses simply obtain this form. The nurse may do so, but the patient has not, in fact, been informed by the physician. The patient thus has ample grounds for objecting, even eventually in the legal arena.

The appropriate process involves the hospital only to the extent that it needs to be assured that the patient has had the opportunity to meet with the physician and talk about the alternatives and risks. This hospital verification of consent may be summarized in a document that it requires the patient to sign before surgery. This may be witnessed by any other competent adult. The hospital has the limited legal responsibility of making an attempt to assure that the patient has had a chance to talk with the doctor prior to surgery or invasive diagnostic or therapeutic procedure. This is as far as it goes. The hospital cannot legally obtain, through any of its personnel, any type of informed consent since it is not a "practitioner."

Risk managers also can help define the role of the nursing staff. This role cannot include the obtaining of informed consent. Nursing staff members may be actively involved in patient education but that is not the same as a conversation and dialogue between a licensed medical professional and a patient concerning a planned intervention. Only physicians who are licensed to exercise their specific form of clinical judgment are empowered by law to obtain such consent. Nurses may assist in the process and may witness the patient's signature to documents but may not get informed consent.

This whole area provides many opportunities for the risk manager to become involved on a one-to-one basis with physicians and nurses in order to provide extensive education. The risk manager also can assist groups of physicians and other health providers to clarify and delineate their roles.

SUMMARY

Risk management in the modern hospital requires the commitment and involvement of the medical staff organization as well as individual doctors as leaders and as practicing physicians. The medical staff organization participates in risk management as it discharges its function to (1) assure the quality of patient care and (2) advise hospital management concerning policy, procedures, and operations.

Physicians play a significant role as individuals and as leaders/managers within their staff organization but they ordinarily are not trained to behave in managerial roles. This may pose problems for risk managers in achieving their desired ends.

The risk management components in the hospital that involve the medical staff include physicians' participation on medical staff audit and departmental committees, as individuals in patient care, and in communications with administration.

The responsibility and authority for the different aspects of risk management derive from the board of trustees through the hospital administration to the risk manager and through the bylaws of the medical staff to the executive committee and departments of the medical staff organization. This organizational structure, involving the delegation of authority, responsibility, and the acceptance of accountability, is an area of frequent misunderstanding among medical staff members. It needs to be dealt with directly and skillfully by risk managers who understand conflict management.

Medical staff members' effectiveness as peer review participants is an area of difficulty for many quality assurance and risk management programs. Supporting this activity and participation requires the risk manager to have a clear understanding of change and an ability to support and effect it with the medical staff.

Chapter 16

Nursing and Risk Management

Janine Fiesta

Nurses as professionals are becoming increasingly more aware of their legal accountability. This is partially in response to the legal system's increasing awareness of the nurse as a professional who may be individually liable for acts of malpractice. It also is a recognition by nursing itself of the translation of moral-ethical-professional standards into legal rule and dictum. The individual professional nurse has always felt morally responsible for patient care. This responsibility in many instances has been interpreted through judicial decisions into a legal standard.

The recognized status of nurses as professionals means that society is recognizing them as having something unique to offer to the health care delivery system. To characterize nurses as the handservants of the physician or employees of the institution is to recognize only a portion of the role they play in meeting the needs of patients and consumers of health care. This so-called "dependent" aspect of the profession may lead to instances of nursing malpractice. But nurses also may be liable for violations of the "independent" aspects of the profession.

For instance, a failure to exercise reasonable professional judgment in notifying a physician when a patient's condition is worsening is a violation of the nurse's independent judgment in assessing a patient's status. It is not necessary for the doctor to write as an order on the patient's medical record "please notify physician if patient's condition worsens." This assessment of the patient, as well as the nursing judgment that the physician should be notified, is part of the constant process of diagnosis and intervention that marks the practice of independent professional nurses.

NURSING LIABILITY

Deviations from appropriate dependent and independent practice may result in nursing liability. In recent years, cases in which nurses are involved as defendants have increased markedly. The scope of nurses' accountability also has broadened, corresponding to the expansion in the professional practice itself. To meet these growing legal responsibilities, nurses need to be aware of and participate in active, institutionwide risk management systems.

Risk management is a systems approach to preventing malpractice claims. It is used basically to assess areas in which claims can be prevented. This process includes the identification, analysis, and treatment of risks.[1]

The process of risk management is familiar to nurses even though the terminology may not be as well known. Traditionally nurses as a profession have participated in an active component of the risk management system known as the incident reporting system. This system is a foundation of many risk management programs, although it has developed and been transformed from its original purpose.

Nurses who have practiced for a decade or longer will recall incident reports as punitive tools used by the Nursing Department largely for disciplinary and counseling purposes and as a personnel tool rather than a patient identification tool.

The use of the incident report has changed as risk management has developed. The language describing this form also is changing. In many locales, it is known as an event report, a situation report, or an occurrence report. All of these terms are an attempt to remove the prior negative stigma attached to these reports because of their original use.

All of these terms are used to describe events that are not consistent with the usual operation of a health care institution or the standard care of a particular patient. Certainly patient injuries caused by the acts or omissions of health care providers must be identified, but this definition also is meant to encompass potential areas of risk for patient injury.

Incident reports, no matter what they are called, are a vital element of the risk management system. They are not, however, limited to use by nurses. A good program receives such reports from all departments of the hospital, including members of the medical staff.

In some states, incident reports are discoverable and may be admitted into testimony during a malpractice case. Therefore, the author of the report should be as objective and factual as possible when documenting the situation. In some particularly sensitive situations, an incident report may not be the appropriate vehicle of communication and documentation. When questioning a medical judgment in which there has been no patient involvement or injury, the nurse may wish to document this in an informal memorandum to the supervisor. Physicians reporting their own errors in patient care may be reluctant to use the formal incident reporting procedure. To insist on the formality of the procedure may result in the loss of significant patient care information necessary to the functioning of an integrated hospitalwide system.

RISK MANAGEMENT GOALS

The goals of the risk management system are twofold: (1) to identify where systems are failing and (2) to identify potential claimants. Systems may fail in any department of the institution.

On the first goal, all hospitals and agencies are built on procedural systems, many of which are designed to prevent injury to patients and others. For example:

- Housekeeping has a system or procedure for keeping floors clean that includes posting signs when floors are wet.
- Engineering has a system for snow and ice removal, often specifying how often and under what circumstances this should be performed.
- Nursing and pharmacy have an overlapping system for checking medication orders.
- The hospital has an overall system of patient identification.

The classic system breakdown in a hospital is the wrong patient having the wrong surgery. When such a drastic event happens, an entire system has failed. Not just one person is solely responsible for correctly identifying patients for surgery; in most institutions, this is a shared responsibility. The purpose of analyzing systems is to attempt to intervene before an injury occurs to a patient. For example, if the patient is noted to be wearing an incorrect identification bracelet, an incident report should be initiated. In addition to correcting the problem for that particular patient, the problem should be addressed as a generic one for the benefit of all patients. The risk manager will question how the event happened and what steps can be taken to prevent its recurrence. It will be noted that no injury has occurred to the patient in this example. The best level of risk management is the identification of a potential problem before an injury occurs.

The second goal of risk management is to identify potential claimants. These may be patients who actually have been the victims of malpractice or those who believe they have been. If a patient does have a valid malpractice case, early identification of the claim is extremely important for risk management purposes. Valid claims can be settled before the patient seeks an attorney's advice. For all parties, the cost of litigation (which can be substantial) may be reduced or even eliminated. Nursing plays an important role in this identification process. It frequently is the nurse who realizes that the patient has an injury that may have been caused by the actions or inactions of a health care provider. The nurse then has a professional responsibility to communicate this information to the nursing supervisor and to the risk manager.

Sometimes patients believe they have been victims of malpractice even though they have not. These may be patients (or families) who are unhappy with their care (or with their illness), who have unexpected outcomes (a neurological deficit on discharge that was not present on admission such as sciatic nerve injury secondary to injection), who have unexpected complications (such as infections), or who have had an accident (a fall or burn). Any of these categories, among others, may contain the No. 1 requirement for a malpractice case.

The essential requirement for a malpractice case is not malpractice; it is an unhappy patient or family who believes that malpractice has occurred and visits an attorney to determine whether this is a valid assumption. Sometimes the patient's misconception results from erroneous information, lack of information, or negative communication from one health care provider regarding another's delivery of care. One positive intervention by risk management is to facilitate accurate and complete communication. Many risk managers work with a patient representative or patient advocate. This individual may intervene on behalf of administration or risk management. In addition, the patient representative provides valuable information to the risk management office.

THE NEED FOR DOCUMENTATION

The risk manager assists in the prevention of claims by providing assistance with documentation. Adequate documentation can prevent malpractice claims from being initiated and is invaluable in a successful defense against them. Nurses and physicians most frequently request information regarding documentation. How a note is worded for the record may be significant. The rules for appropriate documentation emphasize factual information presented as completely and as honestly as possible. A fraudulent record is difficult to defend in a malpractice case. Therefore, all health care providers are encouraged to alter records only if absolutely necessary for patient care purposes and only with the greatest of care to prevent even the appearance of misrepresentation. Accurately timing and dating nurses notes and progress notes is especially important.

The omission of material from the record sometimes forces the settlement of claims. For example, the nurse's failure to document notification to a physician when a patient's condition is worsening may lead to a dispute in the future as to when the doctor was notified. A nurse who charts ''Doctor notified'' should then proceed to document specifically what information was relayed to the physician.

REASONABLE STANDARDS OF PRACTICE

The nurse's failure to document may lead to an erroneous judgment by a jury that the nurse failed to practice in a reasonable manner. Practicing in a reasonable professional manner and documenting that factor are the two best defenses to malpractice claims.

Risk management cannot prevent all malpractice claims. Those that cannot be prevented can be defended successfully by reasonable standards of practice. Nurses frequently ask what the standard of care is. This is a significant question since the nurse's behavior in a specific malpractice case will be measured against reasonable standards of care.

These standards are formulated by the nursing profession. In fact, one of the characteristics of a profession is the ability to set its own standards. Nurses formulate their standards as they practice nursing on a day-to-day basis. Some standards are part of the custom of nursing practice and therefore are not necessarily in written form. Other standards are written, including job descriptions, policies, procedures, association guidelines, textbook material, and the Nurse Practice Act. All of these may be admissible in a malpractice case to establish deviations from customary practice. An expert witness testifies in a malpractice case to assist the court in understanding the standard against which the nurse's actions should be measured. All nurses should familiarize themselves with professional standards. Over time, standards may change or new ones may become necessary. Nurses must accept the professional responsibility of staying current with such changes.

HOSPITALS' CORPORATE LIABILITY

While the general principles of individual accountability continue to expand, making nurses increasingly liable, the responsibility of hospitals also has increased. Historically, following the end of charitable immunity, hospitals became liable for the malpractice acts of employees through the principle of vicarious liability. Thus the employer-employee relationship was sufficient to hold the hospital responsible even though it had no direct relationship with the act of malpractice. This liability still exists but has been expanded by the doctrine of corporate liability.

Corporate liability means that the hospital, as a corporate entity, has a separate and distinct duty to assure that all patients receive safe, quality care. This means the corporate entity has the responsibility for providing safe premises and adequate equipment and personnel.[2] It also includes the responsibility for assuring that independent contractors (physicians who are not employees but who have been granted privileges by the institution) provide safe, competent care.

To assist the hospital board and administration in meeting their corporate responsibility, nurses frequently become the eyes and ears of the risk management and quality assurance programs. Patient care information at the staff level must be channelled into the system appropriately so that action can be taken if necessary.

For example, if the nursing staff became aware of a physician who was impaired by alcohol (or drug) abuse that was interfering with the ability to care for patients, such information must be communicated through appropriate departmental channels as well as to risk management and quality assurance. This not only helps the institution to meet its corporate responsibility, it also allows nurses to meet their own professional, legal, ethical, and personal accountability for patient care. Once a staff nurse communicates the information, it then becomes a management or institutional issue to be resolved. If management or administration fails to pursue appropriate action, the issue becomes one of institutional liability. The same principle applies when the nurse notifies the supervisor that equipment is deficient or unsafe for patient care or that staffing is inadequate.

While it is well recognized that such events will occur on an isolated basis in even the best of institutions, the repetitiveness of such problems with no attempted intervention may signal the failure of reasonable standards of care for the institution. The difficulty with resolving these problems, particularly in a large institutional structure, is failure to communicate significant information from the staff level to the administrative level. Nurses who do so often become frustrated because their efforts do not seem to result in correction of the problems. Sometimes this is because the information has not reached the level of management at which action can be taken.

An individual nurse who is concerned about a repeated significant problem that is not being addressed should recognize that an alternate method for problem solving is the risk management system. The risk manager, who usually is directly responsible to the chief executive officer, has direct access for problem solving. Therefore, problems that are not otherwise resolved may be brought to the specific attention of the risk manager. In other words, while the nurse provides valuable assistance to the risk management program, the risk manager, in turn, may provide assistance to the nurse.

While information collection and problem identification are the cornerstones of a successful risk management program, it also must emphasize the investigation, analysis, and treatment of risks. Because of nurses' unique relationship with patients, they frequently are in the best position to assist the risk manager with the investigation and analysis of potential claims. This might involve a review and understanding of policies and procedures applying to the claim. For example, if a patient has fallen, received an injury, and threatened to initiate a malpractice suit, the risk manager may need to become familiar with nursing policies regarding the use of siderails and restraints. The nurse also may be able to analyze the patient's and family's response to an incident. Frequently patients feel most comfortable expressing their concerns to the nurse who has developed rapport and is attempting to meet their emotional as well as physical needs.

The nurse's role in the treatment of risks may extend to participation in a specific medical malpractice case, testifying as an expert witness. The expert witness appears as an educator, to assist the court in understanding the standards that the profession has established for itself. Nurses who deviate from reasonable professional standards should be held accountable for their actions; conversely, those who have not deviated should not be held liable even though a patient injury may have occurred. The expert witness assists the judge and the jury in distinguishing between cases that are valid and those that are not. The expert provides opinion testimony; that is, based on an analysis of the facts, the witness gives an opinion as to whether the nurse is liable for deviating from reasonable standards of care.

The nurse also may be asked to be a witness to specific facts. This occurs when the nurse has participated in the care of the patient who subsequently sues. In such a case, the nurse will be testifying as to personal knowledge regarding the care. For example, if the patient has fallen and received an injury and Nurse A finds the patient on the floor and notifies the physician, Nurse A may be called to testify regarding those actions. In this situation, as a fact witness, the nurse is assisting the institution in its defense of the case.

THE NURSE AS DEFENDANT

The nurse also may be a named defendant. In such an instance, legal counsel will be assigned to guide the process and vigorously defend the nurse's action. Counsel may recommend settlement if the nurse has breached reasonable standards of care. Sometimes settlement may be the preferred course even though the nurse's actions seem reasonable and defensible. Other factors that counsel may take into account when making this decision will include: (1) the possible sympathy effect on the jury (e.g., paralysis in a young child), (2) lack of documentation, and (3) violation of written policy and/or procedure (even though nurse's actual conduct may seem reasonable).

Usually when a nurse is a named defendant in a malpractice case, the employer also is a named defendant. Under the legal theory of vicarious liability the employer is held responsible for the acts of employees. Therefore, it is in the employer's best interest to defend the actions of its nurses vigorously. If the defense is successful, the hospital will not be automatically liable under vicarious liability but may be under the corporate liability theory for its own acts of malpractice.

The nurse-defendant in a malpractice case usually is not treated punitively by the institution simply because of being a named defendant, even if there is an ultimate finding of liability. The malpractice system was not established as a punitive method; rather, its purpose is to compensate injured patients who have received an injury because health care providers have deviated from reasonable standards of care. Exceptions to this general rule occur when the provider is found to be grossly negligent; in those circumstances, a punitive damage award may be justified.

Sometimes nurses become involved as defendants simply because they happen to be in the wrong place at the wrong time. In other cases, they may be involved because a deviation from standard procedure unfortunately has resulted in a patient injury. For example, medication errors occur often in hospitals but fortunately do not usually result in injuries to patients. The wrong medication may be given to the wrong patient, an extra dose of the correct medication may be administered to the right patient, or a single dose may be omitted. These deviations usually do not result in malpractice cases or in injured patients.

Occasionally, however, such errors do produce a patient injury. The nurse-defendant generally is not treated punitively by the institution if this is an isolated occurrence for that individual. However, if a particular nurse is responsible for repeated medication errors, the hospital will respond appropriately whether or not malpractice cases are involved. The nurse-defendant should cooperate as fully as possible with the institution and insurance company to facilitate a successful defense.

OTHER AREAS OF LIABILITY

While risk management focuses primarily on malpractice claims, there are other areas of potential liability for nurses.

A growing area of concern is the more frequent involvement of nurses and physicians in suits involving criminal allegations. These may involve termination of treatment or failure to initiate treatment. For example, the deliberate removal of life support systems when not appropriate medically or failure to resuscitate a viable fetus following an abortion may be the basis for a criminal action. When the nurse becomes aware of a potential criminal issue, the nursing supervisor and the risk manager should be notified to provide guidance and direction.

Other legal issues may involve patients' belief that their constitutional rights have been violated in some manner. Improper searches in the Emergency Department may lead patients to believe that their Fourth Amendment rights against search and seizure have been violated. Refusing to follow the decision of Jehovah's Witnesses who will not permit blood transfusions in a life-threatening situation may result in a legal challenge by patients based on a belief that their First Amendment rights to practice their religion have been violated.

Disclosing confidential information about a patient in an authorized manner may lead to litigation involving the right to privacy. As consumers become more aware of the Patient's Bill of Rights,[3] cases involving a breach of confidentiality or invasion of privacy are appearing more frequently. These may involve unauthorized disclosure of the patient's medical record but are more likely to be based on oral disclosure of information that is inappropriate. This may include casual conversations with family and friends outside the health care delivery system or within the system involving providers not directly involved with the patient and therefore without a need to know the information.

Informed consent cases also may include the nurse. Unlike the previous examples of liability that demonstrate the nurse's expanded legal role, these cases consistently view informed consent as a physician liability rather than a nurse or hospital liability issue. The informed consent doctrine is based on the right of self-determination. Thus, a patient who is a competent adult should decide whether to accept the treatment. This should be an informed decision. Therefore, informed consent is meant to be an educational process—a sharing of knowledge from physician to patient (legally, not from nurse to patient) in order that the patient may make a knowledgeable decision. The consent form is a document used to verify that this educational process has occurred. Unfortunately, the form itself sometimes is given higher priority than the information it is meant to document.

The informed consent doctrine requires the physician to explain to the patient the nature of the procedure; its risks, benefits, and complications; and any alternatives. The nurse, in the role of health teacher, may supplement this explanation by answering the patient's questions or providing clarification. The hospital may play a role in monitoring the process and verifying that consent has been given. These roles do not stand in place of the physician's legal duty to obtain the informed consent.

REFUSAL OF TREATMENT

Refusal of treatment is an issue with legal and ethical dimensions. In general, the competent adult patient may choose to refuse or terminate treatment. However, the issues in this area are as yet not well defined and the answers, in many instances, are ambiguous. Therefore a case-by-case determination based on each patient's individual circumstances may be the best (or only) course of action. For example, whether a living will has been signed and whether it is legally binding in a particular state may influence the appropriate response to a patient's request. In any event, the staff nurse caring for this patient may seek advice from the nursing supervisor and the risk manager.

Of special concern to nurses is the "Do Not Resuscitate" order and its legal ramifications. It is well-accepted medical practice that a No Code or Do Not Resuscitate Order is appropriate in many patient care situations. For example, a patient who is dying of terminal cancer with no hope of recovery may be a candidate for a No Code order. As long as the physician is acting in accord with reasonable standards of medical care and judgment, this order will produce no more liability than any other.

The nurse's dilemma arises because a minority of physicians will not document this order on the patient's record because of an erroneous belief that doing so may result in their liability. Once the physician makes the medical determination that the patient should not be resuscitated, this judgment should be documented as an order on the record just as any other patient care order would be. The physician who gives a verbal order not to resuscitate places the nurse in a difficult dilemma from a legal, moral, and professional standpoint. Without a specific written order to the contrary at a time a patient's death may be near, the nurse should begin resuscitation. However, the nurse may realize that this is a patient who has expressed the desire not to be resuscitated. Without a doctor's order the nurse must decide whether to violate the patient's rights or to violate legal standards of reasonable care.

A simple solution to this problem is a hospital policy that requires physicians to document this order on the patient's medical record as they do any other order. The risk manager may assist the Nursing Department in the formulation and implementation of this policy. This is only one example of policy formulation that may result from an interaction between the Nursing Department and the risk manager.

The risk manager will be most effective with optimum input from the Nursing Department. In turn, the risk manager will provide valuable assistance to the department in the identification, analysis, and treatment of nursing liability situations.

NOTES

1. Janine Fiesta, *The Law and Liability: A Guide for Nurses* (New York: John Wiley and Sons, Inc., 1983).
2. John Horty, *Action Kit for Hospital Law* (Pittsburgh, Pa.).
3. American Hospital Association, *Statement on a Patient's Bill of Rights* (Chicago: American Hospital Association, 1975).

Chapter 17

Physicians' Office Liability Exposure

John R. Tanner

A claim or a lawsuit over an injury or problem in a physician's office often is received with great surprise and apprehension for fear of a loss that might exceed available coverage. Such a response is symptomatic of office staff attitudes in that, as with an auto accident, one tends to look at such an adverse event as happening only to someone else.

Attitude determines performance in most tasks that people perform. Attitude not only applies to the performance of the expected duties of the office staff but also determines the success with which the office avoids loss exposure and reduces risk to patients and employees themselves. The tone of the office and the employees' attitude are established by the owner-operator physician(s) and requires an affirmative, specific statement by such individual(s) as to what is expected of the staff and how certain situations will be handled in dealing with patients.

How to utilize staff attitudes in loss reduction and prevention of claims and lawsuits in the office is specifically addressed as each area of office liability and exposure is discussed.

OFFICE DESIGN AND FUNCTION

Office design is subject to many forces when it is being laid out. These include the personal tastes of the owner-operator, sometimes the feelings and desires of that individual's spouse, and, on occasion, the requests and suggestions of longtime employees. Occasionally a physician will find it necessary to take over an office that was designed by prior tenants and has flaws in its layout, resulting in inefficient function and sometimes, frankly, raising the risk of injury because of door movements, hallway turns, and the like.

The initial design of a medical office in an existing building naturally incorporates certain architectural considerations based upon the outside structure and constrained by utilities and structural components. In a building being built specifically for physicians' offices, these constraints may be somewhat less but are ever-present in the planning process.

Once the architectural considerations and limitations have been determined, the office design should consider four major areas:

1. the types of patients who will be visiting
2. the visibility patterns within the office
3. the equipment and furnishings
4. the maintenance aspects.

The type of medical practice, of course, will determine the sort of patients seen and will relate to their ages, stage of debility or agility, and mental status. Offices expecting elderly persons should have rails along the walls, corridors wide enough to allow wheelchairs to be moved in and out easily, and toilets with those accommodations. Carpeting should be thick and well padded in case of falls and there probably should be no areas that are uncarpeted or that provide a hard surface, which can result in a fracture if an elderly person should fall. The type of carpet is a consideration, with a tight, hard pile used where the infirm and elderly may be walking and would be less likely to trip than in a shag type of carpet. These are areas in which conflict may arise between the interior designer or decorator, who is attempting to produce a visual and possibly a tactile masterpiece, and the physician owner-operator, who knows the types of patients expected.

Mental status of patients is important. In psychiatric offices there should not be items that can be thrown or used to harm the patient or others; once again, the floors should be well padded and the waiting area should be clearly visible to the staff in attendance so that rapid action can be taken if an emergency should develop with a psychiatric patient.

Visibility within the office is a vital consideration and involves particularly the ability to observe patients in waiting areas as well as those in examination areas where observation is appropriate and socially acceptable. Visibility in hallways and turns in the office are important considerations so that persons do not constantly collide in hallways or have to look at mirrors at intersections. Traffic patterns should be projected and considered when the design is being laid out to minimize visibility problems and associated risks.

Equipment and Maintenance

Office equipment should be in protected alcoves where possible, and the layout should provide this. Where this is not possible, the equipment should be placed behind semiprotective barriers that are smooth and have nondangerous sharp corners. In addition, the equipment should be tested according to manufacturer's instructions and serviced regularly to avoid electrical shocks or improper functioning that could cause injury to a patient or a staff member. Maintenance is a necessity and must be performed with appropriate care to avoid damaging carpets, which could result in a slip, fall, or trip. After servicing, equipment should be restored to its original position and maintenance personnel should be advised to handle it carefully so that any adjustments are not disrupted and electrical connections are not damaged.

Staff members should be instructed never to pull plugs from the wall by holding the cord because that could damage the connection, resulting in injury not only to a patient using the equipment and to an employee attempting to reconnect it to the electrical source but also in damage to the equipment itself. Maintenance services should be evaluated carefully when they are hired and their methods of handling the equipment and the office furnishings should be monitored periodically, simply because of personnel turnover at the maintenance company and techniques may change with new service persons.

Premises Liability

Premises liability is given little consideration by most office owners and operators but may be a source of considerable expense and/or litigation if not maintained carefully. Where the owner-operator is a tenant in a building, the premises liability as to that individual in most states would begin with entrance to the physician's office. Maintenance of the floor surfaces, chairs, and seating areas, and movement of doors and other equipment, must be observed carefully. Insurance coverage for premises liability is always available and usually is reasonably low cost in comparison with the office operating expenses but it is an absolute necessity.

Should the owner-operator lease a larger portion of the building or areas including hallways and parking places or should that person own those same areas, then premises liability becomes of greater concern since control is more remote and requires careful monitoring as to how those areas are maintained. In climates where snow is a factor, snow removal is a vital aspect, as is maintenance of the surfaces of the driveways and hallways and assurance that they all are free of obstructions and in a condition in which persons of ordinary intelligence and observation would not be injured without negligence on their own part.

WORKERS' COMPENSATION AND STATE STATUTES

Most states require Workers' Compensation coverage, either through an insurance company or (in some states) self-insurance. This coverage usually begins when the number of employees reaches a specified level. It also is influenced by whether the office is operated by a corporation, a sole physician, or a partnership of physicians. Information on these factors is specific to each state and should be obtained from legal counsel in the state in which the physician is practicing.

Some physicians feel that they can self-insure since they see themselves as being available to treat persons who work for them who might be injured. Unfortunately, this theory is not realistic in that it does not take into consideration differences of opinion between employee and physician and payments to the injured staff member that might continue for years and involve considerable sums of money. It also fails to consider legal expenses involved, should the self-insured physician decide that there is no viable claim (known as controverting the claim) but the staff member seeks legal counsel and brings suit.

Workers' Compensation insurance premiums are relatively low so self-insurance, where it is legally permissible, should be a last resort in the case of a medical office of small to medium size. A large clinic with numerous specialties and with sufficient money reserves or in which money can be invested at reasonable interest rates to provide for the coverage of Workers' Compensation might be considered but, again, would seem to be too risky in today's litigation climate.

PROFESSIONAL LIABILITY

Loss exposure is greatest for a physician and staff in the area of professional liability. Some 20 percent of all medical malpractice cases arise at the office and not at the hospital. That percentage represents a large dollar amount and a significant area of exposure that for the most part is preventable and controllable by the physician owner-operator.

Patient Processing

Areas of risk associated with patient processing include the making of appointments and the taking of phone messages, observation of waiting and patient care areas, medical recordkeeping, follow-up procedures, follow-up on appointments and medical revisits, and medical relationships with the hospital as to patients who are hospitalized.

Appointments are an area of potential risks that is easily addressed and monitored. The importance of the appointment book is that it establishes that appointments were, in fact, made at the time and not entered into the book at some later date, following a lawsuit or a claim. The credibility of the appointment book depends upon how it is maintained. For example, many office persons feel it appropriate to make appointments in pencil and, when one is cancelled, erase it and write a new one in its place. The legal problem is that the erasure forever removes from the book any evidence that an appointment had been made and cancelled by the patient.

In lawsuits, a patient may claim that an appointment was not made when persons in the office recall specifically that one had been made but cannot prove it since the appointment has been erased from the book. This weakness in preserving evidence can be overcome simply by keeping the appointments in ink and, when one is cancelled, marking through it with a single line and noting that the cancellation was by the patient. Naturally, the appointment book will have to be larger than the standard model since it may be necessary to appoint another patient into the same time slot and there must be space in which to write it.

Phone messages are another source of claim litigation so evidence of such messages should be maintained in some detail and documented accurately. When patients call in to complain of a problem and declare that it is associated with the care that the physician is providing, that information should be noted in the patient's medical record in a handwritten note that is dated, timed, and signed by the person who took the message so it will be a permanent part of the record. To do this, of course, requires a few extra minutes because it means pulling the file and making sure to write in a specific dated note. The time necessary to do this will pay dividends later because it will provide contemporaneous proof that the message was received, and the information given will be written in the record.

The value of the contemporaneous note, of course, is that it is made without contemplation of a lawsuit and thus has more believability should a claim involve that note or the issues it covers. Such notes also serve as memory refreshers when employees are asked to testify as to the facts involving the message.

Employees should be ordered to never give patients medical advice over the phone. The only advice they can give is to tell the patient to come in and see the physician or to make an appointment. All employees, of course, should be educated as to emergencies that can occur and should be alerted to transfer such calls to the physician immediately. The owner-operator physician, of course, must answer such calls when asked by the employee; otherwise, after a few turndowns, the staff member will either begin to make decisions or will put the caller off, which could result in injury to the patient and a claim or lawsuit.

An example of such a situation was a case in which a man who was known to have been ill for several days with a high fever and chills called to report that he was then passing blood through the urinary tract. Such an event, coupled with continued fever and chills, was not recognized by the office staff as being an emergency. When the man finally was seen, he died shortly thereafter.

Phone contacts with physicians' offices or answering services must be monitored carefully. It is always a temptation for physicians to advise answering services to refer to them only calls that are emergencies and to allow the others to wait for office hours. Such a system presumes that the answering service person is able to take a history from the patient sufficient to determine what is and what is not an emergency for that particular situation. Such a presumption rarely is valid and occasionally can result in a claim or medical malpractice action because of the failure of the answerer to identify a problem as a true emergency and therefore failure to notify the physician. Obviously, at a trial of such a lawsuit, the answering person must testify that the physician did not teach or explain what to do. The simple solution, of course, is to not give that advice to the answering service but to accept all phone calls immediately. The physician then can determine what is an emergency and what is not, and act accordingly.

Waiting Areas—Visibility and Safety

Waiting area safety is a vital concern since patients who may be urgently ill may be required to stay in such an area for a short time. Some of these patients may collapse, suffer seizures, fall out of chairs, or otherwise have a medical emergency and it is important that staff persons in the office be able either to see the waiting room in order to identify any such problems promptly or be required to monitor the area frequently to make sure patients there are all right. This is particularly vital when they are aware of a patient who may have a propensity for seizures, fainting, and so forth.

The design of new offices or the remodeling of older ones should include the visibility and observation requirements noted earlier. This can be accomplished with one-direction mirrors, if the staff prefers not to be sitting in a fishbowl but still needs to see what is happening in the waiting area. Some offices use open reception areas, which have the psychological advantage of extending open arms to the patients. However, they have disadvantages for staff members because they must limit their conversations because misunderstandings might arise if waiting patients hear certain candid comments.

Recordkeeping

The medical record is the physician's prime defense in any kind of malpractice action because it is information written contemporaneously with the event and, from the legal point of view, does not represent information that was prepared in anticipation of litigation. Although some physicians might argue with that concept, it is legally viable. The medical records should be filed alphabetically rather than by number since greater misfiling is possible in the latter system. Medical records should detail all known allergies. They also should reflect requests to previous physicians for prior records unless these records are so voluminous as to create a storage problem. In such cases the physician should review the records if they are located locally, either at another physician's office or in a hospital. The new treating physician should obtain selected portions of voluminous medical records, including the face sheet, discharge summary, admission notes, operative notes, pathology reports, x-ray reports, and the like.

The medical record of the first examination is extremely important and should detail the patient's height, weight, temperature, blood pressure, and, of course, the date and time of the visit. The history should be reasonably detailed. Terms such as "review of systems negative" should be avoided since such a statement is difficult to define later. Records should reflect the tentative diagnosis, the proposed treatment plan, the reasons for it, and the expected outcome.

Consent by a patient for certain diagnostic procedures and/or treatment is just as vital at the office as it is at the hospital. Consent issues in a lawsuit are basically swearing-under-oath matches between the physician and the patient. The doctor's best defense is an adequately documented record describing any substantial risks and alternatives available that were described to the patient and including the patient's signature as acknowledgement of receipt of the information. Even with such records, the patient still may deny knowledge of the conversation or may deny understanding the information presented. Nevertheless, a contemporaneously prepared written consent with the patient's signature will carry strong weight in favor of the physician should the issue come to litigation.

The distribution of devices such as IUDs, braces, and prescription medications should be recorded on the patient's record as part of the prescribed treatment. This also should be listed in a separate log so that if there is a recall or problem with the device or the medication, all patients who have received such articles or medications can be identified. For example, a log should be kept of all IUDs given, the name of the patient, the date the IUD was first inserted, and its removal if that occurs. Otherwise, if there were an IUD recall, physicians' offices would have no alternative but to examine everyone of their records to identify all persons who had received them and who should be notified of any defect. It is far easier to set up the log in advance so that all such patients can be identified promptly.

Follow-Up Procedures

Care of a patient involves history, physical examination, laboratory, treatment, and follow-up. Many lawsuits revolve around whether or not a physician in fact requested a patient to be reexamined within a certain time, so such follow-up should be documented in the record.

This again points up the importance of the properly maintained appointment book, in ink, to prove that an appointment was, in fact, on the book and that the patient either cancelled or did not appear, which of course also should be noted.

Back-up systems for follow-ups and for referrals should be established just as they are in emergency rooms so that the physician to whom a patient was referred can be contacted to determine whether that person did in fact appear as instructed. Patients seen in the office who are advised to return at a specific time should be called again at home the evening before the follow-up visit to remind them of the appointment or to establish with them that their condition has improved and that an immediate visit is not necessary.

Although failure to establish these types of follow-up procedures probably is not indicative of negligence by the physician's office, such systems reduce risk and improve the quality of care.

Wait Relationship with the Hospital

Occasionally a patient must be admitted immediately to a hospital and the urgency is determined by the treating physician. Some hospitals tend to cater to certain physicians more than others, which can be detrimental to the care of a patient. An owner-operator physician who knows such a system is in operation should link up with another hospital or meet with the admissions persons and administration to break down those barriers so that cases can be admitted properly for the patients' safety and for risk reduction.

Telephone contacts with hospitals' outpatient and inpatient services must be recorded in the patient's file the same as other phone messages in order to establish the purpose of the messages and the issues involved. Considerable malpractice litigation has involved the issue of whether the hospital inpatient or outpatient service or the doctor's office was responsible for the care of a particular patient.

Patient processing—from the initial phone contacts through appointments, waiting, recordkeeping, follow-up procedures, and hospital relationships—is crucial to the quality of care and to the reduction of risk and of potential loss exposure in a physician's office. Adherence to the concepts presented thus far should have a positive effect in risk reduction and improve relations between office staff and patients.

PATIENT CARE BY OTHERS THAN THE PHYSICIAN

Patient care by others than the physician includes advice, which will be given occasionally by a nonphysician and is a high-risk activity that should be avoided but does occur nevertheless. Direct patient care such as the drawing of blood, electrocardiograms and x-rays, and certain medical procedures, including injection of medications and intravenous fluids, usually is performed by persons other than the physician in the office (or hospital). Persons such as nurses, practical nurses, laboratory technicians, aides, and lay persons who have been trained by the physician and/or other members of the office staff are invaluable members of the medical team. However, they must be attuned to office policies and procedures and particularly to the attitudes necessary to provide good care while at the same time prevent the raising of risk and loss exposure.

Nonphysicians must be careful to avoid making statements that imply inadequacies on the part of the office staff or the physician. Comments that reflect delays because the office was busy or that problems in patient care are related to office difficulties are highly detrimental. They also are of little or no interest to the patient until that person files a lawsuit. Then such information is likely to be used against the office staff and the physician. Statements should be affirmative and pleasant, should not make promises that cannot be kept, and should not be defensive.

A patient complaint about care in the office, whether it relates to delays or treatment the person feels is substandard, should be received in a constructive manner, discussed among members of the staff, and should be followed up with a letter of apology to the patient. Patients are not interested in why the event occurred; they are interested only in knowing that steps have been taken to prevent its recurrence, so any correspondence or verbal statements should not attempt to offer explanations.

Technical care by other than physicians is, in a legal sense, under the supervision of the physician and therefore should be observed by the doctor for quality and technical excellence. Injection sites should be reviewed periodically with the persons who are giving injections so that nerves are not injured; so, too, should methods of drawing blood from veins and arteries where that is appropriate.

The use of procedures that are invasive such as sygmoidoscopy, colonoscopy, cystoscopy, etc., which ordinarily are performed by the physician but with nonphysicians in attendance, should be reviewed with the latter as to their technical aspects and complications for which they should watch. The office staff should be well apprised of the complications possible with certain invasive procedures, how to recognize those complications while a patient is still in the office, or if the patient calls to complain after having left the office.

All office staffs have seen patients who return with a dripping hand or arm when blood has been drawn but adequate hemostasis has not been applied. The physician in charge of the persons providing such patient care must review them thoroughly as to their technical performance. Keeping records of such reviews as part of the employees' file is essential should a lawsuit arise later because of an IV or arterial stick problem or invasive procedure that resulted in a complication. Such information will attest that the physician has taken reasonable steps to ensure the quality of care provided. Although negligence on the part of a nonphysician still will be imputed to the employer-physician, in most cases the fact that reasonable steps to prevent such measures have been taken may have a mitigating effect on a jury's decision.

CREDENTIALING OF EMPLOYEES

All employees who work for the physician, including other physicians, must be credentialed adequately. The cost is minimal. Phone calls to other employers or written requests for information to other employers or state agencies require only a brief time. If an employee is needed immediately, that person can be hired upon employers' or agencies' verbal statements but the credentialing process should continue and the individual informed of probationary status until the information is obtained.

Although experience and education can be measured by objective means, the attitude of the employee in dealing with patients is not measurable in advance and must be observed over time. No matter how technically excellent a particular employee is, a person whose attitude is negative or destructive should not be retained in a medical office but should be discharged. Such employees can create disasters, instilling into patients ideas and feelings that are negative and can cause them to become highly critical of all problems that may occur subsequently in the office and also make them litigation prone.

TRANSFER OF CARE TO OTHER PHYSICIANS

Frequently in the practice of medicine the care of a patient may be transferred to another physician. This usually occurs when the patient moves to a different area of a large city or out of the community entirely. Unfortunately, human nature tends to stimulate the next treating physician in some cases to be critical of the care by the former physician. Therefore, it is vital that adequate narrative summaries, including copies of office records and laboratory data, be forwarded to the new physician and be referred when possible under separate confidential cover.

When patients want to take their own records, and the law of the state permits that, it may be necessary to fill in the next treating physician verbally with details that the original doctor may not wish to have reflected in the written records but that are important and that the new physician should be aware of. This also provides for some unanimity of direction and care in order to avoid misunderstanding on the part of the transferring patient. This contact does not preclude changes in the care by the subsequent physician but at least should alert the latter to take such actions in a tactful and appropriate manner so that they do not reflect adversely on the transferring physician.

A lack of communication and of tact and diplomacy between two such physicians is a frequent cause of medical malpractice actions. This can occur when sudden changes in care by the second physician sometimes are associated with statements by the latter that imply to the patient that the first physician was not providing proper treatment.

Transfers between physicians within the same office may occur when a patient is not content with the care, attitude, or manner of the first physician. If a patient insists on a transfer, an internal one should be encouraged since it eliminates the problem of communications and treatment changes that occur when the patient is transferred totally out of the office. The argument for retaining the care but with another physician in the same office is that all the records are there and the patterns of treatment are well established, which can be shown to the patient to be an advantage. Occasionally patients may really be looking for some encouragement to stay and possibly seeking some attitude adjustment or changes in approach with which they can feel more comfortable.

CONSULTATIONS INVOLVING OTHER PHYSICIANS

Consultations for other physicians place the consulting doctor in the position of being closely associated with the one who requested the aid. In the case of a medical malpractice action, a complaint probably would be brought against both physicians. Nevertheless, consultation is an opportunity to correct diagnostic and/or treatment mistakes by the referring physician in a tactful and diplomatic way. These, of course, must be handled with the patient in the same manner. At no time should errors be described to the patient unless they have resulted in actual damage or injury, in which case the consulting physician may feel some obligation to discuss it with the referring physician first and then inform the patient and outline a solution.

The Catch-22 aspect of this situation is that the patient may well sue upon learning that there has been a problem; on the other hand, if that information is concealed but is discovered later, some courts may consider it a fraudulent concealment, which can be devastating at trial. Honesty, as usual, appears to be the best policy, but the consultant first should discuss the situation with the referring physician before sitting down with the patient and the family and explaining the problem. If there has been good communication and rapport with that patient, then the likelihood of a lawsuit is diminished considerably, although it still is present, depending primarily on the degree of damages—that is, the amount of injury.

Sending patients to other physicians for consultation carries with it a risk similar to that of transfer of a patient except that the referral patterns usually generate a certain amount of respect and social communication between doctors. That will tend to reduce considerably the risk of the consultant's advising the patient that the referring physician in some way has committed a malpractice act or provided improper diagnosis or treatment. In any situation, consultations with the patient should be done with both the referring and consulting physicians together with family members. The meeting should be well documented in the patient's record.

BILL COLLECTIONS

Bill collections are a problem in all medical offices but are a necessity and a reality of life. Patients usually do not object to paying medical bills, provided they feel that a reasonable quantum of care has been delivered with an affirmative pleasant attitude so that they believe they received their money's worth. Failure to pay a bill in a timely fashion most frequently reflects some patient dissatisfaction with the attitude of the office or the actual care received. An occasional patient may be short on funds and be delaying the payment while awaiting adequate funds; others routinely do not pay bills for several months, and such people can be identified fairly quickly.

Collection of delinquent bills has been approached over the years in a variety of ways but most frequently has consisted of a series of cute or serious notes accompanying each monthly statement requesting payment, with each note becoming more firm until threatening collection or possibly legal action. Since the money is owed to the physician, it is suggested that the doctor speak to the delinquent patient and establish why the bill is not being paid. Many a patient will refuse to speak to office personnel and will ignore monthly notices but will be highly receptive to a conversation with the physician. Rarely will that delinquent patient ever make the first move, so that is up to the physician.

Delegating bill collection to the staff without the physician's attempting to determine the problem usually is doomed from the start since the patient will pay only if sufficiently frightened or if some factor arises that was not present when the bill was first submitted.

LOSS PREVENTION AND LOSS REDUCTION

Loss prevention and loss reduction refer to the loss of money and the reduction of the amount that would be or will be lost in a particular claim or medical malpractice suit. Loss prevention generally is thought of as encompassing concepts described as quality assurance. One aspect of this involves improving the quality of care in the office as manifested by better recordkeeping, appointment systems, phone message handling, follow-up procedures, etc.

The medical aspects of quality assurance include periodic reviews of certain diagnoses that are seen in the office on a recurring basis to determine whether adequate diagnostic steps were performed, given the history and physical examinations, and that the treatment was appropriate, based on the history and physical and laboratory data developed. Criteria have been established for those reviews. For example, the patient who appears in a medical office with lower abdominal pain should undergo not only a general physical but also abdominal and rectal examinations and, in the case of women, of the vagina, in order to meet basic quality assurance criteria. It is presumed that failure to perform a rectal under the circumstances of lower abdominal pain is evidence of substandard care and would represent negligence in most instances. If the patient cannot tolerate a rectal examination for some reason, that information should be documented in the record; this would excuse the failure to perform the test. Similar circumstances would apply for vaginal examinations. Review of the criteria for a number of specific conditions, such as abdominal pain, will help an office avoid or reduce substandard care and thus improve the quality of treatment patients receive.

Periodic review of all office procedures and policies, along with attitude adjustment by the office staff and the physician, will improve the quality of care, guide improvement in relations with the public, and enhance the safety of the patient as it relates to administrative and paperwork matters.

RISK MANAGEMENT

Risk management represents, in the pure sense of the term, the reduction of loss already known to have occurred. Such information is vitally necessary, particularly in larger organizations where systems of detection of adverse events are necessary because such occurrences may escape the view of the persons who should be identifying them. In a medical office, adverse events usually are obvious when they occur unless they have a delayed effect, which may be identified by the patient's return to the office because of a complication or to another physician or to an outpatient or emergency service, where criticism is likely to be voiced without hesitation.

Situations such as the last-named, of course, are preliminary to medical malpractice actions, whereas returning to the same office generally is not, even if the treatment was negligent and resulted in an injury. As noted earlier, follow-up procedures become vitally important in these circumstances and patients should be encouraged to return to the office promptly and not be forced to delay because that very waiting may result in their going to an emergency room or to another physician.

Risk management in an office also involves a periodic review of physical premises and equipment for potential hazards. All occurrences of a medical administrative nature must be reviewed with the entire staff, and particularly with those involved in an incident.

Staff members must be encouraged to report all problems or mistakes that they identify. They must understand that such reporting will not be treated punitively unless, of course, the error is of such a gross nature that punitive action is the only reasonable remedy. Most problems are not that severe and should be used as teaching experiences. Should the staff perceive the process as a means of eventual punishment, then reporting will not occur and any attempts to reduce loss by starting early legal defense will be lost and the lawsuit will come as a total surprise.

SUMMARY

Office policies and procedures should be in writing and should reflect attention to the details covered in this chapter. Attention to attitudes of employees and physicians is crucial since they are keys in determining performance and are the aspect of patient care most likely to precipitate legal action. Human nature is such that when a patient feels true empathy and caring by the physician and staff that person ordinarily will be far less critical of mistakes. By the same token, a patient who is aggravated and upset at the handling of making the appointment or after contacts in the office is far more likely to judge attitudes and performance as detrimental and, in fact, probably causative of any errors that might occur.

All of the factors discussed here as pertaining to physician office exposure also are applicable to any ambulatory, outpatient, or emergency service operated by a hospital or other institution.

Chapter 18

Management and Leadership for Risk Managers

Clayton W. Boringer

This chapter provides a capsule view of some of the many facets of management and managing. Each topic discussed, of itself, has been the focus of one or more books so, at best, only a broad-brush treatment is presented here. The chapter summarizes the development of the management process over the years, outlines theories that have emerged with those processes, and analyzes the role of the manager, common leadership styles, and characteristics of effective managers. Human behavior theories and styles as they relate to managers and the managed are touched on.

It may seem a bit unusual that management and managing concepts merit coverage in a book on risk management. In most instances, risk managers will have limited, or no, staff to manage and direct. Why, then, devote attention to the management process and managing? Could not the risk manager learn from experience and exposure all that is necessary to know to supervise the small staff? The material here presents managerial insights that may ease superior-subordinate relationships, however small, whenever they need to be addressed.

Another circumstance is important. The risk manager is in a unique position, working in an organizational environment dissimilar to that in typical business, industry, and governmental settings.

The hospital organizational hierarchy itself is unusual. Analysis of the organization chart, Figure 2–3 in Chapter 2, reveals that many of the critical operating relationships are not in the typical line-staff structure. One of those relationships, for example, includes the medical staff. While its physicians, dentists, and surgeons are part of the operational structure, they are not actual employees of the hospital and indeed constitute a relatively self-governed group. Of course, the group must cooperate and coordinate with hospital management and policies but it is not organizationally obligated to do so.

Risk managers must work with members of the medical staff, for their support and assistance are needed. In case of disagreement, appeals are to the administrator and then to the board. Managers should do all in their power to resolve issues with the medical staff.

Risk managers should learn to judge the managerial and leadership styles of the various members of the medical staff and to note, in particular, how they relate to their peers and subordinates. This is of great assistance in deciding the best courses of action when dealing with such individuals.

Parallels can be drawn for relations with employees in the nursing services, fiscal affairs, professional services, and support services groups. Risk managers will need to interface with these employees—some sooner, some later—if they are to be successful. Some basic insights into human behavior theories can help risk managers to improve their working relationships with others and maximize the effectiveness of their results.

MANAGEMENT STRUCTURE: THEORIES AND MODELS

Industrial Revolution Concepts

The Industrial Revolution established roots during the 19th century. Inventors were busy conceiving, developing, and designing an entirely new breed of consumer and durable goods and products. At the same time, new technologies were being created. Small factories were replaced by large ones. Long-established methods of producing goods were found to be inadequate, ineffective, and obsolete. New production concepts and practices were devised. Production line operations became the order of the day.

These innovations demanded skills, knowledge, and attitudes far beyond those possessed by the workers, owners, and managers of the day. Work settings and working conditions became much different. New and revolutionary concepts of management emerged. All these changes not only were considered consistent with the "new order," they were viewed as absolutely essential if it were to succeed.

The management process and managers came to be recognized as distinct and identifiable disciplines. Some of the more prominent management theories and models of management structure are analyzed next, starting with the latter part of the 19th century. It is not possible, in a single chapter, to cover all the theories and structures that were propounded, or in-depth treatment of those that are discussed.

Bureaucratic Form of Management

A unique schematic representation of the chronology of the management movement is given by Tosi and Carroll in Figure 18–1, "Sources of Modern Management Ideas."[1]

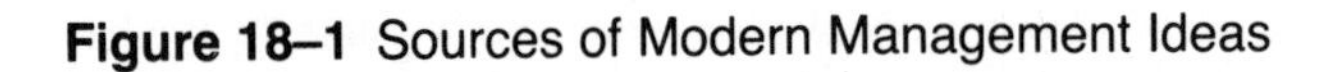

Figure 18–1 Sources of Modern Management Ideas

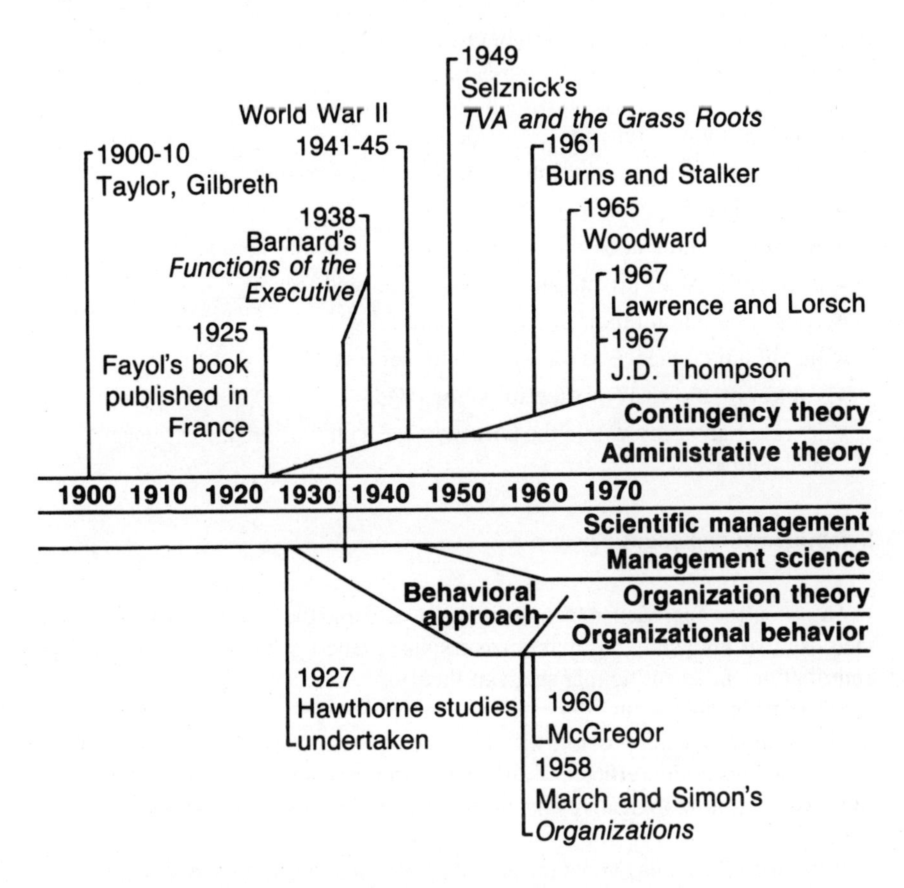

Source: Reprinted from *Management: Contingencies, Structure, and Process* by H.L. Tosi and S.J. Carroll, p. 33, with permission of St. Clair Press, © 1976.

Max Weber was the proponent of the bureaucratic form of management, based on his 19 concepts of power relationships.[2] In a bureaucracy, the power is concentrated in and dominated by the leader. Weber believed organizational positions should be arranged in a hierarchy, with definite and specific authority, responsibility, and accountability assigned to each. He advocated extensive use of procedures and rules, purposely but rationally designed to control workers' behavior on the theory that the organization had the right to control its employees and that they had no alternatives but to accept and obey. Promotion to higher levels would be based on technical competence.

With this type of structure, Weber believed it would be possible to predict behavior and results and to assure great organizational stability over time. To him, the bureaucracy was the most efficient form of organization for large, complex operations. The elements of the bureaucracy in his plan involve:

- specialization of function
- authority implemented through a hierarchical structure
- impersonality
- worker recruitment based on rational criteria such as ability and knowledge
- differentiation of private and official power and income
- control based on rational procedure and rules
- maximum efficiency as the measure of success
- control on the basis of superior knowledge
- levels of authority within the bureaucracy, with the real power concentrated at the top.[3]

Scientific Management Theory

The scientific approach to management seeks to find the best way to do any task, then use that knowledge to maximize results. Frederick Taylor is noted for his contributions to scientific management theory.[4]

Scientific management advocated a ''one best way'' to perform any type of work and urged that all possible effort should be expended to find that way. If the search was successful, efficiency and output would increase, maximization of results would follow logically, and higher wages then would be possible for the workers.

With scientific management the activities of managing would be separate from actual task performance, the allocation of resources would be more efficient, and there would be a better climate in which to analyze both the manager's and workers' jobs.

Taylor believed management should plan the work and be responsible for revising work methods as necessary. He was convinced that workers would perform their tasks in a mechanical fashion and would accept higher wages in return for cooperating and agreeing to play the role of ''tools of management.'' He thought in terms of individuals rather than groups.

Characteristics of the scientific management approach are:

- Management must assume responsibility for the traditional knowledge of workers. The ''one best way'' must be discovered for each job. Higher production results in higher profits that, in turn, will produce higher wages.

- Workers must be scientifically selected and trained for their jobs.
- Scientifically selected workers must be paired with scientific work methods to achieve maximum results.
- Management and labor should divide the work of the organization almost equally, with management assuming the responsibility for planning and coordination and labor performing the work.[5]

Taylor's methods increased production in industry but also alienated workers from their jobs. The growth of unions may be explained as a partial reaction of workers against their role as tools of production.

Opposition to the bureaucratic approach had developed because of the belief that the principles of management and organization covered by Taylor's theory were much too limited; while it could work in some organizations, it certainly would not work in all. The bureaucratic critics believed rigid job specifications, rules, and policies stifled workers' creativity, growth, development, and general effectiveness.

Administrative Theory

During the first quarter of the 20th century, the emphasis began to shift away from the workers and their performances and toward the people who controlled and directed their activities. Organizational designs were being given closer scrutiny. As a result, the administrative theory movement emerged.

Two of those who were most prominent in developing this movement were Henry L. Tosi[6] and Chester I. Barnard.[7]

The Fayol Concepts

Fayol believed that the organization's management function should be divorced from its technical or operational segments. He theorized that management responsibilities at the lower tiers were not as important as the technical or operational ones and that in moving to higher tiers, the activities of management continued to increase. He contended that the converse was true of technical activities—their importance would decrease in moving up through management levels.

Fayol considered theories of management to be important and, because none existed in the mid-1920s, he set out to develop some. Among others, he proposed that:

- The specialization of labor was important if the best use of human resources was to be realized.
- Responsibility must increase as authority increased.
- Discipline or obedience was essential in any prosperous enterprise.

- Organizational members should receive orders from only one superior.
- The proper organizational level at which managerial decisions were made should be determined.
- Equal treatment for workers was important.
- The wage payment system must fit the type of job and situation in order to facilitate motivation.
- Supervisors must encourage initiative among their subordinates.[8]

Fayol believed it was essential first to design the organization in a logical and systematic fashion, then fit the workers into it.

The Barnard Concepts

Barnard dealt with the same two elements—organization design and allocation of human resources.[9] Interestingly, though, he saw the human factors as being the more important, so he preferred to give them priority. The design of the organization would then follow.

Barnard, a former president of New Jersey Bell Telephone Company, developed two concepts:

1. the theory of cooperation and organization
2. the study of the functions and methods of executive operation.[10]

His main contribution to the movement was the first point, his "theory of cooperation." He viewed organizations as systems of coordinated activities and cooperative effort and held that they should be created so that the limitations on a worker's capacity to do the job would be minimized, if not eliminated. Employees could overcome their limitations if they worked cooperatively with others. This theory dealt with groups and noneconomic motives.

His conclusion was that the use of cooperative behavior in an organization was a more effective management technique than authority by position. He summarized the causes of cooperation:

- The human individual has a limited power of choice.
- Each individual has limitations.
- Cooperation lessens these limits by group action.
- Persistence in cooperation depends on effectiveness and efficiency.
- Survival of a group depends on effectiveness and efficiency.
- Group failure is the result of dysfunction in the foregoing points.[11]

Barnard also believed the need existed for a formal, specific, organizational structure, one with procedures, organization charts, and job specifications.

He defined a formal organization as a system of consciously coordinated activities or forces of two or more persons. He said the principles of cooperation applied to large, small, simple, and complex formal organizations because large and complex entities were composed of small, simple ones.[12]

He also believed that within every enterprise, informal forces were working along with the formal organization. These informal forces were born of workers' need to address various human needs with which the formal system could not or would not deal.

The second of Barnard's concepts, the study of the functions and methods of executive operation, involved analyzing the structure of the organization based on the decision-making process. What he proposed is still in vogue today: objectives are set by top management, plans to achieve the objectives are established by the next lower echelon, more detailed plans and planning are the responsibility of the next lower management, and so on until the worker level is reached.

Barnard conceptualized the executive functions (that is, what they must do to manage an organization) as:

- maintaining organization communication
- obtaining the essential services of individuals
- formulating purposes and objectives.[13]

Some of the more important doctrines of the administrative theory are:

- Principles of management: Establish a guide to action for managers to produce high performance.
- Organization structure: Provides an organizational framework and establishes duties and responsibilities so that they are, to the greatest extent possible, functionally similar.
- Emphasis on objectives: Needed in order to develop a rational relationship among activities.
- Authority and responsibility: Should be defined precisely because they are the rights and obligations of employees and managers; no person should be responsible for things without authority over them.
- Unity of command: Requires that a person receive orders from only one superior.[14]

Behavioral Approach

Those who espoused the behavioral approach to management (including J. March, Herbert A. Simon, and those involved with the Hawthorne Studies) sought to learn how human psychological processes interact with what people do.

They attempted to combine rational management with the needs of the workers in order to integrate their needs with those of the organization. More simply put, they wanted to know how motivation and attitude affect performance.

There was not as much agreement among the behavioral approach proponents as there was among those of the scientific management and administrative theories. This lack of unity is explained by the fact that the behavioral approach exponents come from several social science disciplines and this heterogeneity of backgrounds produces marked differences in what they believe to be most important and in what they prefer to stress.

However, for categorical purposes, the management scholars found validity in dividing the behavioral approach practitioners into two groups: (1) those who were organizational behavioralists and (2) those who were organizational theorists.

Organizational Behavioralists

Those of the organization behavior bent concentrated on the human behavior of individual workers. A good part of the thinking of this group stemmed from the 1920 Hawthorne Studies at the Western Electric Company's Hawthorne Plant in Chicago.[14] The second group, organizational theory, focused on managerial activities and organizational design.

Organizational behavioralists focused on individuals and, early on, were concerned with worker problems such as job design, fatigue, and boredom. Their perspective was dramatically redirected as a result of the Hawthorne Studies. Several follow-up studies also were made.

The investigators in the Hawthorne Studies:

- concluded that leadership practices and work group pressures were important to employee satisfaction and performance
- discounted the importance of economic incentives in worker motivation
- stressed the importance of examining the effect of any one factor in terms of a whole social system, pointing out that employees react to an entire complex of forces together, not to just one factor alone.

Organizational Theorists

Two organizational theorists, James March and Herbert Simon, believed individual decision making was a sound basis for understanding behaviors in organizations.[15] But they were not satisfied with all the findings of their fellow theorists. They considered some of those theories to be oversimplified and inconsistent in some respects. One in particular to which they took exception was Taylor's "one best way."

They developed a "sound rationality" concept as a result of their disagreement with Taylor. They reasoned that managers rarely would be able to make optimal decisions. Taylor said those kinds of decisions resulted only when the manager selected the best of all possibilities. Simon and March contended that managers seldom had total knowledge of an issue, and without knowledge of all alternatives, they could not make optimal decisions.

Simon himself also believed a person must be understood as a worker in an organization and as a human being outside that entity.[16] He analyzed the decision-making processes of people in that light because he believed a link existed between understanding organizations and worker decision making.

What he found was that workers placed values on their decisions. In making decisional choices, they selected one future situation over another, and the ends they sought by making decisions tended to form a values hierarchy. Workers gave top priority to ends that were more important to them. Simon explained his "Hierarchy of Ends" theory as follows:

> The clearest way to determine which ends are sought for their own sake and which for their usefulness as means to more distant ends is to place the subject in situations where he must choose between conflicting ends. . . . The fact that goals may be dependent for their forces on other more distant ends leads to the arrangement of these goals in a hierarchy—each level to be considered as an end relative to the levels below it, as a means relative to the level above it.[17]

"Linking Pin" and Other Elements

In addition to his contributions to the administrative theory, Barnard made significant behavioral concept offerings to the organizational theory movement. Most notable of these were what he called the "linking pin," "zone of indifference," and "acceptance of authority."[18]

The "linking pin" theory was applied to group problem solving. The group, usually composed of one manager from each of several organizational units, would become sort of a management task force. One other person would be named to head the group and direct its activities. Barnard saw the task force members as contributing to two units in the organization: (1) their regularly assigned working unit and (2) the manager task force unit. Each member of the task force became linked to decision-making activities in two units.

The "zone of indifference" and "acceptance of authority" concepts related to how workers complied with authority. Barnard believed that workers often obeyed mainly because they were willing to do so, or as Barnard described it, the superior's communication would fall within the worker's "zone of indifference."

The workers really did not care, so they just complied. The ''acceptance theory of authority'' principle means the workers complied because they respected the manager's authority to give orders and believed it was their duty to carry them out. Managers' assumptions about people provided a basis on which to decide how they would deal with superiors, peers, and subordinates. Effectiveness as managers would depend on how correctly they had made those assumptions.

Theory X and Theory Y

Douglas McGregor, another organizational theorist, in 1976 declared that most managers made a set of incorrect assumptions about those who worked for them. He considered it desirable to develop representative traits of workers, which he then clustered into two sets: Theory X and Theory Y.[19]

Theory X assumed that workers had personal goals that ran counter to those of the organization and that they were basically lazy individuals. Workers with those traits had to be given close supervision and guidance to ensure high performance.

Theory Y assumed the workers to be self-controlled, self-motivated, and more mature than the Theory X types. These kind of traits justified greater trust and, therefore, little need for either bureaucratic supervision or interpersonal controls.

McGregor believed these two basic management philosophies were held by most managers in organizations today. He summarized his Theory X and Theory Y assumptions as follows:[20]

Theory X

1. Average human beings have an inherent dislike of work and will avoid it if they can.
2. Most people, because of this human characteristic of dislike of work, must be coerced, controlled, directed, or threatened with punishment to get them to put forth adequate effort toward the achievement of organizational objectives.
3. Average human beings prefer to be directed, want to avoid responsibility, have relatively little ambition, and desire security above all.

Theory Y

1. The expenditure of physical and mental effort in work is as natural as play or rest.
2. External control and the threat of punishment are not the only means for bringing about effort toward organizational objectives. People will exercise self-direction and self-control in the service of objectives to which they are committed.

3. Commitment to objectives is a function of the rewards associated with their achievement.
4. Average human beings learn, under proper conditions, not only to accept but to seek responsibility.
5. The capacity to exercise a relatively high degree of imagination, ingenuity, and creativity in the solution of organizational problems is widely, not narrowly, distributed in the population.
6. The conditions of modern industrial life only partially utilize the intellectual potentialities of average human beings.

According to McGregor, Theory X assumptions were those traditionally held by management; a Theory X system of management was highly production-oriented and centered on the top manager; and Theory X was compatible with Taylor's scientific management in that it concentrated the thinking and planning with management and left the employees with the task of performing the work but gave them no input into the planning phases.

To McGregor, under Theory Y, the integration of individuals' goals with those of the organization could produce better quality and quantity results; when the individuals' attitude was positive, they would provide the organization with their best work; and a positive attitude could be achieved when the individuals were being involved in the formulation of the organization's goals and objectives.

Drucker and MBO

Peter F. Drucker devised a practical guide to solving the problem of integrating the behavior of an individual into the organization's attainment of objectives. He called the program Management by Objectives (MBO).[21] He said the program, if applied throughout the organization's hierarchy, would provide uniformity of direction and substance without necessitating uniformity of the methods and procedures to achieve that direction.

MBO provided a framework in which the entire organization could operate in a results-oriented direction. When it was thus applied, the result would be uniformity of direction and substance without necessarily having uniformity of method and procedure. The MBO process may be summarized as follows:

1. Top management translates broad organizational purposes into several operational objectives.
2. The system is explained to all managers.
3. Top management sets guidelines for the objectives—all of which must be approved by the superior and subordinate.

4. Objectives are set for all employees, from the bottom of the organization to the top.
5. The objectives set by each individual or group are translated into performance and position description standards.

The procedure required an open atmosphere in the organization, and individuals and groups must be rewarded for achievement.

Drucker's MBO was not a total system in itself; rather, it was a method for achieving results within a total organizational framework. It must be related to the larger purposes and values of an organization to be effective. If it ran counter to an entity's goals, it would cause organizational dysfunctions.

The misuse of MBO could cause great problems in terms of morale and long-term effectiveness. If used as a Theory X pressure tactic rather than as a Theory Y integrative approach, it could be self-defeating in the long run. Harry Levinson contended that improper use of MBO could cause great internal hostility and that such misuse probably was the rule rather than the exception.[22]

HUMAN NEEDS AND LIFE STYLE THEORIES

Human needs can be categorized as (1) basic biological and psychosocial and (2) educational. Educational needs require little explanation other than that they relate to expanding people's knowledge base by whatever means—formal education, travel, cultural involvements, personal relationships, and the like.

As for basic biological and psychosocial needs, one of the more familiar theorists is Abraham Maslow.

Maslow's Hierarchy of Needs

There is some similarity between Knowles[1] categorization and *Maslow's Hierarchy of Needs*. Maslow visualized five basic needs: (1) physical, (2) safety, (3) love, (4) self-esteem, and (5) self-actualization. He refined these into the following segments in his ranking in order of importance:

Physical Needs

- food and thirst
- sleep
- health
- body needs

- exercise and rest
- sex

Safety Needs

- security and safety
- protection
- comfort and peace
- no threats of danger
- orderly and neat surroundings

Love Needs

- acceptance
- feeling of belonging
- membership in group
- love and affection
- group participation

Self-Esteem Needs

- recognition and prestige
- confidence and leadership
- achievement and ability
- competence and success
- strength and intelligence

Self-Actualization Needs

- self-fulfillment of potential
- doing things purely for the challenge
- intellectual curiosity and fulfillment
- creativity and aesthetic appreciation
- acceptance of reality.

Maslow believed the needs he listed first, physical, were the basic, important ones. They must be satisfied before the next set, safety needs, could be addressed; and not until safety needs were fulfilled should effort be exercised toward fulfilling the love needs; and so on.

Conversely, Maslow's theory was that the next higher order of needs would become important only when those underlying it were satisfied. He believed that people not only had these needs but were motivated by all of them. He viewed biological and psychosocial needs in the motivational sense; that is, a deficiency in one area could initiate a motivation on the part of the individual to rectify it. The tension caused by the deficiency resulted in the person's wanting to do something to alleviate the void.

Maslow was clear on the point that his principles were not absolute—they were general guidelines on human behavior. He also believed that the level of needs differed from person to person and was not the same for everyone.

Life Style Doctrines

Another interesting insight into human behavior was provided in 1972 by Frank Friedlander and his life style theories.[24] He proposed three life style doctrines: formalistic, sociocentric, and personalistic.

His formalistic doctrine involved strict adherence to prescribed or external forms. Formalistic persons:

- take direction from and have respect for authorities and others in charge
- are guided by, comply with, and have faith in rules, laws, order, precedents, and policies
- are contented when pathways are clear
- learn from and follow the established order
- strive for advancement and prestige
- consider the incentives in life to come from security and comfort
- feel responsible to those higher up
- believe feelings and emotions should be channeled and made rational.

Friedlander's personalistic doctrine emphasized the significance, uniqueness, and inviolability of personality. Personalistic individuals:

- receive direction from within themselves, know what they want to do, and guide their lives
- want freedom to choose how they live, and strive for independence and freedom
- learn from personal experiences, act on their own awareness, and feel responsible only to themselves
- have faith in their own sense of justice and believe in self-determination and self-realization

- are rewarded by experimentation and discovery and believe feelings and emotions are to be experienced.

The sociocentric doctrine has society, people, and social consciousness as its center or core. Friedlander identified sociocentric people to be those who:

- get direction and guidance in life by discussion and agreement with others and through close relationships with others
- seek out friends and colleagues who are committed; believe growth and progress come from learning from and sharing with others; and have faith in group norms—what close friends say and advise
- strive for collaboration, agreement, and consensus, and for acceptance and intimacy
- believe incentives in life come from personal relationships and sharing values; feel responsible to those with whom they have personal relationships; and believe feelings and emotions should be shared with others.

Behavioral characteristics can have a marked effect on the managerial style of the individual. Having some understanding of these behaviors can be helpful in identifying and explaining managers' behavior or personal demeanor.

An understanding of all these basic human behavior concepts could provide risk managers with some guidelines they may use to develop plans of action for dealing with others in the organization, and outside it as well.

MANAGERS AND THE MANAGEMENT PROCESS

It is common for the terms "leader" and "manager" to be used synonymously. The same may be said of "leadership" and "management." Although such usage may be valid in some cases, more often it is not. The differences are important.

To some, the meaning of management is the efficient use of resources, i.e., personnel, money, materials, plant, equipment, time, energy, and other resources. The supply of one or more of these resources is never without limitations, for one reason or another. Therefore, it is important that the most advantageous use be made of each and all of them. Even though at times there may be a surplus of one or more of them, it still is just good business judgment and practice not to be unwise in their applications. To others, management means a group of employees. And to still others it may mean one of these at one time and another at another time.

Tosi and Carroll addressed the problem by using the terms "management process" and "manager" and pointed out that:

> . . . the management process is the set of activities carried out in an organization for the purpose of achieving objectives in an efficient way. Managers are those individuals in the organization who have the right to decide how resources are allocated and who have supervisory responsibility for other people. . . . The basic task of the manager is to seek to make efficient use of resources.[25]

This differentiation is accepted for the discussion here.

Tosi and Carroll explained that the management process occurred when people in organizations attempted to achieve objectives through efficient utilization of resources and that the process included activities that:

- established organization objectives
- developed plans to attain these objectives
- assembled resources to carry out the plans
- supervised the execution of the plans by proper direction, providing help and training to those carrying them out, and giving other support where required
- evaluated whether or not satisfactory progress toward objectives was being made and initiated corrective action, if necessary.[26]

The Managers and the Managed

An organization is composed of two kinds of employees: (1) managers, those who direct subordinates and make decisions about resources, and (2) workers, those who perform the work necessary to produce the goods or provide the services of the organization.

The first group consists of the managerial team and has general responsibilities to plan, organize, control, and evaluate. The second is the group of operative employees, those who do the actual work when the plans, practices, and procedures are ready for implementation.

The manager group customarily is divided into three levels:

1. Top Management: This is the policy-making group, responsible for the overall direction and success of all company activities.
2. Middle Management: This group acts under policies and directives of top management and is responsible for their execution and interpretation throughout the organization and for the successful operation of assigned divisions or departments.
3. Supervisory Management: This is the group directly responsible to middle management for final execution of policies by rank-and-file employees.

Table 18–1 Managers' Functions and Time on Each

Function	*% of Workday*		
	Low Mgr.	*Mid Mgr.*	*High Mgr.*
Supervisor	51	36	22
Planner	15	18	28
Generalist	9	10	20
Investigator	8	8	6
Negotiator	6	8	3
Multispecialist	6	8	5
Coordinator	5	7	8
Evaluator	2	5	8

For purposes here, the term "manager" applies to anyone within the three levels of management ranks. Thus, the first-level supervisor is a manager, as is the president. However, there are differences (often major ones) between the respective manager jobs. These relate to what they do, how they do it, the kinds of decisions they make, and the calibre of employees they supervise.

About 10 percent of the working population in the United States is categorized as managers.

Decisions and Resources

A manager, any manager, will make decisions about how subordinates use the available resources to make the product or provide the service. The subordinates then become the implementers of such decisions. Managers are responsible for the work of others, for ensuring that the tasks are well done, and for making sure that effective use is made not only of human resources but of physical resources (plant and equipment) as well.

Research by Mahoney, Jerdee, and Carroll (1963) involving 450 managers in a variety of companies set about to identify what managers did and how much time they spent doing it.[27] The results as reported by Tosi and Carroll are set forth in Table 18–1.[28]

In addition, the research identified the following areas of technical knowledge in which these functions were performed:

- personnel
- money and finance
- materials and goods

- marketing
- methods and procedures
- facilities and equipment.[29]

As Tosi and Carroll point out, managers would not be expected to have high levels of skills in all these technical areas. They usually would be proficient in one or two, with at least limited knowledge of the others.

LEADERSHIP AND LEADERSHIP STYLES

Managers basically are responsible for getting work done through other persons. In doing this, they have great influence on, and responsibility for, assuring that the human needs of subordinates are satisfied to the greatest extent possible. Under the circumstances, having an understanding of leadership and leadership styles is of special value to managers if they are to fulfill their role as the catalysts who motivate employees and maximize their human needs satisfactions.

A number of approaches to the study of leadership have been made over the years. The early thinking was that to be a successful leader, one need only emulate successful leaders. When the supporters of this theory set out to identify and list the special traits and characteristics of those leaders, they learned it was difficult, if not impossible, to get any two researchers to agree on what the list should contain. This movement never gained much momentum.

Four Leadership Types

A more practical approach evolved which, quite appropriately, explained leadership in terms of types of leaders. The most commonly accepted of these types are: (1) the dictatorial leader, (2) the democratic leader, (3) the participative leader, and (4) the laissez-faire leader.

Dictatorial leaders, as the name implies, believe they are endowed with absolute power and authority. They use that power and authority in accordance with their own will and desires. They believe managerial decisions are theirs alone to make. When they issue directives, they expect subordinates to accept them as law and to carry them out in strict compliance and without question. They condone nothing less than total obedience.

Dictatorial leaders are domineering. They get work done through fear. Their workers will almost always do their bidding because they know that if they do not, they probably will be deprived of wage increases, promotions, job security, and other such economic benefits. Such workers believe that without these advantages, they probably will not be able to satisfy some of their very basic human needs. The dictatorial type of leader usually achieves better-than-average work results but generally at the expense of employee frustration and discontent. Their demeanor may even produce aggression and hostility among workers. It is not uncommon for group productivity to decline when this leader leaves the work site.

This type of superior, who neither seeks nor permits subordinate involvement in making decisions and solving problems, also is known as an autocratic leader.

Democratic leaders consult with subordinates on appropriate job-related matters they and their work group face. They encourage and permit subordinates' involvement in solving problems and making decisions. They define the problems to subordinates, set the limits within which they are to proceed, and give them the latitude to reach solutions within those defined boundaries. They sponsor team effort and build an atmosphere of group identification among subordinates, opting for their group to function as a unit.

Democratic leaders capitalize on the talents and capabilities of their workers, so it is not uncommon to identify high levels of performance and individual subordinate satisfaction within such groups.

Participative leaders also consult with subordinates on work-related matters. However, they usually are less generous about decision-making latitude than are democratic leaders. Participative leaders describe the problem and give a tentative decision, acknowledging it as being subject to change. They permit the workers to offer input and suggestions and the tentative decision but make the final decision themselves.

Subordinate identification with the organization is common in participative leaders' groups. These leaders also are able to foster an acceptance of change among members of their work team.

Laissez-faire leaders allow their group to have complete autonomy. They usually avoid contact with it and rarely give it any supervision. They permit subordinates to find their own limits, set their own goals without guidance or direction, set their own work pace, and decide what kind of operational climate they will adopt.

Under this type of leadership, maximizing the fulfillment of work goals becomes a problem. Work group productivity is not high. A disproportionate amount of time is spent on activities not directly related to performance. Valid evidences also exist that many members of the laissez-faire work group find this type of working arrangement to be neither favored nor gratifying.

Management Philosophies

Organizations also began to develop management philosophies in an effort to accommodate better the human side of the business. These organizational theories also became categorized as democratic, participative, and laissez-faire. Each placed varying emphasis on human values and employee involvement in the work and planning for it. The difference in emphasis was consistent with the descriptions of the respective leader types.

Although entities could be broadly characterized, as noted, it is highly improbable that an entire organization will operate according to any one style. To expect all managers to follow the leadership mode most descriptive of the organization's style is fallacious and fanciful. Managers are individualistic and their basic managerial styles are going to be different—and that is as it is expected to be.

How, then, may effective leaders be identified? Successful managers are analytical and adaptive. They learn that a single style of leadership will be inadequate. They thus practice all styles of leadership in order to accommodate the different supervisory situations they will encounter. They learn they may have to deal with each subordinate differently and may have to use different styles of leadership with each worker at various times and depending on circumstances.

Successful managers will be able to diagnose each situation in terms of its particular circumstances. They will be in a position to identify and understand the differences and be sensitive to them. They will be capable, then, of deciding on and proceeding with what they consider to be the proper plan of action. Here are other attributes characteristic of effective leaders:

- They will set a creditable personal example.
- They will not expect more commitment from subordinates than they themselves are willing to give and, therefore, will not condone or practice the "don't do as I do, but do as I tell you" philosophy.
- They will have a deep commitment to achieve results through the actions of employees.
- They will establish the climate necessary to stimulate each worker to give maximum effort to achieve the group's and organization's goals and objectives.
- They will understand that they must believe in their workers before the workers will believe in the leaders.
- They will show genuine interest in and concern for the individual members of the group as persons and encourage them to develop close and mutually satisfying relationships.
- They will promote job relationships that are indicative of mutual trust, respect for subordinates' ideas, and consideration of their feelings.
- They will have good rapport and two-way communications with subordinates.
- They will plan, organize, coordinate, and control the activities of the group and play an active role in scheduling work activities, directing group efforts, communicating information, and trying out new ideas.
- They will realize that their style of leadership will have a significant influence on the group's spirit, productivity, and effectiveness.

At some point, managers, appropriately, should have a curiosity about and desire to test the effectiveness of the group and its activities. McGregor lists what he considers important characteristics that effective groups should possess:[30]

- They operate in an informal, relaxed atmosphere.
- Each member participates.
- The group's objective is understood by all.
- Members listen to one another.
- Members disagree but in a comfortable manner.
- The group reaches decisions by a kind of consensus.
- Criticism within the group is frequent, frank, and comfortable.
- Members express opinions and are concerned about the group's operation.
- Members respond to a clear assignment when action is required.
- The group has a kind of informal leadership that tends to rotate as circumstances dictate.

LEADERSHIP AND RISK MANAGERS

Amplifying the preceding sections, the emphasis now shifts to the relevance of the information to risk managers and how they may benefit from its application on the job. The discussions of human needs and leadership can enable risk managers to gain at least some understanding of the forces that tend to motivate individuals and how those forces can affect the attitudes and behavior of work associates.

The identification of some basic human needs and how individuals address them was provided in a layman-type description of Maslow's Hierarchy of Needs concepts. That analysis, superficial as it is, should help risk managers discover, if they will, where various individuals stand in that hierarchy at any one time. Such knowledge can offer clues on how then to motivate and deal with them.

Similarly, Friedlander's theories are useful guidelines for assessing, in general, which of three life style classes individuals may occupy.

Neither of these two assessing processes should be difficult for risk managers who are curious, perceptive, and analytical. But before evaluating others, risk managers should start with themselves. This self-appraisal should be done conscientiously and critically. It is important that managers have an appreciation of where they fit on Maslow's hierarchy and into which life style category they fall before they can apply their appraisals of others effectively to advance the objectives of the risk management program.

It certainly is worthwhile for risk managers to consider the behavioral and leadership information as they develop meaningful working relationships with subordinates and as they search for the leadership style or styles to be used in that process. At the early stages of their careers, they probably will have limited need to apply such information, primarily because in most instances they will have no staff of their own to supervise, or at best one aide. However, as the staff enlarges, they will find greater need for the information in strengthening their supervisory skills and performance.

An immediate application of this human needs and leadership information may be found in risk managers' normal, everyday work activities. They interface daily with many persons in the hospital in establishing and implementing risk management programs. These individuals will represent all levels of education and every hospital entity—medical staff, nursing, professional services, support services, and fiscal affairs.

To say the least, this is a diverse array. If they want to do so, risk managers can find ample rationale to support a contention that theirs is a difficult and, at times, frustrating job. But if they are optimistic and industrious, they can use this diversity as a base for building a challenging and rewarding career.

Risk managers will find the total range of human behavior traits and leadership styles represented in this group of work associates. They may find it productive to develop a variety of personal leadership styles to use in working with these people. Being flexible, adaptive, and judicious can help them maximize their relationships with co-workers.

For example, the Maslow Hierarchy of Needs theory can be applied in a work situation. Risk managers are attempting to gain fellow workers' agreement on an important risk management matter. The managers have identified themselves as being at the self-esteem level. They have perceived the workers to be somewhere above the physical needs level and just into the safety needs category. Should such workers be dealt with on the self-esteem level? Should the managers structure their approach in a manner consistent with one of the four other levels of the hierarchy? If so, which might offer the best chance to win agreement of the proposal: physical needs, safety needs, love needs, or self-actualization needs?

Friedlander's life style theories can be useful in a work relationship. The risk managers have determined that they are personalistic individuals. They are dealing with employees they see as being formalistic. Would it be desirable for the risk managers to use a personalistic approach? If not, might it be more advantageous to adopt the sociocentric or the formalistic style? What would workers' reactions be to each of these styles?

Taking the exercise further, what kinds of risk manager and worker reactions are predictable with the following other kinds of relationships?

Risk Manager	*Worker*
Formalistic	Sociocentric
Formalistic	Personalistic
Personalistic	Sociocentric

Sociocentric	Formalistic
Sociocentric	Personalistic

The picture broadens considerably and the process becomes increasingly complex when risk managers qualify the work positions according to educational and experience levels.

The earlier section on theories and models of management structure relates particularly to hospitals (or service organizations, as they are commonly called). Large hospitals operate on all four models of organization:

1. bureaucratic or structured—characterized by organization charts, policies, procedure books, and other structured rules and formal practices
2. scientific management—characterized by time studies and other scientific management methods and techniques
3. administrative, or humanistic, theory—characterized as a value-based rather than a profit-based type of operation, with emphasis on the manager's adopting a more humanistic style of handling workers
4. behavioral or integrated—characterized by emphasis on human behavioral influences that affect motivation and productivity and on motivational techniques, such as MBO.

In service organizations, motivations other than economic ones are important. An objection to Frederick Taylor's scientific approach as it applies to hospitals is that it ignores the human feelings of workers and causes their disenchantment with job and organization.[31] This has a negative influence on productivity and employee morale. However, the Taylor concept can be used properly in service organizations to gather task analysis data for use in developing the most desirable and effective job procedures.

Chester Barnard believed that the use of cooperative behavior in an organization was a more effective management technique than authority by position and developed a list of six causes of cooperation to support his theory.[32] His theories are useful in hospitals because as service organizations they need high levels of cooperation in order to function. Service-oriented employees not only consider it important to be paid for their work, they also want job satisfaction at the same time. The combination of both is the appropriate reward for their cooperation.

Herbert Simon believed that in hospitals and other value-based service-type organizations, decisions should be based on values that are consistent with the organization's goals and objectives.[33] When decisions are not so based, professional employees can become alienated. It is important, therefore, to establish an agreed-upon set of values or guidelines on which to base decisions of substance and procedures.

Amitai Etzioni cautioned that the use of symbolic, prestigious, or artificial rewards to reinforce employee cooperation and participation, if carried too far, could have an opposite effect to the intended one.[34] When an employee is praised for a job well done, it may not be considered as such if it is given insincerely or if it is stated too lavishly. Etzioni pointed out this was particularly true in service organizations.

According to Douglas McGregor, the use of Theory X methods of stimulation in service organizations brings about productivity increases in the short run.[35] The weakness is in the long run. The better employees will become displeased with the environment and leave for jobs where the personal rewards and job satisfactions will be more in line with their needs. McGregor believes this to be particularly true in hospital/service organization settings.

Peter Drucker sees MBO as useful to service organizations because it will help them to prevent the disease of "bureaucracy" in which rules and procedures become ends in themselves, rather than a means to the organization's needs.[36] This disease develops because the service organization's outputs are services rather than material objects. Drucker offers other suggestions on the need for MBO in service organizations:[37]

- Service institutions need to define what their business is and should be.
- Clear objectives need to be derived from the previous point.
- Priorities need to be set, targets selected, standards of performance developed, deadlines set, and someone needs to be made accountable for the results.
- Measures of performance must be defined.
- Measurements need to be used for feedback and self-control.
- An organized audit of objectives and results is essential; the results of this evaluation help in setting new objectives.

In service organizations, the need for and benefit from involvement of staff in decision making cannot be overestimated. People feel most important when they feel most involved in the work and directing an organization.

Drucker also propounded the thesis that service institutions lack effectiveness more than efficiency. Effectiveness is not smooth functioning—it is the reaching of program objectives. The idea that the goals of a service organization are intangible does not mean that they cannot be set. The reaching of an objective, set in the proper way, equals effectiveness. The smooth functioning of an organization in procedural matters equals efficiency. The two should not be confused.[38]

The role of change agent is one risk managers must be able to play, and play well, if they are to effectuate a viable risk management program. As change agents, they will need to move forward on risk management matters and take steps that will get things started. They will need to offer risk management solutions and assist others in adapting those solutions to their individual situations. They will need to help fellow employees identify their own particular risk management problems and give them a hand in solving them. It is evident that the success of their performance as risk managers will revolve around their being able to motivate meaningful behavior change.

SUMMARY

This chapter has reviewed basic information on a number of topics impacting on the behavioral change process. This knowledge can be useful and valuable to risk managers in understanding hospital management behavior and providing clues on how to modify it. Unless steps are taken to understand and use this knowledge, however, risk managers' chances of building and implementing an effective and successful risk management program will be questionable.

NOTES

1. Henry L. Tosi and Stephen J. Carroll, *Management: Contingencies, Structure and Process* (Chicago: St. Clair Press, 1976), 33.
2. Max Weber, *The Theory of Social and Economic Organizations* (New York: The Free Press of Glencoe, 1947), 39.
3. Nicos P. Mouzelis, *Organization and Bureaucracy* (Chicago: Aldine Publishing Co., Inc., 1976), 39.
4. Frederick W. Taylor, *Scientific Management Theory* (New York: Harper and Brothers, 1947), 30.
5. Ibid., 41.
6. Henry L. Tosi and Stephen J. Carroll, *Management: Contingencies, Structure and Process* (Chicago: St. Clair Press, 1976), 41.
7. Chester I. Barnard, *The Functions of the Executive* (Cambridge, Mass.: Harvard University Press, 1968), 65–81.
8. Tosi and Carroll, *Management,* 40.
9. Barnard, *Functions,* 3.
10. Ibid., xxxi.
11. Ibid., 60.
12. Ibid., vii–viii.
13. Tosi and Carroll, *Management,* 43–44.
14. Ibid., 44–45.
15. James G. March and Herbert A. Simon, *Organizations* (New York: John Wiley & Sons, Inc., 1958), 42.
16. Herbert A. Simon, *Administrative Behavior* (New York: The Free Press, 1976), 59.
17. Ibid., 63.
18. Barnard, *Functions,* 167–170.

19. Douglas McGregor, *The Human Side of Enterprise* (New York: McGraw-Hill Book Company, 1976), 30.
20. Ibid., 34, 47–48.
21. Peter F. Drucker, "What Results Should You Expect? A User's Guide to MBO," *Public Administration Review* 36 (January-February 1976): 12.
22. Harry Levinson, "Management by Whose Objectives?" *Harvard Business Review* 48 (July-August 1970): 125.
23. Abraham Maslow, *Motivation and Personality* (New York: Harper & Row, 1954), 35–46.
24. Frank Friedlander, *Life Style Questionnaire* (1972), 1.
25. Tosi and Carroll, *Management,* 5.
26. Ibid., 4.
27. T.A. Mahoney, T.H. Jerdee, and Stephen J. Carroll, *Development of Managerial Performance: A Research Approach* (Cincinnati: Southwestern Publishing Co., 1963), 10.
28. Tosi and Carroll, *Management,* 8.
29. Ibid., 8.
30. McGregor, *The Human Side,* 232–235.
31. Frederick C. Thayer, *Productivity: Taylorism Revisited (Round Three).*
32. Barnard, *Functions,* 60.
33. Herbert A. Simon, *Administrative Behavior* (New York: The Free Press, 1976), 80–81.
34. Amitai Etzioni, *The Comparative Analysis of Complex Organizations,* rev. ed. (New York: The Free Press, 1975), 34–36.
35. McGregor, *The Human Side,* 47–48.
36. Drucker, "Results," 12.
37. Peter F. Drucker, *Management* (New York: Harper and Row, 1974), 158.
38. ———, "Meaningful Reorganization," *The Wall Street Journal,* 4 February 1977.

Chapter 19

Quality Assurance and Risk Management

Steven L. Salman

Hospitals have had the moral obligation to assure that quality of care is provided to their patients, most likely from the day that the first hospital was opened. However, moral obligations often are not met as fully as they could be. Hospitals also probably have had a legal duty to assure that quality of care is provided. However, that duty has been evolving and, for all practical purposes, began with the *Darling*[1] decision in 1965 and was clarified in *Gonzales v. Nork and Mercy Hospital*[2] in 1973. It has continued to develop since that time.

Even so, hospitals still were not meeting moral and legal obligations. As a result, the Joint Commission on Accreditation of Hospitals (JCAH) in 1980 published standards that for the first time defined quality assurance and the requirements on hospitals for assuring quality care. Hospitals that may not have understood those obligations could comprehend the JCAH standards. The quality assurance concept thus had its more formalized birth in 1980.

THE AHA TASK FORCE

Since the medical malpractice crisis of the mid-1970s preceded those standards, by 1979 a number of hospital risk managers of varying degrees of expertise and backgrounds were practicing their profession. It became clear that hospitals' loss prevention activities in risk management and quality assurance operations overlapped. That overlap produced uncertainty over the two functions. In turn, this led many national organizations, most prominently the American Hospital Association, to search for ways to distinguish the two and to establish clearer guidelines, by forming a task force in 1980.

The task force decided there were three possible relationships between hospital quality assurance and risk management (Figure 19–1). The first was that these

Figure 19–1 Possible Relationships Between Quality Assurance and Risk Management

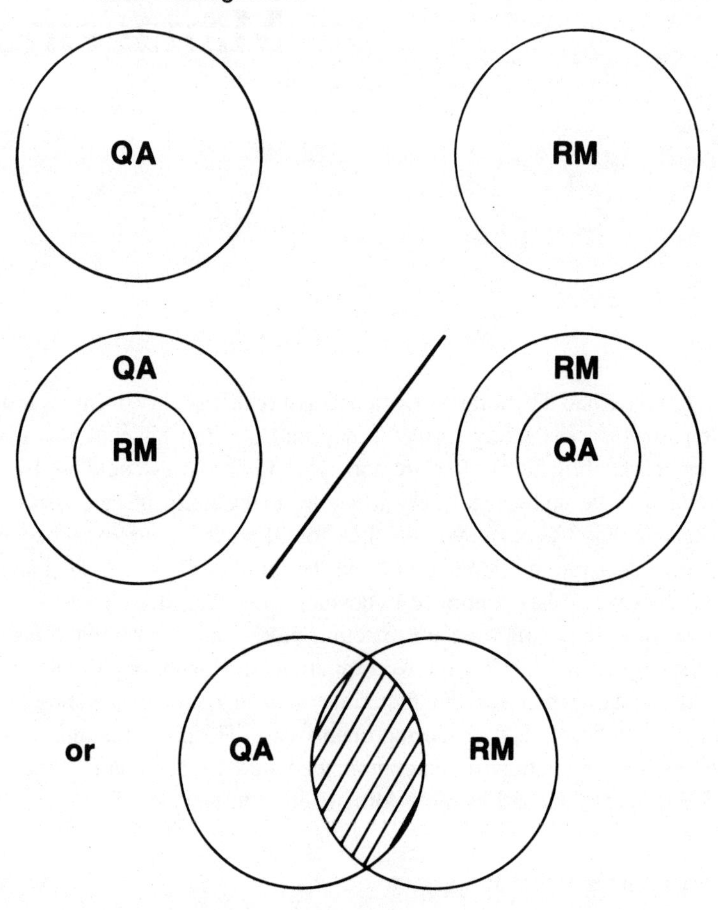

QA = quality assurance; RM = risk management.

Source: Steven L. Salman, © 1980.

---

were independent functions and had no relationship with each other. This was not a realistic alternative since the loss prevention activities of risk management overlapped substantially with quality assurance. The second was that one was a subfunction of the other—risk management a subfunction of quality assurance or vice versa. The task force felt that each of these functions had too many of its own independent responsibilities to be classified as a subfunction of the other. The end result was the third model—each as a separate function with wide overlap and a certain amount of independent activities and responsibilities. This, the most viable alternative, is depicted by the third example at the bottom of Figure 19–1.

THE CIRCLES AND THEIR ROLES

The next issue was: What were these circles composed of and what shape and form did they take? Figure 19–2 is a visualization of that form. The next question was: What are areas *A, B*, and *C* composed of? (The *A* areas were unique to quality assurance, *B* the common areas, and *C* those unique to risk management.) It was determined that many items in *C* (the area unique to risk management) had either no, or minimal, overlap into quality assurance:

- Workers' Compensation: If employees are being injured to the degree there are none or too few remaining to handle patients, obviously there is some impact on the quality of care, but this is a minor overlap.
- Property preservation and protection: This is considered a risk management function but is of minimal concern in quality assurance. If equipment is

Figure 19–2 Quality Assurance and Risk Management Relationships

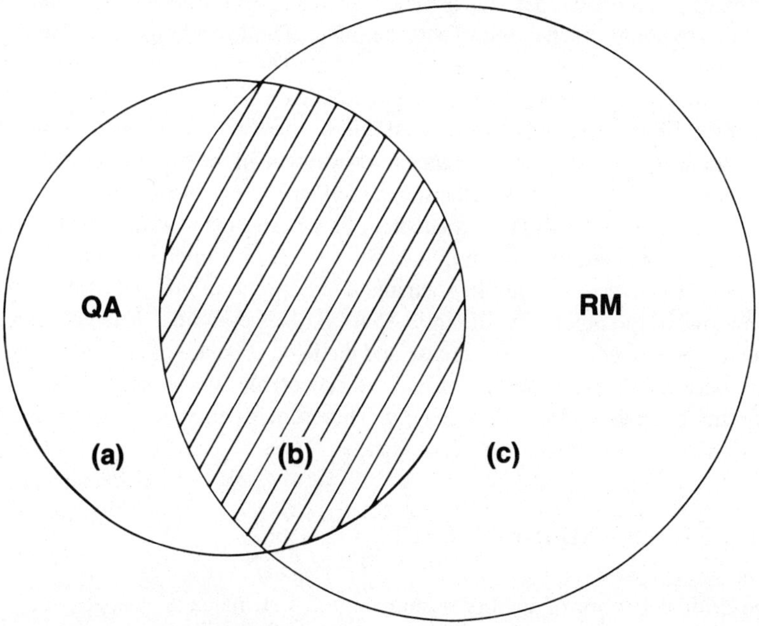

Source: Steven L. Salman, © 1980.

malfunctioning or being lost through theft or fire to the degree that none is left for patient care, obviously there is an impact (but minimal) on the quality of care.

- General liability insurance: This clearly is a major risk management factor.
- Directors' and officers' liability insurance: Without adequate coverage of these persons, the hospital probably would be unable to attract competent management and board members. (Though not a major quality assurance concern, it ultimately would have an impact on the care provided.)
- Employee benefits: If these are not competitive with other institutions, the hospital cannot attract and maintain a high-quality, competent staff. (This, too, has an impact on quality of care, but it is relatively minimal.)
- Other activities include: Risk financing, all other insurance, managing claims, etc., are included. (None of these has more than minimal impact on quality assurance.)

In the common area, *B*, loss prevention and quality assurance are closely related. Loss prevention is an attempt to identify potential sources of substandard care in an effort to increase them to the legal standard of care. However, the standard for purposes of loss prevention may well differ from the one for quality assurance.

For example, the arc separating areas *B* and *A* can be considered to be composed of millions of points, each of them representing the legal standard of care for one of the millions of functions performed in a hospital. The farther away one moves to the left of that line, the more the legal standard of care is exceeded. The farther one gets above the legal standard of care, the less interest loss prevention and risk management personnel have in further improvement in the quality of care.

As long as it can be shown that the standard of care has been met, or exceeded by a small margin, the risk manager is satisfied. From a risk management perspective, there is no real benefit in exceeding it by 10 percent or 20 percent rather than by 5 percent. However, as technology changes, any point on this line is constantly moving toward the outer edge of circle *A*. As skills and abilities change, the goal for quality of care continues to increase and the legal standard of care as shown by the arc between *A* and *B* no longer may be acceptable from a quality assurance standpoint, even though it may be legally. Therefore, quality assurance is striving constantly to achieve better care for patients.

SIMILARITIES AND DIFFERENCES

The critical factors of quality assurance and risk management also may be similar in certain aspects and different in others. The reason for having a quality assurance program may be the requirements of the JCAH or other accrediting bodies, licensing in the states, and reimbursement. These are in addition to a hospital's potential liability exposure for not having a competent quality assurance program. However, the risk management program deals with the hospital's dollar exposure from the increased frequency and severity of lawsuits. These are based primarily on negligence, and the loss prevention function attempts to identify those potential sources of liability and avert their happening. The hospital does have corporate liability for adverse effects on patients that can be attributable to it.

The quality assurance program is designed to protect patients, to improve the providers' care, and to assure compliance with optimally achievable standards. However, risk management's primary purpose is to protect the resources of the hospital and its professional staff(s). Those resources are not only financial, they also include human and intangible elements. Intangible resources include factors such as position in the community and relations with the public.

The methods used by the two functions vary as well. Under quality assurance, care is measured against standards for both effectiveness and efficiency. When patterns of substandard care are identified, remedial action can be taken. Under risk management, managers attempt to identify all risk exposures, not just those for patients' exposures but many of those discussed earlier in section *C* of Figure 19–2. These include property insurance, Workers' Compensation, directors' and officers' liability coverage, employee benefits, claims management, and many others of little or no concern to quality assurance. The main programs for these are:

- loss prevention, an attempt to prevent losses from occurring
- loss reduction, an attempt to reduce a loss once an event has occurred
- protection of the hospital's resources by risk financing, such as transfer of risk through the purchase of insurance or other techniques.

The quality assurance program focuses on groups of patients with similar types of situations in an effort to detect patterns that could be improved; risk management involves individual events that could occur to a patient, employee, visitor, medical staff, volunteer, or student. Under quality assurance, an event that happens only once probably would lead to little action; however, under risk management that same event could lead to a multimillion dollar lawsuit. Therefore, the concerns under risk management can be considerable, even though there may be only minimal or no quality assurance issues.

Quality assurance has dealt with retrospective review of charts of discharged patients to determine care patterns. Risk management ideally would want to know about the event as it occurs so steps can be taken to preserve evidence, develop a case file, and work with the family or patient before litigation begins. An alternative, and certainly not the advisable one, is to learn about it only after the hospital is sued. Quality assurance and risk management functions thus have some similarities as well as some differences.

TOOLS FOR JOINT USE

Some tools can be used jointly by risk management and quality assurance, such as generic outcome screening. These criteria were developed in the California Medical and Insurance Feasibility Study of the mid-1970s (see Chapter 6).[3] This study produced a list of 17 criteria. Today there are many other lists, with many more elements as indicators. These do not necessarily indicate substandard or negligent care; they list events that should be evaluated to determine whether there are problems with the care or whether there is negligence.

When one of these indicators is picked up either on concurrent or retrospective review of the chart, it should be analyzed promptly to determine whether it indeed represents a potentially compensable event or an adverse patient occurrence. If the answer is no, then records should be maintained for statistical purposes to determine whether there are any patterns or trends. This gathering of information may be all that needs to be done. If repeats, patterns, or trends develop, quality assurance can begin to take corrective measures. If the answer is yes, and there is a potentially compensable event, then risk managers must take loss-reduction steps, which means trying to reduce the event to its lowest possible cost through sound claims management and other loss control types of activities.

The generic outcome screening criteria discussed in Chapter 6 have progressed to specific screens by departments, several of which are included in Chapter 6. Instead of having generic applications to all patients in the hospital, the specific screens have specific applications to individual departments such as obstetrics-labor and delivery, surgery and postanesthesia recovery, emergency, psychiatric, and a number of other high-risk areas.

ROLE OF THE BOARD OF TRUSTEES

How does the board of trustees fit into the quality assurance and risk management activities and does it have responsibilities in these areas? If so, how does it meet these responsibilities? The courts in virtually every state began, starting in 1965, to place such a responsibility on boards to assure that their hospitals provide quality care.

A hospital typically is a corporation, which can be defined as ". . . an artificial person or legal entity created by or under the authority of the laws of a state or nation."[4] Corporations do not exist in nature. They are created by the legislatures of the states. The boards of the corporations, be they for profit or not for profit, derive their authority and existence from the state statutes and their articles of incorporation, which provide for the bylaws and the rules and regulations.

Board members normally serve in a fiduciary capacity to the corporation and thus are legally responsible for its activities. Therefore, they must meet their obligation to act with utmost good faith and loyalty and must use reasonable care and prudence in all matters affecting the operation of the corporation. The utmost good faith requirement often is addressed in cases of conflict of interest or self-dealing.[5] The trustees' obligation to exercise reasonable care and diligence looks to certain duties that are nondelegatable. The test normally used here is whether the action or inaction met the standard of care that a reasonable and prudent business person would exercise under the same or similar circumstances.

This duty is described in *Moore v. Trustees of Carson-Tahoe Hospital*.[6] This case involved the removal of a physician's privileges for unprofessional conduct. The appellate court discussed the duty of a hospital board:

> Today, in response to demands of the public, the hospital is becoming a community health center. The purpose of the community hospital is to provide patient care of the highest quality. To implement this duty of providing competent medical care to the patients, it is the responsibility of the institution to create a workable system whereby the medical staff of the hospital continually reviews and evaluates the quality of care being rendered within the institution. The staff must be organized with proper structure to carry out the role delegated to it by the governing body. All powers of the medical staff flow from the board of trustees, and the staff must be held accountable for its control of quality.

It was fairly clear from the Nevada court in *Carson* that the hospital board had the obligation to protect the public. The court said: ". . . licensing, per se, furnished no continuing control with respect to a physician's competence and, therefore, does not assure the public of quality patient care. The protection of the public must come from some other authority, and that, in this case, is the Hospital Board of Trustees. . ." This is only one of the numerous cases that describe the hospital's responsibility and liability for the quality of care it provides.

The board has been held responsible for protecting patients from malpractice by the hospital's independent staff physicians.[7] Even though the medical staff is the body that possesses the clinical skills to take corrective actions, it normally does not have the motivation to do so. The peer review concept possesses numerous economic, social, and financial conflicts for physicians and typically is not handled effectively, if it is voluntary.

The same thing is true of administration, which typically is composed of nonphysicians. The animosity that may exist between the administrative and medical staffs does not position the former in such a way that it can deal effectively with the protection of patients from malpractice at the hands of the medical staff or accurately evaluate and correct problems involving quality of care at that staff level.

However, the board is in a different position. It has the legal obligation to meet its duty to the public to make sure that quality of care is provided, not only by physicians but by nurses and other clinical practitioners in the hospital, be they employees, students, independent contractors, or others. The board has continuing oversight function involving the management of patient care provided in its institution.

There is no reason why this function cannot be handled by a committee, with adequate staff, as long as it includes direct representation from the board and the board in turn receives direct reports on the activities adequate to assure it that it has met its obligation of overseeing the activities in the institution.[8] However, hospital boards seldom meet this type of continuing oversight responsibility. The board typically consists of business, financial, and community leaders. They seldom have the expertise or desire to provide the level of continual monitoring that may be necessary in clinical areas.

In addition, they have not been very successful at confronting the medical staff. The trend to professional board members for hospitals may change this reluctance in the next decade. In the meantime the hospital more frequently is being held accountable for its lack of a competent quality assurance program. The courts are increasingly less willing to rely upon the board's delegation of these activities to the clinical departments, be they medical or nursing. The courts have found this to be a responsibility of the board, which has an obligation to assure itself that these activities are being taken care of adequately on a constant basis.

This omnipresent obligation for quality assurance certainly overlaps into risk management, as discussed earlier. The board's responsibility to protect the organization's financial resources lends itself to the establishment of an obligation to make sure risk management and loss prevention activities are taking place in an effort to protect the institution.

The hospital has an obligation to make sure quality assurance and risk management are performing their functions.

NOTES

1. *Darling v. Charleston Community Memorial Hosp.*, 33 Ill.2d 236, 21 N.E.2d 253 (1965).
2. *Gonzales v. Nork and Mercy Hosp.*, Case 228566, Super. Ct. of Cal., Sacramento County (1973).
3. CMIF.

4. *Black's Law Dictionary*, (rev. 4th ed., 1968) 409.
5. *Stern v. Lucy Webb Hayes Nat'l Training School for Deaconesses and Missionaries*, 381 F.Supp. 1003 (D.C.D.C. 1974); *U.S. v. Thompson*, 366 F.2d 167 (6th Cir. 1966); *Gilbert v. McLeod Infirmary*, 64 S.E.2d 524 (S.C. 1951).
6. *Moore v. Trustees of Carson-Tahoe Hosp.*, 495 P.2d 605 (Nev. 1972).
7. *Purcell v. Zimbelman*, 500 P.2d 335 (Ct. of App. Ariz. 1972); *Joiner v. Mitchell County Hosp. Auth.*, 189 S.E.2d 412 (Ga. 1972); *Corleto v. Shore Memorial Hosp.*, 350 A.2d 534 (Sup.Ct. N.J. 1975).
8. Glenn Troyer and Steven L. Salman, "How Boards Can Meet Their Quality Assurance Responsibilities, *Trustee* 34, no. 6 (June 1981).

Chapter 20

Patient's Personal Items and Valuables: The Bailment Issue

Steven L. Salman

Every hospital risk management program, or each administration in a facility that lacks such an operation, spends a fair amount of time dealing with the problem of patient's valuables and personal items that are reported lost, misplaced, or stolen. During a hospital stay, items such as hearing aids, dentures, and clothing are frequently lost. The risk manager is usually called upon to deal with the patient or the patient's family when this occurs. Sometimes this involves an insurance claim and other times the losses are paid for out of the hospital's operating budget. Either way there is an impact on the financial resources of the hospital and therefore the control and/or prevention of such losses is of great concern to the risk manager.

This subject can be divided into two issues: (1) legal and (2) policy.

LEGAL ISSUES

The legal issues often involve the area of law titled bailments. The word bailment comes from the French word bailler, which means to deliver. It implies a delivery of personal property by one person to another in trust for a specific purpose under a contract, with the obligation to account for that property when the specific purpose has been accomplished.[1]

In a hospital, a bailment can be defined as the presentation or delivery of personal property for some purpose by one person, the bailor (the patient), to another person, the bailee (the hospital), under a contract express or implied. After that purpose has been fulfilled, the property is to be redelivered to the bailor, otherwise dealt with according to the bailor's direction, or kept until reclaimed.[2]

Historically, the law of bailment was neither fish nor fowl. It was uncertain whether it fell under tort-based or contract-based liability. Many states now have clarified this situation by adopting specific statutes dealing with bailment.

Historically, common law broke bailments into three types:

1. bailments for the benefit of the bailor
2. bailments for the benefit of the bailee
3. mutual benefit bailments.

The amount of care required of the bailee depends upon which category the bailment fits into. If the bailment is for the sole benefit of the bailor, then the bailee is responsible to provide only slight care. If the bailment is for the sole benefit of the bailee, then extraordinary care is required of the bailee. If the bailment is for the parties' mutual benefit—that is, a benefit to both bailor and bailee—then ordinary care is required of the bailee. To put it another way, the bailee is liable for ordinary, slight, or gross negligence.[3]

These distinctions are important in states that have not enacted bailments statutes. The distinctions establish the degree of care a hospital must undertake in handling and protecting the patient's personal property once a bailment relationship has been established. This relationship may take many forms. For example:

- It may involve taking the clothes of an obstetrical patient who shows up at the hospital in active labor.
- It may involve the removal of patient's dentures in surgery before the induction of anesthetic.
- It may involve a patient who arrives alone and in the admitting area checks valuables with the hospital through its regular process for protection of such articles.

These do not constitute an exhaustive list of potential bailments but are examples of situations that occur daily in the average hospital.

In determining whether a bailment exists, it is necessary to look first at the factual situation. Inherent in the concept of bailment is the transfer of the possession of personal property without any transfer of ownership, usually for a particular purpose. The bailor remains the owner of the item even though the item has been left with the bailee.[4] A classic example: A person who leaves clothes with the dry cleaners does not transfer title to the cleaners but gives them the possessory right to possess, clean, and press the clothes and return them once this has been accomplished. The importance of determining the existence of a bailment becomes clearer once the policy issues are discussed.

POLICY ISSUES

Policy issues concerning patient's valuables and personal items usually involve an administrative decision on at least one of two points:

1. how to handle a patient's valuables and personal items before a loss or disappearance
2. how to handle this disappearance or loss once it has taken place.

Appendix 20–A is a sample policy on how a hospital can handle the issue of patient's valuables and personal items.

Handling Before a Loss

Obviously, the ideal way of handling this problem is to not allow it to occur. Patients in the preadmission process should be encouraged to leave their personal items and valuables at home. They have no need to bring a large amount of money, jewelry, or other valuable items to the hospital. Nor is there a need for the average patient to bring an extensive amount of clothes, particularly expensive ones.

Notwithstanding this lack of need, hospitals find many patients arriving with some rather unusual items. This may include a briefcase with everything from life insurance policies to large sums of cash to titles to their cars, stocks, bonds, and other bearer-type negotiable instruments. Therefore, hospitals must have a procedure on how to identify and handle such situations. When this happens, the ideal action, if the patient is being escorted by a spouse, parent, or adult child, is to have that person take the items home so they do not remain in the hospital.

If there is no way of sending the items home, patients should be categorized into one of two groups:

1. those who are conscious and oriented with sufficient use of their facilities to understand and take care of their own property
2. those who are unconscious or disoriented and/or do not have the facilities to take proper care of their personal items.

If patients are unconscious or disoriented and unattended at admission, the valuables should be inventoried and sealed in an envelope by two employees and taken to the hospital safe. If they are conscious and no one is with them to take the items home, the articles should be inventoried by the patient and an admitting person. Items that are to go into the safe should be placed in an envelope, sealed, and taken there. Personal items such as clothing and a small amount of money kept with the patient should be so noted on a form such as the patient's "Personal Items And Valuables Checklist" (see Exhibit 20–1).

Exhibit 20–1 Example of Patient Valuables Checklist

PATIENT'S VALUABLES/PERSONAL ITEMS CHECKLIST

Valuables Envelope # 1007 Page 1 of 1

(Addressograph)

Use additional pages, if necessary.

ITEM	BRIEF DESCRIPTION	ADMITTING			UNIT: 5-west		TRANSFER			
		WITH PATIENT	PLACED IN SAFE				1		2	
			DATE IN	DATE OUT	DATE IN	DATE OUT	DATE IN	DATE OUT	DATE IN	DATE OUT
MONEY AMOUNT	$ 71.00		1/29/81							
	$ 3.00	✓		1/29						
JEWELRY: Rings	Gold color — NO OF RINGS 1	✓		1/29						
	Wedding Band									
Watch										
Necklace										
Bracelet										
Earrings	Gold color Loop	✓		1/29						
PROSTHETICS: Dentures	Upper / Lower / Partial									
Glasses	Silver Wire Rim	✓		1/29						
Contacts	Hearing Aid									
Crutches	Walker / Wheelchair / Cane									

MISCELLANEOUS	Credit Cards	American Express	* CREDIT CARDS 3		1/29							
		VISA, & Sun oil										
	Checkbook											
	Keys											
	Papers											
		Red Billfold			1/29							
							Patient Initial	SS				
							Employee Initial	PM				

UPON ADMISSION:

Employee Signature Ron Smith Dept. Area Registration Date 1/29/81

I understand that Hospital will not be responsible for personal or valuable items I wish to keep with me during my treatment/or hospital stay.

Patient or Responsible Party Signature: Sarah Johnson Date 1/29/81

UPON DISCHARGE:

I hereby acknowledge that I am in receipt of all personal items which were kept in patient's possession or which were kept in the Hospital safe during hospital stay/treatment.

☐ Items kept in patient's possession — Patient or Responsible Party Signature(s) ______ Date ______

☐ Items kept in hospital safe — ______ Date ______

Comments

Exhibit 20–1 continued

DATE	TIME	AMT/ITEMS ADDED	AMT/ITEMS WITHDRAWN	BALANCE	EMPLOYEE SIGNATURE	PATIENT OR RESPONSIBLE PARTY SIGNATURE

Since clothing or any items that remain with the patients can easily be taken home and new items brought in by family members, it should be made clear that the hospital has no way of maintaining control of these articles and that a bailment is not established, with the hospital taking no responsibility. If patients insist upon keeping valuable items and are conscious and oriented, it should be made clear to them that the hospital does not recommend this and that if they choose to do so then they assume all risk for loss.

This includes items such as fur coats, watches, expensive luggage, rings with large stones, and other types of jewelry. (It should be noted that the cost of items always seems to increase once they are lost.) If at any time the patients' status changes, that is, they become something other than oriented and conscious, the items should be taken from them by two employees, inventoried, and placed in the safe so that they are available upon discharge.

Hospitals have many problem areas. One is emergency services. This includes patients who come in on an emergency basis and those who are dead on arrival and are taken to the hospital morgue or a mortuary. The hospital often is blamed for loss of items that the family believed such patients had with them. However, these losses may have taken place long before the patient arrived at the hospital. Therefore, Emergency Service patients and DOAs should have their valuables inventoried and disposed of, as discussed, as soon as possible.

The general guidelines in the sample policy and procedure shown in Appendix 20–A are the first step in protecting the hospital from patient claims for lost articles. The policy puts the burden back on conscious, oriented patients to handle their items in the advisable way—sending them home with a family member.

Once an item is inventoried and put in the safe, a bailment relationship most likely has been created in nearly every jurisdiction. At that point, it may be assumed that the bailment is for the benefit of the bailor—that is to protect the bailor's goods during the stay at the hospital. If that is the case, then at least slight care should be taken to protect the items.

It often is argued that this bailment really is for the benefit of bailee (the hospital) to protect it from having to pay for items that disappear from the facility. This argument is strengthened when the patient is brought to the hospital on an emergency basis and has no intent to create a bailment. A third argument is that this is a mutual benefit bailment, with each party benefiting. Certainly the hospital, at the least, should be able to demonstrate that "ordinary care" was taken to place these items in a safe or other security area and that the process was maintained.

Handling After a Loss

Items not placed in the safe that patients choose to keep with them, such as large sums of money, jewelry, clothing, etc., that end up lost must be dealt with. These can be handled through a policy decision. The hospital must decide whether it wants to replace them when they are reported missing by a conscious, oriented patient or whether it wants to establish a procedure that it will not pay. Hospitals that have extensive experience in dealing with this from a policy position find that the public relations aspects of not replacing items can be somewhat distasteful as the erstwhile patients tend to write letters to the local newspaper, call the action editors of the local TV or radio stations, etc. However, the other side of the problem is that if conscious, oriented patients are held responsible for their own personal items, then this is a means of:

1. placing the accountability with the patient, who has made the decision to keep the items and has the most control over them and
2. reducing health care costs.

It is argued that the hospital, for public relations reasons, could replace every item reported lost. Some have done this but have found that they had to increase their budget for such replacements up to 100 percent each year. Once patients realize that they can get a new pair of shoes or a new hearing aid by claiming that the items were lost during their hospital stay, it becomes a popular way of supplementing their wardrobe. However, once patients no longer have the capacity of protecting their own items, the hospital's obligation increases to protect those articles from loss. The hospital should establish a method for handling such items as its accountability goes up considerably.

This problem is particularly true for prosthetics, such as dentures, hearing aids, glasses, contact lenses, etc. It is common for elderly patients to place their dentures wrapped in a napkin on their tray at dinner. A dietary aide picks up the tray and it is taken downstairs, where the dentures inadvertently end up in the garbage disposal, never to be seen again. The question then is, "Was this a conscious and oriented patient, able to take care of the person's own dentures?" If the answer is no, then the hospital may have had an obligation to protect such patients from themselves. If the answer is yes, i.e., a 38-year-old conscious and oriented who is in for diagnostic purposes and is conscious at all times loses contact lenses or dentures, the hospital probably has a minimal obligation to protect such property. The hospital probably could substantiate its refusal to replace those items when they are lost through the patient's own acts.

The threshold questions that should then be asked are:

1. What ability do patients have to protect and take care of their own goods while they are at the hospital? If the answer is that they do have full capacity to do so, then they should be accountable for doing so. If they do not have that capacity, the hospital most likely does have accountability for replacing them.

2. Regardless of patients' status, once the hospital takes those possessions from them, either voluntarily from a conscious, oriented patient or unbeknownst to an unconscious or disoriented one, the hospital most likely has responsibility for the items.

Going back to the conscious and oriented patient who loses one or more items, the hospital, even if not legally accountable, must make a policy decision as to whether or not to replace them anyway. This is strictly a financial decision that could have far-reaching implications as cases and replacement costs begin to grow over the years.

SUMMARY

The one message that should be gleaned from this recurring problem is that the best time to deal with it is before it emerges. The hospital should develop a policy and procedure and educate the admitting, nursing, and medical staffs as to how the procedure operates. It should be reviewed by counsel to make sure it meets local laws involving property and bailments. The hospital (and counsel) must be prepared to have a patient test it in both the courts and the press. However, if these steps are followed, the hospital will be in a good position to defend the policy it has established.

NOTES

1. *Black's Law Dictionary* (rev. 4th ed. 1968), 179.
2. J.E. Cribbet, *Principles of the Law of Property*, 2nd ed. (Mineola, N.Y.: The Foundation Press, Inc., 1975), 83.
3. C. Donahue, T.E. Kauper, and P.W. Martin, *Property: An Introduction to the Concept and the Institution—Cases and Materials* (St. Paul: West Publishing Company, 1974), 77.
4. W.L. Prosser, *Law of Torts*, 4th ed. (St. Paul: West Publishing Company, 1971), 96.

Appendix 20–A

Policy and Procedure Handling of Patients' Valuables/Personal Items

Purpose

To establish procedures for reducing the number of patients' valuables/personal items misplaced or lost during hospital stay or treatment.

Policy

The following are the policies of the Hospital:

1. To encourage patients, during preadmission procedure, to leave personal items at home.
2. To encourage patients, during admission procedure, to give personal items to a responsible adult accompanying them at the time of admission.
3. If the patient is conscious and oriented at the time of admission, the hospital *will not* be responsible for articles of clothing lost or misplaced during the patient's hospital stay or treatment.
4. If the patient is unconscious and not accompanied by a responsible adult at the time of admission, the patient's valuables will be placed in the hospital safe; personal items will be placed in a labeled bag and transferred with the patient to the unit.

Your Hospital *will not* be responsible for personal items or valuables a conscious/oriented patient chooses to keep with him/her during treatment and/or hospital stay.

Emergency Service personnel or Admitting personnel will be responsible for initiating this procedure.

Text

A. *Examples/Definitions*
   1. Valuables include, but are not limited to, the following:
      a. Money (patients should not keep more than $5 with them during their hospital stay or treatment).
      b. Jewelry (rings, watches, necklaces, earrings, bracelets, anklets, cuff links, tie tacks, etc.).
   2. Personal items include, but are not limited to, the following:
      a. Prosthetic devices (dentures, glasses, contact lenses, hearing aids, crutches, walkers, wheelchairs, canes, etc.). *Where possible*, such devices should be left at home or sent home with a responsible adult at the time of admission.
      b. Clothing. The hospital will not be responsible for patient clothing during hospital stay or treatment.
      c. Miscellaneous items (credit cards, checkbooks, keys, personal papers, etc.). These should not be kept in the hospital.
   3. Volunteer: A member of the Your Hospital Volunteer Services Department.
   4. Employee: A Your Hospital employee.

B. *Preadmission:* The text of preadmission materials will encourage patients to leave valuables/personal items at home.

C. *Admission Procedure*
   1. In Admitting, and before the interview, a volunteer/employee will help the patient complete a Personal Items Checklist, form #A–1, of articles that will remain with the patient. The volunteer/employee will encourage the patient to send valuable and/or personal items home with a responsible accompanying adult. After the checklist form is completed, the patient and an employee will review and sign the form. The checklist becomes a part of the patient's record.
   2. For those items not sent home with a responsible adult and/or not sent to the nursing unit with the patient, the volunteer/employee will complete the personal items checklist, as in the above paragraph, and Admitting will place the valuables/items in an envelope with a copy of the checklist reviewed and signed by the patient and the employee completing the admission. The envelope will be placed in the hospital safe. The third copy of the checklist will be stapled to the numbered envelope stub and given to the patient so that valuables/items may be reclaimed at the Business Office between 8 a.m. and 5 p.m. on the day of discharge.
   3. The inventory (personal items checklist) on unconscious patients will be reviewed and signed by two appropriate employees in the area of the patient's admission and sealed in an envelope with a copy of the

checklist inside the envelope. The original and one copy of the checklist will be placed in the patient's record; the copy will be given to the patient upon discharge so that the patient may reclaim valuables/items.

4. In all cases, the sealed envelope will be hand-carried to the safe by an employee.
5. The "Your Hospital" patient guide publication placed beside the patient's bed will remind the patient that the hospital is not responsible for lost items. Patients should be encouraged to read the publication.
6. Patients going directly to the nursing unit will have the personal items checklist and valuables envelope completed on the nursing unit. Upon the patient's arrival on the nursing unit, the personal items checklist will be reviewed with the patient and then signed by the patient and a Your Hospital staff member/employee.

D. *Emergency Services Procedure*

1. Patients arriving at Emergency Services will be encouraged by an employee at reception and/or triage station to give all valuable and personal items to a responsible adult accompanying them in the emergency room. If the patient is unconscious, *Policy* statement #4 and *Admission Procedure* item C (3) will be followed. Conscious patients who are admitted from the emergency room will have the procedure followed as in item C (2) by Admitting personnel.
2. Valuables of emergency patients will be removed in accordance with this policy as soon as possible without deterring treatment.
3. All nonemergency patients will have valuables handled in accordance with this Policy & Procedure prior to treatment.

E. *DOAs*

DOAs will have all valuables other than clothing listed on the personal items checklist and signed by the emergency room employee checking in the body. These items may then be claimed and signed for as itemized by the proper individual through normal channels. If there is any question as to "proper individual," contact the Security Department.

F. *Patient Transfer*

Before a patient is transferred to another room, the personal items checklist will be reviewed with the patient and then countersigned and dated by the patient and an employee/volunteer facilitating the transfer. Upon arrival in the new room, the same procedure is repeated, with the patient and a hospital staff member/employee again signing the checklist.

G. *Discharge*

Prior to discharge, the personal items checklist is reviewed again with the patient and countersigned and dated by the patient and an employee facilitating the discharge. Any item(s) placed in the hospital safe may be retrieved by the patient, a responsible member the patient's family, or a proper individual at the Business Office between 8 a.m. and 5 p.m. If there is any question as to "proper individual," contact Safety and Security.

H. *Miscellaneous*
   1. The hospital will not be responsible for nonclothing items acquired by conscious/oriented patients after admission, unless those items have been added to the personal items checklist and deposited in the safe.
   2. If prosthetic devices or other items are given to the family to take home during the patient's hospitalization or treatment, the patient is encouraged to ask Nursing Service personnel to delete those items from the checklist.

I. *Articles Left by Patient*
   1. Articles left in patient rooms upon discharge are to be taken immediately to Lost and Found by Nursing Service personnel who will obtain a Receipt For Item(s). The item(s) and the receipt will be kept for 30 days and then disposed of in accordance with administrative approval.
   2. Identifiable articles for which ownership can be established are mailed each Monday morning by volunteers who pick up the articles at the Lost and Found.
   3. This Policy and Procedure is in concurrence with Policy & Procedure XYZ, "Lost and Found."

Chapter 21

Computers in Risk Management

Steven L. Salman

By the mid-1980s there could be no denying that the nation had fully entered the computer age. Society is computer driven. There are computers in cars, in homes, and most certainly at work locations.

In risk management, a computer can be a tremendous asset. The kind of functions it can perform lend themselves particularly well to the risk management type of activities. Hospitals, until relatively recently, have been either noncomputerized or, if they were (as most were), they used a big mainframe with terminals throughout the facility. This was particularly true in the financial areas, billing and patient accounts, and admitting, as well as in pharmacy and material management areas. However, with the onset of microcomputers, the devices became both smaller and less expensive, so departments within the hospital—such as risk management—could have their own machines.

USES IN A HOSPITAL

Many of the functions that can be performed on the microcomputer in risk management are similar to those in other areas of hospitals or business—for example, word processing. With the tremendous number of reports that hospitals must provide to their insurers, to boards of trustees, and to administrative and medical staffs, frequently requiring two, three, or more drafts, the word processing function can be most beneficial to risk managers.

With a spreadsheet program, many kinds of data can be managed: renewal dates of coverages, needs to increase coverages as values change, and property values. Many items needed in managing the insurance portfolio can be handled by computers.

CASE FILES AND OTHER MATERIALS

Self-insured hospitals, or those that have captive insurers, have a critical need for managing their own case files and sound claims management, both of which lend themselves well to a computer. The risk managers can keep a computerized file of all the key factors of a case in litigation and tie it into a diary system, so as they go through the legal process, there is a check and balance between defense counsel and the risk management office to make sure critical dates are met for filings, etc. The ability to maintain a claims history for the institution is a valuable tool at the time of insurance renewal, not to mention its importance as a loss prevention and quality assurance tool.

Electronic data storage simplifies the gathering of materials for going to market for professional liability and all the other risks. It can be used as a loss prevention tool, in pinpointing in loss runs where there are common problems, by department, by type of service, or any other ways in which the data are analyzed. Managers thus can focus loss prevention and quality assurance activities in the areas that appear to have the most activity, from both frequency and severity standpoints.

Statistical analyses of such data, by frequency and severity, can be used for histograms and other types of graphic displays for department use and for presentations to meetings of administrative, medical, and nursing staffs, and of the board. When shown to prospective insurers, excess insurers and/or reinsurers in today's volatile environment, these can cause a difference in their feelings about the hospital's competency.

Many hospitals and other industries are using computers to develop risk models for calculating future losses as well as future needs in risk financing. Software for actuarial modeling and projections is available from many independent actuarial firms. These allow mangers to run, on a microcomputer, programs that will help them make actuarial studies based on their own data and assumptions. This can be a valuable tool for self-insured or captive insured organizations and for working with insurers, where hospitals are commercially insured.

EQUIPMENT MANAGEMENT

Microcomputers can help a large risk management program with much capital equipment under its insurance program keep track of its location. This is particularly true of much of the movable patient care equipment that may need to be evaluated and/or appraised on a regular basis to make sure that insurance values are adequate in case of loss. Biomedical equipment also can be managed through a computer system.

Computer management of equipment can be useful:

1. at the time of a loss-producing event, to preserve the evidence and identify the exact piece of equipment involved
2. by biomedical managers to determine the cost of ownership, logistics, and spare parts inventory
3. to make sure preventive maintenance schedules are met and to record repair activities; this is helpful not only in meeting accreditation requirements but in maintaining safe working conditions and equipment
4. for prepurchase evaluation and institutional support
5. in evaluating contract services to make sure that they are meeting the requirements under the contract (i.e., preventive maintenance schedules).

If the risk management office is responsible for hospital employee benefits, this can be managed with a computer. It is critical to keep records of such factors as pension plans, health insurance benefits, and claims management involving health, life, and disability insurance, Social Security withdrawals, etc. Software programs are available to manage the employee benefits program from commercial vendors and major brokerage houses, such as the Benonet computer program from Johnson & Higgins.

INCIDENT REPORT ANALYSIS

One of the most common uses of computers in hospitals is in incident report analysis. Studies by many groups, including the American Institute of Hospital Risk Management, have shown that incident reports are not always the most valuable tool for identifying loss-producing events on a timely basis. This lack of effectiveness is a function of the system itself. However, hospitals have found that a large percentage of all cases that end up as claims or lawsuits can be identified early through an incident reporting system. The effectiveness of this method is strictly a function of the sophistication of the program and the cooperation of the hospital staff. If the hospital has an effective program, then the ability to analyze the data is of paramount importance. Even a 100-bed hospital will have more incidents per year then a normal person could analyze by spreading them on a table and trying to find common problem areas. The computer can be valuable in analyzing incidents and in identifying problem areas so that loss prevention and quality assurance activities can be undertaken to reduce the potential for loss-producing events to occur.

Incident reporting analyses are available from commercial insurers and from organizations such as the American Institute of Hospital Risk Management and some brokerage houses, such as the Annistics Program at Alexander and Alexander. However, for any incident reporting program to be effective it must include a total system approach, as addressed in Chapter 6. A computer analysis program for incidents without the other necessary elements will not be effective.

Many hospitals keep patient profiles in the risk management office so they can discern whether any individuals are habitual complainers or are subject to three or four incidents every admission. This kind of common knowledge can be helpful in dealing with patient complaints or incidents once they do occur.

Closely related to the incident analysis usage, and based on reports of the California Medical Insurance Feasibility study in the mid-1970s, occurrence screens today, whether generic or special, are common. The type of data found in such screens can be entered into a data analysis system that can help identify common trends or patterns, by location in the hospital, or by provider. Occurrence screens analyzed by provider may determine, for example, a particular physician whose lengths of stay are excessive, who typically has problems with tissue, or who has a higher infection rate. That type of information can be valuable not only in provider credentialing and recredentialing, but in preparing for loss prevention and claims activities if they were to materialize.

CREDENTIALING, LEGAL, INSURANCE

Much of the actual credentialing and recredentialing process is nothing more than a data base management system that can be handled on the computer. This allows risk managers to enter and analyze much more data than can be effectively analyzed manually. Therefore, analysis of medical staff recredentialing applications can take into account not only risk management and incident reports involving particular providers but also quality assurance activities, occurrence screens, patient complaints, and many other factors that together develop a profile that may be valuable as the process becomes more sophisticated.

Hospitals that have a risk management program tied to an in-house legal program can do case research through the West Law or Lexsis programs. This will provide identification of patterns and trends in case law, including in other states, long before they emerge in individual hospitals or states.

For those that have captive insurance companies or are involved in the investment portfolio of the self-insured trust, many financial services are available through the computer that can provide everything from current quotes on a given stock to long-term financial planning. Software allows managers to communicate with their insurers and, if they have some form of telex, they can receive binders on insurance through that medium. Documents can be transmitted from one office to another.

Hospital risk managers using computers can expect further expansion of claims history information. Most self-insured and captive insured programs are or will be managing case files on a computer. Many good software packages are available for analyzing and managing claims, including those from Control Data and one that Indata has designed in cooperation with the MSJ Insurance Company. These constantly are becoming more sophisticated, providing more electronic claims file programs. Some companies may be (or already are) using paperless files.

CLAIMS MANAGEMENT AND SETTLEMENTS

The newest use of computers in risk management involves claims management and the design and preparation of settlement presentations, including the use of structured settlements. The Structure One software program from Brokers' Service and available through American Settlement Consultants allows persons with a moderate amount of training to design and redesign actual structured settlements on a portable computer in settlement conferences, using actual guaranteed rates from several top-rated carriers. This permits settling a case quickly and for fewer dollars, so it is financially far more advantageous than the previous cumbersome system.

Insurance portfolio management and bid preparations through computers will be the way of handling the tremendous amount of data required for these activities in the future.

Word processing is commonplace in most hospitals. However, one of the more creative applications may be key word associations. This can be done when all or part of the patient's chart is on the computer. The computer automatically reviews the chart to pick up anomalies or mismatches for evaluation. Much like the occurrence screen, the mismatch would not mean that there had been substandard or poor care, only that an anomaly exists and should be reviewed by a person with sufficient clinical experience to determine whether the care was appropriate. An example of key word association could occur in hospitals in which the entire Emergency Room record is on a computer. For example, when a patient is admitted for abdominal problems, the computer would look for key words in the ER chart, e.g., bowel sounds. The simple absence of key words would not indicate that the care was bad but it might show that documentation in the medical record needs to be improved.

Litigation often hinges on chart documentation, and its absence can cause as many problems for hospitals as actual bad care does. Chart review may be a step in the future when hospitals adopt paperless charts. When the hospital uses electronic charts for patients, a chart review can be done by computer to pick up all sorts of problems. An example would be medications that were not given or a mismatch between what was ordered and what was given. Inconsistencies between nurses' and doctors' notes could be detected.

Claims managers who have handled many malpractice cases have had instances in which they read a nurse's note and the physician's note on the same patient for the same time period. It was more than a little disturbing when, except for the heading at the top of the page, it was impossible to even guess that the chart entries were for the same patient. The nurse's note says the patient is going straight downhill, the physician's note says everything is going along well and the patient should be going home tomorrow.

SUMMARY

This chapter is only a superficial exploration of some current and potential risk management applications of computers. The technology is changing so fast that there will be applications in the near future that are completely unheard of or thought of today. Risk managers who not only can cope with and accept computers but thrive on that kind of application will have an advantage in the emerging environment.

Chapter 22

The Predisposition To File Claims: The Patient's Perspective

*Irwin Press**

The years since the mid-1970s have witnessed an astounding rise in costs relating to the prevention and management of medical malpractice claims. Not surprisingly, a crisis of trust also has been building over the same period. Public interest in alternatives to traditional health care has increased, as has the plethora of defensive medical procedures in hospitals. In addition, those years have seen the rise of such hospital professions as risk management, patient representation, quality assurance, and utilization review. The current high interest in "patient services" and "patient relations" is just that—*current:* a reflection of low priority until gathering crises made such interests relevant.[1]

The cost crisis has led to both reactive and preventive behaviors on the part of hospital personnel. Reactive behaviors are those designed to respond to errors and claims after they occur. Examples are incident investigation, adjustment decisions, and insurance reserve manipulation. Preventive behaviors are designed to head off incidents before they occur by identifying and reducing sources of clinical error, legal liability, and patient aggravation. Many risk management or quality assurance newsletters include as a regular feature a column listing examples of clinical error (including errors of documentation) that "could have been prevented." Books and articles wholly devoted to examples of clinical error are of particular interest to concerned risk managers.[2] Workshops on informed consent and documentation have drawn packed audiences.

All these books, articles, workshops, and symposiums share the assumption that claims can be prevented, or payout minimized, through *mechanical* means—that is, via a reduction of medical error or an improvement in documentation.

**Source:* Reprinted from *Law, Medicine & Health Care,* Vol. 12, No. 2, pp. 53–62, with permission of the American Society of Law & Medicine, © 1984.

EMPIRICAL EVIDENCE LACKING

Unfortunately, this assumption has little empirical basis. There is no evidence that indicates that a significant drop in overall clinical error has occurred since the malpractice crisis began, despite the growth of such hospital departments as risk management and quality assurance. Indeed, the increasing rate of litigation has been accompanied by increasing attention to clinical practices and errors. Nor is there evidence suggesting that particular types of error invariably lead to claims, while others do not. Hospital administrators are well aware of the highly idiosyncratic nature of claims and patients' responses to maloccurrences. Similarly, a well-constructed, witnessed, and signed consent form may not protect health care providers from suits.

In recent years, cases such as *Canterbury v. Spence*[3] (1972) and *Wilkinson v. Harrington*[4] (1968) have demonstrated the courts' growing "material risk" approach—a view that the patient's perception of the exchange of information determines whether consent was informed, and that what is a reasonable disclosure in one instance may not be reasonable in another.[5] Thus, at least in the case of informed consent, a narrow focus upon the mechanical aspects of patient management may not even have a secure legal, let alone empirical, basis.

Given the questionable results thus far produced by an exclusive focus upon the mechanics of harm (whether via an act of medicine or documentation), it would seem that a new approach is required to supplement existing efforts to reduce medical and legal risks. This approach should focus upon patient perception of clinical care and harm.

The opinion that patient perceptions might indeed be relevant to malpractice claim prevention is now being tentatively expressed by some physicians and administrators.[6] The call for greater physician "rapport" with patients, however, does little good if the content and mechanism of establishing rapport are not specified. It is impossible to plan a strategy for overcoming such vague problems as poor "patient relations" or "lack of sensitivity." The goal here is to add to the beginning discussion of specifics in patients' perceptions and evaluations.

ERRORS NOT THE SOLE CAUSE

The cause and continuation of the malpractice crisis cannot result solely from errors by hospitals and physicians, waiting time in emergency rooms, interior decoration, or the legal profession. Rather, patients are perceiving more events and outcomes as negative or claimable. An analysis I made of closed claims at one large inner-city hospital revealed that close to half reflect ambiguous causes or damages: scars from emergency surgery considered unsightly; residual minor impairments from major life-saving treatment; unexpected medical or surgical outcomes when all procedures were routine.[7] These are not clear-cut errors and harm, but were perceived as such by patients or their families. These are formal claims (usually via legal representation), and for every such claim, risk managers usually receive a dozen or more "nuisance complaints" that never get to court, yet require staff time, legal consultation, and, occasionally, bill write-offs.

Risk managers also have a thick file of serious incidents that never result in claims. Indeed, the number of harmed patients who actually enter a claim appears to be less than 5 percent.[8] This figure appears even smaller when one considers the rate of iatrogenic injury to hospital patients. Some estimate that as many as one-third of all patients may experience an iatrogenic incident.[9]

Here, again, it is logical to assume that the operation of patient (or family) perception is a major factor in the genesis of claims. The rather simplistic phrase "Incidents don't sue—patients do" is a fair distillation of the notion that a mal-occurrence in itself generates nothing. Rather, incidents (actual or imagined) must be transformed into lawsuits, and this transformation is a socioemotional process, not a medical or legal one per se.[10]

The transformation process can begin with either patient or family, and the role of family perceptions of management and interactions cannot be underestimated in the genesis of suits. As Horsley notes: "One thing is certain—if a patient is weighing the question of whether or not to sue, the doctor's indifference to the family in their time of stress can be the deciding factor."[11] "Injury by itself," comments Lander, "does not translate into the intense hostility that a lawsuit expresses. The objective sign must be joined with the subjective state of being angry. . . . "[12] Indeed, "without anger, an act as hostile as a lawsuit, particularly against as well-established an authority figure as a physician, is impossible to contemplate."[13] In short, the incident—the mechanical event itself—is insufficient to explain claims, and thus can only be a partial element in their prevention.

PATIENT PERCEPTION AND CLAIMS

Unfortunately, little research has been directed specifically to the operation of patients' perception and attitudes in the decision to seek a claim. Most data on the motivation to seek a claim are inferential only, and derive largely from studies that were not related to claims but that focused on general "patient satisfaction" or observations of doctor/patient interaction.

In one study, 65 percent of patients experiencing a "bad medical outcome" still expressed satisfaction with the medical care they had received.[14] The authors conclude that patients' evaluations of medical care are influenced primarily by "their assessment of the physician's effort. . . . "[15] A seminal study by Cay and his colleagues suggests that patients evaluate successful outcomes of peptic ulcer surgery more on the basis of psychosocial and interactive factors than upon physical outcome.[16] Segall and Burnett conclude that patients, lacking medical competence themselves, ''must rely on the affective dimension of the doctor-patient relationship in evaluating the physician's role performance.''[17] Ben-Sira finds that ''mechanical'' factors, such as waiting time and adequacy of staffing, seem unrelated to patients' reported satisfaction.[18] As Larson and Rootman put it, ''satisfaction with medical care is influenced by the degree to which a doctor's role performance corresponds to the patient's expectations.''[19] Patients' expectations of physicians' roles are based almost wholly upon patient beliefs, attitudes, and psychosocial needs—not knowledge of appropriate professional behavioral standards.

Unfortunately, patient attitudes and evaluations of care generally do not receive administrators' attention unless the hospital has a ''hot line'' or mail-out questionnaire with adequate returns. Questionnaires, however, almost invariably use Likert-scaled items, which produce vague results (such as ''nursing staff were *fairly* courteous'') that are useless in pinpointing problems. Questionnaires, furthermore, often fail to contain items about physicians. One study found no correlation between patient satisfaction and staff merit raises, or nurse morale measured on the same services experienced by these patients.[20] Indeed, higher nurse morale was correlated with lower patient satisfaction. Researchers here concluded that hospitals and patients evaluate staff performance on very different bases.[21]

Physicians, too, often have little idea of their personal or medical impact upon patients. In observations of physicians' visits with their hospitalized patients, Waitzkin and Stoeckle noted that during an average 20-minute stay, less than one minute was spent by the physician informing the patient about the medical problem or treatment.[22] Patients, following such visits, were quite aware of this, while physicians reported spending 10 to 15 minutes in giving information.[23] Another researcher directly observed that physicians tend to talk more than patients during medical history-taking.[24] For their part, physicians so observed denied having talked more than their patients. Golden and Johnston noted that many physicians are unaware that patients experience ''massive amounts of anxiety'' during sickness and treatment.[25] Further, physicians tend to be unaware of the part played by their insensitivity to patients' socioemotional needs in patients' noncompliance,[26] and are generally unaware of the extent to which their patients are noncompliant.[27] Indeed, findings of 50 to 60 percent noncompliance are common. This study also found physicians to be unable to judge which of their patients were or would be noncompliant.[28]

While research does not directly demonstrate a relationship between the patient's perception of the medical event and the transformation of incidents (again, real or imagined) into claims, there is sufficient suggestion of this connection. Certainly, the very possibility of such a connection demands that it be discussed and investigated seriously. The following sections offer a preliminary discussion of some specific factors that can affect patients' perceptions and their predisposition to claim. These factors most intimately define the patients' sickness and trigger their response to it and to the healing process.

PREDISPOSING AND PRECIPITATING FACTORS

Patients are the final judge of how well they are treated, how well they are healed, and whether they have been harmed in the process. Before entering a claim, patients must first perceive an injury. Such a perception, of course, is never automatic. It depends upon the degree to which the patient is predisposed to view treatment—and incidents—negatively.

Predisposing factors include consciously or subconsciously perceived events, interactions, and phenomena that the patient evaluates negatively and that affect the patient's perception and evaluation of subsequent treatment and mistreatment. These factors, major or minor, accumulate during the patient's stay in the hospital—the wake-up call for medications at 2 a.m.; the cold lunch because of tests scheduled near noon; the walks in corridors where strangers of both sexes can see the catheter dangling from beneath the short gown and the urine-filled bag clutched in the patient's hand; the physician's quickly passing over the patient's ideas of what the sickness might be. These are all predisposing factors, and essentially condition the patient to expect negative events or to search for them.

Precipitating factors, in contrast, are specific, usually single incidents that trigger a predisposed patient's desire to make a claim. These include the more familiar errors and events that risk managers traditionally emphasize. Frequently, however, the precipitating factor is merely the last in a chain of events perceived negatively (and often unconsciously) by the patient. Predisposing factors are complex, involving subtle interactions between hospital and patient. Each responds to the other on the basis of long-established value systems, and each confronts sickness from its own perspective and with its own agenda.

PATIENT-GENERATED PREDISPOSING FACTORS

As an anthropologist working in clinical settings, I have found that consciously or subconsciously, every hospitalized patient asks a multitude of questions about his experience. These questions range from why he is sick, to how his family can manage the complex treatment once he is discharged, to worries about the discomfort of the treatment.

Patients ask: Will the physician and staff take my ideas and worries seriously? How emotional will they allow me to be? Will the sickness diminish me in terms of sexual, economic, and other roles? Will anyone consider that I will miss events and obligations because of my sickness and hospitalization? Is there an alternative to this mode of treatment?

It should be noted that the patient also wonders about the housekeeping and hotel functions that figure so prominently in most patient-satisfaction questionnaires. Yet housekeeping elements are the least important problems confronting the sick patient. It is likely, however, that patients complain heavily about these hostelry phenomena simply because they are intimidated by the health professional staff, dependent upon (and thus afraid to antagonize) them, or embarrassed at demonstrating their fears, inexperience and weakness.[29]

THE MYTH OF MEDICAL PERFECTION

The manner in which the hospital answers or handles these typical concerns contributes to the patient's perception of treatment. The concerns themselves reflect a number of underlying predisposing factors. The most significant of these (and those with broadest impact) are: (1) the general concepts and stereotypes of medicine that patients bring with them to the hospital; and (2) the manner in which the patient's *illness* is managed by the hospital.

The first—general stereotypes—reflects the public image of medicine. Chief among the elements of this image is the "myth of medical perfection." Both hospitals and physicians foster this notion of medical infallibility. Admission of susceptibility to error is viewed by health professionals as terrifying to potential patients—and likely to trigger malpractice suits. From the patient's perspective, medical perfection is desirable (as well as expected) for several reasons. First, one's life may depend upon it. Second, because biomedicine is a monopoly and prevents all competition, it should be perfect. Third, in an era of high technology and mechanical miracle, error becomes intolerable.[30] The "deification" of physicians is probably both a byproduct and a cause of the myth of perfection, and stems from their monopoly over health resources. Whatever the reason, deification is an additional source of unreasonably high expectations about performance, which are further fostered by television programming's idealized image of the selfless, warm, and sensitive health professional. No hospital, nurse, or physician can meet these constantly and publicly reinforced standards, but the average patient is predisposed to expect them.

ILLNESS VERSUS DISEASE

It is necessary in this analysis to make a convenient distinction between illness and disease.[31] "Disease" is the physical manifestation of sickness, as well as the official medical interpretation and labeling of sickness. "Illness" is the behavioral, emotional, and expressive component of sickness. Since patients' worries, comments, responses, interactions, and beliefs about sickness far outnumber the disease components themselves, the bulk of any sickness episode is perceived as illness, not disease, by the patient. All discussions, recollections, comments, and opinions, as well as the medical history, given by the patient constitute illness—perceptions and sensations heavily affected by culture.

Symptoms and Culture

Symptoms are largely cultural constructs, from the initial act of identifying sensations as suggestive of sickness, to grouping them as a meaningful syndrome. An aching joint can be interpreted as stiffness resulting from a vigorous tennis game or as a symptom of sickness such as arthritis. Pain tolerance itself has been shown to be affected by reference group values.[32] Complaining about pain is strongly affected by ethnic definitions of sickness as cues for social cohesion versus social isolation.[33] Different ethnic groups may focus attention upon symptoms in differing body locations as indicators of sickness.[34]

If symptoms have a large cultural component, responses to symptoms are pure culture. Symptoms almost invariably are discussed and evaluated with family and friends.[35] Decisions to self-treat, e.g., with patent medicines, old prescription drugs, or dietary shifts, are pure culture. Most sicknesses (whether or not seen by physicians) are self-limiting, and most never are seen by doctors.[36] Decisions to seek professional care stem as much from symptom-caused social inconvenience, e.g., disruption of everyday life or income or threat to self-image, as from purely physical discomfort. One study concludes that what underlies the final decision to seek medical care is still unknown—but it certainly is not the disease alone.[37]

In sum, by the time the patient even sees a physician, his initial *disease* has been sifted through a fine-meshed screen of culture, and converted largely into the *illness* with which the person finally presents. This illness is then expressed to the physician as verbal statements about symptoms, feelings, and worries. The interaction with the clinical professional thus constitutes yet another cultural element in the evolution of sickness. It is affected by the doctor's and the patient's expectations of one another, social class and ethnic congruence, and other symbolic factors. These factors determine the content and style of the patient's presentation.

While the patient presents with illness, clinical medicine looks exclusively for disease. During research in Bogotá, Colombia, I found that patients of folk healers present with only one-half to two-thirds of the number of symptoms as do patients at the outpatient clinic of the city's major hospital (both groups of patients were identical socially, and many in each group used both healers and physicians regularly).[38] The reason for the difference is that folk healers accept any symptom offered by the patient while clinical physicians accept only those symptoms that fit official biomedical syndromes, or that fit the disease that the physician believes the patient may have. Thus, by presenting with "extra" symptoms, clinical patients in Bogotá increase the possibility that at least one of them will be validated by the physician's attention—thereby giving the patient some proprietary ownership of his own sickness. Patients may thus resent having several symptoms ignored or given cursory attention.

Explanatory Models (EMs)

Illness consists of more than symptoms, decisions to seek relief, and presentation strategies. All individuals arrive at the hospital with full-blown explanations for their sickness. This explanatory model consists of explanations for what the patient has, why the person is afflicted, why at this time, and what the treatment should be.[39] The fact that all patients have such explanatory models (EMs) reflects the significant anxiety and threat caused by all episodes of sickness.

Such EMs may or may not conform to official orthodox biomedical models, but they enable the patient to understand and attack the unpredictable and threatening. All humans (whether jungle primitives or American urbanites) have a large repertoire of explanatory models. Most self-treat and most do not seek medical help. Because most sickness episodes are self-limiting, there usually is a return to health, thus reinforcing the EMs employed.

EMs can have multiple origins. In the United States population, explanatory models derive from archaic biomedical beliefs, contemporary mass fads, individual family traditions, ethnic group repertoires, and "common sense."[40] Examples of EMs that I obtained at a major inner-city hospital include: "Hypertension is reflected in tenseness and irritability; so when you feel calm, the pressure is down;" "I think I lost my baby because I started having sex when I was only 14;" and "Diabetes is a sweetness of the blood; eating sour things (lemon, aloe, vinegar) will cure it."

Popular and/or folk EMs are employed for each bout of sickness, and vary by region, rural or urban residence, ethnicity, race, generation, and social class. They affect decisions to seek medical care, interaction and expectations during care, and compliance afterward. It is easy—and misguided—to assume that a white, English-speaking, nonethnic "standard American" patient will have EMs generally conforming to the biomedical paradigm and that such a person's response to sickness will be "rational." Unfortunately, there is no such thing as a standard response to sickness and hospitalization. Lower and middle class nonethnic WASPs may differ significantly in EMs and strategies of resort to treatment; the literature on class and response to illness is huge.[41]

Where ethnicity is involved, EMs may vary dramatically from official biomedical concepts and practices. Latin American, African, and Asian peasant and tribal medical traditions are generally humoral in nature, with disease causal concepts linked to maintenance of balance between body, personality, environment, and social context. In such systems, diseases can be caused by such factors as other humans, social and ritual dysjuncture, weather, supernaturals, and purely mechanical means. Health and healing are as much social as physical phenomena, and are inseparable from everyday events and places.[42] Where disease is linked to social, religious, and economic life, it threatens a broad spectrum of human concerns and cannot be perceived as being treated effectively if such human concerns are not addressed. The United States has many migrants who still adhere to such variant medical systems or to remnants of them. Elsewhere, I have indicated the broad range of social, economic, and psychological functions that ethnic or folk EMs can play, even for urbanites in United States cities.[43]

In conclusion, explanatory models—whether mundane or exotic—are logical and meaningful to the patient, and are invariably mobilized when sickness occurs. EMs form a significant part of the cultural baggage that all patients bring to the clinical setting.

Other Affective Factors

There are additional factors. All humans—particularly adult ones—fill numerous societal and private roles that are generally threatened by sickness. Self-image suffers when sexual, parental, collegial, and other obligations are faced with curtailment. Threats to one's role and image are even greater in the clinical setting, where the already threatened individual is isolated from even the familiar physical trappings of control and competence. The hospital environment provides no potential for the maintenance or the resumption of the obligations, identities, and rewards now undermined by sickness. First-time hospital patients can be severely traumatized by this new experience, thus exacerbating the already significant anxieties created by the disease and its effects on one's role and self-image. Lewis notes:

> For certain medical purposes it might be just as relevant to classify illnesses according to the social attributes of the people affected . . . or by social effects of the illness (stigma, interference with obligations at work, in the home, job performance, chronic or fleeting social inconvenience). Such features as these may correlate better with differences in the behavior of people ill (for instance, delay in seeking advice, readiness to comply with treatment, liability to relapse after discharge) than features that are intrinsic to the kind of disease they suffer from.[44]

Cassell has recently decried modern medicine's inattention to patients' "suffering" (a socioemotional response to disease, not to be confused with "pain"). People, he comments, "are their roles" and, when sick, "suffer from what they have lost of themselves in relation to the world of objects, events, and relationships. . . . Although medical care can reduce the impact of sickness, inattentive care can increase the disruption caused by illness.''[45]

All of these factors—the symptom sensations and definitions, the attitudes toward health providers, the perceptions of healers and hospitals, the explanatory models, and threats to roles—comprise illness. It is always brought to the hospital along with the disease. Often the elements of illness far outnumber the perceived symptoms of disease. Hospitals and biomedical health care professionals, however, are trained to deal with disease, not illness. Yet, it is the perceived attention to illness that predisposes the patient to a positive or a negative evaluation of the treatment—often long before any maloccurrence.

HOSPITAL VALUES

It is not that patients enter the hospital already predisposed to evaluate its treatment and personnel negatively. Of course, the myth of medical perfection affects prehospitalization expectations, but the patient's overall predisposition depends largely upon the manner in which the hospital interacts with the illness. The illness, in short, is the raw material, and the hospital's response can convert this raw material into a negative predisposition. The hospital's response reflects basic clinical predisposing factors that, no less than the patient's illness, are cultural in nature and reflect values, roles, and legal and economic decisions that are no more scientific, valid, or natural than those of the patient. By implication, therefore, they are open to modification.

There are two ways in which hospital predisposing factors are culturally generated: through common medical and clinical values and through the organization of clinical care. Major values include the assumption that only physicians with their specialized training know medicine. Nurses may know a little about medicine, but generally not enough to diagnose, call for tests, or prescribe medications in the physician's absence. The patient, however, knows nothing; in effect, ''the customer is always wrong.'' This value, of course, puts a minimal premium upon eliciting (let alone negotiating with) the patient's explanatory model.[46] It also tends to suppress the provision of information to patients: there is no reason to provide this information if patients do not have the special knowledge to evaluate it properly. While many physicians do ask patients if there is anything they would like to know, patients are often intimidated and incapable of articulating specific queries that can make sense of the strange information just given by the physician. Information-providing often occurs only as part of the mandated informed consent. As such, it is usually one-way, with the providers selecting the agenda.

A corollary value holds that because modern medicine is scientific and true, it works independently of patients' thoughts, desires, and personalities. There are two major consequences of this assumption. One is that patients' anxieties and explanatory models may be considered irrelevant to medical management. The second is that if a patient is noncompliant or insists on a personal EM, that individual is considered to be "acting out" and is a potential candidate for a psychiatric consultation. This consequence is reflected in a 1980 study by Ries and his colleagues, who report that nearly half of all calls by medical staff for psychiatric consultations result from poor interaction and understanding between patients and staff, rather than from patients' problems.[47]

Another basic clinical value leads to the assumption that patients are able to leave their daily life outside when they enter the hospital. This life is not considered to be the concern of the hospital, nor is it expected to be the patient's. Physicians' sensitivity to the threats made by illness to patients' roles and identities is generally low.[48] History-taking (the basic tool of doctor/patient interaction) is not heavily stressed in medical schools, and doctors frequently talk more than their patients.[49] Inter personal factors are downplayed in favor of clinical indicators; if the patient has a legitimate problem to address and does not complain, nonmedical data are not usually elicited.[50] Where social, economic, familial, and other role problems are expressed, nonmedical consultation is frequently sought. By giving these problems to social workers, chaplains, or psychiatrists, clinical medicine is clearly separating disease from illness, and patients from their social and emotional selves.

Another value (which also diminishes the clinical importance of socioeconomic and emotional factors) results in the view of the hospital patient as mainly concerned with diagnosis and treatment of the disease, not with such matters as personal dignity. This leads to such hospital conventions as shared rooms, short gowns, public x-ray areas (which often contain outpatients in street clothes) and other assaults on patients' sensitivities. It is a cornerstone of hospital values that the patient leaves all identity and dignity behind when entering the world of sickness and healing.

Patients also must surrender their autonomy—yet another clinical value. Knowing nothing, and being the legal responsibility of the hospital, they must conform to clinical schedules, treatment modes, and behavioral requirements. Lifelong habits and ego-reinforcing modes of environmental control must be abandoned.

A final value reflects the notion that medical professionals are too busy for "trivia," which usually refers to what they regard as minor medical problems or irrelevant behavioral manifestations. Here patients are placed in a double bind. On one hand, they are expected to know enough about medicine to engage in the self-triage of unimportant symptoms so as to avoid presenting trivia to the physician or, once in the hospital, to avoid requesting nursing care for them. On the other hand, patients are expected to "have no knowledge and to passively accept what the physician (or hospital) offers."[51] The result for the patients can be confusion and resentment. Knowing neither medicine nor hospital protocol, they must relinquish control over their own sickness and medical management, voicing few questions and worries, or risk being labelled a "crock," which frequently results in slower patient care.

CLINICAL ORGANIZATION

Aside from the values themselves, the ways in which medical care and hospitals are organized significantly affect interactions with patients and their illnesses. One significant organizational aspect concerns the fact that only physicians are licensed to diagnose, test, and treat patients. Patients are aware that nursing and other staff members have only limited managerial powers. As a result, when the physician leaves, patients can easily feel abandoned or have anxiety.

The Role of Families

Another organizational aspect is that hospitals generally are geared to deal with sick people, not their healthy retainers. This is reflected in the lack of planned space in sickrooms for families, if not in the visiting policies. The fact that increased room size and more comfortable furnishings undoubtedly will affect hospital revenue is not at issue here, because malpractice claims, successful or not, also affect revenue.

Because our medical system generally downplays the effect of symbolic or social phenomena upon either sickness or healing, it tends to view the family as a socially, but not a medically, necessary factor in patient management. Whereas families of young children and the elderly usually are brought into dicsussions of treatment and postdischarge strategy, the kin of alert, competent adult patients often are neglected.

A study of emergency room nurses reveals more tolerance for patient emotional outbursts than for emotional demonstrations of family members who accompany them.[52] This is not surprising; the patient, of course, is the sick one. But it reflects a common view that the patient's family is, at best, peripheral to the state of sickness and the process of healing. If the patient's emotionalism is suspect and distracting, the family's demonstrations of anxiety are unacceptable. This study noted emergency room nurses' tendency to view any emotionalism as more appropriately attended by psychiatric nurses than by themselves.

Underestimation of the effect of family upon patients' attitudes can have serious consequences, with patient compliance and healing directly affected.[53] Equally significant, patients rarely initiate lawsuits without consulting first with significant family members. Where the family as well as the patient have experienced negative interaction with the hospital, the predisposition to claim may be higher.[54]

Inpatients and Outpatients

Another organizational aspect that generates hospitals' predisposing factors concerns the fact that clinical treatment involves only inpatient or outpatient modes. Although a number of hospitals now offer significant outpatient services and such innovations as same-day surgery, inpatient philosophy is still largely "all or nothing."

Procedures for releasing patients temporarily are nonexistent or poorly articulated. Patients frequently languish over weekends for tests scheduled on a Monday morning, or are hospitalized for entire days for one or two one-hour diagnostic procedures. It is easy to ignore the fact that patients may be more inconvenienced by the hospitalization than by the sickness itself, once acute symptoms have subsided. Policies that accommodate some patients' needs to be elsewhere for periods during hospitalization might significantly alleviate role stresses that could otherwise lead to a negative predisposition.

Specialized Language

The specialized training and skills required of hospital staff necessitate a specialized language for efficient, minimal-error communication. This language also serves, however, to reinforce the hospital staff's higher level of status and competence, and it can confuse and frighten the patient. More important, clinical language is not designed for healer-client interaction, negotiation, or consensus. It is a one-way language that conveys inadequacy along with (and often instead of) information to the patient.

Because patients do not know the medical language, it is easy for clinical personnel to fall into the erroneous assumption that patients thus do not have their own terms and concepts for body parts, conditions, or symptoms. Actually, patients are vast repositories of terms for body parts, diseases, causes, and effects.[55]

Use of Complex Equipment

The increasing dependence of modern hospitals upon complex machinery places them increasingly beyond the comprehension and everyday experience of patients. The machinery depersonalizes and intimidates the patient who has received little or no information. The symbolic effect of clinical procedures upon patients cannot be ignored.

For example, fetal heart monitors and IVs are employed routinely in labor rooms around the country. They are used just in case something should happen (e.g., an irregularity in the fetal heart beat or a blood pressure crash). In most cases, there is no incident; yet not to utilize them (and document the use) is to ask for a claim in the event of complications. Thus, they are used for legal as much as medical purposes.

Such measures also have the effect of telling the maternity patient that she is sick and dependent and that birth is not a natural process, but one that requires active intervention by specialists and specialized machinery. The procedures imply that she is a dependent. It stands to reason, therefore, that *any* complication is the hospital's fault, not hers.

Stimuli for Claims

This raises the general issue of the claim-generating potential of patient management modes that have high dependency-producing impact. The implications of this extend beyond obstetrics to all clinical patients. It would be useful to investigate the postdischarge claim rates of patients who had varying degrees of invasive and regimented procedures while hospitalized (particularly procedures that kept them bed- or room-ridden), and how patients perceive clinical procedures in the first place. Such routine invasive techniques as IV might be found extremely dependency-producing to an average patient.

Hospitals, unlike families, operate on shifts. This necessarily results in discontinuity of personnel. Patients may feel reluctant or resentful of having to reestablish sick roles and modus vivendi with personnel who at the very least have not seen them for 16 hours. Discontinuity also is significant in teaching hospitals when resident rotations occur.

A different sort of discontinuity is created by staff specialization, which guarantees that the patient will be functionally dismembered, with the parts distributed to a variety of staff members with differing ranks and tasks. This is unquestionably the most depersonalizing aspect of the entire clinical encounter. It could easily outweigh a host of other factors that make patients dislike their clinical experiences.

The anxiety created by this lack of continuity in care may have a significant impact upon predisposition to claim. The most obvious effect upon the patients is their suspicion that no single person is wholly "in charge" and their concern that the attending physician is not keeping track of the data generated and procedures delivered by diverse specialists during the clinical stay. Most attending physicians visit patients for only a few minutes per day. That the attending physician may already have perused the charts and spoken with staff in the nursing station is not obvious to the patient, who sees the physician's brief visit as the day's medical highlight.

It thus seems that time should be focused on major treatment strategies and prognoses, for physician visits do not usually seem appropriate for minor queries, gripes, or rambling interrogative sessions. The question of who is in charge is easily converted into a question about who is responsible. The lack of a coherent personal relationship with the clinic can result in the most impersonal of quests for remedy—the claim.

A final element is related to both hospital values and organization. The very efficiency of the modern clinic, its mechanical wizardry, and its never-ending stream of minimally to spectacularly sick patients foster an understandably blasé attitude on the part of staff. To staff members, upper chest infections are routine. But to hard-breathing patients, this new and terrifying problem is life-shattering (not least because it threatens their values and roles). Errors or incidents caused by apparently blasé attendants—as opposed to obviously concerned collaborators in the treatment of a serious and anxiety-provoking condition—are more likely to predispose patients to claim.

RECOMMENDATIONS

These are but some of the factors ostensibly generated within the clinical milieu that predispose patients to file claims. These phenomena appear to operate apart from outright error and incident to affect the patient's evaluation of his clinical experience. These factors, I suggest, involve the interaction of the cultures of both the patient and the clinic. The relationship between this interaction and the predisposition to file claims begs for extensive research. There is enough information at present to look to such research less for actual corroboration than for specific mechanisms and linkages.

In the meantime, the likelihood that the illness/perception model is reflected significantly in the generation of claims suggests the utility of applying even tentative insights to the present problem. What, however, should be applied where, and by whom? As the interaction between patient and clinical culture occurs within the physician's or hospital's, rather than the patient's, bailiwick, the largest "burden of modification" lies with professional medicine and its own configuration of predisposing factors. After all, little can be done about patients' predisposing factors before they are brought into contact with the clinic's.

Unfortunately, patient culture is not immediately or easily perceived and comprehended by clinical staff. It's not simple common sense. Nor are patient perception and satisfaction so simplistic as to be readily manipulated by "guest relations" programs that are based primarily on marketing principles. Sick patients whose lives, appearance, roles, and self-images are threatened, and who are disoriented and frightened by the unfamiliar hospital setting, are only peripherally comparable to the relaxed TV buyer or hotel guest. I suggest that patient satisfaction programs be based first on sensitivity to the patient/hospital value systems (including illness/disease distinctions) enumerated herein, and only secondarily on the more obvious elements of courtesy, etc., which underlie traditional customer relations.

The following is a partial list of suggestions for programs that could affect patient perception of the clinical experience:

1. *Hospitals should implement continuing education workshops for physicians on history taking and the medical interview.*[56] Studies indicate severe inadequacies in the doctor/patient interview. Platt and McMath refer to this lack of interview skills as "clinical hypocompetence."[57] Other data have indicated the actual (not simply potential) impact of poor interaction upon patient compliance, satisfaction, and evaluation of both clinical care and physician competence.[58] Kurella warns clinicians against underestimating the "social character of all diagnosis, therapy, and prophylaxis."[59]

2. *Hospitals should implement continuing education workshops for all clinical staff on patient illness content and on the importance of eliciting and responding appropriately to patients' perceptions of their symptoms,* "explanatory models" (EMs), role and image disruptions, etc. Local medical anthropologists and medical sociologists are appropriate facilitators for such workshops. EMs are quick and easy to elicit, and their elicitation can have significant impact on patient trust.[60,61]

Physicians and nurses should also be sensitized by social workers, chaplains, patient reps, consultation liaison psychiatrists, and others who deal regularly with the emotional, economic, social, and other "outside" disruptions that normally accompany sickness and hospitalization.

3. As a corollary, *all patients should be routinely visited by a patient rep, chaplain, counselor, or other nonstigmatizing professional.* (Note: many patients are of the opinion that only "crazy," "poor," "indigent," or other stigmatized people need psychiatrists or social workers.) The purpose is to elicit and express empathy with anxieties and inconveniences caused by the sickness and hospitalization (some hospitals already do this with good results).[62] It should be stressed that most patients do *not* complain about such matters, rather suffer them silently. If these are elicited before they become problematic, patients will be calmer and more trusting, and staff will have useful information with which to maximize treatment planning.

4. *Patient information needs must be met.* Again, workshops can sensitize staff to such needs. Staff take equipment and procedures for granted. To a typical patient, however, all hospital equipment is threatening, and a common procedure such as IV can produce much anxiety. Changes in drip rate, run-out of fluid, and other routine events can terrify patients who are unused to having their veins and life-blood invaded. Explanations of machinery, treatment, tests, and scheduling are essential to making patients feel part of the medical management, rather than outside it. As part of their own management, patients thus share responsibility in it and are less likely to take an adversarial view of events. If ward staff and physicians cannot provide adequate information, the role of patient educator must be enhanced and expanded.

5. *Schedules must be adhered to.* In the hospital, the patient is isolated from normal events that pace his day. Thus, meals and repetitive tests become signposts

that mark significant portions of the day. Late or early meals, promised tests undone, all contribute to disorientation of the patient who has been wrenched from his familiar routines and places.

6. *Quality interaction with family must be given high priority.* Information exchange must be enhanced. Family must receive ongoing news of tests, proposed treatments, schedules, etc., even where these are minor events. The more closely family is integrated into the patient's management, the less likely is an "us vs. them" orientation to develop. Family must be made to feel welcome. When visiting at meal time, family members must be given complementary food trays. It must be stressed that no patient decides to initiate a claim without consulting family.

7. *Hospitals must have adequate measures of patient satisfaction, and effective means for quickly tapping complaints and problems.* Thus, quality data gathering is essential, and it must be diversified. A serious questionnaire (as opposed to a "schizophrenic" instrument, part public relations and part questionnaire) must be designed for tapping existing problems. A convenient hot line must be established, offering inpatients a phone number to call for any problem, question, or gripe. Hot lines are usually manned by the patient rep department, and also serve the important function of defusing acute dissatisfaction while the patient is still in the hospital and experiencing it. Patient focus groups are another essential data-gathering device. Here, a group of recent ex-patients exchange opinions and comments on their hospital experience. Such focus groups provide narrative compliments and complaints to flesh out quantitative questionnaires, and which help staff identify and solve specific problems. Ex-patients are usually delighted and flattered when asked to participate in such sessions.[63]

A centralized office should concentrate and analyze complaint data from all sources—questionnaires, patient reps, focus groups, and risk management. Each source provides different kinds of data, and by such centralization, the hospital can gain an overview of its performance. By combining claims with gripe data, an astute analyst may be able to identify patterns of dissatisfying experiences (not incidents) that seem to be shared by patients who subsequently make claims against the hospital. This is a major means of discovering the predisposing factors discussed earlier.

SUMMARY

Most of the points stressed here have been made previously by numerous scholars and clinicians. The time has clearly come for the clinical professional to give credence to the growing body of insights into patients' perception, to recognize the practical implications, and to attempt to convert them into workable policy.

The epigram "incidents don't sue—patients do" recognizes the parts played by both hospitals' and patients' value systems, behavioral patterns, and expectations in the processes of incident perception and predisposition to claim. The implications of the importance of these forces go beyond claims to the far more common decision by patients to return to or recommend a hospital or physician. In an era of increasing competition for bed-filling patients, administrators may see the latter as important as claim prevention.

Errors and incidents will always occur. It is folly to focus exclusively upon these as the basis of claim prevention or upon better recordkeeping and documentation, which are reactive mechanisms and thus do not prevent claims, as the answers to a continuing negative press and barrage of malpractice suits.

There are many roadblocks to implementation of new programs. Vested interests in existing procedures will resist change. Pecking orders will be threatened. Physicians will balk at being told to take additional training in history-taking; nurses will argue that they already are sensitive to patients' EMs and threats to patients' roles. New duties for new or existing personnel will increase budgets. Requiring physicians to take workshops would be insulting and could send them (and their patients) to competing hospitals.

I cannot imagine a service or office that would not be threatened by such suggestions. However, it is imperative to rethink policies and habits that may be born not out of "scientific medical truth" but out of such purely cultural factors as values, organization, and turf. It is essential to consider innovative shifts in clinical patient management and risk management. That such shifts may have to occur gradually is understandable, but they must begin.

My purpose here has not been to belabor the insensitivity of physicians or hospital administrators to patients' cultural and emotional needs. Patients are equally unaware of and insensitive to the complex needs and pressures experienced by harried health professionals and the realistic limitations to their healing abilities.

Health care professionals and patients represent cultures relatively unknown to each other. These cultural elements rather than mechanical ones appear to underlie patient dissatisfaction with clinical medicine, and—by logical extension—the decision to make a claim. These cultural elements and their specific relationship to claims are still poorly understood, although sufficient data exist to suggest their function and significance.

Incidents, like seeds, may fall on sterile or fertile ground. Hospitals and health professionals can affect the propensity of patients to make claims by addressing attention to patient management strategies, patient-staff interactional styles, the physical plant, and organizational policies that affect patients' perception and thus have the potential to predispose them toward negative evaluation of the healing experience. The result is likely to prove to be not only good business—but good medicine as well.

NOTES

1. The crisis is still growing. Contrary to the belief that the peak of 1973-75 is past, claims are costing more than ever. St. Paul Fire and Marine Insurance Company (the nation's largest malpractice insurer) estimates that while the actual number of suits may be dropping, cost per exposure is increasing dramatically—up 63 percent between 1976 and 1981. ST. PAUL FIRE AND MARINE INSURANCE, PERSPECTIVE SPECIAL #1 (February 1981).
2. *See, e.g,* N.M. DAVIS, et al., MEDICATION ERRORS (George F. Stickley, Publisher, Phildelphia, Penna.) (1981); Furrow, B.R., *Iatrogenesis and Medical Error: The Case for Medical Malpractice,* LAW, MEDICINE & HEALTH CARE 9(5): 4–7 (October 1981).
3. Canterbury v. Spence, 464 F.2d 722 (D.C. Cir.), *cert. denied,* 409 U.S. 1064 (1972).
4. Wilkinson v. Harrington (Wilkinson v. Vesey), 243 A.2d 745 (R.I. 1968).
5. Miller, L.J., *Informed Consent, Parts I-IV,* JOURNAL OF THE AMERICAN MEDICAL ASSOCIATION 244(15): 2100–03 (November 7, 1980); 244(20): 2347–50 (November 21, 1980); 244(22): 2556–58 (December 5, 1980); 244(23): 2661–62 (December 12, 1980).
6. *See* Vaccartino, J.M., *Malpractice: The Problem in Perspective,* JOURNAL OF THE AMERICAN MEDICAL ASSOCIATION 238(3): 861–63 (August 22, 1977); Ladenburger, M., *quoted in* OCCURRENCE 3(6): 4 (1983).
7. Press, I., Report to the Department of Risk Management, Jackson Memorial Hospital, Miami, Fla. (1982).
8. St. Paul Fire & Marine Ins. Co., Property and Liability Division Report (1982) (claims per physician were 3.4 percent; hospital claims per exposure were 2.5 percent).
9. Steel, K., *et al., Iatrogenic Illness on a General Medical Service at a University Hospital,* NEW ENGLAND JOURNAL OF MEDICINE 304(11): 638–42 (March 12, 1981).
10. Felsteiner, W., Abel, R., Sarat, A., *The Emergence and Transformation of Disputes: Naming, Blaming, Claiming . . . ,* LAW AND SOCIETY REVIEW 15(3 & 4): 631–54 (1980/1981).
11. Horsley, J., *Turning Off the Patient's Family Can Turn On a Lawsuit,* MEDICAL ECONOMICS, 56: 119, 129 (January 22, 1979).
12. Lander, L., *Why Some People Seek Revenge Against Doctors,* PSYCHOLOGY TODAY 12(2): 88, 90–91 (July 1978).
13. *Id.* at 91.
14. Woolley, F.R., *et al., Research Note: The Effects of Doctor-Patient Communication on Satisfaction and Outcome of Care,* SOCIAL SCIENCE AND MEDICINE 12A(2): 123, 127 (March 1978).
15. *Id.*
16. Cay, E.L., *et al., Patients' Assessment of the Result of Surgery for Peptic Ulcer,* LANCET, pp. 29, 30 (January 4, 1975).
17. Segall, A., Burnett, M., *Patient Evaluation of Physician Role Performance,* SOCIAL SCIENCE AND MEDICINE 14A(4): 269, 277 (July 1980).
18. Ben-Sira, Z., *The Function of the Professional's Affective Behavior in Client Satisfaction: A Revised Approach to Social Interaction Theory,* JOURNAL OF HEALTH & SOCIAL BEHAVIOR 17(1): 3–11 (March 1976).
19. Larson, D., Rootman, I., *Physician Role Performance and Patient Satisfaction,* SOCIAL SCIENCE AND MEDICINE 10(1): 29 (January 1976) (emphasis added).
20. Taylor, P.W., *et al., Development and Use of a Method of Assessing Patient Perception of Care,* HOSPITAL AND HEALTH SERVICES ADMINISTRATION 26: 89–99 (Winter 1981).
21. *Id.*

22. Waitzkin, H., Stoeckel, J., *Information Control and the Micropolitics of Health Care: Summary of an Ongoing Research Project,* SOCIAL SCIENCE AND MEDICINE 10(6): 263, 264 (June 1976).

23. *Id.*

24. Bain, D.J., *Doctor-Patient Communication in General Practice Consultations,* MEDICAL EDUCATION 10(2): 125–31 (March 1976).

25. Golden, J., Johnston, G., *Problems of Distortion in Doctor-Patient Communications,* PSYCHIATRY IN MEDICINE 1: 127–49 (1970).

26. Hulka, B., *et al., Communication, Compliance, and Concordance Between Physicians and Patients With Prescribed Medications,* AMERICAN JOURNAL OF PUBLIC HEALTH 66(9): 847–53 (September 1976); Sackett, D.L., Snow, J., *The Magnitude and Measurement of Compliance,* in COMPLIANCE IN HEALTH CARE (R. Haynes, *et al.,* eds.) (Johns Hopkins University Press, Baltimore, Md.) (1979).

27. Norrell, S.E., *Accuracy of Patient Interviews and Estimates by Clinical Staff in Determining Medication Compliance,* SOCIAL SCIENCE AND MEDICINE 15E(1): 57, 59 (February 1981).

28. *Id.*

29. A study I recently completed in three hospitals in South Bend, Indiana, revealed that hostelry items constitute approximately 45% of total complaints, while 25% of the patients complained about quality of interaction with physicians and nurses.

30. B. MARKS, THE SUING OF AMERICA (Seaview, New York, N.Y.) (1981) at 21.

31. Eisenberg, L., *Disease and Illness: Distinction Between Professional and Popular Ideas of Sickness,* Culture, Medicine, and Psychiatry 1(1): 9–23 (April 1977) at 9.

32. Lambert, W.E., *et al., The Effect of Increased Salience of a Membership Group on Pain Tolerance,* JOURNAL OF PERSONALITY 38: 350–57 (1960).

33. Zborowski, M., *Cultural Components in Responses to Pain,* JOURNAL OF SOCIAL ISSUES 8: 16–30 (1952).

34. Zola, I.K., *Culture and Symptoms: An Analysis of Patients' Presenting Complaints,* AMERICAN SOCIOLOGICAL REVIEW 31(5): 615, 630 (October 1966).

35. *See generally* Suchman, E.A., *Stages of Illness and Medical Care,* JOURNAL OF HEALTH AND HUMAN BEHAVIOR 6(3): 114–28 (Fall 1965); E. FREIDSON, PATIENTS' VIEWS OF MEDICAL PRACTICE: A STUDY OF SUBSCRIBERS TO A PREPAID MEDICAL PLAN IN THE BRONX (Russell Sage Foundation, New York, N.Y.) (1961).

36. Alpert, J., *et al., A Month of Illness and Health Care Among Low-Income Families,* PUBLIC HEALTH REPORT 82(8): 705, 713 (August 1969); White, K., *et al., The Ecology of Medical Care,* NEW ENGLAND JOURNAL OF MEDICINE 265(18): 885, 890–91 (November 2, 1961).

37. Zola, I.K., *Studying the Decision to See a Doctor,* ADVANCES IN PSYCHOSOMATIC MEDICINE 8: 216–36 (1972).

38. Press, I., *Urban Illness: Physicians, Curers, and Dual Use in Bogotá,* JOURNAL OF HEALTH AND SOCIAL BEHAVIOR 19: 209–18 (1969). *See* Good, M.J., Good, B., *Patient Requests in Primary Care Clinics,* in CLINICALLY APPLIED ANTHROPOLOGY (N. Crisman, T. Maretzky, eds.) (D. Reidel, Dordrecht, Holland) (1982) at 292.

39. A. KLEINMAN, EXPLANATORY MODELS IN HEALTH CARE RELATIONSHIPS (National Council for International Health: Health of the Family, Washington, D.C.) (1975) at 159–72.

40. *See* Press, I., *Problems in the Definition and Classification of Medical Systems,* SOCIAL SCIENCE AND MEDICINE 14B(1): 45–57 (February 1980) (discussing the difference between popular and folk medical beliefs and systems). *See also* Weidman, H., *"Falling-Out": A Diagnostic and Treatment Problem Viewed from a Transcultural Perspective,* SOCIAL SCIENCE AND MEDICINE

13B: 95–112 (1979) (southern black "falling out"); L. COHN, CULTURE, DISEASE, AND STRESS AMONG LATINO IMMIGRANTS: RILES SPECIAL STUDY (Research Institute on Immigration and Ethnic Studies, Washington, D.C.) (1979) (hypertension beliefs); Snow, L., *Folk Medical Beliefs and Their Implications for Care of Patients,* ANNALS OF INTERNAL MEDICINE 84: 82–96 (1974) (black American medical concepts); Blumhagen, D., *Hyper-Tension: A Folk Illness with a Medical Name,* CULTURE, MEDICINE AND PSYCHIATRY 4(3): 197–227 (September 1980) (hypertension beliefs); Helman, C.G., *"Feed a Cold, Starve a Fever"—Folk Models of Infection in an English Suburban Community and Their Relation to Medical Treatment,* CULTURE, MEDICINE AND PSYCHIATRY 2(2): 107–37 (June 1978) (non-ethnic beliefs about cold and fever treatment).

41. *See, e.g.,* E. KOOS, THE HEALTH OF REGIONVILLE (Columbia University Press, New York, N.Y.) (1954); Hinkle, L.E., *et al., An Examination of the Relation Between Symptoms, Disability, and Serious Illness in Two Homogenous Groups of Men and Women,* AMERICAN JOURNAL OF PUBLIC HEALTH 50(9): 1327–36 (September 1960); Rosenblatt, D., Suchman, M., *Blue Collar Attitudes and Information Toward Health and Illness,* in BLUE COLLAR WORLD: STUDIES OF THE AMERICAN WORKER (A. Shostak, W. Gomberg, eds.) (Prentice-Hall, Englewood Cliffs, N.J.) (1964); R. DUFF, A. HOLLINGSHEAD, SICKNESS AND SOCIETY (Harper & Row, New York, N.Y.) (1968); *A Month of Illness and Health Care Among Low-Income Families, supra* note 36; J. KOSA, *et al.,* POVERTY AND HEALTH: A SOCIOLOGICAL ANALYSIS (Harvard University Press, Cambridge, Mass.) (1969); Rosenstock, I., Kirscht, J., *Why People Seek Health Care,* in HEALTH PSYCHOLOGY: A HANDBOOK: THEORIES, APPLICATIONS, AND CHALLENGES TO THE HEALTH CARE SYSTEM (G.C. Stone, *et al.,* eds.) (Jossey-Bass, Inc., San Francisco, Calif.) (1979).
42. H. FABREGA, JR., DISEASE AND SOCIAL BEHAVIOR (MIT Press, Cambridge, Mass.) (1974) at 247–56; Foster, G., *Disease Etiologies in Non-Western Medical Systems,* AMERICAN ANTHROPOLOGIST 78(4): 773–82 (December 1976).
43. Press, I., *Urban Folk Medicine: A Functional Overview,* AMERICAN ANTHROPOLOGIST 80(1): 71–84 (March 1978).
44. Lewis, G., *Cultural Influences on Illness Behavior: A Medical Anthropologist Approach,* in THE RELEVANCE OF SOCIAL SCIENCE FOR MEDICINE (L. Eisenberg, A. Kleinman, eds.) (D. Reidel, Dordrecht, Holland) (1981) at 156.
45. Cassell, E.J., *The Nature of Suffering and the Goals of Medicine,* NEW ENGLAND JOURNAL OF MEDICINE 306(11): 639, 642 (March 18, 1982).
46. Waitzkin, J., *Medicine, Superstructure, and Micropolitics,* SOCIAL SCIENCE AND MEDICINE 13A(6): 601–09 (November 1979).
47. Ries, R., *et al., Psychiatric Consultation-Liaison Service: Patients' Requests, Functions,* GENERAL HOSPITAL PSYCHIATRY 2(3): 204–212 (September 1980).
48. Cassell, *supra* note 45, at 639.
49. Bain, *supra* note 24.
50. Platt, F., McMath, J., *Clinical Hypocompetence: The Interview,* ANNALS OF INTERNAL MEDICINE 91(6): 898–902 (December 1979).
51. Twaddle, A., *Sickness and the Sickness Cancer: Some Implications,* in THE RELEVANCE OF SOCIAL SCIENCE FOR MEDICINE, *supra* note 44, at 124. For further discussion of the double bind, *see* Bloor, M., Horobin, G., *Conflict and Conflict Resolution in Doctor/Patient Interactions,* in SOCIOLOGY OF MEDICAL PRACTICE (C. Cox, A. Mead, eds.) (Collier-MacMillan, London, Eng.) (1975) at 271–84; FRIEDSON, *supra* note 35.
52. Yoder, L., Jones, S., *The Family of the Emergency Room Patient as Seen through the Eyes of the Nurse,* INTERNATIONAL JOURNAL OF NURSING STUDIES 19: 29–36 (1982).
53. DiMatteo, M., Hays, R., *Social Support and Serious Illness,* in SOCIAL NETWORKS AND SOCIAL SUPPORT (B. Gottlieb, ed.) (Sage Publications, Beverly Hills, Calif.) (1981) at 117–48; Pisarcik,

G., *et al.*, *Psychiatric Nurses in the Emergency Room,* AMERICAN JOURNAL OF NURSING 79(7): 1264–66 (July 1979).

54. Horsley, *supra* note 11.
55. *See* Boyle, C.M., *Differences Between Patients' and Doctors' Interpretations of Some Common Medical Terms,* in SOCIOLOGY OF MEDICAL PRACTICE, *supra* note 51, at 299–308.
56. Press, I., *Witch Doctor's Legacy: Some Anthropological Implications for the Practice of Clinical Medicine,* in CLINICALLY APPLIED ANTHROPOLOGY, *supra* note 38, at 179–98 (suggesting relatively simple changes in physicians' style, and suggesting that folk healers have been successful by fitting their paradigms to the social/emotional needs of patients and, in particular, by their overwhelming attention to the patient's illness).
57. Platt, McMath, *supra* note 50.
58. *See generally* A. CARTWRIGHT, PATIENTS AND THEIR DOCTORS (Atherton Press, New York, N.Y.) (1967); Davis, M.S., *Variations in Patients' Compliance with Doctors' Advice: Empirical Analysis of Patterns of Communication,* AMERICAN JOURNAL OF PUBLIC HEALTH 58(2): 274–99 (February 1968); Golden, Johnston, *supra* note 25; Barnlund, D.C., *The Mystification of Meaning: Doctor-Patient Encounters,* JOURNAL OF MEDICAL EDUCATION 51(9): 716–25 (September 1976); Wachsman, P., *The Significance of Reducing Malpractice Claims,* MEDICAL MALPRACTICE COST CONTAINMENT JOURNAL 1(1): 40–47 (Spring 1979); Hauser, S., *Physician-Patient Relationships,* in SOCIAL CONTEXTS OF HEALTH, ILLNESS AND PATIENT CARE (E. Mishler, *et al.*, eds.) (Cambridge University Press, Cambridge, England) (1981) at 5–140; P. BYRNE, B. LONG, DOCTORS, TALKING TO PATIENTS (Her Majesty's Stationery Office, London) (1976); Larson, Rootman, *supra* note 19.
59. Kurella, S., *The Social Needs of Patients and Their Satisfaction with Medical Care: A Survey of Medical Inpatients in the County Hospitals of the German Democratic Republic,* SOCIAL SCIENCE AND MEDICINE 13A(6): 737–42 (November 1979) (emphasis added).
60. Kleinman, A., Eisenberg, L., Good, B., *Culture, Illness, and Care: Clinical Lessons from Anthropologic and Cross Cultural Research,* ANNALS OF INTERNAL MEDICINE 88(2): 251–58 (February 1978).
61. Lazare, A., *et al., Studies on a Negotiated Approach to Patienthood,* in THE DOCTOR-PATIENT RELATIONSHIP IN THE CHANGING HEALTH SCENE (E. Gallagher, ed.) (National Institutes of Health, Washington, D.C.) (1978) at 119–39.
62. Personal communication with directors of Holy Cross Shared Services, a hospital management organization.
63. Patient committees may be used in handling, in addition to identifying, complaints. Dr. Milton Seifert, Jr., a family practitioner in Excelsior, Minnesota, formed an ''advisory council'' from among his patients, apparently with such empathy and success that Seifert's insurance company has reduced his malpractice premium by 10 percent (personal communication with author).

Appendixes

Miscellaneous Sample Policies and Procedures

The following are sample policies and procedures actually used by various hospitals. Before risk managers attempt to use these in their hospital, they should consult with legal counsel to make sure they meet with local requirements.

Appendix A

Nursing Policy and/or Procedure: Charting

One of Your Hospital's goals is to keep accurate, authentic, and permanent records of patients' hospitalization. Charts can be admitted as evidence when summoned by the courts. They should state the facts that communicate essentials. Charting should be objective, i.e., patient status as determined by nursing assessment, care, and instructions rendered, patient behavior, and your response to same.

The following guidelines and basic requirements should be used in recording or charting nursing notes:

1. Chronological sequence is important.
2. If an error is made on the chart, for example, "right arm" is charted instead of "left arm," the chart should not be altered once it is written. The proper way to correct it is as follows: Begin on the next open line in the chart and note that the entry on a particular date and time was entered as "left arm" when it should have been "right arm." A thin line may be placed through the error as long as it is still readable to indicate that further clarification will follow. Your name should be written above the line. Only the person who wrote the original entry may do the correcting. Erasing is not permissible. The courts are more willing to accept the fact that hospital employees are human and make mistakes than they are that a chart has been altered.
3. It is essential to be brief and concise, avoiding the repetitious use of the term "patient." Only approved abbreviations should be used to avoid misunderstanding.
4. It is imperative that the unusual be recorded along with normals in areas of patient assessment that pertain to an individual patient, e.g., for CHF—good skin turgor, absence of pedal edema.
5. Ambiguity makes interpretation liable to error.

6. Vague statements, e.g., "turned at intervals," usually are meaningless.
7. Statements that are authentic and explicit may avert needless litigation.
8. Omissions are considered as inaccurate as incorrect insertions.
9. Charting should not be done for another person. If one signs a document the person is attesting to personal knowledge of the information.
10. Written notes must be identified by date, time, first initial and last name and appropriate title, e.g., 10/1/78—2PM—L. Smith, R.N.
11. Documentation in the nursing notes should include (but not be limited to) pertinent observations regarding:

    a. diagnostic studies, treatment medications
    b. therapy prescribed, patient's response to therapy
    c. refusal to submit to therapy, refusal reason
    d. patient responses to teaching attempts
    e. nursing measures designed to meet patient needs and results of nursing intervention
    f. reason for treatment and medications omitted
    g. accurate description of patient/family complaints, measures taken, any follow-up
    h. documentation of events in proper sequence, noting time, name of person if message is left, etc.
    i. documentation of safeguards taken to protect patients, i.e., siderails up, restraints used or instructions given, etc.

12. The applicability of both physical/mental health assessment factors should be evaluated. If an item is important enough to spend time assessing, it should be charted. Otherwise, it is not worthwhile spending time assessing it. The key is documentation.
13. Nursing Assistants are responsible for recording information on the clinical graph sheet, the sugar and acetone results on the appropriate record, intake and output on I & O record, and may complete the first page of the nursing admission sheet. The following Nursing Assistants are expected to document patient care:

    a. long-term care
    b. mental health/psychiatric units
    c. OB units
    d. named technicians.

Exhibits A–1, A–2, and A–3 are examples of charts filled out (1) correctly, (2) incorrectly, and (3) with an error corrected properly.

Exhibit A–1 Correct Chart Entry

NURSES' OBSERVATIONS

Up in Chair	Up Ad Lib	Ambulated	Turned	Shower	Bath	H.S. Care		Time	FRIDAY JAN 30 1981
								4pm	IV started in Ⓛ hand c̄ #18 angio. M. Smith R.N.

Exhibit A–2 Incorrect Charting

NURSES' OBSERVATIONS

Up in Chair	Up Ad Lib	Ambulated	Turned	Shower	Bath	H.S. Care		Time	FRIDAY JAN 3 0 1981
								4pm	IV started in (R) hand c̄ #18 angio. M. Smith R.N.
								6pm	Pt. tolerated diet well M. Smith R.N.
								8pm.	Open-heart pre-op teaching done. Pt. then
									was prepped for OR in AM. M. Smith R.N.
									WRONG

Exhibit A–3 Chart with Error Corrected Properly

NURSES' OBSERVATIONS

Up in Chair	Up Ad Lib	Ambulated	Turned	Shower	Bath	H.S. Care		Time	FRIDAY JAN 30 1981
									error MS
								4pm	IV started in (L) hand c̄ #18 angio. M. Smith R.W.
								6pm	Pt. tolerated diet well M. Smith R.W.
								8pm	Open-heart preop teaching done. Pt then was
									prepped for OR in A.M. M. Smith R.W.
								9pm	4:00 p.m. Charting c̄ error. IV was started in
									(R) hand but was charted "(L) hand." M. Smith R.W.

Appendix B

Nursing Policy and/or Procedure: Informed Consent

Informed consent for all surgical and special procedures is a requirement of the Joint Commission on Accreditation of Hospitals. For this hospital to maintain its accreditation, it must ascertain that completed informed consent forms are in the chart prior to surgical or special procedures. Before the nursing procedure is stated, it is important to define several terms:

1. *Informed Consent:* Informed consent is the explanation by the physician of the surgery, surgical or special procedures to be performed. It should cover certain topical areas. The informed consent must be obtained by a physician—preferably by the physician who will be performing the procedure.
2. *Informed Consent Form:* The informed consent form is a piece of paper that the patient signs confirming that the informed consent, as defined above, was performed by the physician. A hospital nurse/employee may be involved in the informed consent process to the extent of obtaining the patient's signature on the informed consent as described below:

Unit Responsibility

1. Nursing personnel on the unit will review the patient's chart to make sure that the fully completed informed consent form is present.

   a. This will take place during the admission process on the unit for patients being admitted the day prior to surgery.
   b. For patients already in-house who are being scheduled for surgery, this process can take place any time up to the evening before surgery.
   c. For patients having outpatient surgery who are in-house patients, this audit process will take place some time prior to the patient's being sent to outpatient surgery for the procedure.

d. Whenever possible this audit should take place 24 hours or more prior to the scheduled surgery/procedure.

When the informed consent form is absent from the chart during this audit, nursing personnel on the unit will notify the operating/administering physician of this deficiency.

2. In cases where the informed consent form has been sent to the hospital with the preadmission packet or sent with the patient to the hospital and for some reason has not been received in the hospital, the operating/administering physician may sign the affidavit form #_______ stating that the consent form has been completed and that the form was signed and a copy will be sent or brought from the physician's office to the hospital within 24 hours for placement on the chart. In these cases, the physician may proceed with the surgery/procedure.
3. Nurses/employees may be involved in an informed consent procedure under the following conditions only:

   a. The operating/administering physician wishes the nurse/employee to witness the entire informed consent process and to witness the signature by the patient, or
   b. The operating/administering physician has obtained the informed consent and wants the nurse/employee to witness the patient's signature only, or
   c. The operating/administering physician has obtained the informed consent and places a specific written order stating that the specific surgery/special procedure has been explained to the patient and requests that the nurse/employee obtain and witness the patient's signature on the informed consent form.

4. The nurse/employee will *NOT* answer *ANY* questions relating to the informed consent. The questions will be referred back to the physician doing the consent/explanation. If the patient refuses to sign the form until these questions are answered, the physician will be notified immediately by the nurse/employee.
5. Nurses/employees who participate in the informed consent process to the extent of responding to the patient's questions about the surgery/special procedure jeopardize their protection under the hospital's liability program.
6. The hospital-provided informed consent form # _______ is the minimum requirement of placement on the chart. Physicians or group practices preferring to use a special form that they may be using currently or wishing to develop may do so once the form has been approved by the Risk Management office to make sure that it meets the minimum requirements of the Joint Commission. Once these have been approved, a letter will be sent

to nursing service listing the physicians and the forms that have been approved in addition to the # ______ form.

7. In the case of outpatient surgery or special procedures the informed consent form # ______ or the affidavit form # ______ must be used the same as in in-house procedures. In all cases, the patient must possess the capacity to consent to the procedure, meaning that the consent should be obtained prior to preoperative medications.
8. In case of an emergency procedure, please refer to Policy & Procedure XYZ for guidelines.
9. Either the consent form # ______ or the affidavit form # ______ must be in the chart prior to the operation/procedure or the operation/procedure will be postponed.
10. Any problems with this procedure or with a particular patient or physician should be referred to the Risk Management office if it cannot be handled directly by the floor and/or nursing personnel.

Exhibits B–1 and B–2 are samples of (1) a consent form and (2) an affidavit form attesting that informed consent was obtained.

Exhibit B–1 Example of a Consent Form

CONSENT FORM

I, Sara Johnson, hereby request the performance of Extracapsular cataract extraction Left eye.
(patient's name) (operation or procedure)

The operation or procedure will be performed by Dr. Ralph P. Watson. I understand that
(operating/administering physician)
the operation/procedure is performed by an operating/administering team which may consist of (1) (an) operating/administering physician(s); (2) other physicians participating in the operation/procedure; (3) the anesthesiologist and his associates; (4) nurses and technicians; (5) other necessary personnel.

I consent to the administration of anesthetics as deemed advisable by the physician or anesthesiologist performing or assisting in the operation or procedure.

It has been explained to me that during the course of the operation or procedure, unforeseen conditions may be revealed that necessitate an extension of the original procedure or different procedures. I therefore authorize and request the above-named individuals to perform such surgery/procedures that are necessary in the exercise of their professional judgment. I authorize the administration of blood or blood components or derivatives. I request the disposal by authorities of ____________ Hospital of any tissues or parts which it may be necessary to remove. The only exceptions to the above are as listed below:

none
____

(If none, write "none.")

I acknowledge that I have had an opportunity to discuss with and have explained to my satisfaction by the operating or administering physician the operation or procedure, its purpose and nature, as well as reasonably foreseeable risks. I have been advised as to the reasonable alternatives, possible consequences of remaining untreated, and risks and possible complications of each alternative.

I understand that the practice of medicine is not an exact science, that it may involve the making of medical judgments based upon the facts known to the physician at the time, and that it is not reasonable to expect the physician to be able to anticipate nor explain all risks and complications, and further, that an undesirable result does not necessarily indicate an error in judgment and that no guarantee as to results has been made nor relied upon by me. I expressly wish to rely on the physician to exercise his judgment during the course of the operation or procedure which he feels at the time, based on the facts then known, are in my best interest.

REMARKS

none

(If none, write "none.")

Exhibit B–1 continued

I do hereby consent to the above operation/procedure and anesthetic and accept all the risks inherent to the operation/procedure and/or anesthetic.

September 5, 1978
date signed

signature of patient or responsible person

Witness to patient/family signature

relationship to patient

Dr. Frank S. Jones
name of physician administering consent

1st copy: Hospital Copy (place in chart)
2nd copy: Physicians Copy

Exhibit B–2 Example of Affidavit Attesting Informed Consent

INFORMED CONSENT AFFIDAVIT

Patient Addressograph

I, Ralph P. Watson, M.D. , have scheduled
operating/administering physician (print)

Sara Johnson for Extracapsular cataract extraction
patient's name operation/procedure

on September 6, 1978 at 9:00 a.m. (a.m.) (p.m.).
date time

The informed consent for the procedure was completed in my office and the consent form was signed by the patient. For reasons beyond our control this form has not yet been received in the hospital. I will send/bring a copy of the aforementioned form to Hospital within 24 hours for placement in the patient's chart.

operating/administering physician (sign)

September 6, 1978
date signed

witness (sign)

Appendix C

Standard Policy and/or Procedure: Authorization for Emergency/Outpatient Treatment

Statement of Purpose

The purpose of this Standard Policy and Procedure is to establish guidelines for acquiring authorization for emergency/outpatient treatment.

Policy

It is the policy of Your Hospital that authorization be obtained prior to treatment of a patient.

Text

A. All emergency/outpatient treatments will be categorized into two classes:
   1. *Emergency:* Patients who have a problem that can be categorized as life threatening.
   2. *Nonemergency:* Patients whose medical problems are *NOT* threatening to life.

B. All patients who in the determination of *two medical doctors* can be categorized in classification 1 should be treated immediately regardless of whether there has been an authorization for treatment signed. The effort to obtain authorization for treatment should continue simultaneously with the treatment.

C. Patients in classification 2 (nonemergency) are divided into two areas:

1. For patients age 18 or over, an authorization for treatment must be signed by the patient, the patient's spouse, or next of kin,* prior to the initiation of treatment.
2. For those under age 18, treatment may begin when:

   a. The patient's parent(s)** are with the patient and have signed authorization for treatment.
   b. The authorization for treatment, signed by the parent, was supplied by the patient's school, camp, etc. A copy of the form supplied by the organization may be used.
   c. The patient arrives with a signed authorization from the parent, i.e., a teenager with authorization signed by parent for lab tests. The written authorization or a copy should remain in the chart.
   d. The patient arrives with no authorization nor with a parent. The patient should be encouraged to contact the parent(s) and have them come to the hospital to sign authorization. If this is impossible, because of the parents' location or other extenuating circumstances, a verbal authorization may be taken over the telephone. This authorization should be witnessed on the phone by two employees and should be legibly noted on the patient's chart/file and signed by both employees.
   e. If a patient claims to be independent of parental guidance and wishes to sign authorization for treatment, the Risk Management Office must be consulted for assistance in determining the patient's ability to authorize the treatment. (The hospital operator should be called after hours.)
   f. If the child/patient is in legal custody of an institution, the director of the institution should be contacted, if possible, for consent.
   g. If the patient is within a group that may be treated without consent, per state statute, then the person may be treated without consent. (See Section E. below.)

D. Any patient who either cannot or will not meet the above criteria should wait or be rescheduled for treatment until such time as those criteria can be met, with the exception of classification A-1 (Emergency) patients. In the rare

*If there is no surviving spouse, the right vests in the next of kin. Order of kinship per state statute is:

1. spouse
2. child
3. parents
4. brother and sister
5. other relatives
6. person authorized by a written instrument as legal guardian.

**Parent(s)/guardian(s).

instances when an exception may be necessary, the administrator on call and/or the Risk Manager should be contacted to assist in the decision.

E. Exceptions:

1. Under recently enacted state law, a minor (under age 18) may give consent for treatment of:

   a. drug-related conditions
   b. venereal disease
   c. suspected rape
   d. suspected abuse

   However, in these cases the parents are not financially liable unless they elect to be.

2. Active military personnel who are minors may consent for minor procedures.

Appendix D

Standard Policy and/or Procedure: Private Duty Nurse Policy

Purpose

To order and assign Private Duty Nurses with the full consent of the patient and/or the family. Intensive Care, Coronary Care, Cardiovascular Thoracic, NICU, or Maternity units do *NOT* permit Private Duty Nurses.

To assure that all Private Duty Nursing requests meet the hospital's requirements as specified by the Risk Management Department.

Text

I. *Nursing Unit Responsibility for Order*

A. When a patient or family requests a Private Duty Nurse:

1. The requesting party must sign a request form # ______. Imprint the upper right-hand section with the patient's Addressograph.

a. *One form (#   ) must be signed for each shift of nurses ordered.* (It is important to be sure the party understands that the signing of the form denotes the person's responsibility to pay the Private Duty Nurse and that the order will be in effect until cancelled by the patient or family).

b. The level of Private Duty Nurse desired is indicated by noting the choice and a second choice on the request form. The date/time the nurse/sitter is to start and the approximate length of the case also are noted.

c. It is essential to write a complete diagnosis, condition, and special care needs, i.e., a respirator, trach, CVP line, TPN, special equipment. *BE SPECIFIC*.

2. Forms ## ______ are forwarded to the nursing office during open hours. At other times, the Nursing Coordinator is notified and will order the nurse(s).
3. Unit will be notified if the request is or is not filled; the charge nurse should notify the family or patient and record the shift and nurse's name on patient care Kardex.
4. Private Duty Nurse/sitter must report to the nursing office when starting the case. It is not necessary to sign in each day, only the first working shift. However, each replacement or relief nurse must sign in for the first relief shift. The nursing office will notify the unit that a relief Private Duty Nurse/sitter has signed in and has been approved.
5. It is the unit charge nurse's responsibility to notify the Nursing Coordinator when a Private Duty Nurse or sitter reports for duty without a previous Kardex notation or verbal communication from the nursing office.
6. The charge nurse should give each Private Duty Nurse a patient report and review Your Hospital's Policies and Procedures that may be applicable to the patient.
7. The head nurse or shift charge nurse should complete the Private Duty Nurse evaluation form and return it as soon as possible to the nursing office.
8. Employees should *NOT SIGN* the Private Duty Nurse's vouchers. The patient or family should sign these vouchers. If the patient is unable to sign and the family is not present, the unit charge nurse may initial the margin, including date and time, to verify that the nurse was on duty.
9. Notify nursing office clerical staff or Nursing Coordinator when a nurse is cancelled, or the patient expires.

II. *Nursing Office Responsibility*

When the request for a Private Duty Nurse is received, the order will be processed by the nursing service clerical staff, staffing clerk, or Nursing Coordinator. Requests may be filled only from agencies approved by the Risk Management Department. A current list is kept on file in the nursing office. Your Hospital employees who contract to provide Private Duty service during off-duty hours must follow the guidelines under Section III.

A. Procedure for ordering nurses:

1. Request is recorded in Private Duty request log and action taken is noted (i.e., request called, not called, or filled). Requests are placed only with agencies that have met the hospital's minimum requirements.

2. Calls to and from agencies are recorded on log. When request is filled, this is noted on log, entered on Kardex form, and unit is notified and asked to notify the family and/or patient.
3. Kardex form and request form(s) are placed in Private Duty Nurse file according to the area.
4. The person receiving a call from the agency filling a Private Duty request *MUST* verify that each nurse (R.N., L.P.N.) has attended the orientation program. (Sitters are not required to attend orientation). A Rolodex file will be kept in the nursing office containing name, agency, and date of orientation of each nurse (R.N., L.P.N.). Unfilled requests are carried over automatically until filled or cancelled.

B. Related Duties:

1. Nursing office clerical staff must check nurses' license, orientation attendance, and Workers' Compensation (when applicable) when the Private Duty Nurse reports to the nursing office for duty.
2. An evaluation form (Private Duty Evaluation) should be initiated by filling in the name of the Private Duty Nurse, date, and shift, and placed in the head nurse box or taken to the unit by the Nursing Coordinator. Log and Kardex must be marked to indicate that the form was sent.
3. Nursing office staff or Nursing Coordinator will review the Kardex each morning and follow up or order any unfilled requests; they also will remove any original cancelled Private Duty Nurse request forms and forward to Medical Records to be placed with the patient's chart.
4. When Private Duty Nurses are cancelled by the patient or family, if the patient dies, the agency should be notified and the occurrence marked appropriately on log.
5. A Nursing Coordinator of appropriate shift or area will review the returned evaluation forms. Forms indicating satisfactory performance will be filed in the nursing office for six months, then discarded. Unsatisfactory forms will be on file for a year.
6. All unsatisfactory evaluations or those denoting a problem should be followed up with a letter to the agency from the area Nursing Coordinator. A copy of the letter should be filed with the evaluation and a notation made on the nurse's Rolodex file.

III. *Private Duty Nurse Responsibility*

A. Private Duty Nurses (including sitters) must report in person to the nursing office at the beginning and *ending* of their case.
B. Additional requirements:

1. Private Duty Nurses must have attended Your Hospital's Orientation Program. (Sitters are not required to attend.) Former employees who wish to waive the orientation must send this request to the Office of Risk Management; if approved, the name will be added to the Rolodex in the nursing office.
2. The nurses from the R.N. Registry must show evidence of current liability and Workers' Compensation coverage each time. A photocopy of the Workers' Compensation Certificate or Liability Policy is acceptable.
3. Family-ordered nurses must meet the above criteria; otherwise, they can attend only as a family member.
4. Private Duty personnel are responsible for their own parking. There is no special discount or area for parking.
5. Private Duty personnel are expected to wear a name pin with title included and to dress appropriately according to their position.
6. Employees who contract for Private Duty nursing cannot accept a case on their scheduled working unit and must:

   a. Provide proof of current malpractice liability insurance with minimum limits of $100,000 per occurrence.
   b. Provide proof of current Workers' Compensation coverage by showing a valid Certificate of Insurance on an Accord form.
   c. Provide items a & b above to the Risk Management Office prior to accepting Private Duty nursing assignments; a list of qualified nurses will be provided to the nursing office.

C. Private Duty Nurses may perform the following duties:

1. R.N.s

   a. May give all bedside personal care.
   b. May give patient medications (see _______, Medication Administration Policy). May hang IVs, and blood or blood derivatives, but *MAY NOT START IVs* (see _______ Intravenous Therapy).
   c. May chart.
   d. May do patient treatments.

   When unfamiliar with procedure, equipment, or therapy, the Private Duty Nurse must seek the guidance and assistance of the unit charge nurse.

2. L.P.N.s

   a. May give bedside personal care.
   b. May do treatments.

   c. May chart.
   d. May *NOT GIVE MEDICATIONS OR IVs*.

3. Sitters

   a. May assist with the patient's personal care (bath, oral hygiene), feed patient, give the bedpan, change linen.
   b. May *NOT GIVE ANY MEDICATIONS, TREATMENTS, OR CHART*.

Exhibit D–1 is a sample nursing evaluation form to be filled in by a qualified outside source.

Exhibit D–1 Example of a Nurse Evaluation Form

NURSING SERVICE DEPARTMENT

Nurse Evaluation from an Outside Source

NAME OF NURSE ____________________ DATE ____________
AGENCY ____________________ UNIT ASSIGNED ________
SHIFT ____________

As one of the means of fulfilling our responsibility for the nursing care of our patients and in keeping with our quality assurance program, the Head Nurse or Charge Nurse on each tour of duty is responsible for evaluating the following factors as they relate to the tour of duty indicated above:

O = Outstanding G = Good I = Needs Improvement U = Unsatisfactory

Factor:	*O*	*G*	*I*	*U*
1. Interpersonal Relations (patient, unit staff medical team)	1	2	3	4
2. Job Performance (nursing process, organization, knowledge, accuracy, quantity)	1	2	3	4
3. Adaptability (stress, new situation)	1	2	3	4
4. Communication (directing, documentation, patient teaching, reporting, observations)	1	2	3	4
5. Physical Care/Safety (patient, treatments)	1	2	3	4
6. Observance of Working Hours				

Write a brief paragraph including pertinent specific information regarding the performance of this agency nurse.

____________________ R.N. DATE RETURNED ________
SIGNATURE OF R.N. EVALUATOR

NOTE:

1. Hospital nursing assistants may not be employed by patients as sitters.
2. If sitters come from home with the patient but are not from an approved agency, the family must be referred to the Nursing Coordinator for clarification.
3. Sitters from special facilities (state mental hospital, prison, etc.) are not required to sign in or out. These sitters are with the patient for safety and/or security reasons and do not provide nursing care.

Index

A

Acceptance of authority (organizational) theory, 393-394
Accountability
  in bureaucratic form of management, 387
  CEO, for code of ethics, 76
  individual, as increasing, 365
  institutional, and governing board, 63
  legal, of nurses, 361, 362, 367-368
  managerial definition of, 58
  on fiduciaries, 195
Accounting formula
  allowances and provisions, 83
  beginning fund balance, 85
  contributed capital, 85
  ending fund balance, 85
  excess (deficit) of revenues over expenses, 85
  gross patient service revenue, 82-83
  hospital, 82-86
  net operating income, 84
  net patient service revenue, 83
  nonoperating items, 84-85
  operating expenses in, 84
  other operating revenue, 83
  as profit calculation, 85
  risk management implication of, 85-86
  for statement of revenues, expenses, and changes in fund balance, 90
  total operating revenue, 83
Accounting, patient, 95
Accounts payable, 96, *97*
Accreditation, effect on health care system, 29
Active medical staff, defined, 67-68
Actuarial studies, computerized, 436
Administration
  and the CEO, 74-77
  commitment to risk management, 314
  as input for risk identification, 162
  and risk evaluation, 180
  risk insurance for, 196
  role in quality assurance, 418
  role in risk management, 305-306, 315, 418
Administrative management theory, 389-391

Note: Page numbers in *italic* indicate entry is found in an exhibit, figure, or table.

Administrator
  role in community hospital, 75
  See also Chief executive officer
Admissions
  hospital, numbers of, 32, *35*, 36
  inpatient, as secondary care, 2
  procedure for handling patients' valuables and personal items, 430-433
  short-stay hospitals, *35*
Admitting clerks, as input for risk identification, 163
Advertising, health care, 51
Aged, Medicare/Medicaid coverage for, 22, 24-26
Agency
  liability, special issues of, 117-121
  ostensible, and hospital liability, 118
Age, of population, effect on nursing home expenditures, 11
AHA task force, 411-413
Aid to Families with Dependent Children (AFDC), 22
Air Force, health services for, 17
Air pollution control, as public health care, 12
Allowances, and provisions, in accounting formula, 83
All-risk coverage insurance, 188
Almshouses, as early hospitals, 6, 27
A.M. Best and Co., insurer ratings, 205
Ambulatory care
  components and levels of, 2-4
  liability exposure in, 384
  for low-income patients, 15
  for middle/upper income patients, 13
  VA, 21
Ambulatory surgery, 2
American Academy of Hospital Attorneys, 154
American College of Hospital Administrators, code of ethics, 76
American College of Surgeons, 29
American Hospital Association (AHA)
  for data on hospitals, 30
  task force, 411-413
American Institute of Hospital Risk Management, 164, 437
American Medical Association (AMA), 29, 301
American Society of Law and Medicine, 154
Analysis, budget preparation, 93-94
Anger, patient, and claim filing, 443
Annuities
  annuity certain, 263
  cash refund, 264
  compound, 264
  as funding vehicle for structured settlements, 262
  increasing, 264
  installment refund, 263
  joint and survivor, 264
  life, 262-263
  as life and health insurance, 186
  lump sum certain, 263
  lump sum life contingent, 263
  period certain and life, 263
  pricing settlement, 264-265, 267-279
  standard life, 262
  step-increasing, 264
  substandard life, 262-263
  types of, 262-264
Annuity certain policy, 263, 265
Answering services, as source of claims litigation, 375-376
Anticipated loss
  catastrophic, insuring levels for, 211
  insuring for, 209-216
  low, as level of deductibles, 211
  middle level, as optional zone of risk retention, 211
Antitrust laws, 103
Anxieties, patient, and predisposition to file claims, 451
Apparent authority, legal principle of, 118
Appointments, patient, and liability exposure, 374-376
Apportionment of liability in
  comparative negligence, 127-128
  contribution and, 130-131
  in contributory negligence, 127-128
  hospital, 127-131
  indemnity and, 129-130
  in joint and several liability, 128-129

Arbitration, 137, 235
Army, health services for, 17
Assault and battery, as hospital liability, 107-108
Assets, defined, 87
Assignments, use in structured settlements, 284-285
Associate medical staff, defined, 68
Attitudes
  effect on loss exposure, 371, 383
  group and individual, effect on risk, 145
Attorney
  defense, in claims management, 250
  defense, involvement in claims management, 250
  fee, structured settlements, 270
  hospital, and risk manager, 333-334
  legal opinions file from, 342
  plaintiff's, sample letter to, 298
  risk evaluation and, 180
Audit
  by financial committee, governing board, 65
  medical, committee of the medical staff, 72
Authority
  acceptance of, 393-394
  apparent, legal principle of, 118
  in bureaucratic management, 387
  defined, 57
  in general systems theory, 62
  in matrix organization, 60
  organizational, delegation of, 57-59
  structure, 57
Automobile
  insurance, 193-194
  liability, 86
Autonomy, patients' surrender of, 451
Average length of stay, 36, *38*

B

Bailment
  contract, as risk transfer, 229
  hospital liability in, 421-433
  legal issues, 421-422
  patients' personal items and valuables, 421-433
  policy issues, 423-429
  post-loss procedures, 427-429
  preventive procedures, 423, 427
  sample hospital policy and procedure for, 430-433
Balance sheet, 87-88
  sample, *89*
Barnard, Chester I., administrative theory of, 389, 390-391
Basic financial statements, 86-91
Battery, assault and, as hospital liability, 107-108
Baylor University Hospital, first hospitalization plan from, 29
Bed control clerks, as input for risk identification, 163
Beds
  in community hospitals, *39*
  hospital personnel per, 40, *42*
  long-term hospitals, *44-45*
  numbers of, 32
  in nursing homes, 46, 47, *48*
  population ratio-geographic distribution, 36, 40
  in short-stay hospitals, *33*
Beginning fund balance, defining, in accounting formula, 85
Behavioral management, 391-396
Best's policyholder ratings, *205*
Bidding
  insurance, 204, 206-208
  preparation by computer, 439
Bill collections, physician liability exposure in, 381-382
Billing department, role in risk management, 308
Biomedical engineering, 163
Biomedical equipment, computer managed, 436
Blind patients, Medicaid for, 22
Blood types, discovery of, 28
Board of trustees
  and quality assurance, 416-418

role in hospital's organizational structure, 63-66
role in risk management, 306, 314, 416-418
See also Governing board
Boiler and machinery insurance, 189
Bonds, for structured settlements, 26
Borrowed servant/employee issue, in hospital liability, 120-121
Bottom line, excess (deficit) of revenues over expenses, 85
Breach of duty, as measure of negligence, 105
Brief, claim, 240, *242-244*
Broker of Record Letters, 207
Brokers
and agents, 203
insurance, selecting, 203-206
for structured settlements, 288
Budgeting, as administrative role, 77
Budgets
and budget process, *94*
hospital, 93-94
types of, 93
Business, general, regulation of, 102-104
Business interruption
insurance coverage, 86, 189
as risk, 85
Business office director, role in risk mangement, 335
Bylaws, hospital, as claims information, 338-339

C

California Medical Insurance Feasibility Study (CMIFS), 158-160, 197
Canterbury v. Spence, 442
Capital
budget, 93
working, defined, 91
Capital budget, 93
Captive insurance companies, 153, 176, 217, 222, 260
Care
ambulatory, defined, 3
appropriateness of, 66
breach of duty of, 106
components of, 2-4
inpatient hospital, defined, 3
level of, risk screens to determine, 161
levels of, 2-4
long-term, defined, 3
mental health, defined, 4
preventive, defined, 3
primary health, defined, 2
public health, defined, 3
quality, hospital requirements for assuring, 411
secondary, defined, 2
standard of, and risk manager, 414
tertiary, defined, 2
transfer, to another physician, 380-381
Case files, computer managing of, 436
Case-finding services, 2
Cash flow budget, 93
Cash refund annuity, 264
Casualty insurance, 152-153
Catastrophic insurance, 152-153
Catastrophic loss, anticipated, 210
Cell boundaries, size-of-loss distribution table, 212-216
Centralization, organizational, defined, 59
CEO. *See* Chief executive officer
Certificate of Need, 103
Cervical cancer examinations, as preventative health care, 13
Chain of command
and span of control, 55-56
See also Scalar differentiation
CHAMPUS, 5, 17
CHAMPVA, 5
Channeling, as insuring alternative, 226-227
Chaplain service, as input for risk identification, 163
Charting
and documentation, computer, 439

forms, *467-469*
nursing policy and/or
procedure for, 465-469
physician and nurses, compared, 439
Chart review, by computer, 439
Chicago Hospital Risk Pooling
Program (risk screens), 160-161
Chief executive officer (CEO)
and the administration, 74-77
commitment to risk management,
314
and delegation, 58
and division of work, 54-55
and governing board, 74
and medical staff, 76-77
responsibilities, 74, *75*
role in risk management program, 315
See also Administrator
Chief financial officer (CFO), role in
risk management, 316
Chief of staff, role in risk
management, 315
Child abuse, reporting requirements
for, 104
City hospitals, for care of
low-income patients, 15-16
Civilian Health and Medical Program
(Veterans Administration Program), 5
Civilian Health and Medical Program of
the Uniform Services (CHAMPUS)
as payer, 5
Civil rights laws, 103
Claim brief, 240, *242, 243-244*
Claims
brief, 240, *242, 243-244*
closed, for risk identification, 320, 332
control, education in, 317
development, 240
development flow sheet, *241*
evaluation of, 249-250,
file, 238
fraudulent, 248
handling of, 238-242
history, computerized, 436
information, in risk management
system, 310-311
log, 332-333
management, 235-260
manager, 236-245, 332-333
model program for, 236-245
patients' predisposition to file,
441-462
phone messages as source of
litigation, 375-376
prevention, by mechanical vs.
nonmechanical means, 441-442
reserves, 251-252
stimuli for, 454-455
surveys, 154
See also Claims management
Claims made insurance, 192
Claims management
captive concept in, 260
claims evaluation, 249-250
defense attorney involvement, 250
development of, 235-236
hospital, 235-260
and incident reports, 322-323
legal aspects, 248
and liability, 245-248
primary commercial insurance
coverage in, 253-254
reserving process in, 251-252
as risk management, 99
self-insuring under, 254-259
settlement and release in, 252-253
system, 236-245
taking of statements, 248-249
use of computers, 436, 439
year-ending reports, 253
See also Claims; Claims manager
Claims manager
claims model for, 236-245
information from, 332-333
Clinical patient management, and
risk management, shifts in, 458
Closed systems, defined, 62
Coast Guard, health services for, 17
Code of ethics, and CEO, 76
Commissioned Corps of National
Oceanic and Atmospheric
Administration,

health services for, 17
Commissioned Corps of Public Health Service, health services for, 17
Common law
bailment types in, 422
indemnity, 129
Communication
hospital liability in, 115-116
patient-physician, as confidential, 133-135
and risk evaluation, 181
Community general hospital
defined, 53
traditional structure, *75*
Community homes, nursing homes as, 43, 46
Community hospitals
beds, by region, *39*
FTE employees per patient, *42*
general, organization and structure of, 53-79
general, structure of, *75*
occupancy rates for, 40, *41*
Comparative negligence, 127-128, 245
Compound annuities, 264
Comprehensive all-risk insurance policies, 188
Computers
in risk management, 435-440
Concept of risk, 141-148
Conference, for structured settlements, 288-290
Confidentiality
disclosure by nurses, 368
hospital, and investigations, 135-136
and hospital liability, 133-136
patient, 133-135
and risk manager, 334
waived, 134
of work product, 136
Consent
basic, assault and battery and, 107-108
in emergencies, 110-111
familial, 111
forms, written, 108, 112
as hospital liability, 107-114
incapacitated adults and, 108
informed, 111-114, 131, 357-359, 369, 471-475
by minors, 108-110
patients' perception and material risk approach to, 442
in physicians' offices, 377
refusal of, 110
See also Informed consent
Consequential loss or time element insurance, 188-189
Consolidation, in budget preparation, 93-94
Construction
contract, as risk transfer, 229
and research, expenditures for, *9*
Constructive receipt doctrine, in structured settlements, 266
Consultants
guidelines for use of, 323
for structured settlements, 288
use for smaller hospitals, 323
Consulting medical staff, defined, 68
Consumer
choice in health care, 14
mentally indigent as, 15
Consumerism, role in health care change, 101
Contractual indemnification, as risk management tool, 129, 152
Contractual transfer, 152
Contributed capital, defined, in accounting formula, 85
Contribution, apportionment of, 130-131
Contributory negligence, 127-128, 245
Control Data, 164
Conversion process, in open systems, 62
Cooperation, theory of, 390
Coordination, of hospital activities, 56-57
Corporate liability
doctrine defined, 365

hospital, 102, 121-125, 365-367
joint and several, 128
See also Hospital law; Liability
Cost-benefit analysis, insurance, 209-216
Cost-containment, 75
County homes/hospitals, 15-16, 46
Courtesy medical staff, defined, 68
Credentialing
by data base management system, 438
of physician's office employees, 379-380
records, as information source for medical staff, 340-341
corporate liability and, 121
medical, by governing board committee, 65
Credentials committee, medical staff, 70-71

D

Daily admitting log, as source input, 336
Damages, as hospital liability, 105
Data base management system, 438
Death
and bailment, 427
liability evaluation in, 247
Debt service reserve funds, 87
Decentralization
defined, 59
and delegation of authority, 57
Deductibles, levels of, 211
Defensive medicine, 235
Deferred structured settlement, 282
Delegation
advantages/disadvantages, 59
in general systems theory, 62
of organizational authority, 57-59
role in management, 58
Democratic leaders, 403
Dental services, 2, 8
Department of Defense medical service, 17
Departments
committee structure in, 74
effect of microcomputers on, 435
in hospital structure, 54
Diagnosis
patient involvement in, 451
periodic review as quality assurance, 382
physician errors in, 355
as primary health care, 2
Dictatorial leaders, 402-403
Difference in conditions (DIC) insurance, 190-191
Differentiation, organizational, 54-59
Directors' and officers' liability, 86, 150, 194-195
Disabled patients, Medicaid for, 22
Disabled veterans, homes for, 21
Disclosure
attorney-client privilege and, 136
compulsory, 133
physician's duty of, 112
Discovery
of incident reports, 156
of risk analysis data, 169-171
Discovery rule, in statute of limitations issues, 132
Disease and illness, compared, 446-450
Dishonesty insurance, 189-190
Division of work, 54-55
Dix, Dorothea, 28
Doctrine of emancipation, in hospital liability, 108-109
Documentation
need for, 364
See also Medical records
Domiciliaries, veterans', 21
Do Not Resuscitate order, nurses dilemma with, 369-370
Drucker, Peter F., organizational theorist, 395-396
Drugs
and alcohol abuse, 134
medical staff committee on, 73-74
usage, as personal health care, 8
See also Medication

Duty
as measure of negligence, 105

E

Education
hospital and medical staffs, in risk management, 307-308
medical, effect of Flexner Report of Medical Education on, 28
and risk evaluation, 181
risk management, four components in smaller hospitals, 317
in risk management model, 151-152
workshops for clinical staff on patient illness content, 456
Education fund structured settlement, 280-281
Elderly, nursing homes for, 46-48
Electrocardiogram, discovery of, 28
Electronic data processing equipment and media insurance, 190
Electronic data storage, of professional liability materials, 436
Electronic medical equipment, insuring, 189
Emancipation, doctrine of, 108-109
Emergency care
consent in, 110-111
as secondary health care, 2
Emergency department
authorization for outpatient treatment, 477-479
bailment and, 427
improper searches in, 368
liability exposure in, 384
patient valuables/personal items procedure for, 430-433
Employee benefit legal insurance, 196
Employee benefits, 186, 195-196, 414, 437
Employee Retirement Income Security Act of 1974 (ERISA), 195-196
Employees
benefit insurance plans for, 186, 195-196
benefit legal insurance, 196
benefits, as area of risk management, 414
benefits, computer-managed, 437
and contractual indemnity, 129
full-time equivalent (FTEs), 40, *42*
health and safety, risk management program and, 325
hospital liability for actions of, 120-121
managers as, 400-402
in physicians' offices, 375, 379
risk education of, 151
workers as, 400
Employment
and civil rights law, 103
in health care system, 6
EMs. *See* Explanatory models
Ending fund balance, defined, hospital accounting formula, 85
Epidemiologist, on medical staff infection control committee, 73
Equipment
capital, computer-monitored, 436
complex, effect of use on patients, 453
electronic, 189, 190, 435-440
hospital liability for, 126
management, by microcomputer, 436-437
Erasures, in medical records, 374-375, 465
ERISA. *See* Employee Retirement Income Security Act of 1974
Error, as financial risk, 81
Evaluation
of physician services, 69-71
of risk management, smaller hospitals, 324
Excess (deficit) of revenues over expenses, in accounting formula, 85
Excess-specific life and health insurance, 186-187
Executive committee
governing board, 64

medical staff, 69-70
Expenditures
health care, U.S., 6-11
for hospitals, 29-30
military health care, *18*, 19-20
for nursing homes, 46, *47*, *49*, *50*
See also Health care expenditures
Experiences, personal, effect on risk, 144
Explanatory models (EMs), 448-449
Exposure, liability, defined, 86
Extra expense insurance, 189
Eyeglasses, as personal health care, 8

F

Facilities, CEO responsibility for, 74
Family
and medical staff, quality interaction between, 457
Family planning, as preventative health care, 13
Fayol management concepts, 389-390
Federal hospitals, 30
Fiduciary liability, 100, 195-196
Finance, and the CEO, 74
Financial committee, governing board, 65-66
Financial management
hospital, 81-100
and risk management, compared, 100
role of governing board in, 65
systems, 91-99
Financial management systems
accounts payable, 92, 96
budgets, 92, 93-94
general ledger, 92, 99
hospital, *92*
management reporting, 92, 99
materials management, 96
patient accounting, 92, 95
payroll and labor distribution, 95-96
property records, 92, 98
statistical records, 92, 98
Financial manager
goal and responsibilities, 81
and risk manager, 99-100
Financial risk, managing, 99-100, 174, 175-179
Financial services, computer, 438
Financial statements
balance sheet, 87-88
basic, 86-91
of changes in financial position, 90-91
revenues, expenses, and changes in fund balance, 89-90
Financing, of risk, 99-100, 174, 175-179
Fire and extended coverage insurance, 188
First-party insurance, types of, 187-191
Flat structure, defined, 55-56
Flexner Report of Medical Education, 28
Flow charts in risk identification, 165, *166*, *167*
Flowsheet, claim development, *241*
Fluoridation and purification of water, as public health care, 12
Folk healers, and physicians, 447
Follow-up procedures, liability exposure of, 377-378
Food sanitation, as public health care, 12
Formalistic life style doctrine, 398
Four Ps, the, defined, 4-5
Frauds, statute of, and hospital liability, 131
Fraudulent concealment, and limitation of liability, 132
Friedlander, Frank, life style theorist, 398-399
Fronting
as insuring alternative, 177, 222-225
Full-time equivalent (FTE)
hospital employees, 40, *42*
Functional structure, of medical staff, 69-74
Fundamental risk, defined, 146

Fund balance, 87
Funded depreciation accounts, 87
Funded self-insurance
  and claims management, 235, 254-259
  as insuring alternative, 217, 220-221
  to retain risk, 176
  See also Self-insurance

G

General business regulation, 102-103
General hospital
  AHA defined, 30
  community, organization and structure of, 53-79
  community, structure of, *75*
General ledger, 99
General liability
  as exposure, 86
  insurance, 194, 414
General systems theory, 61-63
Generic model, risk management, 150-153
Generic Occurrence Screening Criteria, 158-160
Generic occurrence screening
  computerized, 438
  criteria, 158-160
Generic outcome screening, 321, 336
Geographic distribution
  of bed/population ratios, 36, 40
  of community hospital beds, *39*
  FTEs per patient, *42*
  nursing home care by, *47*
  of occupancy rates, 40, *41*
Going bare (noninsurance), 217, 220
Governing board
  and the CEO, 74
  chairman, 64
  executive committee of, 64
  fiduciary responsibilities, 65
  financial committee of, 65-66
  joint conference committee of, 66
  personnel committee of, 66
  professional committee of, 64-65
  role and responsibilities, 63-66
  role in quality assurance and risk management, 416-418
  See also Board of trustees
Government bonds, for structured settlements, 261-262
Government-provided health care system, 5, 11, 16-21
Government public health expenditures, personal health care, *9*
Gross national product (GNP), health care expenditures as percentage of, 6, *7*
Gross patient service revenue, defined in accounting formula, 82-83
Group attitudes, effect on risk, 145
Group behavior, as riskier than individual behavior, 145
Groups, effective, characteristics of, 405
Guarantor contract, 230

H

Harvard Medical Group/Crico channeled program, 227
Hazard logic tree, risk analysis, *167*
Health and life insurance, 186-187
Health care delivery system, U.S., 1-16
Health care expenditures, 6-11, 16-23, 27, 29, 46-48, *49, 50*
Health care industry, 6-11
Health care practitioner, 4-5
Health care system
  ambulatory care in, 2
  defined, 2
  effect of private health insurance, 29
  expenditures, 6-11
  expenditures for hospitals, 29-30
  expenditures for nursing home care, 47, *49, 50*
  financial objectives, 95
  government-provided, 11, 16-21
  growth of, 28

history, 6-11
institutional, 2, 5
for low-income patients, 11, 14-16
for middle/upper income patients, 11-14
military, 11, 16-21
patients' perspective, 11-26
special regulation of, 103-104
U.S., 1-16
Health insurance
government, defined, 5
private, defined, 5
Health maintenance organizations (HMOs), 14
Health supplies, national expenditures for, *9*
Hierarchy of ends theory (Simon), 393
Hierarchy of needs, Maslow's, 396-398
Hierarchy, vertical, and delegation of authority, 57
Highly protected risk (HPR) insurance, 153
History taking, physician, 456
Hold-harmless contracts
as risk management tool, 152
between hospitals and third parties, 231-233
and indemnification, 230
as noninsurance risk transfer, 229-231
Home health care, 2, 20-21, 24
Homes, veterans, 21
Honorary medical staff, defined, 68
Horizontal organizational differentiation, 54-55
Hospital
accounting formula, 82-86
admissions, numbers in, 32, *35*, 36
American, history, 26-29
apportionment of liability, 127
bailment in, 421
banding together of, 48
changing numbers and size, 29
colonial, 6
community, beds in, 27, *39*, 53
confidentiality, 135-136
cooperative efforts among, 51
corporate negligence, 121-125
federal, number of, 29
financial goals of, 82
financial management in, 81-99
as formal entity, 53-54
general, AHA defined, 30
and general business regulation, 102
hierarchical structure, 63-77
history, 6, 26-29
"hotel" exposure, insurance for, 101, 197-198
inpatient services, 13, 15-16
as landowners, premises liability, 126-127
large, organizational models of, 407
larger, risk management in, 327-346
law, theory and application, 101-139
liability, 104-127
licensure requirements for, 103, 104
long-term, 40-45
managing loss exposures in, 301-311
matrix organization, 59-*61*
mental, AHA defined, 30
microcomputer uses in, 435-440
multi-, captive insurance companies and, 153
number of, 30-32
number of beds in, 32
obligation for quality assurance and risk management, 418
occupancy rates in, 32
as open system, 61-63
organization of, 53-79
ownership categories of, 30
personnel per bed, 40, *42*
physicians' wait relationship with, 378
policies and procedures, miscellaneous sample, 463-486
present status, 29-40
public and private, 30

review function, and confidentiality, 135
risk and financial management, 81-100
self-insured, microcomputer use by, 436
share of costs, personal health care, 8, *10*
short-stay, admissions, 31-35
size, defined, 30
smaller, organizing risk management program in, 313-326
specialty, AHA defined, 30
staff, blase, 455
structure of, 53-79
teaching, risk manager's role in, 308
triad, board, medical staff, and administration as, 66
tuberculosis, AHA defined, 30
types of, 30
VA, 19, 20
values, and patient predisposition to file claims, 450
voluntary, 27
Hospital and medical benefit plans, 186
Hospital corporate negligence, doctrine of, 121-125
Hospital general liability, 100
Hospital law
apportionment of liability, 127-131
confidentiality and, 133-136
hospital liability, 104-127
investigations and, 133-136
regulation, 102-104
special statutes, 131-133
Hospital professional liability. *See* Professional liability
Hospital risk manager. *See* Risk manager
"Hotel" exposure, hospital, 101, 197
HPR (highly protected risk) insurance, 153
Human needs and lifestyle theories, 396-399

I

Iatrogenic injuries
occurrence, 443
prevention of, 235
Illness
and diseased, compared, 446-450
hospital's response to, 450
perception model, claims generation and, 455
Immunizations, as preventative health care, 13
Incident
defined, 156, *157*
vs. patient perception, 458
Incident reports
and claims management, 237, 322-323
computer-analyzed, 437-438
encouragement of, 156-158
evaluation of, 180
example of, *170*
nursing use of, 362
policy/procedure for, *157-158*
and problem sheets, 310
purposes, 164
requirements of, 320-321
as risk identification tool, 155-161
in risk management system, 309-310
smaller hospital, to identify risk, 320
Indemnification, and release covenant, 293-297
Indemnity
agreements, 229-231
apportionment of, 129-130
common-law, 129
contractual, 129, 230-231
and hold-harmless contracts, 230
Individualized settlement. *See* Structured settlement
Industrial Revolution, management structure of, 386
Infection control
committee, 73
director, role in risk management, 335

as input for risk identification, 163
Infections, reporting requirements for, 104
Infirmaries, as early hospitals, 6
Informed consent
affidavit, *475*
form, nursing, *474-475*
as hospital liability, 111-114
hospital verification of, 358
and medical staff, 357-359
nursing policy/procedure for, 471-475
nursing role in, 358-359, 369
physician vs. hospital liability, 113-114
and special statutes, 131
subjective standard for, 112
See also Consent
Inpatient
admission, as secondary care, 2
hospital care, 3, 24
or outpatient, effect on patient attitude, 453
Installment refund annuity, 263, *274-275*
Institutional care, components and levels of, 2-4
Insurance
analysis of efficiencies in, 209-216
automobile, 193-194
bidding, 206-208
boiler and machinery, 189
brokers and insurers for, 182, 203-206
business interruption, 86
captive, 217, 222, 260
casualty, 152-153
commercial, as favored method of risk financing, 177
contract elements, 199-203
defined, 183-185
difference in conditions (DIC), 190-191
directors' and officers' liability, 194-195
dishonesty, 189-190
electronic data processing equipment and media, 190
employee benefit legal, 196
fiduciary liability, 195-196
to finance unexpected large losses, 209-216
fire and extended coverage, 188
first-party, 187-191
funded, unfunded, self-, and pooled, 176-177
general liability, 194
government health, defined, 5
HPR (highly protected risk), 153
liability, contractual indemnity as, 129
life and health, 186-187
malpractice liability, 196-197
options, smaller hospital, 324
partial, 176-177
portfolio, evaluation of, 324
portfolio, microcomputer managed, 435
private health, defined, 5
product liability, 194
professional liability, 196-197
property, 151-152
property, professional liability, and other, 177-178
purchased, advantages/disadvantages, 219
purchased, alternatives to, 216-219
purchased, for smaller hospitals, 322
purchased, primary commercial, 253-254
purchasing, 206
requirement of physician, 130
and risk evaluation, 181-182
as risk transfer, 152
self-, 153, 176-177
social, 198-199
third party, 191-198
time element or consequential loss, 188-189
types of, 177-178, 186-199
umbrella liability, 197-198
unemployment compensation, 199

Workers' Compensation, 198-199
See also Insurance companies; Insurance contracts; Insurance coverage
Insurance companies
captive, 217, 222, 260
risk manager and, 332
selecting, 203-206
Insurance contracts
components, 200-203
conditions, 201-202
declarations, 202-203
definitions, 202
exclusions, 201
insuring agreements, 201
legal background, 199-200
See also Insurance; Risk financing
Insurance coverage
for accounts receivable, 88
for patient accounts, 88
property, 88
for theft and burglary, 88
Insurers, selecting, 203-206
Internal Revenue Code, revenue ruling 79-220, for structured settlements, 281-282
Invasive procedures, liability exposure of, 379
Investigations
in claims management, 238-239
and hospital confidentiality, 135-136
hospital liability and, 133-136
Investment income, as nonoperating income, 84-85
Investment portfolio, and financial committee, 65
Investor-owned (proprietary) hospitals, AHA defined, 30

J

JCAH. *See* Joint Commission on Accreditation of Hospitals
Joint and several liability, 128-129
Joint and survivor annuity, 264
Joint Commission on Accreditation of Hospitals (JCAH)
effect on hospital industry, 29
medical staff requirements, 67
quality assurance standards of, 411
Joint conference committee, governing board, 66

K

Key word associations, for anomalies in patient medical records, 439
Kidnapping insurance, 190

L

Labor, specialization of, 54
Labor unions
and governing board personnel committee, 66
and hospital regulation, 102
Laissez-faire leaders, 403
Last treatment rule, in statute of limitations, 132
Law. *See* Hospital law
Law of Large Numbers, and insurance pooling, 185
Lawsuits
in claim management process, 240
as detection system, 331
physician behaviors affecting probability of, 354
prevention, physician concern for patients as, 356, 442-446
Law titled bailments, 421
Lawyer. *See* Attorney
Leaders
democratic, 402-403
dictatorial, 402-403
effective, characteristics of, 404
laissez-faire, 402, 403
participative, 402, 403
Leadership
and leadership styles, 402-405

management and, 385-410
and risk managers, 405-409
types of, 402-403
Legal discovery
of incident reports, 156
of risk analysis data, 169-171
Legal opinions file, 342-343
Legibility, of physician records, 355
Lewin, Kurt, model for change, 353
Liabilities
in balance sheet, 87
defined, 88
See also Liability; Liability exposure
Liability
apportionment of, 127-131
and claims management, 245-248
confidentiality and, 133-136
corporate, 121-125, 365-367
evaluation, 246-248
hospital, 104-127
insurance, contractual indemnity as, 129
joint and several, 128-129
of nurses, 361-362, 367-369
premises, 126-127, 373
product, 150
risk financing of, 178
special statutes relating to, 131-133
vicarious, 118-120, 367
Liability
See also Liabilities; Liability exposure
Liability exposure
auto, 100
directors' and officers', 86, 100
fiduciary, 100
hospital general, 100
physicians' office, 371-384
special facility, 100
types, 100
types of, 86
See also Liabilities; Liability
Librarian, role in risk management, 335
Licensure, liability from, 131
Life and health insurance, 186-187
Life annuity
and lump sum, example, *272-273*
parent's, example of, *276-277*
pricing of, 264-265
types of, 262-263
Life-extending procedures, liability with, 110
Life insurance companies, 287
Life style doctrines (Friedlander), 398-399
Lifetime income structure settlement, 279-280
Limitations, statute of, and hospital liability, 131
Linking pin (organizational) theory, 393-394
Litigation
and computer chart documentation, 439
computer management of, 436
management, education in, 317
Living will, and refusal of treatment, 369
Long-term care
defined, 3
See also Long-term hospitals
Long-term hospitals
beds and occupancy rates, *44-45*
general, 43
for low-income patients, 16
for middle/upper income patients, 13-14
military, 19
psychiatric, 43
U.S., 40-43
Loss
anticipated, and insurance efficiency, 209-216
avoidance or minimization, 99-100, 302
catastrophic, 197-198, 210
characteristics, in risk analysis, 165-167
control programs, 151
detection, 345
exposure, attitudes and, 371

exposures, managing, 301-311
financial, prevention of, 302
insured's participation in, 187
large, unexpected, insurance for, 209-216
and risk control, 174-175
runs, computer analyzed, 436
size of, distribution table, 212-216
See also Loss prevention; Loss reduction
Loss funding
education in, 317
evaluation in smaller hospitals, 324
Loss prevention
computer use in, 436
defined, 415
education in, 317
as identifying potential sources of liability, 415
and incident reports, 164
in physicians' offices, 382-383
as risk management, 99
as risk treatment, 174
Loss reduction
claims management as, 236
defined, 415
in physicians' offices, 382-383
risk management as, 383
staff attitudes and, 371
Low-income patients
health care system for, 11, 14-16
Medicaid/Medicare for, 21-26
Lump sum certain annuity, 263

M

Machinery and boiler insurance, 189
Maintenance department, as input for risk identification, 163
Malpractice. *See* Medical malpractice
Management
behavioral approach to, 391-396
bureaucratic form of, 386-388
by objectives, 146
claims, 99-100, 235-260
cooperative, 390-391
financial, governing board and, 65
of financial risk, 99-100
ideas, sources of modern, *387*
leadership and, 385-410
open systems concept of, 61-63
and organizational structure, role in risk management, 62-63
of patient care, CEOs responsibility in, 74
patient care team, 60
patient care team, defined, 60
philosophies, 403-405
process, defined, 400
process, managers and, 399-400
project, 60
of quality of care, credentials committee and, 70-71
risk, 62-63, 99-100, 146-147
role of delegation, 58
role of hospital's external environment in, 63
role of integration and coordination in, 56
span of, defined, 55
structure, theories and models, 386-396
Management by Objectives (MBO), 395-396
Management-by-objectives system, as risk management, 146-147
Management reporting, 99
Management structure
administrative, 389-391
behavioral, 391-396
bureaucratic, 386-388
of Industrial Revolution, 386
scientific, 388-389
theories and models of, 386-396
Managers
decisions, resources and, 401-402
functions and time on each, *401*
and the managed, 400-401
and the management process, 399-400
matrix, 60
successful, characteristics of, 404

March, James, organizational theorist, 392-393
Marine Corps, health services for, 17
Marketing
as administrative role, 75
health care, 51
Markets, insurance, 207
Maslow, Abraham, human needs theorist, 396-398
Maslow's hierarchy of needs, 396-398
Massachusetts General Hospital, as first voluntary hospital, 27
Material risk approach, consent and, 442
Materials management system, 96, *97*
Matrix organization
defined, 59
hospital, 59-60, *61*
McGregor, Douglas, organizational theorist, 394-395
Mediation, 235
Medicaid (Title 19) programs (P.L. 89-97)
eligibility, 22
expenditures, *23*
medical services under, 23-24
and Medicare, 21-26
for nursing home charges, 48, 50
patients in, 21-24
Medical affairs committee, governing board, 64-65
Medical and hospital benefit plans, 186
Medical assistance, as defined by Medicaid, 23
Medical audit committee, medical staff, 72
Medical director, role in risk management, 315
Medical education director, 335
Medical incident review committee (MIRC), 322-323
Medical interview, physician, 456
Medical language, specialized, effect on patients, 453
Medically indigent patients
health care system for, 11, 14-16
Medicare/Medicaid for, 21-26
Medical malpractice
claim arising from patient transfer between physicians, 380-381
crisis, 235, 301, 411
information to physicians, 344
insurance for, 196-197
no-fault system, 158
ostensible agency and, 118
patient perceptions and, 442
physician behaviors affecting, 354-356
reference materials on, 344
requirement for case, 364
and risk management, 149-150, 347
Medical office, liability exposure in, 371-384
Medical perfection, myth of, 446
Medical records
altering, 364
copies for risk manager, 338
defined, 71
director, 316, 335
effect of statute of limitations on, 133
hospital liability in, 114-115
importance to physicians, 355-356
inclusions in, 337-338
as input for risk identification, 163
legal nature of, 71-72
in physicians' offices, 376-377
procedure for nursing notes, 465-469
purpose of, 114
right-of-access laws for, 135
See also Documentation
Medical records committee, medical staff, 71-72
Medical records director, role in risk management, 316, 335
Medical school, admissions, 29
Medical staff
active, 67-68
associate, defined, 68
attitude of, 455

board of trustees and, 418
categories of membership in, 67-69
and CEO, 76-77
consulting, 68
courtesy, 68
credentialing, 64-65, 70-71, 340-341, 438
credentials committee, 70-71
educational programs for, 304
executive committee of, 69-70
functional structure of, 69-74
functions of, 347-348
honorary, 68
in hospital organization and structure, 66-74
infection control committee, 73
informed consent and, 357-359
medical audit committee, 72
medical records committee, 71-72
model for change in, 353-354
peer review committees of, 353
pharmacy and therapeutics committee, 73-74
physicians' role on, 350-351
provisional status, 68-69
recredentialing applications, computerized, 438
responsibilities, 66
risk evaluation of, 180
risk management and, 304, 314, 341-344, 347-359
special concerns of, 354-356
temporary status, 69
tissue committee, 73
utilization review committee, 72-73
See also Physician

Medicare (Title 18) programs (P.L. 89-97)
and Medicaid, 21, 24-26
for nursing home charges, 48, 50
services under Part A, 24-25
services under Part B, 25-26
and utilization review committees, 72

Medication
documented in patients' records, 377
errors, hospital liability in, 117, *166*, 368
order, physician, risk analysis of, *166*
See also Drugs

Mental health care
acute, 4
chronic, 4
for low-income patients, 16
for middle/upper income patients, 14

Mental hospital, AHA defined, 30

Microcomputers, effect on hospital departments, 435

Military health care system
expenditures, *18*
facilities, *18*
personnel, *18*
trends in, 20
U.S., 11, 16-21
VA, characteristics of, *22*

Miscommunication, legal implications of, 116

Multihospital systems, captive insurance companies and, 153

Multiowner captive insurer, 217
as insuring alternative, 217

N

Named perils coverage, 188

National Association of Insurance Commissioners' Closed Claims Study, 154

National Center for Health Statistics (DHHS), 30

National Health Lawyers, 154

Navy, health services for, 17

Need analysis, structured settlements, 269-271

Needs, human, and lifestyle theories, 396-399

Neglected child statutes, 109

Negligence
bailment, 422
comparative, 127-128, 245
contributory, 127-128, 245
hospital corporate, 121-125

as hospital liability, 105-106, 415
legal liability in, 245-246
liability evaluation in, 246-248
plaintiff, in malpractice case, 128
presumption of, 106-107
Negotiation, budget preparation, 93-94
Net operating income, defined in accounting formula, 84
Net patient service revenue, in hospital accounting formula, 83
Neurosurgery, as tertiary care, 2
Nightingale, Florence, 28
No Code orders, nurses dilemma with, 369-370
No-fault medical malpractice system, 158
Noninsurance
as insuring alternative, 217, 220
risk transfer, 229-233
Nonoperating items, defined in hospital accounting formula, 84
Nonprofit hospitals, 30-32
Nurse Practice Act, 365
Nurses
assistance in risk investigation, analysis, and treatment, 366
as defendants, 367-368
duty of hospital through, 123
evaluation form for, *486*
and informed consent, 358-359, 471-475
notes, charting, 465-469
and physicians, criminal allegations against, 368
private duty, standard policy and/or procedure for, 481-486
as professionals, 361
and risk manager, 366-367, 370
role in patient relations, 366, 456
See also Nursing
Nursing
early development, 28
liability, 361-362
policy and/or procedure for charting, 465-469
policy and/or procedure for informed consent, 471-475
and risk management, 305, 334-335, 361-370
schools, early, 28
See also Nurses
Nursing director, role in risk management, 315-316
Nursing home
care, as personal health care, 8
care, Medicaid/Medicare paid, 22, 24
charges and expenditures for, 11, 8, 10, 46, 47, 49, 50
history, 43, 46
for middle/upper income patients, 13-14
private, and Social Security, 46
size, 47
U.S., 43-48
VA provided, 17

O

Occupancy rates
geographic distribution, 40, *41*
hospital, defined, 32
by hospital type, 32
long-term hospitals, *44-45*
in short-stay hospitals, *34*
Occupational Safety and Health Administration (OSHA), as regulators, 102
Occurrence
based insurance policies, 191
generic screening criteria for, 158-159
of an incident, 155-156
report, 155, 237
report, claims management system for, 237
screens, 158-161
screens, computerized, 438
Office equipment, physician, liability, exposure of, 372-373
officers' and directors' liability, 63, 86, 100

Open heart surgery, as tertiary care, 2
Open system, hospital, 61-63
Operating budgets, 93
Operating expenses, in hospital accounting formula, 84
Operating revenue, other, 83
Optional zone of risk retention, 211
Organization
  clinical, effect on patients, 452-455
  delegation role in, 58
  differentiation in, 54-59
  formal, defined, 53, 391
  integration and coordination in, 56-57
  matrix, 59-60, *61*
  and structure, hospital, 53-79
Organizational behavioralists, 392
Organizational differentiation
  defined, 54-59
  division of work, 54-55
  vertical (scalar) and horizontal, 54
Organizational theory
  classical, span of control in, 55-56
  theorists, 392-393
Organ transplants, as tertiary care, 2
Ostensible agency
  joint and several liability and, 128
  legal principle of, 118
Outpatient
  authorization for emergency treatment, 477-479
  clinic, VA, 17
  departments, as physician visits, 29
  services, liability in, 384

P

Pain tolerance, cultural effects on, 447
Parent's life annuity, example, *276-277*
Participative leaders, 403
Particular risk, defined, 146
Pasteur, Louis, 28
Patient
  advocate, risk manager as, 364
  anger, and lawsuits, 443
  as bailor, 421
  blind, Medicaid for, 22
  confidentiality, 133-135
  consent and, 107-114, 131, 357-359, 369, 471-475
  disabled, Medicaid for, 22
  DOA, bailment issues and, 427
  education, as risk management tool, 152
  escorts, as input for risk identification, 163
  and health care system, 4, 11-26
  illness content, 456
  information needs, meeting, 456
  injuring self or others, hospital liability in, 116-117, 125
  injury, prevention of, 302, 363
  low-income/medically indigent system, 11, 14-16
  and Medicaid/Medicare, 21-26
  mentally ill, nursing homes for, 46
  middle/upper income, 11-14
  minors, consent by, 108-110
  motivation for malpractice claims, 363-364, 441-462
  in nursing homes, 47, *49*
  as payer, 11-14
  perceptions, and medical malpractice, 442-447
  personal items and valuables, bailment, 421-433
  predisposition to file claims, 441-462
  processing, liability exposure in, 374-376
  relations, 325, 335-336, 345, 450-452
  safety, early risk management and, 347
  satisfaction, 455, 457
  self-harm, 116
  significant other of, 151
  stimuli for claims, 454-455

total risk disclosure to, 113
transferring, liability exposure in, 380-381
valuables, checklist, *424-426*
valuables/personal items, policy and procedure for handling, 430-433
veterans as, 19-20
See also Patient care; Patient relations
Patient accounting, 88, 95, 162
Patient accounts, as input for risk identification, 162
Patient accounts receivable, insurance coverage for, 88
Patient billing department, 308
Patient care
CEO responsibility for, 74
equipment, computer monitoring, 436-437
information, from nurses, 365
management, board of trustees function in, 418
systems, financial objectives, 95
Patient care team, 59-60
Patient education, as risk management tool, 152
Patient relations
and bailment issues, 428
importance, 335-336, 441
nurses role in, 366
risk management program improving of, 325
risk manager and, 345
Patient's Bill of Rights, 368
Payer
defined, 5
patient as, 11-14
Payroll and labor distribution, 95-96
Peer review committees, physicians' role in, 353
Perception, patient, and claims, 442-447
Period certain and life annuity, 263
Periodic Payment Settlement Act of 1982 (P.L. 97-473), for structured settlements, 281-282, 286
Personal dignity, patient, 451
Personal health care
components of, 8
expenditures by source of payment, *10*
expenditures by type of care, 9
expenditures for, 8, 11
government share of, 8, *10*
See also Health care; Health care system
Personalistic life style doctrine, 398-399
Personnel
CEO's responsibility in, 74
committee, governing board, 66
FTE, numbers per bed, 40, *42*
Pesthouses, as early hospitals, 27
Pharmacy and therapeutics committee, medical staff, 73-74
Phone messages, physicians' offices, and liability exposure, 374-376
Physician
access to legal opinion file, 343
accreditation of, 29
behaviors affecting malpractice suits, 354-357, 443
as co-defendant, 116
as coordinator of patients' health care system, 12
credentialing questions for, 340-341
diagnostic errors by, 355
duty of disclosure, 112
duty to third party, 125
education in loss prevention, 318
evaluation, 69-71
follow-up procedures, liability in, 377-378
hospital vicarious liability for, 118-120
importance of medical records for, 355-356
indemnification hold-harmless clause from, 232
involvement, risk management program, 341
medical recordkeeping by, 356

medication order, flow chart for
risk analysis of, *166*
nonemployed, vicarious liability
for, 118-120
nonemployee, involvement of,
341-344
offices, risk management in,
371-384, 383
patient awareness of, 444
patient care by others than the,
378-379
and patient communication, as
confidential, 133-135
peer disciplinary actions, 352-353
rapport with patient, claim
prevention by, 442
on risk management committee, 304
role on medical staff, 350-351
sensitized to patients, 456
services, as personal health care, 8
specialization, 28
staff, lawsuits for wrongful staff
privilege by, 123
therapeutic privilege defense for,
113
See also Medical staff;
Physicians office
Physician audit committees
and risk manager, 355
Physicians' office
bill collection liability, 381-382
credentialing of employees in,
378-380
equipment and maintenance,
liability exposure of, 372-373
liability exposure, 371-384
liability for patient care
by nonphysicians, 378-379
liability from design and
function of, 371-373
liability from transfer of care to
other physicians, 380-381
liability in consultations with other
physicians, 381
loss prevention in, 382-383
loss reduction in, 382-383
patient processing in, 374-376
premises liability, 373
professional liability in, 374-378
risk management in, 383
waiting areas as source of claims
litigation, 376
Workers' Compensation and state
statutes liability, 373-374
Planning, strategic, 75, 77
Policies and procedures, hospital, and
risk evaluation, 180-181
Policies and procedures, miscellaneous
sample of, 463-486
Pooling
insurance, 184-185
programs, 225-226
risk, as insuring alternative, 217
Population/bed ratio-geographic
distribution, 36, 40
Postanesthesia recovery, risk screen
for, 160-161
Postloss objectives, risk management
program, 147
Preloss objectives, risk management
program, 147
Premises liability, 126-127, 373
Prepaid items, as operating expenses,
84
Prepayment expenses, *9*
Presumption of negligence, 106-107
Preventive health care
defined, 3
for low-income patients, 15
for middle/upper income
patients, 12-13
as primary health care, 2
Primary commercial insurance
coverage, 253-254
Primary health care, defined, 2
Prior acts insurance coverage, 193
Private duty nurse, standard policy
and/or procedure for, 481-486
Private health insurance
effect on health system, 29
as payer, defined, 5
Private hospitals, AHA defined, 30

Private letter ruling 8333035, for structured settlements, 291-292
Private nursing homes, and Social Security, 46
Probability
in risk analysis, 165
as risk concept, 142-143
and uncertainty, 144
Problem sheets, and incident reports, 310
Product liability, and risk management, 150
Product standardization committee, 96
Professional committee, governing board, 64-65
Professional liability
insurance for, 196-197
as liability exposure, 86
physician, as risk management focus, 347
physicians' office, 374-378
risk financing of, 175-177
and risk management, 149-150
and risk manager, 100
Profit
calculation, accounting formula as, 85
for debt service, plant replacement, fixed costs, 85
Project management, as matrix organization, 60
Property
exposure, types of, 100
insurance coverage for, 88
patients' personal, bailment of, 421-433
preservation and protection, 413-414
records, 98
Property insurance
as risk financing, 177-179
as risk management tool, 152-153
Proprietary hospitals, 30
Provider, defined, 4-5
Provisional medical staff, 68-69
Proximate causation, as measure of hospital liability, 105
Psychiatric long-term hospitals, 43
Public defined, 5
Public health care
for middle/upper income patients, 12-13
defined, 3
expenditures, *9*
for low-income patients, 15
Public hospitals, AHA defined, 30
Public relations
as input source for risk identification, 162
and bailment issues, 428
Pure risk, and insurance, 145, 183-184

Q

Qualified assignments, in structured settlements, 285
Qualified funding assets, in structured settlements, 285
Quality assurance
computer use, 436
medical staff responsibility in, 352-353
nurses role in, 365
program, goals, 415
review, 163
risk management and, 309, 411-419
role of board of trustees in, 416
standards for, 411
tools for, 416
Quality assurance committee, and hospital liability, 115
Quality of care
board of trustees responsibility for, 314
cost-effective, 104
credentials committee and, 70-71
and medical staff audit committee, 72
as medical staff responsibility, 347
in physicians' offices, 383
role of professional (medical affairs) committee in, 64-65
and standard of practice, 104

See also Care; Quality assurance
Questionnaires, for patient perceptions, 444
Quinlan, Karen Ann, an alleged incompetent, case of, 110

R

Radiation safety committee, as input for risk identification, 163
Railroad Retirement Acts, Medicare coverage under, 24
Recredentialing, using computers, 438
Referrals, physician, documentation of, 377
Regulation
  general business, 102-103
  and hospital law, 102-104
  role in health care, 51
  special, health care, 103-104
Regulations, hospital, as claims information, 338-340
Reinsurance, 153, 176, 260
Releases
  and indemnification covenant, 293-297
  and settlement, claims management process, 252-253
  in structured settlements, 285
  See also Settlements; Structured settlements
Reporting endorsement insurance coverage, 192
Reports
  claims, 253
  computerized, 164-165
  for identification of risk, 164
  informal, and incident reports, 310
  from larger hospitals, 336-337
  staff, example of, *339*
Research
  and construction, expenditures for, *9*
  human patients for, 103
Reserving process, claims management, 251-252
Res ipsa loquitur (presumption of negligence), 106-107
Restatement, budget preparation, 93-94
Retention, risk, 176-179, 211
Revenue, types of, 82-83, 85
Risk
  avoidance, 175
  classifications of, 145-146
  concept of, 141-148
  control, functions, 302
  dynamic, 145
  effect of values and experiences, 144
  evaluation, 179-182
  fundamental, 146
  identification and analysis, 150-151
  insurance, 183-184
  of loss through error, 81
  of loss through theft, 81
  management of, 99-100, 141, 146-147
  models, computer-developed, 436
  particular, 146
  and probability, 142-143
  pure, 145, 183-184
  retained or assumed, 175-179
  speculative, 145
  spreading, 176
  static, 145
  transfer, 152-153
  treatment, 151
  and uncertainty, 143
  and variation, 143
  See also Risk analysis; Risk financing; Risk identification; Risk management; Risk manager
Risk analysis
  probability in, 165
  protection of information in, 169-171
  risk management committee for, 167-169
  in risk management process, 165-174
Risk financing
  alternative methods of, 209-227
  analysis of efficiencies in, 209-216

commercial insurance as
favored method of, 177
education in, 317
fronting arrangements in, 177, 222-225
functions, 303
protection of hospital's resources by, 415
risk assumption/retention, 176
as risk management, 414
in smaller hospitals, 324
Risk identification
and analysis, 150-151
California study of, 158-160
Chicago screens for, 160-161
claims history in, 154-155
costs of, 161-162
described, 153-165
education in, 317
incident report for, 155-161
information sources for, 155-164, 321
likely areas for potential loss, 319-320
by nurses, 366
in smaller hospital, 319-321
statistics and reports for, 164-165
Risk management
basic components, 153-182
and clinical patient management shifts in, 458
commitment to, 314
committee, 167-169, 306-307
common misconceptions about, 317-318
communication role with patients, 364
components of, 351-352
computers in, 435-440
educational programs, 151-152, 307-308, 317, 456
and financial management, 100
functions, 302-303
goals, 151, 302, 363-364
implication of accounting formula in, 85-86
integration in all hospital functions, 313
keys to effective, 301
management and leadership theories applied to, 405-409
managing loss exposures by, 301-311
medical components of, 348-349
medical staff and, 347-359
microcomputer use in, 135
model of, 150-153
nontechnical definition, 149-150
and nursing, 361-370
objectives, preloss/postloss, 147
and organizational structure, 62-63
in physicians' offices, 383
policies and procedures, sample, 463-486
process, defined, 149
processes and functions, 149-182
processing patient care information for, 309-310
program, establishing, 146
program, scope and objectives, 318-319
and quality assurance, 309, 411-416
reactive, 441
as reduction of loss, 383
risk analysis component, 165-174
risk control in, 302
risk evaluation component, 179-182
risk identification component, 153-165
risk treatment component, 174-179
role of board of trustees in, 416-418
role of medical staff in, 304
for smaller hospital, 313-326
staff involvement, 314-316
system, elements in, *179*
tools for, 416
Risk management committee, 304, 306-307
Risk management system
comprehensive, 323
evaluation of, 324-325
formal authority of, 327-331
goals of, 415
informal authority of, 331
information sources for, 321
with in-house legal program, software for, 438

for larger hospitals, 327-346
nursing in, 362
planning for smaller hospital, 317-323
See also Risk management
Risk manager
advice to physicians on medical recordkeeping, 356
and the bailment issue, 421
clinicians and, 349-350
curiosity of, 344
documentation assistance by 364
duties in corporate negligence, 124-125
duties of, 333-334
duty in fraud and limitation of liability, 131-133
duty in indemnity, 131
and duty to third parties, 125
early detection system by, 331
education and experience, 303
goal and responsibilities, 81
and hospital confidentiality, 133-135
and hospital law, 136-137
and hospital's insurers, 332
interpersonal skills, 303
and leadership, 405-409
management and leadership for, 385-410
management and leadership theories applied to, 405-409
on medical staff committees, 304
as patient advocate, 364
and physician audit committees, 355
relations with hospital attorneys, 333-334
role in communication with patients, 115
role in informed consent, 114
role in physician malpractice, 119
on rounds to patient care units, 304
selection of, 303
selection of insurance broker, 204
support of medical staff peer review committees, 353
visibilty of, 332
word processing by, 435
Risk retention, 176-179, 211
Risk transfer
commercial insurance for, 177
defined, 229
noninsurance, 229-233
as risk management tool, 152-153
Risk treatment
education as tool in, 151-152
loss/risk control, 174-175
by nurses, 366
priority chart, 171-174
risk financing as, 174, 175-179
in risk management model, 151
Risk treatment priority chart, 171-174
Roentgen, Wilhelm Conrad, 28

S

Safety
patient, early risk management and, 347
programs, as risk treatment tool, 151
Scalar differentiation, 54-55
Schedules, hospital, adherence to, 456-457
Scientific management theory, 388-389
Screening services, 2
Screens
computerized, 438
generic outcome, for smaller hospitals, 321
for larger hospitals, 336-337
risk identification, 158-161
Secondary health care, defined, 2
Self-appraisal, risk manager, 405
Self-harm, patient, 116
Self-image, and predisposition to file claims, 449-450
Self-insurance
advantages/disadvantages, 220-221
in claims management process, 254-259
concept, 254-256
excess coverage above, 256-258

funded and unfunded, 176
and insured's participation in loss, compared, 187
an insuring alternative, 217
potential conflicts in, 258-259
programs, 153
for smaller hospitals, 322
for structured settlements, 261
See also Funded self-insurance

Self-insured hospitals, case file and claim management in, 436

Self pay, 5, 12

Self-treatment, as culturally motivated, 447

Services, contractual, and risk transfer, 152

Settlements
cash, structuring, 267-271
conference for, 288-290
pricing of, 264-279
and releases, claims management process, 252-253
and releases, structured settlements, 285-286
structured, 261-300
use of computers for, 439

Short-stay hospitals
admissions, *35*
numbers of, *31*
occupancy rates, *34*
outpatient visits, *37*

Sibley Hospital, Washington, D.C., financial management in, 65-66

Sickness and health policies individual, 186

Significant other, patient's, education of, 151

Simon, Herbert, organizational theorist, 392-393

Single-owner captive company, as insuring alternative, 217

Size cells, size-of-loss distribution tables, 212-216

Size, of hospital, defined, 30

Size-of-loss distribution table, 212-216

Social insurance, 198-199

Social Security
Medicare benefits under, 24
and private nursing homes, 46

Social services
as input for risk identification, 163
direction, role in risk management, 335

Sociocentric life style doctrine, 398

Sound rationality (management) concept, 393

Span of control
and chain of command, 55-56
for coordination in scalar chain organization, 57
in hospital structure, 54

Speculative risk, defined, 145

Spreadsheet software, risk management uses of, 435

Standard life annuity, 262

Standard of care, and risk manager, 414

Standard of practice
reasonable, in nursing, 364-365
statutes defining, 131

State Closed Claims Studies, 154

State hospital associations, captive insurance companies and, 153

State hospitals, numbers of, 30

Statement of changes in financial position, 90-91

Statement of revenues, expenses, and changes in fund balance, 89-90

Statements, in claims process, 248-249

State veterans' homes, 21

Static risk, defined, 145

Statistical analyses, computerized effect of, 436

Statistical beds. *See* Beds

Statistical records
as financial management, 98
for identification of risk, 164
statistics accumulation system, 99

Statute
of frauds, 131
of limitations, 131-133

Stay, average length in short-stay
hospitals, 36, *38*
Step-increasing annuities, 264
Sterilization, discovery of, 28
Stop-loss life and health insurance,
186-187
Strategic planning, administrative,
75, 77
Structure
defined, 53
flat or tall, 55, *56*
functional, of medical staff, 69-74
management, theories and models,
386-396
and organization, hospital, 53-79
organizing hospital's, 54-56
traditional, community general
hospital, *75*
Structured settlements
advantages, 266-267
agreements or releases, 285-286
analysis and approach, 267-279
annuities for, 262-265
attorney, sample letter to, 298
closing of, 290
conference for, 288-290
consultants, brokers, and specialists
for, 288
defined, 261, 299-300
explanation in simple terms,
299-300
first-time offer, 278-279
funding vehicles for, 261-262
life insurance companies for, 287
private letter ruling 8333035, 291-292
release and indemnification covenant,
293-297
tax guidelines and principles,
281-284, 286
third party assignments, 284-285
value analysis, 267-269
varieties of, 279-281
Students, as input for risk identification,
163
Substance abuse treatment, 134
Substandard life annuity, 262-263
Surety contract, 230
Surgery
Chicago risk screen for, 160-161
minor (ambulatory) as primary health
care, 2
quality, and medical tissue
committee, 73
schedule, as input source, 336
Symptoms, cultural component of, 447
System
defined, 62

T

Tail (insurance) coverage, 192-193
Tall structure, defined, 55-56
Tax principles, structured
settlements, 281-284, 286
Taylor, Frederick, scientific
management theory of, 388
Telephone messages, as source of
claim litigation, 375
Temporary medical staff status, 69
Tertiary health care, defined, 2
Theft, 81, 88
Theory X and Theory Y (McGregor),
394-395
Therapeutic privilege, and informed
consent, 113
Therapeutics and pharmacy committee,
medical staff, 73-74
Third parties
duty to, and hospital liability,
125-126
hold-harmless contracts
between hospital and, 231
Third party assignment
release and indemnification covenant,
296-297
in structured settlements, 284-285
Third party insurance, 191-198
Third party payment
for middle/upper income
patients, 12
for personal health care, 8, *10*

Time element or consequential loss insurance, 188-189
Tissue committee, medical staff, 73
Tosi, Henry L., administrative theory of, 389
Total operating revenue, in hospital accounting formula, 83
Transfer of care, between physicians, liability exposure of, 380-381
Transfer of risk, 415
Treasurer, governing board, 65
Treatment
  authorization for emergency, outpatient, 477-479
  documented in patients' records, 377
  patient refusal of, 369-370
  termination or failure to initiate, 368
  of uncomplicated illness and disease, as primary care, 2
Tree, hazard logic, *167*
Triad, hospital, board, medical staff, and administrative as, 66
Trusts, for structured settlements, 261-262
Tuberculosis hospitals, 30, 43

U

Umbrella liability insurance, 197-198
Uncertainty, as risk concept, 143-144
Unemployment compensation, as social insurance, 199
United States
  health care system, 1-16
  military health care system, 11, 16-21
Utilization review
  committee, 72-73
  as input for risk identification, 163

V

Vaccination, as preventive health care, 13
Valuables, patient, and the bailment issue, 421-433
Values, effect on risk, 144
Variation, as risk concept, 143
Vertical organizational differentiation, 54-55
Veterans
  as patients, 19-20
Veterans Administration
  health care system, 16, 17-22
  expenditures, *18*, 19-20
  hospitals, 20
  nursing homes, 20
Vicarious liability
  with nurse defendants, 367
  for staff physicians, 118-120
Visibility
  in physicians' offices, as liability factor, 372, 376
  of risk manager, 332, 343-344
Visitor education, as risk treatment tool, 151
Voluntary hospitals
  for care of low-income patients, 15-16
  early, 27
Volunteers, as input for risk identification, 163

W

Waiting areas, physicians' office, as source of claims litigation, 376
Wait relationship, physician and hospital, liability exposure in, 378
Waste disposal, as public health care, 12
Wasting assets. *See* Prepaid items
Water purification and fluoridation, as public health care, 12
Weber, Max, as proponent of bureaucratic form of management, 387-388
Well-baby examinations, as preventive health care, 13

Wellness programming, 51
Word processing, for risk managers, 435
Work, division of, 54-55
Workers' Compensation
as business regulation, 102
financial risks, 100
as liability exposure, 86
and risk management, 150, 413
as social insurance, 198-199
Working capital, defined, 91
Work product, confidentiality of, 136

Z

Zone of indifference (organizational) theory, 393-394

About the Editors

STEVEN L. SALMAN is the Director of Risk & Insurance Management for Sisters of Charity Health Care Systems, Inc., Cincinnati, Ohio, a national multihospital system. In addition, he is president of MSJ Insurance Company, Denver, Colorado and a partner in the law firm of Fischer, Klimon, Salman & Harpster. Prior to his position with Sisters of Charity Health Care Systems, he was the risk manager for Riverside Methodist Hospital, Columbus, Ohio, a 1000-bed teaching hospital. Mr. Salman is the current president of the Cincinnati Chapter of Risk and Insurance Management Society and chairman of the Subcommittee on Malpractice Legislation of the Ohio State Bar Association. He was selected Hospital Risk Manager of the Year by the Ohio Hospital Association in 1983. He is past president of the American Society for Hospital Risk Management of the American Hospital Association, and past president of the Ohio Association of Hospital Risk Managers. He is a director of the American Institute of Hospital Risk Management and American Settlements Consultants, Inc. He has been listed in *Who's Who in Risk Management* every year since 1980. Mr. Salman is the author of many articles and a lecturer on risk management health care law and medical malpractice. He is a member of numerous health care and legal organizations. He is a graduate of Indiana University School of Business Administration and Capital University Law School.

GLENN T. TROYER received a bachelor of arts degree in sociology from Wittenberg University in 1967, a master's degree in health administration from Indiana University in 1971, and a juris doctorate degree from Capital University in 1975. Since beginning his career in health care in 1967, Mr. Troyer has held numerous administrative positions in Illinois, Indiana, and Ohio. Prior to his current position as a member of the firm of Locke Reynolds Boyd & Weisell, Counsellors at Law, Indianapolis, Indiana, he was general counsel for Methodist Hospital of Indiana, Inc., Indianapolis, Indiana.

About the Contributors

CLAYTON W. BORINGER received a bachelor of science degree in business from Ohio Wesleyan University. He is an organization development consultant who has had extensive corporate experience in human resource development activities, including management training and development, management processing, manpower planning, and personnel and labor relations.

GREGORY G. DRUTCHAS is a principal of the law firm of Kitch, Saurbier, Drutchas, Wagner & Kenney, P.C., which directly or through insurers represents a majority of the hospitals in Michigan in medicolegal matters. He is active in various legal organizations and a frequent lecturer on hospital and medical risk management issues. Mr. Drutchas's practice is directed toward insurance law and consultation on hospital risk management matters. He is chairman of the Committee on Insurance Law of the State Bar of Michigan, a participant in the development and operation of several hospital captive insurance programs, and the author of published articles on hospital law.

JANINE FIESTA is vice president of legal services, HealthEast, Inc., Allentown, Pennsylvania. She received her law degree from Duquesne University, Pittsburgh, and her nursing degree from Carlow College, also in Pittsburgh. Ms. Fiesta is the author of *Law and Liability: A Guide for Nurses* (John Wiley & Sons, 1983). She is a member of the founding board of the American Hospital Association Society for Risk Management.

CHARLES M. FISCHESSER is vice president—claims of the M.S.J. Insurance Company and a partner in American Settlement Consultants Inc. He has thirteen years of experience in settlement negotiations, particularly in medical malpractice cases, and has utilized structured settlements extensively.

WILLIAM H. GILL is an account executive with Gerald L. Sullivan & Assoc., Inc., insurance brokers, Chicago. He has been involved in casualty work with the United States Fidelity and Guaranty Company of Baltimore; Fred S. James & Co., Chicago; and The Wyatt Company, Chicago. He is a graduate of Rice University, Houston. Gill has been a faculty member of seminars for the American Management Association and CPCU and has addressed numerous professional organizations.

PAUL A. GREVE, JR. received his undergraduate degree from Ohio Wesleyan University and his juris doctor degree from Capital University School of Law. He was employed by the Cleveland Clinic Foundation and subsequently was a claims administrator for the Joint Underwriting Association, an insurance company legislatively created to provide professional liability coverage for physicians, nurses and hospitals. He is President of the Ohio Society for Hospital Risk Managers and currently serves as a member of the Hospital Law Committee of the Columbus Bar Association. Mr. Greve is an associate of Galen Systems Corporation of Dallas, Texas, and is a consultant in the areas of quality assurance, risk management and health care legal liability exposure. Mr. Greve is a member of the adjunct faculty, Ohio State University, School of Allied Medical Professionals. He has made numerous presentations to nursing schools and hospital nursing departments. Mr. Greve is currently employed as the Director of Legal Services, Children's Hospital, Columbus, Ohio.

MICHAEL B. GUTHRIE, M.D., is vice president for medical affairs and medical director for Penrose Hospitals, Colorado Springs, Colo. He has been active as a consultant, including being technical medical adviser for "Kids Corner, LTD.," national producer of patient education films. Guthrie has written for numerous professional journals and publications. He received his B.A. from Amherst College and his M.D. from the University of Pennsylvania School of Medicine and an M.B.A. from the University of Colorado School of Business.

GERALD J. MCHUGH, D.B.A., is Director of the Graduate Program in Health Administration, and Chairman of the Health Sciences and Administration Faculty at Indiana University in Indianapolis, Indiana. Dr. McHugh has coauthored several articles concerning health administration and has had operational hospital experience. He received his D.B.A. and M.B.A. from George Washington University, Washington, D.C.

ALAN J. MITTERMAIER is administrator of Valle Vista Hospital, Indianapolis. He previously held administrative positions at Methodist Hospital, Indianapolis; Children's Medical Center, Dayton; and Children's Hospital, Columbus, Ohio. A member of the American College of Hospital Administrators, Mittermaier holds a B.A. from Capital University, Columbus, Ohio, and an M.H.A. from Ohio State University.

RONALD T. NELSON began his career in 1955 in accident and health insurance with the CNA Insurance Companies, involving underwriting, marketing, and field positions, and became regional manager of special risks.

He joined a major brokerage firm in 1959, serving in the employee benefits and property and casualty fields. He became involved in medical/health professional liability during the crisis of the mid-1970s, serving as a consultant/broker to the American Hospital Association and the Illinois State Medical Society. Other professional activities since then have been almost exclusively in the design, implementation, and administration of insurance programs with commercial carriers.

JOSEPH M. O'REILLY was graduated from Providence College with a bachelor of science degree, cum laude, in business administration. He is currently a candidate for a master's degree in business administration. Mr. O'Reilly began his insurance career in 1970 with the Kemper Insurance Company and then moved to American Universal Insurance Company in 1974. In 1978, he was appointed Claims Superintendent of both the Rhode Island and New Hampshire Medical Malpractice Joint Underwriting Associations. In this capacity, he handled the designing and structuring of individualized claim settlements for the association. Mr. O'Reilly is in charge of the Settlement Annuity Division and is a partner in Brokers Service Corp.

MALCOLM S. PARSONS serves as risk manager at Doctor's Hospital in Columbus, Ohio. He has designed, written and implemented claims management systems specifically tailored toward controlling professional and general liability claims. Additionally, he has assisted agents, brokers and insurance companies in designing and implementing claims control programs. Mr. Parsons has served as vice president of claims for Personal Service Insurance Company and Anson B. Smith and Company, with an emphasis in casualty and professional liability claims. In addition to his other duties, he serves as president of the Doctor's Hospital Management Association which provides continuing education on management related topics. Mr. Parsons has participated in numerous professional liability and risk management seminars sponsored by insurance agents and companies as well as health care organizations.

IRWIN PRESS, PH.D., is a professor of anthropology at the University of Notre Dame. He received his Ph.D. from the University of Chicago in 1968. He has published extensively on the style and function of folk healers and on the clash between folk healing and modern health care. Dr. Press is currently engaged in research on patient satisfaction in both emergency and inpatient care. He is the author of three books and numerous articles and has lectured widely on the implications of attitudinal factors for patient relations and risk management. Dr. press is president of Press, Ganey Associates, Inc., a firm specializing in patient satisfaction monitoring.

RICHARD F. RAIL is senior vice president for corporate services at the St. Joseph Hospital, Inc., in Albuquerque, New Mexico. He graduated from the University of Rhode Island with a B.S. in business administration in 1961 and he is a Certified Public Accountant. Before joining the St. Joseph group in 1980, Mr. Rail was associated with Peat, Marwick, Mitchell & Co., Certified Public Accountants. Mr. Rail is a member of the Board of Directors of the New Mexico Hospital Association and Chairman of its Joint Unemployment Compensation Program Committee.

ROBERT M. SAYWELL, JR., Ph.D., M.P.H. is an associate professor in the graduate program in health administration, School of Public and Environmental Affairs, Indiana University—Indianapolis. He received his Ph.D. in economics from Colorado State University and his M.P.H. in public health administration and medical care organization from Johns Hopkins University. He has been a consultant in many health care organizations and has published in a variety of health journals in the areas of cost containment strategies, quality assurance, and technology assessment. He is a member of the American Public Health Association, the American Hospital Association, and the American Economic Association. He is also on the board of directors of several health organizations.

LAYTON C. SEVERSON received his degree from Idaho State University and served as an adjuster for the General Adjustment Bureau specializing in medical malpractice for several years. He subsequently served as the claims manager of the Ohio Medical Protective Liability Underwriting Association and was responsible for investigation and resolution of professional liability claims involving physicians, hospitals, nurses and other health care professionals. He is a founding member of the Ohio Association of Hospital Risk Managers and the American Society of Hospital Risk Managers. He is a member of the American Society of Law and Medicine and past president of the Columbus Claims Club. Mr. Severson is President of the Advisory Board of the School of Certified Registered Nurse Anesthesists at Ohio State University and is a frequent lecturer at several schools of nursing. He has appeared on programs sponsored by the American Nursing Association, Association of Operating Room Nurses, American Association of Nurse Anesthesists and the American Hospital Association. Mr. Severson has served as a consultant to hospital and health care professional organizations throughout the United States.

John R. Tanner graduated from the Ohio State University College of Medicine in 1955. He was board certified to practice internal medicine in 1967 and has practiced it for 27 years. He graduated from Nova Law Center, Nova University, Fort Lauderdale, Florida in 1978 and was admitted to the Florida Bar the same year. Dr. Tanner has consulted nationally in risk management and quality assurance issues for inpatient and outpatient facilities, and in medical staff credentialing and by-laws matters. He is currently practicing medical malpractice law in Miami, Florida.

Ralph F. Valitutti is a principal of the law firm of Kitch, Saurbier, Drutchas, Wagner & Kenney, P.C., which directly or through insurers represents a majority of the hospitals in Michigan in medicolegal matters. He is active in various legal organizations and a frequent lecturer on hospital and medical risk management issues. The focus of Mr. Valitutti's practice is the defense of hospitals and physicians in malpractice litigation. He is past chairman of the Medical-Legal Committee of the State Bar of Michigan and a past member of the Michigan Medical Schools Council of Deans.

Charles B. Van Vorst is president and chief executive officer of the Carle Foundation, Urbana, Ill. He previously was vice president-operations, Methodist Hospital, Indianapolis. He is an officer or member of numerous professional concerns or associations. A fellow of the American College of Hospital Administrators and a personal member of the American Hospital Association, Van Vorst received a B.S. from the University of Evansville (Ind.), and an M.B.A. from The George Washington University, Washington, D.C. He was a recipient of the 1973 World Health Organization Fellowship under which he studied ambulatory care systems in Denmark, Sweden, and Germany.

James A. White is director-risk management and insurance at the Carle Foundation, Urbana, Ill. He previously was risk manager for the board of governors, State Colleges and Universities, based in Springfield, Ill., and covering five midwest universities. Other prior positions included the University of Illinois, the Hartford Insurance Group, Florist Mutual Insurance, and Franklin Life Insurance Co. White is a graduate of the University of Illinois.